THE MAPS
OF CHICKAMAUGA

An Atlas of the Chickamauga Campaign,
Including the Tullahoma Operations,
June 22 - September 23, 1863

David A. Powell

David A. Friedrichs (Cartography)

SB

Savas Beatie

New York and California

The Maps of Chickamauga: An Atlas of the Chickamauga Campaign, Including the Tullahoma Operations, June 22 - September 23, 1863

Cataloging-in-Publication Data is available from the Library of Congress.

ISBN-13: 978-1-932714-72-2

10 9 8 7 6 5 4 3 2
First Edition, First Printing

SB

Published by
Savas Beatie LLC
521 Fifth Avenue, Suite 1700
New York, NY 10175

Editorial Offices:

Savas Beatie LLC
P.O. Box 4527
El Dorado Hills, CA 95762
Phone: 916-941-6896
(E-mail) editorial@savasbeatie.com

Savas Beatie titles are available at special discounts for bulk purchases in the United States by corporations, institutions, and other organizations. For more details, please contact Special Sales, P.O. Box 4527, El Dorado Hills, CA 95762. You may also e-mail us at sales@savasbeatie.com, or click over for a visit to our website at www.savasbeatie.com for additional information.

This book is lovingly dedicated to our wives,
Anne Powell and Laura Friedrichs

1 LA

8 AR

2&15 AR

Govan

*Fowler

6&7 AR

Liddell

exander Bridge Road

5 IN

93 OH   6 IN

24 MS

27 MS

29 MS

30 MS

34 MS

Walthall

Baldwin

5 KY

1 OH

49 OH

Winfrey
Field

Willich

15 OH

Johnson

32 IN

89 IL

A
1 OH

30 IN

79 IL

Dodge

20 OH

Brotherton Road

29 IN

77 PA

Jackson

21 IN

Smith

Smith

Cleburne

18 KY

36 OH

Glln

92 OH

11 OH

Stanford

OH

Brock
Field

Strahl

Vegetation					Features	Troops	Map
Field	Orchard	Woods	Cedars	Stumps	Road	Federal	Scale

Features
Road
Track
Building
Fence

Troops
Federal
Confederate
Advance
Retreat

Map

Scale

0   60   120   18

3:30 p.m., September 19, 1863

Contents

Contents (continued)

The Battle of Chickamauga
(September 19 - 20, 1863)

Contents (continued)

Contents (continued)

Introduction

By any definition this book you now hold in your hands is a labor of love. The general idea germinated in 1997, when I first began researching the battle of Chickamauga for an entirely different project.

Back then I was designing historical war games (paper games, not computer simulations) and wanted to tackle Chickamauga as my next subject. For those of you who aren't familiar with the rather arcane hobby of historical board games, they are highly detailed (some say overly complicated) manual simulations of past events. Printed maps represent the terrain, overlaid with a hexagonal grid that acts as a sort of chessboard, with die-cut cardboard counters portraying the regiments, battalions, batteries, and leaders who fought these epic encounters. Players use these tools to recreate the struggles of the event portrayed or to explore alternative outcomes. Think of them as a step between reading about the event and participating in a Civil War reenactment of it. My goal was to produce an epic of the genre, including as much detail as I could about Chickamauga. Accurate maps of the battlefield—and lots of them—were of prime importance, as were accurate numbers and losses for the organizations that fought there. The project took about a year to complete, and when the game was finally published it was well received. As I soon discovered, I was not yet finished with Chickamauga.

Like so many other people with a strong interest in the Civil War, I spent many years studying Gettysburg (for which I had also designed a board game). The July 1863 battle was the largest of the war. Much of it was fought across generally open terrain, and neither side was broken or driven from the field. Chickamauga was a very different affair. The combat in North Georgia in September 1863 was the Confederacy's only clear-cut victory in the Western Theater (and a barren one at that, rendered so by the crippling Rebel defeat just two months later at Chattanooga). The dark forests and

limited clearings triggered a host of unexpected combats, flanking maneuvers, and direct assaults that left commanders on both sides confused as to the exact ebb and flow of the battle. Commanders William Rosecrans (Army of the Cumberland) and Braxton Bragg (Army of Tennessee) exerted only limited control over the action, groping for whatever meager details of the fighting that came their way. Unlike so many battles, Chickamauga was largely fought by brigade, regimental, and sometimes even company commanders; senior officers often remained frustrated spectators to the chaos swirling around them. Thirty years later when the National Park was created, veterans of the battle recognized this truth when they decreed Chickamauga to have been the quintessential "soldiers' battle." No statues honoring individual generals are to be found on the field.

There were other significant differences. One consideration that drew me to Gettysburg was the wealth of published and easily accessible primary and secondary resources on the battle. I could learn about it in as much detail as I wished. There was always another letter or diary or newspaper account coming to light, or another book being published. I remember at one point many years ago counting nearly ninety Gettysburg-related titles on my personal library shelf. Hundreds more were in print and/or easily available. Gettysburg is—and will likely continue to be—a publishing mainstay.

The opposite is true about Chickamauga. Nearly all of the primary sources penned on the battle are in archival holdings and old newspapers, and so are not readily available. The secondary literature is remarkably sparse. Despite the battle's size and importance to the course of the Civil War, only two modern battle studies exist: Glenn Tucker's *Chickamauga* dating from the centennial era, and Peter Cozzens' *This Terrible Sound*, published in 1992. In the "micro-tactical" genre (such as the multiple monographs that exist for each of Gettysburg's three days) Archibald Gracie published in 1911 *The Truth About Chickamauga*, a detailed study of the September 20 afternoon fighting on Horseshoe Ridge. Unfortunately, Gracie's narrative is jumbled, poorly organized, and deeply confusing, and his analysis remains questionable at best. The redeeming aspect of Gracie's work is that he used extensive quotations from actual participants.

At the campaign level, there are several studies available that place Chickamauga in the larger context of the war, including Steven Woodworth's *Six Armies in Tennessee* and William G. Robertson's excellent five-part series recently published in *Blue & Gray Magazine*. As of this writing, Dr. Robertson is finishing a new monograph on the campaign, a much-anticipated work those of us fascinated with Chickamauga have long wished to see.

My own interest in Chickamauga continued unabated even after I finished my game design. I started collecting every primary source I could find, visiting or contacting archives and repositories across the country. I also scanned hundreds of period newspapers looking for letters home and casualty reports from men and regiments that had fought at Chickamauga. Somewhere along the line I developed the idea of assembling a map atlas that would explain the battle at the regimental level, tracking all movements at fifteen minute intervals. I knew my computer graphic talents weren't up to that challenge, so I sought a partner for this ambitious project. David Freidrichs was a fellow wargamer and good friend who had the digital and artistic skills I lacked. When I pitched the project to him he signed on quickly. Although we did not yet have a publisher or even a product, at least we had the concept and the means to execute it.

Originally (and foolishly) I estimated it would take about one year to finish the atlas. It was more than a decade later before I understood enough about the battle to begin sketching out draft maps. The time in between was spent reading primary accounts, walking the battlefield, and trying to integrate often conflicting recollections with the terrain under my feet. It was an often frustrating, but ultimately very rewarding, experience.

Hopefully, readers of this book own one of Brad Gottfried's excellent volumes in the Savas Beatie Military Atlas Series: *The Maps of Gettysburg* (2007) and *The Maps of First Bull Run* (2009). If so, you appreciate the wholly unique approach of this series that Brad thought up and Ted Savas (Savas Beatie) helped develop. Full-page maps with facing explanatory text convey simultaneity and clarity in a way that traditional battle narratives simply cannot accomplish. Chickamauga was a very confusing series of nearly non-stop combats driving in and falling back from every point of the compass. This format provides a markedly different view and understanding of this chaotic fighting than heretofore available.

Acknowledgments

Many people have had a hand in bringing this work to publication. First and foremost is my wife Anne, who has lived with Chickamauga as long as I have. Too much of my free time and days off have been spent traveling for this project or writing it up. Anne has given me the space and time to bring everything to completion without a word of complaint.

Two men have been instrumental in developing my understanding of the battle, and they know more about Chickamauga than anyone else alive: Dr. William Glenn Robertson, head of the Combat Studies Institute, and James Ogden, Chief Historian at the Chickamauga-Chattanooga National Military Park. When Dr. Robertson was first tasked by the U.S. Army to develop a modern staff ride program to use history to instruct young officers, he selected Chickamauga. Over the years he has developed that curriculum through an in-depth study of the battle and the campaign, collecting a wealth of resources along the way. I first met Dr. Robertson by tagging along on a staff ride. He has since shared many of his sources with me as I tried to bring this project to fruition. He is the dean of Chickamauga studies, and I thank him for his kindness.

Jim Ogden has been equally gracious with his time, granting me full access to the park library. Jim is always willing to discuss or argue points of contention. He read and offered suggestions on the text and has commented on the maps. For the past six years he has supported and helped guide our annual battlefield tours each March, when we break down the larger battle into detailed tactical segments and explore significant aspects of a given action. Much of my understanding of how events unfolded in 1863 came from these walks with Jim and the discussions that ensued. There is no better time spent than with Jim Ogden on the field at Chickamauga.

A number of friends have lent helping hands. Dan Cicero accompanied me on my first research trip to the park, sharing the driving duties with me from Chicago one rainy weekend to explore the park's library and map materials. Zack Waltz has been invaluable, lending me his time and copying talents on research trips to both the Combat Studies Institute at Fort Leavenworth, Kansas, and to what is now the Army Heritage and Education Center in Carlisle, Pennsylvania. Copying page after page of transcriptions and regimental histories is a tedious task, but Zack's enthusiasm never flagged. John Reed opened his doors to me in Atlanta, accompanied me (along with Zack and others) on numerous trips to the park, and endured monsoon-like rains more than once. Rick Manion of White Star Tours led me on my first exploration of Chickamauga, a day-long walk that provided the foundation of my understanding of the fighting of September 19. Rick has been an enthusiastic supporter of our yearly March tours. Sam Elliott of Chattanooga, Tennessee, and Scott Day of Birmingham, Alabama, offered support and encouragement as we shared our mutual interest in and love for the field. All of us will miss our weekend lodgings at the Log House on the grounds of the Gordon-Lee Mansion in the town of Chickamauga, our base for many excursions to the battlefield.

Park Ranger Lee White has become a good friend over the course of my numerous trips to Chickamauga. Lee is always alert to new resources on the battle, especially in electronic format. He has graciously read much of the text and has offered both praise and criticism. Lee caught and corrected errors on the maps and in the text, and this book is much the better because of his help.

Dr. Keith Bohannon of the University of West Georgia has an equal passion for archival research, and shared many finds with me over the years. Dr. Stephen Wise, director of the Marine Corps Museum at Parris Island, South Carolina, has also been a great booster of my efforts.

Numerous librarians, archivists, and scholars who maintain collections at so many of the institutions where I have spent time poring over old documents have been invaluable to this project. Over the years I have visited or contacted more than 200 archival repositories ranging from major university collections to local regional libraries and historical societies. Everyone was tremendously helpful in unearthing obscure collections and providing copies, and I am indebted to them for their efforts.

Every author eventually realizes that writing is the first stage of a project. I want to thank my first real editor, Terry Johnson, for accepting my articles in *North and South* magazine and helping me hone my prose into something worthy of publication. I also want to thank Terry for putting me in touch with Theodore P. Savas, Managing Director of Savas Beatie the publisher of this book. Ted helped translate my idea into a concrete product that fits nicely as the third book in the Savas Beatie Military Atlas Series. I would also like to thank some of the great Savas Beatie staff—Sarah Keeney (marketing director), together with Tammy Hall and Veronica Kane (marketing assistants), and Alex Savas (summer marketing assistant)—who worked hard to position and promote this book before its release.

If you helped me along the way and I forgot to mention you here, please accept my apology and know that I appreciate your efforts. Human nature dictates that mistakes will inevitably slip through the final editing process. For any errors that remain, I take all responsibility.

David Powell

Prelude: The Strategic Situation in 1863

Viewed solely from the microcosm of Virginia, by the summer of 1863 the Civil War appeared to be at a stalemate. Confederate forces had frustrated repeated Federal offensives through two long years of war and occupied roughly the same ground they had held in 1861. The primary reason for this success was the rise of Gen. Robert E. Lee. As long as he commanded the Army of Northern Virginia, the South seemed to have little to fear from any general President Abraham Lincoln could find to oppose him.

The proximity of the opposing capitals (Washington and Richmond), coupled with major media centers (Boston, New York, Philadelphia, and Charleston) lining the Eastern seaboard, focused much of the nation's attention on the largely static war in the narrow corridor between the District of Columbia and northern Virginia. In reality, the conflict covered a much wider front.

The Western Theater, running from the Appalachians to the Mississippi River, spanned hundreds of miles (as did the Trans-Mississippi Theater west of the Mississippi). There, the war was anything but static and by nearly any measure was turning decisively against the Confederacy. The vast spaces and plethora of navigable rivers offered Union forces access into the interior of the rebellious states. As the South learned early and often, waging a successful defense there was much more difficult than it was in Virginia.

By 1863, a trio of the South's most important cities—Memphis, Nashville, and New Orleans—containing much of what passed for heavy industry in the South were under Federal control. Their loss significantly damaged the Rebel cause. The Lincoln administration expected that renewed offensive operations that summer would bring more success and perhaps crush the rebellion and end the war.

President Lincoln anxiously anticipated two decisive victories in the West in 1863: the reopening of the Mississippi River with the capture of the Southern stronghold at Vicksburg, and a strong move into East Tennessee. Federal control of the Mississippi from Cairo to the Gulf of Mexico would reestablish a trading route

critical to the survival of the Midwest and divide the Confederacy in two (geographically if not in terms of raw population). Two Union armies were poised to conduct these operations. Maj. Gen. Nathaniel P. Banks was ordered north from New Orleans to clear the river of Rebel defenses from south to north, an operation aimed largely at Port Hudson, while Maj. Gen. Ulysses S. Grant would do the reverse, clearing the river from north to south from Memphis to Vicksburg. By May, both operations were well under way.

Maj. Gen. Ambrose E. Burnside was expected to move on Knoxville, Tennessee, from Kentucky. East Tennessee was important because it was a hotbed of Unionism deep in the heart of "Secessia." Pro-Union citizens had long been abused by Confederate authorities. Liberating them would be a major political triumph for Lincoln and demonstrate that the rebellion lacked sustained popular support among the people. The loss of East Tennessee would also sever the Confederacy's only direct rail connection between the Eastern and Western theaters, complicating Confederate troop and supply movements.

At Nashville, Maj. Gen. William S. Rosecrans led the Army of the Cumberland, the Union's largest army in the theater. Rosecrans had been inactive since the bloody stalemate of Stone's River the previous winter. His objectives were Middle Tennessee and Chattanooga. Success would return Tennessee to Federal control and set the stage for an invasion of Georgia.

Confederate President Jefferson Davis faced a serious dilemma trying to confront these various Union threats. Only two Rebel armies of any size were available to defend this vast region: Gen. Braxton Bragg's Army of Tennessee facing Rosecrans outside Nashville, and Lt. Gen. John C. Pemberton's Army of Mississippi at Vicksburg. Smaller garrisons held East Tennessee and other areas. Short of troops, Davis envisioned shifting men between armies to deal with the Union offensives individually—a strategy that would prove much less feasible if the Federal armies advanced simultaneously.

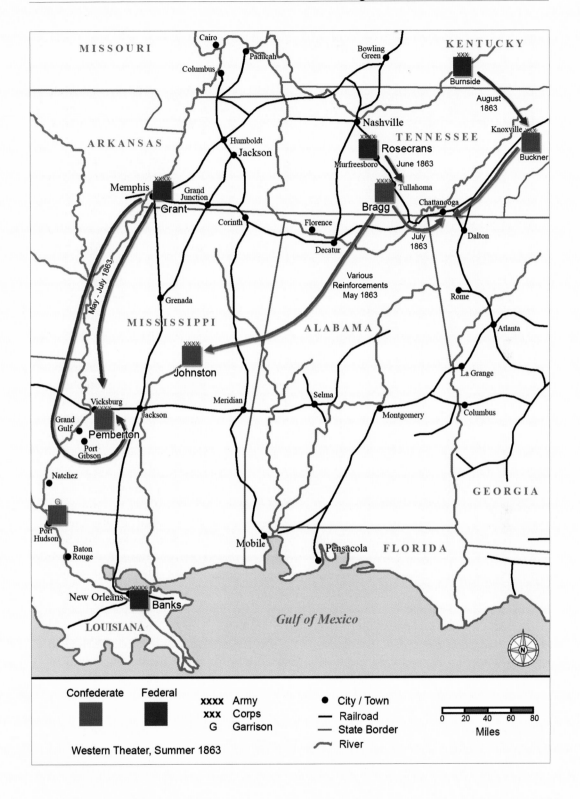

Western Theater, Summer 1863

William S. Rosecrans
(September 6, 1819 – March 11, 1898)

William Starke Rosecrans was born to Crandell Rosecrans and Jane Hopkins in Delaware City, Ohio. His great-grandfather was a governor of Rhode Island, a signer of the Declaration of Independence, and a co-author (with John Adams) of a draft of the Articles of Confederation.

Like many during his age, Rosecrans received only an informal education, but he demonstrated his intelligence and intellectual curiosity early and read everything he could get his hands on. He landed an appointment to West Point, and graduated from the military academy in the Class of 1842. His standing (5th out of 56) placed him near the top of one of the most notable classes in the institution's illustrious history. His classmates included future Civil War generals John Newton, James Longstreet, Richard H. Anderson, George Sykes, Abner Doubleday, Seth Williams, Alexander P. Stewart, Lafayette McLaws, Mansfield Lovell, John Pope, Daniel Harvey Hill, and Earl Van Dorn. Rosecrans roomed at West Point with Longstreet and Stewart, two generals who would later play a major role in ending his tenure as an army commander.

Because of his class standing, Rosecrans entered the engineers but resigned in 1854 in order to pursue a civilian career path that would include stints as an architect, civil engineer, mining management, and running a navigation company launched to haul coal. "Old Rosy" was also a prolific inventor. Unfortunately, he was working in a coil-oil production laboratory in 1859 when a lamp exploded, burning much of his body. Somehow he managed to walk more than one mile home. His injuries were so severe that he was confined to bed for the better part of two long and painful years. The scars on his forehead remained visible for the rest of his life.

Within days after the Civil War broke out in 1861 he was on the staff of Gen. George B. McClellan with the rank of colonel of engineers. Two months later he was the colonel of the 23rd Ohio Infantry—the regiment included two future presidents, Rutherford B. Hayes and William McKinley—and was made a brigadier general in the Regular Army, to date from May 16, 1861. Some of his early duties included the drilling of troops and working as an engineer to help design Camp Dennison in Ohio.

Rosecrans was appointed a brigadier general in June in the Regular Army (to rank from May 1861). His well-crafted plans for the campaign in western Virginia resulted in the victory at Rich Mountain, and set the stage for a later successful campaign against Confederate Robert E. Lee that drove the Rebels from the region. Transferred to the Western Theater, Rosecrans led a wing of John Pope's Army of the Mississippi, participated in the siege of Corinth, and was given command of the army in June of 1862.

After demonstrating solid fighting skills at Corinth and Iuka (and being criticized by his superiors for a lackluster pursuit, a concern that would surface later in the war), Rosecrans was given command of the XIV Corps (soon to be the Army of the Cumberland). He was also promoted to major general, to date from March 1862, so that he would outrank George Thomas. At the end of

1862, Rosecrans led his army (technically the XIV Corps) at Stone's River, where Confederate Braxton Bragg's Southern army nearly overwhelmed him in a series of attacks. The tactical stalemate ended with Bragg's retreat, leaving Rosecrans complete control of the battlefield. Thereafter, the XIV Corps was renamed the Army of the Cumberland.

Rosecrans had thus far displayed a good grasp of strategy, but had a tendency toward micromanagement of his troops, and a mercurial temperament. He was generally well-liked by the men in the ranks.

Braxton Bragg
(March 22, 1817 – September 27, 1876)

A native of Warrenton, North Carolina, Bragg spent his early years there before entering West Point in 1933. Like William Rosecrans, he graduated 5th in his class (of fifty) four years later. There were several notable future Civil War generals in his class, including Jubal Early, William H. French, John Sedgwick, Joe Hooker, and John C. Pemberton.

Bragg entered the artillery branch, fought the Seminoles Indians in Florida, and performed distinguished service in the Mexican War (three brevets). His handling of artillery at the battle of Buena Vista in 1847 against a numerically superior enemy was particularly noteworthy and helped

seal the victory. This success helped catapult Jefferson Davis, an infantry officer, out of the ranks of the anonymous.

The common wisdom is that Bragg and Davis became close friends—largely as a result of their shared Mexican War experiences—and that is why Davis refused to remove him from command during the Civil War. While Davis bore no great animosity toward Bragg, he was also not a particularly close friend, either. In fact, Davis played a major role in Bragg resignation from the army in 1856.

Bragg was upset over the disbanding of horse artillery batteries after the Mexican War. When Davis was appointed Secretary of War in the Franklin Pierce administration, Bragg wrote to Davis and urged changes that would restore the batteries and make other modifications to the artillery arm to improve its overall efficiency. Davis rejected his suggestions outright, and ordered Bragg's battery to the Texas frontier—a move that infuriated Bragg and convinced him the order was retaliatory in nature. Bragg resigned. Both he and his wife viewed Davis as personally hostile. In 1860, at a dinner party with William Sherman, Elise Bragg told Sherman that her husband was "no particular favorite" of Davis'.

Bragg was tending to a plantation in Louisiana when that state left the union, and he was given command of the Louisiana army. He was promoted to brigadier general in the Confederate Army in March 1861 and accepted a Gulf Coast command that included Pensacola, Florida, and Mobile, Alabama. That September, Bragg was made major general. He eventually reached the conclusion that Davis kept him in Pensacola, considered a backwater of the war, out of sheer spite. In fact, Davis was not being petty or vengeful, and had formed an early favorable opinion of Bragg's abilities—an opinion not reciprocated by Bragg.

In early 1862, Bragg offered to take his troops north to Corinth, Mississippi. Davis agreed. There, Bragg assisted Gen. Albert S. Johnston in organizing a motley command that would eventually become the Army of Tennessee.

Bragg's first major combat in the war was at Shiloh in April of 1862, where he directed a corps and served capably. Although the Confederates lost the battle (and Johnston lost his life) and retreated into Mississippi, Bragg was promoted to full general less than one week later. When Gen. P. G. T. Beauregard proved unable to fulfill his role as army commander, Bragg was elevated as his successor. That August, Bragg led what was then called the Army of Mississippi north into Tennessee and then into Kentucky, triggering several combats including the large but indecisive battle at Perryville on October 8. The manner in which he conducted the campaign resulted in harsh criticism from his subordinates, laying the seeds for future discord within the South's primary Western army.

On December 31, Bragg moved to meet a Union advance southeast of Nashville near Murfreesboro. His attack nearly destroyed William Rosecrans' army. The next day, January 1, 1863, the combatants remained largely (and curiously) inactive. Bragg renewed the attack on January 2, but was repulsed with heavy losses. Although a draw, Bragg withdrew, giving up Middle Tennessee and opening the door to another round of divisiveness within the ranks of his army. His corps commanders openly expressed a lack of confidence in his ability to lead the army and asked President Davis to relieve Bragg.

Davis sent Gen. Joseph E. Johnston to inspect Bragg's army and report on the true state of affairs, including the dangerous problems within the officer corps. Davis gave Johnston the authority to relieve Bragg, if necessary. Johnston, however, was worried about how it would look if he relieved Bragg and took command himself, so he gave Davis an unrealistically favorable report concerning Bragg and the army—so much so that Davis could not relieve Bragg without completely disregarding Johnston's advice.

Ben Cheatham, one of Bragg's division commanders, vowed to never serve under Bragg again, and John C. Breckinridge, whose division was cut to pieces by the Union artillery in a nearly suicidal attack on January 2, challenged Bragg to a duel. These and other major confrontations were left unresolved when the summer of 1863 arrived,

and with it the Tullahoma Campaign and the maneuvering that would trigger the bloodshed at Chickamauga.

Bragg was a walking contradiction. Unlike Joe Johnston, he was perfectly willing to commit his army to decisive combat, but his uniquely unhealthy relationship with not only his chief lieutenants but a good percentage of the men in his army made it doubly difficult for him to plan and execute a successful campaign.

THE MAPS
OF CHICKAMAUGA

An Atlas of the Chickamauga Campaign,

Including the Tullahoma Operations,

June 22 - September 23, 1863

Map Set 1: Middle Tennessee: The Tullahoma Campaign

1.1: Opposing Deployments (June 22)

It was the third summer of the war, and momentous events were unfolding across the country. Gen. Robert E. Lee's Confederate thrust into Pennsylvania was well underway. Union Maj. Gen. Ulysses S. Grant was tightening his grip on the Rebel bastion of Vicksburg, Mississippi, a siege now into its second month. On the main Western front in Tennessee, however, Federal inactivity cast a long shadow.

By June of 1863, Maj. Gen. William S. Rosecrans and his Army of the Cumberland had been inactive for six months, encamped in and around Murfreesboro following the bloody and nearly disastrous battle fought there at the end of 1862 and on the first day of 1863. In Washington, D.C., President Abraham Lincoln and his cabinet—including the brilliant but ill-tempered Secretary of War Edwin M. Stanton—carefully followed every scrap of news. To Lincoln and his subordinates, Rosecrans' inaction was both frustrating and inexplicable.

Rosecrans had reasons for waiting, some good and some less so. He needed to stockpile supplies. Moving southeast from Nashville against Braxton Bragg's Army of Tennessee would require the passage of land known as "the Barrens." Forage there would be scarce. The Federal army also needed more cavalry. In March, Rosecrans' mounted arm numbered just 6,000 troopers, while Bragg could count on more than 16,000.[1] Facing such a disparity, Rosecrans could not hope to successfully screen his movements or divine Bragg's response. By June, the number of Federal horsemen had doubled to about 12,000, including a brigade of mounted infantry armed with Spencer repeating rifles commanded by Col. John T. Wilder. This combination of mobility and firepower suggested that if properly utilized, Wilder's roughly 2,000 men would play a role in the looming campaign far beyond their numbers.

Still, Rosecrans showed little desire to move against Bragg despite armies marching in Pennsylvania and waging a siege in Mississippi. Rosecrans suggested that by doing nothing, he was keeping Bragg from sending men to other theaters, and that if he were to move, it might violate a "great military maxim not to risk two . . . decisive battles at the same time."[2] In fact, Bragg was sending troops to Mississippi. As Union Maj. Gen. Henry Halleck pointed out, it was in Bragg's interest not to fight, not the other way around.

By June, Bragg had lost roughly two cavalry and one infantry divisions. Brig. Gen. John H. Morgan led his three horse brigades on a raid into Kentucky, exceeded his orders, and rode into Ohio. Brig. Gen. William Jackson took a mounted division to Mississippi, as did former vice president (and now major general) John C. Breckinridge, who left with his infantry command. Rosecrans' strength was growing; Bragg's was dwindling. By June 22, Rosecrans had roughly 80,000 men, while Bragg counted fewer than 50,000 of all arms.

When the final week of June arrived, Rosecrans decided he was ready to move. Bragg's two infantry corps occupied Wartrace and Shelbyville, with his main depot at Tullahoma on the Nashville and Chattanooga Railroad—the same line Rosecrans had to possess in order to sustain his army on an advance. Brig. Gen. Nathan Bedford Forrest's 4,000-man mounted division guarded Bragg's left at Spring Hill, Tennessee. Brig. Gen. Joseph Wheeler's 8,000-man mounted corps was supposed to be protecting the right. Wheeler, however, was ever alert for a shot at glory. With Bragg's approval, he shifted one of his two divisions (Brig. Gen. William T. Martin) to Forrest's front, from there intending to raid Federal supply lines. This left only Brig. Gen. John A. Wharton's men to screen an extended front.

Bragg's army was deployed behind a series of hills. Three narrow gaps (Hoover, Liberty, and Guy, from east to west, respectively) would prove critical in anticipating any Union moves, and they could serve as choke points to stymie the Federals—if they could be held.

Rosecrans concentrated nearly his entire force around Murfreesboro: nine infantry divisions (three-fourths of the XIV Corps, and all of the XX Corps and XXI Corps) and one of cavalry. Ten miles west, Maj. Gen. Gordon Granger's Reserve Corps held Triune with Brig. Gen. Absalom Baird's division of his own corps, Brig. Gen. John M. Brannan's Third Division of the XIV Corps, and one cavalry division. Strong garrisons from the Reserve Corps also guarded heavily fortified Nashville and other points along the railroad to ensure that the Union rear remained protected.

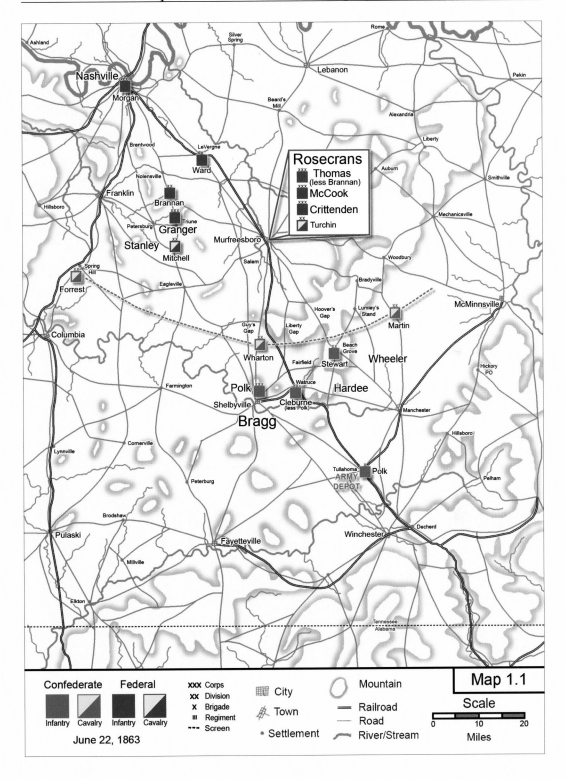

Map 1.1

1.2: Opening Moves (June 23-24)

Instead of attacking Braxton Bragg head-on behind his entrenchments at Wartrace or Shelbyville, Rosecrans elected to outflank the Southern army. While part of the Army of the Cumberland moved south to demonstrate against the Rebel front, the Union XIV Corps and XXI Corps would move rapidly southeast, brushing aside limited Confederate opposition and advancing to Manchester, Tennessee. Once at Manchester, the Federals would be closer to Tullahoma—and Bragg's supply base—than most of Bragg's own men. A rapid march to seize Tullahoma before the Rebels could adequately defend it would trap the Army of Tennessee north of the Elk River where it might then be destroyed. It was a sound plan, and Bragg was about to increase its odds of success.

On June 21, Union activity convinced cavalryman Joseph Wheeler, in charge of two-thirds of Bragg's mounted command, that an enemy advance was imminent. Leaving John Wharton's Division to guard the direct approaches to Shelbyville, Wheeler sent Martin's command to Spring Hill. There, combined with some of Forrest's troopers, Wheeler intended to "dash around Rosecrans' rear, capture his [Rosecrans'] trains, and make a diversion."[3] The entire idea was ill-conceived. Not only were the important Federal supply points well garrisoned and likely to be immune to any attack Rebel raiders might be able to mount, but Wheeler was stripping Bragg's right flank of an all-important cavalry screen at precisely the moment Bragg would need it the most (to discover and report Rosecrans' movements). Martin's Division spent the 23rd and 24th in transit from the army's right flank to its left, and did not arrive at Spring Hill until late on the 24th.

Rosecrans initiated his own movements on the 23rd. That day, Brig. Gen. Robert Mitchell's First Cavalry Division of Maj. Gen. David S. Stanley's Cavalry Corps rode south from Triune, passing through Eagleville to Rover, Tennessee. This advance drew resistance from Col. C. C. Crews' Confederate cavalry brigade, and also attracted Wheeler's attention, who rode to the front and personally directed operations for a time.[4] Several sharp encounters resulted, with

Mitchell eventually falling back a short distance at nightfall.

Simultaneously, Gen. Granger, who had been given overall responsibility for directing the diversionary movement now underway, took Baird's First Division, Reserve Corps (all of the field force that could be spared from the reserve) and, reinforced by Brannan's Third Division, XIV Corps, occupied Salem a few miles southwest of Murfreesboro. Wheeler reported that he had repulsed the Union cavalry thrust, and that Union infantry was also stirring. It was enough information to alert Bragg that a major movement was probably underway.

The next day, June 24, Rosecrans increased the pressure. While Mitchell's cavalry division moved northeast to join Granger at Salem, Granger's own column moved south from Salem toward Guy's Gap, threatening Shelbyville from the north. At the same time, Maj. Gen. Alexander McCook's XX Corps departed Murfreesboro. Sending Maj. Gen. Philip Sheridan's Third Division to cooperate with Granger's move toward Guy's Gap, McCook directed the rest of XX Corps toward Liberty Gap. Simultaneously, Maj. Gen. George Thomas and his XIV Corps struck at Hoover's Gap. Col. John T. Wilder's newly mounted infantry brigade led Thomas' column. With their horses and recently acquired Spencer seven-shot repeaters, Wilder's men had a significant edge in both firepower and mobility. Both Hoover's Gap and Liberty Gap were lightly defended and seized quickly by the Federals.

The XXI Corps comprised Rosecrans' trump card. Maj. Gen. Thomas Crittenden's divisions marched southeast to Bradyville, where they were beyond the Rebel picket line. It was Crittenden's task to take Manchester (deep behind the Confederate right-rear) before Bragg could react. Initially, all of Brig. Gen. John Turchin's Second Cavalry Division led this move, but with Mitchell encountering such stiff Rebel resistance, on the 24th Stanley directed Turchin to detach Col. Robert H. G. Minty's First Brigade and send it to Granger's front. This left only a single brigade of Federal troopers supporting Crittenden and Thomas.[5]

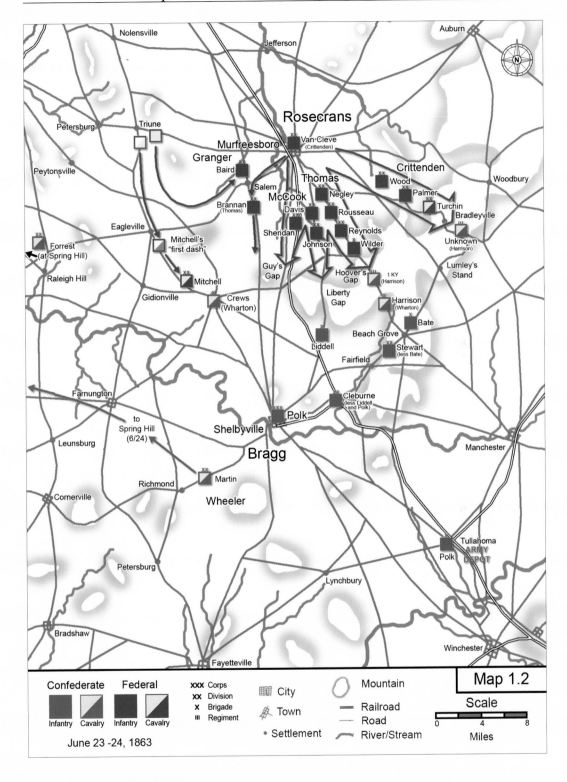

Map 1.2

Scale

Confederate   Federal

Infantry Cavalry Infantry Cavalry

June 23 -24, 1863

XXX Corps
XX Division
X Brigade
III Regiment

City
Town
Settlement

Mountain
Railroad
Road
River/Stream

Miles

1.3: Liberty Gap (June 24 and 25)

On June 6, Brig. Gen. St. John Liddell was at Bell Buckle, Tennessee, an advanced outpost of Maj. Gen. Pat Cleburne's Division in roughly the center of Bragg's long line. Liddell's small command was divided, with a picket force at the mouth of Liberty Gap three miles north of his position.[6] There was already a small cavalry picket of unknown size from John Wharton's command there, reinforced by a section of Capt. Charles Swett's Mississippi battery and the 5th and combined 13th/15th Arkansas of Liddell's Brigade, all under the immediate command of Col. Lucius Featherston of the 5th Arkansas.

Excluding the cavalry picket (which cannot be firmly identified) Featherston mustered 540 men and two guns. Quiet prevailed at Liberty Gap until noon on June 24, when a courier brought word of the cavalry fight between the Union First Cavalry division and Col. Crews' Georgians some miles to the northwest. Featherson soon had more immediate problems. A second messenger arrived to inform the Arkansas colonel that Federal infantry was "directly in front of Liberty Gap."[7]

The enemy in his front belonged to Brig. Gen. Richard W. Johnson's Second Division, XX Corps. Featherston and Col. Joseph Josey of the 15th Arkansas moved their small force into prearranged defensive positions, scattered across the hills in skirmish order at the mouth of the gap. Featherston wanted to fight a delaying action until the rest of Liddell's men could arrive.

Union Brig. Gen. August Willich's brigade led Johnson's division, its advance covered by part of Thomas Harrison's 39th Indiana Mounted Infantry. At first contact Willich deployed his men, extended his skirmishers, and asked for support. Harrison's mounted Hoosiers moved to Willich's left, while Johnson deployed Col. John F. Miller's brigade on Willich's right. Once arranged, the Federals edged south. Gen. McCook could "see at a glance the immense advantage the enemy would have over our troops" from their positions on the heights.[8]

Fortunately for the Yankees, Featherston lacked the strength to do more than delay things. With his flanks threatened, he slowly fell back through the gap as the afternoon hours ticked past. Once through the gap, Johnson added Col.

Philomon Baldwin's four regiments to the movement, maneuvering them up and through Willich's line to drive the Razorbacks farther south. Johnson's men halted at Liberty Church for the night.[9]

Liddell hurried two more regiments up that evening and deployed them opposite Johnson, hopeful that additional support would soon arrive. On the morning of the 25th, division commander Patrick Cleburne arrived from Watrace. After Cleburne informed Liddell that Brig. Gen. S.A.M. Wood's Brigade was en route, Liddell filled him in on the situation. When Liddell told him that the Yankees might be retreating, Cleburne ordered him to find out. Liddell's skirmishers advanced only to discover that the Federals were not withdrawing and in fact were likely reinforcing.[10] Most of the Yankees recalled Liddell's move as a dramatic attack instead of a skirmish advance that cost Liddell only a slim handful of casualties.

That afternoon, Johnson renewed his own attack, now supported by Brig. Gen. Jefferson C. Davis' First Division, XX Corps. Once again the Federals advanced cautiously across the imposing terrain, triggering a prolonged firefight. Willich and Miller had switched places, with Willich advancing on the right and Miller on the left. Even with rein-forcements, Liddell fielded no more than 1,000 men. Late in the day, Brig. Gen. William P. Carlin's regiments of Davis' division replaced some of Johnson's men when their ammunition gave out.[11]

The most dramatic moment of the day occurred when Willich committed the 49th Ohio from his reserve and sent his entire force forward. The decisive move drove Liddell's left (the 5th and 13th/15th Arkansas) from the hills. The attack, boasted Capt. Alexis Cope of the 15th Ohio, was a complete success brought about by a drill of Willich's own invention designated "Advance, Firing." The regiments formed in four ranks instead of two, with each rank marching forward, firing and reloading in succession. The tactic allowed a command to move steadily forward and still produce a nearly constant stream of rifle fire. Liddell fell back and linked up with Wood's newly arrived infantry.[12]

McCook's XX Corps had fulfilled its mission of focusing Bragg's attention to the north and away from his right. Cleburne's troops would maintain their position through the following day until Bragg ordered his army to retreat.

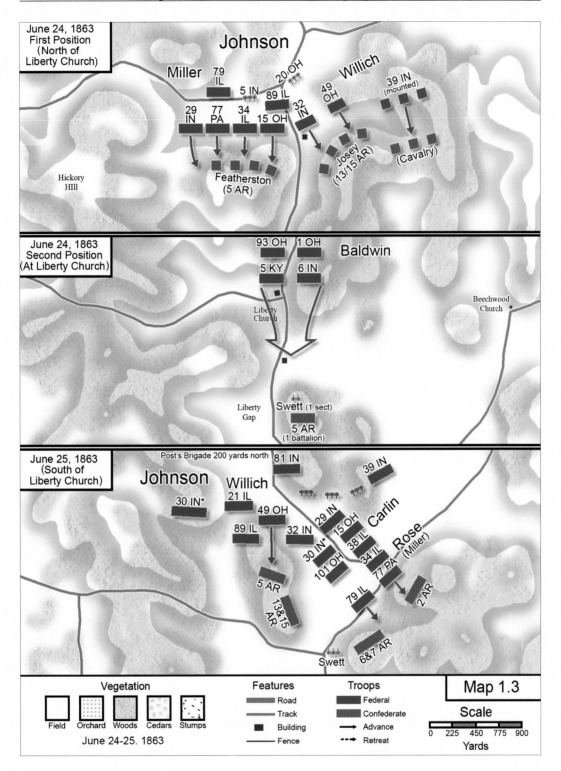

June 24, 1863
First Position
(North of
Liberty Church)

Johnson

Miller   79
           IL

20 OH

Willich

5 IN   89 IL   49   39 IN
              OH   (mounted)

32
IN

29   77   34
IN   PA   IL   15 OH

Featherston
(5 AR)

Josey
(13/15 AR)

(Cavalry)

Hickory
HIll

June 24, 1863
Second Position
(At Liberty Church)

93 OH   1 OH   Baldwin

5 KY   6 IN

Beechwood
Church

Liberty
Church

Liberty
Gap

Swett (1 sect)

5 AR
(1 battalion)

June 25, 1863
(South of
Liberty Church)

Post's Brigade 200 yards north

81 IN

39 IN

Johnson   Willich

30 IN*   21 IL

49 OH   29 IN   15 OH   Carlin

89 IL   32 IN

30 IN*   38 IL   Rose
                        (Miller)

101 OH   34 IL

5 AR   77 PA

13&15
AR   79 IL   2 AR

Swett   6&7 AR

Vegetation

Field   Orchard   Woods   Cedars   Stumps

June 24-25. 1863

Features

▬ Road
— Track
■ Building
— Fence

Troops

■ Federal
■ Confederate
→ Advance
--▸ Retreat

Map 1.3

Scale

0   225   450   775   900

Yards

1.4: Wilder at Hoover's Gap (June 24)

Col. John T. Wilder's Mounted Infantry Brigade was a unique organization in the Federal army. Wilder, only thirty-three years old in 1863, had already achieved success as an Indiana entrepreneur operating his own iron foundry before the war. He had no military experience but quickly gained plenty, rising to command the 17th Indiana in 1862. As post commander at Munfordville, Kentucky, during Bragg's invasion that fall of 1862, Wilder was forced to surrender his garrison when it was besieged by most of the Southern army. Upon his return to service, Wilder turned his enterprising nature to finding a new way to make war. He submitted a plan to mount his brigade with local livestock, and arranged for the purchase of several thousand Spencer seven-shot repeating rifles. Rosecrans, in his quest to increase his cavalry arm, approved the unusual request. Wilder also forged a relationship with a young Hoosier druggist named Eli Lilly, who commanded a battery of six three-inch rifles. Lilly was the perfect fit for Wilder's command. On his own hook, Lilly had scrounged up four mountain howitzers drawn by mules. His was now the only ten-gun battery in the entire Union army.[13]

With the mobility of cavalry and firepower equal to at least twice their number of conventional infantry, Wilder's regiments were the natural choice to lead Thomas' column to Hoover's Gap on June 24. Despite scorn from the army's Regular mounted establishment—Maj. Gen. Stanley referred to Wilder's men as "tadpole cavalry" and feared they would all be captured by the Rebels—Wilder's troops were primed for action.

Hoover's Gap was seven miles long but very narrow, in places no more than a few hundred yards wide. Wilder's orders directed the First Brigade to seize the north end of the gap and wait for the infantry to close up behind. Confederate cavalry screening the gap believed that entrenched infantry was behind them. Breaking camp at 3:00 a.m. in a dismal rain, Wilder's 2,000 men encountered Rebel pickets well north of their objective. Wilder pushed forward aggressively, scattered elements of the 3rd Confederate and 1st [3rd] Kentucky Cavalry regiments, and captured the Kentuckians' flag.

Once they entered the gap, Wilder realized that the Rebel infantry had not yet been alerted, and the Confederate defenses, situated about mid-gap at one of its narrowest points, were unmanned. "Believing that it would cost us at least a thousand men to retake the ground we now held," Wilder reported, "I determined to take the entire gap."[14] By midday, it was firmly in Union hands.

At the southern end, Wilder deployed his men on the hills overlooking the Garrison Fork of the Duck River. About 3:00 p.m., Rebel infantry finally appeared. The 20th Tennessee and 37th Georgia of Brig. Gen. William B. Bate's Brigade deployed on the east side of the creek south of Beechgrove. They waited there until the 4th Georgia Sharpshooter Battalion came up. Bate decided to try and outflank the Federals to the left (west). The 20th Tennessee and 4th Sharpshooters bore the brunt of the effort. Together they drove in the Yankee skirmishers, but received a nasty surprise when Wilder reinforced his right regiment (the 72nd Indiana) with the 17th Indiana and 98th Illinois. The Federal fire inflicted a punishing twenty-five percent loss and ended Bate's attack.[15]

Federal commanders celebrated at how easily the gap had fallen. Maj. Gen. Reynolds arrived at 5:00 p.m. with the other two brigades of the division. Gen. Thomas followed, congratulating Wilder fulsomely: "You have saved the lives of a thousand men . . . today," exclaimed the corps commander, pumping Wilder's hand. "I didn't expect to have this gap for three days."[16] Rosecrans and his chief of staff, Brig. Gen. James A. Garfield, soon arrived as well and proudly surveyed the scene of Wilder's success.

Rain was still falling when Bushrod Johnson's four Tennessee regiments arrived that night to replace the regiments holding Bate's right. Given the nature of the terrain and the strength of the Federal position, no further attacks were attempted. June 25 was consumed with limited skirmishing. Confederate division commander Maj. Gen. A. P. Stewart was under orders to fall back on Fairfield or Wartrace if the Federals were too strong. By that afternoon it was clear that Thomas' men held Hoover Gap in strength.

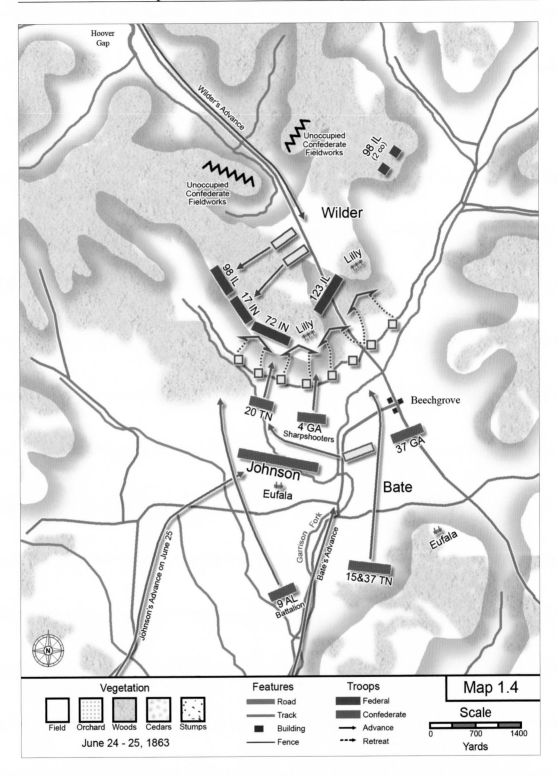

Hoover
Gap

Wilder's Advance

Unoccupied
Confederate
Fieldworks

98 IL
(2 co.)

Unoccupied
Confederate
Fieldworks

Wilder

98 IL

Lilly

123 IL

17 IN

72 IN   Lilly

20 TN

4 GA
Sharpshooters

Beechgrove

37 GA

Johnson

Eufala

Bate

Johnson's Advance on June 25

Garrison Fork

Bate's Advance

Eufala

15&37 TN

9 AL
Battalion

N

Vegetation

Field   Orchard   Woods   Cedars   Stumps

June 24 - 25, 1863

Features

Road
Track
Building
Fence

Troops

Federal
Confederate
Advance
Retreat

Map 1.4

Scale

0   700   1400

Yards

1.5: Rosecrans Unleashes a Left Hook
(June 25 - 26)

William Rosecrans' efforts at misdirection thoroughly fooled Braxton Bragg. Wheeler's reports of heavy Federal activity to the northwest and the Union attack at Liberty Gap convinced Bragg that Shelbyville (on his left) was the Federal target. That decision froze Bragg in place and set the stage for Rosecrans' next move: the seizure of Manchester.

And then the weather intervened. The light rain and drizzle that had begun on June 24 grew heavier on the 25th. The downpour, observed Gen. Crittenden, continued "incessantly for fifteen days," turning the roads into a quagmire.[17] One soldier in the Federal Reserve Corps remembered the mud was from "1 to 6 [inches] deep."[18] Union movements everywhere were hindered, and Crittenden's XXI Corps slowed to a painful crawl. The route from Bradyville to Manchester passed through rough country, the roads climbing out of the Nashville basin up to the Cumberland Plateau. The steep ascents, coupled with the slippery mud, made it virtually impossible for the draft animals to haul the corps and divisional trains. Details of men, fifty to a wagon, spent their time shoving buried wheels out of the mud. Crittenden made virtually no progress on either the 25th or 26th.

As Crittenden tried to move forward, the rest of Thomas' XIV Corps slogged its way through Hoover's Gap on the 25th. Thomas recalled Brannan's Third Division, detached earlier to support Granger, reuniting Rosecrans' most powerful corps. The next day Thomas deployed three of his divisions for a move on Fairfield, but the Confederates declined to make a fight of it.

A. P. Stewart's Confederates of Lt. Gen. William J. Hardee's Corps had the unfortunate duty of trying to hold back Thomas' relentless advance. After Bate was soundly repulsed by Wilder late on the 24th, Stewart spent the 25th skirmishing and reporting the Federal activity—including the threat to Manchester—to Hardee, who in turn ordered Stewart to fall back toward Wartrace if the Yankees attacked. By the 26th Stewart was in full retreat. His lone division was no match for Thomas' three Federal divisions.[19]

Liddell was fighting a similar action at Liberty Gap, this time against McCook's XX Corps. Liddell's heavily outnumbered command (part of Cleburne's Division, also of Hardee's Corps), attempted to retake Liberty Gap on the 25th but was easily repulsed. The next day Liddell was also retreating to Watrace.

By this time Bragg's command structure was beginning to break down. Joe Wheeler's move to strip Martin's Division from the Army of Tennessee's right flank had denuded that sector of adequate reconnaissance just when Bragg needed it most, and information that should have easily reached Bragg's headquarters was getting lost in the shuffle. Bragg was informed enough about Liddell's fight at Liberty Gap to conclude that it was the Federal main effort. Somehow, he was not informed about A. P. Stewart's problems at Hoover's Gap—an error that would have serious repercussions. Stewart was not the problem. As the surviving message traffic between him and Hardee shows, Stewart kept his corps commander well informed about ongoing developments on his front. Nor does all the blame rest with Hardee, for Bragg was kept in the loop concerning Liberty Gap. Whatever the reason, the lack of information about the loss of Hoover's Gap and the threat to Manchester led Bragg to make a serious mistake.

On the morning of June 26, Bragg ordered Lt. Gen. Leonidas Polk to move his entire corps north through Guy's Gap (still controlled by Wheeler's troopers), bypass the Federal force in Liberty Gap, and swing around and attack the Federals from the rear at dawn on June 27 while Hardee's men struck the Yankees from the front and east. The orders astounded Polk, who described the move as "nothing short of a man-trap."[20] Despite his objections Bragg insisted, and Polk spent much of the 26th readying his force for the complicated and dangerous movement. At 5:00 p.m. on the 26th, however, news of the loss of Hoover's Gap and Stewart's subsequent engagements fell upon the Rebels at Shelbyville like a thunderclap. Bragg cancelled Polk's planned move and by 11:00 p.m. ordered the entire Confederate army to fall back on Tullahoma.[21]

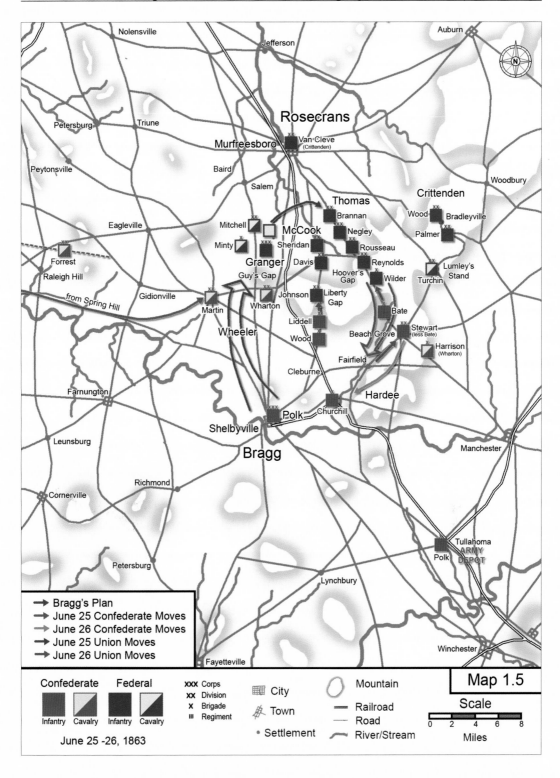

Bragg's Plan
June 25 Confederate Moves
June 26 Confederate Moves
June 25 Union Moves
June 26 Union Moves

Confederate		Federal		
Infantry	Cavalry	Infantry	Cavalry	

June 25 -26, 1863

XXX Corps
XX Division
X Brigade
III Regiment

City
Town
Settlement

Mountain
Railroad
Road
River/Stream

Map 1.5

Scale

0   2   4   6   8
Miles

1.6: Retreat to Tullahoma
(June 27 and 28)

The withdrawal forced the Confederates to fight their own battle against the rain and torturous mud. June 27 became a slow-motion race between the two armies: the Federals struggling to reach Manchester and the Rebels slogging their way to Tullahoma. Bragg's men, who had a shorter distance to cover, won the exhausting footrace.

Bragg had ordered the retreat on the night of June 26, but the last elements of Hardee's Corps and Polk's Corps did not reach Tullahoma until late on the afternoon of the 28th. Elements of desperation marked the march. When some of Polk's trains blocked Cleburne's men, Cleburne complained that Polk's officers stopped the whole train whenever a wagon broke down, instead of pushing it aside. "Orders," insisted one officer, required him to leave no wagon behind. "This policy will risk the safety of this army," complained Cleburne at 6:45 p.m. on the 27th, still just a few miles south of Wartrace. Cleburne's message prompted Bragg to angrily rebuke Polk for his lack of urgency. Polk denied that he had ordered any such thing, and sent out his own chastising dispatches.[22]

Bragg reached Tullahoma about noon on the 27th, where word arrived that the Yankees had occupied Manchester. Despite the upsetting of his plans, Bragg was determined to give battle and set about arranging Tullahoma's defenses. Meanwhile, Rebel cavalry was still north of the Duck River on June 27. Joe Wheeler sent Wharton's Division to cover Hardee's retreat from Watrace while holding Shelbyville with Martin's troopers. Wheeler was determined to hold Shelbyville until Forrest's Division, en route from Spring Hill, arrived.

Forrest and Wheeler did not get along well. After a confused and bloody action at Dover, Tennessee, back in February 1863, Forrest vowed never to take orders from Wheeler again. Forrest was by nature a combative and confrontational man, and not just with Yankees. He was still suffering from a June 13 gunshot wounded inflicted by a disgruntled Confederate lieutenant during a quarrel that quickly got out of hand. Physically impaired, Forrest was not at his best as June prepared to give way to July.[23]

Forrest was ordered to join the main army on June 25, but the incessant rains spilled creeks, streams, and rivers out of their banks. By the 26th he was still far from the army. An order from Wheeler reached him late that day directing Forrest to move his troopers to Shelbyville, where Wheeler would hold the crossing open for him. Forrest never arrived. Unable to drive through the Union cavalry, Forrest instead found a crossing over the Duck River four miles upstream. Spearheaded by Col. Robert Minty's Federal cavalry brigade, the Union horsemen quickly overwhelmed Wheeler's perimeter defense and charged hell-for-leather through the streets of Shelbyville in an effort to capture the bridge at the southern end of town. The Rebel cavalry was overwhelmed, losing 400 men in the action, with Wheeler himself nearly captured. The entire affair was but another sticking point in the troubled relationship between the two cavalry commanders. Forrest finally reached Tullahoma on the 28th.[24]

Leading elements of the Union army might have reached Manchester by the 27th, but the bulk of the XIV and XXI Corps was still on the march. Ascending the heights to reach the Cumberland Plateau proved more difficult than anyone imagined. Brig. Gen. Thomas J. Wood, commanding the First Division, XXI Corps, recorded the details. His division did not start its climb until 2:00 p.m. on the 27th, having already been detained forty-eight hours waiting for other Federals to clear the road. It took eleven hours to move the division up the steep grade, and Wood had to stop four miles short of Manchester on the afternoon of the 28th to let his exhausted men rest. "It has scarcely ever been my ill-fortune in eighteen years of active service . . . to have to pass over so bad a road," he wrote.[25]

The rest of the Federal army followed. Rosecrans ordered McCook's XX Corps to move back though Liberty Gap and, via Hoover's Gap, join the rest of the army at Manchester. Mitchell's First Division of the Cavalry Corps, still reinforced by Minty's troopers, attacked Shelbyville on the 27th, routing Wheeler and forcing Forrest into his detour, but the Yankees occupied the town and did not pursue south of the Duck River.

It had been a grueling two days for both armies.

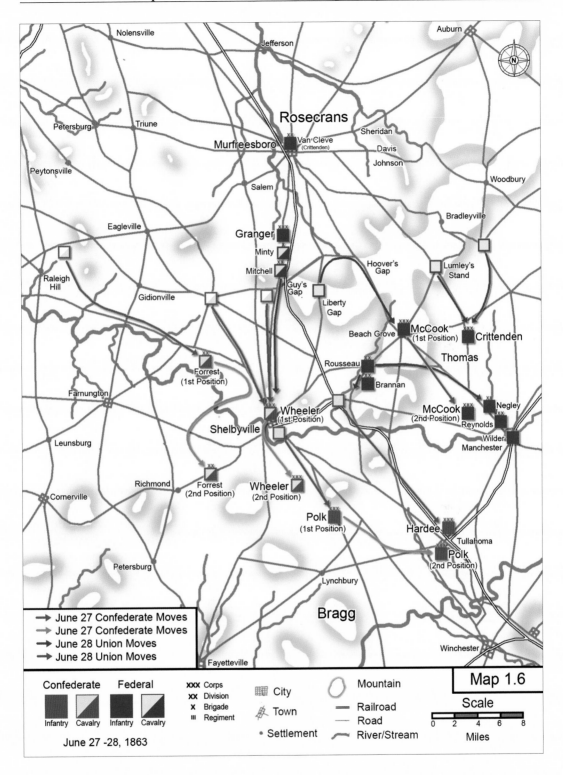

Map 1.6

Scale

June 27 -28, 1863

1.7 Bragg Escapes Across the Elk River (June 29-July 1)

Bragg intended to give battle at Tullahoma. Liddell reached the village after bringing up the rearguard of Pat Cleburne's Division and called on Bragg. Liddell emerged from the meeting completely flummoxed. As badly outnumbered as the Army of Tennessee was, concluded Liddell, Tullahoma "offered no natural advantages . . . for a weak force to contend with a strong one."[26] Bragg's principal lieutenants, Polk and Hardee, offered mixed opinions. Polk believed the army should retreat at once, before the Federals repeated their outflanking maneuver and cut the Rebels off from Chattanooga. Hardee adopted a more cautious wait-and-see posture. For the Confederate rank and file, June 29 offered a day of needed rest.

Despite the success of the campaign thus far, Rosecrans was frustrated that the Rebel army had somehow managed to reach the defensive works around Tullahoma ahead of his own men.[27] His intention was not just to force Bragg to abandon the Shelbyville defenses and retreat, but to cut off the Rebel army and bring it to battle in circumstances favorable to the Federals. Rosecrans was not inclined to launch a frontal attack against the Tullahoma lines. Instead, he organized his three corps carefully and began a cautious advance on the town from the east while Wilder's mounted infantry embarked on yet another expedition, this one to Decherd, Tennessee, to wreck the rail line there.

Wilder reached and damaged Decherd on June 29 after a difficult crossing of the swollen Elk River. Deep in enemy territory and pursued by Rebel horsemen, Wilder rode on to University Place and finally returned to Manchester on July 1, his command exhausted but without having sustained any losses.[28] While Wilder was occupying his enemy's attention, Rosecrans was shifting troops for another flanking march around Bragg's rear.

Wilder's raid did not inflict any lasting damage, but it did convince Bragg that the Army of Tennessee was vulnerable at Tullahoma. On June 30, with Rosecrans again threatening to move around his right flank, Bragg ordered a retreat eight miles south behind the Elk River. By now, the Confederate command was in disarray.

Bragg was no longer consulting his corps commanders. He also appeared dazed by the Union maneuvers: halting, preparing to fight, and then within hours ordering a new retreat. Finally, on July 2, Bragg ordered the entire army back to Chattanooga.

Bragg had escaped Rosecrans' trap, but at the expense of demoralizing his army and surrendering all of Middle Tennessee to the Union.[29]

The rest of July and most of August were slow months for the Federals. The Tullahoma advance pushed the Army of the Cumberland well beyond normal operating range of its railhead at Murfreesboro. With Bragg in retreat to Chattanooga, Rosecrans set his engineers to restoring track, repairing bridges, and creating the depots he would need for the next campaign. The task was daunting. The Elk River Bridge, for example, had been destroyed down to its stone abutments; the 500-foot wooden span had to be reconstructed, and new track put down. The bridge was finished in just five days, but there were more bridges and more miles to repair before the Federals reached the banks of the Tennessee River.

Once there, Rosecrans had to stockpile supplies for his next operation. This task was complicated because he had to both feed his army and build up a surplus, all over a single track running southeast from Nashville. The Federals had little option but to halt for the summer.

The Army of Tennessee also needed a respite. Desertions spiked when the army retreated and all but abandoned the state to Federal occupation. Command problems increased. In mid-July, Gen. Hardee transferred to Mississippi, preferring to take command of the paroled remnants of Gen. John Pemberton's surrendered Vicksburg army than continue serving under the despised Braxton Bragg. Many other officers voiced their growing frustration at Bragg's apparent indecisiveness. Hardee's replacement, Lt. Gen. Daniel H. Hill, was shocked at Bragg's haggard, careworn appearance. Gen. Thomas C. Hindman arrived at this time to replace division commander Jones M. Withers in Polk's Corps, whose failing health made it difficult for him to cope with life in the field.

The Southern army needed time to recover from its latest defeat as it dug in and prepared to defend Chattanooga.

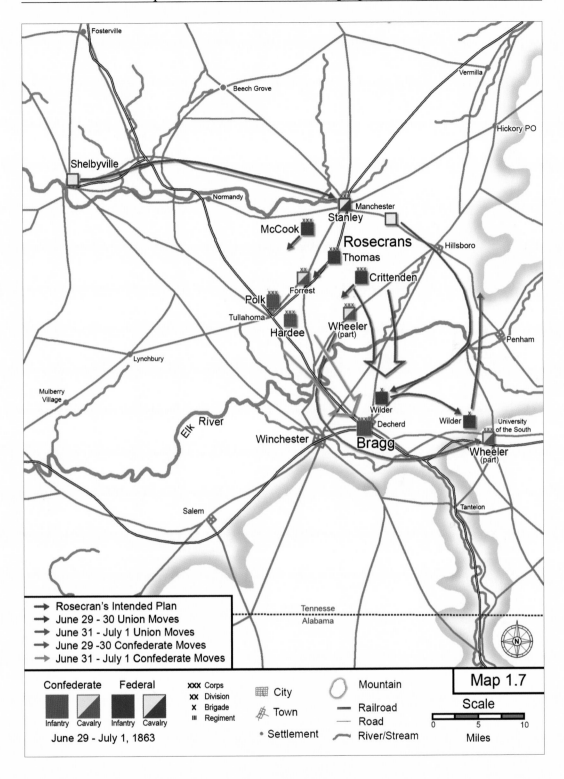

Legend:
→ Rosecran's Intended Plan
→ June 29 - 30 Union Moves
→ June 31 - July 1 Union Moves
→ June 29 -30 Confederate Moves
→ June 31 - July 1 Confederate Moves

Confederate   Federal

xxx Corps
xx Division
x Brigade
III Regiment

Infantry   Cavalry   Infantry   Cavalry
June 29 - July 1, 1863

City
Town
Settlement

Mountain
Railroad
Road
River/Stream

Map 1.7

Scale
0   5   10
Miles

Map Set 2: William Rosecrans Crosses the Tennessee
(August 29 – September 18)

Map 2.1: Union Plans

Despite a few limited forays across the Tennessee River in the last half of August 1863, the Army of the Cumberland's main offensive did not commence until the end of the month.

The two previous months had been largely devoted to stockpiling supplies and arranging the complicated logistics that Maj. Gen. William S. Rosecrans' 70,000 men would require to maneuver Gen. Braxton Bragg's Confederate Army of Tennessee out of Chattanooga. The rail line had been restored through Stevenson and as far as Bridgeport, Alabama. Both towns became supply depots for the Federal army. On the 16th of August Rosecrans also began moving troops closer to the north bank of the river. Full-scale crossings would begin on the 29th.[1]

Two divisions of Maj. Gen. Alexander McCook's XX Corps were ordered to cross at Caperton's Ferry, near Stevenson, and another at Bridgeport. Brig. Gen. Jefferson C. Davis' First Division and Maj. Gen. Richard W. Johnson's Second Division were assigned the Caperton's Ferry site. Davis' mission was to immediately climb Sand Mountain and clear that dominating height, while Johnson's men moved north along the river and established contact with Maj. Gen. Phil Sheridan's Third Division, spearheading the Bridgeport crossing. Sheridan's instructions were to secure Trenton, Georgia, on the far side of Sand Mountain.[2]

Maj. Gen. George H. Thomas' XIV Corps was slated for three crossing sites. Brig. Gen. Absalom Baird's First Division would support Sheridan at Bridgeport. Brig. Gen. John M. Brannan's Third Division would cross at the mouth of Battle Creek, moving up through Taylor's store while Maj. Gen. Joseph J. Reynolds' Fourth Division crossed at Shellmound, with both commands joining the general move to Trenton. Maj. Gen. James S. Negley's Second Division, camped near Stevenson, would wait for the other various

Union columns to clear the bridges before it crossed.[3]

Maj. Gen. Thomas L. Crittenden's XXI Corps had a dual mission. Two of its infantry brigades, a cavalry brigade, and one of mounted infantry had already crossed Walden's Ridge and, as early as August 22, were dropping artillery fire in Chattanooga. These four brigades were intended to deceive Bragg into thinking they presaged a major crossing of the river upstream from the city. In the meantime, the bulk of Crittenden's three divisions were to move south through the Sequatchie Valley to Jasper, Tennessee, and from there follow the XIV Corps across the river. With Walden's Ridge in Union hands, the XXI Corps' movements would be concealed from Confederate observers.[4]

The Union Cavalry Corps did not lead the move across the river. Rosecrans elected instead to get as much infantry across as possible during those critical first few days before Bragg could react. The cavalry would instead follow the XX Corps and cross at Caperton's when the traffic allowed. The corps trains would follow their respective commands, with the cavalry protecting them and the army trains during this initial phase of operations. The mounted troops would also be expected to escort supply wagons to and from the primary depots as the army moved deeper into Georgia, securing them from guerrillas or raiding Rebel cavalry.

Nor would the critical depots of Bridgeport and Stevenson be left unguarded. Once the first line infantry and cavalry was across, Rosecrans intended to bring up elements of Maj. Gen. Gordon W. Granger's Reserve Corps to hold these critical points. More of Granger's men could be brought forward as needed as the Federals advanced, precluding the need to detach elements from the main body to guard rear areas.[5]

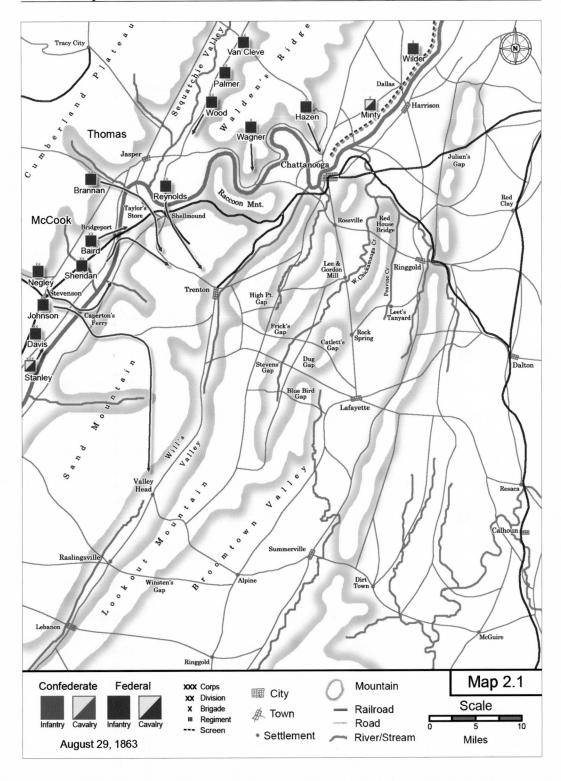

Map 2.1

Confederate   Federal

Infantry Cavalry Infantry Cavalry

xxx Corps
xx Division
x Brigade
lll Regiment
--- Screen

City
Town
Settlement

Mountain
Railroad
Road
River/Stream

Scale

0   5   10
Miles

August 29, 1863

Map 2.2: Confederate Reactions (8/29 to 9/4/63)

Braxton Bragg stationed the bulk of his army in and around Chattanooga, with his cavalry spread in a wide net. With two separate cavalry corps (nearly 16,000 troopers), Bragg could station one corps on each flank and cover a vast amount of territory. His patrols ran from Kingston, Tennessee, as far south as Gadsden Alabama, a front stretching more than 150 miles. The authorities in Richmond had promised him reinforcements from other theaters, but they were not yet on their way to him. At this stage of the campaign, with fewer than 50,000 men, Bragg was substantially outnumbered.

Union activity picked up in earnest in mid-August. On August 21, Union troops appeared opposite Chattanooga (see Map 2.1) and opened fire in a move that took the Confederates completely by surprise.[6] That same day, Rebel Maj. Gen. Simon B. Buckner, commanding at Knoxville, Tennessee, reported that Union Maj. Gen. Ambrose Burnside was advancing on that city and that he would have to move to join Bragg.[7] Bragg did not believe that Rosecrans would "sever himself from Burnside," so Federal activity upstream came as no surprise to him.[8]

Rebel infantry watched the crossings from the mouth of the Hiawassee to Shellmound. Maj. Gen. Joseph Wheeler's cavalry was tasked with patrolling the river from Shellmound to Gadsden, including the critical sites of Bridgeport and Caperton's Ferry. A native of Augusta, Georgia, Wheeler graduated from West Point in 1859 and was commissioned a brevet second lieutenant in the 1st U. S. Dragoons. He resigned shortly after Fort Sumter and threw his lot in with the Confederacy. After service along the Gulf coast, Wheeler moved north and engaged in his first significant combat during the Shiloh campaign in April of 1862, where he demonstrated bravery and a dashing spirit. He later clashed with Gen. Forrest, and the two men grew to dislike one another.

Despite orders to watch the important river crossings, Wheeler left only two regiments to patrol the waterway, and only one of these, Col. William N. Estes' 3rd Confederate, was stationed opposite the main Federal thrust.[9] Wheeler

carelessly sent the bulk of his men to rest camps far from the scene of any potential action.

On August 29, when Rosecrans began his main crossings downstream, Bragg had little word of the size or scope of these movements. Still wedded to the idea that Rosecrans would maintain a connection with Burnside, he dismissed the downstream efforts as a feint.[10] On the 30th, Bragg discovered the extent of Wheeler's mistaken deployments and ordered him to move his whole force back to the army, but even those instructions suggest where Bragg's attention was focused. Wheeler and Brig. Gen. John A. Wharton's large division reinforced Lt. Gen. Daniel H. Hill's Corps upstream; only Brig. Gen. William T. Martin's small 2,500-man division was sent to watch the downstream movements.[11]

Because both cavalry divisions were two days' ride away, Wheeler sent the 3rd Alabama ahead in a forced ride, but it would not arrive at Trenton until the 31st. By then, Estes' 3rd Confederate had been badly scattered and Sand Mountain was in enemy hands, allowing the Union troops to screen Rosecrans' movements.[12] When he finally realized that a major Federal movement was underway, Bragg changed Wheeler's orders, sending his full corps to LaFayette, Georgia, which it would not reach until September 2.[13] Rosecrans' thrust across the river had taken Bragg completely by surprise.

By September 2, Bragg grasped Rosecrans' intentions downstream, but he was not yet ready to give up on operations north of Chattanooga. On September 3, with Buckner's command fast approaching from Knoxville, Hill proposed that the Confederates cross the Tennessee and launch their own attack against the Federal diversionary force. Cavalryman Nathan B. Forrest supported the plan. Bragg briefly entertained the idea, but by this time events were moving swiftly beyond his control.[14]

Bragg also received reports on September 3 that placed Union troops in Will's Valley, with rumors noting enemy scouts as far east as Summerville, Georgia. If true, Rosecrans might be in position to cut the Western and Atlantic Railroad, which served as Bragg's supply line running north from Atlanta. What to do?

Bragg decided to let Martin's cavalrymen hold at LaFayette. Wheeler, with Wharton's cavalry division, would watch Summerville.[15]

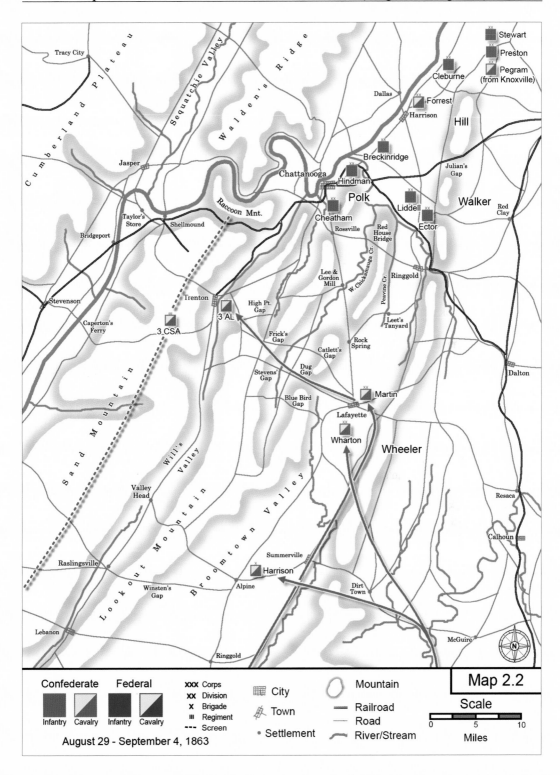

Stewart

Preston

Pegram
(from Knoxville)

Cleburne

Forrest

Dallas

Harrison

Hill

Breckinridge

Julian's
Gap

Chattanooga

Hindman

Polk

Walker

Liddell

Red
Clay

Cheatham

Rossville

Red
House
Bridge

Ector

Jasper

Tracy City

Sequatchie Valley

Walden's Ridge

Cumberland Plateau

Taylor's
Store

Shellmound

Raccoon Mnt.

Bridgeport

Stevenson

Caperton's
Ferry

3 CSA

Trenton

3 AL

High Pt.
Gap

Lee &
Gordon
Mill

W. Chickamauga Cr.

Peavine Cr.

Ringgold

Frick's
Gap

Leet's
Tanyard

Catlett's
Gap

Rock
Spring

Dalton

Dug
Gap

Stevens'
Gap

Blue Bird
Gap

Martin

Lafayette

Wharton

Wheeler

Sand Mountain

Will's Valley

Valley
Head

Lookout Mountain

Broomtown Valley

Resaca

Calhoun

Raslingsville

Winsten's
Gap

Alpine

Summerville

Harrison

Dirt
Town

Lebanon

McGuire

Ringgold

N

Confederate		Federal		
Infantry	Cavalry	Infantry	Cavalry	

XXX Corps
XX Division
X Brigade
III Regiment
--- Screen

City
Town
• Settlement

Mountain
Railroad
Road
River/Stream

Map 2.2

Scale

0   5   10
Miles

August 29 - September 4, 1863

Map 2.3: Bragg Outflanked

By September 5, Rosecrans' initial move to get the Army of the Cumberland across the Tennessee River safely before Bragg could react was a compete success. Firmly established in Will's Valley, the Federals could now begin a three-pronged advance eastward to either trap the Confederates inside Chattanooga or fall upon a divided enemy as Bragg retreated southward.

While opportunity beckoned, there were also risks: the Federals were scattered across heavy terrain on a broad front some forty miles wide, making coordination between the advancing prongs very difficult.

The most exposed of these columns was Alexander McCook's, concentrating at Valley Head. Two of McCook's XX Corps divisions and Maj. Gen. David S. Stanley's Cavalry Corps were gathered there. One of the fourteen "Fighting McCook's" from Ohio (and the highest ranking of them all), Alexander McCook was a graduate of West Point (1852), a veteran of the 3rd U. S. Infantry, and a former instructor of tactics at his alma mater. He knew enough about military affairs to be worried about pressing on aggressively without Sheridan's Third Division, which was just reaching Trenton on September 5 with the corps trains in tow. It would take several more days before Sheridan joined the corps at Valley Head.[16] Crossing Lookout Mountain (the next natural obstacle) would be a major undertaking, and both McCook and Stanley were reluctant to push too far forward too soon. Stanley was also ill, which may have compounded his caution. Ill or not, by September 7 Rosecrans was vigorously prodding both commanders to move more aggressively.[17]

Rosecrans and the other two corps were clustered around Trenton. George Thomas' XIV Corps was ordered to move directly across Lookout Mountain to LaFayette. By September 7, James Negley's division was atop the prominent mountain near Stevens Gap, with Baird's men in support.[18] All three of Crittenden's XXI Corps divisions were moving on Chattanooga directly, northeast of Trenton, with orders to seize the city should Bragg abandon it.[19]

Bragg, meanwhile, was growing increasingly anxious. The long mountain ridges shielded Union movements, and his cavalry was not providing him with adequate intelligence. Daniel H. Hill described the effect on Bragg as being "bewildered by the 'popping out of the rats from so many holes.'"[20]

Joe Wheeler was especially troublesome. Each of his cavalry divisions opposed a prong of the Union advance, but none controlled the gaps cutting through Lookout Mountain. As a result, Wheeler could not provide his commanding general with detailed information on the Union movements. In frustration, Bragg ordered Wheeler to find out what was occurring in Will's Valley "even at the sacrifice of troops." Wheeler flatly refused.[21]

With unconfirmed reports that there might be an entire Federal corps at Valley Head, Bragg could not afford to ignore the threat. His army was still concentrated around Chattanooga, now reinforced by Simon Buckner's men and also Maj. Gen. William H. T. Walker's large division from Mississippi. But it was becoming clear that the city could easily become a trap. On September 6, Bragg issued a circular alerting the army to an impending movement south. He also ordered Forrest, whose troopers were still watching the river north of town, to take "Dibrell's Brigade and such other cavalry as he [Forrest] may deem necessary" and move south, leading this new advance.[22] If Wheeler couldn't get the job done, perhaps Forrest could.

Bragg put his plans in motion on the night of September 7. Hill led the march to LaFayette, followed by Polk, Walker, and then Buckner.[23] Chattanooga would be abandoned to the Federals without a fight.

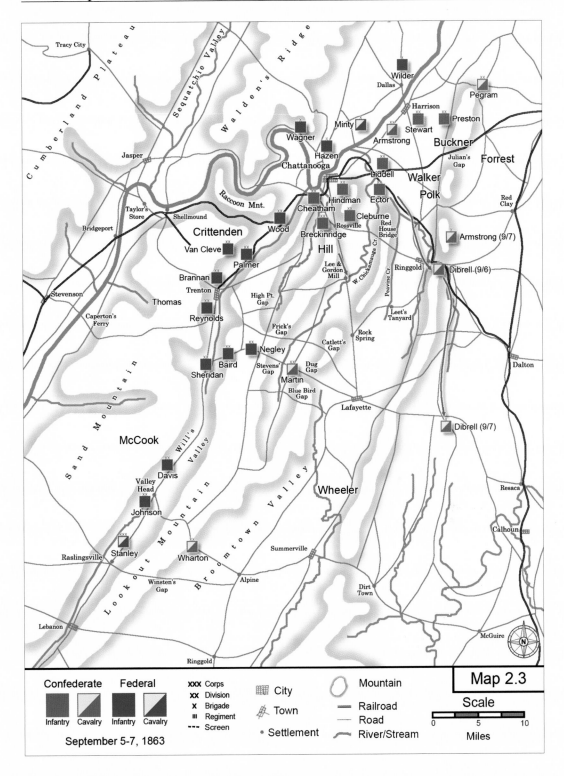

Map 2.3

Map 2.4: Chattanooga Falls (9/8 – 9/9)

By the morning of September 8, Chattanooga was almost free of Confederates. Only one cavalry regiment, Col. Edmund W. Rucker's Legion of Brig. Gen. John Pegram's Brigade remained in the city, while a 75-man detachment from the 3rd Alabama Cavalry clung to Lookout Mountain.[24] A Federal patrol from the 92nd Illinois Mounted Infantry reported these facts up the chain of command. Rosecrans ordered Crittenden's XXI Corps to seize the city the next morning.[25]

Kentucky native Tom Crittenden was the son of United States Senator John J. Crittenden, the brother of Rebel Gen. George B. Crittenden, and the first cousin of Gen. Thomas T. Crittenden. A pre-war attorney, Thomas enlisted during the Mexican War and served as an aide for Zachary Taylor. When the Civil War broke out, the Kentuckian remained with the Union, led a division at Shiloh in Gen. Don C. Buell's Army of the Ohio, and was promoted the major general a couple months later. Now in command of a corps, he was more than pleased to have the honor of marching the first troops into the important city of Chattanooga.

Plenty of other Federals were also stirring on the 8th. Negley's division of the XIV Corps, now leading Thomas' column, pushed its way across Lookout Mountain to Cooper's and Stephen's gaps. From the mountain's summit, they had a clear view of Bragg's columns kicking up immense dust clouds in the valley below as they marched toward LaFayette.[26] Thomas' other divisions, still marking time near Trenton, prepared to follow Negley and support the Federal advance on LaFayette.

Another twenty miles to the south, McCook's command was stirring. Energized by Rosecrans' prodding, Stanley sent Brig. Gen. George Crook's cavalry division across Lookout Mountain to drive off the Rebels and seize Alpine. By noon, despite some sharp skirmishing and a little axe-work required to clear trees felled by the enemy, the Federal cavalry had driven Wharton's Confederate troopers back nearly to Summerville.[27]

By nightfall on the 8th, the last units of the Army of Tennessee were straggling into their new camps. Bragg's infantry halted on a line running from LaFayette north as far as Lee and Gordon's Mills, the site of Gen Leonidas Polk's Corps. Wheeler's cavalry continued to oppose Union threats developing from the south and west.

Forrest had only officially been made a corps commander five days earlier on September 3, when the two mounted brigades of Simon Buckner's command were combined into a new division and assigned to him.[28] This new division was given to John Pegram, the senior brigadier. Pegram's Brigade was given to Brig. Gen. Henry B. Davidson, but Davidson would not arrive to assume his new position for two more weeks, leaving Pegram to handle both brigade and divisional command for the time being.

Pegram's other brigade was commanded by Col. John Scott. As recently as last spring Pegram arrested Scott for insubordination and the incident still rankled with both men.[29] Accordingly, Pegram led his old command and paid little attention to Scott. Now both brigades were guarding the retreat, with Scott at Graysville, Tennessee, and Pegram deployed between Rossville and Ringgold, Georgia. Polk's command at Lee and Gordon's Mills had no cavalry screen at all. Upon receipt of Bragg's orders of September 7 to go south, Forrest took his old division, now under Brig. Gen. Frank Armstrong, and hurried off without giving much thought to Pegram, the other half of his new corps. With Pegram under pressure, Bragg ordered Forrest back north to help screen the retreat. Forrest hurried back to Dalton, intending to establish his corps headquarters there.[30]

The next day, September 9, Chattanooga officially fell into Union hands. The transfer of ownership was signified by the fluttering of the 92nd Illinois' flag atop the Crutchfield House, the finest hotel in town.[31] Most of Rosecrans' diversionary force—the brigades of Brig. Gens. William B. Hazen, George D. Wagner, and Col. John T. Wilder—crossed into the city as well, linking up with Brig. Gen. Thomas J. Wood's division of the XXI Corps.

At the other end of Rosecrans' operational line, McCook and Stanley continued to advance, emboldened by their easy success against Wharton's troopers the previous day. Stanley sent each of his cavalry divisions on a parallel course toward LaFayette, while Davis' infantry division moved up to Alpine.[32]

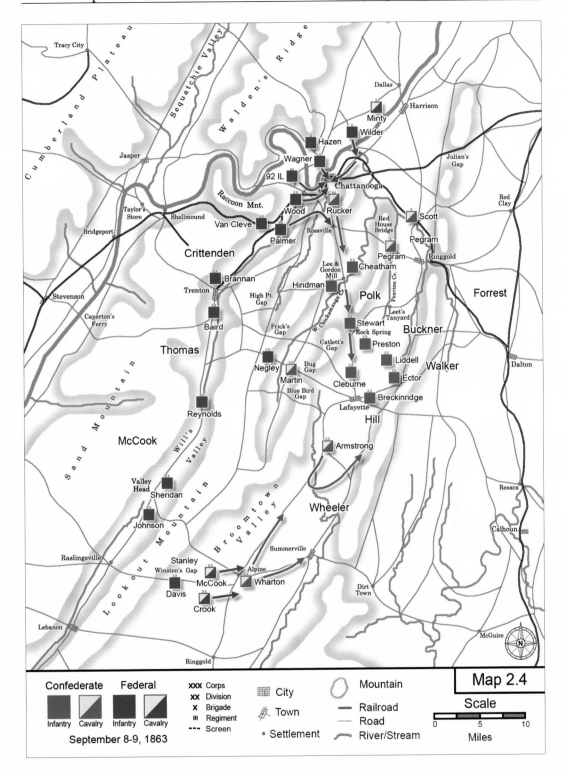

Map 2.4

Map 2.5: Bragg Counterattacks (9/10 – 9/11)

By the morning of September 10, Rosecrans was almost euphoric. Chattanooga, a logistical hub and one of the most important cities in the South, had fallen with barely a shot fired and Bragg appeared to be in full retreat. William B. Hazen, leading the forces deployed to the north bank of the river, thought that Rosecrans now "expected to drive Bragg into the sea."[33] Brimming with optimism, the Union commander intended to keep up the pressure.

His next objective was LaFayette. By seizing it, Rosecrans could reunite his scattered columns and advance east toward Dalton and Resaca, or southeast toward Rome. To secure his rear without detaching troops from the main army, he had ordered Granger to bring up all the men that could be spared from the Reserve Corps. By September 11, the two brigades of Brig. Gen. James B. Steedman's First Division and Col. Daniel McCook's Second Brigade of the Second Division were concentrated at Bridgeport.[34]

Crittenden's XXI Corps advanced on two fronts. Maj. Gen. John M. Palmer's division continued toward Ringgold. When Bragg ordered Polk to abandon Lee and Gordon's Mills late on September 10, Tom Wood's division occupied that location.[35] Wagner's infantry and Minty's cavalry brigades remained behind to garrison Chattanooga. On September 10, Palmer's leading brigade clashed with some of Forrest's men at Graysville, coming off the worse for the encounter. The next day, reinforced by Wilder's mounted infantry and Brig. Gen. Horatio Van Cleve's division, the Federals swept into Ringgold, with Wilder's men driving the Rebels as far as Tunnel Hill. However, the farther south his men moved—the country was rough and wooded—the more isolated Crittenden felt.

McCook's XX Corps continued toward LaFayette from the south, expecting to meet Thomas' XIV Corps there. Still advancing in parallel columns, the Federal cavalry pressed within several miles of the town, which intelligence reports indicated contained a large number of Rebels, and perhaps the bulk of Bragg's army.[36] On September 11, Stanley elected to concentrate his own strength. He moved Crook's division from the Summerville Road to rejoin the main column on the Alpine-LaFayette Road, and advanced more cautiously.

Not fully convinced that Bragg was in full retreat, Thomas also proceeded with caution. On September 10, his advance ground to a halt in front of Dug Gap in Pigeon Mountain, where James Negley's division found stiffening enemy resistance. Calling for support, Negley deployed at Davis' Crossroads and waited for Baird's division to join him.[37]

Thomas was right in his suspicions: Bragg was done retreating. At LaFayette, his Army of Tennessee was concentrated between Rosecrans' widely separated Federals and in perfect position to attack the columns one at a time. Forrest reported that Crittenden's Federals were scattered and vulnerable to the north; Martin's information made it clear that Negley's column was even more exposed just to the west. An opportunity to deliver a crippling blow had fallen into Bragg's lap.[38]

On the night of the 10th, Bragg ordered Maj. Gen. Thomas C. Hindman's Division of Polk's Corps to lead a dawn attack on Negley in conjunction with Maj. Gen. Patrick R. Cleburne's Division of D. H. Hill's Corps, the whole supported by Buckner's Corps (Map 2.7). Bragg, with Hill and Cleburne, waited in vain for Hindman's attack. By the time the Confederates finally converged on Davis' Crossroads late on the 11th, Negley and Baird had slipped away. Instead of a crushing blow, only a brief sputtering rearguard action ensued (see Map 2.7 for more details). Understandably, Bragg was furious by the breakdown in command.[39]

Several reasons explain this failure. First, most of Bragg's key general officers had little experience working together. Buckner, Hindman, and Hill had only recently joined the army, and all three had transferred in from other theaters. Next, Bragg was not a popular commander and was often quick to find fault with his subordinates. His tendency to come down hard induced caution among his officers, which partially explains Hindman's reluctance to act decisively. Finally, Bragg's orders contained just enough leeway to create a lingering uncertainty among his key subordinates.

There would be time for repercussions and recriminations later. Already contemplating another attack, Bragg turned his attention northward.

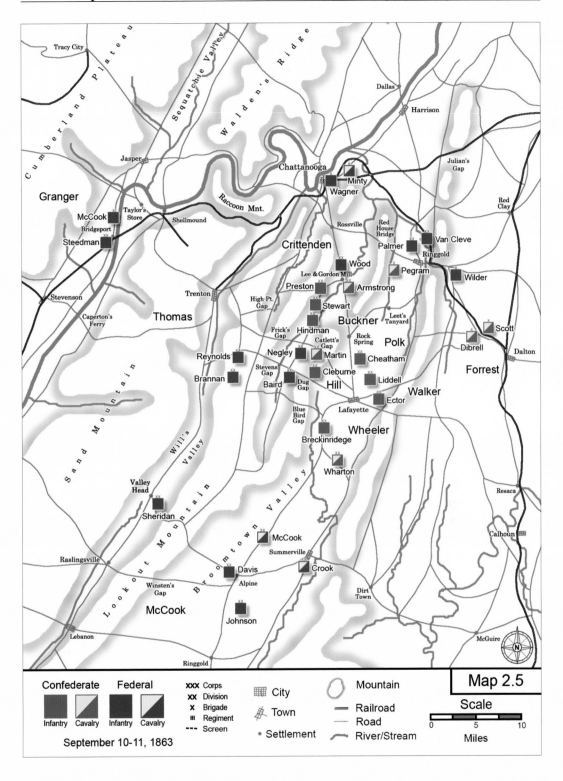

Tracy City

Sequatchie Valley

Walden's Ridge

Dallas

Harrison

Cumberland Plateau

Jasper

Chattanooga

Minty

Wagner

Julian's Gap

Granger

McCook

Taylor's Store

Bridgeport

Shellmound

Raccoon Mnt.

Red Clay

Rossville

Red House Bridge

Van Cleve

Steedman

Crittenden

Palmer

Ringgold

Stevenson

Trenton

Wood

Pegram

Wilder

Lee & Gordon Mill

Caperton's Ferry

Thomas

High Pt. Gap

Preston

Stewart

Armstrong

Leet's Tanyard

Buckner

Scott

Sand Mountain

Frick's Gap

Hindman

Catlett's Gap

Rock Spring

Polk

Dibrell

Dalton

Reynolds

Negley

Martin

Cheatham

Forrest

Brannan

Stevens Gap

Baird

Dug Gap

Cleburne

Liddell

Hill

Will's Valley

Blue Bird Gap

Lafayette

Ector

Walker

Wheeler

Breckinridege

Valley Head

Sheridan

Wharton

Resaca

Lookout Mountain

Broomtown Valley

Raslingsville

McCook

Summerville

Calhoun

Davis

Alpine

Crook

Dirt Town

Winsten's Gap

McCook

Johnson

Lebanon

McGuire

N

Ringgold

Confederate		Federal		
Infantry	Cavalry	Infantry	Cavalry	

September 10-11, 1863

xxx Corps
xx Division
x Brigade
III Regiment
--- Screen

City
Town
Settlement

Mountain
Railroad
Road
River/Stream

Map 2.5

Scale

0   5   10

Miles

Map 2.6: Graysville and Leet's Tanyard (9/10 – 9/12)

Graysville: 9/10

On the morning of September 10, Gen. John Palmer's Second Division of the XXI Corps pushed toward Ringgold after the retreating Rebels.

Leaving Rossville at 6:00 a.m., his leading brigade under Brig. Gen. Charles Cruft advanced cautiously down the Old Federal Road until it reached a range of hills overlooking Pea Vine Creek. Here, Cruft and Palmer had a good look at the terrain ahead where the road dipped to cross the stream and then rose to disappear over the next ridge line to the east. Clouds of dust spiraled in the distance, marking the presence of enemy cavalry behind those hills.[40] Borrowing the small Federal mounted force of Palmer's divisional escort—Company C of the 7th Illinois Cavalry, augmented by a company of the 4th Michigan—Cruft added them to the four companies of the 1st Kentucky Infantry and ordered the entire group to conduct a reconnaissance across the creek.

Opposing them were troopers from the 6th Georgia and 6th North Carolina cavalry regiments of Pegram's Brigade, supported by Capt. Gustave Huwald's Georgia Battery.[41] Most of the Rebel troopers fought on foot, but Pegram retained two companies of Georgians as a mounted reserve. Pressing forward aggressively, the Union troopers made a costly mistake when they overlooked the grade of an unfinished railroad bed cutting laterally across the road from the north. Sensing an opportunity, Pegram ordered Col. John R. Hart to attack with the 6th Georgia reserve.[42] The railroad allowed Hart's men to outflank the 1st (Union) Kentucky, routing the Federal advance and sweeping up fifty-eight prisoners to boot.[43]

Forrest arrived just as this action was winding down and watched as the enemy prisoners were herded past him. "He only regretted, in his blunt way, that they had not been killed in the fight," recalled Huwald.[44]

Leet's Tanyard: 9/12

After Graysville, the XXI Corps pressed on, driving the Confederates from Ringgold the next day. By September 12, it was obvious that Bragg was no longer retreating. Crittenden recalled his command to Lee and Gordon's Mills. Covering this movement, Wilder's mounted infantry departed Ringgold that morning, riding southwest toward the crossroads at Leet's Tanyard. Unbeknownst to Wilder, Pegram's Southern cavalry was riding for the same point.

Pegram arrived first and took a mid-morning break. Fodder was gathered and fed to the horses, and some of his men took the chance for laundry or a rare bath in the springs. A patrol was sent out on the road to Ringgold, but no word was sent back that any Federals were in the area. When Pegram's men resumed their march, they discovered why: the entire cavalry patrol had fallen into Union hands, and Pegram's column nearly blundered into an ambush set by Wilder. The Confederates fell back in disorder, pursued aggressively by the 17th Indiana. Pegram detailed the 6th North Carolina and Huwald's artillery to defend a ridge east of the crossroads while the rest of the brigade reformed on a second ridgeline a short distance to the southwest.

Wilder found himself in a bit of a bind. Scott's Rebel brigade reoccupied Ringgold when Wilder left, forcing him to detail the 123rd Illinois to protect his rear. As Pegram's opposition stiffened, Wilder sent the 72nd Indiana to reinforce the pursuing 17th Indiana. The Hoosiers overlapped the Southern line, and four companies of the 72nd flanked the Confederate right.[47] Unable to hold their position, Huwald and the Tar Heels fell back to Pegram's second line.

The Federals aggressively pursued. At the second ridge, Wilder's entire brigade (except for the 123rd Illinois) engaged the enemy. The 72nd attempted to repeat the outflanking move with the same four companies. This time, however, the Southern line was longer and the Hoosiers were repulsed with loss.[48] Still, Wilder's main objective was fulfilled: the Confederates had abandoned the crossroads, allowing his Federals to break contact easily and retreat to the northwest toward Lee and Gordon's Mills.

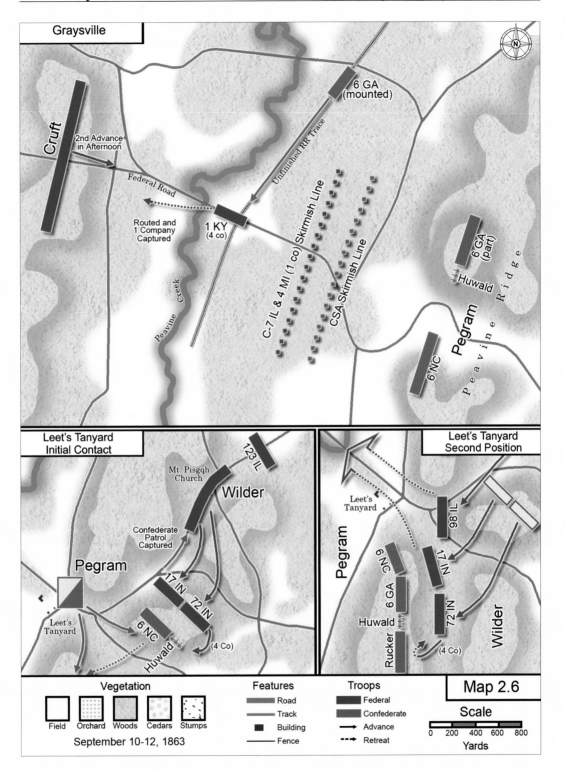

Graysville

6 GA
(mounted)

Cruft

2nd Advance
in Afternoon

Federal Road

Unfinished RR Trace

Routed and
1 Company
Captured

1 KY
(4 co)

Peavine Creek

C-7 IL & 4 MI (1 co) Skirmish Line

CSA Skirmish Line

6 GA
(part)

Huwald

Pegram

6 NC

Peavine Ridge

**Leet's Tanyard
Initial Contact**

123 IL

Mt. Pisgqh
Church

Wilder

Confederate
Patrol
Captured

Pegram

17 IN

72 IN

Leet's
Tanyard

6 NC

Huwald

(4 Co)

**Leet's Tanyard
Second Position**

Leet's
Tanyard

98 IL

17 IN

Pegram

6 NC

6 GA

72 IN

Huwald

Rucker

(4 Co)

Wilder

Map 2.6

Vegetation					Features	Troops	

Field   Orchard   Woods   Cedars   Stumps

September 10-12, 1863

Road
Track
Building
Fence

Federal
Confederate
Advance
Retreat

Scale

0   200   400   600   800

Yards

Map 2.7: Davis' Crossroads
(9/10-9/11)

On September 10, Negley's division advanced into McLemore's Cove toward LaFayette, control of which was vital to Rosecrans' continued offensive plans. Unlike Rosecrans, Thomas was not convinced that Bragg was still retreating, and so did not press Negley into undue haste. Negley's division did not get started until 10:00 a.m.[49] Col. William Sirwell's brigade led the column and, after moving fewer than three miles, met the first enemy skirmishers at Bailey's Crossroads.

Sirwell's men drove Martin's Rebel cavalry across the valley to the foot of Dug Gap. There, with resistance stiffening, Negley ordered a halt. Lt. Col. William Ward, commanding the 37th Indiana, reported that enemy infantry had fortified the gap, and Southern prisoners confirmed the "proximity" of Bragg's army.[50] A friendly local added to Negley's worries by reporting that a Confederate column was approaching from the northeast.[51] To Negley, it appeared as though he had just stuck his head into a trap.

With Rebel columns reportedly closing in from different directions, the Second Division commander cast about for defensible ground and called upon Thomas for reinforcements. Beatty's brigade halted west of Davis' Crossroads to protect the divisional trains. Sirwell, holding an extended line near the Shaw house, was the most exposed. At sundown, Negley ordered Sirwell and Stanley's brigades to "make a strong demonstration" in order to drive the enemy skirmishers back into the gap and mask his own subsequent movements.[52] At 3:00 a.m., both Stanley and Sirwell were quietly withdrawn to a ridge around the Davis house.

Help reached Negley at 8:30 the next morning in the form of two brigades from Baird's First Division, Thomas' XIV Corps. Scribner's brigade replaced Sirwell's command, which allowed Negley to shift Sirwell's troops farther left, while Starkweather's regiments pressed forward to support Stanley.[53] In the meantime, Negley started his trains back toward the passes in Lookout Mountain, hoping to get them away safely before the Confederates decided to attack him. Negley fully expected a serious fight to open at first light, and when it did not he remained puzzled—if grateful—about the lack of Rebel activity. He had no way of knowing the degree of confusion and uncertainty that paralyzed the enemy that morning.

Neither D. H. Hill nor Thomas Hindman was optimistic about an assault. In fact, both men operated under the assumption they were badly outnumbered and were themselves about to be attacked (Map 2.5). Hindman started his march early, and by 6:00 a.m. was within four miles of the Union position. By this time rumors reached him that a Federal force was beyond his left flank. That news, coupled with no word from Hill and concern that his own retreat could be blocked, conspired to stop Hindman in his tracks.[54]

When Hill established contact with Hindman, he had no good news to convey. In response to Bragg's attack order of the night before, Hill offered up a series of reasons why he could not support Hindman. Sensing opportunity slipping through his fingers, Bragg ordered Buckner's Corps (two divisions) forward because it was close at hand. Unfortunately for the Confederates, Buckner's troops would not be up before noon.[55] Half the day was already lost.

Hindman compounded the delay when he decided to let Buckner's men take the lead. Once in front, Buckner deployed Brig. Gen. A. P. Stewart's Division in line, arranged Brig. Gen. William Preston's Division behind Stewart, and sent out reconnaissance parties.[56] This activity consumed more precious time. It was late in the afternoon when Hindman, Buckner, and the other officers met for a council of war. The officers voted to retreat. Only the news that the Federals had beaten them to it and were retreating first changed their minds. At 5:00 p.m. Stewart's Confederates finally advanced on Davis' Crossroads.[57]

Infuriated by the delay and its potential consequences, Gen. Martin—who probably had the clearest picture of the opportunity now lost—dispatched his cavalry to dog the retreating Federals. A volley from the 19th Illinois threw back his advancing troopers.[58] The "battle" of Davis' Crossroads was over.

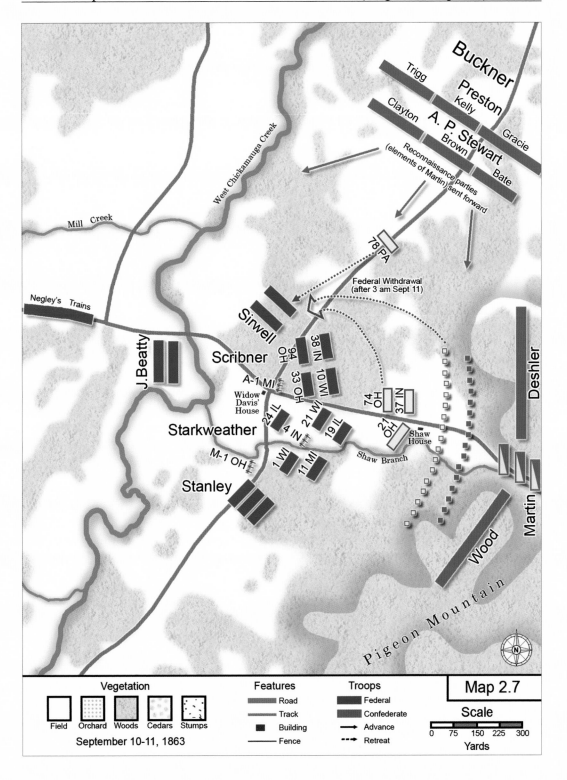

Buckner

Trigg

Preston

Kelly

Clayton

A. P. Stewart

Gracie

Brown

Bate

Reconnaissance parties
(elements of Martin) sent forward

West Chickamauga Creek

Mill Creek

78 PA

Federal Withdrawal
(after 3 am Sept 11)

Negley's Trains

Sirwell

J. Beatty

Scribner

38 IN

94 OH

33 OH

10 WI

A-1 MI

Widow
Davis'
House

74 OH

37 IN

Deshler

Starkweather

24 IL

4 IN

21 IL

19 IL

21 OH

Shaw
House

M-1 OH

1 WI

11 MI

Shaw Branch

Stanley

Martin

Wood

Pigeon Mountain

Vegetation

Field   Orchard   Woods   Cedars   Stumps

September 10-11, 1863

Features

Road

Track

Building

Fence

Troops

Federal

Confederate

Advance

Retreat

Map 2.7

Scale

0   75   150   225   300

Yards

Map 2.8: Bragg Turns North; Rosecrans Reacts (9/12 – 9/13)

The Union army went over to the defensive on September 12. On the XXI Corps front, Crittenden ordered the divisions of Palmer and Van Cleve to abandon Ringgold in order to unite the entire corps at Lee and Gordon's Mills, which was now held by Thomas Wood's division. Wilder's brigade covered the move by striking southwest to Leet's Tanyard. The Federal infantry reached the mills without incident, but Wilder had a spirited skirmish with John Pegram's Confederates at Leet's.[59] Rebuffed at Davis' Crossroads, Thomas' XIV Corps moved to defend the eastern face of Lookout Mountain, behind which the army's trains could escape to Chattanooga if the need arose.[60] Granger's Reserve Corps was shifted farther to the front as Col. McCook's brigade occupied Shellmound.[61]

McCook's XX Corps and the cavalry, far to the south, were slower to get word of the change of attitude. Still expecting to meet Thomas at LaFayette, Crook's cavalry pressed on despite stiffening resistance until, on the afternoon of the 12th, Wheeler's cavalry was replaced by a division of Confederate infantry under John C. Breckinridge, part of D. H. Hill's Corps.[62] Additional Federal probing confirmed that LaFayette was strongly held by the enemy, and Thomas was nowhere to be found. With this discovery, McCook ordered his entire command back over Lookout Mountain to Valley Head.[63] That night a note from Rosecrans, sent via Thomas, confirmed McCook's decision and ordered the XX Corps to rejoin the XIV Corps as soon as possible.

Crittenden's XXI Corps' movements during September 12 did not go unnoticed by the Confederates. Forrest, back with the army after his diversion toward Alpine, reoccupied Ringgold. A dispatch from cavalryman John Pegram, one of Forrest's commanders, reporting a lone Federal division camped near Pea Vine Church stirred Bragg to action.[64] Corps commander Leonidas Polk, reasoned Bragg, should be perfectly situated to take advantage of the widely dispersed Federals if he could be reinforced quickly. In a flurry of orders Bragg directed Maj. Gen. William H. T. Walker's

Reserve Corps and Hindman's Division to rejoin Polk in time for an attack at dawn. "I shall be delighted," Bragg wrote, "to hear of your success."[65]

Polk saw things differently. Crittenden's converging infantry columns could as easily be aimed at him, and for a time he expected to be the target of a Union attack.[66] When Bragg's order arrived, Polk realized it was no longer applicable to the situation in his front. Crittenden's men were now concentrated behind West Chickamauga Creek at Lee and Gordon's Mills, and they outnumbered him. Even the arrival of Walker and Hindman would give Polk only a modest edge in numbers.[67] Polk informed Bragg of these details in an 11:00 p.m. dispatch. In response, Bragg promised additional reinforcements in the form of Buckner's Corps, and impressed upon Polk the need to strike: "[I]t is highly important that your attack in the morning should be quick and decided. Let no time be lost."[68]

Before sunrise on the 13th, Bragg left LaFayette expecting to hear the sounds of Polk's battle. Once again he was disappointed. In fairness to Polk, Bragg's expectations were unrealistic. At dawn, Hindman and Walker were just coming into position, while Buckner's men were only leaving LaFayette, eight miles south.[69] Bragg had asked too much of his men, marching them hither and yon in an effort to catch Rosecrans off balance. Had Polk attacked at first light as ordered, he would have thrown one division against the entire Union XXI Corps, strongly posted behind the Chickamauga waterway.

Bragg could at least take heart that still more reinforcements were on the way. Brig. Gen. Bushrod R. Johnson's Brigade, detached from A. P. Stewart's Division (Buckner's Corps) now occupied Dalton, and the railroad to the south was humming with activity. The leading elements of Brig. Gens. Evander McNair's and John Gregg's brigades from Mississippi were reaching Resaca, Georgia. Better still, thousands of more troops were also on their way from Robert E. Lee's Army of Northern Virginia.[70]

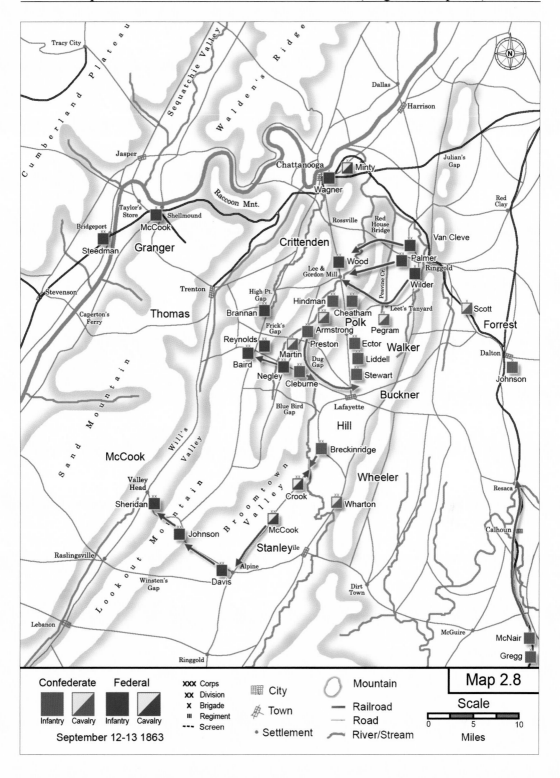

Map 2.8

Map 2.9: The Armies Regroup (9/14-9/17)

Leonidas Polk's aborted attack forced Bragg to reconsider his plans. The Union probe toward LaFayette from the south on September 13 had alarmed the Confederates almost as much as it did McCook's Federals, and even though the Union troops retreated, late on the 13th Bragg ordered Buckner to march south yet again to reinforce John C. Breckinridge's Division; Polk and Walker would follow overnight.[71] By the next day, September 14, Bragg's main force was again concentrated around LaFayette, exhausted by a week of nearly constant marching.

While his men rested, Bragg accumulated information. Early on the morning of the 15th, Wheeler reported that Alpine (beyond Bragg's left) was deserted; McCook had retreated over Lookout Mountain and the Union threat from the south had evaporated.[72] On the same day, a Confederate cavalry patrol to the north confirmed that Rosecrans' Army of the Cumberland and Maj. Gen. Ambrose Burnside's command from eastern Tennessee had not yet affected a juncture.[73] More good news arrived: heavy reinforcements were on their way. James Longstreet's long-anticipated First Corps, troops dispatched from Gen. Lee's Army of Northern Virginia, were beginning to arrive in Atlanta.[74] Bragg directed them north to Resaca.

Although Bragg had paused, Rosecrans could not afford to do the same. Between September 14 and 17, the Federal commander hurried his forces north to close up on Crittenden's XXI Corps. McCook was the farthest away, especially now that McLemore's Cove was no longer occupied by Thomas' troops; he would have to fall back to Valley Head and use Will's Valley.[75] By dint of prodigious marching, McCook's column was out of danger by September 17. All three of his infantry divisions had moved up Lookout Mountain and reentered McLemore's Cove via Steven's Gap to connect with the XIV Corps' right flank. Only a brigade of infantry and cavalry remained at Valley Head with orders to bring up the rear, escorting supply wagons and the sick.

Both Thomas' XIV Corps and Crittenden's XXI Corps remained mostly inactive during these four days. Thomas brought his corps into line on Crittenden's right, watching the crossings of the Chickamauga and waiting for McCook to make contact. Crittenden's three divisions did the same as far north as Lee and Gordon's Mills. There was still a gap between Crittenden's left and the garrison at Chattanooga, however. Rosecrans screened this area with Col. Minty's cavalry brigade, ordered to Pea Vine Valley on the 15th. Wilder's brigade reinforced Minty on the 17th.[76] To backstop this outpost line, Rosecrans also ordered Granger's Reserve Corps to march for Rossville. Also on the 17th, Granger went as far as to order Brig. Gen. James B. Steedman's First Division to make a reconnaissance to Ringgold. The move discovered the enemy in strength.[77]

The growing concentration of troops at Ringgold was central to Bragg's newest plan. If Rosecrans was no longer so widely scattered as to be vulnerable to piecemeal destruction, there was still a chance the Confederates could get between the Union army and Chattanooga, forcing the Federals to either make a harried retreat back over the mountains or be exposed to destruction in McLemore's Cove. Following a late-morning conference with his generals on September 15, Bragg issued Special Orders No. 244, which designated Ringgold as the army's new supply depot and began shifting troops back to the north.[78] Special Orders No. 245 followed the next day, outlining Bragg's intention to bring the army into line facing Rosecrans across the Chickamauga. Bragg briefly suspended this movement in the dark hours of early September 17 when Maj. Osmun Latrobe of Longstreet's staff arrived with the first hard news of that command's imminent arrival.

By noon that day the march was resumed. By nightfall, the three corps of Walker, Buckner, and Polk were arrayed between Rock Springs and Leet's Tanyard. D. H. Hill's Corps was still guarding the approaches to LaFayette, and the force assembling at Ringgold placed Longstreet's Corps well north of Rosecrans' left flank.[79]

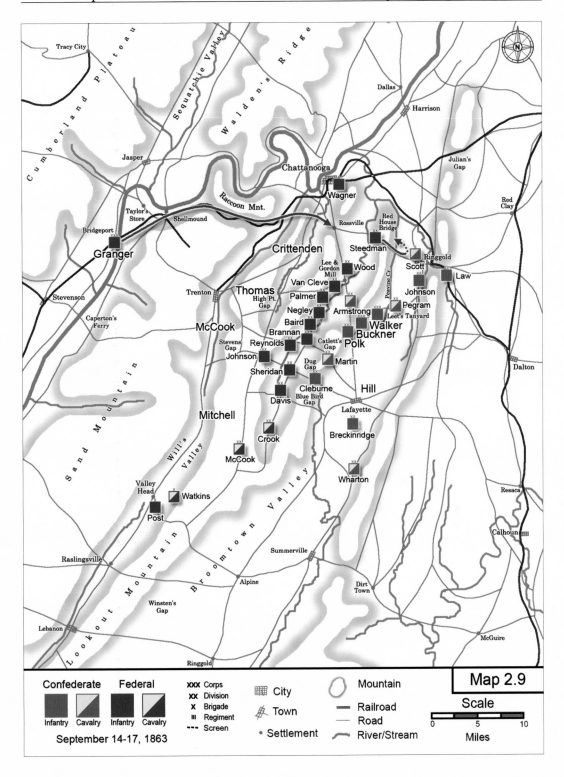

Map 2.9

September 14-17, 1863

Scale

0   5   10
Miles

Map Set 3: Braxton Bragg Strikes Back at Rosecrans
(September 18)

3.1: Confederate Plans and Union Dispositions

Despite the miscarriage of his earlier plans, by September 16 Gen. Braxton Bragg still sought to take the offensive. It would be possible, assuming they moved quickly, for Bragg to insert a large force between Maj. Gen. William Rosecrans' Army of the Cumberland and Chattanooga. Doing so would force Rosecrans to make an unpalatable choice: retreat across the mountains toward Bridgeport and Stevenson, try and force his way through Bragg's men to the relative security of Chattanooga, or retreat south into the wilderness of McLemore's Cove in North Georgia. The Federal army was potentially in great peril.

Freshly reinforced, and with more men still on the way, Bragg also had the resources to commit substantial numbers of men to this plan. Three of his five small infantry corps and Brig. Gen. Nathan B. Forrest's cavalry—in all, 22,000 infantry and 6,500 horsemen—would form the blocking force, maneuvering across West Chickamauga Creek.[1]

Bragg's complicated, multi-stage plan, was as follows: (1) Brig. Gen. Bushrod R. Johnson, commanding a provisional division consisting of his own brigade and the van of the newly arrived Army of Northern Virginia's First Corps, would advance from Ringgold and cross the Chickamauga at Reed's Bridge. Maj. Gen. John B. Hood (of the Army of Northern Virginia) would assume command of this column once he arrived; (2) Johnson (or Hood), along with those additional elements of the First Corps that arrived in time, would sweep southwest toward the LaFayette Road, blocking the way to Chattanooga and moving astride Rosecrans' flank at Lee and Gordon's Mills; (3) Maj. Gen. William H. T. Walker's Reserve Corps, advancing from Leet's Tanyard, would cross at Alexander's Bridge, wait for the First Corps to pass, and then (4) close up behind Johnson to add support to the blocking force; (5) Maj. Gen. Simon B. Buckner's two divisions under Maj. Gen. Alexander P. Stewart

and Brig. Gen. William B. Preston (6) would cross at Thedford's Ford and Dalton's Ford, respectively, to fall in on left flank of the advancing First Corps (7) adding yet more weight to the column. In order to prevent the Federals from reacting to the growing threat, Maj. Gen. Benjamin Cheatham's Division (8) was ordered to move up and support Maj. Gen. Thomas C. Hindman's Division, thereby uniting Lt. Gen. Leonidas Polk's Corps in front of Lee and Gordon's Mills, fixing Rosecrans' attention there. With a 6:00 a.m. start, Bragg expected rapid movement and an early crossing of the Chickamauga, leaving him ample time to cut the Federals off from Chattanooga or launch his own attack.[2]

Forrest's troopers were expected to screen these movements, speeding the infantry across the creek and preventing Union interference. Unfortunately for Bragg's plans, Forrest's troopers were widely scattered. Instead of being able to concentrate both cavalry divisions for the movement, Forrest had only Brig. Gen. John Pegram's Brigade at hand.

Rosecrans was not unaware of the peril, although thus far he and his senior commanders dismissed news of the arrival of Lt. Gen. James Longstreet's men as nothing but unsubstantiated rumor.[3] In an effort to provide some warning of exactly the kind of maneuver Bragg contemplated, Rosecrans placed Brig. Gen. Robert H. G. Minty's cavalry brigade in Pea Vine Valley with instructions to watch Reed's Bridge, while Col. John T. Wilder's powerful brigade of mounted infantry deployed to watch the crossings between Alexander's Bridge and Maj. Gen. Thomas Crittenden's XXI Corps at the Mills. Minty, however, had only three regiments, and Wilder another four—fewer than 3,000 Federal troops directly in the path of Bragg's proposed three-corps juggernaut.

Behind this screen, Rosecrans had only a few scattered forces. Chattanooga was garrisoned by one brigade of infantry, occupying the earthworks recently erected by Bragg's own men. Maj. Gen. Gordon Granger also had three brigades of troops in and around Rossville, defending that gap in Missionary Ridge and with it, the most direct route into Chattanooga. None of these forces, however, were strong enough to materially disrupt Bragg's intentions.

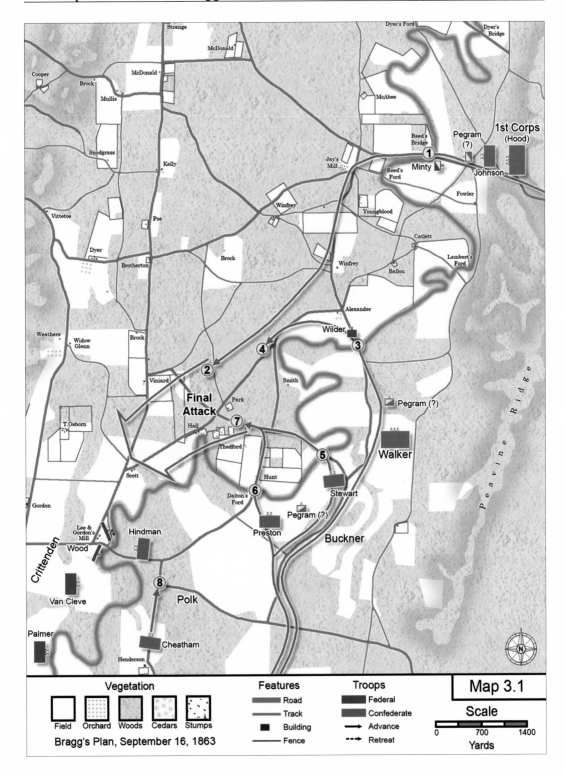

Map 3.1

Bragg's Plan, September 16, 1863

Map 3.2: Reed's Bridge: Morning Phase

On September 15, Minty's Federal cavalry established a camp at Peeler's Mill along Pea Vine Creek, guarding the Ringgold Road. By September 17, as the Confederate force in Ringgold increased daily, Minty prudently withdrew his camp two miles west to Reed's Bridge.[4] From there, he sent out daily patrols to the east and south, alert to an enemy advance. On the 18th, with the Confederates stirring, Minty established an initial defensive line atop Pea Vine Ridge overlooking his former campsite. His force consisted of the 4th Michigan Cavalry, a section of guns from the Chicago Board of Trade Battery, and a battalion of the 4th U.S. The line was reinforced a short time later by an additional battalion of the 7th Pennsylvania Cavalry, just returned from a early morning patrol.[5]

Despite Bragg's intentions for an early start, the Rebel plans misfired almost immediately. Following an outdated order, Bushrod Johnson took the wrong road and had to be rerouted. He did not encounter Minty on Pea Vine Ridge until almost 11:00 a.m., many hours later than Bragg envisioned.[6] Neither Forrest nor any other Rebel cavalry were present, orders to the contrary notwithstanding. Uncertain of the opposition he faced, Johnson halted his division, deployed a Tennessee infantry brigade under Col. John S. Fulton into line of battle, and began to probe the Federal defenses. At this juncture Forrest finally arrived, accompanied by only a handful of troopers. He promptly took charge of the advance.[7] Before long, Confederate infantry began to work around Minty's flanks atop the ridge. (See facing map, first position.)

Just before noon, Minty withdrew to a second position closer to the bridge. Spotting a dust cloud rising to the northeast, he requested additional support from Wilder's brigade upstream at Alexander's Bridge. Minty wanted reinforcements to cover Dyer's Bridge and Red House Bridge to his north. Wilder responded generously, sending the 72nd Indiana, 123rd Illinois, and a section of guns to Minty's aid.[8]

Minty formed his second line carefully. The 4th Michigan covered the road, with the 7th Pennsylvania forming in the open ground just to the south. Two battalions of the 4th U.S. moved into the mixed timber on the Michiganders' left. Half of these commands were dismounted, but the 4th Michigan and the Pennsylvanians each retained at least a squadron on horseback, in reserve. As a final backstop the artillery, supported by the remaining battalion of Regulars, took up position in an orchard just south of the Reed house with their backs to what one soldier described as a "bad ford."[9]

The Confederates took their time crossing the ridge. Leading his detachment and the 17th Tennessee, Forrest swung south, ostensibly in a flanking move, but also with an eye toward striking what Forrest thought was Minty's camp.[10] From atop the ridge Johnson got his first good look at the Federals and realized just how small a force he faced.[11] He brought Brig. Gen. John Gregg's large brigade up on the right, extending Fulton's line and threatening to outflank Minty's position. (See facing map, second position.)

Once Gregg was in place Fulton's three remaining regiments (the 17th was still absent with Forrest) moved out from the gap at the foot of the ridge. The Union artillery immediately opened fire, and the aggressive-minded Minty ordered squadrons from the 4th Michigan and 7th Pennsylvania to deliver what one called "a terrific saber charge."[12] The Federals might have been impressed, but the Confederates were not. Not a single Southern report mentioned the charge as a distinct event or reported losses from it. However, Minty's belligerent posture reinforced Johnson's overall sense of caution. The Rebels took their time forming. Johnson elected to extend his line even more by bringing up Brig. Gen. Evander McNair's command—which was deploying as a reserve behind Fulton and Gregg—on Fulton's left, in lieu of the absent Forrest.

While these events were unfolding, Col. Abram O. Miller of the 72nd Indiana arrived with the reinforcements sent by Wilder. They halted on the west side of the creek and observed the early stages of the fight.[13] Minty, still worried that he would be outflanked from the north and encircled, reiterated the order to cover the two-mile gap between his own line and that of the Union Reserve Corps, which should be holding Red House Bridge.[14]

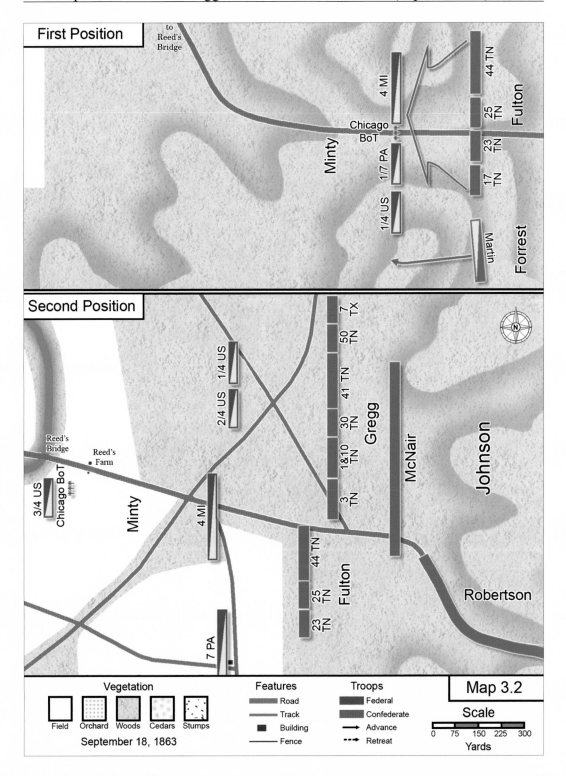

First Position

to Reed's Bridge

4 MI

44 TN

Fulton

Chicago BoT

25 TN

23 TN

17 TN

Minty

1/7 PA

1/4 US

Martin

Forrest

Second Position

7 TX

50 TN

41 TN

1/4 US

2/4 US

Gregg

30 TN

1&10 TN

McNair

Johnson

Reed's Bridge

Reed's Farm

3 TN

3/4 US

Chicago BoT

Minty

4 MI

44 TN

Fulton

25 TN

23 TN

Robertson

7 PA

Vegetation

Field   Orchard   Woods   Cedars   Stumps

September 18, 1863

Features

Road

Track

Building

Fence

Troops

Federal

Confederate

Advance

Retreat

Map 3.2

Scale

0   75   150   225   300

Yards

3.3: Alexander's Bridge

While the morning action was developing east of Reed's Bridge, Confederates also began to make their appearance at Alexander's Bridge. The night before, Col. Wilder established his brigade camps on the high ground around the Alexander house several hundred yards north of the bridge, and posted pickets at the various crossings between there and Lee & Gordon's Mills. Small patrols and foragers ranged farther afield, bringing back warning of approaching Confederates about mid-morning.[15]

This first contact was with some of John Pegram's Confederate cavalry chasing a band of mounted foragers from the 72nd Indiana. Pegram's men rushed the bridge but were driven off by a flurry of rapid Spencer fire. In order to preclude further thrusts, Company A of the 72nd tore up the bridge flooring and threw up a small earthwork in the road about 100 yards to the north.[16] Quiet settled onto the field.

About noon, a more substantial Confederate threat developed. Infantry from Maj. Gen. Walker's Reserve Corps—Brig. Gen. Edward C. Walthall's Mississippians of Brig. Gen. St. John R. Liddell's Division—arrived, triggering another collision with Wilder's Spencer-armed Federals.[17] Walker was an old Army Regular who had been wounded in the Seminole and Mexican conflicts (he was nicknamed "shotpouch" by his comrades for his propensity to collect enemy lead). Liddell and Walthall, by contrast, were not professionals. The former attended West Point for only one year (he was Bragg's plebe classmate) before resigning due to poor grades, while the latter was a promising young Mississippi lawyer. All three, however, were determined to fight for the bridge. Walker's mission was to force the bridge and link up with Johnson's troops, moving southwest from Reed's Bridge. The handful of Federals opposing Walthall suggested that his task should not be a daunting one.

Only three companies of the 72nd Indiana held the creek bank opposite Walthall's advancing brigade, and half of the 98th Illinois was away guarding crossings upstream. Worse still, Wilder had already sent away the better part of two regiments to help Minty farther north at Reed's Bridge. This left him with only the 17th

Indiana, the remaining half of the 98th Illinois, and two-thirds of Lilly's battery.[18] Undeterred by the steep odds, the men of Company A manned their hastily constructed work and prepared to hold off the Mississippians.

Walker and Liddell ordered Walthall to form his five Mississippi regiments in line (34th, 30th, 29th, 27th, and 24th, from left to right) and force a crossing. Things went wrong almost from the start. Walthall's line was disrupted by both the underbrush and the curving nature of the roadway, so that individual regiments reached the creek separately. The creek itself, reported Walthall, "was narrow, but deep, the banks steep and impassable."[19] The bridge, now floorless and swept by Union artillery and small arms fire, proved unusable. Despite their overwhelming numbers, the Confederates found themselves stalemated by the terrain and intrepid defenders.

The Spencer repeaters more than made up for the manpower disparity, their rounds cutting through the Mississippi ranks. Walthall's losses were surprisingly heavy, something Liddell attributed to "the efficiency of this new weapon." He described the Union artillery, however, as "relatively harmless."[20]

Not everything went in favor of the Federals. Confederate skirmishers managed to ford the creek and threatened to rush Company A's breastwork from the rear. Under heavy fire—one Hoosier was hit five times at about thirty yards—the Indianans fell back, shooting down their own horses rather than letting them fall into enemy hands.

At 2:00 p.m. Wilder responded to Walthall's attack by sending the remaining five companies of the 98th forward to reinforce the defense of Alexander's Bridge. The Mississippians lined the bank and traded shots with the well armed Federals while Rebel artillery lining the crest overlooking the creek from the south threw shells toward Wilder's brigade trains. No additional assaults across the creek were launched.

Walker's crossing was by this time hopelessly delayed, and there seemed no way to break the stalemate anytime soon.[21]

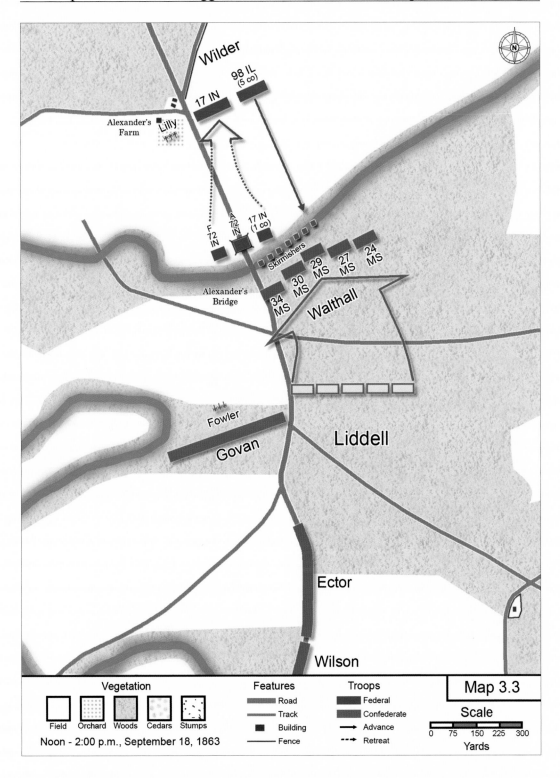

Wilder

98 IL
(5 co)

17 IN

Alexander's
Farm   Lilly

F
72
IN

A
72
IN

17 IN
(1 co)

Skirmishers

29
MS

27
MS

24
MS

30
MS

Alexander's
Bridge

34
MS

Walthall

Fowler

Govan   Liddell

Ector

Wilson

Vegetation					Features	Troops	Map 3.3

Field   Orchard   Woods   Cedars   Stumps

Noon - 2:00 p.m., September 18, 1863

Features
Road
Track
Building
Fence

Troops
Federal
Confederate
Advance
Retreat

Map 3.3

Scale

0   75   150   225   300
Yards

3.4: Reed's Bridge: Afternoon Phase

Despite the fleeting success of his earlier charge, Minty was under no illusions about his ability to hold on west of Reed's Bridge. Bushrod Johnson, still moving with care, deployed three Confederate brigades to face Minty's troopers. The Federals quickly figured out just how outmatched they were. Instead of standing and fighting, Minty intended to delay the Rebels as much as possible. Each time they organized into a line of battle to attack, he gave ground. The time had come to retreat across the creek, moving via the bridge and a couple of fords, to establish a new line on the far side.

This time, retreat was a riskier proposition. The first to fall back was the 4th Michigan, with orders to take up a skirmish line on the far bank and provide covering fire for the rest of the brigade. The first difficulty was the bridge itself, so narrow (and rickety to boot) that each regiment had to cross in column of twos.[22] Once across, the Wolverines dismounted and lined the west bank. The next to move was the artillery, falling back via a nearby ford. Now it was the turn of the Regulars and the 7th Pennsylvania.

Thus far, the Confederates had not significantly interfered with the withdrawal. The 4th U.S.—still divided with two battalions north of the road and one squadron covering the artillery's retreat—broke enemy contact without too much trouble, but as the 7th made for the bridge, the Confederates finally took a hand in affairs. Col. Fulton's three regiments (23th, 25th, and 44th Tennessee—the 17th Tennessee was still with Forrest) rushed for the bridge. Lt. Wirt Davis of the 4th Regulars was alert to the approaching danger. His squadron, which had been covering the artillery, charged the oncoming Confederates and checked their advance. This pause granted the Pennsylvanians enough time to finish crossing the bridge. Davis then ordered his own troopers across, halting briefly on the far bank long enough to rip up the flooring and hurl the planks into the creek, where the wood was carried away downstream.[23] Until new planking could be found, the bridge was unusable. Having made a successful escape, Minty deployed his new line on rising ground about 700 yards behind the creek, pulling his skirmishers back about half that distance.

Directly opposite the bridge, the 23rd Tennessee made another rush for it, followed by the rest of the brigade and the balance of the division (the brigades of Evander McNair, John Gregg, and Jerome Robertson). Heavy ranks of Confederate infantry lined the east bank, firing on the Federals. Capt. William D. Harder of the 23rd Tennessee soon had the bridge re-floored, tearing planks off the Reed house and barn to do so. Forrest rejoined the main attack column at this time. Harder watched admiringly as the cavalry general coolly crossed the newly re-planked bridge to examine Minty's new line.[24]

Here fell one of the battle's civilian casualties. An unknown woman and her children occupied the Reed house. Against his better judgment, Minty did not have her forcibly evacuated, though he did order her to stay inside. As the men of the 23rd Tennessee pounded their way past, she ran out onto the porch cheering, only to be swept away by a burst of canister from a Confederate battery supporting Fulton's advance.[25]

Once again, Johnson looked to flank the Federals. While Fulton's Brigade, including the newly returned 17th Tennessee, crossed at the bridge and squared off against Minty's line, Gregg's Brigade waded the creek downstream and formed on Fulton's right.[26] McNair's regiments fell in behind in support, while Forrest's troopers forded the creek upstream looking for Minty's flank.[27] Robertson's Brigade continued to bring up the rear.

About 3:00 p.m. Johnson received an impatient note from Bragg urging him to hurry across. The Confederate timetable, however, had crumbled beyond repair. Almost immediately after Johnson received the message, Maj. Gen. John B. Hood arrived and assumed overall command.[28] The young major general, his crippled arm still in a sling from his Gettysburg wound, had reached Ringgold that morning ahead of his corps commander James Longstreet. Hood conferred with Johnson for a few minutes and approved his plan to envelop Minty's line, but it was nearly 4:00 p.m. before the Confederates were once again moving forward.

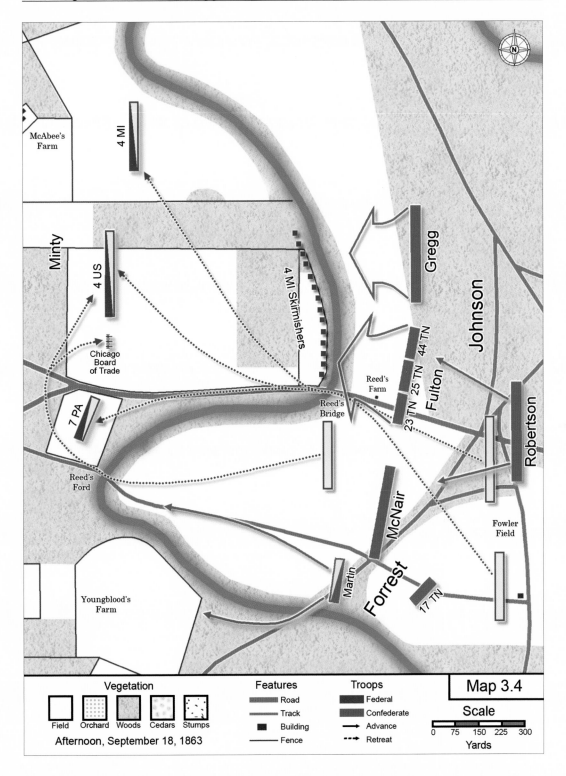

McAbee's Farm

4 MI

Minty

4 US

Chicago
Board
of Trade

7 PA

Reed's
Ford

Youngblood's
Farm

4 MI Skirmishers

Gregg

Johnson

44 TN

25 TN

23 TN

Fulton

Reed's
Farm

Reed's
Bridge

McNair

Robertson

Fowler
Field

Martin

Forrest

17 TN

Vegetation

Field   Orchard   Woods   Cedars   Stumps

Afternoon, September 18, 1863

Features

▨ Road
— Track
■ Building
— Fence

Troops

▨ Federal
▨ Confederate
→ Advance
--▸ Retreat

Map 3.4

Scale

0   75   150   225   300

Yards

3.5: The Federals Retreat

By 4:00 p.m., both Wilder and Minty were more than satisfied with their day's work. Together, their small commands had delayed vastly superior Confederate columns for hours, and by extension, threw the timetable for Braxton Bragg's attack plan off schedule an entire day. But the Federals could not defend every crossing, and likely realized that eventually the Confederates would find a way around them.

Gen. Walker broke the stalemate. Realizing the futility of trying to force a passage at Alexander's Bridge, he moved downstream where Bryam's and Fowler's fords offered access to the Union flank.[29] About 3:00 p.m., as Bushrod Johnson's Confederates were trying to force their way across Reed's Bridge to the north, a local guide led Walthall's Mississippians to Lambert's Ford, where they crossed without trouble.[30] Although not in enough strength to oppose the crossing, Federal scouts sent word to their brigade commander that the enemy had gained his flank. About 4:00 p.m., Wilder ordered his men to "fall back up the creek if possible," intending to withdraw slowly to Crittenden's Union infantry position at Lee and Gordon's Mills. [31] Wilder also sent word of his retreat to Minty.

Minty was about ready to pull out anyway. Johnson's Rebels were obviously preparing to deliver another attack, and for the first time that day, significant numbers of Forrest's cavalry were making their presence felt. Pegram's Brigade, which had begun the day with Gen. Walker, probed Alexander's Bridge early before riding to find Forrest, who was now in the vicinity. It was late by the time Pegram crossed West Chickamauga Creek at Fowler's Ford, but he was now moving up toward Jay's Mill, threatening Minty's rear.[32] His Southern troopers had not yet made contact, but their presence could not be ignored.

This was the deteriorating situation facing Minty when messages from Wilder and Lt. Joseph G. Vale—commanding Minty's baggage train—arrived outlining Wilder's withdrawal.[33] Minty held the line long enough to allow Col. Miller of the 72nd Indiana to be recalled from Dyer's Ford and Red House Bridge before retreating to the LaFayette Road. From that point he could safely move south to join Crittenden, "making a circuit round the Confederates who had crossed near Alexander's Bridge."[34] Miller's retreat was made in some haste, and several men from his column were captured. By 5:00 p.m., the Federals were gone from Johnson's front.[35]

Johnson's (Hood's) Confederates advanced to Jay's Mill, where they were joined by Pegram's troopers. There, Hood and Johnson faced a choice: which road to take? On the right lay the Brotherton Road, angling southwest. Two miles on it struck the LaFayette Road well north of Crittenden's Federals. Straight ahead ran the narrow Jay's Mill Road, which led directly toward the Alexander House where Walker's Rebels were expected to be. Johnson wanted to follow the Brotherton Road, but Hood overruled him. The column would head due south to link up with Walker.[36] Each choice had its own merits and drawbacks. Striking out on the Brotherton Road would have allowed the Confederates to reach—and cut—the LaFayette Road more quickly, while moving south ensured a timelier meeting with Walker. Since all the other Confederate columns would be waiting on Johnson's movement, Hood elected to find Walker first.

The Confederate schedule, however, was already so delayed that speed was now less important. Walker's four brigades were still struggling to cross the creek at Lambert's Ford, which would take most of the night.[37] Gen. Simon Buckner's two divisions had reached their respective crossing sites by mid-afternoon and had engaged in some long range artillery fire, but halted there in accordance with their orders. Buckner's relationship with Bragg was already troubled for a number of reasons, including a lingering resentment over Bragg's assumption of Buckner's own departmental authority after departing Knoxville. Buckner was content to fulfill the letter of his orders and wait for contact with Walker or Johnson—but he was unlikely to push forward aggressively on his own initiative. As a result, one brigade each from Brig. Gen. William Preston's and Maj. Gen. Alexander Stewart's divisions crossed on the 18th; the rest of Buckner's men would not pass over the stream until the next morning.[38]

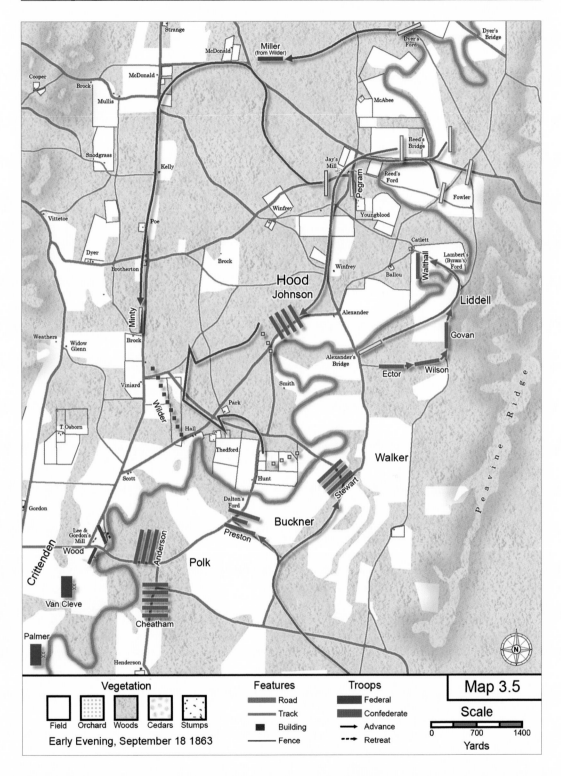

Vegetation

Field Orchard Woods Cedars Stumps

Early Evening, September 18 1863

Features
Road
Track
Building
Fence

Troops
Federal
Confederate
Advance
Retreat

Map 3.5

Scale

0   700   1400
Yards

3.6: Final Clash: Johnson vs. Wilder and Dick

Years later, both Col. Wilder and Gen. Minty claimed the other retreated first, though the issue never really became a serious point of contention between the veterans. In reality, both commands retired about the same time to avoid what they perceived as imminent encirclement. The leading elements of Simon Buckner's Confederate corps, crossing at Dalton's and Thedford's fords, added to Wilder's growing concerns. "Fearing I should be surrounded," he wrote, "[I] moved the command to a ridge in the woods . . . covering three [converging] roads . . . about a half mile east of Vineyards."[39] When Col. Miller's detachment of the 72nd Indiana arrived, Wilder fed it into the line until four of his five regiments—the 92nd Illinois was serving with the Union XIV Corps—presented a solid front facing west. About the same time, Minty rode up. "Where do you want me?" he asked Wilder. "I think your best position will be on my right," replied the Hoosier colonel.[40]

The Federals to their front having departed, Johnson's Confederates (with Hood's blessing) were ready to resume their march. Johnson let John Gregg's Brigade take the lead, and with the 41st Tennessee in skirmish formation, it set off.[41] The men advanced more than two miles without finding opposition, passed the burning Alexander cabin en route before colliding with Wilder's new line. Despite the day's action and everyone's expectation that the fighting wasn't over, the encounter was a surprise to both sides.

With the first crackling volley, Johnson deployed the rest of Gregg's Brigade "under a sharp fire" that inflicted several losses. Col. Fulton's men moved up to the right, extending their front to match Wilder's, while Gen. McNair's troops closed up in support. Jerome Robertson's Texans, having trailed the column all day, were deployed in the rear facing northwest as a hedge against an enemy flank attack. It was now past 7:00 p.m., and these last manuevers were executed in the growing darkness; within minutes it would be full night.[42]

While the Confederates were deploying into line, several Union officers gathered for an impromptu council of war. Minty recalled that both Maj. Gen. Thomas Crittenden and one of his division commanders, Brig. Gen. Thomas J. Wood, were present. Both were dubious that Confederate infantry were across the creek in force, Crittenden especially so. Two nights before, when Minty reported that elements of James Longstreet's Confederate Corps were arriving at Ringgold, Crittenden dismissed the report as a rumor, arguing instead that Longstreet was in Virginia. Further, scoffed Crittenden, the XXI Corps alone could whip every Rebel within a twenty-mile radius. Minty found the generals no less skeptical now. When he recounted details of his daylong fight to Wood, the officers rode forward to Wilder's line, with Wood joking that they would soon send the Confederates back "across to their own side."[43] Just as they reached Wilder's position, Johnson's Confederates arrived in Wilder's front. Muzzle flashes brightened dusk's shadows. With a look of what Minty later described as "blank astonishment," Wood galloped back to his lines for support as the fire quickly became general.

The nearest Federal infantry belonged to Col. George F. Dick's Second Brigade, Maj. Gen. Horatio Van Cleve's Third Division, Crittenden's XXI Corps. Dick's 44th Indiana and 59th Ohio were hustled forward to reinforce Wilder, with orders to "hold the road at all hazards."[44] The Ohioans initially deployed behind Minty. When the Federal cavalry skirmishers were driven in, the Buckeyes reported that Johnson's Confederates closed to within fifty yards of their line until a volley and a quick charge checked the enemy advance.[45]

Like most night actions, this engagement produced few losses. The woods, the deepening gloom, and the spreading confusion added up to a lot of noise but little else. Johnson, however, was surprised at the intensity of the Federal resistance, enough so that he believed he was facing "the whole Yankee army" with just his lone division.[46] As far as he was concerned, this was no place for a prolonged fight. With Hood's agreement, Johnson pulled his brigades back to a defensible line in the woods, scraped out some hasty entrenchments, and ordered at least one-third of his men to remain awake and alert at all times. Johnson and Hood hoped the morning would see the rest of the Confederate army come up to their support.

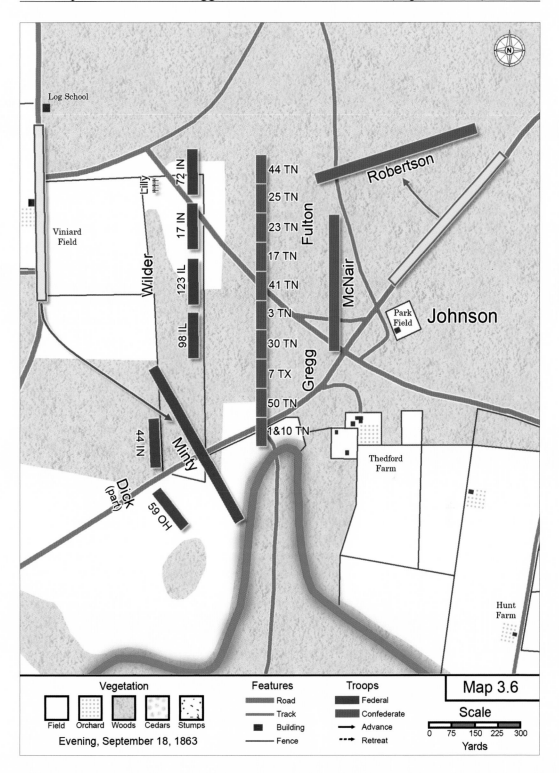

Log School

72 IN

17 IN

123 IL

98 IL

Lilly

Wilder

Viniard
Field

44 TN

25 TN

23 TN

17 TN

41 TN

3 TN

30 TN

7 TX

50 TN

1 & 10 TN

Fulton

Gregg

McNair

Robertson

Johnson

Park
Field

Thedford
Farm

44 IN

Minty

59 OH

Dick
(part)

Hunt
Farm

Vegetation

Field   Orchard   Woods   Cedars   Stumps

Evening, September 18, 1863

Features

Road
Track
Building
Fence

Troops

Federal
Confederate
Advance
Retreat

Map 3.6

Scale

0   75   150   225   300

Yards

3.7: McCook Advances to Reed's Bridge

Unbeknownst to Minty, another Union force was moving toward Reed's Bridge even as he was deciding to pull out. Union Maj. Gen. Gordon Granger's Reserve Corps—not to be confused with the similarly named Confederate Reserve Corps under Gen. Walker—was stationed at Rossville just a few miles to the northwest. With only three of his seven brigades present, Granger's force was really more of a division than a corps. His other brigades were guarding the Federal army's supply lines nearly all the way back to Nashville. The portion of the corps at Rossville was tasked with keeping open Rosecrans' line of retreat to Chattanooga, guarding the LaFayette Road where it cut through Missionary Ridge at the Rossville Gap. The three brigades at Granger's disposal for this task numbered 5,894 officers and men. Another 2,000 or so, detached from other elements of the Union army, garrisoned Chattanooga proper.[47]

Minty had maintained contact with Granger during the past few days, updating the Reserve Corps leader as the fight progressed on the 18th. About 4:00 p.m., just when Minty was deciding whether or not to withdraw, Granger sent one brigade to Red House Bridge and a second under Col. Daniel McCook to backstop the Federal cavalry at Reed's Bridge.[48] Minty, who apparently never received word that the help was coming, withdrew before McCook arrived.

Dan McCook (yet another member of the famous "Fighting McCook" family of Ohio) was an ambitious officer determined to wear a general's straps before the war ended. Two of his brothers had already beat him to that lofty rank. Alexander M. McCook was commanding the XX Corps, while Robert L. McCook had earned his star early in the war at the Battle of Mill Springs before being killed by bushwhackers in August of 1862. Dan, tall and whipcord thin, had impressive connections—the former law partner of no less a figure than William T. Sherman and the influential Ewing family of Ohio. Despite this, the chances of war had thus far kept him removed from significant combat, and there had been little chance to prove his mettle on a battlefield.

His five regiments marched cautiously down the Reed's Bridge Road, arriving within a mile of the bridge "just as the sun was setting."[49] There was no sign of Minty or any sound of combat. McCook halted his brigade, formed a double line astride the road, and sent his brigade scouts ahead to reconnoiter the heavy terrain. Within a few hundred yards they found Rebels. Rear echelon elements from Gen. McNair's Brigade of Bushrod Johnson's division were still in the area. Rashly, Federal Pvt. Eli Shields ordered the Confederates to "halt!" in a loud and clear voice. "Keep your damn mouth shut!" retorted an annoyed Confederate, worried that the Federals might hear the loud order.[50] Shields' comrades shushed him, slipped back into the woods, and proceeded to stake out the roadway. The pickets quietly captured Rebel after Rebel until they had twenty-two prisoners, including members of the brigade band complete with instruments, a Confederate major who immediately lost his horse, and several doctors from the brigade field hospital who had lingered behind in search of rations.[51] The medical staff would be particularly missed over the next few days. With Confederates so near, a more cautious officer might have retreated, but McCook ordered his men to sleep on their arms and keep noise to a minimum. Pickets were sent out far enough to watch both the Reed's Bridge and Jays Mill roads.

An hour or so later, Granger reinforced McCook with four more regiments under Col. John G. Mitchell, who placed his brigade behind McCook. This force augmented McCook's total strength to nine regiments and two batteries, in all about 3,200 men. Still, the uncertainty of their situation preyed on the Federals.

Curiously, the Confederates were as ill-informed as their opponents about the true situation in their front. Forrest, with Pegram's Brigade now at hand, had responsibility for scouting the area and should have moved aggressively to secure it. Unfortunately, after Hood and Johnson moved on, Forrest rode his troopers back across the Chickamauga at Alexander's Bridge to camp on the south side of the creek a mile or distant.[52] Confederate cavalry apparently made no provision to picket the Reed's Bridge Road, which allowed McCook to approach unmolested. The 1st Georgia Cavalry picketed the road south of Jay's Mill, but the Georgians were not deployed far enough forward to offer any protection to McNair's potentially vulnerable men.[53]

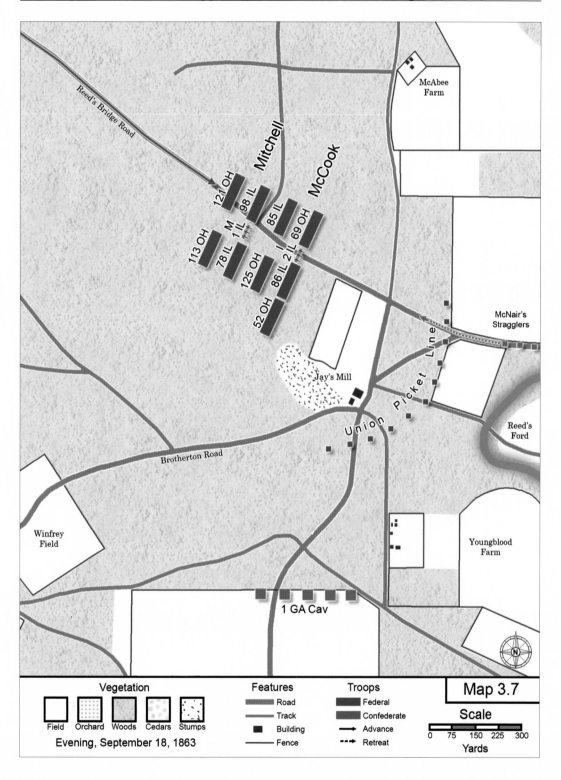

Reed's Bridge Road

McAbee
Farm

Mitchell

McCook

121 OH

98 IL

85 IL

69 OH

113 OH

1 IL M

78 IL

125 OH

86 IL 2 IL

52 OH

Jay's Mill

McNair's
Stragglers

Union Picket Line

Reed's
Ford

Brotherton Road

Winfrey
Field

Youngblood
Farm

1 GA Cav

Vegetation					Features	Troops	Map 3.7

Vegetation
Field   Orchard   Woods   Cedars   Stumps

Features
━━ Road
━━ Track
■ Building
— Fence

Troops
■ Federal
■ Confederate
→ Advance
╍╍▸ Retreat

Map 3.7

Scale
0   75   150   225   300
Yards

Evening, September 18, 1863

Map Set 4: Battle Begins in Winfrey Field
(Morning, September 19)

4.1: Overall Situation (7:00 a.m.)

As the last hours of September 18 waned, Gen. William Rosecrans knew two vital pieces of information: Gen. Braxton Bragg's Southern army had been heavily reinforced, and it was farther north than he had supposed. Strong enemy columns had crossed West Chickamauga Creek at both Reed's and Alexander's bridges, well beyond Maj. Gen. Crittenden's XXI Corps' left flank at Lee and Gordon's Mills. The Union commander turned to his most trusted subordinate, Maj. Gen. George H. Thomas, to address the problem. Rosecrans ordered Thomas to move north with half of his XIV Corps, leapfrogging behind Crittenden to the Kelly farmstead on the LaFayette Road.[1]

By dawn Thomas was at the Kelly house with the divisions of Brig. Gens. Absalom Baird and John M. Brannan. Baird had only recently stepped into command of the First Division. His was a temporary appointment during the absence of Maj. Gen. Lovell Rousseau. Baird had large shoes to fill. Rousseau, a politically active Kentuckian, had shown considerable military ability in a number of battles and was popular with his command. He was absent on a political lobbying mission, petitioning Congress to supply Rosecrans with more cavalry. Baird had been called forward from a rear area garrison to lead the division during Rousseau's absence. Baird and Brannan had marched their men most of the night and were preparing breakfast when Union Col. Daniel McCook appeared on the scene.[2]

McCook's two brigades were in the process of withdrawing to Rossville from their forward position along the Reed's Bridge Road. Because all his captives appeared to be from one command—Gen. Evander McNair's Brigade—McCook conceived the idea that a lone Rebel brigade was isolated on his side of the creek and so was ripe for the taking.[3] Bagging the entire lot would be an ideal way to win his coveted stars. McCook's chance was frustrated at dawn when Gen. Gordon Granger ordered him back to Rossville, denying the young officer—or so McCook thought—a golden opportunity.

McCook complied with Granger's recall, ordering the 69th Ohio to creep forward to burn the bridge and fall back to join his command in the withdrawal. The attempt proved a dismal failure. The Buckeyes managed to pile some brush on the planks and set the piles alight, but nearby Confederates extinguished the flames before they could do any real damage.[4]

As his men departed the area, McCook informed Thomas of the "lone" Confederate command isolated by the "destroyed" bridge. Despite the defensive nature of his orders, Thomas responded to the news aggressively by ordering Brannan's men away from their breakfast and into the woods to find the enemy.[5]

Bragg was equally concerned. He expected his command to have overlapped the Union left flank. Reports of Union activity near Jay's Mill, in what should have been his rear area, were disturbing. Gen. Nathan Forrest's cavalry should have been in position to prevent just this kind of activity, but the troopers had retired across Alexander's Bridge, and so were not in front of the Confederate infantry.

Bragg ordered Forrest to return to Jay's Mill and assess the nature of the threat there. With Col. John S. Scott's men still guarding the approaches to Ringgold, and Brig. Gen. Frank C. Armstrong's Division still serving with Lt. Gen. Leonidas Polk near Lee and Gordon's Mills, Forrest had only Gen. John Pegram's men at hand. There was also a command change, at least nominally. Brig. Gen. Henry B. Davidson finally arrived that morning to take charge of the brigade, per his appointment back on September 3 when Forrest's Corps was created. It had taken Davidson (who had been post commander at Staunton, Virginia) more than two weeks to reach the army. Pegram continued to accompany the brigade and, for all intents and purposes, remained in command. In later years, few of the troopers even recalled that Davidson was present at Chickamauga.

Taking the lead, members of the 1st Georgia Cavalry moved north from Alexander's Bridge and collided with McCook's skirmishers in the pre-dawn twilight. A lively little skirmish broke out until it was cut short when, per his orders, McCook began falling back.[6]

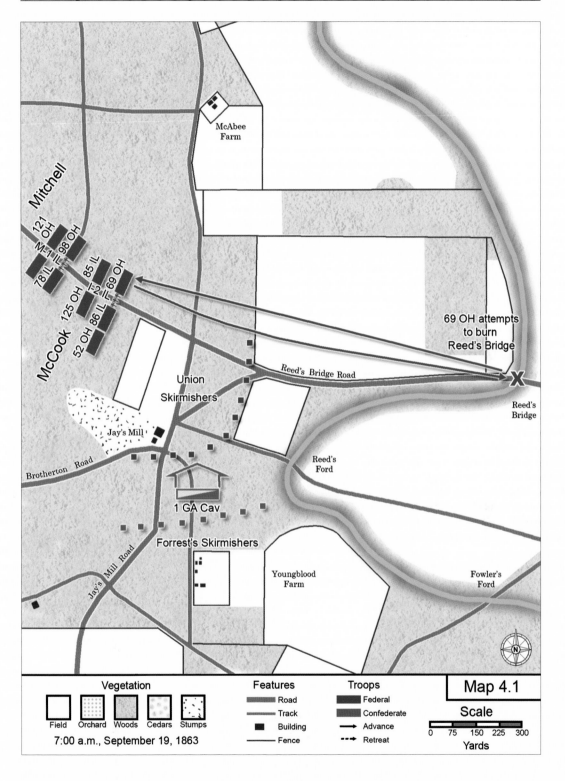

McAbee
Farm

Mitchell

121
OH
M-1
78 IL
98 OH
85 IL
125 OH
I-2
86 IL
69 OH
52 OH

McCook

69 OH attempts
to burn
Reed's Bridge

Reed's Bridge Road

X

Reed's
Bridge

Union
Skirmishers

Jay's Mill

Brotherton Road

Reed's
Ford

1 GA Cav

Forrest's Skirmishers

Jay's Mill Road

Youngblood
Farm

Fowler's
Ford

N

Vegetation

Field   Orchard   Woods   Cedars   Stumps

7:00 a.m., September 19, 1863

Features

Road
Track
Building
Fence

Troops

Federal
Confederate
Advance
Retreat

Map 4.1

Scale

0   75   150   225   300

Yards

4.2: Croxton Finds Confederates
(7:30 a.m.)

At the forefront of Brannan's division, Col. John T. Croxton's large brigade of 2,200 men left their unfinished breakfasts and marched east along a narrow logging road in the direction of Jay's sawmill. About one mile in, Croxton's men formed a double line and, with skirmishers thrown well forward, advanced cautiously through the open woods.[7]

In the spring of 1863, the Army of the Cumberland embraced Casey's new tactics wholeheartedly. These called for a brigade to form its regiments in two lines instead of one long single rank. This more compact formation was easier to handle in most terrain and gave the brigade commander more flexibility to respond to unexpected threats. Its primary disadvantage was that an opponent still using the single lines called for in Hardee's or Scott's manuals enjoyed a longer front, and could bring more firepower to bear during the initial collision.

Moving to support Croxton, Col. Frederick Van Derveer's brigade marched north to the intersection of the LaFayette and Reed's Bridge roads, turned right, and paralleled Croxton's command on the latter's left. Leaving the 9th Ohio near the McDonald House to guard the division's ammunition train, Van Derveer deployed his remaining three regiments and set off, his front lagging some distance behind Croxton's advance.[8]

Col. Gustav Kammerling was not pleased that his 9th Ohio was detailed to guard the train. The 9th was an ethnic German regiment, recruited mostly from the immigrant community in Cincinnati. Even drill commands were issued entirely in German. Kammerling was always sensitive to slights concerning their ethnicity or fighting spirit, real or perceived, and looked for any opportunity for his men to prove their mettle.[9]

Col. John T. Connell's First Brigade followed Croxton and Van Derveer. Connell was new to brigade command. Edward H. Phelps, the brigade's senior colonel, and his 38th Ohio regiment were absent escorting the divisional baggage train and the next ranking colonel, Moses B. Walker of the 31st Ohio, was under arrest due to a dispute with Phelps over a matter

of military protocol. This left Connell in charge of the brigade. Brannan rode along with him to keep an eye on things.[10]

About 7:30 a.m., Davidson's (Pegram's) Rebel troopers were taking their breakfast in the open fields around the mill when firing broke out to the west. A picket line from the 1st Georgia Cavalry was still guarding the Reed's Bridge Road after seeing off McCook's departing Federals that morning. Earlier probes into the timber had not discovered any signs of the enemy.[11]

The scattered firing was triggered by a collision between the 10th Confederate, a sizable command of some 250 men, and pickets screening Croxton's advancing Federals, who were making a mounted reconnaissance into the woods west of Jay's Mill. The Confederates charged and scattered the Federals pickets. Within minutes the horsemen discovered Croxton's main line halted behind a rise. The Federals delivered a volley at less than 100 yards. Stunned by the size and proximity of the Federal line, and with a number of saddles emptied, the 10th Confederate broke and fled. In full retreat, the troopers pushed their way through the rest of Pegram's men, throwing the brigade into disorder.[12]

Croxton moved his two reserve regiments into the front line and sent word of the encounter back to Brannan, while Forrest ordered Pegram to dismount his entire command and hold the Federals back until Confederate infantry could be brought forward. Capt. Gustave A. Huwald's Battery anchored the new Confederate line, unlimbering on "a rocky ridge in a piece of woods between saplings so thick that it was difficult to see far forward."[13] Limited lines of sight proved to be less of a problem than the gunners may have believed when the Federals soon pressed within canister range, driving the Confederate cavalry before them.

Forrest's decision to slug it out was in keeping with his combative nature, but it may not have been the best response. Pegram's cavalry were both outnumbered and at a tactical disadvantage. Forrest could have avoided going toe-to-toe with the Yankees and fallen back slowly, delaying Croxton with skirmishers while the situation developed. This might have given Bragg a clearer understanding of the threat so he could respond in a more coherent manner instead of being dragged into a major action from an unexpected direction.

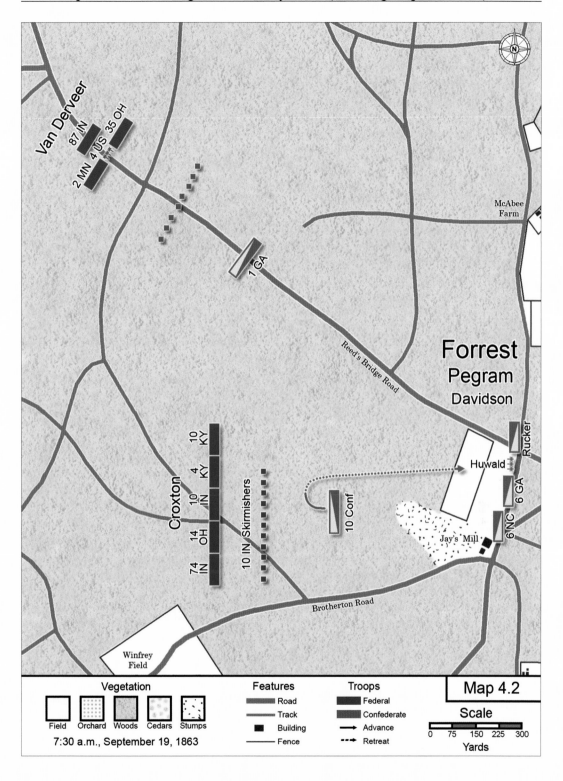

Map 4.2

7:30 a.m., September 19, 1863

4.3: Wilson's Brigade Attacks
(8:30 a.m.)

Facing a strong body of Federals (more than 2,000), Forrest's first inclination was to bolster Pegram's line in any way possible. The Rebel troopers could not hold for long in the face of aggressive Union infantry pressure. Even the horse-holders—normally every fourth man—were needed on the firing line. "You go right over there," Forrest yelled to a staff officer, "and tell the holders to hold ten or twelve horses, and *fetch* the balance right here."[14]

Additional help would have to come from farther afield. George Dibrell's Brigade of Armstrong's Division was on the way, but would not arrive for some time, having been on duty the night before with Polk's Corps. What Forrest really needed was not more cavalry but infantry. Fortunately, there were plenty of Confederate foot soldiers near at hand.

The closest were a pair of brigades belonging to Maj. Gen. William H. T. Walker's Reserve Corps. Forrest sent couriers to army commander Bragg as well as Walker and both brigade commanders requesting immediate help. Walker responded quickly, ordering Col. Claudius Wilson to take his brigade to support the embattled cavalry.[15]

Hurrying up the Jay's Mill Road, Wilson's five regiments formed into line well south of the mill and angled northwest through the woods toward Winfrey Field, seeking to come into action alongside the cavalry to take Croxton's Federals in the flank. Behind him, Brig. Gen. Matthew D. Ector did not even wait for Walker's approval. Instead, he moved his brigade forward in column a few minutes after Wilson's regiments filed past, marching farther north to prolong Pegram's other flank.

The woods where much of this battle would be fought did not look like it does today. It was an old-growth forest in 1863, with large mature widely spaced trees. Local farmers fenced their fields but let their animals roam free. Thus, most of the forest had little underbrush, leaving lines of sight in the middle of the woods up to 100 and even 200 yards.

For his part, Croxton was not pressing his reconnaissance very hard. He was waiting for Van Derveer to come alongside him to the north and outflank the Confederates instead of driving headlong into the enemy line opposing him. So far the fight had been a fairly static affair lasting a half-hour or more. Other than nearly emptying the Confederate cartridge boxes, little else had been accomplished.

The fighting was still underway when Wilson's Confederate line of battle appeared. With his right flank suddenly menaced, Croxton ordered Col. William Hays to move his 10th Kentucky, earlier shifted from reserve to the left front, to the extreme right. Croxton intended to refuse his exposed flank and extend a new line southwest, almost perpendicular to his original position. While Hays' Kentuckians were passing behind the firing line, however, the 74th Indiana gave way. Misconstruing an order to refuse part of the regiment as one for a general retreat, the Hoosiers broke and fell back about 200 yards. Hays proved equal to the crisis. The intrepid colonel quickly arranged his 10th regiment into line and charged into the advancing enemy in a move that, momentarily at least, checked Wilson's advance and allowed the 74th to reform behind the Kentuckians.[16]

With the Hoosiers safely behind him and the Southern enemy knocked on their heels, Hays fell back to the brigade line. Croxton's entire command slowly gave ground several hundred yards westward to a new position on a small ridge. There, the opposing lines came into contact again in a stubbornly contested fight. The fluid fighting between Croxton and Wilson had two major consequences: it effectively reoriented the combat from an east-west axis to one facing more north-south, and it opened a considerable gap in Brannan's divisional front.

The repulse of Croxton's reconnaissance meant Forrest's troopers only had to deal with the developing threat along the Reed's Bridge Road, where Van Derveer's men were still feeling their way cautiously eastward. When Matt Ector arrived, Forrest directed the Texan to form his brigade in the fields around Jay's Mill and attack up the road.

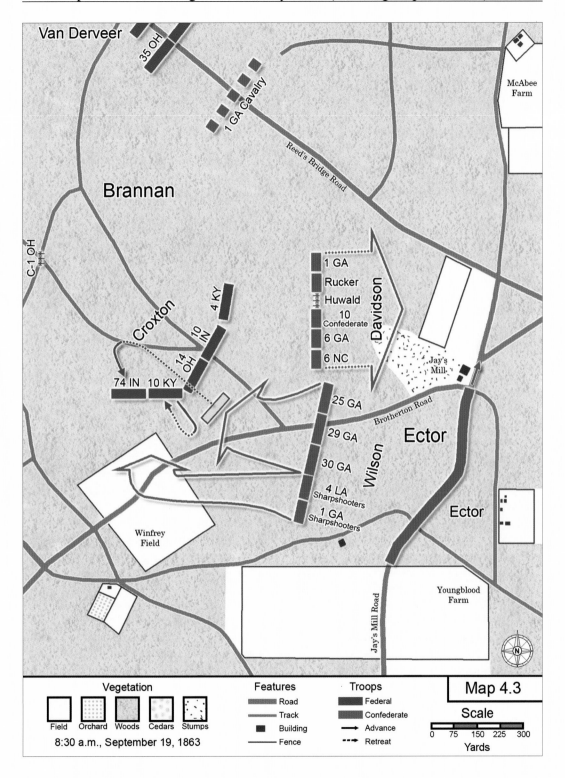

Van Derveer

35 OH

1 GA Cavalry

Reed's Bridge Road

McAbee Farm

Brannan

C-1 OH

Croxton

4 KY

10 IN

14 OH

74 IN   10 KY

1 GA

Rucker

Huwald

10 Confederate

6 GA

6 NC

Davidson

25 GA

29 GA

30 GA

4 LA Sharpshooters

1 GA Sharpshooters

Brotherton Road

Ector

Wilson

Ector

Jay's Mill

Winfrey Field

Jay's Mill Road

Youngblood Farm

N

Vegetation

Field   Orchard   Woods   Cedars   Stumps

8:30 a.m., September 19, 1863

Features

Road
Track
Building
Fence

Troops

Federal
Confederate
Advance
Retreat

Map 4.3

Scale

0   75   150   225   300

Yards

4.4: Ector Goes In (9:15 a.m.)

Like the Federals opposing them, Matt Ector's troops had little chance to rest the night before and were still at breakfast when Forrest's peremptory order to move arrived. "Their boots were still wet from wading the creek," remembered one eyewitness, when the mixed brigade of Texans, North Carolinians, and a small battalion each of Alabamians and Mississippians left their morning meal behind and marched rapidly up the Jay's Mill Road.[17]

Matt Ector's command was a well-traveled one by the fall of 1863. A Georgia native, attorney, politician, and transplant to Texas, Ector began the war as a private in the 3rd Texas Cavalry, was appointed an adjutant to another brigadier, and thereafter elected colonel of the 14th Texas Cavalry. He assumed command of his own brigade in August of 1862. His current command was cobbled together in the wake of the army's reorganization following the battle of Stone's River. In May 1863, Ector's men boarded trains for Mississippi in response to the unfolding crisis around Vicksburg. Fortunately for them, they arrived too late to join the Confederate garrison there (and so avoided capture) and instead hooked up with Gen. Joseph Johnston's Army of Relief at Jackson, Mississippi. There, Maj. T. O. Stone's and Capt. M. Pound's battalions joined the brigade. Both units were formed from men whose regiments were trapped inside the citadel, rendering them military orphans. In early September, when Ector's troops rejoined Bragg, the orphan battalions went along. They would not meet their comrades again until that November.

Replacing the thin skirmish line of the 1st Georgia Cavalry that had thus far performed sterling service in discouraging Van Derveer's advance, Ector's 1,199 men moved forward in a single line of battle. They did not have far to go before they struck the two regiments forming Van Derveer's brigade front. With only 775 troops in the first line, Van Derveer's front was outnumbered, but the four Napoleons of Lt. Frank Smith's Battery I, 4th U.S. Artillery proved to be a substantial equalizer. From the ranks of the 2nd Minnesota, Jeremiah Donahower recalled the first attack by Ector's veterans: "Soon over the little rise . . . the heads of a solid line of men in gray coming toward us in something like a rush. . . . We greeted them with a telling volley."[18]

Samuel H. Sprott was one of those on the receiving end of that initial volley. Sprott recalled the opening barrage as a "murderous fire" that checked Ector's advance. A static firefight developed for a few minutes before the Rebels fell back to reorganize and try again.[19]

With both of his leading brigades engaged, John Brannan decided to divide Connell's brigade to provide reinforcements for the other two commands. Brannan personally led the bulk of the brigade (Connell, the 82nd Indiana, 17th Ohio, and the 4th Michigan Battery) to reinforce Van Derveer on the left (north), while the 31st Ohio's 465 bayonets moved to the right (south) to reinforce Croxton.[20]

With two more regiments and another battery, Van Derveer easily overmatched Ector, whose second attack fared no better than the first. Southern casualties were heavy. Ector was lightly wounded four times (he would later lose a leg in the fighting around Atlanta in July of 1864), every mounted officer in the brigade lost a horse, and two regimental commanders went down with severe wounds. Several color bearers also fell, and losses among the rank and file were heavy. One of the stricken regimental leaders was the well-liked Col. William H. Young of the 9th Texas, who was badly wounded in the chest. It was his second serious injury, the first coming in the form of a bullet in the shoulder at Murfreesboro the previous December while rallying his command. Young would recover and eventually be promoted to brigadier, but would also be wounded three more times before the end of the war.[21]

In addition to committing his own reserves, Brannan had earlier appealed to Thomas for additional help. The XIV Corps commander had already ordered Brig. Gen. Absalom Baird's First Division to follow Brannan and support him as needed. Now, Thomas ordered Baird to "push rapidly forward" and join Brannan.[22]

The two beleaguered Confederate infantry brigades under Wilson and Ector would soon to find themselves face-to-face with no less than five brigades of Federals.

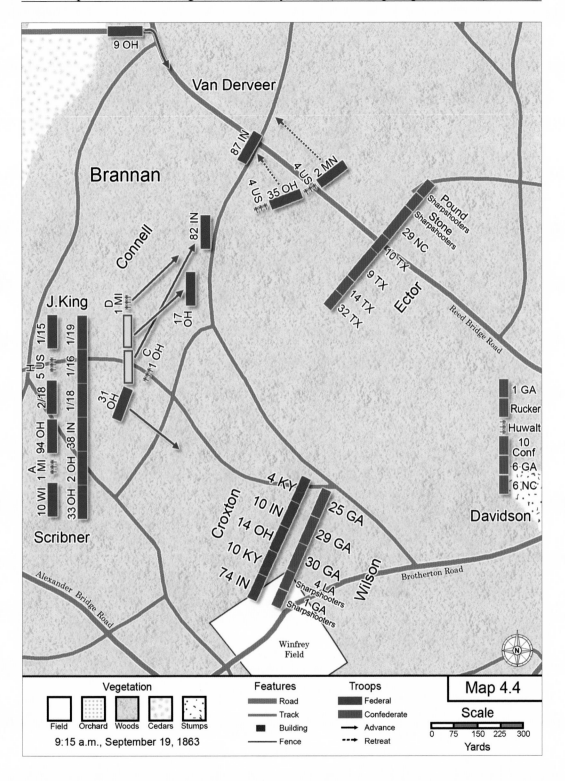

9 OH

Van Derveer

87 IN

Brannan

4 US 2 MN

4 US

35 OH

Pound
Sharpshooters
Stone
Sharpshooters
29 NC

Connell

82 IN

10 TX

9 TX

J. King

D
1 MI

17
OH

14 TX

32 TX

Ector

Reed Bridge Road

1/15

1/19

C
1 OH

1/16

5 US

1/18

38 IN

31
OH

1 GA

Rucker

Huwalt

10
Conf

6 GA

6 NC

Davidson

2/18

94 OH

A
1 MI

33 OH

2 OH

10 WI

Scribner

4 KY

25 GA

Croxton

10 IN

29 GA

14 OH

30 GA

10 KY

Wilson

Brotherton Road

Alexander Bridge Road

74 IN

4 LA
Sharpshooters

1 GA
Sharpshooters

N

Winfrey
Field

Vegetation					Features	Troops	Map 4.4

Field   Orchard   Woods   Cedars   Stumps

9:15 a.m., September 19, 1863

Road — Federal
Track — Confederate
Building — Advance
Fence --▸ Retreat

Scale

0   75   150   225   300
Yards

4.5: Baird Attacks (10:00 a.m.)

Following Brannan's command into the woods, Gen. Baird's division adopted a formation similar to that of the Third Division. His first line was composed of his First Brigade under Col. Benjamin F. Scribner and Brig. Gen. John H. King's Third Brigade, while Brig. Gen. John C. Starkweather's Second Brigade trailed as a reserve. Like Brannan's men before them, Baird's troops also headed due east.

The nature of the terrain and the direction from which the Confederate infantry appeared caused Brannan's line, as it became engaged, to pivot and face more south than east. While unplanned, this directional shift provided Baird's division with a perfect opportunity to turn the flanks of both Confederate brigades.

Claudius Wilson was probably not aware of any threat to his left. The area was thickly wooded, and he had already come in on the Union flank. In addition, there was no sound of combat to his left or rear. The former lawyer from Georgia, thirty-two years old in 1863, had recently served with Joe Johnston in Mississippi, and so was new to the Army of Tennessee. His performance in the hours ahead would earn him a bump up to brigadier general, but a fever would kill him in November.

Farther north, Matt Ector was not unaware of how exposed his men were. Separated from Wilson's right flank by several hundred yards of timber, Ector's only support was the thin line of cavalry his men had just replaced. During his first charge, Ector sent a courier to Forrest expressing concern about dangling right flank. The aide, Capt. Constantine B. Kilgore, returned with Forrest's reply: "Tell General Ector that he need not bother about his right flank, I'll take care of it."[23]

Wilson's Brigade was struck first when Scribner's fresh troops appeared at the northwest edge of Winfrey Field. Their charge, as vigorously delivered as it was unexpected, routed Wilson's already battered command. His leftmost regiments (1st Georgia and 4th Louisiana) quickly tumbled rearward through the field and into the woods to the east, threatening to peel apart the whole line from left to right. The 30th Georgia managed to reorient its fire for a time, and Wilson ordered the Georgians to hold

while he rallied his shattered left, but the 1st and 4th could not be halted short of Jay's Mill. When Col. Thomas W. Mangham fell with a severe wound in the thigh, the 30th also broke. While trying to rally his left Wilson lost track of his right, and the 25th and 29th Georgia also retreated. Lt. Lucius D. Hinkley of the 10th Wisconsin recalled the Federal advance as an "impetuous rush" of one-half mile, "capturing many prisoners." Hinkley also noted that the charge scattered Scribner's five regiments almost as badly as it did the Confederates, with the 94th Ohio advancing so far that it lost contact with the rest of the brigade.[24]

Wilson's rout alerted Ector to yet another flank threat, this time to his left and rear. Once again he sent Capt. Kilgore to find Forrest. The staff officer returned with the cavalry leader's angry, shouted reply: "Tell General Ector that, by God, I am here, and I will take care of his left flank as well as his right!"[26]

Unfortunately for Ector and his men, Forrest had no troops with which to fulfill that promise. While Wilson was being routed, John King's five battalions of U.S. Army Regulars were advancing almost due east, past Wilson's right flank and directly into Ector's exposed left. As the Regulars drove ahead, the brigade's battery unlimbered and poured fire into the surprised Confederates from a convenient ridge. C. B. Carlton of the 10th Texas Dismounted Cavalry reported home that the brigade was "flanked on the left & commenced falling back in confusion," only to discover that "Federals . . . had got in [our] rear." Later, 138 of Ector's men were reported missing, almost all of them captured by the Regulars in this portion of the fight.[27] After enduring two costly failed charges and a shocking Union counter-thrust, Ector's losses approached fifty percent. His brigade was finished as a organized combat force that day. Claudius Wilson's men suffered similar losses.

With Ector and Wilson both routed, the Confederates were for the moment out of the fight. Brannan's and Baird's Federals paused and reorganized their ranks. Croxton's brigade moved back to obtain more ammunition. Scribner's men replaced them, aligned along the northern edge of Winfrey Field. King's Regulars formed at right angles to Van Derveer's line, along the ridge where their battery unlimbered, while Starkweather's brigade went into reserve behind Scribner. A short lull settled on the field.

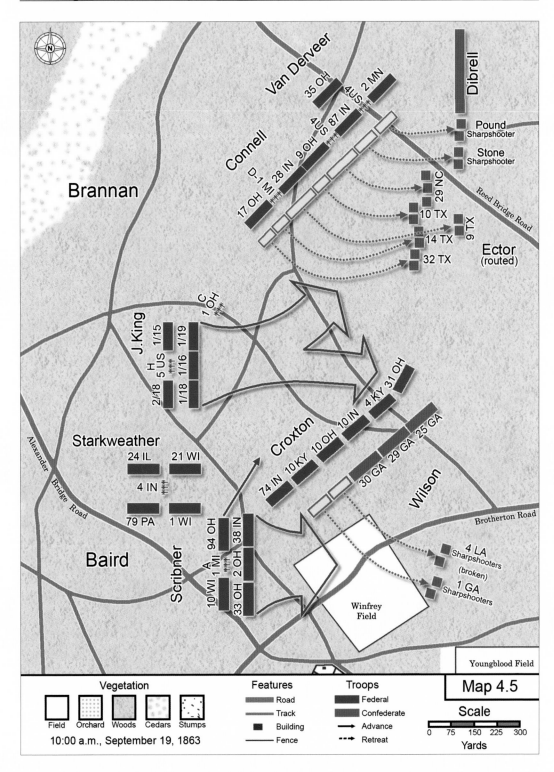

Brannan

Van Derveer

Dibrell

35 OH

4 US 2 MN

4 US 87 IN

Connell

4 US 9 OH

D-1 MI 28 IN

17 OH

Pound
Sharpshooter

Stone
Sharpshooter

29 NC

10 TX

9 TX

14 TX

32 TX

Ector
(routed)

Reed Bridge Road

1 C OH

1 OH

J.King

1/15 1/19

H 5 US 1/16

2/18 1/18

4 KY 31 OH

10 IN

10 OH

Croxton

4 IN

10 KY

30 GA 29 GA 25 GA

Starkweather

24 IL   21 WI

74 IN

79 PA   1 WI

Wilson

Baird

Scribner

10 WI 1 MI A 94 OH

33 OH 2 OH 38 IN

Brotherton Road

4 LA
Sharpshooters
(broken)

1 GA
Sharpshooters

Alexander Bridge Road

Winfrey
Field

Youngblood Field

Vegetation

Field   Orchard   Woods   Cedars   Stumps

10:00 a.m., September 19, 1863

Features

Road
Track
Building
Fence

Troops

Federal
Confederate
Advance
Retreat

Map 4.5

Scale

0   75   150   225   300

Yards

4.6: Overall Situation (11:00 a.m.)

While the combat developed and spread near Jay's Mill, both armies set events in motion that would expand what was so far a limited fight into a full-scale battle. Rosecrans originally sent Thomas north to Kelly Field to outflank the Confederates and frustrate any enemy plans to turn his own flank. Thomas had unilaterally converted that defensive movement into an attack on what was presumed to be an isolated Confederate brigade. In fact, the "isolated" unit turned out to be the right flank of Braxton Bragg's Army of Tennessee. When Thomas called for more troops, Rosecrans obliged him.[29]

Brig. Gen. Richard W. Johnson's Second Division, XX Corps, was already en route. Johnson's men were passing directly in front of Rosecrans' headquarters, newly relocated that morning to the Widow' Glenn's house, when the commanding general personally ordered Johnson to report to Thomas, informing XX Corps leader McCook of the detachment.[28] Thomas intended that Johnson's brigades advance parallel to and south of Baird's line, prolonging the Union front. At this time Rosecrans also ordered Maj. Gen. Thomas L. Crittenden, commanding the XXI Corps, to detach Maj. Gen. John M. Palmer's Second Division and send it to Thomas as well. These reinforcements were helpful, but Thomas was thinking more ambitiously. While Rosecrans was sending the divisions of Johnson and Palmer to him, Thomas suggested that Crittenden's entire corps attack northeast toward Jay's Mill. Despite Thomas' confident predictions of success, Rosecrans rejected his plan.[29]

If quick reinforcements were desired, Palmer's division was the logical choice. Not only was it the farthest north of the XXI Corps' three divisions, but Palmer's Third Brigade under Col. William Grose was already moving up the LaFayette Road on orders to patrol the gap between Crittenden's left and Thomas' newly established right flank in the vicinity of Kelly Field.

Another of Thomas' own divisions was also nearby. Maj. Gen. Joseph J. Reynolds' two brigades of the Fourth Division, XIV Corps, were temporarily halted in the woods northeast of the Widow Glenn's, resting after their night march. Thomas had ordered Reynolds there earlier, holding his men in reserve.[30] With word that both Johnson and Palmer would be attached to his command, Thomas decided to leave Reynolds in place.

Gen. Minty's troopers, meanwhile, had been without a mission since their earlier fight at Reed's Bridge. Rosecrans ordered them to fall back to Rossville in order to guard the steady stream of Union wagons that were hurrying back toward Chattanooga.[31]

On the Confederate side of the line, Braxton Bragg was beginning to realize the fight was slipping away from him. As Ector and Wilson were being fed into the combat, William Walker joined Forrest and assumed overall command of the developing combat. Walker ordered up his other division under Brig. Gen. St. John Liddell. While Ector and Wilson were being repulsed, Liddell's men were advancing northward in a long battle line, about to descend upon an unsuspecting Union flank near Winfrey Field. Liddell's position and direction of advance could not have been more fortuitous for Bragg—had he only realized it.

Instead, Bragg was worried about the spreading conflagration west of Jay's Mill. It was exactly where he did *not* want to fight, since it undermined his previously conceived plan to drive in the Federal left flank and force the Federal army south, away from Chattanooga. Perhaps unsure of how to proceed, Bragg decided to hold the bulk of his available infantry in check and see how things developed.

He did, however, decide to support Walker with one more division. Maj. Gen. Benjamin F. Cheatham's large five-brigade command (Polk's Corps) had crossed the Chickamauga at Hunt's Ford that morning and was resting behind Simon Buckner's and John Hood's concentration of infantry that comprised Bragg's main striking power. With two full corps already in line here, Cheatham's Division could be spared to move north to support Walker's small command.[32]

While tapping Cheatham's men made sense (given their current inactivity and location), Bragg was creating a break in his chain of command that would have larger implications later in the battle. Cheatham's corps commander, Leonidas Polk, also assumed command of the developing battle on the army's right flank, where Bragg expected to make his main effort.

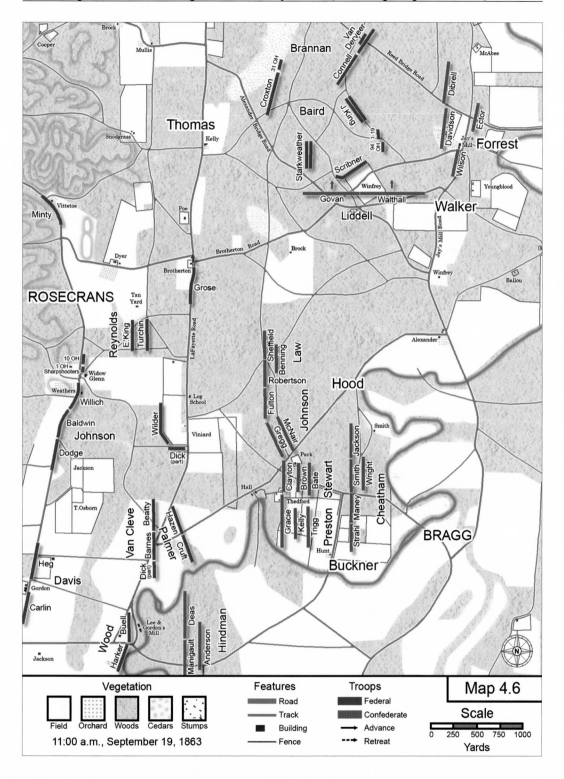

Vegetation

Field   Orchard   Woods   Cedars   Stumps

11:00 a.m., September 19, 1863

Features
Road
Track
Building
Fence

Troops
Federal
Confederate
Advance
Retreat

Map 4.6

Scale

0   250   500   750   1000

Yards

4.7: Liddell Attacks (11:00 a.m.)

So far, Col. Scribner's fight had been both successful and relatively cost-free. His advance caught Wilson's Confederates in the flank and drove them easily (with little loss to his own men) from Croxton's front. The last thing Scribner was expecting was an attack from the south. He had been informed that William Grose's brigade was coming up on his right flank, and had been cautioned not to fire in that direction "lest I should fire into our own men."[33]

Instead of Grose approaching from the south it was the remaining Rebels of Walker's Reserve Corps. Walker's command had only recently been cobbled together, and Gen. St. John Liddell's relationship with Walker was not a good one. Walker's reputation for argument was legendary, and he seemed driven to have the last word. He so annoyed his superiors that Bragg, in the wake of the campaign, confessed that even he had become "worn out and disappointed" with Walker. "This was the man Bragg placed over me," lamented Liddell.[34] Right now, however, both men were more focused on fighting Federals than each other.

Leaving his division, Liddell accompanied Walker when the corps commander rode forward and took control of the developing battle from Forrest about 10:00 a.m. Both men soon realized that the Federals were much stronger than Ector and Wilson. Liddell asked for and received prompt permission to bring up his two large brigades.[35]

With his 3,800 infantry deployed in a single line of battle, Liddell's command advanced northward undetected toward Winfrey Field. The Confederate blow fell with almost no warning. Scribner and his officers were still celebrating Wilson's retreat when the brigade surgeon stumbled into the Union line. "The enemy is in your rear and on your right," he exclaimed to Scribner. The Federal colonel tried desperately to get the brigade faced about, but there was no time.[36]

The Mississippians under Brig. Gen. Edward C. Walthall struck first. The brigade held the right of Liddell's advancing line, deployed from left to right as follows: 34th, 30th, 29th, 27th, and 24th Mississippi regiments. As they burst across the field, one Confederate recalled

an unusual tactic: the Rebels went to ground briefly in a "slight depression" mid-field, waited to receive the first Federal volley, and then charged the final distance. "The scheme worked like a charm . . . and the enemy were swept away."[37]

Despite a brief and valiant stand around Battery A, 1st Michigan Light Artillery, Scribner's brigade collapsed. Adjutant Angus Waddle of the 33rd Ohio remembered artillery commander Lt. George W. Van Pelt dying amidst his pieces, "fighting a regiment with his single saber" and refusing to surrender the guns. August Bratnober fought with the 10th Wisconsin supporting the battery. When Walthall's Confederates appeared and Van Pelt ordered his guns turned to face them, Bratnober and his comrades dropped to the ground in front of the muzzles instead of going prone behind the battery (the normal position for supporting infantry). The Badgers fired one volley into the advancing Mississippians, but without time to reload for a second, broke and fled northward. When they finally reformed, Bratnober recalled, half the regiment was gone.[38]

Liddell personally led his own Arkansan brigade (under the command of Col. Daniel C. Govan since the creation of the Reserve Corps) into the fight. Govan advanced on Walthall's left, with the 6th/7th Arkansas on the left, followed on the right by the 2nd/15th, 8th, 1st, and 5th/13th. The Arkansans struck Starkweather's unsuspecting Northerners almost without warning. As each regiment came into line, they fired into the Federal brigade "at point blank range [and] did awful execution in the Federal ranks," as a modern historian of the 6th Arkansas described the scene.[39]

Like Scribner, Starkweather desperately tried to pivot his troops under fire, but his men only managed to fire three or four rounds before they, too, were overrun. They did manage to inflict some losses on Govan's men. Lt. Col. John E. Murray, commanding the 5th Arkansas, reported that the fight here was "a short but sanguinary struggle," leaving the Confederates in victory nearly as disorganized as the Federals in defeat.[40]

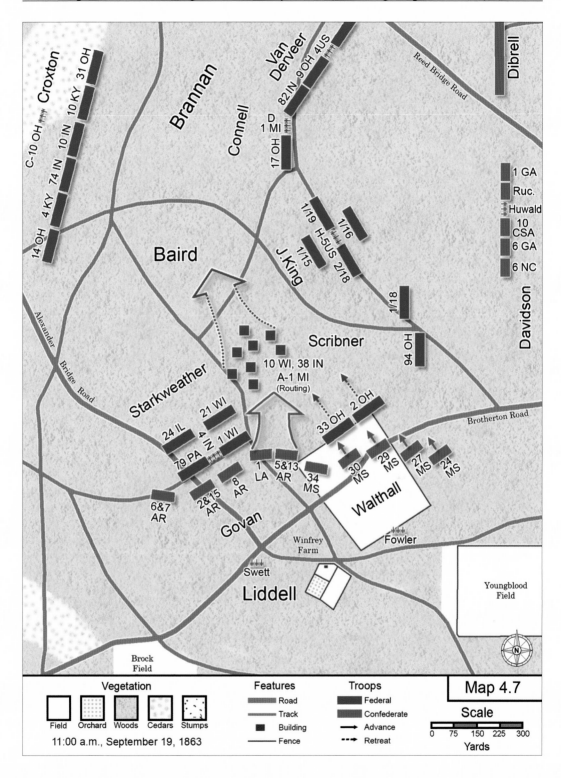

Brannan

Croxton

C-10 OH

14 OH 4 KY 74 IN 10 IN 10 KY 31 OH

Connell

Van Derveer

82 IN 9 OH 4 US

D 1 MI

17 OH

Reed Bridge Road

Dibrell

1 GA

Ruc.

Huwald

10 CSA

6 GA

6 NC

Davidson

1/19 1/16

H-5 US 2/18

J. King

1/15

1/18

94 OH

Baird

Scribner

10 WI, 38 IN
A-1 MI
(Routing)

Alexander

Bridge Road

Starkweather

24 IL 21 WI

4 IN

79 PA 1 WI

33 OH 2 OH

Brotherton Road

30 MS 29 MS 27 MS 24 MS

1 LA 5&13 AR

34 MS

6&7 AR 2&15 AR 8 AR

Govan

Walthall

Winfrey Farm

Fowler

Swett

Liddell

Youngblood Field

Brock Field

Vegetation						Features		Troops		Map 4.7

Vegetation

Field Orchard Woods Cedars Stumps

11:00 a.m., September 19, 1863

Features

Road
Track
Building
Fence

Troops

Federal
Confederate
Advance
Retreat

Map 4.7

Scale

0   75   150   225   300

Yards

N

4.8: The Rout of Baird (11:15 a.m.)

With Scribner and Starkweather shattered, only King's Regulars were still in good order, but they too faced the wrong way. The swell of battle to the southwest, directly in King's rear, alerted him that trouble was brewing from an unexpected quarter.

King's Regulars were not, by and large, pre-war soldiers but instead were comprised of men enlisted at the outbreak of war into a newly expanded Regular Army. They had enough of a leavening of pre-war officers and NCOs to create a sense of discipline distinctly different than that found among the volunteers, and so held themselves out as an elite force. Moreover, their brigade commander, Brig. Gen. John H. King, was an exemplar of the old army breed. He received a direct commission as a second lieutenant in the Second Infantry in 1838, and was a captain by 1846. He had fought Seminoles, Mexicans, and Plains Indians. Stationed in Texas in 1861, he carried his troops safely to New York and was later tasked with raising the 15th U.S. Infantry. King did well at both regimental and brigade command, seeing action at Shiloh, Corinth, and Murfreesboro.

Within minutes his worries were confirmed when Baird appeared and ordered him to form a new line at right angles to his existing position. King was trying to reorient his brigade even as the thundering noise of combat rushed through the trees to greet him. According to Capt. Henry Haymond, commanding the 2nd Battalion, 18th Infantry, "[W]e at once changed front to the rear and marched to the edge of the ravine and formed a hasty line. We had scarcely got into position before a division of [the enemy] advanced upon us on the run . . ."[41]

These Confederates were largely Walthall's troops. The Mississippians were in only slightly better order than Govan's Arkansans, but in the wake of their triumph over Scribner's troops, they were not about to halt. King reported after the battle that he had only managed to turn the battery and the 16th Regulars to face the enemy before "being assailed by an overwhelming force."[42]

The surprise was as complete as it was devastating. Baird's divisional losses were staggering, the majority of which were suffered in just a few minutes. The captured proved especially heavy, with Scribner reporting about 400 men missing, and Starkweather another 250. King listed 500 missing or captured—more than one-third of the 1,400 Regulars he marched into the timber. Virtually all the men of the 1st Battalion, 16th U.S. Infantry, were made prisoners.[43] Scribner's and Kings' batteries were captured outright, while Starkweather's 4th Indiana escaped with only one of its six guns.

The Regulars had no choice but to run for their lives, following the spine of the ridge north toward Van Derveer's brigade line astride the Reed's Bridge Road. Walthall's men remembered this encounter as the scene of their fiercest action, with dead and wounded men carpeting the ground all around the guns. The cannon themselves were the focus of great excitement. Robert Jarman of the 27th Mississippi remembered that he and several of his fellows "bounced astride of a gun and yelled our loudest. Then we turned the loaded guns on the Yanks and gave them their own grape."[44]

Two regiments from Baird's division emerged largely unscathed from this maelstrom. The 94th Ohio, from Scribner's command, and King's 1st Battalion, 18th Infantry, were both detached from their respective brigades when the Confederates struck, and so avoided the initial attacks that proved so disastrous for their comrades. Maj. Rue P. Hutchins, commanding the 94th, discovered the presence of the Confederates when he heard the firing behind him and dispatched a staff officer to find out what was happening. The staffer returned with the alarming news that the enemy was indeed in their rear, and that the 94th should fall back and support King's struggling soldiers. Together, the 94th and the 1/18th covered the retreat of King's routed brigade.[45]

After routing a second Union brigade in less than thirty minutes, Walthall's Mississippians pursued the fleeing Regulars with wild abandon. The 94th Ohio and 1/18th U.S. lacked the strength to stop or even slow the attack, and soon followed King's men, albeit in somewhat better order. Shoved northward, the Federals soon found themselves running through Van Derveer's and Connell's lines.

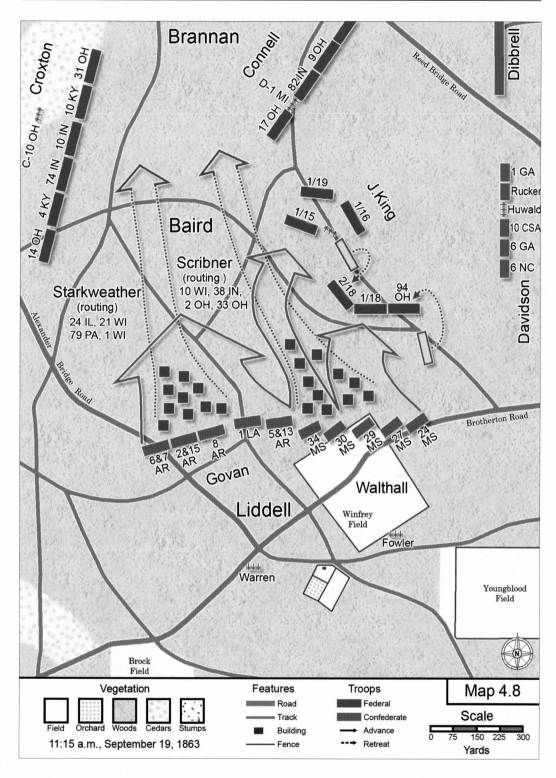

Map 4.8

11:15 a.m., September 19, 1863

Vegetation

Field   Orchard   Woods   Cedars   Stumps

Features
- Road
- Track
- Building
- Fence

Troops
- Federal
- Confederate
- Advance
- Retreat

Scale

0   75   150   225   300

Yards

4.9: Brannan Strikes Back (11:30 a.m.)

Van Derveer's troops had little love for the Regulars now pouring through their ranks. In March of 1862, when the two units were camped near each other, the volunteers grew outraged after witnessing the severe discipline enforced by Regular Army officers to the point that a small riot ensued. Since that time, Van Derveer's men showed a pointed disdain for Regular Army troops and their inexplicable ways. Witnessing Kings' current plight did nothing to improve their opinion.[46]

Judson Bishop of the 2nd Minnesota described the moment: "a straggling line of blue appeared, coming toward us in wild retreat, their speed accelerated by the firing and yelling of the exultant Confederates." This "appalling spectacle" momentarily alarmed Bishop. The Minnesotans held firm with "grim composure" until the routed men passed over them, at which point they stood and unleashed a killing volley into the Confederates, "which abruptly ended the yelling and the charge."[47]

At this point in the crisis Van Derveer's 9th Ohio Germans appeared. Called forward from wagon train guard duty, the Buckeyes plunged into the swirling combat without any hesitation. "Col. Kammerling, chafing like a wounded tiger that he had been behind at the opening, ordered his men to charge." Describing that advance, Constantin Grebner recorded that the 9th "hurled back the front rank, penetrated to the second and third, and . . . [re-]captured several cannon belonging originally to . . . the 5th U.S. Artillery."[48]

Kammerling's impetuous counterstroke pulled the 87th Indiana and 17th Ohio into the attack with him. This sudden riposte by three Federal regiments proved too much for Walthall's exhausted and disorganized Rebels. The Mississippians retreated, abandoning all but one of their trophy cannon from the 5th U.S. They fell back several hundred yards, with all formation lost. Walthall was attempting to reorganize his regiments when he discovered that Govan's Brigade was also retreating beyond his left (to the west). Worse, the Federals were threatening to turn Walthall's own left flank.[49]

The change in circumstances was because John Croxton's large brigade had returned to the fight. Croxton was a Kentuckian who had graduated from Yale in 1857 and practiced law before the war. He enlisted in the fall of 1861 as a lieutenant colonel in the 4th Kentucky Mounted Infantry, served under George Thomas at Mill Springs, and participated in the Tullahoma operations. His men had moved to the rear an hour earlier, replaced by Scribner and King's troops, to take stock of their early and significant losses and to obtain more ammunition. Croxton's regiments had shot away more than sixty rounds apiece in the earlier fight against Claudius Wilson's Southern infantry. Resupplied and having caught their breath, they were now in an ideal position to deal with Govan's attacking Arkansans.[50]

With a remarkably good grasp of the relative positions of both friends and opponents in this confusing and rapidly changing fight, Croxton deployed his regiments—augmented by the 31st Ohio on his own left—in a single line and marched south several hundred yards until he was astride Govan's left flank. Fronting eastward, Croxton advanced.[51]

Govan was aware of this new threat, but his brigade was in poor condition to meet it. His losses had been heavy, even in success. Several of his regiments had suffered casualties approaching one-third. Breaking off pursuit of Starkweather's men, Govan turned the combined 6th/7th Arkansas to face west to provide some flank protection. However, with only 250 men left in its ranks, the 6th/7th was far too weak to cope with Croxton. With no other choice than to fall back or risk being destroyed, Govan ordered his entire brigade to retreat by the right flank.[52]

As far as Croxton's Federals were concerned, the Rebel retreat was considerably less orderly than Govan later tried to make it appear in his report. With his brigade line too long for one man to fully command, Croxton took personal charge of the three regiments on the right and appointed Col. Charles W. Chapman of the 74th Indiana to lead those on the left. Then, recalled Pvt. Henry G. Davidson from amidst the ranks of the 10th Kentucky (Union), "[Croxton] ordered a bayonet charge, which was performed in a style never surpassed and scarcely ever equaled . . . driving them in the wildest confusion, actually running clear through their lines [and] capturing many prisoners."[53]

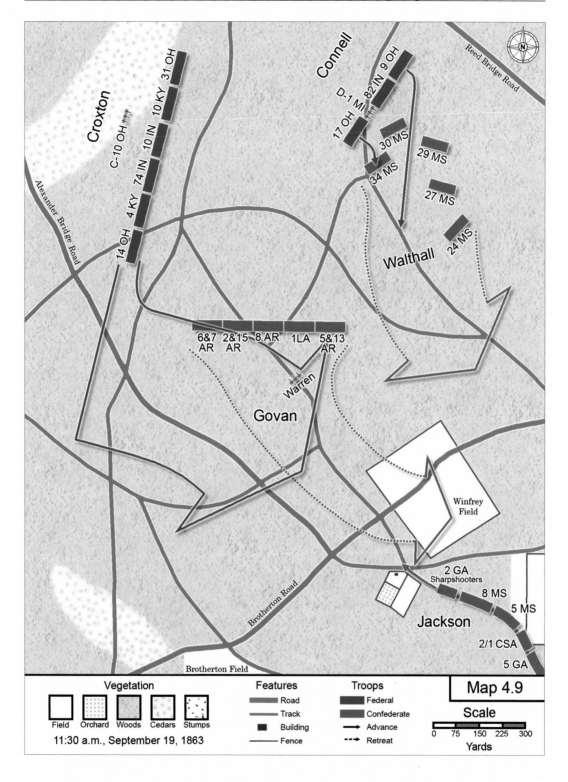

Croxton

C-10 OH 14 OH 4 KY 74 IN 10 IN 10 KY 31 OH

Connell

D-1 MI 82 IN 9 OH

17 OH

30 MS

29 MS

34 MS

27 MS

24 MS

Walthall

Alexander Bridge Road

Reed Bridge Road

6&7 AR 2&15 AR 8 AR 1 LA 5&13 AR

Warren

Govan

Winfrey Field

Brotherton Road

2 GA
Sharpshooters

8 MS

5 MS

Jackson

2/1 CSA

5 GA

Brotherton Field

Vegetation

Field   Orchard   Woods   Cedars   Stumps

11:30 a.m., September 19, 1863

Features

Road
Track
Building
Fence

Troops

Federal
Confederate
Advance
Retreat

Map 4.9

Scale

0   75   150   225   300

Yards

4.10: Van Derveer Defends the Reed's Bridge Road (Noon)

With the retreat of Liddell's Rebel division (Govan and Walthall), Gen. Walker's entire Reserve Corps was now out of the fight and, once again, the Confederates were nearly out of troops. Only one Southern brigade was still fresh enough to make a final effort to locate and turn the elusive Federal left flank. Col. George G. Dibrell's cavalry reached Jay's Mill about 10:30 a.m., just as Matt Ector's mauled Southern command was pulling back.

Thus far, Forrest had been fighting with troops new to him. Davidson's Brigade—indeed, Pegram's entire division—was only placed under Forrest at the beginning of September, and all of the infantry had been borrowed from Walker's Reserve Corps. Dibrell's troopers, however, were long familiar with "Old Bedford." Prior to his promotion, Dibrell's command was Forrest's own and still known officially as "Forrest's Brigade" on the army's rolls. Tennesseans all, Dibrell's six regiments and two batteries had complete faith in their former commander, a confidence he heartily returned. After all, these men had run twice their number into the ground chasing Union Col. Abel Streight's raiders across northern Alabama back in May 1863. This mutual confidence encouraged Forrest and Dibrell to attempt a more creative tactical solution than a mere frontal attack.

Dibrell deployed astride the Reed's Bridge Road facing that part of Van Derveer's line Walthall's men had not reached. Ector's Confederates had already discovered that Van Derveer's position was a strong one, and not likely to fall to a frontal assault. When an initial probe by Dibrell's troopers bore out the fact that Van Derveer's men were still there, Forrest and Dibrell worked out an alternative strategy.

Forrest brought forward Huwald's guns again, this time reinforced by four more of Capt. Amariah L. Huggins' Tennessee battery, ordering them to open on the Union line.[54] Shifting Dibrell's dismounted troopers north of the road and using low ground to shelter the move, Forrest intended to strike Van Derveer with a flank attack. Moving several hundred yards into the woods, Dibrell turned and brought his men forward in a heavy skirmish line.[55]

Unfortunately for the Rebels, Van Derveer was alert to the danger. The enemy "suddenly appeared on my left and rear, he reported, "but not before I had changed my front to receive him." Union skirmishers had spotted the movement and the 2nd Minnesota was shifting into position to receive it.[56] The 2nd and one section of Battery I, 4th U.S. Artillery, took up a line on the north side of the road facing northeast. Together they repulsed Dibrell's first effort, a limited attack to conceal the larger movement.[57]

Meanwhile, Van Derveer was still trying to recall the 87th Indiana, and the 9th and 17th Ohio, involved in Kammerling's charge, and restore his line. The first regiment to rush back to aid the embattled 2nd Minnesota was the 87th Indiana. Sgt. Benjamin Brown of Company D described the circumstances for friends at home: "They came very near to surrounding us here, so near that we had to change front to the rear in order to get at them again."[58]

Using the 2nd Minnesota as an anchor, Van Derveer built up the rest of his new line. The 87th went in alongside and west of the 2nd, with the 35th Ohio placed next to the 87th. The entire line was studded with artillery from both Lt. Frank Smith's Battery I, 4th U.S., and Capt. Josiah W. Church's Battery D, Michigan Light Artillery. These units went into line successively, working from east to west, as they rushed up to meet Dibrell's developing attack from the north.

Federal accounts exaggerated the scope and ferocity of Dibrell's thrust. The 35th Ohio, for example, reported seeing the "rapid approach of the enemy in four lines," and described the assault as "terrific." The 2nd Minnesota's regimental history described it this way: "Here they come— ranks after ranks—emerging from the sheltering trees . . . we opened with file firing that soon broke up . . . the first line, [who] . . . commenced firing wildly. . . . Our big guns . . . opened great gaps in the enemy's columns with every discharge."[59]

In fact, Dibrell's men advanced mostly in skirmish order, and losses were remarkably light. Out of the approximately 2,200 men in his large brigade, Dibrell reported only ten killed and forty wounded for the *entire* battle, losses that clearly do not square with the dramatic Federal descriptions of the encounter.[60]

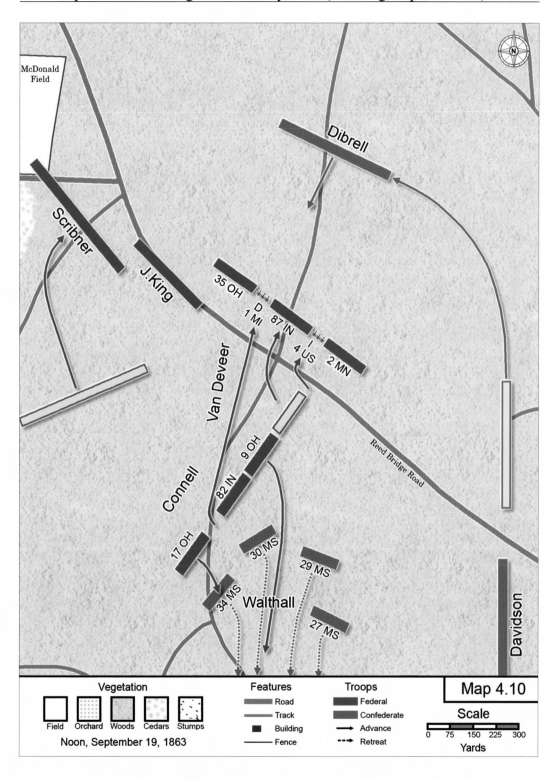

McDonald Field

Dibrell

Scribner

J. King

35 OH

D
1 MI

87 IN

I
4 US

2 MN

Van Deveer

9 OH

82 IN

Connell

17 OH

30 MS

29 MS

34 MS

Walthall

27 MS

Reed Bridge Road

Davidson

Vegetation

Field Orchard Woods Cedars Stumps

Features

Road
Track
Building
Fence

Troops

Federal
Confederate
Advance
Retreat

Map 4.10

Scale

0   75   150   225   300

Yards

Noon, September 19, 1863

Map Set 5: The Fight for Brock Field and LaFayette Road
(Midday, September 19)

5.1: Overall Situation (Noon)

With Col. George Dibrell's repulse, the fighting on the north end of the field drew to a close around noon. Both armies had traded exploratory jabs. Maj. Gen. William Walker's Reserve Corps was about fought out. Brig. Gen. Matthew Ector and Col. Claudius Wilson had sustained losses approaching fifty percent. Brig. Gen. St. John R. Liddell's divisional casualties weren't as severe, but both his brigades (Col. Daniel C. Govan and Brig. Gen. Edward C. Walthall) had been bruised and disorganized by Union counterattacks.

On the Union side, Brig. Gen. Absalom Baird's division (the brigades of Col. Benjamin Scribner and Brig. Gens. John Starkweather and John King) had been roughly handled and was withdrawing up the Reed's Bridge Road to recuperate. Two brigades from Brig. Gen. John M. Brannan's division (Cols. Ferdinand Van Derveer and John Connell) covered Baird's withdrawal. Only Col. John T. Croxton's brigade (Brannan), augmented by the 31st Ohio, pressed the retreating Rebels astride the Alexander's Bridge Road.

Still concerned about Federal attacks from this unexpected quarter, Braxton Bragg decided to continue fighting. At midday, he still had two infantry corps—more than 17,000 men—massed in the woods south of Brock Field about one-half mile east of the LaFayette Road. These troops faced the lightly defended Federal center. Bragg, however, did not know how lightly defended the enemy front was, and he was not about to send them forward without a better understanding of the threat to the north.[1] Between 7:00 a.m. and 9:00 a.m., Maj. Gen. Benjamin F. Cheatham's large division, about 7,000 men and twenty guns arrayed in five brigades, had crossed the Chickamauga at Hunt's ford and filed into position behind Maj. Gen. Simon Buckner's Corps. At 11:00 a.m., Bragg sent Cheatham to help Walker.[2] Moving north and forming his division along the Alexander's Bridge Road, Cheatham was ready by noon.

By now, both Brig. Gen. Richard Johnson's and Maj. Gen. John Palmer's Federal divisions were also ready to advance. Col. William Grose's brigade had finished its excursion up the LaFayette Road, making contact with the Maj. Gen. George Thomas' XIV Corps near the Kelly farm. It was returning south when it met the rest of its division marching toward it. Union Army commander William Rosecrans was still hesitant about launching a major attack, but Thomas was thinking aggressively. About 9:30 a.m., he sent a note to Palmer: if his troops were to "advance as soon as possible on [the Rebels] in front, while I attack them in flank, I think we can use them up."[3] Some time later, when Rosecrans authorized Palmer to move to Thomas' aid, attacking was still on the XIV Corps commander's mind.[4] With Grose falling in at the rear of the column, Palmer reached the vicinity of the Poe farm and faced east.

At the same time, Johnson's leading divisional elements were forming a line at the south end of Kelly Field, neatly filling the gap between Thomas' line and Palmer's men. Thomas ordered both divisions to replace Baird and Brannan's exhausted troops. These six fresh Union brigades were now poised to clash with Cheatham's five Rebel brigades, opening the second phase of the battle.

Thomas was now in command of units from all three corps, as Rosecrans elected to reinforce him with whatever troops were closest without regard for the formal chain of command. Perhaps it mattered little at the moment, with Thomas on hand to control the fight directly, but the decision would lead to serious confusion over the next two days with substantial ramifications.

Thomas had at least one more division he could call on quickly, as the two brigades of Maj. Gen. Joseph Reynolds' Fourth Division, XIV Corps (Cols. Edward A. King and John B. Turchin) resumed their march to join him. The rest of the field remained quiet. Wilder's "Lighting Brigade" watched Vinyard Field from its vantage on the low rise west of the LaFayette Road. They were the only Federals at that time facing Bragg's main column, had the Rebel leader but known it. Farther south, the other two divisions of Thomas Crittenden's corps remained in position west of Lee and Gordon's Mills, protecting the crossing there and awaiting the arrival of the balance of McCook's XX Corps.

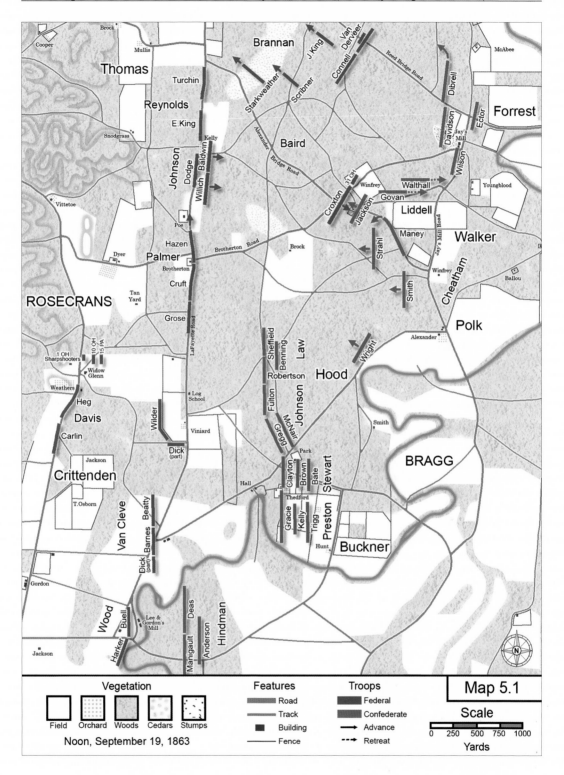

Vegetation

Field   Orchard   Woods   Cedars   Stumps

Noon, September 19, 1863

Features

Road
Track
Building
Fence

Troops

Federal
Confederate
Advance
Retreat

Map 5.1

Scale

0   250   500   750   1000

Yards

5.2: Cheatham Enters the Fight
(12:15 p.m.)

Ben Cheatham's large division didn't have time to halt and dress lines to enter the battle as a cohesive attacking mass. Instead, each of Cheatham's five brigades advanced rather haphazardly as circumstances dictated. Gen. Walker, who had been calling for support all morning, was more than happy to see fresh veteran troops. Almost all of Cheatham's men were from Tennessee, and most were disheartened after the disastrous Tullahoma campaign forced them to leave their homes and families to suffer under Federal occupation. As a result, desertion plagued the division during the retreat. At the end of April, Cheatham's (then) four brigades numbered more than 8,000 effectives. Now, in September, those same four brigades numbered just 5,200 men. The addition of Brig. Gen. John K. Jackson's command only brought Cheatham's strength up to 7,000. Although their units were understrength, these Tennesseans were good fighters determined to strike back at the enemy, all with an eye toward returning to Middle Tennessee.[5]

The Reserve Corps' chief of staff, Capt. Joseph B. Cumming, was sent to warn Cheatham's leading brigade under Jackson that Federals had scattered Liddell's line. Jackson's men were still in road column on the Alexander's Bridge Road looking for friendly troops to support when Cumming galloped up with the news that Federals were just ahead. The Confederates quickly fumbled into a line of battle where they stood. From left to right, the brigade was aligned as follows: 5th Georgia, 2nd Battalion, 1st CSA, 5th Mississippi, 8th Mississippi, and 2nd Georgia Sharpshooters.

Uncertainty marked the deployment. Col. Charles P. Daniel of the 5th Georgia, on the brigade's left flank, was instructed by Jackson not to deploy skirmishers because Walker's men were still in their front. In fact, Walker's men were falling back east of Winfrey Field to reorganize. Daniel soon discovered that Jackson was mistaken when his regiment stumbled into a line of enemy infantry a few hundred yards in their front. The Federals leveled their rifled muskets and opened fire. "This confused my command considerably," admitted Daniel.[6]

The Federals belonged to John Croxton. After routing Col. Daniel Govan's Brigade, Croxton recovered seven pieces of artillery around Winfrey Field, guns the 1st Michigan and 4th Indiana had lost earlier when Baird's line was overrun.[7] Croxton's brigade was moving forward cautiously along the Alexander Bridge Road when it encountered Jackson's advancing Rebels. Croxton (and the 31st Ohio) occupied a wide frontage in this wooded and hilly terrain—so much so that Croxton operated the brigade as two wings, one commanded by himself and the other by Col. Charles W. Chapman of the 74th Indiana. By the time the last of Walker's Confederates were driven away, a gap of 200-300 yards yawned wide in the center of Croxton's line.[8]

If Jackson's troops were surprised by the collision, so were Croxton's men. There seemed to be no end to the Confederates, and these new Rebels were no less willing to fight than their earlier counterparts. Jackson ordered his brigade to charge, and it did so with a will, driving Chapman's portion of the brigade a considerable distance.[9] Croxton's "wing" was still attempting to rescue the abandoned Union guns on its front when Jackson's regiments struck. Capt. I. B. Webster of the 10th Kentucky (Federal) had just deployed his company I as a skirmish line to cover the detachments of men hauling off the recovered artillery when, "Suddenly, rapid musket-firing commenced on our right . . . and rear."[10]

Once again fearing for his right flank, and with Chapman's three regiments in considerable disorder, Croxton left the guns and ordered the entire brigade (both "wings") back about 300 yards to a wooded ridge where, reunited, all six regiments halted Jackson's advance.[11] Confederate Maj. John B. Herring, whose 8th Mississippi held the center of Jackson's line, believed they "failed to move them, owing to the want of ammunition . . . and the bad condition of [some of our] guns."[12] The action devolved into a static firefight.

Behind this struggle, more troops from both sides were maneuvering to extend the fight. Johnson's Federals were moving in to relieve Croxton's tired troops for the second time that morning, while more of Cheatham's brigades were swinging into line on Jackson's left, extending the front southward. The battle was about to widen yet again.

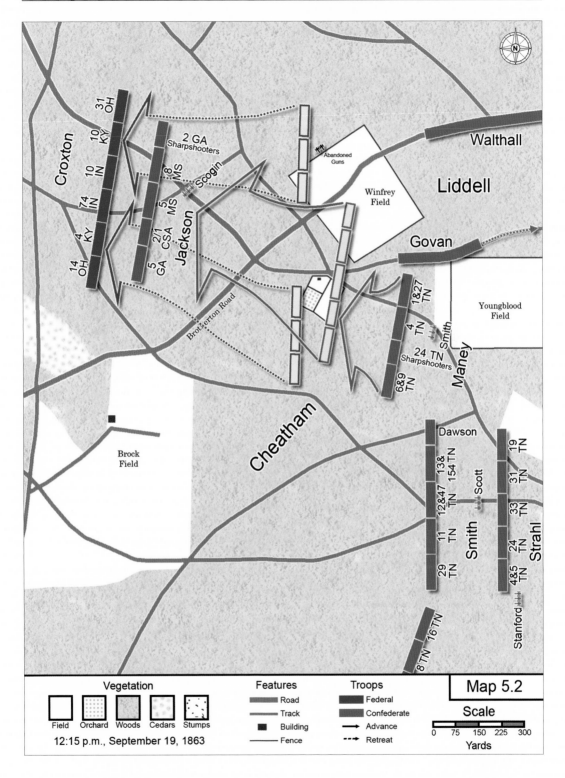

Croxton
31 OH
10 KY
10 IN
74 IN
4 KY
14 OH

2 GA
Sharpshooters

8 MS
5 MS
2/1 CSA
5 GA

Scogin

Jackson

Brotterton Road

Abandoned Guns

Winfrey Field

Walthall

Liddell

Govan

Youngblood Field

1&27 TN
4 TN
24 TN Sharpshooters
6&9 TN

Smith

Maney

Cheatham

Brock Field

Dawson

13& 154 TN
12&47 TN
11 TN
29 TN

Scott

Smith

19 TN
31 TN
33 TN
24 TN
4&5 TN

Stanford

Strahl

8 TN
16 TN

Vegetation

Field   Orchard   Woods   Cedars   Stumps

12:15 p.m., September 19, 1863

Features

Road
Track
Building
Fence

Troops

Federal
Confederate
Advance
Retreat

Map 5.2

Scale

0   75   150   225   300

Yards

5.3: Johnson and Palmer Engage (12:45 p.m.)

Despite the combat racket rising from the woods ahead, Sgt. Isaac Young of the 89th Illinois, Brig. Gen. August Willich's brigade, recalled an oddly peaceful scene in Kelly Field as troops from Johnson's Federal division deployed for action. "The birds were singing, the butterflies were fluttering about, and a cow stood under a tree to our right," Young recalled, "lazily chewing her cud."[13] Within minutes, Young and his comrades in the 89th, together with the rest of the division, left this bucolic scene behind and stepped off into the woods.

Johnson deployed in what by mid-1863 was a standard Federal formation: two brigades abreast (Willich on the right and Col. Philemon P. Baldwin on the left), each with two regiments in front and two behind in support, with a third brigade (Col. Joseph B. Dodge) formed behind, also with two forward and two supporting regiments. Artillery trailed the center of each brigade, alert for possibilities to bring the guns into action. Johnson's orders were to find and attack the enemy, though Thomas could not sketch out a clear picture of the Southern deployment. The best he could do was instruct Johnson to move in an "oblique to the general line" angling off to the south.[14] Thomas was still looking for that elusive Rebel flank.

August Willich's men were the first of Johnson's troops to find the enemy. Willich was another German immigrant, but no ordinary one. Once an officer in the Kaiser's army, he became an ardent communist as a young man, leaving the service to pursue a political life. He was fiercely committed to the ideals of socialism, so much so that he scorned those who failed to live up to his ideals. He quarreled with Karl Marx over the future of the movement, and once challenged Marx to a duel. No one questioned Willich's military skills. He had proved his worth in the revolution of 1848-49 in Europe, and after that uprising was crushed moved to Cincinnati, Ohio, to edit a German-language newspaper. In the current conflict, he proved himself anew, becoming one of the best brigade commanders in the Army of the Cumberland.

Passing Croxton's exhausted Federals, Willich made contact when his skirmish line, well to the front of his main battle line, encountered "a murderous fire of musketry and artillery."[15] The lead and iron was being hurled by Gen. Jackson's Confederate brigade. Willich responded by bringing up his own battery and, after a short engagement during which he felt his fire had "sufficiently shaken the enemy's infantry line," ordered a charge.[16] Now it was Jackson's turn to fall back. Once again the abandoned guns of Baird's division changed hands, and this time Willich's brigade claimed the honors.

Some distance to the south and west, Palmer's division, XXI Corps, was also coming into action. As Palmer deployed, Rosecrans sent him orders that may have saved his division from the same fate that plagued Union troops all morning: constantly being flanked on the right. Just as his men were finished deploying and about to head east through the woods, reported Palmer, Rosecrans "suggested an advance *en echelon* by brigades, refusing the right."[17] This change, immediately adopted, allowed Palmer to shift his front more easily when, as will be seen, Cheatham's Division began groping for the Union flank around Brock Field.

This maneuvering left Brig. Gen. William B. Hazen's brigade leading Palmer's advance on the left side of his line. Hazen was a Regular Army man, and one of the more competent Union brigadiers on the field. His command advanced about three-quarters of a mile before he struck the Rebels. "A terrific contest here was added to the already severe battle [Willich's] on our left," he wrote. When Willich charged, Hazen did as well, and "the enemy gave ground freely."[18] Hazen pushed forward until he reached Brock Field, a large L-shaped open area. He halted his command on a small rise in the middle of the field and engaged in a heavy exchange with Brig. Gen. Preston Smith, one of Cheatham's brigades.[19]

Smith's six Tennessee regiments and a sharpshooter battalion had advanced on Jackson's left and met little opposition until finding Hazen. Col. William Watkins, commanding the combined 12th and 47th Tennessee, reported he made contact "about 400 yards from the enemy, who seemed to [be] entrenched, having an open field between us, except a few yards of timber next to the enemy's line."[20] Capt. Alfred T. Fielder of the 12th remembered that here "[we] were engaged in an awful fight the enemy disputing every inch of the ground."[21]

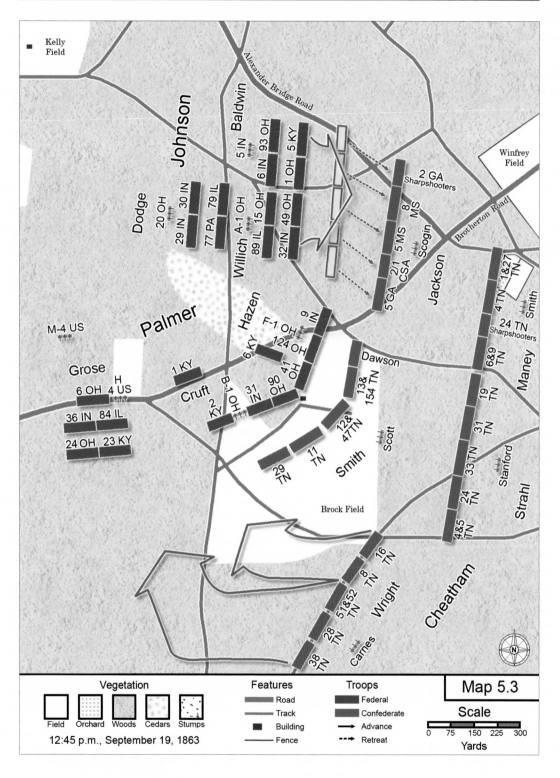

Kelly
Field

Alexander Bridge Road

Johnson

Baldwin

5 IN   93 OH

6 IN   1 OH   5 KY

Winfrey
Field

2 GA
Sharpshooters

Dodge

20 OH

29 IN   30 IN

77 PA   79 IL

89 IL   15 OH

32 IN   49 OH

Willich   A-1 OH

8
MS

5 MS   Scogin

5 GA   2/1   CSA

Brotherton Road

Jackson

1&27
TN

4 TN   Smith

24 TN
Sharpshooters

Palmer

Hazen

9
IN

F-1 OH

124 OH

6 KY

M-4 US

Dawson

6&9
TN

19
TN

Grose

1 KY

41
OH

31   90
IN   OH

13&
154 TN

31
TN

Maney

H
6 OH   4 US

Cruft

B-1 OH

2
KY

12&
47TN

Scott

33 TN

Stanford

36 IN   84 IL

24 OH   23 KY

29
TN

11
TN

Smith

24
TN

Strahl

Brock Field

4&5
TN

16
TN

8
TN

51&52
TN

Wright

28
TN

Cheatham

38
TN

Carnes

5.4: Cheatham Becomes Fully Engaged (1:15 p.m.)

Initially, Ben Cheatham intended to advance with three brigades on line and two following in support. In practice, the hurried commitment of his leading elements, coupled with the unusual formation of Palmer's division, meant that Cheatham's troops advanced into action piecemeal. Because Confederate doctrine called for forming all regiments in a brigade in a single line (recall the Federals had by now adopted a doubled formation, two regiments in front and two in support), each Southern brigade had roughly twice the frontage of its Union counterpart. Shortly after 1:00 p.m., Cheatham's three leading brigades (Jackson, Smith, and Brig. Gen. Marcus J. Wright, from right to left) were moving to engage two full Union divisions.

As noted, Jackson's success in driving Croxton ground to a halt when Croxton consolidated his command, and was converted into a slow retreat when Willich's Federals entered the fight. Jackson's men fell back until they came into line alongside Smith's troops near the northeastern edge of Brock Field's northern leg. Once aligned, both commands began a steady exchange of fire with parts of four Union brigades. On Willich's left, Col. Baldwin's two front-rank regiments—the 1st Ohio and 5th Kentucky—arrived and added their firepower against Jackson's right front. Levi Wagner, a private in the 1st Ohio, remembered this moment: "We advanced some distance through the heavy timber, driving the Rebel skirmish line as we advanced, until our regiment came up to a rail fence, with an open field to our front. . . . The enemy were in heavy force beyond this field." Despite enemy inducements, thought Wagner, the 1st Ohio proved too canny to launch a charge into the open, and instead "halted at this fence and as the two lines were in good shooting distance . . . they promptly opened fire."[22]

A similar scene played out on Hazen's right. Brig. Gen. Charles Cruft's brigade extended Hazen's line on the right, preventing Smith's longer frontage from wrapping around Hazen's flank. Due to the staggered or *en echelon* nature of the advance, however, Cruft's line faced more south than east, so angled to cover the other leg of the "L" comprising Brock Field. Reduced to three regiments by the detachment of the 1st Kentucky to support the divisional artillery, Cruft placed his brigade in a single line, with his battery positioned to fire on the brigade's front and flanks as needed.[23]

With both Jackson and Smith stymied, Cheatham again groped for an exposed Union flank to turn. On his left, Marcus Wright was still advancing unopposed. Wright was new to brigade command, still uncertain in his authority, and confused about the deployment of the rest of the division. He took over the brigade in January 1863 after Brig. Gen. Daniel Donelson resigned for health reasons. The officers of the brigade expected the promotion to go to one of their own, most likely Col. John H. Savage of the 16th Tennessee. Cheatham instead promoted Wright, who had previously served on his staff. Savage resigned in protest, and resentment toward Wright lingered within the ranks.

Wright's command of five regiments of Tennesseans passed west through the timber south of Brock Field before turning at an oblique angle toward the northwest. Wright mistakenly believed he was holding the center (and not the left flank) of Cheatham's long line because he expected Cheatham's remaining two brigades to move in on his left (south of him). Until they could come up, however, Wright sent Carnes' artillery battery out to his left to protect his line from being turned from that direction.[24] Within minutes Wright's advancing infantry struck the enemy.

Carroll H. Clark, a member of the 16th Tennessee on the brigade's right, recalled the moment of first contact: "Advancing through the woods, Jim Martin said 'Yonder they are.' & Col. Donnell said 'don't shoot they are our men,' but Jim said 'Our men hell' and bang went his gun. . . . The Yanks were swinging around and never saw us, as their attention was directed to the firing on our right."[25]

Regiment by regiment, Wright's line became engaged, initially against Cruft, and then against Grose's brigade, which had been bringing up Palmer's rear. As the fight developed, Wright's line stretched several hundred yards facing generally north, a brigade front at roughly a right angle to Smith's and Jackson's men.

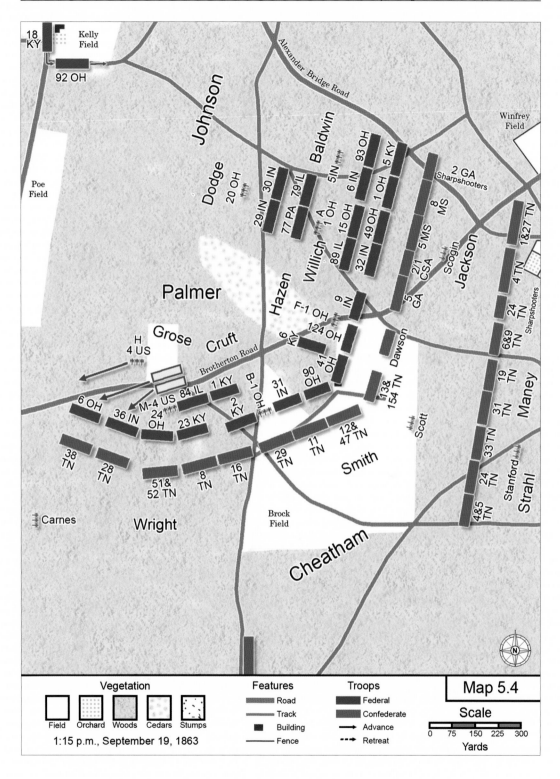

Map 5.4

Scale

1:15 p.m., September 19, 1863

5.5: Jackson and Smith Fall Back
(1:45 p.m.)

By the time Wright's Brigade completed what was essentially a drift toward the sound of the guns and engaged troops from Palmer's division, the Confederate brigades of Jackson and Smith were beginning to feel overmatched.

Preston Smith's Tennesseans made an effort to drive the Federals by advancing across Brock Field, but as the brigade advanced its line fragmented. The various regiments tried to re-orient individually to face the angled Federal line, but in doing so lost cohesion. Col. Watkins, whose 12th/47th Tennessee struck the Yankees where Hazen's right connected with Cruft's left at a sharp angle, lost touch with the 13th/154th Tennessee on its right when that command wheeled to the right.[26]

On the left of Smith's line, Col. Horace Rice of the 29th Tennessee reported an even more difficult movement as he tried to keep pace and engage the enemy. "Having double-quicked some distance over rough ground, studded in some places with thick, short undergrowth," reported the colonel, "the line of the regiment was considerably broken and some confusion prevailed at the time we halted. A volley from the enemy at that moment added still more to the confusion."[27]

Smith soon saw the folly in attacking an enemy superior in numbers across exposed ground and ordered his brigade to fall back to the southern and eastern sides of the field, where his men took cover behind a fence. After fighting from behind this protection for a short time, their ammunition began to run low. About 1:30 p.m., Smith sent word to Cheatham that he was nearly out of bullets and needed support, adding that he could hold his current line until relief arrived.[28] Cheatham ordered Brig. Gen. Otho F. Strahl's Brigade to replace Smith's men, with orders to "make no attempt to advance."[29] Cheatham also sent Brig. Gen. George Maney's command forward to replace Jackson, on Smith's right, who was also running low on ammunition. Instead of attacking an exposed Union flank, Cheatham found himself struggling just to maintain a cohesive line of battle.

The switching of brigades did not go as smoothly as Cheatham hoped it might. Strahl's line moved through Smith's men and then, contrary to Cheatham's orders, stepped out into Brock Field. By doing so, it exposed its right flank (19th and 31st Tennessee regiments) to enfilade fire from some of Hazen's men.

By now visibility was becoming an issue. On Strahl's left, William Dillon of the 4th Tennessee recorded that as the infantry moved forward, "some old dry fences had taken fire and the wind blew the smoke in the faces of our men completely blinding them."[30] Many of Strahl's men were cautioned not to fire for fear of hitting Smith's troops, so several of Strahl's regiments suffered the enemy's fire without being able to return it.[31] When he realized his error, Strahl pulled his troops back to the fence line recently vacated by Smith's regiments, but not before his command had suffered considerable loss.

Despite Cheatham's involvement, Smith's retreat caught Jackson off-guard. "Seeing troops on the left retiring," Jackson wrote, "I sent to inquire the meaning of it."[32] When he was informed of Smith's disengagement, Jackson asked Maney to come forward quickly before his own line fell apart. Pvt. Sam Watkins, a member of the 1st Tennessee of Maney's command, remembered the moment: "Even then the spent balls were falling amongst us with that peculiar thud so familiar to your old soldier. . . . We debouched through the woods, firing as we marched, the Yankee line about two hundred yards off. Bang, bang, siz, siz. It was a sort of running fire. . . . In ten minutes we were face to face with the foe."[33] Behind Watkins and his comrades, Jackson's men fell back into the woods, following Smith's battered regiments to find a place to rest and reorganize.

Cheatham's troops had at least managed to halt the advance of Johnson and Palmer, who if left unchecked might have crushed Walker's battered command. But if Bragg expected Cheatham to turn the tables on the Federals yet again, he was disappointed. Every man the Confederate army commander sent into action seemed to find twice the number of Yankees, all appearing from exactly the wrong direction.

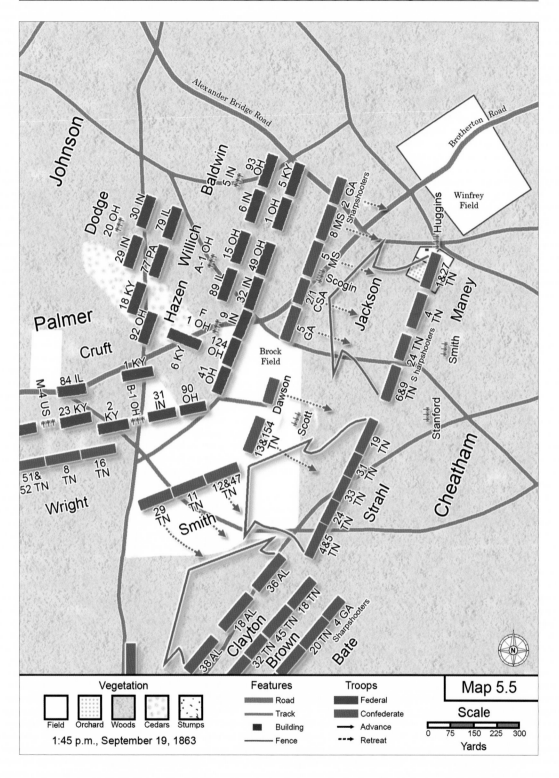

Alexander Bridge Road

Brotherton Road

Johnson

Baldwin

Dodge

20 OH

30 IN

29 IN

77 PA

79 IL

18 KY

92 OH

Willich

A-1 OH

89 IL

F 1 OH

9 IN

124 OH

41 OH

Hazen

5 IN

93 OH

5 KY

6 IN

1 OH

15 OH

49 OH

32 IN

Winfrey
Field

Huggins

2 GA
Sharpshooters

8 MS

5 MS

2/1
CSA

Scogin

5 GA

1&27
TN

Maney

4 TN
Sharpshooters

Smith

24 TN

6&9
TN

Jackson

Palmer

Cruft

84 IL

1 KY

6 KY

M-4
US

23 KY

B-1 OH

2
KY

31
IN

90
OH

Brock
Field

Dawson

Scott

Stanford

Cheatham

51&
52 TN

8
TN

16
TN

Wright

29
TN

11
TN

138&154
TN

12&47
TN

Smith

24
TN

33
TN

31
TN

19
TN

Strahl

4&5
TN

18 AL

36 AL

Clayton

38 AL

32 TN

45 TN

18 TN

Brown

20 TN

4 GA
Sharpshooters

Bate

Vegetation

Field   Orchard   Woods   Cedars   Stumps

1:45 p.m., September 19, 1863

Features

Road
Track
Building
Fence

Troops

Federal
Confederate
Advance
Retreat

Map 5.5

Scale

0   75   150   225   300

Yards

5.6: Wright is Outflanked, Stewart Approaches (1:45 p.m.)

While Maney and Strahl were attempting to stabilize the Southern line in Brock Field on his right, Marcus Wright's left flank remained completely exposed. Capt. William W. Carnes' four guns held the far left of Wright's line, posted behind the 38th Tennessee in an effort to find a position from which to engage the Yankees arrayed to their north. As the gunners were going into action, enemy fire broke out to their left and rear. Unbeknownst to Wright, two Federal brigades from Brig. Gen. Horatio P. Van Cleve's Third Division, Crittenden's XXI Corps, were moving to turn his vulnerable left flank.[34]

When he learned that Palmer's division of his corps was hotly engaged, Gen. Crittenden ordered Van Cleve to move north along the LaFayette Road with two of his brigades.[35] Leaving one brigade under Col. Sidney M. Barnes behind as part of the dwindling force guarding Lee and Gordon's Mills, Van Cleve quickly marched Brig. Gen. Samuel Beatty and Col. George F. Dick to Brotherton Field. There, following the template the Yankees had thus far taken all morning, Van Cleve faced his men to the right and moved into the timber east of the road. They were in a perfect position to turn Wright's flank.

In Beatty's brigade, Marcus Woodcock of the 9th Kentucky remembered the moment he entered the fight: "We were almost completely exhausted by the long run we had been compelled to make [nearly two miles]. . . . Our brigade fronted . . . [a] regiment at a time[,] those that fronted first commencing a musketry fight with the enemy . . . and then the whole brigade made a general charge."[36] Alongside them, struggling to keep up, hustled Dick's four regiments. Initially, Dick expected to fall in behind Beatty's men, "But," he reported, "the First Brigade having obliqued to the left . . . my front line . . . was immediately engaged and gallantly drove the first line of the enemy."[37]

Carnes' gunners and the men of the 38th Tennessee bore the brunt of the attack, but had very little time to prepare for it. Carnes reported the crisis to Cheatham, who replied, "hold [your] ground for as long as possible." When Federal fire began cutting down his artillerymen, Carnes ordered the drivers up to work the cannon, "and, giving the enemy double charges of canister at close range," held the Yankees in check.[38] The return fire, however, remained very intense. Confederate Lt. L. G. Marshall remembered the open lid of a limber chest drawing the fire of "hundreds of hostile . . . shots" so that it "made the chest resemble a huge grater." The battery was doomed. Alongside the artillery, the men of the 38th suffered a heavy fire from two directions and within a short time gave way. Col. John C. Carter did his best to rally the fleeing infantry, but they fled all the same, leaving him amidst the cannoneers.[39] Without any infantry support, Carnes ordered his gunners to abandon their pieces and limbers and save themselves.

Help was on the way. Shortly after committing Cheatham, Bragg decided to reinforce him with another Confederate infantry division, also plucked out of the middle of the line. He chose Maj. Gen. Alexander P. Stewart's three brigades (Brig. Gens. William B. Bate, John C. Brown, and Henry D. Clayton) of Simon Buckner's Corps. After crossing the Chickamauga that morning, Stewart's men occupied Buckner's right near the Park House, with John B. Hood's Corps massed just to the north. Bragg decided that Buckner could spare Stewart's troops, and around noon instructed Stewart to "move to a point where the firing had commenced . . . a considerable distance to the right . . . and rear."[40]

Unsettled by the vague nature of the directive, Stewart rode to Bragg to seek clarification. The commanding general could not offer much more in the way of specifics: Walker had been engaged, Polk was now in command on that wing, and Stewart should head for the sound of the guns and "be governed by circumstances."[41] Preserving his tactical formation—column of brigade—while he moved, Stewart pulled his men out of line, passed behind Hood's command, and advanced through the woods southeast of Brock Field. Just then, one of Marcus Wright's aides found Stewart and filled him in on the nature of the unfolding crisis. With Clayton's Alabamians leading the column, Stewart advanced to restore the situation.

Once again, Bragg had split one of his infantry corps by removing Stewart's Division from Buckner. The confused nature of the battle was playing havoc with the Southern chain of command.

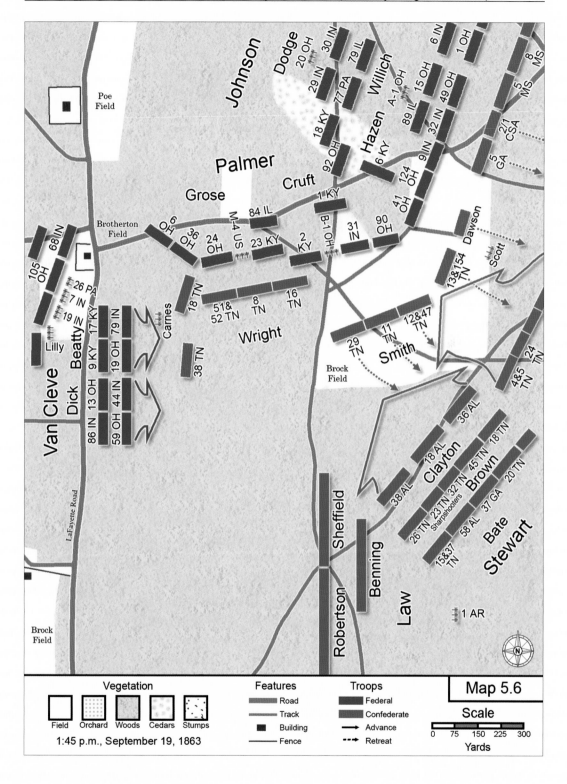

Map 5.6

Scale

1:45 p.m., September 19, 1863

Vegetation

Field   Orchard   Woods   Cedars   Stumps

Features

Road
Track
Building
Fence

Troops

Federal
Confederate
Advance
Retreat

0   75   150   225   300
Yards

5.7: Johnson's Division Advances (2:15 - 2:45 p.m.)

While Cheatham's left (Wright) was being turned, his center and right (Strahl and Maney) were subjected to increasing Union pressure. George Maney's 1,300 Tennesseans faced double their number of Federals in August Willich's and Philemon Baldwin's brigades. Matters were about to get even more lopsided.

On Willich's right, Hazen's men were running short of ammunition after their extended firefight with first Preston Smith's and then Strahl's men. Fortunately for Hazen, help was on the way. First to arrive were two regiments from Brig. Gen. John B. Turchin's Third Brigade, Fourth Division, Thomas' XIV Corps. The 18th Kentucky and 92nd Ohio were commandeered from Turchin's column by Gen. Reynolds and sent to help out in Brock Field.[42] When they appeared behind Hazen, he moved them into his front line to replace tired troops who were nearly out of bullets.

More help was on the way. Alerted to Hazen's concerns, Johnson also dispatched Col. Joseph B. Dodge's brigade, which was still in reserve and as yet unneeded on his own front. Dodge, a school teacher before the war rather than a professional soldier, was instrumental in raising two companies of the 30th Indiana Infantry in 1861. He was elected lieutenant colonel soon after the regiment's organization, and assumed command of the 30th after Col. Sion S. Bass was mortally wounded at Shiloh. When Brig. Gen. Edward Kirk was struck down at Murfreesboro, Dodge inherited the brigade. So far his men had been spared the ordeal of combat, but that was about to change.

Dodge remembered it was relatively quiet on his own front, "but off to our right it was evidently 'red-hot.'"[43] Dodge's regiments moved quickly, brushing past Hazen's surprised line to charge rapidly across Brock Field toward Strahl's Tennesseans. The weight of the attack fell primarily against the 19th Tennessee, Strahl's right-most regiment. The 19th had just extended its ranks to cover a gap between its right and Maney's left when Dodge struck. It could do little to stop the onslaught. Among those who fell was Capt. S. J. A. Frazier, shot in the throat

and left behind as the Tennessee regiment "fell back under the murderous fire."[44]

Willich, Johnson's most trusted brigade commander, believed the moment was ripe for another charge. The former Prussian officer, intellectual, and devoted communist who had fled Europe in the wake of the failed 1848 revolution was also a tactical innovator. As far as Willich was concerned, the standard two-rank infantry line was insufficient, so he developed a technique he called "advance fire." With each regiment formed in four ranks instead of two, the front rank advanced a few steps and fired, then reloaded while the next rank passed through it to do the same, and so on in turn. The result was a rolling wall of fire that could advance or retreat with equal ease.[45] Willich used his tactical innovation to great effect at Chickamauga. With Dodge's Federals driving a wedge between himself and Strahl, and menaced with Willich's determined advance against his own front, Maney could no longer hold his ground.

In addition to the threats of Dodge and Willich, Maney also had to contend with Johnson's last brigade (Baldwin) threatening his right. Only a skirmish line of Rebel cavalry protected Maney's northern flank, hardly sufficient to stop Baldwin's advance. Sam Watkins of the 1st Tennessee remembered seeing Forrest ride up at the height of the crisis and yell out to Col. Hume R. Field, the regimental commander, "'Col. Field, look out. You are almost surrounded: you had better fall back.' The order was given to retreat. I ran through a solid line of bluecoats as I fell back."[46]

The troopers were more of Col. Dibrell's men, who covered the retreat of infantry. Prominent among them were the gunners of Capt. A. L. Huggins' Tennessee Battery, whose six pieces dropped trail along the Alexander's Bridge Road in front of the Winfrey House. There, "they kept up a constant and destructive fire upon the enemy until they were within 50 yards of the guns, getting off the field with all their pieces, notwithstanding the loss of horses," reported one witness.[47] After driving the Rebels some distance, Johnson ordered his brigades to halt since there were no troops supporting his left and Palmer's division could not advance on his right. Shortly thereafter, Johnson's men fell back to their previous line, well pleased with their success.

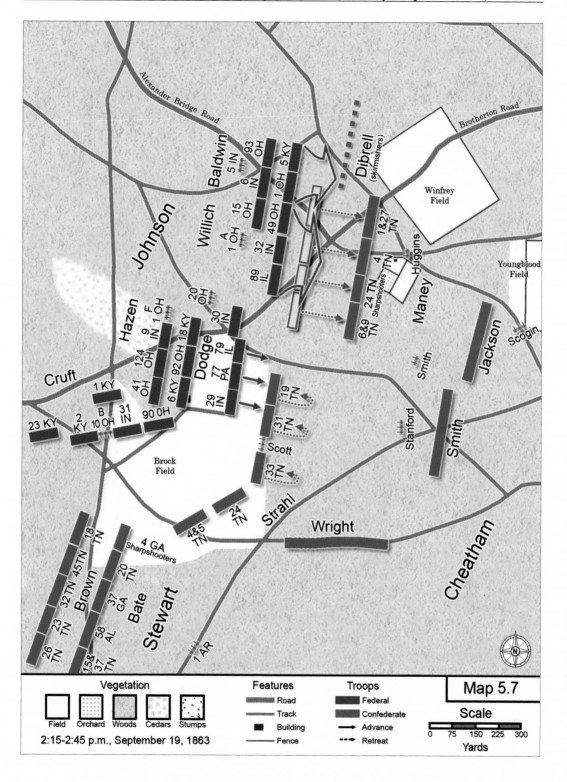

Map 5.7

Scale

2:15-2:45 p.m., September 19, 1863

5.8: Stewart Enters the Fight
(2:15 – 2:45 p.m.)

A. P. Stewart, an 1842 graduate of West Point, served only three years in the peacetime army before resigning to become a college professor. Although he was not in favor of secession, when Tennessee left the Union he volunteered first for state, and then for Confederate, service. He had not forgotten his military skills, and proved himself a capable brigade-level officer. Stewart's newly created division had shouldered the brunt of Col. John T. Wilder's attack at Hoover's Gap back in June 1863. Nicknamed "Old Straight" by his men, Stewart prepared to enter this fight in a more cautious manner than his predecessor. Cheatham had spread out to cover a wide frontage; Stewart advanced his brigades in a column, one behind the other, hoping to maintain an adequate reserve.

Henry Clayton's large Alabama brigade led Stewart's Division into action, passing through the wreck of Marcus Wright's command as the Tennesseans fell back in disorder. Clayton had been wounded at Murfreesboro and promoted to brigade command when he recovered. He had been commander of the 39th Alabama, so his brigade was entirely new to him. Despite having only three regiments, with 1,446 men Clayton's command was the largest in the division, but also the least experienced.[48] The 18th Alabama saw action at Shiloh, but the 36th and 38th Alabama regiments were garrison troops from Mobile and had yet to hear a shot fired in anger.

The Federals still enjoyed the advantage of position that had brought Wright's Brigade to grief. With Grose's men to the north and Van Cleve's brigades (Beatty and Dick) lined up facing east, the Rebels were subjected to flanking fire no matter which direction they faced. In an effort to respond to the threat that had turned Wright's flank, Clayton decided to advance northwest. As he went in, Stewart passed on Bragg's advice, vague as it was: "After having more definitely located the enemy," explained Clayton, "I would have to act for myself and be governed by circumstances."[49]

Cpl. Edgar W. Jones, marching in the ranks of Company G, 18th Alabama, recalled the experience. "Standing in line the firing began seemingly without any command," he wrote years later, "and in three minutes the engagement was something awful. The slaughter was dreadful. We discovered that we were within perhaps fifty yards of the enemy's main line."[50]

Still, the Alabamians made headway, driving back the front rank of both Beatty and Dick. "We had made one charge and drove the Rebs but was not able to hold our ground," recalled John J. Warbinton of the 59th Ohio. "As we was falling back and just before I passed the line that was in our rear, I was hit."[51] Beatty's and Dick's second lines, however, were solid bedrock upon which to rally, and both Yankee brigades held there. Clayton's Alabama regiments recaptured the remains of Carnes' battery, minus several of the guns dragged away the 79th Indiana, but beyond that they could not go.[52]

Fortunately for the Alabamians, the fire from Grose's Federals on Clayton's right proved more annoying than deadly. The range was farther, with Grose's men about 300 yards distant through the woods. Any Federal advance from that quarter was precluded by the curving nature of Palmer's divisional front. Just as Hazen couldn't advance east alongside Johnson without breaking contact with the rest of the division, Grose could not advance south without doing the same. Tied into this formation, Grose's regiments contented themselves with long range fire at whatever targets they could make out through the trees.

Grose's inability to effectively engage him allowed Clayton to focus his attention on the Yankees to his front. A static firefight developed, with every man loading and shooting as rapidly as possible—as it turned out, too rapidly for Clayton. "The firing seeming to be too much at random," he reported. "I passed down and up the line, calling the attention of officers to the fact." After regaining control of the brigade's rate of fire, Clayton decided to renew the attack. "I then directed my staff to inform [the] regimental commanders that I was about to order a charge."[53] The idea foundered when his officers informed him that they were rapidly running out of ammunition. With his options limited, Clayton decided to disengage and resupply. He sent word to Stewart of his problems and asked for relief.

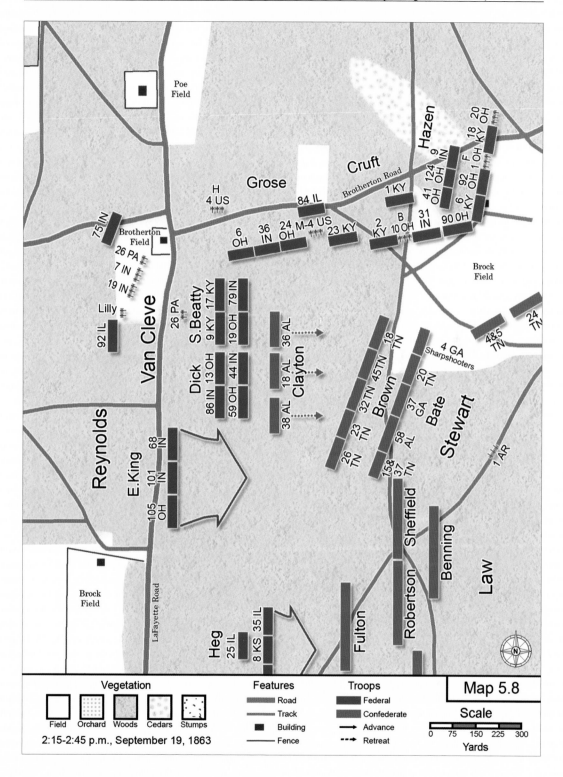

Poe Field

Hazen

Cruft

Grose

Brotherton Road

H 4 US

84 IL

1 KY

18 OH 20 OH
9 OH IN
124 OH
41 OH
92 OH 1 OH KY
6 KY

75 IN

Brotherton Field

26 PA

7 IN

19 IN

Lilly

92 IL

6 OH   36 IN   24 OH   M-4 US   23 KY

2 KY   B 10 OH   31 IN   90 OH

Brock Field

Van Cleve

26 PA

S.Beatty
9 KY 17 KY
19 OH 79 IN

36 AL

4 GA
Sharpshooters

18 TN

48 5 TN   24 TN

Dick
86 IN 13 OH
59 OH 44 IN

18 AL

Clayton

38 AL

32 TN 45 TN

Brown

20 TN

37 GA

Bate

Stewart

Reynolds

E.King

68 IN

101 IN

105 OH

23 TN

26 TN

15 & 37 TN

58 AL

1 AR

Sheffield

Robertson

Benning

Law

Brock Field

LaFayette Road

Heg

25 IL   8 KS   35 IL

Fulton

Vegetation

Field   Orchard   Woods   Cedars   Stumps

2:15-2:45 p.m., September 19, 1863

Features

Road
Track
Building
Fence

Troops

Federal
Confederate
Advance
Retreat

Map 5.8

Scale

0   75   150   225   300

Yards

N

5.9: Brown Replaces Clayton (3:00 p.m.)

Clayton's courier found division leader A. P. Stewart with Brig. Gen. John C. Brown, a Tennessee lawyer and by 1863 a veteran brigade commander. Brown had seen action at Fort Donelson, led a brigade into Kentucky in the fall of 1862, and fought at Murfreesboro. His men were supporting the Alabamians so closely that Brown reported taking casualties while waiting behind Clayton's line, though without being able to return fire. With Clayton coming out of the fight, Stewart ordered Brown to go in.[54]

Brown's was another all-Tennessee outfit, his four regiments (18th, 26th, 32nd, and 45th) and a battalion (23rd) totaling 1,340 men. His broad front covered both Dick's and Beatty's opposing lines. Despite terrain difficulties, limited visibility, and "no position from which my artillery could be served with advantage," Brown ordered his men to charge.[55] T. I. Corn of the 32nd Tennessee wrote that "the battle was now on in dead earnest, and it was like a cyclone of fire."[56] The woods were ablaze in many places, and smoke made it difficult to see far in any direction. According to N. J. Hampton of the 18th Tennessee, the smoke was so dense "we could not distinguish the enemy from our own men ten steps away."[57] As the 32nd passed through Carnes' position, Corn spotted thirteen dead horses in a single pile. "[W]ith the shouts of the men, the boom of the cannon, and the roar of the small arms," he recalled, "[it] was an event never to be forgotten."[58]

The Federal line had the dual advantage of position and numbers, but lacked command coordination. No single officer directed Grose's brigade and Van Cleve's two brigades in the bitter close-in combat. Moreover, elements of a third division—Reynolds' command, Thomas' XIV Corps—held the open field behind them. Reynolds already had one of the smallest divisions in the army, made even smaller when one of his two brigades under Turchin was sent to support Hazen. Earlier, as the fighting swelled in the woods to the east, Reynolds met Thomas near the Brotherton farm. Thomas was worried about the spreading battle and seeking reinforcements. "I asked [him] distinctly," recalled Reynolds, "if our people could maintain themselves and he said he was not sure."[59]

Thomas also counseled Reynolds not to send his artillery into the woods, for too many guns had already been lost there. Shortly after this meeting, Reynolds sent three regiments of his last brigade under Col. Edward A. King into the timber on Dick's right flank, extending the line well past Brown's left flank. At forty-nine, King was one of the older brigade leaders on the field, and perhaps the only one who had fought in the Texas War for Independence. He was commissioned into the Regular Army and accompanied Winfield Scott to Mexico City. It only made sense he would return to the colors again in 1861. Although an Ohio resident, he secured command of the 68th Indiana. The 68th was raised in August 1862, rushed to the front during the Perryville Campaign, and captured less than a month later at Munfordville. The men had seen little action since.

Reynolds retained only the 75th Indiana and the 92nd Illinois of Wilder's brigade, plus a line of artillery, gathered haphazardly, to hold Brotherton Field. About thirty minutes later, or roughly 3:00 p.m., the disorganized 6th Ohio from Grose's command appeared looking for ammunition. Reynolds added the Buckeyes to his reserve line.[60] When Palmer requested the loan of another regiment to replace the 6th Ohio, Reynolds committed the last of his own regiments, the 75th Indiana, sending it forward to take up a position between Beatty and Grose.[61] The 75th reached a point where it could pour enfilade fire into Brown's 18th and 45th Tennessee regiments, checking the advance and allowing time for Van Cleve's men to rally.[62]

Had the move been better coordinated, King's arrival might have decisively crushed Brown's Tennesseans. Uncertain of Van Cleve's exact location in the smoky woods, King's three regiments extended themselves too far to the south. When King halted the brigade, placed all three regiments in a single line, and started moving eastward into the timber, his left was nearly one-quarter mile beyond Dick's right.[63] While this gap precluded any immediate support for Dick's regiments, it still would have allowed King's 1,138 men to sweep around into the Rebel rear, had they advanced unchecked.

By 3:00 p.m. the battle was expanding rapidly, and Bragg was finally ready to commit John B. Hood's troops to the fight.

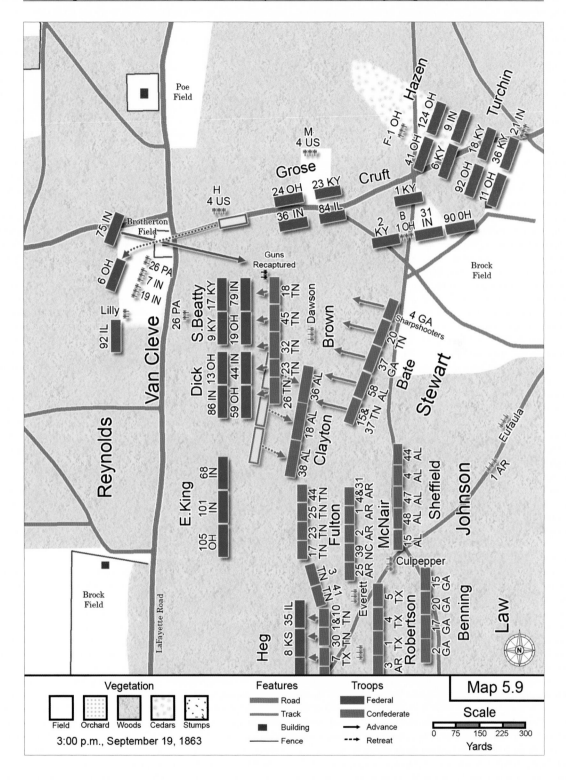

Poe Field

M 4 US

Grose

Cruft

Hazen

Turchin

F-1 OH

41 OH

124 OH

6 KY

9 IN

18 KY

36 KY

2 IN

24 OH   23 KY

H 4 US

1 KY

92 OH

11 OH

Brotherton Field

36 IN   84 IL

75 IN

2 KY

B 1 OH

31 IN

90 OH

Brock Field

6 OH

26 PA

7 IN

19 IN

Guns Recaptured

Lilly

26 PA

S.Beatty

9 KY 17 KY

79 IN

18 TN

45 TN

Dawson

92 IL

Van Cleve

Dick

19 OH

32 TN

Brown

86 IN 13 OH

44 IN

26 TN 23 TN

36 AL

4 GA Sharpshooters

20 TN

37 GA

Bate

Stewart

59 OH

18 AL

58 AL

Eufaula

Reynolds

38 AL

Clayton

15& 37 TN AL

1 AR

E.King

68 IN

44 AL

4 AL

47 AL

Sheffield

101 IN

105 OH

25 44 TN TN

48 AL

Johnson

Fulton

1 4&31 AR AR

15 AL

McNair

Culpepper

Brock Field

17 23 TN TN

2 39 AR NC

AR AR

Law

LaFayette Road

3 NI

4 NI

Everett

25 AR

5 TX

15 GA

Benning

8 KS 35 IL

30 1&10 TIN TN

4 TX

20 GA

Heg

7 TX TN

3 AR

1 TX

Robertson

17 GA

2 GA

Vegetation	Features	Troops	Map 5.9

Vegetation: Field Orchard Woods Cedars Stumps

3:00 p.m., September 19, 1863

Features: Road Track Building Fence

Troops: Federal Confederate Advance Retreat

Map 5.9

Scale

0   75   150   225   300

Yards

5.10: Overall Situation (3:00 p.m.)

By mid-afternoon the fighting had all but ceased on the northern end of the battlefield. Walker's Confederate Reserve Corps was recovering from its morning engagements. Dibrell's cavalry covered the retreat of George Maney's Brigade, which was the last of Ben Cheatham's units to break contact. Cheatham would spend the next two hours reforming his division in the woods east of Brock Field. While his losses had not been as severe as Walker's, his five brigades needed to be rested and resupplied.

For their part, the Federals were glad to see them go. Thomas aligned Absalom Baird's and John Brannan's divisions along the open clearing of the cedar glade east of the LaFayette Road, with Ferdinand Van Derveer's brigade still covering the Reed's Bridge Road. Each division had lost about one-third of its complement during the morning's action, with total losses approaching 3,000 men. Additionally, fourteen of Baird's eighteen artillery pieces had been captured or abandoned.

In the center, the Union forces controlled Brock Field, but their lines were disorganized. When Johnson's division advanced, Dodge's brigade, on the right, never regained contact with Hazen on Palmer's left. A gap of several hundred yards yawned between the two formations, even after Johnson's men fell back to a line roughly anchored on Winfrey Field. As an additional complication, Hazen's regiments were being relieved. Turchin and his remaining two regiments came up about this time, affording Hazen the opportunity to pull his entire brigade out of line and move back to Poe Field and the divisional trains, where he replenished his ammunition.[64] Had Hazen remained in place, he might have been more alert to Dodge's failure to reconnect on his left, but Turchin's arrival interrupted that continuity. The rest of Palmer's troops still faced south, aligned roughly parallel to the Brotherton Road behind them, but played little part in the fight still raging between Van Cleve and A. P. Stewart.

South of Brock Field, six Rebel brigades comprising Hood's First Corps were, at 2:00 p.m., still massed in the woods awaiting orders. About 2:30 p.m., Union troops of Brig. Gen. Jefferson C. Davis' First Division, McCook's XX Corps, entered the woods near the Viniard House and collided with Brig. Gen. John Gregg and Col. John Fulton's men, who comprised Gen. Bushrod Johnson's (not to be confused with Richard C. Johnson's Union division) front line. Shortly after this contact, Hood ordered Johnson's men forward in a general attack, supported by Brig. Gen. Evander Law's three brigades to their rear.[65] Whether by accident or design, these 7,000 Southern troops were aimed primarily at the gap that still existed in Rosecrans' line between Brotherton Field and the Viniard farm.

For his part, Rosecrans was acutely aware of the gap and had been trying to fill it for much of the day. It was at the Union commander's personal direction that Davis' division was sent forward, triggering the collision with Hood. Rosecrans was still looking to turn the elusive Rebel flank, and thought he was sending Davis' men into the trees alongside Van Cleve's troops, but Davis' two brigades—amounting to only 2,500 men—were too few to fill the wide space.

More Federals, however, were on the way. Van Cleve's last brigade under Col. Sidney M. Barnes was halted just south of Viniard's. Barnes had lost touch with his division commander, but was in proximity to support Davis. Brig. Gen. Thomas J. Wood's First Division, XXI Corps, was also en route, ordered forward by Gen. Crittenden to join the fight.

Once again, the battle's center of gravity was shifting south. All of these commands, Union and Confederate, were about to collide in and around the Viniard farmstead.

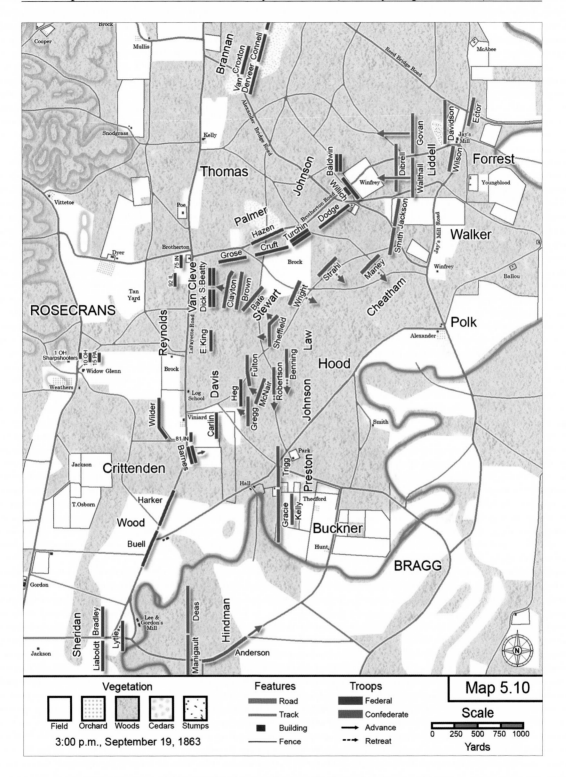

Vegetation

Field | Orchard | Woods | Cedars | Stumps

Features

Road
Track
Building
Fence

Troops

Federal
Confederate
Advance
Retreat

Map 5.10

Scale

0   250   500   750   1000

Yards

3:00 p.m., September 19, 1863

Map Set 6: Back and Forth in Viniard Field

(Afternoon, September 19)

6.1: Davis Deploys (2:15 p.m.)

As the fighting swelled around Brock Field, the two brigades of Brig. Gen. Jefferson C. Davis' First Division, Maj. Gen. Alexander McCook's XX Corps, reached the field.

That morning Davis' men were camped at Pond Spring, where they received word from McCook to move north and report to either Thomas or Rosecrans. A dusty morning march carried the First Division to the Widow Glenn's, where it found Union army commander Maj. Gen. William Rosecrans. Here, at midday, Rosecrans ordered Davis "to move forward as speedily as possible in the direction of the heaviest firing, and to make an attack with a view, if possible, to turn the enemy's left flank."[1] The threat was obvious. Overshots from enemy artillery and even a few musket balls were dropping around the cabin or whistling past overhead.[2] A competent officer, Davis' shooting of fellow general William Nelson in Louisville the previous year cast a long shadow over his career. Although charged with murder, the indictment was suspended and ultimately ignored. Leaving one battery on the forward slope of the knoll at the Glenn house, Davis immediately started for the front.

The men in Brig. Gen. William P. Carlin's brigade had led Davis' division that morning and were already tired. They had double-quicked about three miles to reach the field on a warm afternoon, their only break a pause at Crawfish Springs to refill the canteens.[3] Capt. William E. Patterson of the 38th Illinois was impressed by the combat racket as they drew closer to the action. "The firing," he wrote, "seemed to increase and become terrific. Volley after volley broken by continual and incessant peals of artillery resounded through the woods and over the fields."[4]

Now Col. Hans Heg's four regiments took the lead. Heg's force was a mixed bag of Midwesterners: the 8th Kansas, 15th Wisconsin, and 25th and 35th Illinois. The Kansans were the only representatives of their state serving in the

Army of the Cumberland, and the Badgers from Wisconsin enjoyed the distinction of being the only Norwegian regiment in Federal service. Col. Heg had led the 15th until recently, when the regiment was transferred out of Carlin's brigade in order to allow the talented Heg to rise to brigade command.[5]

When Heg reached the road, he deployed his small brigade facing the woods, his line of 1,200 centered on a small structure known later as the "Log School."[6] Heg departed from standard tactics by leaving only one regiment (the 25th Illinois) in the second line. His front line was held by the 8th Kansas in the center, the 35th Illinois on its left, and the 15th Wisconsin on its right. Carlin moved his brigade into position on Heg's right, deploying his regiments facing the open expanse of Viniard Field. His front line, from left to right, consisted of the 38th Illinois, 101st Ohio, and 81st Indiana. The 21st Illinois aligned itself behind the 81st Indiana on the right side of the line. With an eye toward supporting the infantry's advance, Davis planted the 2nd Minnesota's guns on the right side across the road in the southern end of the field.[7]

Davis could be a bit of a meddler, and Carlin—who had his hands full—felt keenly his superior's interference. While forming a line of battle, the 81st Indiana appeared to be in distress. Because the Hoosiers were commanded by a captain inexperienced at regimental control, Carlin dispatched Maj. James E. Calloway of the 21st Illinois to take charge of the regiment.[8] Davis stepped in, took the 81st Indiana away, and shifted it south to support the 2nd Minnesota. After issuing his order, Davis rode along Carlin's line and instructed the men to lie down, "without giving me or them additional instructions," complained a bewildered Carlin.[9] Finally, Davis ordered Carlin to give up the 21st Illinois to act as a divisional reserve, a move that left his disgruntled brigadier with only two regiments.

Heg, meanwhile, was not waiting for Carlin and Davis to finish deploying. After forming his lines, the Norwegian colonel plunged into the timber and scrub oak east of the road. Within a short time Heg's line uncovered and drove back a line of enemy skirmishers. Lt. Col. Ole C. Johnson, in command of the 15th Wisconsin, found the firing heavy and the timber so thick that "we could but imperfectly see the enemy." Still, the Norwegians pressed forward rapidly.[10]

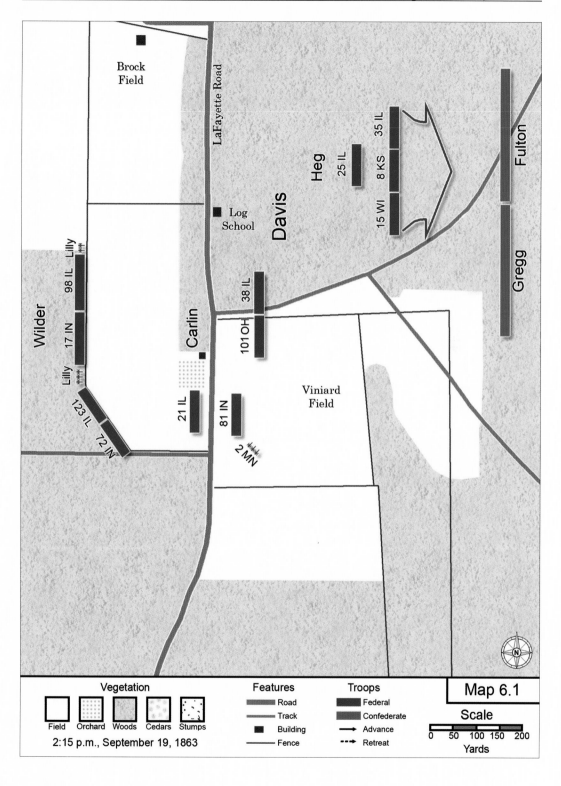

Map 6.1

2:15 p.m., September 19, 1863

6.2: Heg Finds the Rebels (2:45 p.m.)

The Union army was noted for its ethnic regiments. As war frenzy swept the country in 1861, many nationalities rushed to prove their patriotism by recruiting regiments of their countrymen. Most prominent within the Army of the Cumberland were regiments of Germans and Irish. Hans Heg represented another—much rarer—breed of immigrant: Norwegian.

Active in Wisconsin state politics and the pre-war militia, Heg recruited the 15th Wisconsin from the many Norwegians who had settled in the state beginning in the 1840s. Since Swedes and Danes also filled out the ranks, the 15th became known as "The Scandinavian Regiment." With two companies on detached duty and much hard service already behind them, the 15th was smaller than most regiments on the field that day, mustering only 176 men. Small numbers did not deter them from hurrying through the open timber toward the Rebel line.

Heg's attack fell upon Brig. Gen. Bushrod Johnson's main divisional line a few hundred yards into the woods. The Norwegians struck the front of most of Brig. Gen. John Gregg's Brigade, as well as the left portion of Col. John S. Fulton's command. Despite the retreat of their skirmish line, most of the Rebels were surprised by the sudden encounter. Capt. William H. Harder of the 23rd Tennessee, fighting in the center of Fulton's line, recalled the racket that suddenly arose to the south: "We sent a skirmish line to our left center, which was no sooner deployed . . . than they were attacked with great fury and by overwhelming force driven back."[11]

Clarence Malone of the 10th Tennessee, squarely in the middle of Heg's attack, was surprised by the ferocity of the initial encounter. "The whole line was engaged," remembered Malone, "and in less than ten minutes our regiment had lost one hundred men out of 168."[12] Losses during this stage of the fighting were lower than Malone recalled. Although many Rebels were surprised, the sudden attack did little to dampen their fighting spirit. The Federals, recalled John Goodrich, another of Gregg's men, "were handsomely repulsed."[13]

The Yankees found the fight equally brutal. Capt. Mons Grinager of the 15th Wisconsin reported they "received a heavy volley from the enemy's line. . . . We held our position for some minutes, and fired about 6 or 7 rounds, when we were ordered back 10 or 15 paces."[14] As Heg quickly discovered, his brigade front was too short for the numbers opposing him: Fulton and Gregg overlapped Heg's line on both flanks, and had artillery support close at hand. To James Love, adjutant of the 8th Kansas (holding Heg's center), it seemed the Confederates' "superior numbers found several gaps in the line . . . and flanking us . . . we had to fall back."[15] Capt. Grinagar added that the brigade also faced a devastating crossfire "from infantry on our right and a rebel battery on our left."[16] Heg's Federals slowly gave ground, edging westward toward the LaFayette Road. The capable colonel called up the 337 men of the 25th Illinois into the front line to bolster his ranks, and appealed to Davis for more help.

Despite his superiority in numbers, thus far Bushrod Johnson had done little more than maintain his position. With two of his batteries engaged, he brought forward his remaining artillery—Capt. James Culpeper's South Carolina battery—from the reserve line and directed all his guns to fire toward the Viniard House, west and slightly to his south. Wary of breaking formation, Johnson did not allow Fulton and Gregg to advance far, and indeed, for a while Federal pressure appeared to be absent from Fulton's front and Gregg's right. Not so for Gregg's left, where the 7th Texas and 50th Tennessee seemed to be "suffering severely."[17] These troops were facing the newly arrived 25th Illinois, dispatched to the firing line by Heg.

One other Confederate brigade entered the picture about this time, if only on the periphery. When Stewart's Confederate division moved out for action farther north, its departure left a gap between the commands of Maj. Gen. John Hood and Maj. Gen. Simon Buckner. Buckner filled that space with Col. Robert C. Trigg's Brigade from Brig. Gen. William Preston's Division. Trigg, in turn, covered his entire front with the 271 men of the 1st Florida Cavalry (dismounted), who deployed as skirmishers at the eastern edge of Viniard Field. There, the Floridians settled in to fire at long range in the direction of Carlin's distant regiments.[18]

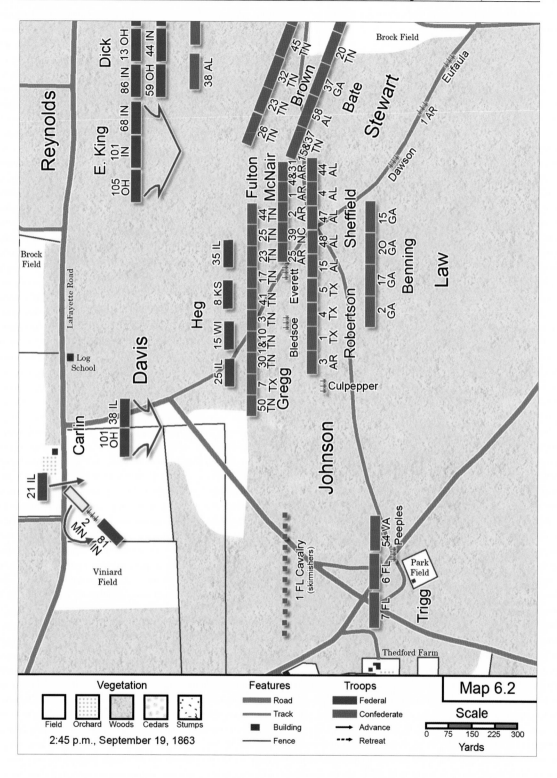

Map 6.2

Vegetation

Field Orchard Woods Cedars Stumps

2:45 p.m., September 19, 1863

Features

Road
Track
Building
Fence

Troops

Federal
Confederate
Advance
Retreat

Scale

0   75   150   225   300
Yards

6.3: Carlin Advances (3:00 p.m.)

William Carlin watched the developing combat with growing frustration. The brigade leader's men were still lying prone in the bed of the LaFayette Road, left there—and apparently forgotten—by Davis. As Col. Heg collided with the main Rebel line, the firing swelled with new intensity, but still no orders arrived. Capt. William C. Harris of the 38th Illinois, Carlin's brigade, was also distressed by the vexing state of affairs. According to the captain, the men of the 38th were "very much exposed," and no one could figure out why the regiment had been "ordered not to fire." Still, he added proudly, "they stood their ground without flinching."[19]

Carlin was Regular Army, a West Pointer (1850) who had already seen a decade of hard service on the western frontier when war arrived in 1861. He didn't get along with Davis, an attitude that hardened into outright dislike after Stone's River. Davis' division had suffered severely in that fight, and Carlin believed that Davis' official report was a rebuke of his (Carlin's) performance. Thereafter, Carlin harbored a deep grudge against his division commander.

By now, Viniard Field was a beehive of Union activity. What that activity lacked, however, was a single organizing hand. About 200 yards behind Carlin, four regiments of Col. John T. Wilder's brigade were deployed on a slight rise at the edge of the field. Armed mostly with Spencer rifles and supported by Capt. Eli Lilly's 18th Indiana battery, Wilder's troops represented a powerful backstop to any Union force in the vicinity. Unlike the other organizations on the field, Wilder was acting independently and took his orders directly from Rosecrans. The brigade leader was tasked with the vague assignment to take up a position "on the right fighting flank of our army."[20] Wilder cautioned Carlin to be especially aware of two of his regiments holding the woods behind Carlin's right rear.

Wilder's troops were of less immediate impact to the unfolding battle than another Union brigade deployed and ready to advance in the woods just south of the field. These men belonged to Col. Sidney M. Barnes, who was still wondering where Van Cleve, his division

commander, could be found. Left behind when the division was dispatched north, Barnes had been relieved by other troops and was trying to rejoin his command, which was then engaged with Stewart's Rebels east of Brotherton Field. Barnes knew little of the fluid situation unfolding in the woods to his front. When ordered forward, he later explained, "I asked to whom I should report, and upon whom I should form, and where was the enemy." Like so many responses that day on both sides, a courier from Thomas Crittenden, his corps commander, provided only the sketchiest of information. Barnes was informed that "our army was driving them," and that "I could take them in the flank," and "to go in and act on my own judgment."[21]

At this time, in response to Heg's appeals for help, Davis ordered Carlin's 21st Illinois forward. Moving north about 200 yards, the Illini came into action just at the edge of the timber to Heg's right, "where the enemy was engaged in great fury."[22] The 21st added enough weight to stabilize Heg's line. Within a few minutes, the aggressive colonel renewed his advance. Six days after the battle, Pvt. James G. Watson, Company I, 25th Illinois, recorded the moment his regiment stepped into the fight: "The first thing we knew the Rebels were firing on us; we returned the compliments, and then charged and drove them for a while."[23]

Carlin was aware of the presence of Wilder and Barnes but paid them little heed: Heg was in trouble, and Davis had finally ordered Carlin to move forward. With the 38th Illinois on the left and the 101st Ohio alongside on the right, Carlin led his men into action. Instead of charging headlong across the field they commenced a methodical advance, facing at first only the lively but long-range fire of the 1st Florida's skirmish line and whatever attention John Gregg's right wing regiments could pay them. If Bushrod Johnson's Rebels had been alone in these woods, Carlin's attack might have unraveled the entire Rebel line in a repetition of the ongoing flanking attacks that had thus far characterized much of the day's fighting. Johnson, however, was not alone. Behind his line was John Hood's veteran division from the Army of Northern Virginia, under the command of Brig. Gen. Evander Law. A skilled tactician and often impatient man, Hood quickly grew tired of waiting. After all, he had been doing that all day. Accordingly, he ordered his entire command into action.

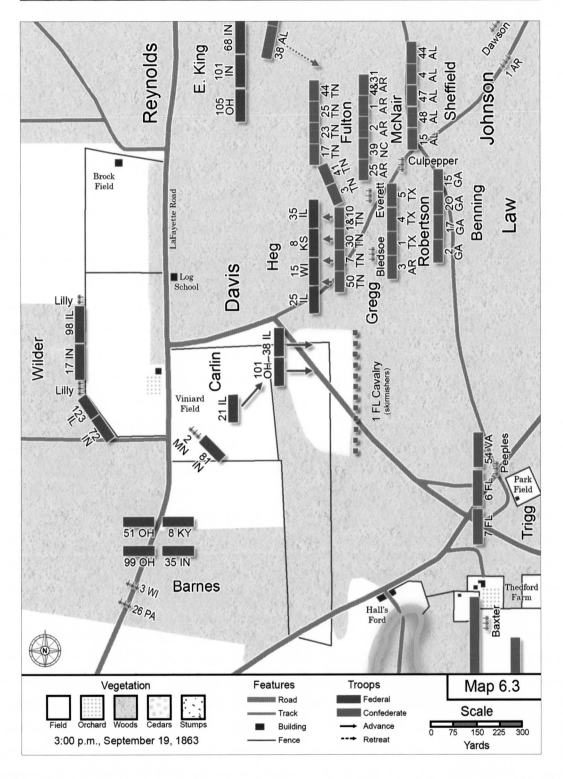

Vegetation

Field Orchard Woods Cedars Stumps

3:00 p.m., September 19, 1863

Features

▓▓▓ Road
— Track
■ Building
— Fence

Troops

▓ Federal
▓ Confederate
→ Advance
⇢ Retreat

Map 6.3

Scale

0   75   150   225   300

Yards

6.4: The Rebels Advance (3:30 p.m.)

John Hood led only the rump of an army corps on the 19th. James Longstreet's absence elevated Hood to corps command, which now included three brigades of his own division, temporarily led by Evander Law, and Bushrod Johnson's provisional division of three brigades. Maj. Gen Lafayette McLaws' Division was en route, as was Longstreet himself. Neither would arrive in time to participate in what would include some of the most confusing movements and combat of the entire day.

Initially, Law's and Johnson's two divisions were deployed in two lines: each division alongside one another, with two brigades abreast and one in reserve. As noted, Johnson was bearing the brunt of the Union attack. When he moved against Col. Heg, his line angled northwest—in effect moving up and in front of Law's men. This was problem enough, but as the Rebels started to move west, Hood added an additional complication. Law's Division began on the left. Stewart's troops moved close by Law's left brigade (under Col. James Sheffield) as they marched to replace Marcus Wright's disorganized and battered Tennesseans. Johnson's men were in line on Law's right. Hood apparently wanted Law and Johnson to switch places, and ordered Law's entire command to move southwest while Johnson's men angled northwest. This crisscross disrupted both divisions. Sheffield's Brigade immediately lost contact with the rest of Law's Division and moved to his right instead of his left (ultimately fighting amidst Stewart's men instead of his own organization) while Johnson's front split apart between Gregg and Fulton. Ultimately Hood's orders dissipated his striking power. Why he attempted the maneuver (or if he even ordered it) remains unclear.[24] It is possible that he intended to form a column by moving Law into position behind Johnson, but if he did, it failed.

Johnson's front was the first to fracture. With Fulton's front clear and McNair behind him in reserve, the two brigades struck off for the northwest, moving toward the sound of the fighting near Brotherton Field. John Gregg's command, however, faced an impossible task. He was ordered to "keep the connection to the right" with Fulton, while at the same time part of his command was still hotly engaged with Heg's Federals.[25] Not surprisingly, his brigade broke into two pieces. The 3rd and 41st Tennessee kept their connection with Fulton and followed his men fully 600 yards before encountering opposition. Gregg's left, pulled apart by the widening gulf between Fulton and Buckner's Corps, lost contact with both friendly flank forces. The 50th Tennessee, was attenuated almost to a skirmish line trying to maintain this impossible contact.

Despite not being in immediate contact with the enemy, Law's troops suffered much the same fate as Gregg. Brig. Gen. Jerome B. Robertson's Texans and Arkansas, on the division's right, advanced only a short distance when the brigade's skirmishers found Carlin's 38th Illinois and 101st Ohio regiments menacing their flank as they advanced to support Heg. Law immediately ordered Robertson to change front to the left to deal with the unexpected problem.[26] The tactic severed Robertson's right flank from Law's own advancing brigade under Sheffield. Robertson sent a courier to inform Sheffield of the shift, but either he never reached Sheffield or he misunderstood, for his 1,457 Alabamians continued straight ahead in A. P. Stewart's wake and eventually joined the conflict raging near Brotherton Field.[27] A Georgia brigade under Brig. Gen. Henry Benning, tasked to support Robertson, followed him southwest.

Holding Robertson's left was the 3rd Arkansas, the first of Robertson's men to make contact with Carlin's Federals. The brigade's change of direction put the Arkansans on a line facing southwest. As the Razorbacks moved forward the men emerged from the trees in the northeast corner of Viniard Field and glimpsed "a low, wooded hill on the left, a house and barns on the left front . . . [and] the all too familiar glint of bayonets."[28] Facing the 3rd Arkansas was the 38th Illinois, whose Capt. Patterson recalled that the Federals "immediately opened fire on the advancing Rebels but were unable to check them. They continued to advance slowly, concealing themselves behind the trees and keeping up a destructive fire upon us."[29]

Now it was Carlin's turn to hesitate and fall back.

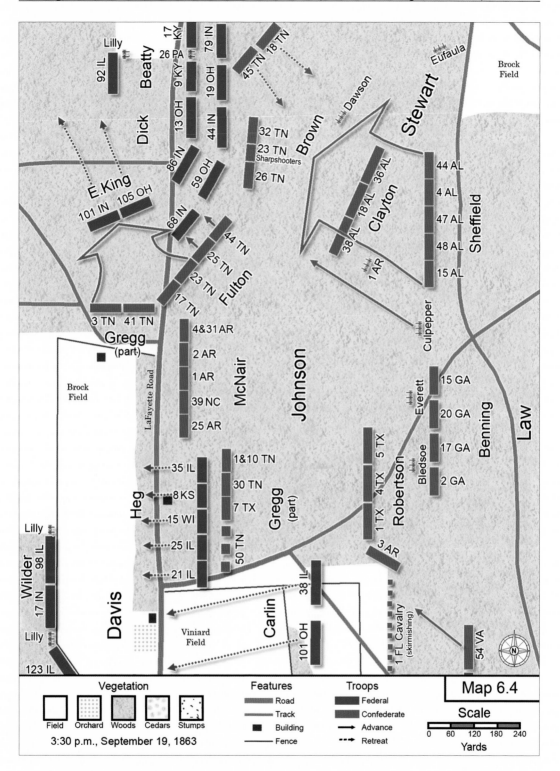

Map 6.4

Vegetation

Field   Orchard   Woods   Cedars   Stumps

3:30 p.m., September 19, 1863

Features
Road
Track
Building
Fence

Troops
Federal
Confederate
Advance
Retreat

Scale
0   60   120   180   240
Yards

6.5: Wood's Division Deploys, Viniard Field North (3:45 p.m.)

While Heg and Carlin were waging their unequal battle against John Hood's Corps east of the LaFayette Road, even more Federal troops were moving up that road behind them. About 3:30 p.m., Brig. Gen. Thomas J. Wood's First Division, XXI Corps, arrived in the Viniard Field area from Lee and Gordon's Mills.

Tom Wood was one of the Army of the Cumberland's more experienced divisional commanders, having led his current command at Shiloh, Perryville, and Stone's River. In the latter combat, Wood's men fought with grim tenacity, and he won no small degree of distinction for his performance. By any measure he was a solid officer. Like Davis' command, Tom Wood's division was smaller than normal. Brig. Gen. George Wagner's brigade was left to garrison Chattanooga, leaving Wood short one-third of his command. Since Davis was also short a brigade, this left only four Federal brigades to contend with a much larger number of Rebels. The looming action promised to be a hard fight.

Wood's two brigades represented the last of Crittenden's men to enter the battle. (Palmer's Second Division was already well engaged up in Brock Field under George Thomas' direction, Van Cleve's Third Division, less one brigade, was facing growing Confederate pressure in the Brotherton Field area.) Crittenden originally intended to place Wood on Van Cleve's right, extending the latter's line far enough south to connect with Davis and keep at least part of the corps working together in mutual support. The corps commander's concept was commendable, but the execution of his idea left something to be desired. Wood later reported that he was "totally ignorant of [Van Cleve's] position in the battle, and met no one on the field . . . to enlighten me, I found my self much embarrassed for the want of information."[30] Just before 4:00 p.m., Wood halted his men in the road and formed into line facing east, with Col. Charles G. Harker's Third Brigade on the left and Col. George P. Buell's First Brigade on the right in front of the Viniard cabin.

Here Wood met Davis, who explained Heg's troubles and the general nature of the fighting thus far. As the two officers conferred,

one of Heg's aides arrived with the alarming news that Heg could not hold his position and was falling back. Within moments the aide's report was confirmed by the sight of Federals pouring out of the trees in complete disorder just north of Harker's left flank. "It was evident," Wood recalled, "that a crisis was at hand."[31]

The routed Federals belonged to the 35th Illinois, Heg's left flank regiment. While facing the right regiments of Gregg's Confederate brigade on its front, the 35th watched helplessly as the better part of first Fulton's and then McNair's brigades swept past their north flank and through the gap between Heg's and Van Cleve's positions. Fulton's men angled to the northwest, and thus did not threaten Heg's rear, but as Gregg's front fractured, McNair saw a opportunity. His mixed brigade of Arkansans and North Carolinians comprised Bushrod Johnson's second line. In an effort to bridge the rapidly growing gap between Fulton and Gregg, McNair ordered Col. David Coleman to take his own 39th North Carolina and the 25th Arkansas forward into the yawning fissure. Their advance was more than enough to send the Illini of the 35th running. Coleman's two regiments—about 380 strong—pursued vigorously, crossing the LaFayette Road and driving several hundred yards west.[32]

When Wood realized what was happening, he ordered Harker's four regiments into the fight. He originally intended for Harker to attack northeast in an effort to turn the tables and take the Rebels in the flank, but that idea quickly foundered when Coleman's troops poured across the LaFayette Road in strength. Wood reoriented Harker again, directing him to drive due north up the road. Wood hoped the attack would strike the advancing Rebel flank and eventually locate Van Cleve or some other Federals believed to be fighting near the Brotherton Field.

Like nearly everyone else, Harker had only the vaguest of notions of his exact mission. "About this time there was very great confusion among the troops which had been engaged," he later wrote, "and no one seemed to have any definite idea of our own lines or the position of the enemy."[33]

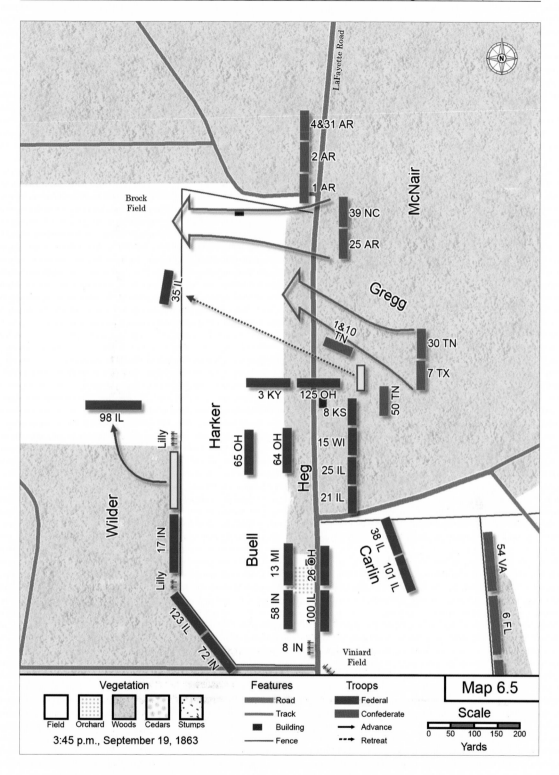

Map 6.5

Scale

3:45 p.m., September 19, 1863

6.6: Barnes Enters the Fight, Viniard Field South (3:45 p.m.)

While Gens. Wood and Davis were deciding what to do, the situation on Davis' own front was deteriorating quickly. Carlin had just been checked by the 3rd Arkansas while the rest of Jerome Robertson's Brigade—the 1st, 3rd, and 4th Texas—swung around to engage Heg's crumbling line of battle in the timber north of Viniard Field. Heg's renewed advance had all but destroyed the 50th Tennessee. Col. Cyrus A. Sugg reported that of the 186 men who entered the fight that afternoon, only 54 emerged unscathed after three hours of fighting.[34] Robertson's Texas Brigade proved a timely reinforcement, passing through Sugg's shattered command and driving Heg's line. This was the second or even third time that Heg's troops had been driven back. They had already suffered heavily in the earlier fighting, and the appearance of a fresh and powerful line of battle advancing through the timber in their direction sent them reeling. Heg's problems were compounded by the collapse of the 35th Illinois on his left. Once again the Norwegian colonel fell back to the road and set about rallying his disorganized regiments.

Barnes, who had maintained his position in the woods at the southern end of Viniard Field, judged the moment ripe to enter the fighting. His four regiments—the 35th Indiana, 8th Kentucky, and 51st and 99th Ohio—advanced in textbook formation, angling across the field toward where Barnes assumed the Rebel flank was located: northeast of the open ground. The Federal infantry marched past the 2nd Minnesota artillery and 81st Indiana infantry, which were still holding the low rise mid-field that offered them protection and excellent fields of fire, and swept into the middle of the field. Capt. T. J. Wright of the 8th Kentucky's recollection demonstrates just how limited an individual's view of a battle was when he wrote that he and his men "moved through [the] brush by right of companies, and then into line through a small cornfield." When the initial advance scattered a Rebel skirmish line, Wright believed matters were going pretty well: "Our men appeared in the best of spirits, notwithstanding the heavy fire [the enemy] was pouring on us."[35]

Carlin was not happy to see Barnes' men because they advanced diagonally across his brigade's front, masking the fire of his own regiments and creating the dangerous possibility of killing and maiming friendly troops. In an effort to clear the front of the 101st Ohio, Carlin ordered that regiment to wheel into line alongside Barnes' men in order to orient his own line with the new arrivals.[36] Before that could happen, however, disaster struck.

The oblique nature of Barnes' attack exposed his right flank regiments (8th Kentucky and 35th Indiana) to Col. Robert Trigg's Southerners in the woods along the east side of Viniard Field. Trigg had just received instructions to support Hood's attack.[37] Accordingly, his 1,536 Rebels moved up to the edge of the open ground, leveled their weapons, and opened fire. Barnes knew there were no Federals on his right, but also believed he was entirely on the Rebel flank and—mistakenly—expected "to be supported on the right [soon] by Colonel Harker's Brigade."[38]

As he advanced without skirmishers, the Rebel fire struck with devastating results. Lt. Col. John J. Wade, commander of the 54th Virginia, Trigg's Brigade, reported that when his men reached the fence at the edge of the field, "a volley was fired by the brigade, which drove the enemy from the cleared land in our front."[39] The Federals on the receiving end also recalled that moment. "[T]o our surprise," wrote Capt. Wright of the 8th Kentucky, "we were completely flanked on our right by a heavy force, who opened an enfilading fire on us."[40]

The shock of the volley collapsed Barnes' attack and sent all four of his regiments running through Carlin's pair of regiments, completely disrupting both commands. Pvt. James M. Cole's 101st Ohio lay directly in the path of this stampede, and he was outraged by the sudden rout: "the Rebels flanked them [Barnes] in turn," he wrote, "and instead of their acting like men, they run like cowards, retreating through [our] ranks."[41] Carlin was equally dismayed as he struggled to rally his disintegrating command. Within minutes, both brigades were scrambling for the nominal cover of the road behind them.

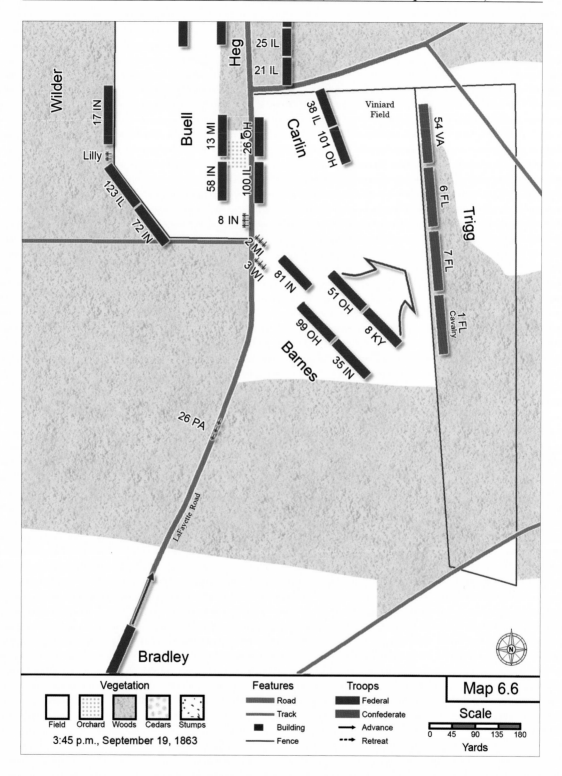

Wilder

Heg

25 IL

21 IL

17 IN

Buell

38 IL

Viniard
Field

54 VA

13 MI

101 OH

26 OH

Carlin

Lilly

58 IN

6 FL

123 IL

100 IL

Trigg

72 IN

8 IN

7 FL

2 MI

3 WI

81 IN

51 OH

1 FL
Cavalry

99 OH

8 KY

Barnes

35 IN

26 PA

LaFayette Road

Bradley

Vegetation

Field   Orchard   Woods   Cedars   Stumps

3:45 p.m., September 19, 1863

Features

Road

Track

Building

Fence

Troops

Federal

Confederate

Advance

Retreat

Map 6.6

Scale

0   45   90   135   180

Yards

6.7: The Union Line Rallies (4:00 p.m.)

When the Union lines in Viniard Field collapsed so abruptly, Col. Trigg decided to press his advantage. While he led Col. Jesse J. Finley's 6th Florida over the fence, the rest of his mixed brigade of Floridians and Virginians advanced hastily into the cornfield—and stopped. As far as Trigg and Finley could see, the only formed Union troops in sight were the 81st Indiana and the 2nd Minnesota Battery. Likely with Trigg's blessing, Finley headed directly for the unlimbered guns.

When he reached the middle of the field, Finley came under fire from the 3rd Wisconsin battery in the road. Undaunted, Finley thought both Federal batteries were ripe for the taking. It was then when he and Trigg discovered that the 6th Florida was alone. "If my regiment could have been supported," wrote Finley, "we could have made a successful charge."[42] Somehow, both colonels failed to realize that the brigade's remaining three regiments had not advanced with the 6th Florida during that regiment's impetuous lunge. According to Pvt. C. O. Bailey of the 7th Florida, he and his comrades were "were ordered to halt, and then right face forward double quick which carried us at a right angle to where we were going before."[43]

Shocked to discover that his other three regiments were moving in the wrong direction, Trigg galloped back to find out the reason. Lt. Col. Wade of the 54th Virginia (on Trigg's right) later explained how the confusion arose. While the Virginians were crossing the fence, Gen. Robertson rode up and informed Wade that he was in the wrong place, and wanted the brigade shifted north. Wade, "knowing that we were to be subject to Hood's orders . . . suffered the regiment to be conducted by him."[44] The 7th and 1st Florida Cavalry followed suit, but the 6th Florida was not in a position to do so. A critical, if fleeting, opportunity was lost.

By now the LaFayette Road was full of Union officers trying to restore order. Col. Buell's brigade of Wood's division was deployed about sixty feet east of the road. Fugitives from Carlin's and Barnes' commands disrupted Buell's regiments and blocked Capt. George Estep's 8th Indiana battery's field of fire. When Estep's front

was finally clear, Finley's Floridians were so close that their musketry decimated his left section and forced the battery into a hasty retreat, leaving one gun unlimbered on the road. Witnessing the impending loss of his artillery, Wood ordered Buell's 100th Illinois under Col. Frederick A. Bartleson to charge.[45]

Unbeknownst to Bartleson, he and his men were not alone. Wilder also proved equal to the developing crisis, ordering his 72nd Indiana and 123rd Illinois forward to support the collapsing Union line. His regiments swept past and through the disorganized Federal infantry "in handsome style" to join in Trigg's repulse.[46] The 72nd's William H. Records remembered pushing past Carlin's and Barnes' men who were "falling back in a demoralized condition, the bullets flying through them and us."[47]

With at least three Federal regiments converging on him, two Union artillery batteries throwing shells in his direction as fast as they could load, and men falling all around him from the converging Federal fire, Col. Finley realized that any window of opportunity for overrunning the Federal line had now closed. There was little recourse left but to retreat for the safety of the distant woods.

Instead of pursuing, however, the tactically nimble Wilder quickly recalled the 72nd and 123rd because he still had a problem on his left flank, where McNair's two Confederate regiments under Col. Coleman (25th Arkansas and 39th North Carolina) were advancing unopposed. This time Wilder pulled the 98th Illinois out of line, turned it ninety degrees and, supported by elements of Lilly's battery and the 17th Indiana, "opened a deadly fire on [the] dense mass of rebels."[48] This fire, coupled with the even more alarming advance of Harker's men north along the LaFayette Road, convinced Coleman that he and his Confederate infantry were on the verge of being surrounded. Like Finley, Coleman had no viable option other than a hasty retreat into the woods east of the LaFayette Road.[49] The retreat of the 25th Arkansas and 39th North Carolina also pulled back the 30th Tennessee and 7th Texas, which had started to follow Coleman into the field.

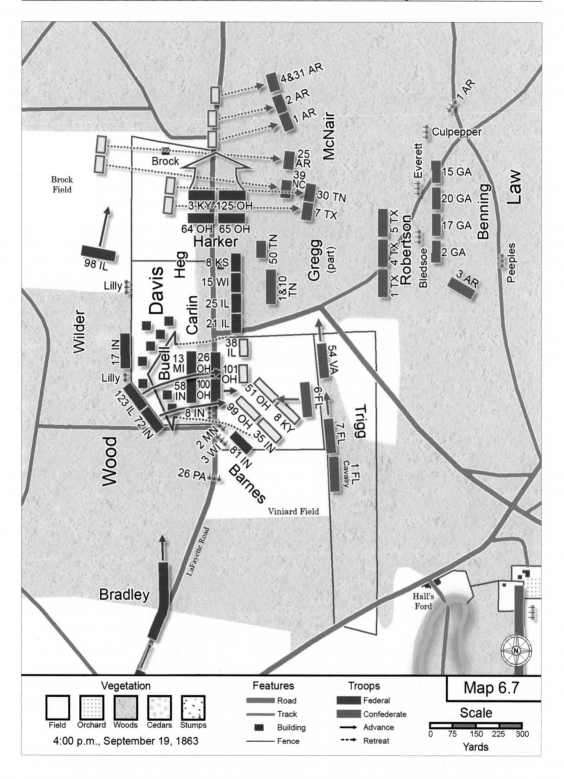

4&31 AR
2 AR
1 AR
1 AR
McNair
Culpepper
Everett
Law
Brock
Brock
Field
25 AR
39 NC
30 TN
7 TX
15 GA
20 GA
17 GA
2 GA
Benning
3-KY 125 OH
64 OH 65 OH
Harker
Heg
Davis
Carlin
8 KS
15 WI
25 IL
21 IL
50 TN
1&10 TN
Gregg (part)
1 TX 4 TX 5 TX
Robertson
Bledsoe
3 AR
Peeples
98 IL
Lilly
Wilder
17 IN
Lilly
Buell
123 IL 72 IN
13 MI
58 IN
26 OH
100 OH
101 OH
38 IL
8 IN
51 OH
8 KY
8 KY
99 OH 35 IN
2 MN
3 WI
81 IN
26 PA
Barnes
54 VA
6 FL
Trigg
7 FL
1 FL
1 FL Cavalry
Wood
Viniard Field
Bradley
LaFayette Road
Hall's Ford

Vegetation
Field Orchard Woods Cedars Stumps
4:00 p.m., September 19, 1863

Features
Road
Track
Building
Fence

Troops
Federal
Confederate
Advance
Retreat

Map 6.7
Scale
0   75   150   225   300
Yards

6.8: Collapse of the Union Line
(4:30 p.m.)

The respite won by the repulse of attacking Rebels under Cols. Trigg and Coleman was short lived. William Records of the 72nd Indiana (Wilder's brigade) observed that the regiment's counterstroke, brief as it was, "reassured Davis' men so that they reformed and advanced towards the foe."[50] That reassurance was not contagious, recalled Carlin, who noticed that many of his men failed to rally, choosing instead to disappear "in the brush and woods west of" the LaFayette Road.[51] Barnes' men to the south were in little better condition, and Buell's brigade line, fighting to hold the western edge of Viniard Field, was ragged but generally intact.

Jesse Finley's 6th Florida was advancing unsupported into Viniard Field, and Robertson's Rebels were pressing forward at an oblique, driving southwest through the timber and sweeping Buell's ranks with enfilade fire. When Gen. Wood ordered Bartleson's 100th Illinois (Buell's brigade) forward in a small tactical counterattack, Buell attempted to advance his other three regiments in support, with varying degrees of success. At one point some of his men withdrew to the west side of the road, reforming along the 8th Indiana's guns. Once Finley's unsupported Floridians retreated, the Federal brigade and battery together returned to their first position. Confederate momentum on this part of the field, however, was building.

North of the Viniard house and east of the Log School, Col. Heg's brigade was about played out. He had reformed his troops two or three times that afternoon. Each time, he renewed his effort to drive deeper into the woods against the Rebels, and each time he had been driven back. Now his command was largely ineffective, and once Harker's brigade moved north, Heg no longer had any support behind him.

And the Rebels were coming again. Jerome Robertson reorganized his line in the shelter of a ravine several hundred yards east of the LaFayette Road. When Heg tried to move east yet again, two of Robertson's regiments on the right side of his advancing line, the 4th and 5th Texas, met the Federals with a withering fire and a charge. The advance of the Texans proved too much for Heg's weakened line. "We came to

close quarters," Texan B. I. Franklin of the 5th regiment recalled, "punishing them severely and driving them in confusion."[52] The Federals quickly fell back near the road, where some of Norwegians from the 15th Wisconsin attempted a desperate stand in and around the Log School, but the pressure was too heavy and they were too few. The Wisconsin men were falling back when Heg was shot down trying to rally his troops. He lingered through the night and, at thirty-three years old, died the next day. He was the highest ranking Wisconsin officer killed in combat during the war.

Success by Robertson's left wing translated into success on his right. The 3rd Arkansas and 1st Texas renewed their advance, striking Buell's, Barnes', and Carlin's combined line. Already wary of his command's morale, Carlin did his best to hold the front together. The added fire from elements of the 4th and 5th Texas into Carlin's left flank only increased the stress on his men. Hoosier William Records observed the action from the right side of Wilder's line (behind Carlin's right-rear). What he witnessed shocked him. "We had scarcely got settled in our places," he wrote, "when Davis' [Carlin's] men gave way and came back in dreadful confusion. They were generally throwing away their knapsacks, in some instances their weapons. They ran over us like sheep."[53]

For the second time in an hour, Capt. Estep found his 8th Indiana battery in peril. Lt. Col. William Young's 26th Ohio fell back across the road to a fence line near the Viniard House, where they rallied and fired at the advancing Texans. The retreat of the Buckeyes, however, convinced Buell's other regiments to give way.[54] Within a short time Estep found himself engaging Rebels less than 100 yards away. Their "musketry fire became so heavy, terrible, and galling" that there was no option but immediate retreat.[55] The Texans captured three more of the 8th's Indiana's guns.

Robertson had swept the field east of the LaFayette Road, routing what was left of Heg, Buell, Carlin, and Barnes. Wilder's line 200 yards west of the road, however, provided the solid backstop upon which Federal artillery and infantry rallied. Unable to advance farther, Robertson called upon Hood for support, seeking both artillery and infantry for the task ahead. No guns were readily available, but Brig. Gen. Henry L. Benning's four Georgia Regiments were close at hand and prepared to fight.[56]

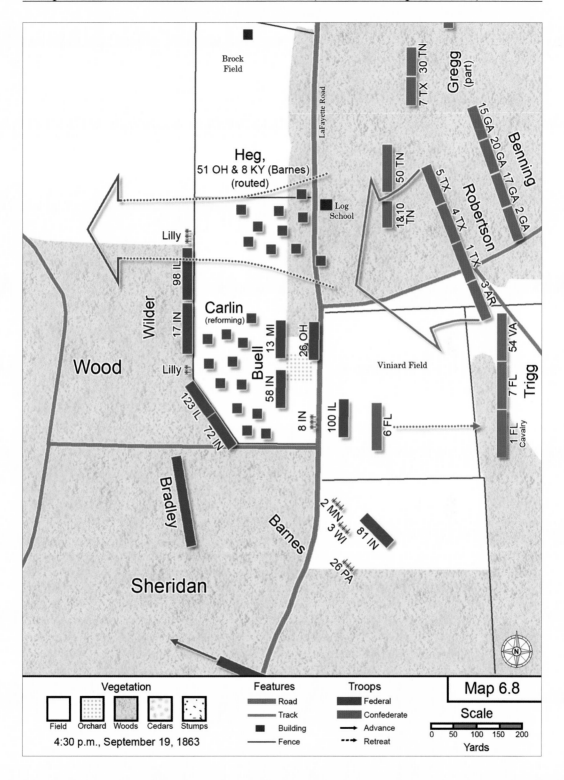

Brock
Field

LaFayette Road

Gregg
(part)

7 TX   30 TN

15 GA 20 GA 17 GA 2 GA

Benning

Heg,
51 OH & 8 KY (Barnes)
(routed)

50 TN

5 TX   4 TX

Robertson

Log
School

1&10
TN

1 TX   3 AR

Lilly

98 IL

Wilder

17 IN

Carlin
(reforming)

13 MI

26 OH

54 VA

Viniard Field

7 FL

Trigg

Wood

Lilly

Buell

58 IN

123 IL   72 IN

8 IN

100 IL

6 FL

1 FL
Cavalry

Bradley

Barnes

2 MN
3 WI

81 IN

26 PA

Sheridan

N

Vegetation					Features		Troops		Map 6.8
Field	Orchard	Woods	Cedars	Stumps	Road Track Building Fence		Federal Confederate Advance Retreat		Scale

4:30 p.m., September 19, 1863

Scale
0   50   100   150   200
Yards

6.9: The Ditch of Death (5:00 p.m.)

Wilder's front was protected by a stream bed about halfway between his defensive barricade at the tree line and the LaFayette Road. The dry weather of the past few weeks had evaporated the water, so most men who described it referred to the bed as a "ditch" or the "dry ditch." The banks were steep, cut into the field about five feet deep. The ditch angled across the field from the southeast to the northwest, growing shallower as it wound its way north. For most of the width of Wilder's front, it made a perfect natural trench.

During the afternoon's action, large numbers of Yankee stragglers and wounded sought shelter in the dry stream bed. Some of Buell's men tried to defend the ditch. Lt. Col. Young reported trying to reform part of his 26th Ohio in it. He must have enjoyed some success, for he dispatched Companies A and F briefly from that position to rescue one of the 8th Indiana's lost guns.[57] However, most of the surviving Federals retreated behind Wilder's line, where the trees provided enough cover to comfort the distressed and defeated regiments. Young and his fragment of a command soon joined them there.

Henry Benning, a former Georgia Supreme Court judge, drove his veteran Georgia brigade forward in response to Robertson's appeal for support. The brigade was not up to its standard combat effectiveness. Heavy losses suffered at Gettysburg earlier that summer had cleaved hundreds of men from the ranks, and a wave of temporary absenteeism swept the companies on their way to reinforce Bragg's Army of Tennessee when the men traveled close by their homes—the first time they had done so in nearly two years. As a result, Benning's 2nd, 15th, 17th, and 20th Georgia regiments carried fewer than 800 bayonets into action. Still, their advance was powerful enough to scatter what remained of the Union defenders.

Sgt. W. R. Houghton of the 2nd Georgia remembered reaching the edge of the timber, where Benning's men poured volley after volley into the fleeing Federals: "We pushed ahead and swung around against the fence just as the Yankee line in the field began to give way. As they ran back . . . we stood there . . . shooting

them down. . . . It was horrible slaughter. The field seemed to be covered with dead and wounded."[58] Benning's infantry swept forward out of the trees near the Viniard house "with open ground for 150 or 200 yards in front."[59] When he spotted Wilder's line on the western edge of the field, Benning ordered his troops to advance against them.

The attacking Rebels, recalled William Records, "moved out into the farm in front of us and formed their lines upon the road. All of the artillery that escaped . . . was now stationed at intervals along the line of our brigade. . . . Our entire line from right to left opened out on them . . . The rapid fire of our seven shooters gave our line the appearance of a living sheet of fire." Benning's troops suddenly found themselves in a lopsided fight they could not win, and their attack quickly fell apart. Records continued: "While we knelt down in two ranks behind our works—Davis' men formed in two ranks, standing behind us and fired over our heads as fast as they could."[60]

Large numbers of Georgians sought shelter in the ditch, hoping the depression would shield them from the intense Union fire. For a time, both sides traded fire from whatever cover they could find. Wilder decided the best way to pry the Georgians out of their natural trench was to enfilade them. He advanced a section (two guns) of Lilly's battery and four companies of the 17th Indiana to the northern end of the field and directed them to fire down the length of the depression at close range. The effect was all he could have desired. Just as the railroad cut at Gettysburg had trapped Joe Davis' unsuspecting Mississippians, the ditch at Chickamauga had become a death trap for Benning's Georgians. When speaking to a reporter after the battle, Wilder stated, "it almost seemed a pity to kill men so."[61] Benning retired his shattered regiments east of the LaFayette Road. Perhaps as much as one-third of his command fell in the ditch.

Benning's repulse offered a large number of scattered Federal regiments the chance to regroup behind Wilder. His seemingly impregnable defensive line gave heart to many hundreds of Yankees whose own regiments had long since dissolved as effective commands. These stragglers, primarily from Heg's, Carlin's, and Buell's brigades, began the slow process of coalescing back into some sort of manageable order.

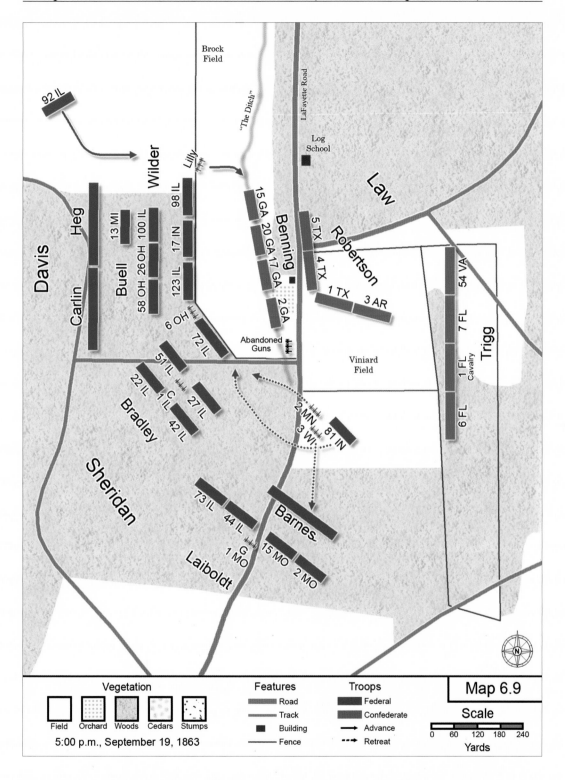

Brock Field

"The Ditch"

LaFayette Road

Log School

92 IL

Wilder

Lilly

Law

Heg

13 MI

98 IL

15 GA

Benning

5 TX

Robertson

Davis

Buell

58 OH 26 OH 100 IL

17 IN

20 GA 17 GA

4 TX

54 VA

Carlin

123 IL

2 GA

1 TX   3 AR

7 FL

Trigg

6 OH

Abandoned Guns

1 FL
Cavalry

72 IL

Viniard Field

51 IL

6 FL

22 IL   27 IL
1 C
1 IL
42 IL

Bradley

2 MN
3 WI   81 IN

Sheridan

73 IL   Barnes

44 IL

G
1 MO   15 MO   2 MO

Laiboldt

Vegetation

| Field | Orchard | Woods | Cedars | Stumps |

5:00 p.m., September 19, 1863

Features
Road
Track
Building
Fence

Troops
Federal
Confederate
Advance
Retreat

Map 6.9

Scale
0   60   120   180   240
Yards

N

6.10: Bradley Enters the Fight
(5:30 p.m.)

All afternoon, Rebels and Yankees surged back and forth across Viniard Field and in the woods just to the north. Losses were heavy on both sides, and real tactical gains remained beyond reach. The Federals faltered several times, but in each case Rebel counterattacks foundered when they reached Wilder's powerful line. Firm control of the LaFayette Road eluded both combatants. Following the repulse of Benning's men, more Union infantry arrived to try and turn the tide on this part of the field.

By 5:30 p.m., only two of Rosecrans' ten infantry divisions had not seen action. Maj. Gen. Negley's Second Division of George Thomas' XIV Corps was marching up the Glenn Kelly Road en route to join Thomas. Brig. Gen. Philip Sheridan's Third Division of Maj. Gen. Alexander McCook's XX Corps was moving north just a mile or so below the Viniard field, tasked with guarding Lee and Gordon's Mills. With the battle consuming fresh troops as quickly as they arrived, McCook ordered Sheridan to leave one brigade to watch the crossing and hurry the other two to Viniard Field to support Wood's embattled division. His instructions were to feed his men into action a "brigade at a time as he needs them."[62]

Leading Sheridan's column was Col. Luther P. Bradley's brigade of four Illinois regiments. Bradley, born in Connecticut, moved to Chicago in 1855 and found work with a local bookseller. He had been active in militia affairs, and carried that interest with him to Illinois. He was only twenty-nine in 1861, but pre-war expertise in things military soon earned him a position as lieutenant colonel of the 51st Illinois. By Stone's River he was in charge of a brigade. Bradley was not a flashy or boastful man, and his men respected him as a capable, efficient, and humane commander.

Bradley's Illinois infantry left the road as they approached the field and moved west through the woods behind Wilder's position, forming in the rear of the 72nd Indiana. Behind Bradley tramped Col. Bernard Laiboldt's mixed Illinois and Missouri brigade, which formed astride the road behind the 81st Indiana and 2nd Minnesota Artillery, both of which were still gamely holding their little corner of Viniard Field. Bradley and Laiboldt were in the process of deploying when Benning's Georgians fled from the "Ditch of Death" and broke for the rear.

A number of Federal officers, Sheridan among them, watched Benning's retreat and believed that the moment was ripe for another attack. The bantam Irishman instructed Bradley to recapture the 8th Indiana battery's abandoned guns littering the roadway and drive the enemy into the woods beyond.[63]

Independently, Carlin and Buell reached the same conclusion. Carlin advanced the 38th Illinois and 101st Ohio, while Buell sallied forth with the 58th Indiana and 26th Ohio. Both Federal officers seemed intent on at least restoring their original lines. Fragments of other commands, including some of Heg's men, rallied and went forward as well, though by now their formations had been reduced to little more than squads.

The Southerners refused to be driven easily, grudgingly giving up their hard-earned ground yard by yard. Bradley described this action as "an old fight and a pretty hot one." Once he and his infantry reached mid-field, he continued, "We had a monkey-and-parrot time of it for a while."[64]

Bradley's regiments had been taken under fire by Robertson's men on the north, and Trigg's Floridians lining the eastern edge of the field. Sgt. John S. Glenn of the 27th Illinois, holding Bradley's right-front, also found the engagement "warm work." Writing home, Glenn continued, "Our brigade entered the fight something over 1,500 strong and . . . they killed and wounded near 300 of us. This was doing bully," he explained, "yet we held our own."[65]

Passing through Estep's guns, scratch detachments of Yankees organized to draw the pieces off by hand, since most of the battery's horses carpeted the ground. Bradley's thrust met with no more success than had previous attempts. Bradley was struck down as his brigade reached mid-field. Wounded in two places, he was helped to the rear. Laiboldt's regiments took up a supporting line but did not move forward. Shortly thereafter, Sheridan ordered Bradley's brigade back to join Laiboldt. This final assault accomplished little other than to add to the growing casualty lists.

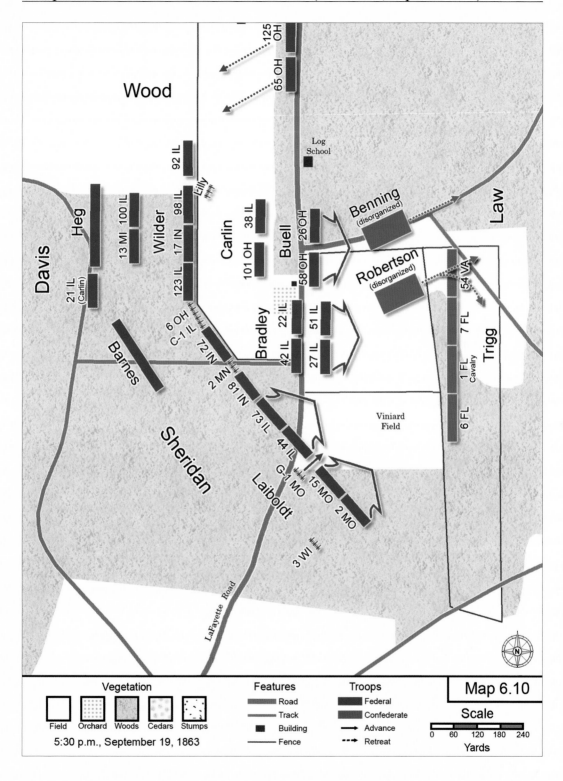

Wood

125 OH

65 OH

Log
School

92 IL

Lilly

13 MI 100 IL

Heg

Wilder

98 IL

17 IN

38 IL

Benning
(disorganized)

Law

Davis

Carlin

101 OH

26 OH

Buell

Robertson
(disorganized)

54 VA

21 IL
(Carlin)

123 IL

58 OH

7 FL

Barnes

6 OH
C-1 IL

72 IN

Bradley

22 IL

51 IL

1 FL
Cavalry

Trigg

42 IL

27 IL

2 MN

81 IN

Viniard
Field

6 FL

Sheridan

73 IL

44 IL

Laiboldt

G-1 MO

15 MO

2 MO

3 WI

LaFayette Road

N

Map 6.10

Scale

Vegetation

Field Orchard Woods Cedars Stumps

Features

Road
Track
Building
Fence

Troops

Federal
Confederate
Advance
Retreat

0   60   120 180 240
Yards

5:30 p.m., September 19, 1863

6.11: Final Positions (6:00 p.m.)

Other than for some fitful skirmish fire, by 6:00 p.m. an eerie silence settled over Viniard Field. Elements of seven Federal and six Confederate brigades had contested for control of this part of the battlefield for most of the afternoon. Losses had been heavy. Details of men from both sides began the painstaking process of evacuating the wounded they could safely reach.

Col. Trigg's three regiments of Floridians and one of Virginians continued holding the eastern edge of the field but retired some distance into the trees, leaving only skirmishers along the fence line. Trigg's 6th Florida had suffered the heaviest losses of any of his regiments during its unsupported charge against Union artillery about 3:30 p.m. Trigg's other three regiments each suffered fewer than ten percent losses, compared to the 6th's butcher's bill that topped forty-six percent.

The Southern brigades under Jerome Robertson and Henry Benning had also suffered significant losses. Casualties for each totaled between one-quarter and one-third of those engaged, though heavy fighting the next day (September 20) makes it impossible to calculate exact losses with precision. Both commands fell back into the woods north and east of Viniard Field, about 400 yards east of the LaFayette Road. Alongside them, John Gregg's battered brigade reformed under command of its senior colonel, Cyrus A. Sugg of the 50th Tennessee. Gregg was down with a wound (Map 7.5) along with some 250 others from his brigade. Sugg formed the command on Benning's right (just off the facing map), anchoring the line with the rest of Bushrod Johnson's troops to form a solid extension north. An estimate of Rebel casualties for this part of the fighting (including Col. Fulton's limited initial involvement) total roughly 1,250 men killed, wounded, and missing.

On the Union side, Col. Wilder's position provided the anchor the Union brigades needed to rally and hold fast along the LaFayette Road around the Viniard Field position. Gens. Jefferson C. Davis, Thomas Wood, and Phil Sheridan shuttled their men behind or around Wilder. Federal losses were higher than Confederate casualties because the Northern infantry had carried the burden of the attack for most of the day. Davis' division was shattered, losing 900 of the 2,500 men he carried into action. Heg's brigade casualties were the heaviest, which is not surprising given the number of times the Norwegian led his four regiments forward, first against Fulton and Gregg, and then against Robertson and Benning. Davis pulled his command into the woods behind Wilder's line and began the arduous process of gathering in wounded and stragglers, reconstituting a division that by the next day would number only the size of an average brigade.

Wood's division split early in the fight, with Col. Harker's men moving north out of the sector (to play a role in fighting soon to be described), while Col. Buell's brigade was repeatedly disrupted by routed Federals from other commands running through its ranks. Wood finally reassembled his two brigades about dusk, pulling both Harker and Buell into the open field leading back to the Widow Glenn House on Wilder's right. Buell, who suffered the bulk of Wood's casualties on the 19th, lost roughly 300 men killed, wounded, and captured, or about one-quarter of his strength. Harker's losses numbered about fifty.

Barnes' itinerant brigade, still detached from Van Cleve's division, joined Sheridan in the woods southwest of Viniard Field on Wilder's right flank. Barnes and Col. Bradley also suffered significant losses, each bleeding away between 250 and 300 men. Wilder's losses were surprisingly light—even taking into account his largely defensive action. Combined losses from his four regiments engaged totaled fewer than fifty men.

All told, in four hours of combat 1,250 Confederates and about 1,800 Federals had been killed, wounded, captured, or were missing. Untold others had straggled or had become confused and disoriented amid the repeated charges and countercharges. For many, the pressure of the intense combat overtaxed their nervous systems. When Carlin found his dead horse—an animal he had grown deeply fond of—amidst the wreckage of combat he removed the saddle and freely admitted that he "seated myself upon it, and then gave way to a long, hysterical crying spell, which I could no more have checked then I could have checked the setting sun."[66]

More eloquently than any words, the general's reaction described the horrors of that day.

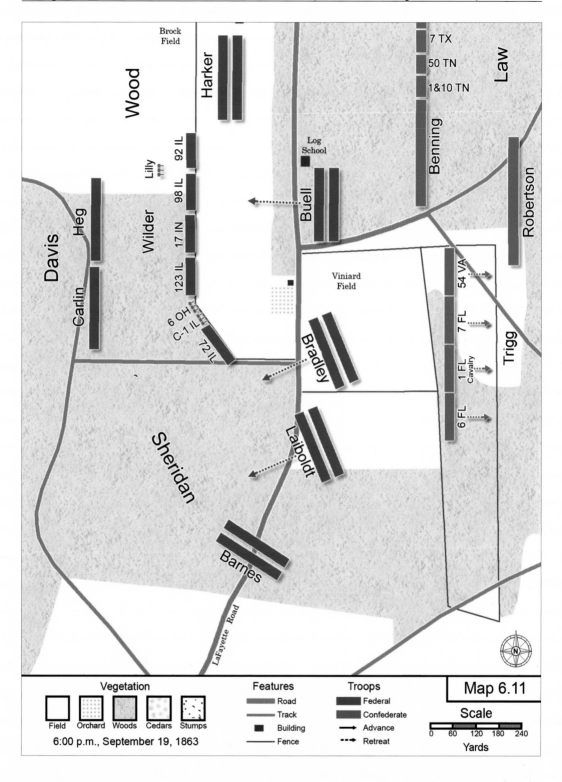

Brock
Field

Wood

Harker

7 TX

50 TN

1&10 TN

Law

92 IL

Lilly

98 IL

Log
School

Buell

Benning

Robertson

Heg

Wilder

17 IN

Davis

123 IL

Viniard
Field

54 VA

Carlin

6 OH
C-1 IL

72 IL

Bradley

7 FL

Trigg

1 FL
Cavalry

Laiboldt

6 FL

Sheridan

Barnes

LaFayette Road

Map 6.11

Vegetation

Field   Orchard   Woods   Cedars   Stumps

6:00 p.m., September 19, 1863

Features
━━ Road
━━ Track
■ Building
── Fence

Troops
■ Federal
■ Confederate
→ Advance
▪▪▶ Retreat

Scale

0   60   120   180   240
Yards

Map Set 7: Fleeting Rebel Success in Brotherton and Poe Fields

(Late Afternoon, September 19)

7.1: Johnson Flanks the Federals (3:30 p.m.)

While Brig. Gen John Gregg's Brigade of Brig. Gen. Bushrod Johnson's Division was entangled with Federal divisions under Brig. Gens. Jefferson C. Davis and Thomas J. Wood near the Viniard farm, the rest of Johnson's troops broke free to fight in the action around Brotherton Field. These Confederate had a significant impact on the combat there.

As will be recalled (Map 5.9), Col. Edward King's three Federal regiments from Maj. Gen. Joseph Reynolds' division were sent into the woods to extend Brig. Gen. Horatio Van Cleve's divisional line and find Maj. Gen. Alexander P. Stewart's Rebel flank. Instead, King's men ran headlong into Col. John Fulton's Brigade. Informally augmented by the 3rd and 41st Tennessee of Gregg's command, who joined his left flank instead of following their own command, Fulton numbered at least 1,700 men and significantly overmatched King's 1,138. It was King's turn to have a flank compromised.

Albion Tourgee, who fought with the 105th Ohio in King's brigade, lamented the disorienting nature of the terrain and the combat. "The winding roads were full of lost staff officers," he wrote. "The commander of a regiment rarely saw both flanks of his command at once. . . . Confusion reigned even before the battle began." And then Fulton's men appeared, their line long enough to threaten King's right and work into the gap on his left, where he should have been connected to Van Cleve's line. "The One hundred and First Indiana began to bend backward . . . like a willow wand," wrote Tourgee, and "presently it broke. Then the line of the [105th Ohio] began to bend in like manner."[1] Within minutes, King's brigade was falling back in chaos.

King's collapse created a domino effect by exposing Col. George Dick's right flank while his brigade was fully engaged with Brig. Gen. John C. Brown's Rebels. As will be recalled, Brown's infantry had replaced Brig. Gen. Henry Clayton's

command about 3:00 p.m. (Map 5.9) and recaptured the wreckage of Capt. William Carnes' Tennessee battery. Now, low on ammunition and with his right flank threatened by the 75th Indiana, Brown needed support. Fulton's arrival could not have been timelier. To the regimental historian of the 44th Indiana, this sudden reversal of fortune proved bewildering: "Confusion seems to have taken possession of our lines, and to add to it, the lines on our right have been broken and the enemy is sweeping past our flank."[2]

These circumstances were repeated in regiment after regiment, as each became infected with the fear of being cut off in the smoky woods. Marcus Woodcock of the 9th Kentucky, Brig. Gen. John Beatty's brigade, described the panic. "We saw away through an opening in the woods, heavy columns of Rebels going to the right," he wrote. "Where are they going?—Is our right properly protected? . . . The enemy's line is advancing almost at right angles with our right and consequently they are subjected to a heavy front and flank fire . . . soon our line begins to waver, and then fall back in great disorder."[3] Within minutes both Dick and Beatty were in full retreat.

The Union situation might have been dire, but just as a lack of coordination had hampered earlier Federal advantages, so too did confusion among the Rebels cripple their efforts to turn the tide of battle. Although their brigades fought side-by-side, Brown seemed unaware of Fulton's intervention on his left. Brown, who had not been informed of the advance of Maj. Gen. John Hood's Corps, thought his brigade was supported only by the brigades of Henry Clayton and William Bate of his own division, both still at least 600 yards behind him. Fulton's men were much closer and came into action on his left, but thinking he was alone, Brown took advantage of the enemy's discomfiture to fall back. Brown also seemed confused about his other flank, thinking there were no friendly troops "upon my right for a mile."[4] In fact, A. P. Stewart was sending Bate's as yet unbloodied brigade of Alabama, Georgia, and Tennessee troops into action against the 75th Indiana, but it would take time to pass them through Brown's ranks. Had Brown pressed the enemy in front while Fulton turned their exposed right, Dick, Beatty, and King might have lost significantly more men during their retreat. As it was, this misunderstanding among the Rebel leaders bought the Federals a brief—but precious—respite.

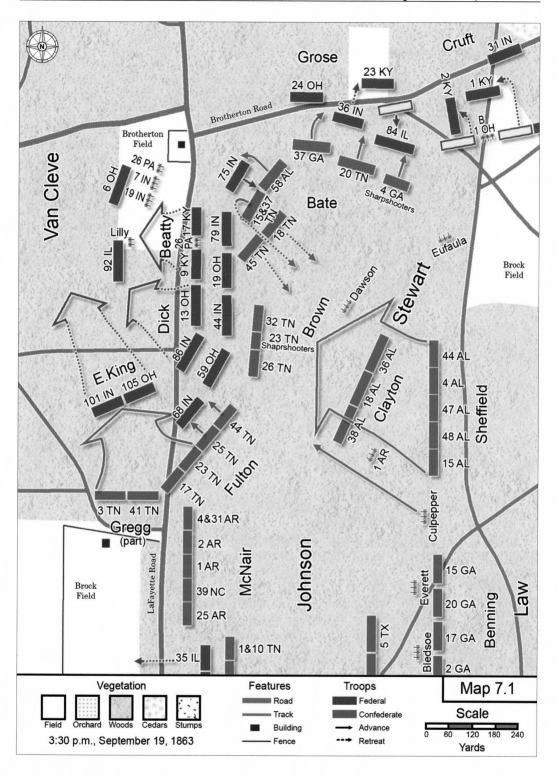

Map 7.1

Scale

3:30 p.m., September 19, 1863

7.2: Rally in Brotherton Field
(3:45 p.m.)

Joseph Reynolds had already built the framework of a reserve line by the time the Federals swarmed back into Brotherton Field, but it was only a framework.

With his own infantry committed elsewhere, Reynolds had only the 6th Ohio (Maj. Gen. John Palmer's division, Col. William Grose's brigade) at his disposal—accumulated more through chance than by design—and the 92nd Illinois from Wilder's brigade, which arrived on the southern end of the Brotherton Field about midday.[5] The bulk of Reynolds' defense consisted of the considerable number of artillery tubes massed on the low ridge crowning the middle of the field. Having been advised by Maj. Gen. George Thomas (XIV Corps) not to let the guns follow their infantry brigades into the woods, Reynolds decided to deploy them here. The artillery amounted to two sections of the 26th Pennsylvania, the 7th and 19th Indiana batteries, and one section of Eli Lilly's battery that accompanied the 92nd Illinois. A few minutes later, the four howitzers of Lt. Harry C. Cushing's Battery H, 4th U.S. Regulars clattered up, also separated from Palmer's division and looking for a place to fight. Reynolds put them into his growing Brotherton Field line.[6] All told, sixteen guns lined the field, a substantial amount of firepower if they could be properly supported.

The sudden stampede of men pouring out of the woods to the east cast in some doubt the wisdom of Reynolds' decision. He had just ordered the 92nd Illinois to support King when the issue became moot: before the Illini could do more than cross the road, according to the 92nd's historian, "King's brigade came out of the woods beyond, in disorder and retreating."[7] Reynolds also described the moment: "I remember seeing Van Cleve telling the boys to go slow . . . trying to stop his men. They were being driven but I could not see who was driving them. They were not firing . . . [but] were going to the northward in the rear of my line."[8] Clearly a crisis was at hand.

The lack of immediate pursuit by Brown's Rebels, however, allowed at least bits and pieces of the three Union brigades (King, Beatty, and Dick) to rally on the gun line. King's men were unable to reform at all, his three regiments retreating another 600 yards before they paused west of the tanyard in South Dyer Field.[9] Elements from the brigades of Beatty and Dick performed better, having been less savaged by Fulton's flank attack. Unfortunately, they also had to endure fire from their own artillery, which was throwing shells indiscriminately into the woods from the middle of the open field. Despite this added aggravation, Jason Hurd of the 19th Ohio, part of Beatty's command, recalled that "men from every regiment in the brigade rallied on the hill with the artillerymen, who but a moment before had thrown such consternation into our own ranks."[10]

Similar dramas were playing out in Van Cleve's other regiments. Among the most prominent were the 44th, 86th, and 79th Indiana, and 9th Kentucky, all of which reformed reasonably intact and deployed amongst the guns. About one-half of the 17th Kentucky reformed at the tree line, where smaller fragments of the 13th, 19th, and 59th Ohio fell in alongside them.[11] Both Brig. Gen. Samuel Beatty (not to be confused with John Beatty) and Col. Dick were present, doing what they could to rally their commands. Several of Beatty's staff officers, however, had been wounded earlier trying to prevent the rout in the timber, and the rest were as badly scattered as the men in the ranks. Straggling and disorganization were severe. Hurd of the 19th Ohio noted that only about one-third of his regiment could be found—roughly 125 of the original 384 men. The 19th had thus far suffered between eighty to ninety losses, which meant that some 200 men were no longer in the ranks.[12] Most would return later that night, but they would be sorely missed in the meantime.

The combat crisis had all but undone the aging Van Cleve. One of the army's oldest officers, the Minnesotan struggled to rally his men, but soon decided that more help was needed. He left his own command to ride north along the LaFayette Road in search of reinforcements until he found Brig. Gen. William B. Hazen's brigade at the Poe Cabin. "Did I have any troops," was how Hazen recalled Van Cleve's query, for "they were wanted badly 'just down there . . . saying he had not a man he could control. He was an elderly, gray-haired man . . . his distress was not feigned."[13]

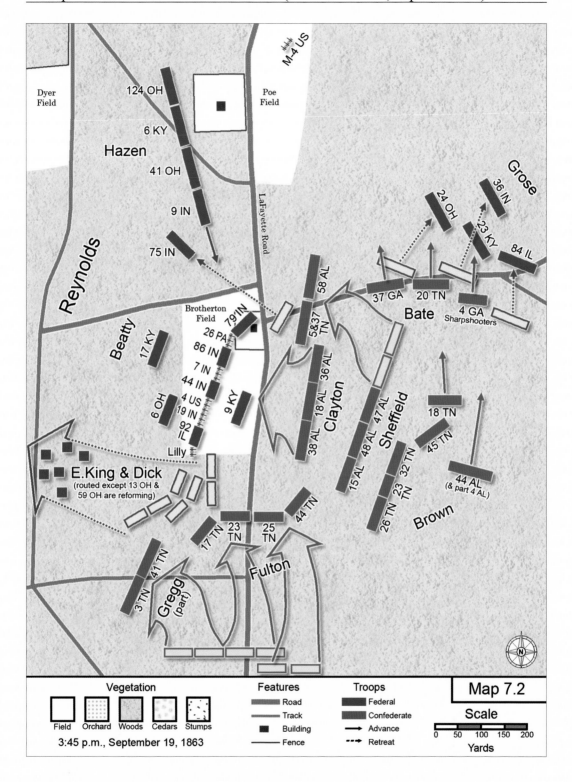

Dyer
Field

Poe
Field

M-4 US

124 OH

6 KY

Hazen

41 OH

9 IN

Reynolds

75 IN

LaFayette Road

Grose

36 IN

24 OH

23 KY

84 IL

58 AL

5&37 TN

37 GA   20 TN   4 GA
Sharpshooters
Bate

Brotherton
Field

79 IN

Beatty

26 PA

17 KY

86 IN

7 IN

36 AL

44 IN

18 AL

Clayton

47 AL

Sheffield

18 TN

6 OH

4 US

19 IN

9 KY

48 AL

92
IL

38 AL

15 AL

45 TN

Lilly

32 TN

44 AL
(& part 4 AL)

E. King & Dick
(routed except 13 OH &
59 OH are reforming)

26 TN

23
TN

Brown

44 TN

17 TN   23
TN

25
TN

3 TN   41 TN

Fulton

Gregg
(part)

N

Vegetation					Features	Troops		Map 7.2

Vegetation

Field   Orchard   Woods   Cedars   Stumps

3:45 p.m., September 19, 1863

Features
Road
Track
Building
Fence

Troops
Federal
Confederate
Advance
Retreat

Map 7.2

Scale

0   50   100   150   200
Yards

7.3: Stewart Attacks, Hazen Defends (4:00 p.m.)

Gen. Hazen's brigade was already heading toward Brotherton Field, drawn there by the sound of the fight. His four regiments entered the field from the northwest corner, deploying diagonally from near the cabin to somewhere along the western edge in a line angled about 45 degrees from the road. The 41st Ohio and 9th Indiana led the line, with the 6th Kentucky and 124th Ohio falling in behind. As Hazen's regiments were hurrying into line, the next Rebel attack broke out of the woods to the east.[14]

William Bate's mixed Georgia and Tennessee brigade made its way through Brown's retreating men and sent the outmatched 75th Indiana back in retreat (though Bate's own front was disrupted as his line turned to face threats from various directions). Intending to renew the attack on a broader front, division leader A P. Stewart also moved up Henry Clayton's resupplied Alabamians. Both brigades were advancing north by northwest. In addition to his own two brigades, Stewart was about to receive more (unsought) support. Col. Fulton's Brigade was still in the vicinity, operating south of Brotherton Field and emboldened by its earlier easy victory. Col. James Sheffield's Brigade, part of Brig. Gen. Evander Law's division, was also coming up from the southeast, though at least two of his regiments—the 4th and 44th Alabama—fell into disarray during their advance. Tactical success had rendered the Rebel condition only slightly less chaotic than the defeat that had thus far been dealt the Federals.

Bate was an ambitious Tennessee politician and a competent and aggressive commander. His brigade, he reported, "moved forward with spirit and zeal."[15] Bate angled northwest, brushing past Brown's right. Clayton moved up in support on Bate's left and they partially intermingled. As Clayton's 36th Alabama moved past and through Bate's 58th Alabama (which by now also included some members of the 4th Alabama, Sheffield's Brigade), Col. Bushrod Jones leading the latter regiment found it "an opportune moment for a charge . . . and the two regiments, commingled, charged in a run with loud and enthusiastic cheers."[16] Clayton's line and the 58th Alabama swept forward into Brotherton

Field. Once in the open they found Hazen's men, led by the 9th Indiana, along the northwestern edge. A bloody close-range slugfest erupted.

After their role in routing Van Cleve's line, Fulton's men occupied the trees south of Brotherton Field directly astride the Yankee right flank. Realizing the danger, the dismounted cavalry of the 92nd Illinois (Wilder) fell back to their horses. The result would have far-reaching consequences. The Illini retreat exposed the right flank of the 9th Kentucky (Federal), some distance east of the main Federal line.[17] With their nightmare of just one-half hour ago reawakened, the Kentuckians fell back, which precipitated the unraveling (from south to north) of the entire Union Brotherton Field line. Capt. Samuel J. Harris of the 19th Indiana battery found his men and guns exposed to "a destructive fire on my right," which he struggled to engage to no avail.[18] The Hoosiers limbered and fled, with Harris wounded, abandoning one gun in the field. William E. Webber and the rest of the 6th Ohio were supporting the guns. The Buckeyes struggled to buy time for the cannon to escape. "After quite a heavy fight . . . the battery being crippled in loss of men and horses . . . we fell back though a little brush and timber and struck the Dyer Field," recalled Webber.[19] With most of the Yankees cleared from Brotherton Field, Fulton halted his regiments, his line occupying the southwest corner of the field and extending partly into the woods.

At the north end of the field, Hazen's Yankees were the only defenders still fighting, though without Hazen. As his troops struggled to hold back Clayton's infantry, Hazen spotted Rebels threatening his left flank as they poured north along and just east of the LaFayette Road. Hazen reprised Van Cleve's earlier ride by galloping north toward Poe Field in search of support for his beleaguered brigade.[20]

Meanwhile, Hazen's men, alone and under heavy pressure, began retreating into the timber north of the field. Col. Isaac Suman of the 9th Indiana admitted that his regiment did so "in some disorder."[21] Col. Aquila Wiley's 41st Ohio covered the Hoosier's retreat. The Buckeyes faced about to deliver volleys to their right and left, "gaining ground to the rear with each change of front . . . until he could take his place in good order upon [the] new line."[22] The center of the Army of the Cumberland had effectively collapsed.

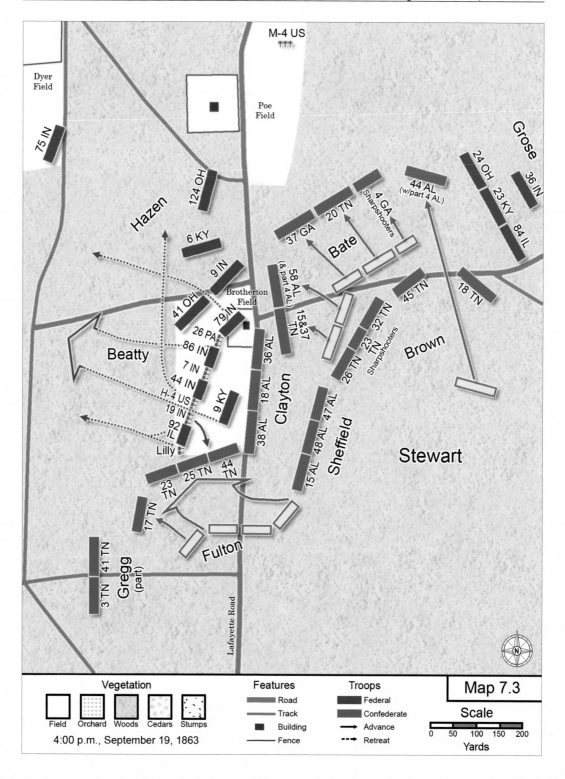

Map 7.3

4:00 p.m., September 19, 1863

Scale

0   50   100   150   200

Yards

7.4: Grose Opens the Door
(4:00—4:30 p.m.)

Col. William Grose, a lawyer from Newcastle, Indiana, led the 36th Indiana to war in 1861. His first action came at Shiloh, where he was slightly wounded. He rose to brigade command, and by the fall of 1863 was an experienced commander. Thus far his brigade had done well, though it hadn't been tested as strongly as it had been in other actions. The nagging worry plaguing Grose was his exposed right flank, where a sizable gap yawned between his own line and that of Van Cleve's division. The 75th Indiana, thrust forward earlier, was simply too small to fill that hole completely.

By 4:00 p.m., Grose's men holding Palmer's right flank on the Brock Field line had not faced a direct Confederate challenge in two hours (since Brig. Gen. Marcus Wright's Tennessee brigade withdrew). A. P. Stewart's attention had focused instead on the threat Van Cleve's attack posed, leaving Grose's regiments to fire into the Rebel flank at their leisure. And fire they did. As previously discussed, the 6th Ohio, one of Grose's regiments, was the first to run out of bullets. Grose sent the Buckeyes to the rear looking for more, where they were commandeered by division commander Joseph Reynolds. Now, with rather unfortunate timing, most of the rest of Grose's infantry was also out of ammunition.

The left flank of the Southern brigade led by William Bate joined with Henry Clayton's to help clear Brotherton Field. Bate's right—the 37th Georgia, 20th Tennessee, and 4th Georgia Battalion of Sharpshooters, 700 men in all—continued their advance to the northwest. In an effort to remain in close support, Brown's Tennesseans attempted to follow. In addition to these two groupings of Confederates, the 44th Alabama of Sheffield's wandering command was advancing on Bate's right, though once again this was a happy accident and not a coordinated movement.

Engaging Bate, Grose added the 36th Indiana from his support line to lengthen his front, leaving only the 84th Illinois in reserve, sitting on a small hill where its members could both observe action and—disconcertingly—catch any stray incoming rounds that sailed over

the heads of the men in front.[23] When the 23rd Kentucky exhausted its ammunition, the 84th moved forward down the slope to the front, adjacent to the 36th Indiana. Both regiments opened fire on Bate's men.

The fight did not last long. The Hoosiers quickly used up their last cartridges and fell back. "Now came the time for the Eighty-Fourth Illinois to come into the breach," Grose reported.[24] It proved a deadly post. James L. Cooper of the 20th Tennessee recalled it as the "prettiest fighting during the whole war. We rushed up on a little hill, and the enemy were just below us, all crowded together in a deep hollow. Our rifles were in prime condition and our ammunition so good that I really enjoyed the fight."[25] With his right flank turned, Col. Lewis H. Waters of the 84th decided to fall back before his regiment was slaughtered.[26]

The 44th Alabama helped speed the Illini on their way. In the ranks of the 84th, Pvt. James P. Suiter noted that more Rebels "came in overwhelming numbers on our left flank" just as the 20th Tennessee was swarming around the right.[27] Alabamian Joab Goodson recounted that "the Yankees fought us manfully as long as we lay and fought them, but when we . . . went at them double quick . . . they went at a double-quicker. I tell you they skedaddled in fine style."[28] With a wild yell, the Alabamians followed, all formation lost, "[like] a broken mass of howling demons," wrote Col. William F. Perry of the 44th Alabama.[29]

Grose's men fell back—not to the north or northwest, but northeast across the Brotherton Road toward their division. Here, the quick thinking of Gens. Palmer and George Cruft came into play. Alert to Grose's danger, Palmer ordered Cruft to shift his second line—the Federal 1st and 2nd Kentucky—into position at right angles to his front and backstop Grose's retreat.[30] The Unionist Kentuckians advanced briefly toward Grose's former position and, finding it swarming with Rebels, just as quickly fell back to form a firm anchor upon which Grose's command reformed.

Palmer's line was intact, and his position for the moment was secure. Grose's retreat, however, opened the door to the Union rear, and Bate's right wing poured through the gap, heading straight for Poe Field.

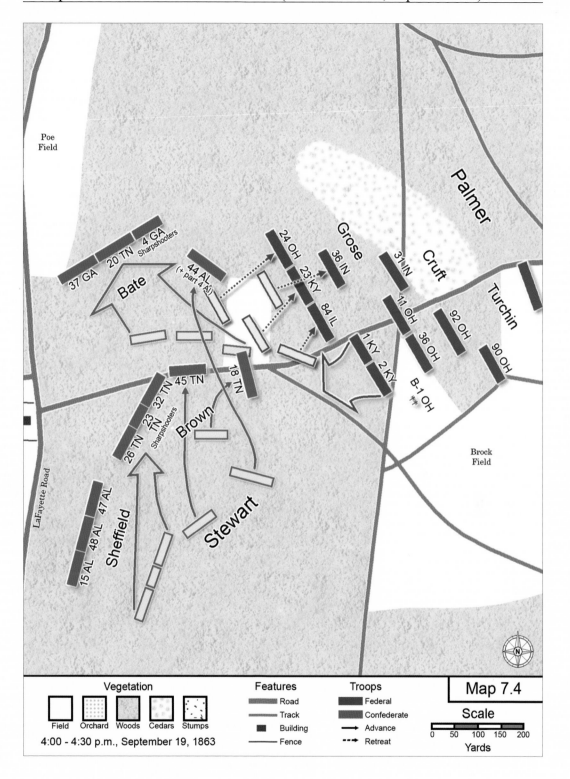

Poe Field

Palmer

37 GA   20 TN   4 GA
Sharpshooters

Bate

44 AL
(+ part 4 Al)

24 OH

23 KY

36 IN

84 IL

Grose

Cruft

31 IN

11 OH

36 OH

92 OH

Turchin

90 OH

1 KY   2 KY

B-1 OH

45 TN

18 TN

26 TN   23 TN   32 TN
Sharpshooters

Brown

Stewart

Brock Field

LaFayette Road

15 AL   48 AL   47 AL

Sheffield

N

Vegetation

Field   Orchard   Woods   Cedars   Stumps

4:00 - 4:30 p.m., September 19, 1863

Features

Road
Track
Building
Fence

Troops

Federal
Confederate
Advance
Retreat

Map 7.4

Scale

0   50   100   150   200
Yards

7.5: A. P. Stewart's Division Advances (4:30 to 5:00 p.m.)

While Bate was sweeping aside Grose, and after Fulton's appearance shattered the Union line, Henry Clayton's Brigade pursued the fleeing enemy west through the timber between Brotherton and South Dyer fields. The 18th and 38th Alabama emerged near the pits the Dyers used for tanning animal hides. With Clayton at their head, the regiments paused. Maj. P. F. Hunley, 18th Alabama, admitted that by now "the regiment . . . [was] a good deal scattered, [and] the pursuit was somewhat in confusion."[31]

The situation was more than "somewhat" confused. Fulton's men were stationary behind Clayton's advance, while John Gregg's two regiments that had managed to cling to Fulton's flank all afternoon (the 3rd and 41st Tennessee) came to rest in the woods to Clayton's left-rear. Despite their proximity, neither Fulton nor Clayton was aware of the other's presence.

Despite not having seen much combat, Sheffield's Brigade was a mess, and its deteriorating situation only added to the growing confusion within the Confederate ranks. The bulk of Sheffield's Alabama command (the 15th, 47, and 48th regiments) arrived in Brotherton Field. These regiments were supposed to be fighting alongside Benning's and Robertson's brigades, which were engaged a mile south around Viniard Field, but had failed to keep that connection, drifting instead northwest. Sheffield had been unhorsed by an artillery round early in the advance, and command should have passed to Col. Perry of the 44th Alabama. However, Perry and the 44th were not with the brigade. As noted earlier, the 44th and the 4th Alabama (also of Sheffield's command) were intermingled with Brown's men, both regiments separated from Sheffield's main line. Command of the remaining three Alabama regiments (15th, 47th, and 48th) devolved to the 15th's Col. William C. Oates, who led them into Brotherton Field shortly after 4:30 p.m. in search of a mission. Oates was aware of Fulton's presence to the south, but had no idea of Clayton's advance to the west, and seemed unconscious of any fight still being put up by Hazen's men north of Brotherton Field (an action that may have been winding down by the time Oates arrived).[32]

All might have seemed relatively quiet to Oates, but Fulton was alert to a new threat. Col. Charles G. Harker's Yankees, advancing cautiously north astride the LaFayette Road, surprised and outflanked the tag-a-long 3rd and 41st Tennessee regiments. Harker, it will be recalled, was part of Brig. Gen. Thomas Wood's division. Harker initially intended to support Jefferson C. Davis's division before Wood redeployed him. All Wood and Harker knew was that Confederates were across the road to their north, threatening the division's left flank, and they had to be dealt with.

Along the way, Gen. Gregg stumbled into Harker's lines while trying to gather up the scattered elements of his brigade. Gregg refused a demand to surrender and attempted to ride away, but was shot in the neck by a 64th Ohio skirmisher. Although many believed he was killed, Gregg survived to lead the famed Hood's Texas Brigade in General Lee's army in 1864. The Ohioans had no time to secure Gregg himself, but they did gather a few trophies, including his sword, which was passed to Col. Alexander McIlvain of the 64th. (Gregg's luck would run out on October 7, 1864, outside Richmond when he was killed leading a counterattack.)[33]

Harker's appearance in the timber south of Brotherton Field checked any additional Rebel advance. The 3rd and 41st Tennessee fell back precipitously, exposing Fulton's 17th Tennessee. Capt. Harder, fighting in the adjacent 23rd Tennessee, recalled that "this was all done so quick that [Lt. Col. Watt W.] Floyd hesitated . . . [and] the federals opened at short range a heavy small arms fire on the left and rear of the 17th."[34] "A general stampede ensued," Fulton admitted, his brigade fleeing into the trees east of the road.[35]

Fulton's retreat alerted Oates to Harker's threat. With some haste, Oates ordered his men to change facing, but by doing so drew Harker's attention and a volley that ripped through the 15th Alabama. Oates ordered a retreat to the LaFayette Road, but "saw that a panic had seized the command."[36] When his regiments reached the road they rallied briefly before falling back into the woods where Van Cleve and Stewart had fought.

Col. Harker's appearance had routed nearly twice his number of Confederates, and in just a handful of minutes.

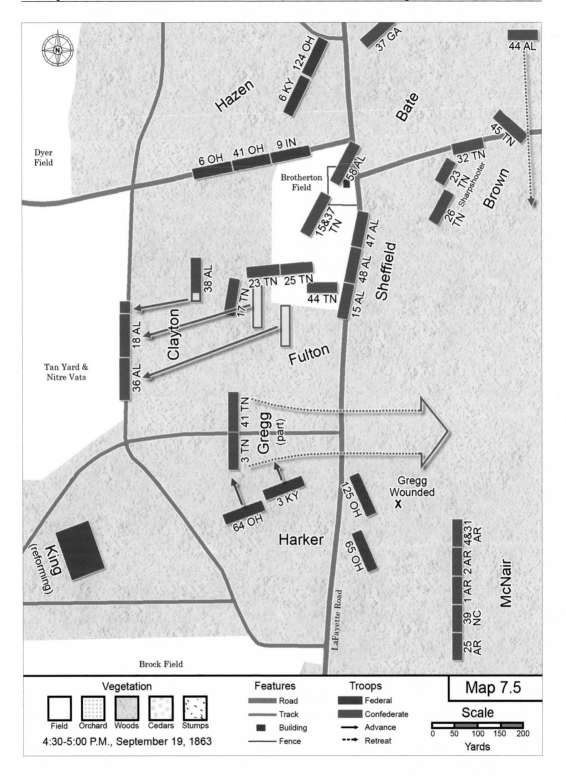

Map 7.5

Scale

4:30-5:00 P.M., September 19, 1863

Vegetation: Field, Orchard, Woods, Cedars, Stumps

Features: Road, Track, Building, Fence

Troops: Federal, Confederate, Advance, Retreat

0   50   100   150   200
Yards

7.6: Stewart's Advance: Bate (4:30 to 5:00 p.m.)

William B. Bate was both a capable soldier and an ambitious man, determined to rise in his military avocation. What he lacked in formal education he made up with drive and determination. Bate served in the Mexican War and commanded the 2nd Tennessee Infantry at Shiloh, where he was badly wounded leading an assault near Shiloh Church. The injury kept him out of combat for many months, but did not diminish his aggressive spirit, as the attack against Grose's Yankees demonstrated.

Flushed with success, Bate's men were willing to charge recklessly upon any Yankees they found, but Grose's withdrawal left few enemies in their path. One such Federal unit, Lt. Francis Russell's Battery M, 4th U.S. Artillery, was at risk of being overrun and promptly withdrew west. Russell's guns had originally supported Grose from a position near the Brotherton Road, but were left exposed when his infantry fled. With a direct path to Battery M visible, Bate's Georgians and Tennesseans made straight for the guns. "I could see them [Rebels] distinctly," Russell reported, "and . . . I fired as rapidly as possible." When the lieutenant realized "that to remain longer . . . would be sacrificing my battery, I limbered up and retired."[37] Col. A. F. Rudler, of the 37th Georgia mistakenly remembered that his regiment "drove [the Yankees] from their guns." In fact, the Georgians would meet Russell again, guns intact, just a few hundred yards farther on.[38]

The retreat of Russell's battery left only the 75th Indiana to hold the gap. Dispatched by Reynolds earlier after Palmer requested help, the Hoosiers had taken a hand in repulsing Brown (Map 5.9). The regiment, which had entered the fight with only 360 men and had already suffered significant losses, could not hope to stop Bate's attack. Still, remembered Company G's William Hilligos, the 75th stood "for some time (it was here we suffered most). . . ."[39] Fellow Hoosier James Essington recorded what happened next: "behold to our right . . . they are flanking us. . . . From our officers— Retreat—Retreat—back we go."[40] Reynolds, who watched as the Indiana troops emerged from the trees, reported that the 75th "returned . . . in some disorder, having relieved an entire brigade."[41]

Pausing only briefly to reform after each of these engagements, Bate's men plunged on. These were the Confederates Hazen had spotted moving north (Map 7.3) past his own brigade's flank (the threat that had sent him galloping back to Poe Field). Hazen found there only a polyglot collection of Federals, mostly artillery. He quickly alerted them to the approach of a large body of Southerners. Among the flotsam were Russell's Battery M and the battered 75th Indiana, both of whom formed on the west edge of Poe Field, which, "A moment later," wrote future writer and satirist Ambrose Bierce, "the field was gray with Confederates in pursuit."[42]

Bate's men ran into a meat grinder in Poe Field. "The artillery (4 batteries)" recalled Hazen, "opening at short range on their flank with canister [and] . . . sent them back."[43] Bierce marveled at the bloody spectacle: "For perhaps five minutes—it seemed an hour—nothing could be heard but the infernal din of their discharge and nothing seen through the smoke but a great ascension of dust."[44] This time Russell, who unlimbered his guns next to Cushing's battery H of the 4th U.S., was not retreating. "Cushing and I opened with canister," Russell reported in satisfaction, "and speedily repulsed them." When the firing stopped and the dust settled only broken bodies, many covered with dirt, could be seen. The tide of Bate's charge crested and receded in Poe Field.[45]

The ferocity of their reception stunned the Rebels. W. J. McMurray of the 20th Tennessee recalled that "some of Bate's regiments were almost annihilated."[46] Indeed, about one-half of the 20th fell there. The 37th Georgia lost 142 of its 425 men on the afternoon of the 19th, most of them during the short punishing action in the field. The 37th's wounded Col. Rudler reported that this fire "was so destructive that the regiment divided, a large portion moving forward to the left and others to the right."[47]

With his ardor temporarily checked, Bate rallied his three regiments and fell back near his line of departure.

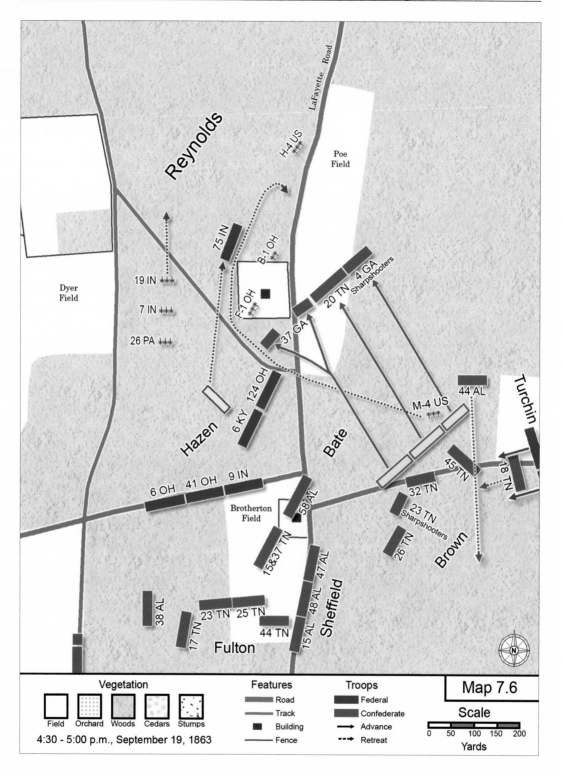

Reynolds

LaFayette Road

H-4 US

Poe
Field

Dyer
Field

19 IN

7 IN

26 PA

75 IN

B-1 OH

F-1 OH

4 GA
Sharpshooters

20 TN

37 GA

Hazen

6 KY 124 OH

Bate

M-4 US

44 AL

Turchin

45 TN

18 TN

6 OH   41 OH   9 IN

Brotherton
Field

58 AL

32 TN

23 TN
Sharpshooters

26 TN

Brown

38 AL

17 TN

23 TN 25 TN

15&37 TN

47 AL

15 AL 48 AL

44 TN

Sheffield

Fulton

Vegetation

Field   Orchard   Woods   Cedars   Stumps

4:30 - 5:00 p.m., September 19, 1863

Features

Road
Track
Building
Fence

Troops

Federal
Confederate
Advance
Retreat

Map 7.6

Scale

0   50   100 150 200
Yards

N

7.7: Brown Halts, Turchin Counterattacks (4:30 to 5:00 p.m.)

After their withdrawal from the firing line, John Brown's Tennesseans fell back several hundred yards to reorganize and draw fresh ammunition. Their losses had been heavy. Brown carried 1,340 men into action, and approximately 400 had been killed and wounded, with many more missing or lightly wounded.[48] Despite these heavy losses, the Tennesseans rallied quickly and moved to rejoin the rest of the division, which was fully re-engaged.

With Henry Clayton driving west toward the LaFayette Road and William Bate driving north and west toward Poe Field, Brown was presented with a dilemma: which brigade should he support? The overall confusion of the field added to his quandary. Fulton's Brigade of Bushrod Johnson's Division was in position to Brown's right south of Brotherton Field. Just as he was "ready again to move forward, a staff officer announced that the enemy had penetrated between Bate's left and Johnson's [Fulton's] right." Changing front, Brown led his battered command into this supposed gap. When his advance failed to find any Federals, Brown realized it was either a false alarm or the enemy had retreated.[49] Unfortunately for the Rebels, the staff officer's message removed Brown's men from A. P. Stewart's attack for the rest of the day. Brown's regiments finally came to rest in a disordered line facing generally northwest in the woods east of Brotherton Field some distance behind Col. Oates' section of Sheffield's Brigade. Eventually, Bate's retreating troops (after their defeat in Poe Field) made their way behind Brown's line and reformed there.

There were in fact Federals threatening a flank at this time, but not where the staff officer believed. John Palmer's Federal division was still deployed on Brown's right, its flank refused to face west after Col. Grose's abrupt retreat. Brig. Gen. John Basil Turchin, a former Imperial Russian officer and a man of strong-willed temperament, held Palmer's left in place of Hazen's brigade, which had been relieved earlier. Grose's withdrawal combined with Gen. Cruft's reorientation alerted Turchin to the suggestion of a larger Union disaster unfolding behind him. Since his own front was now quiet—the enemy

had been driven off when Union Gen. Richard W. Johnson's division advanced before 3:00 p.m., and had not yet returned—Turchin decided he could lend a hand to support Cruft and Grose.

Turchin's men, divided amongst four regiments (18th Kentucky, and the 11th, 36th, and 92nd Ohio) found the order to change front both dramatic and confusing. Initially in the reserve line, Rob Adney of the 36th Ohio found himself and his comrades in the forefront of the new movement. "Suddenly, off to our right there broke out a most infernal din and uproar," Adney recalled. "We changed our course to a direct right angle to our former line of march, and started not at a double-quick, but at a keen run."[50] Moving quickly through groups of Federal stragglers, Turchin's men arrived on line with Cruft's brigade. With both commands now facing east along the Brotherton Road, they lunged forward about 400 yards.

Despite later recollections, Turchin's counterattack struck few Rebels. Bate's men were mostly gone by now, marching to their fate in Poe Field. Brown's men had stopped in the woods farther west, and none of Brown's regiments reported an encounter with anyone at this time. The unfortunate 44th Alabama, part of Sheffield's widely separated brigade, was facing north with its right flank exposed to the onrushing Federal tide.

Col. Perry of the 44th recalled that it was an unknown Union battery, opening at close range, that routed his command.[51] While there is no reason to doubt Perry's recollection, other evidence suggests the circumstances were more complicated. Turchin reported that his command routed Law's (currently Sheffield's) Brigade, which was clearly a reference to the 44th Alabama.[52] The Alabamians were also subject to friendly fire. The historian of the 18th Tennessee, part of Brown's Brigade, admitted that his regiment, in a fit of confusion, fired into the 44th.[53] Regardless of the cause, the men of the 44th bolted for the rear in utter confusion.

Satisfied that order had been restored, Turchin and Cruft agreed to pull their regiments back to Cruft's refused line.[54] In doing so, they unwittingly opened a route for Bate's shattered formations to fall back from Poe Field and reform behind Brown.

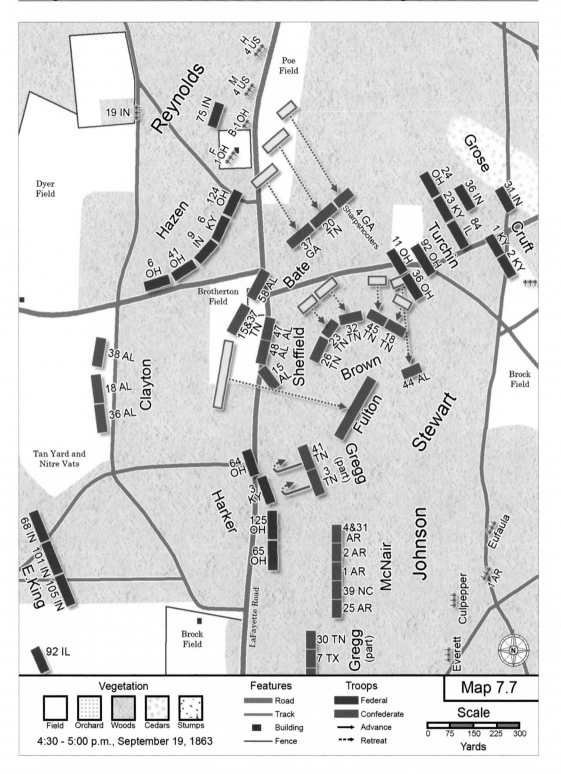

Map 7.7

Vegetation: Field, Orchard, Woods, Cedars, Stumps

Features: Road, Track, Building, Fence

Troops: Federal, Confederate, Advance, Retreat

Scale: 0 75 150 225 300 Yards

4:30 - 5:00 p.m., September 19, 1863

7.8: Brannan and Negley Close the Door (5:30 p.m.)

Isolated actions by Turchin's and Harker's Federals threatened the flanks of the Rebel breakthrough and helped check the advance of A. P. Stewart's Division. A more coherent response, however, was now taking form.

George Thomas (XIV Corps) and army commander William Rosecrans were each sending troops to help. At the height of the crisis in Brotherton Field, Thomas ordered Brig. Gen. John Brannan's division to move from its position on the now quiet left flank astride the Reed's Bridge Road and rush south. Rosecrans also contributed a division: Maj. Gen. James S. Negley's men were en route to the battlefield after finally being relieved near Glass Mill that morning. Two of Negley's brigades under Cols. William Sirwell and Timothy Stanley were at hand, having just reached the Widow Glenn House. These seven regiments sealed the breach torn open by Stewart's Southerners.

Brannan reported that he received orders at 3:00 p.m. to move two of his brigades south to support Palmer. Brannan tapped the commands of Cols. John Connell and Ferdinand Van Derveer for the move, leaving Col. John Croxton's brigade behind near the Reed's Bridge Road.[55] As Brannan and his officers soon discovered, shifting quickly several thousand men proved impossible. Connell reported that his men did not arrive near the Poe Field until "just before sundown."[56] Van Derveer's regiments led the march south halting and deploying somewhere behind Hazen's scratch line. By the time Van Derveer arrived the fighting was over and William Bate's Brigade had been repulsed. None of Brannan's men reported seeing any action after deploying around Poe Field.

Gen. Joseph Reynolds was also active, rallying and forming "into double line ten or twelve other retiring regiments."[57] Some of these were scattered far afield, including Col. King's brigade, which Reynolds located almost a mile to the south and ordered back toward Poe Field. He also rallied Hazen's regiments (9th Indiana, 6th Kentucky, and 41st and 124th Ohio), and the still wandering 6th Ohio of Grose's brigade. John Croxton, belatedly ordered to march after the division, arrived with Brannan's remaining brigade. Reynolds incorporated Croxton's men into this growing mass of Federal soldiers and assigned Croxton the task of controlling the front line. Brannan ordered him and the entire force to sweep from the left, effectively clearing any remaining Rebels from the Union rear.

In the meantime, Negley's men were up, deployed and advancing. Like Brannan, Negley also had only two of his three brigades present (Sirwell and Stanley.) John Beatty's command remained in place as a rearguard at Glass Mill several miles to the south. As Negley's van approached Rosecrans' headquarters at the Widow Glenn's, his troops witnessed the "panorama of war on a grand scale," recalled the regimental historian of the 78th Pennsylvania. "The battle was raging fiercely in the forest along the Chickamauga; batteries of artillery and brigades of infantry were moving on double quick to the support of our forces on the battle lines . . . we could see the smoke of battle rising above the trees, almost shutting out our view of the forest, while the roar of artillery and the rattle of musketry was deafening."[58]

The army commander greeted Negley's arrival with palpable relief as he sketched out a plan: locate Thomas, attack into the teeth of the Confederate advance, and restore the Union line. As Negley hurried past, James Martin of the 11th Michigan recalled that Rosecrans "gave us a few cheering words and told us if we had a fight with the Rebels to give them fits."[59]

Negley placed his artillery in line on the high ground overlooking Dyer Field from the west and formed the infantry in the empty fields below (Clayton's Rebels having fallen back). The woods between Dyer and Brotherton fields, however, were still full of Confederate skirmishers. Unaware of other Union movements unfolding at the same time, Negley's men expected a heavy fight in the gathering gloom of dusk, but their advance proved anticlimactic. Sirwell and Stanley discovered that the Confederates—menaced by Federals on both flanks and now in their front—had retreated. Lt. Col. William D. Ward of the 37th Indiana, Sirwell's brigade, remembered how his men "gained and occupied the position to which we were ordered without firing a gun and with only one man wounded."[60]

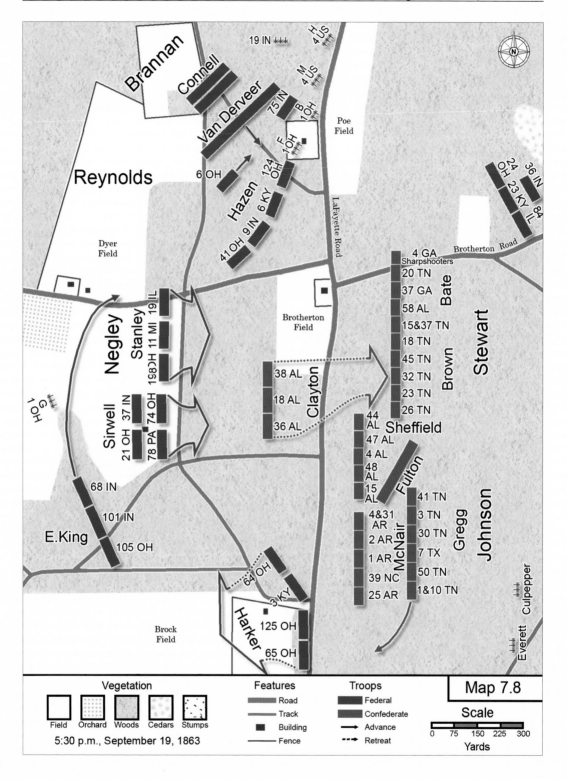

Map 7.8

Vegetation

Field Orchard Woods Cedars Stumps

5:30 p.m., September 19, 1863

Features
— Road
— Track
■ Building
— Fence

Troops
■ Federal
■ Confederate
→ Advance
⇢ Retreat

Scale
0   75   150   225   300
Yards

7.9: Overall Situation (6:00 p.m.)

Negley's advance brought the fighting to a fitful close and largely restored the Union center. Both armies had committed tens of thousands of troops with little regard for chain of command. The result was a haphazardly faced patchwork line bisecting the battlefield from northeast to southwest. The LaFayette Road remained a contested objective. It was well inside Union lines north of the Poe house, but was in no-mans land south of that location.

William Rosecrans had spent most of the 19th reacting to Southern moves, responding to various perceived thrusts rather than attempting to control the action by disengaging his army or orchestrating a larger assault. He fed troops into the fight as they became available, often without regard to the chain of command. The jumbled nature of the army's condition at nightfall was the natural result of these decisions. Only Thomas had a clearly defined sphere of command. McCook and Crittenden tried to help where they were needed, but received no clear direction or defined sectors of responsibility from the army commander.

On the northern end of the field, Thomas still commanded roughly one-half of the Union army. Baird's division stretched to fill the gap left when Brannan moved south, with one brigade on the Reed's Bridge Road and the other starting to move southeast toward the Union flank at Winfrey Field. Having helped stabilize the Union line in Poe Field, Brannan deployed his division near the Dyer house. Reynolds held Poe Field with the reformed and reunited men of King's brigade. Negley's two brigades came to rest on the western edge of Brotherton Field.

The Federal divisions of Johnson and Palmer, with Turchin's brigade still attached, defended a salient well in advance of the rest of the Union line. Johnson's three brigades fronted a compact line just west of the Winfrey farmstead. A dangerous gap of several hundred yards, however, still existed between Dodge and Turchin. Having reoccupied Hazen's old ground, Turchin formed a semi-circular line astride the Brotherton Road along with the brigades of Grose and Cruft of Palmer's division. Hazen, Palmer's last brigade, was ordered to rejoin the division and was still en route.

Thomas Crittenden and Alexander McCook's commands were less clearly defined. Wilder continued to act as the anchor in West Viniard Field, even though as an independent command he answered to neither corps commander. Davis' pair of mauled brigades reformed in the woods behind Wilder. Harker and Buell, comprising Wood's division, withdrew from exposed positions across the LaFayette Road and fell in on Wilder's left. Two of Phil Sheridan's brigades followed suit on Wilder's right. Even though the bulk of these troops belonged to McCook's XX Corps, Crittenden (XXI Corps) was still responsible for this sector. McCook was not personally assigned any current duties. John Beatty's brigade of Negley's division was ordered up from Glass Mill, but would spent much of the night in transit. Lytle's brigade of Sheridan's division currently guarded Lee and Gordon's Mills, but was ordered to rejoin the division.

On the Southern side, all along the line the Confederate troops were located about where they had come to rest after fighting, rather than intentionally redeployed there. John Hood's troops and A. P. Stewart's Division simply fell back into the woods east of the LaFayette Road. Ben Cheatham and St. John Liddell's men did likewise, opposite Palmer' and Johnson's Federals. Matthew Ector and Claudius Wilson of William Walker's Reserve Corps, whose brigades had been out of the fight since that morning, were badly used up. However, many thousands of Rebels had not yet fired a shot, including William Preston's Division of Simon Buckner's Corps, still in place near the Hall house, Thomas Hindman's Division, recently arrived behind Buckner, and D. H. Hill's entire corps. Hill's two divisions under Pat Cleburne and John C. Breckinridge were solid commands. Cleburne's men were even then filing into place behind Liddell's troops. Breckinridge's three brigades were the last to reach the field after spending the day guarding Glass Mill.

One last act remained to be played out on September 19. As Cleburne's infantry marched up, Liddell sensed that there was still an opportunity to inflict some damage on the Federals, if only an attack could be organized in time. He conveyed the idea to Cleburne, and by doing so touched off one of the few large-scale night actions of the entire Civil War.

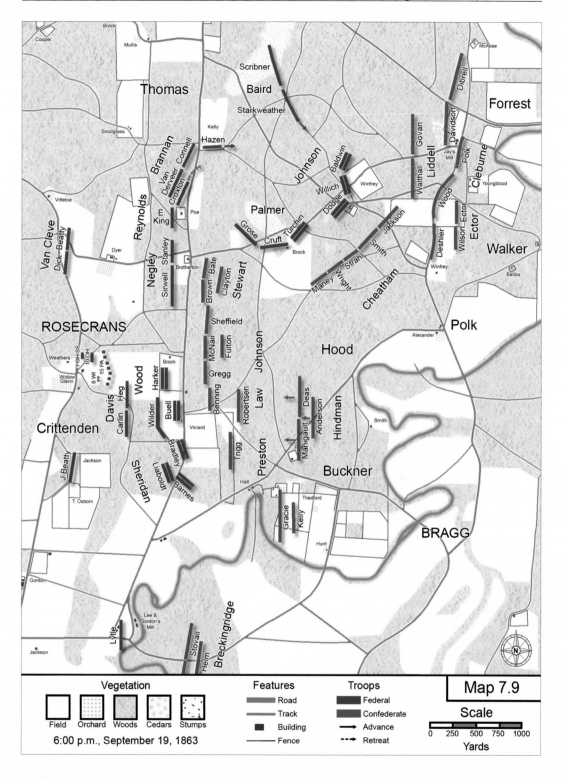

Vegetation

Field   Orchard   Woods   Cedars   Stumps

6:00 p.m., September 19, 1863

Features

▨ Road

— Track

■ Building

— Fence

Troops

■ Federal

■ Confederate

→ Advance

⇢ Retreat

Map 7.9

Scale

0   250   500   750   1000

Yards

Map Set 8: Cleburne Attacks in Winfrey Field

(Night, September 19)

8.1: Walthall Attacks Winfrey Field (3:30 p.m.)

While the battle raged farther south, the Winfrey Field sector remained quiet for several hours. That afternoon, fighting flared up there again, and intermittent action continued well into the evening. About 3:30 p.m., after successfully driving back the Confederates an hour or so earlier, Brig. Gen. Richard W. Johnson's Federal division assumed an irregular line facing east and stretching from a point just south of the Winfrey house and orchard to the northwest corner of Winfrey Field. Unfortunately, both of Johnson's flanks remained exposed.

On Johnson's right, Brig. Gen. John Turchin's brigade marked Maj. Gen. John M. Palmer's flank, slightly south and several hundred yards west. The divisions under Brig. Gens. Absalom Baird and John M. Brannan still guarded the Reed's Bridge Road, but their lines ended three-quarters of a mile north of Johnson's left. Despite their exposed position, Johnson's men remained confident. They had just driven the enemy one-half mile or more, inflicted considerable losses, and had knocked Maj. Gen. Ben Cheatham's division out of the fight for the rest of the day.

Cheatham's abrupt retreat in the face of Johnson's attack at 2:30 p.m. (Map 5.7) caused concern in Lt. Gen. Leonidas Polk's Corps headquarters. The only troops available to stabilize the situation were from Maj. Gen. William Walker's battered Reserve Corps. Brig. Gen. St. John Liddell's two brigades under Col. Daniel Govan and Brig. Gen. Edward Walthall (which had suffered somewhat less than those under Brig. Gen. Matthew Ector and Col. Claudius Wilson) were ordered to support Cheatham's right.[1]

Liddell placed Walthall on the left and Govan on the right, both facing west. Once again, each regiment was deployed in a long single line. When it went into action that morning, the division numbered just more than 4,000 men. Roughly one-quarter of its strength had been swept from the ranks during the earlier fighting. Liddell ordered his men to advance. It was about 3:30 p.m.

The Mississippians made little headway moving into the open and by now grimly familiar ground that was already carpeted with casualties from Walthall's work that morning. This time the brigade moved in from the east on a line perpendicular to its earlier charge. The tactical situation was also very different. Instead of falling on an unsuspecting Union flank, Walthall was moving directly into the leveled rifled muskets of two brigades: Brig. Gen. August Willich's on his left front, and Col. Philemon Baldwin's on his right front. Artillery studded the Federal line: the 5th Indiana had an excellent field of fire across Baldwin's front from the left, Battery A, 1st Ohio guarded Willich's right south of the field, and the 20th Ohio was behind Dodge's center. Walthall came under fire almost immediately after he began forming and advanced 400 yards. "Here the enemy, strongly posted delivered a very heavy fire," he reported.[2] Within fifteen minutes he realized the futility of his effort and ordered his men back into the trees.

Things might have gone much worse for the Yankees defending Winfrey Field. Daniel Govan's line of Arkansans and Louisianans extended well beyond Baldwin's flank and could have rolled up Johnson's entire division. Govan failed to realize the opportunity because of the heavy timber and the rampant confusion circling within the Rebel ranks. While Walthall was falling back, Govan was still moving west, marching past the exposed Federal left. Walthall's retreat, however, sucked the 6th/7th Arkansas regiment on the far left of Govan's line away from its mother brigade, disrupting Govan's formation and severing contact with the rest of the division.

The Federals on the west side of Winfrey Field were well aware of the danger to their exposed northern flank. The always astute Willich suggested that Baldwin face his two reserve regiments north and turn the tables on the advancing Rebels. Govan was thus outflanked, and his line fell back precipitously. Although the attacking regiments belonged to Baldwin, Willich took the opportunity to ride amongst Hoosiers of the 6th Indiana, "carrying his hat in his hand . . . rolled up in a long, club-like shape," recorded the regiment's historian, "and every once in a while he would hit a fellow a crack over the back . . . and say, 'Go in, boys, and give 'em hell,' and was all the time cursing in Dutch."[3]

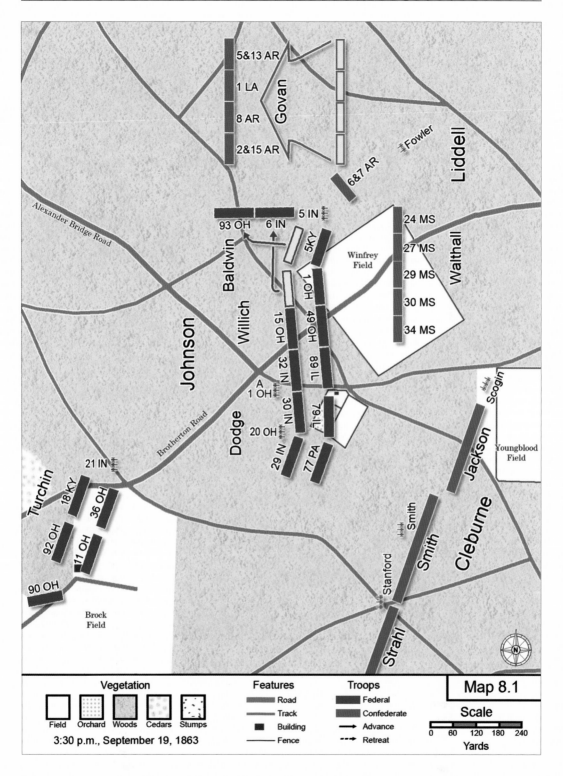

5&13 AR

1 LA

8 AR

2&15 AR

Govan

6&7 AR

Fowler

Liddell

93 OH   6 IN   5 IN

5 KY

24 MS

27 MS

29 MS

30 MS

34 MS

Winfrey
Field

Walthall

Baldwin

1 OH

Alexander Bridge Road

Willich

15 OH

49 OH

Johnson

32 IN

89 IL

A
1 OH

30 IN

Brotherton Road

Dodge

20 OH

29 IN

77 PA

79 IL

Scogin

Youngblood
Field

Jackson

21 IN

Turchin

18 KY

36 OH

92 OH

11 OH

Smith

Cleburne

90 OH

Brock
Field

Stanford

Smith

Strahl

N

Vegetation

Field   Orchard   Woods   Cedars   Stumps

Features

━━ Road
━━ Track
▪ Building
━━ Fence

Troops

Federal
Confederate
→ Advance
⇢ Retreat

Map 8.1

Scale

0   60   120   180   240
Yards

3:30 p.m., September 19, 1863

8.2: Cleburne Deploys (7:00 p.m.)

Despite his earlier repulse, Liddell was still convinced that opportunity beckoned in Winfrey Field. Previous efforts failed for want of fresh troops. Those troops were now at hand with the arrival of a division under Maj. Gen. Patrick R. Cleburne. "I pressed [him] to move to the attack at once . . . and drive the enemy back, as they must be greatly exhausted from our constant fighting," Liddell recalled.[4]

Cleburne and Liddell were well acquainted. The latter general had attended West Point for a year before dropping out (likely because of his low class standing). The Mississippi native proved his ability in the field as a combat leader at Corinth, Perryville, and Murfreesboro, but was frequently ill, first with bronchitis and later with a nearly fatal bout of typhoid. He had led a brigade under Cleburne for nearly a year, and had only recently been elevated to command a division. Despite this familiarity, Cleburne refused the offer to attack. It was now dusk, his troops were moving into unfamiliar ground, and Liddell's own assault had been a bloody failure—all strong reasons for not attacking immediately. When corps commander Lt. Gen. Daniel H. Hill arrived, Liddell reiterated his argument and Hill concurred. Cleburne would attack, despite the growing darkness.

Cleburne's command numbered 5,380 officers and men. After the war his division would enjoy a storied reputation for combat prowess, but in September of 1863 it was just coalescing as a combat unit. His first battle at the head of a division was Murfreesboro (December 31, 1862 to January 2, 1863). In the inevitable post-battle reorganization that followed, two of the four brigades he had led were transferred to other commands. These troops were replaced by one brigade composed of Texans and Arkansans who, captured at Arkansas Post and exchanged, were sent to the Army of Tennessee under a bit of a cloud.[5] The reequipped troops were led by the recently promoted Brig. Gen. James Deshler, "an elegant gentleman . . . everybody in the brigade liked."[6] Cleburne had no doubts about how they would perform. His remaining two brigades were led by Brig. Gens. Lucius K. Polk and S.A.M. Wood. Polk was a solid performer, nephew to the corps commander, and now

heading Cleburne's former brigade. Wood was more problematic. He had stumbled at Shiloh and demanded a court of inquiry to clear him. Returned to command, he was wounded at Perryville and saw action at Murfreesboro.

Cleburne's men initially followed the same route Cheatham's men had tramped, moving up the road past the Alexander House and on toward Jay's Mill. When they finally halted and faced west, the three brigades formed a line more than one mile long, their front covered by parts of both Liddell's and Cheatham's divisions. Cleburne's front also overlapped both of Johnson's flanks, a potential Federal disaster in the making.

Johnson and his men were alert to the pending danger. After Liddell's attack, George Thomas ordered Baird to move two brigades of his division down from the Reed's Bridge Road to connect with and support Baldwin's brigade on Johnson's left. At 5:00 p.m., Thomas made a more dramatic decision: thinking that his lines were "very much extended," he decided to fall back and "concentrate them on more commanding ground."[7] At that hour Thomas was also dealing with the unfolding crisis in Brotherton Field (Map 7.8) and was fully engaged in restoring the shattered Union center. Thomas had little time or energy to spare much attention on the relatively quiet sector around Winfrey Field.

Perhaps these distractions explain why Baird's men were so slow in moving up or why, two hours after Thomas decided to pull back, Johnson's line was still hanging on at the Winfrey farm. In his report Johnson wrote only that he received Thomas' order to fall back after Cleburne's assault was well underway.[8] Baird offers more elaboration. The two brigades he had on the move under Brig. Gen. John Starkweather and Col. Ben Scribner advanced cautiously, halting a few hundred yards behind Johnson's left rear. The sector was still quiet when Baird arrived. His infantry was being posted by a couple of Johnson's staff officers when, "toward dark," Thomas arrived to consult with both division commanders. Baird explained: "Orders were given to have the troops withdraw after nightfall, and Gen. Johnson and myself rode back with [Thomas] to ascertain the position we would occupy."[9]

All three generals were absent when Cleburne's mile-long line stepped off in their direction.

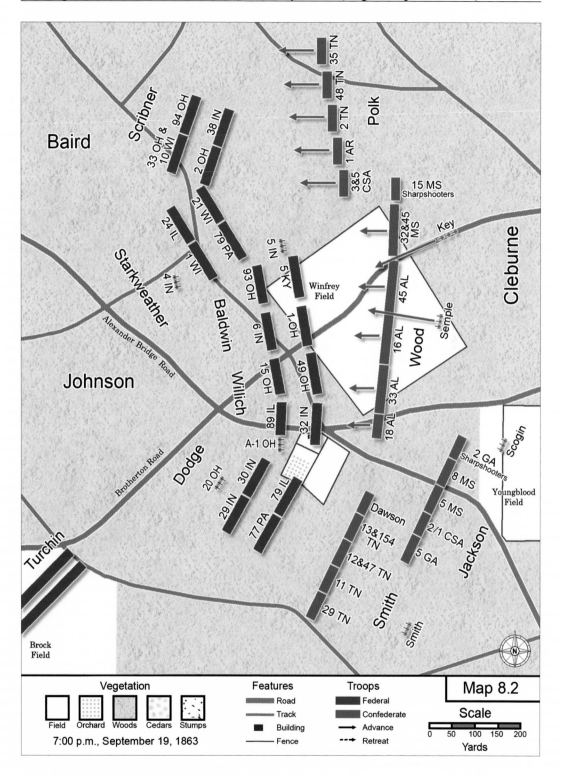

Map 8.2

7:00 p.m., September 19, 1863

8.3: Cleburne's Advance (7:30 p.m.)

While the length of Cleburne's line offered certain advantages over the defending Federals, it also created several difficulties for the Southerners.

Very few night attacks were launched during the Civil War because darkness complicated combat, especially for the aggressor. Controlling a mile-long battle line was hard enough in daylight; cloaked in darkness on unfamiliar ground, it was practically impossible. Cleburne's brigades would also have to pass through Cheatham's and Liddell's stationary troops. The passage of lines was one the most difficult maneuvers in linear warfare, and this attempt would prove no exception. The advance almost immediately disrupted Cleburne's front, with gaps appearing between brigades.

As might be expected, the most difficult resistance came in the center, where S.A.M. Wood's regiments had to cross the open ground of Winfrey Field. Wood lost control of his regiments almost from the start. An Alabama lawyer when the war began, Wood had no military training and apparently little skill at directing the movements of a brigade under combat conditions. The Federal rate of fire was heavy, though as Cleburne noted, "Accurate shooting was impossible . . . and few of the shot from either side took effect."[10]

Some of Wood's regiments halted, while others surged ahead. Col. E. B. Breedlove's 45th Alabama, holding the right-center of Wood's line, drove his regiment up to the fence where Baldwin's Federals were posted. Only then did he discover that he was seventy-five yards ahead of the rest of the Wood's infantry. The confusion increased when the regiment on his right, the combined 32nd & 45th Mississippi, began shooting into Breedlove's exposed flank instead of into the defending Yankee line.[11] Half of the 45th Alabama halted while the other half rushed on. In an effort to reconnect his fractured regiment, Breedlove ordered the entire regiment to fall back. A private "Wilson" in the 16th Alabama—there were eleven Wilsons in the regiment—fighting alongside the 45th on its left recounted what happened next. The men of the 16th had also reached the fence when "the 45th Ala . . . gave way and Maj. McGaughy . . . gave the command to march in retreat." Instead "of marching away in an orderly manner," Wilson continued, "two companies in our right wing . . . ran disgracefully . . . [causing] . . . great confusion in the remainder of our regiment."[12]

The rest of Wood's advance was equally troubled. Complicating the attack was Wood's failure to lead. Instead of controlling his brigade, he was nowhere to be found. After the battle rumors swept the ranks that the general had "acted very badly on the field," remaining well to the rear as his men advanced. True or not, within days the brigadier left the army "in disgrace (emphasis in original)," wrote Robert L. Bliss, serving at brigade headquarters, the taint of cowardice forcing his resignation.[13]

Confusion dogged the Federal defense as well. In the midst of the attack, Hoosiers in the 6th Indiana were stunned to see Col. Baldwin, their former commander now leading the brigade, ride in front of them between the dueling lines of infantry. He seemed intent on launching a counterattack, explained C. C. Briant of Company K. "This of course placed him between the two fires . . . both him and his horse were killed instantly. The Regiment, very sensibly, did not obey an order which never should have been given," continued Briant, "but did just what they should have done: 'Stand fast and give 'em Hell!'"[14]

Baldwin's body was never recovered, and was probably buried as one of the hundreds of unknown dead of Chickamauga. His rash attack order puzzled many in his old regiment. The colonel had begun the war as a company commander in the 6th, was appointed colonel after Shiloh, and led a brigade at Stone's River, so he didn't lack for experience. It was probably fortunate for the regiment that its members did not obey him, because while Wood's line was in difficulty, the rest of Cleburne's Division was still moving forward.

With Wood's line disrupted and falling to pieces, two Confederate artillery batteries, aided by the darkness, unlimbered as close as sixty yards of the Federals and "opened a rapid fire."[15] On the division's flanks, meanwhile, Lucius Polk's and James Deshler's brigades were still advancing.

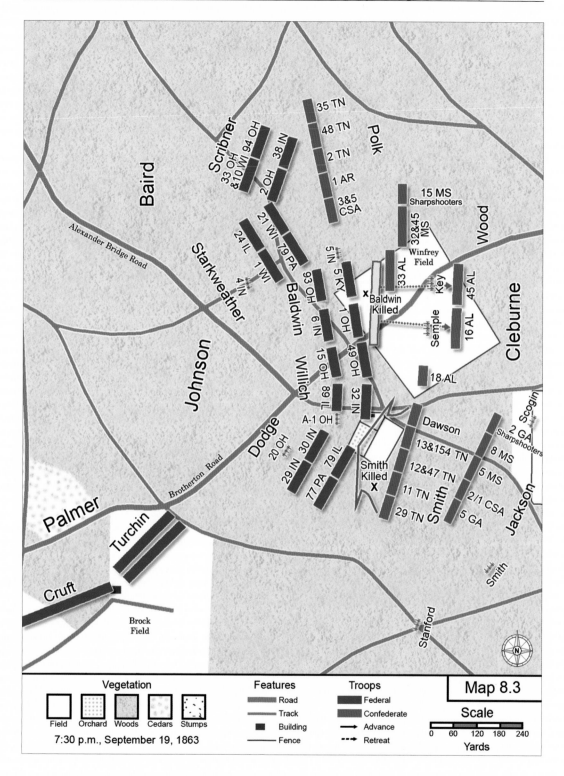

Baird

Scribner

Polk

35 TN

48 TN

2 TN

1 AR

3&5 CSA

33 OH &10 WI 94 OH

2 OH

38 IN

15 MS
Sharpshooters

Wood

32&45 MS

Winfrey Field

33 AL

Key

45 AL

16 AL

Cleburne

Semple

18 AL

Alexander Bridge Road

Starkweather

21 WI 79 PA

24 IL

1 WI

4 IN

Baldwin

93 OH

5 IN 5 KY

6 IN

1 OH

49 OH

X
Baldwin
Killed

Johnson

Willich

15 OH

89 IL

32 IN

A-1 OH

Dawson

Scogin

2 GA
Sharpshooters

8 MS

5 MS

2/1 CSA

5 GA

Jackson

Dodge

20 OH

30 IN

29 IN

77 PA 79 IL

13&154 TN

12&47 TN

11 TN

29 TN

Smith

Palmer

Turchin

Brotherton Road

Smith
Killed
X

Cruft

Brock
Field

Stanford

Smith

N

| Vegetation | Features | Troops | Map 8.3 |

Field   Orchard   Woods   Cedars   Stumps

7:30 p.m., September 19, 1863

Road
Track
Building
Fence

Federal
Confederate
Advance
Retreat

Scale

0   60   120   180   240

Yards

8.4: Collision in the Dark (8:00 p.m.)

S.A.M. Wood's muddled advance was not duplicated along the rest of Cleburne's extended line. Lucius Polk's Brigade pushed north of both Winfrey Field and Baldwin's left flank and collided with the confused Yankees of Starkweather's and Scribner's brigades (Baird's division). These men were expecting to move shortly, either forward to support Johnson's division or backward to a new line designated by XIV Corps commander George Thomas. As a result, they were unready for the heavy attack that hammered them out of the deepening darkness. The fact that Starkweather and Scribner were not aligned correctly—they had come to rest in a shallow V-shaped formation with their exposed flanks angled toward the enemy and their center as likely to fire into one another as fire into the Confederates—only compounded Baird's problems.

Polk's men struck the 38th Indiana first. Lt. Col. Daniel F. Griffin reported that "the enemy came in at this point, advancing in the darkness and pouring a volley of musketry on our flank that caused the line to retire a few hundred yards."[16] W. H. Springer, also of the 38th Indiana, remembered a confused fighting. At one point, he noted, the 2nd Ohio, "just next to us . . . foolishly . . . fired right on us."[17] Things only got worse. To Starkweather, it seemed as though fire was coming from all directions. Scribner's men, continued Starkweather, "having . . . obliqued to the right instead of moving parallel . . . opened . . . fire upon the left regiments of my brigade and the left of Johnson's division, thus destroying my men." In response, "Johnson's troops . . . faced about and fired into my right."[18] The result was a bloody fiasco. It is little wonder that both of Baird's brigades fell back precipitously in confusion.

Polk's success on Cleburne's right flank was being duplicated by James Deshler's Texans, who were busy working their way around Johnson's other flank south of Winfrey Field. When Deshler's line lost contact with Wood, it initially drifted southwest, reoriented itself, and a short time later swung in a wide arc to come up on Col. Joseph Dodge's flank from the south. In an effort to support this attack, Cheatham ordered the brigades under Brig. Gens. John K.

Jackson and Preston Smith to move forward and support Deshler. What Cheatham did not yet realize was that Deshler's shift to the southwest had opened a large gap in Cleburne's advancing line. Fully expecting friendly troops in their front (and so with no need to deploy skirmishers), Jackson and Smith marched westward, confident of their mission.

While leading his men Smith suddenly found himself in the middle of the 77th Pennsylvania regiment. "We rode right into their lines before they discovered us," wrote Capt. John W. Harris, one of Smith's staff officers.[19] Equally surprised by the encounter, little more than thirty Federals managed to set fingers to trigger and fire. Unfortunately for the Confederates, several bullets found their mark. One ricocheted off the gold watch over Smith's heart before penetrating his body; two other officers fell with him. Smith was removed from the field but died within the hour.

Within a short time the Pennsylvanians found themselves mobbed by Smith's rushing infantry. Struck heavily from the front, Dodge's brigade only a moment later was attacked from its right-rear by Deshler's advancing Texans. According to the 77th's historian, "the 17th and 18th Texas filed across the right flank . . . and opened a terrific enfilading fire. The regiment was hemmed in on all sides."[20] In the dark and bloody chaos that naturally followed, seventy-three Pennsylvanians surrendered, including regimental commander Thomas E. Rose. Dozens more were captured from Dodge's other regiments. Harris noted that he personally took custody of thirty Yankees, including a major and a captain.[21] Of Dodge's 532 total casualties, 307 were reported missing, most of them were captured in this night action.

With Rebels on their front, both flanks, and working their way into their rear, Johnson's brigades broke. Col. Allen Buckner of the 79th Illinois, Dodge's brigade, reported that "we fell back under a heavy crossfire from the enemy and our friends. I found the colors of the Thirtieth Indiana and rallied as many as possible . . . constantly moving back until we reached the rear of our battery."[22]

Equally disordered by their stunning tactical success, the Confederates did not attempt to pursue. Johnson's Federals reformed on Baird's line in complete darkness.

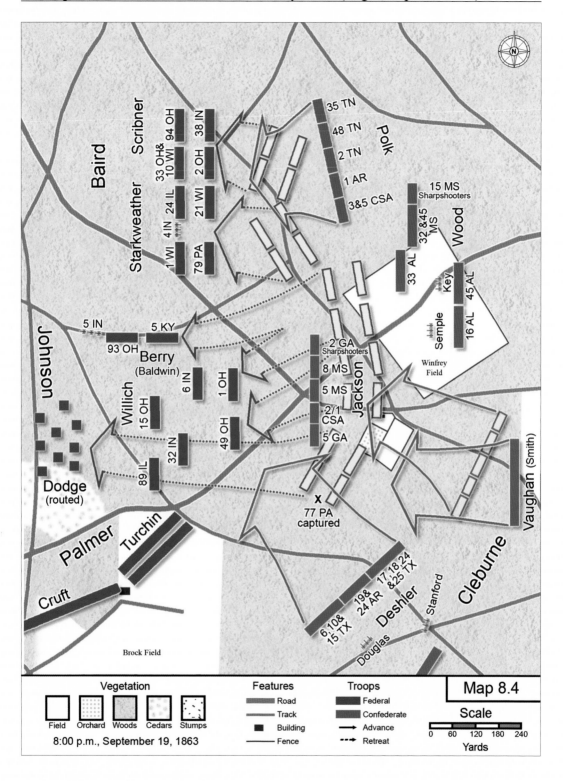

Baird

Scribner

Starkweather

33 OH & 10 WI   94 OH   38 IN

2 OH

4 IN   24 IL   21 WI

1 WI   79 PA

Polk

35 TN
48 TN
2 TN
1 AR
3 & 5 CSA

15 MS
Sharpshooters

Wood

32 & 45 MS

33 AL

45 AL

Key

16 AL

Semple

Winfrey
Field

Johnson

5 IN   5 KY
93 OH

Berry
(Baldwin)

Willich

6 IN   1 OH

15 OH

49 OH   32 IN

89 IL

Dodge
(routed)

2 GA
Sharpshooters

8 MS

5 MS

2/1
CSA

5 GA

Jackson

Vaughan (Smith)

X
77 PA
captured

Palmer   Turchin

Cruft

17, 18, 24
& 25 TX

6, 10 &
15 TX   19 &
24 AR   Deshler   Stanford   Cleburne

Douglas

Brock Field

Vegetation

Field   Orchard   Woods   Cedars   Stumps

8:00 p.m., September 19, 1863

Features

Road
Track
Building
Fence

Troops

Federal
Confederate
Advance
Retreat

Map 8.4

Scale

0   60   120   180   240
Yards

8.5: Overall Situation (9:00 p.m.)

Cleburne's attack marked the denouement of the first day's battle. Cleburne and corps leader D. H. Hill elected not to pursue the enemy. Night fighting was typically marred by confusion and this clash had been no exception. Sporadic picket fire still flared here and there across the battlefield, but the real fighting would wait for the morrow.

Both armies settled on the field where dusk found them. King's Regulars watched the Reed's Bridge Road. In the woods to the south, Baird's other two brigades (Starkweather and Scribner) formed a line facing east. Johnson rallied his division on Baird's right. Still farther south, a dangerous bulge marked the center of George Thomas' front. Turchin (Reynolds' division) curved to the southwest. On Turchin's right, Palmers division was scattered. Cruft's men held Turchin's right facing nearly south. Then Grose's brigade angled to face nearly due west creating a potentially dangerous salient. Hazen's brigade was en route to rejoin the division. Thomas wanted all of these nine brigades back in line along LaFayette Road.

At Poe Field, Reynolds' division—with just Ed King's brigade under his command—sketched a line along the west edge of the field and into the woods to the south. Negley (Stanley and Sirwell) held a similar line on Reynolds' right, but was unaware of Reynolds' presence and did not connect with any Federals to the south. Brannan's three brigades (Van Derveer, Connell, and Croxton) formed at the Dyer House, while Van Cleve was working to reorganize the two brigades of his division (Beatty and Dick) still under his immediate command.

Loosely grouped west of Viniard Field and generally along the LaFayette Road, eight more Union brigades formed a third discrete segment of the Federal line. All of them were under the ad-hoc command of Tom Crittenden, commander of the XXI Corps. This mass included: Thomas Wood's two brigades (Buell and Harker, recalled after their foray up the LaFayette Road); two of Phil Sheridan's brigades (Bradley and Laiboldt); Van Cleve's last brigade, under Barnes; Wilder's utility brigade; and behind them all, Jefferson C. Davis' two mauled brigades under Carlin and Heg. Alexander

McCook's XX Corps troops were parceled out to other sectors and he had no designated command. Lytle's brigade (Sheridan's division) and John Beatty's brigade (Negley's division) were still detached to the south.

The Confederates were similarly disorganized. West of the creek on the Confederate left, William Preston's Division (Gracie, Kelly, and Trigg) of Simon Buckner Corps was in position near the Thedford house. Thomas Hindman's Division of Leonidas Polk's Corps was massed a few hundred yards behind Preston. Hindman crossed the creek late, without enough daylight left to engage. The Confederate center was a jumble of troops. John Hood's Corps and A. P. Stewart's Division were intermingled in the woods on a north-south line facing the LaFayette Road from near Viniard Field stretching as far north as the Brotherton Road. Brock Field represented a kind of no-man's land.

On the northern end of the field (the Rebel right flank), Cleburne's brigades (Deshler, Polk, and Wood) remained in place after routing Johnson's Federals from around Winfrey Field. Cheatham's brigades (Jackson, Vaughan, Maney, Wright, and Strahl) filed in behind Cleburne, while Walker's Reserve Corps (Liddell's Division and the brigades of Wilson and Ector—Gist's brigade had yet to reach the field) massed behind Cheatham south of the Youngblood farm. Forrest's cavalry pulled flank duty, mostly north of the Reed's Bridge Road. Maj. Gen. John C. Breckinridge's Division, part of D. H. Hill's Corps, was marching to join Cleburne. Lt. Gen. James Longstreet and two more of his brigades under Kershaw and Humphreys were also en route from Ringgold.

Although each side had fought the other to a bloody draw on September 19, Bragg held one significant advantage over Rosecrans: fresh troops. Divisions under Hindman, Preston, Breckinridge, and Kershaw (eleven brigades) had yet to see significant action. Cleburne's three brigades had escaped serious injury during their only fighting of the day. Finally, the arrival of James Longstreet on the field provided the Confederates with one of the South's best tactical commanders, and Bragg intended to fully utilize his talents.

Conversely, Rosecrans had only Negley's division and Gordon Granger's three brigades that could be counted as fresh, although a handful of brigades in divisions that had seen combat on the 19th were in reasonably good shape.

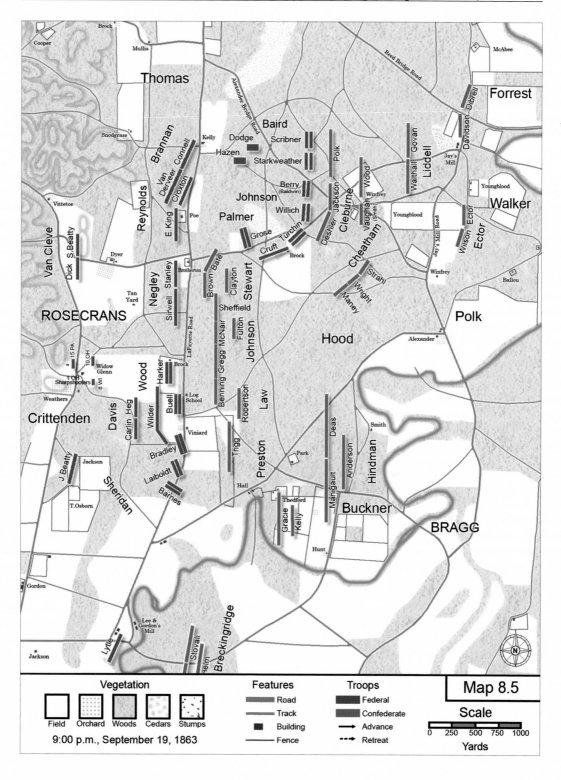

Vegetation

Field Orchard Woods Cedars Stumps

9:00 p.m., September 19, 1863

Features
Road
Track
Building
Fence

Troops
Federal
Confederate
Advance
Retreat

Map 8.5

Scale

0   250   500   750   1000

Yards

Map Set 9: Confederates Dither; Rosecrans Rearranges his Lines

(Night and Early Morning, September 20)

9.1: Confederate Command Crisis (Night, September 19-20)

An enduring image of Chickamauga is the confusion that gripped the Rebels during the night of September 19-20. All of the frustrations, rivalries, personal dislikes, and general bad luck that were the hallmarks of the ill-used and frequently unlucky Army of Tennessee coalesced in one night of command dysfunction.

Bragg was nothing if not persistent. His failed attack plan for the 19th was the fourth or fifth offensive to have miscarried since the Federals crossed the Tennessee River at the end of August. As early as September 4, Bragg had been seeking a way to strike a blow against the Army of the Cumberland. Some of his efforts never went beyond the discussion stage, some went awry because of recalcitrant subordinates, and others were derailed by an uncooperative enemy. Bragg conceived yet another offensive operation for the 20th. On the 19th, Bragg expected to fall on the Union left flank and attack south. On the 20th, Bragg wanted Lt. Gen. Leonidas Polk's Right Wing to attack frontally, overwhelm Thomas' XIV Corps, turn south, and flank the rest of the Union army with Lt. Gen. James Longstreet and the Left Wing helping to complete the victory.[1]

In order to simplify his overburdened command structure and make the best use of Longstreet, Bragg reorganized his five infantry corps into two large command wings. Had the battle followed the course Bragg intended (as outlined on the September 18), Longstreet's men would have been on the army's right (northern end), and Polk's on the left (southern end). However, with the Federals sidling north the Rebels followed suit, reversing those roles. Ideally, Bragg did not want to place the burden of opening the attack on Polk's shoulders yet again, but any other alternative would require the shifting of too many troops to be practical.

Bragg's most consequential mistake that night was not holding a conference with all of his key subordinates at one time, as Rosecrans did in the Widow Glenn cabin. Instead, Bragg met with generals individually and relied on his new wing commanders to relay his orders clearly. Longstreet proved equal to the task; Polk did not.

Once the fighting on the 19th concluded, Bragg and Polk met at army headquarters. Bragg wanted Polk to renew the attack at dawn, and to lead it with Maj. Gen. D. H. Hill's fresh troops. Polk returned to his headquarters, riding past Longstreet, who was just then making his way to see Bragg.[2] For some reason Polk waited for Hill to report to him. When Hill did not show up, Polk sent written orders detailing Hill's mission for the next morning—and then went to bed.[3] Polk assumed that his orders had been properly delivered., In fact, they never reached Hill.

As the night fighting wound down, Hill worked to get Maj. Gen. Patrick Cleburne's men into position instead of reporting immediately to Bragg. About midnight, Hill set out to find Bragg's camp but lost his way, mistaking Lambert's Ford for Thedford's Ford. After hours of fruitless searching, Hill finally gave up and returned to Cleburne's camp.[4] There, Hill was informed that he was now under Polk's command, and about 3:00 a.m. set out on an equally unsuccessful ride to find Polk's headquarters. Unable to do so, Hill returned to Cleburne's position. Maj. Gen. John Breckinridge spent much of the night at Polk's headquarters, but Polk never mentioned that his division (part of Hill's Corps) was expected to lead the attack at dawn. Why Polk did not discuss such a critical fact with Breckinridge remains a mystery.[5]

After hours of wandering en route from Ringgold, Longstreet found Bragg's headquarters about 11:00 p.m. The army commander outlined Longstreet's new duties and provided a rough sketch of where the units now under his command were positioned. Longstreet rose before dawn and, with his customary energy, set out to find his division commanders to assess their deployments.[6]

In sharp contrast to Longstreet's efforts, Polk remained in his camp until after dawn, by which time he realized the attack his "wing" was supposed to launch was not taking place. Only then did Polk discover that his note to Hill had not been delivered. This series of unfortunate events was compounded when Bragg dispatched Maj. Pollack Lee to find out why the attack was not underway. Lee returned to report (falsely) that he found Polk a mile from the front, lounging on a porch while reading a newspaper.

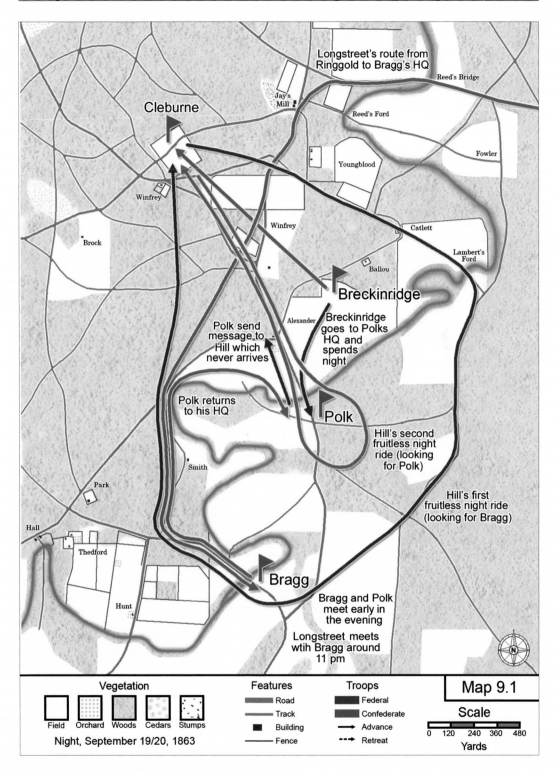

Cleburne

Longstreet's route from Ringgold to Bragg's HQ

Reed's Bridge

Jay's Mill

Reed's Ford

Fowler

Youngblood

Winfrey

Winfrey

Catlett

Lambert's Ford

Brock

Ballou

Breckinridge

Alexander

Breckinridge goes to Polks HQ and spends night

Polk send message to Hill which never arrives

Polk returns to his HQ

Polk

Hill's second fruitless night ride (looking for Polk)

Smith

Park

Hill's first fruitless night ride (looking for Bragg)

Hall

Thedford

Bragg

Hunt

Bragg and Polk meet early in the evening

Longstreet meets wtih Bragg around 11 pm

Vegetation

Field Orchard Woods Cedars Stumps

Night, September 19/20, 1863

Features

Road
Track
Building
Fence

Troops

Federal
Confederate
Advance
Retreat

Map 9.1

Scale

0   120   240   360   480

Yards

9.2: Overall Situation (6:30 a.m.)

Most of the Federal army was in motion during the night of September 19-20, 1863. The divisions under Brig. Gens. Richard W. Johnson and Absalom Baird were the first to fall back, stumbling through the dark in the wake of the messy fight with Cleburne to take up the position Maj. Gen. George Thomas had identified the previous afternoon. Forming on Thomas' chosen ridge, Baird served as the northern anchor, his left resting along the Alexander's Bridge Road. Thomas wanted Baird to stretch all the way to the Reed's Bridge Road, but Baird didn't have the manpower to do so. When informed of that fact, the XIV Corps commander had John King's battered Regulars refuse their line to face northeast.[7] Each brigade in Baird's line formed in a double line of regiments. What was left of his artillery, already battered from yesterday's action, was placed in reserve.

As Johnson came up, Col. Joseph B. Dodge's brigade was detached and placed on King's left, with Dodge's left near the LaFayette Road.[8] Col. Philemon Baldwin's brigade, now under Col. William Berry, deployed on Baird's right. Brig. Gen. August Willich's men formed in reserve.[9] Maj. Gen. John Palmer's men came next, filing in on Berry's right. As Palmer deployed, Maj. Gen. Joseph Reynolds rearranged his own divisional lines to conform to the new position: Turchin advanced to continue the line on the ridge alongside Palmer, while Edward King's men were left about fifty yards to the rear. Several hundred yards south of Turchin, the ridge was in Rebel hands.[10]

About 6:00 a.m. on September 20, Rosecrans left the Widow Glenn cabin to ride the length of his line. When he reached Thomas, Rosecrans agreed with his corps commander that the left flank was a potential problem, and sent orders to both Maj. Gens. James S. Negley and Alexander McCook that Negley's division should come north to lengthen Thomas' left as soon as possible.[11] Negley's division was in line where it came to rest last evening, fronting Brotherton Field, and would have to be replaced before moving north. Rosecrans also made a number of smaller adjustments during his ride along the line that morning. Brig. Gen. Jefferson

C. Davis' division was too far west and had to be brought forward, Palmer's line was shortened (probably by moving Col. William Grose into reserve) and Brig. Gen. John Brannan's brigades were moved forward into line on Reynolds' right at Poe Field.[12] In the reorganization of responsibility that occurred during Rosecrans' command conference several hours earlier, McCook had charge of the army's right, which effectively meant Negley's line, while Maj. Gen. Thomas Crittenden's XXI Corps would be held in reserve.

Despite Bragg's plans, few Confederate troops were stirring early. D. H. Hill moved Breckinridge's Division, which had reached the field well after dark and camped a mile and a half north of Alexander's Bridge, forward into line on Cleburne's right about 5:30 a.m.[13] Still unaware that he was expected to kick off Bragg's main effort, Hill ordered his men to draw rations and prepare breakfast.[14]

If the Rebel troops were largely inactive, most of their commanders were not. In the interest of speed, Polk decided to bypass the stationary Hill and dispatch the attack order directly to Cleburne and Breckinridge.[15] Polk then rode to join Cheatham's line behind Cleburne's position, where he waited for the sounds of battle to reach him. The aide bearing the orders to Cleburne and Breckinridge, Capt. Frank Wheless, found Hill and both division commanders near Winfrey Field. A surprised Hill demanded to see the orders but Wheless refused, handing them instead to Cleburne and Breckinridge, who promptly showed them to Hill.[16] With his men already in the process of preparing breakfast, Hill decided the attack would have to wait.

On the other end of the field, Longstreet remained unaware of the foul-ups plaguing Polk's command. He was, however, keenly aware that time was passing quickly and that the dawn attack ordered by Bragg had not yet begun. Longstreet remained ready to commit his troops when the battle opened, which could begin at any time. Up well before dawn, he made a circuit of his new command, ascertaining its position and readiness. Maj. Gen. John B. Hood, who had already found the relentless pessimism within the Army of Tennessee wearying, took heart from his commander's appearance. Longstreet, recalled Hood, "was the first general I had met since my arrival who talked of victory."[17]

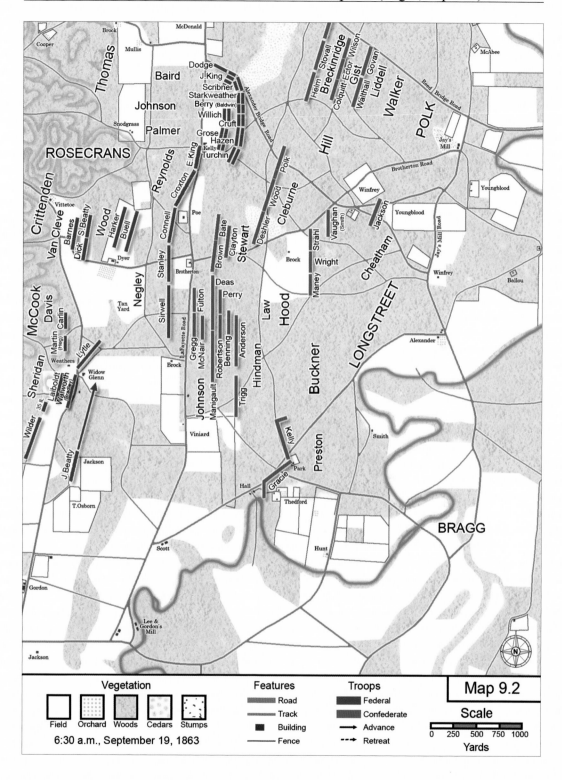

Vegetation

Field Orchard Woods Cedars Stumps

6:30 a.m., September 19, 1863

Features
Road
Track
Building
Fence

Troops
Federal
Confederate
Advance
Retreat

Map 9.2

Scale

0   250   500   750   1000
Yards

9.3: Overall Situation
(8:00 a.m. September 20)

By 8:00 a.m., with his left still unprotected, an increasingly anxious George Thomas sent Capt. J. P. Willard to order Negley to move "without delay" toward the McDonald house.[18] Willard's urgency, coupled with a similar message from McCook just a few minutes later, convinced Negley that he had to leave immediately, even though no other Federals were present to take his place in line. Guided by Willard, John Beatty's brigade led Negley's division. Cols. William Sirwell and Timothy Stanley of the same division started to pull their brigades back from Brotherton field to follow. Beatty was just leaving when Negley commented to an aide that he was "anxious to keep [his] division together" in the forthcoming fight.[19]

Rosecrans returned from his early morning scout to ask where Negley was going, and if he had been relieved. When he learned that no replacements were present, Rosecrans spoke "a little sharply" to Negley about the importance of waiting for relief, and ordered Stanley and Sirwell to shift their brigades back into line.[20] Beatty, however, could continue marching. Rosecrans galloped off to find McCook.

Thus far McCook had done very little. Despite Rosecrans' early morning adjustments, the divisions under Davis and Phil Sheridan were still essentially in their overnight positions. Neither command had received instructions to replace Negley. However, Rosecrans noticed that Brig. Gen. Thomas J. Wood's division was nearby; Crittenden had ordered Wood up to a reserve position near the Dyer House about this time.

Facing Negley in the woods east of the LaFayette Road, Longstreet completed his informal survey of his new command. Like Rosecrans, he too was unsatisfied with the disposition of his men. The divisions of Maj. Gen. Thomas Hindman and Brig. Gens. Bushrod Johnson and Evander Law were intermingled, having simply fallen back haphazardly across the road after the previous day's fighting. (In Hindman's case, he and his men arrived too late for any combat on Saturday.)

James Longstreet has a modern reputation as a defensive-minded general, one who understood the strength of the defense and preferred to receive attacks rather than deliver them. He also had substantial experience delivering large-scale assaults. He prepared his attacks methodically and carefully, and had achieved success on the offensive, most notably with the mammoth assault at Second Manassas in Virginia.

Longstreet wanted his best troops—Hood's former division, now led by Law since Hood was at the helm of the First Corps—to lead the attack, but there was no time for a redeployment because Polk's assault was expected at any moment. Longstreet ordered Maj. Gen. A. P. Stewart to shift his division north several hundred yards to open a gap for Law's brigades to advance westward. Stewart's move would also put his men into closer contact with Pat Cleburne's left flank, increasing the odds of a better coordination on the timing of the attack.[21] While this sounded good in theory, things didn't go as Longstreet planned. When Stewart started to move, Bushrod Johnson noticed the shift and followed suit, sliding his brigades northward into the place Longstreet desired for Law. At the same time, instead of connecting with Cleburne, Stewart's command moved in front of the Irishman's line, masking it for several hundred yards. Because there was no time to move Johnson back to the south, Law's division formed behind Johnson's division.

Each of Longstreet's divisions deployed in two heavy lines. To lend even more weight to the column, Longstreet intended for Brig. Gen. Joseph Kershaw's brigade of South Carolinians and Brig. Gen. Ben Humphreys' Mississippi brigade, both part of Maj. Gen. Lafayette McLaws' Division, to form a fifth line when they arrived. Because McLaws had not yet reached the field, Kershaw assumed command of both brigades. Hood was given overall direction of the assault column.[22]

Despite the confusion that had ensued, Longstreet had reason to be satisfied. By 1863, he had ample experience leading large formations in combat. The final in-depth deployment "Old Pete" adopted at Chickamauga, concludes a recent biographer, "exemplified the evolution of his tactical views during the war."[23] As Longstreet later informed a reporter, "The number of men and the peculiar formation of the force that I sent against the Federal line in this battle could have and would have carried any position except a strongly fortified one."[24]

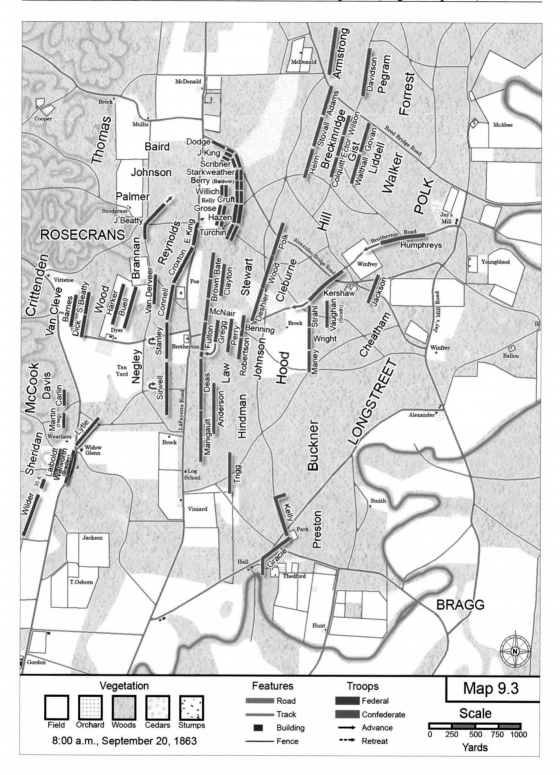

Map 9.3

Scale

Vegetation
Field   Orchard   Woods   Cedars   Stumps

8:00 a.m., September 20, 1863

Features
Road
Track
Building
Fence

Troops
Federal
Confederate
Advance
Retreat

0   250   500   750   1000
Yards

9.4: Overall Situation
(9:00 a.m., September 20)

When 9:00 a.m. arrived without a Rebel attack, many Federals concluded that battle was unlikely that warm Sunday. The senior Union commanders brooked no such illusions, however, and by mid-morning their lines were astir with activity.

Thomas remained concerned about his exposed left flank. When Beatty's brigade arrived, the XIV Corps commander ordered him to move quickly to that flank. Beatty found "a good position" astride the LaFayette Road facing north, prolonging Dodge's line.[25] Whatever the merits of his deployment, however, they failed to meet Thomas' requirement to extend the front as far as the Reed's Bridge Road. More troops would have to be found.

The rest of Negley's men would have been hard on Beatty's heels, solving Thomas' problem, had they not been turned back by Rosecrans. Now, an hour later, the problem of replacing Negley still plagued the Union army commander. After dressing down Negley for moving too quickly, Rosecrans hunted up McCook's headquarters and took the XX Corps commander to task for not moving quickly enough.[26] When he noted Wood's division conveniently at hand, Rosecrans seized on Wood as the solution and dispatched a courier to Crittenden directing Wood into line.[27] A short while later Rosecrans sent Lt. William Moody of Negley's staff to reiterate the order to Crittenden.[28]

Next, Rosecrans—who by now was quite agitated—rode back to Negley. Perhaps he was expecting things to happen more quickly than was reasonable. Finding Negley still in position, and with Wood's men just coming up, Rosecrans rode to meet with the latter division leader. Exactly what happened next has become the subject of much argument and recrimination. Not surprisingly, accounts of what transpired differ. According to Rosecrans partisans, the army leader rebuked Wood for being too slow. According to Wood, the exchange was cordial.[29] In any case, Wood's arrival allowed the rest of Negley's division to at last move out and head north to reinforce Thomas.

Two more Federal divisions were in motion, or soon would be. McCook had finally ordered Davis' two brigades forward (east) to extend Negley's (now Wood's) right flank into the woods south of Brotherton Field.[30] The other was Crittenden's last division under Brig. Gen. Horatio Van Cleve, who was instructed to move his three brigades forward onto the same ground previously occupied by Wood, thus replenishing the army's reserve.[31] In all, roughly one-third of the Union army was in motion between 8:00 a.m. and 9:00 a.m. on September 20.

While the Federals were moving, turmoil was still roiling within the Confederate command structure. Prompted by Capt. Wheless' return, sometime before 8:00 a.m. Leonidas Polk rode to find Hill, who offered up a litany of problems explaining why he could not yet mount an attack. Instead of insisting, Polk "reluctantly acquiesced in a delay of indeterminate length," noted a modern student of the battle.[32]

Shortly after Polk left Hill, Bragg found Polk, having just met with Capt. Wheless at Polk's headquarters. That meeting could not have been satisfying for either general. Nor was the next meeting, when Bragg rode to meet Hill. Each subordinate officer provided Bragg with the same list of excuses for non-performance. To Hill, Bragg complained that he "found Polk . . . sitting down reading a newspaper . . . when he ought to have been fighting"—a variation of Maj. Lee's falsehood.[33] No one, it seemed, was willing or able to follow Bragg's battle orders. It was now 9:00 a.m. and no combat was forthcoming.

While the dysfunctional trio of Bragg, Polk, and Hill argued, Longstreet worked on the final details of his attack plan for the Confederate left (southern) flank. The brigades under Joe Kershaw and Ben Humphreys were just filing into their places. Longstreet intended to support Hood's column with a division on each flank: Stewart on the right (north) and Hindman on the left (south). Simon Buckner's Corps had fought divided all day on the 19th, and the 20th would be no different. There was no time to "to draw Buckner's divisions into reciprocal relations." Brig. Gen. William Preston's Division would once again remain in reserve on the 20th.[34]

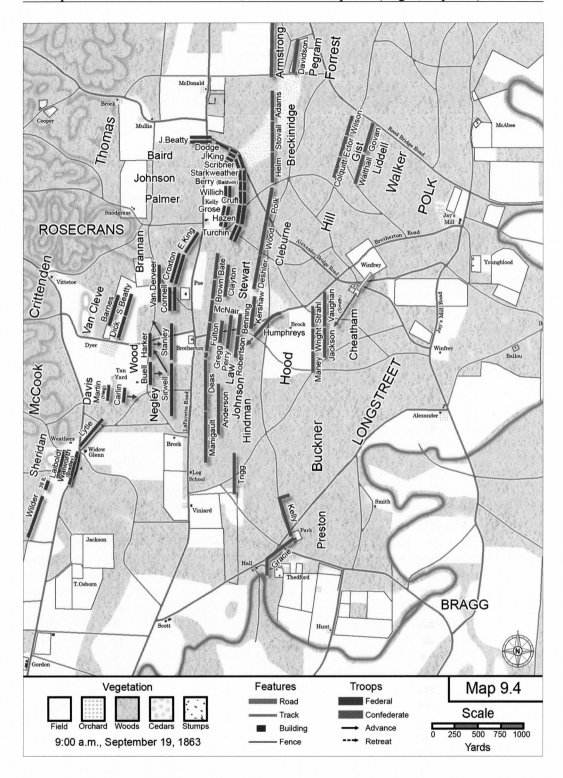

Map 9.4

Vegetation

Field Orchard Woods Cedars Stumps

9:00 a.m., September 19, 1863

Features

Road
Track
Building
Fence

Troops

Federal
Confederate
Advance
Retreat

Scale

0   250   500   750   1000

Yards

9.5: Overall Situation
(9:30 a.m., September 20)

Not all of the frustration bubbling to the surface was found inside the Rebel ranks. John Beatty, a brigade commander under James Negley, was also having a difficult morning. An Ohio banker who had taken well to soldiering, Beatty had enlisted in the 3rd Ohio and led brigades at Perryville and Stone's River. He was a competent and effective brigadier, respected by his men and his superiors. And now, one of the latter, George Thomas, was about to ask the impossible of him.

Shortly after settling into his favored position astride the LaFayette Road, staff officer Capt. W. B. Gaw arrived. Beatty, it turned out, was in the wrong place. Thomas wanted him to stretch his brigade north all the way up to the McDonald house and face west instead of north. That distance, protested Beatty, required a divisional frontage, and his lone brigade could not begin to adequately span it. No matter, insisted Gaw, the order was "imperative."[35] With no other choice, Beatty dutifully advanced. He spread his men across a wide expanse, deploying the 42nd and 88th Indiana regiments near the McDonald House, while the 104th Illinois and 15th Kentucky regiments attempted to extend the line as far as the Alexander's Bridge Road. Beatty was right: his front was more gap than line. However, he reasoned, the rest of the division would be up soon.

Negley was indeed en route. Stanley's brigade led the way, followed at a considerable distance by Sirwell's, which had more trouble disengaging from Longstreet's increasingly active skirmishers.[36] This delay further fragmented Negley's division, slowing the reinforcements Beatty was expecting.

Back in Brotherton Field, Wood assumed Negley's former line, including the rude breastworks scraped together overnight and during the morning. Wood discovered that his two brigades could not entirely fill the frontage Negley's line had occupied. Combined, Stanley and Sirwell deployed 2,747 men in seven regiments, all in a single line. At 2,679 bayonets Wood's brigades—Cols. Charles Harker and George Buell—numbered almost the same, but were instead formed in a double line of regiments.[37] To flesh out his line and connect with Brannan's division on his left, Wood requested the loan of a brigade from Van Cleve, and Col. Sidney Barnes' four regiments advanced to fill the gap.[38]

The rest of Van Cleve's command was, for the moment, without a mission. Rosecrans directed the division to a spot behind Brotherton Field with the vague instruction "to move forward and engage the enemy wherever I [Van Cleve] should find an open space in our front lines."[39]

By now, of course, there was no open space, which forced Van Cleve to cast his eyes about for a place to make himself useful. To his wife he explained that his men were "ordered to march to various points . . . [until] . . . finally placed in rear of some troops and ordered to lie down."[40] Essentially without a command, Crittenden took up whatever role he could. Mindful that many Union guns had been lost while fighting in the timber the previous day, the Federals were more cautious in how they fought their artillery. When Wood reported that "it was useless to bring artillery into the woods," Crittenden directed Maj. John Mendenhall to establish a line of guns well behind the front on an open ridge.[41]

In his unceasing quest to find more troops to strengthen his left and protect the Reed's Bridge Road, Thomas also called upon Brannan's division to support Baird. Thomas was apparently still under the impression that Brannan was in reserve and not in line—despite the fact that the latter's brigades had moved forward at or slightly before dawn.

On the Confederate side of the line, the troops were still marking time while their commanders sorted things out. While they waited, the ominous sounds of ringing axes echoed through the trees: enterprising Federals were constructing breastworks along much of their line.[42] These breastworks were not elaborate, or even ordered by senior Federal leaders. Instead, infantry began piling logs, rocks, and fence posts, having sensibly concluded on their own that even a little protection was better than none. The infantry lacked tools, but managed to borrow axes from the artillery, where such items were standard issue. Accounts differ about where this initiative started, but by mid-morning Thomas' entire line around Kelly Field was the stronger for it, and the price Bragg's Army of Tennessee would pay for the delay would be a dear one.

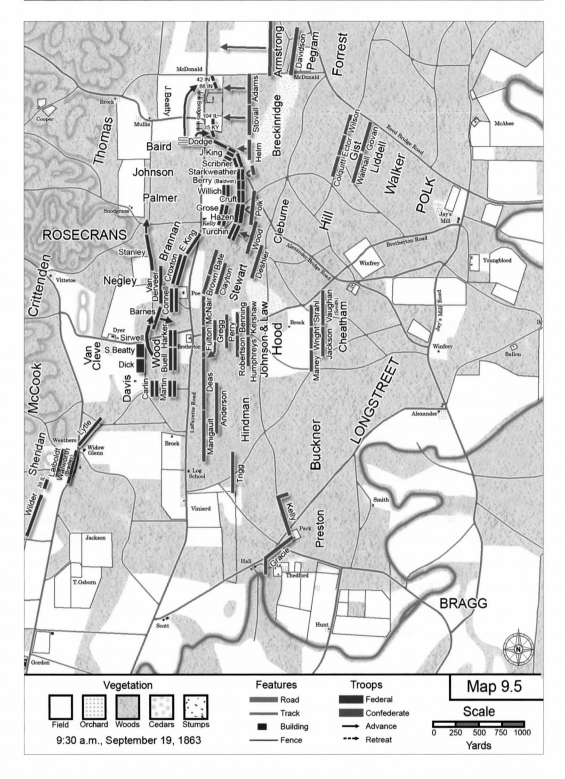

Map 9.5

Scale

9:30 a.m., September 19, 1863

Vegetation: Field, Orchard, Woods, Cedars, Stumps

Features: Road, Track, Building, Fence

Troops: Federal, Confederate, Advance, Retreat

0   250   500   750   1000
Yards

Map Set 10: Turning Thomas' Flank and the Battle for Kelly Field

(Late Morning, September 20)

10.1: Beatty Overwhelmed (9:45 a.m.)

When Brig. Gen. John Beatty redeployed his brigade to cover the Reed's Bridge Road, he knew he had too few men to mount a successful defense. Believing the remaining two brigades in the division would arrive momentarily, Beatty chose deception: he doubled his skirmish line, sending two companies from each regiment forward instead of just one. It was an effort to appear stronger than he actually was, and it was an effort that did not fool anyone.[1]

As their men were finishing hurried breakfasts and filing into attack positions, Maj. Gens. D. H. Hill and John C. Breckinridge, together with Brig. Gen. Nathan B. Forrest, reconnoitered enemy lines. What they saw delighted them. According to Hill, the Federal "flank was covered for a great distance [only] by infantry skirmishers."[2] Despite the morning delay, the first part of Gen. Braxton Bragg's plan—to gain the enemy flank before turning to attack south—looked to still be attainable.

At 9:45 a.m., Breckinridge's three-brigade division stepped off in one long line abreast with Brig. Gen. Benjamin H. Helm on the left, Brig. Gen. Marcellus A. Stovall in the center, and Brig. Gen. Daniel W. Adams on the right. The *en echelon* advance began with Adams' men. As each regiment stepped off, the next on its left followed suit until all three brigades were moving. Brig. Gen. Frank Armstrong's cavalry advanced to the north, protecting Breckinridge's right flank. On Breckinridge's left, Maj. Gen. Patrick Cleburne's division also moved forward when the wave of motion reached the right side of his line. Beatty's overmatched Federals were doomed.

Daniel Adams struck the left side of Beatty's front with devastating results. Within a handful of minutes the withering fire from his Louisianans and Alabamians collapsed the 42nd Indiana. Hoosier Francis Carlisle recalled that the entire Yankee skirmish line was captured almost immediately.[3] The 88th Indiana crumpled just as quickly. The routed survivors of both regiments fled westward as fast as they could across the McDonald farm.

This rout exposed the three guns of Capt. Lyman Bridges' Illinois battery (which had advanced to support the Hoosiers) and the 104th Illinois 200 yards to the south. To the 104th's Col. Douglas Hapeman, it seemed as though Stovall's infantry struck his front and both flanks simultaneously. Knowing he could not hold his position, Hapeman ordered his men to fire one volley and fall back.[4] Bridges' half-battery fared only slightly better, falling back to unlimber near the rest of the unit on Beatty's original line. Almost immediately, however, they were attacked again.

The assailants that struck the right side of Beatty's embattled brigade were from one of the more storied brigades in the Confederate army— Helm's so-called "Orphan Brigade" made up of four regiments of Kentuckians and one of Alabamians. Helm's five regiments had a tougher fight on their hands than the other men in the division. The left side of his line faced the long slow angle where Brig. Gen. Absalom Baird's breastworks curved to face northeast along the Alexander's Bridge Road. The other (right) side faced no opposition for several hundred yards. As Helm advanced, roughly half of his men (the 2nd and 9th Kentucky and part of the 41st Alabama) turned to face this wide smooth part of the enemy line. The other half of his brigade—the 4th and 6th Kentucky, along with several companies of the 41st Alabama—continued westward, slamming into the Union 15th Kentucky. Kentuckian Fred Joyce of the 4th regiment remembered that he and his Southern comrades were moving so impetuously through the timber that the Yankee Kentuckians of the 15th regiment (holding Beatty's right flank) were "almost literally run over."[5] The 15th fell back to Bridges' guns and tried to rally there, along with the 104th Illinois. The men stood briefly before both units fell back another 300 yards into the woods.[6]

The triumphant Orphans rushed the guns from the east while Bridges' attention was still fixed on Stovall's and Adams' Rebels to the north. Beatty ordered Bridges and his gunners to leave, but it was too late to save the guns of the right-hand section, which were abandoned on the field.[7] Helm did not witness this success. The brigadier was fighting with the left half of his brigade, trying to rally it after being repulsed by Baird's Federals.

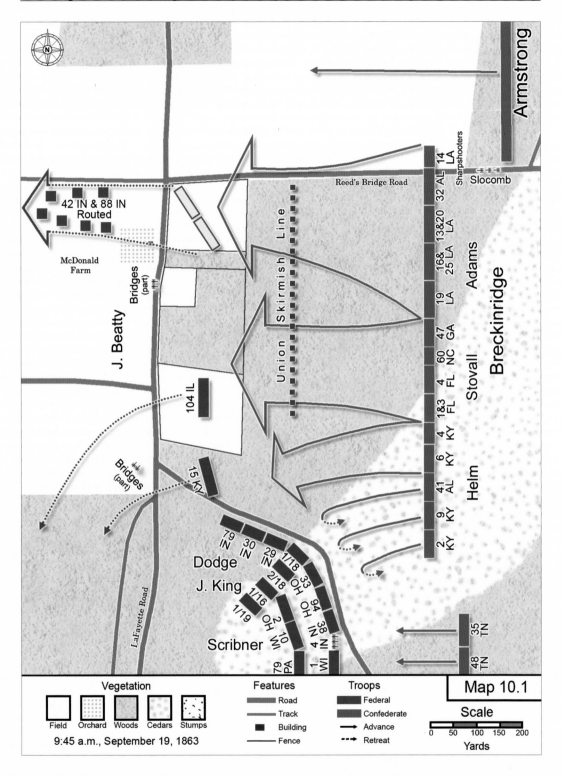

Armstrong

14 LA Sharpshooters

Slocomb

Reed's Bridge Road

32 AL

13&20 LA

16& 25 LA

Adams

19 LA

Breckinridge

47 GA

Stovall

60 NC

4 FL

1&3 FL

4 KY

6 KY

Helm

41 AL

9 KY

2 KY

42 IN & 88 IN
Routed

McDonald
Farm

J. Beatty

Union   Skirmish   Line

Bridges
(part)

104 IL

Bridges
(part)

15 KY

79 IN   30 IN   29 IN

Dodge

1/18 OH

33 OH

J. King

2/18 OH

94 OH

1/16 OH

38 IN

1/19 OH

2 10 WI

4 NI

Scribner

1 WI

79 PA

35 TN

48 TN

LaFayette Road

Vegetation

Field   Orchard   Woods   Cedars   Stumps

9:45 a.m., September 19, 1863

Features

Road
Track
Building
Fence

Troops

Federal
Confederate
Advance
Retreat

Map 10.1

Scale

0   50   100   150   200
Yards

10.2: Breckinridge Turns South and the Federals React (10:15 a.m.)

Ben Helm's difficulties notwithstanding, Breckinridge's initial attack shattered the Union left flank. His men were now poised to strike south in accordance with Bragg's general plan of attack for September 20. The former vice president-turned-battlefield-general struggled to reorient his long line and continue the attack. Leaving Maj. John E. Austin's 14th Louisiana Battalion of Sharpshooters to screen his right flank, Breckinridge posted Capt. C. H. Slocomb's Louisiana artillery near the intersection of the LaFayette and Savannah Church roads, assigned the 32nd Alabama to support the guns, and ordered the rest of Adams' Brigade to reform west of the LaFayette Road.

Adams had no pre-war military experience, but had gained plenty since, all the hard way. At Shiloh, a shot in the left side of his head cost him his left eye. At Murfreesboro, he was struck in the arm by a shell fragment while leading an attack against the Round Forest that he regarded as foolhardy.

Breckinridge also ordered Stovall's regiments to form on Adams' left, east of the road, intending to send both brigades sweeping south deep into the Union rear.[8] For the moment, Col. Joseph H. Lewis of the 6th Kentucky took charge of the portion of Helm's outfit still celebrating its success against Bridges' guns, but with the brigade split, Breckinridge wisely ordered Lewis to find Helm and reform it.

Unlike Adams and Stovall, Helm's men on the left side of his brigade had stirred up a hornet's nest of immovable opposition. When the advance was enfiladed with a heavy fire delivered by Brig. Gen. John H. King's Regulars, Lt. Col. John E. Wycliffe of the 9th Kentucky told Helm that the Orphans were "going into as hot a place as they had even been in, as the Federals were entrenched on the hill."[9] After an initial repulse, Helm was organizing a second effort when a bullet struck him in the right side of the abdomen and knocked him off his horse. His aides carried him to a hospital site, but the wound proved mortal. Mary Todd Lincoln's half-sister's husband died later that night.[10]

The Federals were busy cobbling together a line to oppose Breckinridge. With only half of his command on hand, Beatty placed the mauled 15th Kentucky and 104th Illinois under the 15th's colonel, Marion C. Taylor, before riding off to find more troops.[11] He found them in the form of Col. Timothy R. Stanley's brigade, which was marching up from the south. Beatty led Stanley's troops into the woods west of the road to strengthen Taylor's tenuous line.

With his side of the army in danger of collapsing, George Thomas set about to rectify the deteriorating situation. Close at hand, lying in reserve behind John Palmer's division, were four regiments of Col. Grose's brigade. Although Palmer's front was already taking some fire from an advancing Rebel brigade under Brig. Gen. Lucius Polk, there seemed to be ample strength in the front line. Thomas ordered Grose to move north across Kelly Field and reinforce Baird's left.[12]

Earlier orders were finally bearing fruit. Thomas' request for John Brannan to bring his division up could not be met in full (Map 9.5), but Brannan and Joseph Reynolds concluded that Col. Ferdinand Van Derveer could be spared.[13] His troops were now hurrying north. Another unlooked-for reinforcement came from Thomas' latest appeal to Rosecrans. The army commander had already decided that Horatio Van Cleve's two uncommitted brigades lying in reserve behind Brannan would also be sent, with Col. George F. Dick's men moving first. Breckinridge was realigning his Confederates to begin his southward assault, but it was clear that plenty of troops were on the move to help Thomas.

Curiously, Negley and his remaining brigade under Sirwell were not among them. Even more than Crittenden, George Thomas was mindful of how vulnerable his artillery was while fighting in the woods. About 10:00 a.m., the tireless Capt. Gaw carried a message to Negley, who was en route to reinforce Beatty's lone brigade holding Thomas' all-important left flank, redirecting the division leader to instead establish an artillery reserve position on a high hill about one mile to the rear.[14] Negley commandeered Van Derveer's artillery battery along the way to his new position, and also ordered Sirwell to join him there. Thomas believed that the artillery could make a better contribution to the fight from this rising ground— and perhaps help protect his left flank to prevent its collapse.

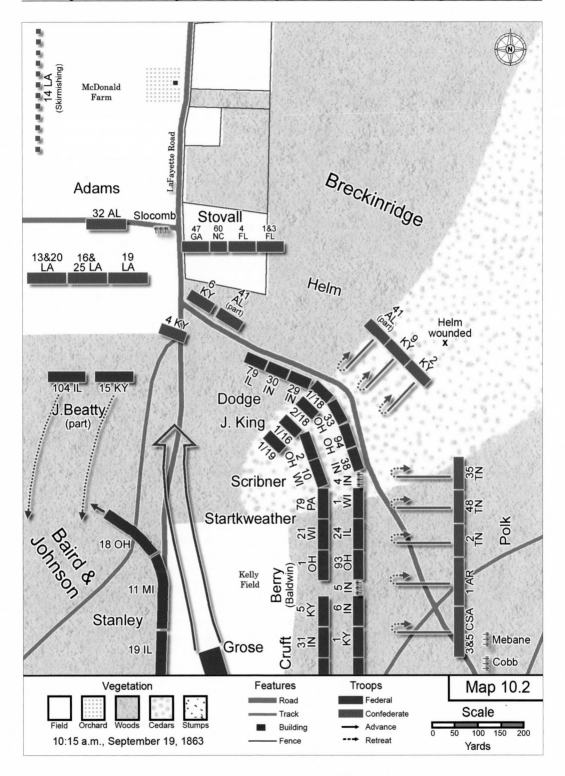

14 LA
(Skirmishing)

McDonald
Farm

LaFayette Road

Adams

32 AL   Slocomb

Stovall

47   60   4   1&3
GA   NC   FL   FL

13&20   16&   19
LA   25 LA   LA

6
KY   41
AL
(part)

Breckinridge

Helm

41
AL
(part)

Helm
wounded
X

KY 6
KY 2

4 KY

104 IL   15 KY

J. Beatty
(part)

79
IL   30
IN   29
IN   1/18
OH   33
OH   94
OH   38
IN

Dodge

J. King

2/18
OH

1/16
OH   2
IN   10
WI   4
IN

1/19
OH

Scribner

79
PA   1
WI

Startkweather

Baird
Johnson

18 OH

21
WI   24
IL

1
OH   93
OH

11 MI

Kelly
Field

Berry
(Baldwin)

5
IN

Stanley

5
KY   6
IN

19 IL   Grose

Cruft   31
IN   1
KY

35
TN

48
TN

2
TN   Polk

1 AR

3&5 CSA

Mebane

Cobb

Vegetation					Features	Troops	Map 10.2

Field   Orchard   Woods   Cedars   Stumps

Features
— Road
— Track
■ Building
— Fence

Troops
■ Federal
■ Confederate
→ Advance
--→ Retreat

10:15 a.m., September 19, 1863

Map 10.2

Scale

0   50   100   150   200
Yards

10.3: Stovall and Adams Smash Grose (10:30 a.m.)

Col. William Grose's four regiments (84th Illinois, 36th Indiana, 6th Ohio, and 24th Ohio—the 23rd Kentucky was left behind with Brig. Gen. William Hazen) double-quicked the length of Kelly Field and into the timber marking its northern limit. A prewar attorney and judge, Grose saw service at Shiloh at the head of the 36th Indiana and as a colonel leading a brigade in the Kentucky campaign and in Vicksburg-related operations in Mississippi. On this day, he knew virtually nothing about either the Union positions or the attacking enemy. All Grose knew was that he was ordered to support Baird's left, wherever that might be.

While his brigade was forming near the LaFayette Road, an officer of the 6th Ohio stole forward to observe Adams and Stovall forming for their own attack not 200 yards distant. Grose was surprised by the news and assumed the man was mistaken: "they *must* be our troops," insisted the colonel, "because there was at least one line ahead of ours."[15]

By now artillery and small arms fire had become general. Friendly fire, falling short, was making Grose's troops increasingly restive, and he shifted his regiments in an effort to avoid it. He was in the process of doing so when the Confederates fell upon him through the trees.

Circumstances had once against unfolded to leave a lone Union infantry brigade to be overwhelmed by superior numbers. Even without the Orphans, Adams and Stovall had a long enough frontage to easily overlap Grose's men, who were not yet completely formed in two lines of two regiments each. The surprise was complete. "Suddenly a gray line burst into view," recalled the Ohioan, "and before we were aware of it, fired into us a terrific volley."[16] The Rebels found the 84th Illinois still forming into line. "The first intimation of their presence was a sharp volley," recorded the 84th's historian, but "a line of battle was however formed under a galling fire."[17] Despite a valiant effort to shoot back, the Federals had little choice but to retire. Grose ordered an immediate retreat, which quickly deteriorated into a rout.

James P. Suiter, also in the 84th Illinois, recorded the collapse. "On they came, and we were compelled to fall back, for we were nearly surrounded," he wrote in his diary. "We became somewhat confused and the regiments were considerably mixed, one with another. But though disorganized," he added with some defiance, "we were not by any means demoralized."[18] Demoralized or not, the brigade all but collapsed. The four regiments—not one of which retained its organization—broke in several directions. Grose would later rally the bulk of the brigade near the southern end of Kelly Field, but by this time most of the 84th Illinois (which fell back more west than south) would end up near Negley's new position on Snodgrass Hill.[19]

The collapse of Grose's brigade on the Union left flank went largely unnoticed by the men in Col. Dodge's brigade just 125 yards to the east. Already mauled by hard fighting and the surprise encounter with Patrick Cleburne's veterans on the evening of the 19th, Dodge's men held a small frontage in the woods between John King's left and Grose's newly forming right—but was not, apparently, in contact with either of them. Like so many others that day, Dodge's command was another detached brigade, and Dodge found himself riding back and forth to Richard Johnson often while Col. Allan Buckner managed the battle line. According to Buckner, the brigade was charged repeatedly, but the rude breastworks constructed during the morning lull rendered their position relatively safe.[20] This appears unlikely, because only Stovall's left flank regiment (1st/3rd Florida) faced Dodge's line directly, and it did not press the issue.[21]

Once again Breckinridge's men seemed on the verge of a significant tactical success. The faulty nature of the deployment used by Gens. Polk and Hill, however, was now becoming apparent. Hill's two divisions (Breckinridge and Cleburne) advanced in a single line with not a man in reserve. Polk failed in his duty as a corps commander to ensure that Walker or Cheatham (or both) advanced with Hill's troops. The upshot was that now, at the moment of potential victory, Breckinridge lacked even a single reserve regiment to commit to the fight. To compound matters, E. John Ellis of the 19th Louisiana (Adams' Brigade) wrote later about an order to halt, which allowed Grose enough breathing space to escape. The order was a grave mistake, thought Ellis, one that "altered the whole face of affairs" and allowed the Yankees time to rally once more.[22]

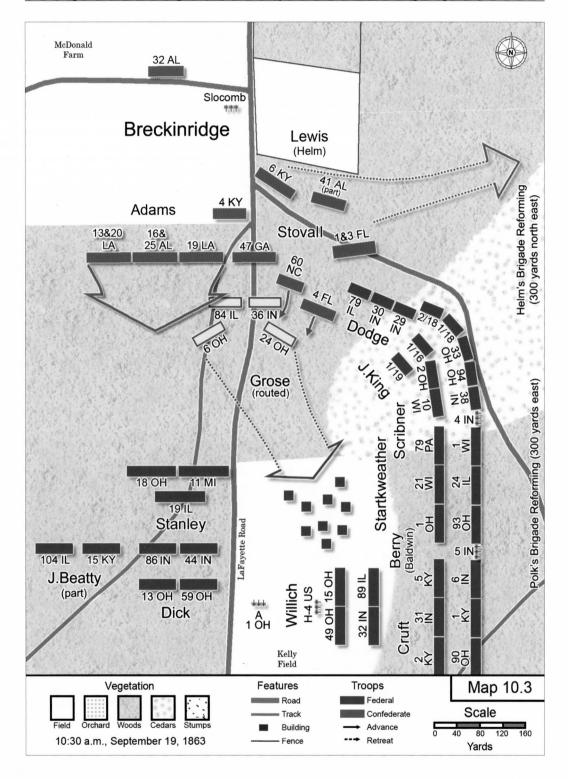

McDonald Farm

32 AL

Slocomb

Breckinridge

Lewis (Helm)

6 KY

41 AL (part)

4 KY

Adams

13&20 LA

16& 25 AL

19 LA

47 GA

Stovall   1&3 FL

60 NC

84 IL   36 IN

4 FL

79 IL   30 IN   29 IN   2/18 1/18

Dodge

6 OH   24 OH

1/16 OH

33 OH

94 IN

38 IN

J.King   1/19

Grose (routed)

Scribner

79 PA

1 WI

10 IN

4 IN

Starkweather

21 WI

24 IL

18 OH   11 MI

19 IL

Stanley

Berry (Baldwin)

1 OH

93 HO

5 IN

104 IL   15 KY

86 IN   44 IN

5 KY

6 IN

J.Beatty (part)

13 OH   59 OH

Dick

Willich

Cruft

31 IN

1 KY

A 1 OH

H-4 US

49 OH 15 OH

32 IN 89 IL

2 KY

90 HO

LaFayette Road

Kelly Field

Helm's Brigade Reforming (300 yards north east)

Polk's Brigade Reforming (300 yards east)

Vegetation

Field   Orchard   Woods   Cedars   Stumps

10:30 a.m., September 19, 1863

Features

Road
Track
Building
Fence

Troops

Federal
Confederate
Advance
Retreat

Map 10.3

Scale

0   40   80   120   160

Yards

10.4: Breckinridge's High Water Mark (11:00 a.m.)

If there was any hesitation by Adams or Stovall, it was of very short duration. Adams' line marched south steadily through the timber west of the road, while Stovall's line (except for the 1st/3rd Florida, stymied by Dodge) followed Grose's routed elements into Kelly Field. The attack threatened Thomas' entire position.

Now it was Adams' turn to be ambushed as his Alabamians and Louisianans worked their way through the woods toward Stanley's recently arrived Yankees. Elements of both Beatty's and Grose's brigades "gave way and came tumbling over us," wrote James Martin of the 11th Michigan, followed by "the Rebels yelling like mad men."[23] Unfazed by this panic, the Wolverines and their comrades in the 18th Ohio on their left rose and delivered a powerful volley with dramatic effect, leaving "the ground . . . covered with their dead and dying."[24]

One of the regiments on the receiving end of this fire was the 13th Louisiana, whose member John McGrath recalled being stunned by the "concentrated fire of the enemy [that] was poured into our ranks. . . . Genl Adams fell wounded from his horse."[25] The bullet that shattered Adams' upper left arm elevated Col. Randall Gibson to the command of the brigade. Breckinridge's advance west of the LaFayette Road was blunted.

Adams' troubles left Marcellus Stovall's men to press forward alone. Stovall, who spent a year at West Point, left because of illness and pursued plantation life in Georgia. He was active in militia affairs, but his Civil War career was undistinguished until Murfreesboro, where his excellent performance won him promotion to brigadier general. By the time his line entered the northern fringes of Kelly Field, it was showing signs of disorder. His regiments—the 4th Florida on the left, 60th North Carolina in the center, and 47th Georgia on the right—advanced into the open area one by one. They found there a swarm of Federals waiting for them. Batteries H and M of 4th U.S. Artillery were already unlimbered mid-field and throwing shells northward. (These guns were the source of the friendly fire that had earlier bedeviled Grose.) To reinforce them, regiments all along Thomas'

support line turned to face the new threat, ringing Stovall's small force with a deadly arc of fire.

August Willich redeployed his battery A, 1st Ohio, alongside the two batteries manned by Regulars and promptly supported it with the 15th Ohio and 89th Illinois regiments, which took up positions "in the brink of time."[26] Others soon joined them. Col. William H. Berry executed a similar maneuver with his reserve line, comprised of his own 5th Kentucky and the 1st Ohio. For a short time Berry found himself directing a fight on two fronts, as his first line was being pressed by some of Cleburne's men even while the 1st and 5th rushed to flank Stovall's stalling attack.[27]

Two of Col. John King's battalions of Regulars also faced about. King's brigade had already had a busy morning, initially advancing to shred Helm's left flank. The 1/15th and 1/19th Battalions were about to do the same to Stovall. The Regulars, however, mistook Grose's collapse as Dodge's, and so assumed their own flank was completely exposed. Here the unusual depth of King's formation came into play: his two rearmost units quickly faced to their left and formed a new line perpendicular to their former position.[28] Both battalions were small, with a combined number of no more than 300 rifles. But they were perfectly situated to rake Stovall's lines.

Likely to the great relief of many Federals that morning, Ferdinand Van Derveer's brigade was marching into the field's southern end. Van Derveer had no orders, and found no single person in charge, but the main problem was obvious: "[Rebels] just then emerging from the woods at a run."[29] Urging his own men to greater speed under long range artillery and small arms fire, Van Derveer led the brigade forward to a slight swale just north of the Union gun line and had them lie down, dropping below Stovall's line of sight.

Col. Lewis, now in charge of the Orphan Brigade after Helm fell mortally wounded, was unaware of the exact position of either Adams or Stovall, and knew next to nothing about whether their attacks were succeeding or on the brink of failure. Clinging to his orders, Lewis rallied the Orphans and led them forward in a third charge, slamming into Baird's front line only to be repulsed in bloody failure. The brigade's final losses would total nearly 500 men, almost all of them felled during this single desperate hour of fighting.

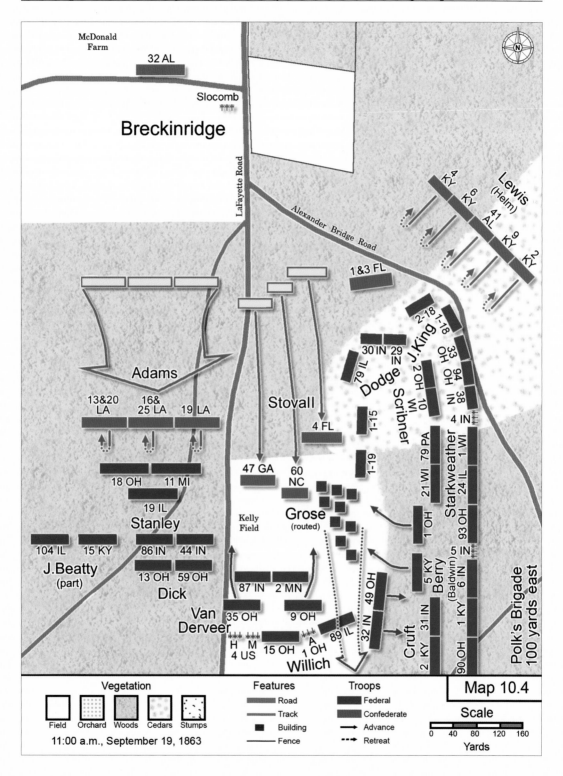

McDonald Farm

32 AL

Slocomb

Breckinridge

LaFayette Road

Alexander Bridge Road

Lewis (Helm)

4 KY
6 KY
41 AL
9 KY
2 KY

1 & 3 FL

2-18
1-18
J. King
30 IN
29 IN
33 OH
94 IN
38 IN
79 IL
Dodge
2 OH
Scribner
10 WI
4 IN

Adams

13 & 20 LA
16 & 25 LA
19 LA

Stovall

4 FL

1-15

1-19

21 WI 79 PA
Starkweather
1 WI
24 IL
93 OH

18 OH   11 MI

47 GA
60 NC

19 IL

Stanley

Kelly Field

Grose
(routed)

1 OH

104 IL   15 KY

86 IN 44 IN

5 KY
Berry
(Baldwin)
5 IN
6 IN

J. Beatty
(part)

13 OH 59 OH

Dick

87 IN   2 MN

49 OH

1 KY

Polk's Brigade
100 yards east

Van Derveer

35 OH   9 OH

32 IN

Cruft

31 IN

2 KY

H   M
4 US
15 OH
A
1 OH
89 IL

90 OH

Willich

Vegetation					Features		Troops		Map 10.4

Vegetation
Field Orchard Woods Cedars Stumps

11:00 a.m., September 19, 1863

Features
—— Road
—— Track
■ Building
—— Fence

Troops
■ Federal
■ Confederate
→ Advance
┅► Retreat

Map 10.4

Scale

0   40   80   120   160
Yards

10.5: Adams and Stovall are Repulsed (11:15 a.m.)

With Daniel Adams down and the Rebels staggered by the ferocity of the Federal fire, Col. Stanley realized it was time to counterattack. Bringing the 19th Illinois up to the front on the right, he ordered his entire line to charge.[30] The Confederates, remembered James Fenton of the 19th, were completely surprised by the swiftness of the attack. The Illini, originally commanded by John Turchin, had been taught French Zouave bayonet drill, and Fenton thought this skill made them the terror of the Rebels.[31] John Beatty, fighting with the remainder of his brigade on Stanley's left, also intended his men to move forward against the enemy. Without notice, Beatty recalled, "[Stanley's] brigade rushed forward with a yell."[32]

Thrust into brigade command by the wounding of Adams, Randall Gibson struggled to control the rebuffed battle line. Pressure seemed greatest from the left, where the 19th Illinois was charging. Gibson ordered the brigade to fall back behind Slocomb's Battery, many hundreds of yards to the north, while he rode to the left flank to rally the line.[33] His efforts were unsuccessful, and within minutes the entire brigade was routed and falling back.

When Stanley's regiments pursued the fleeing Rebels, the wounded Adams fell into Federal hands. A half-dozen or more Union regiments in the vicinity of his fall claimed him as their trophy. The 19th swept past the two abandoned guns of Bridges' battery and reclaimed them. The Illini took special pride in that feat; Bridges' men had originally been designated Company G of the 19th, so the regiment felt a certain kinship with the gunners.[34] Lt. Joseph Chalaron, one of Slocomb's officers, remembered the first evidence of disaster when Adams' men poured north out of the woods, the wounded general's riderless horse leading the way. Within a few minutes the intense fire of Slocomb's guns, supported now by the 32nd Alabama and Maj. Austin's sharpshooters who had rushed over during the crisis, brought the advancing Federals to a halt.[35]

Marcellus Stovall's men suffered a similar fate. Despite the number of Union rifles turned their way as they burst into the clear of Kelly Field, Stovall's regiments pressed gamely on. The Rebels ran forward toward Van Derveer's waiting line, which remained prone in the slight swale ahead of the Union guns. At seventy-five yards, Van Derveer ordered his first line to stand up. "The front line," he reported, " . . . delivered a murderous fire almost in their faces."[36] Hard on their heels, the 9th and 35th Ohio passed through Van Derveer's first line and charged, driving Stovall's impetuous regiments north into the timber and several hundred farther, the fighting intense every step of the way.[37] With Van Derveer's stunning tactical victory, most of the other Federal regiments that had turned west to face the field during the crisis resumed their places in the Federal main line facing east.

Back on the other side of the LaFayette Road, Beatty was trying to reassemble a coherent line from the mass of charging Federals. While Stanley was driving Adams' (now Gibson's) Brigade, Beatty was looking to bring up other troops. His own two regiments, the 15th Kentucky and 104th Illinois, had not joined the charge. During Adams' approach, Col. George Dick's brigade of Van Cleve's division had come up, and Beatty promptly formed it behind Stanley in support. Once the engagement began, however, Beatty discovered that Dick's men had taken off in a panic at the first volley.[38]

Breckinridge was with the mortally wounded Maj. Rice Graves—his artillery commander and close friend—at Slocomb's position when Adam's Louisianans fell back in disorder. Realizing that his attack had failed, Breckinridge issued orders for his men to reform and rode quickly to seek support from Walker's Reserve Corps.[39]

So far, George Thomas had repulsed every Confederate assault, but the penetration of his line by Breckinridge served to confirm his fears about his vulnerable left flank. A jumble of units from various divisions had aided in expelling the enemy, but Thomas was still seeking more troops to reestablish his lines as far north as the Reed's Bridge Road, this time with a more substantial force than John Beatty's lone brigade.

Thomas' constant barrage of requests for troops fixed Rosecrans' attention almost entirely on the army's left flank—with devastating consequences.

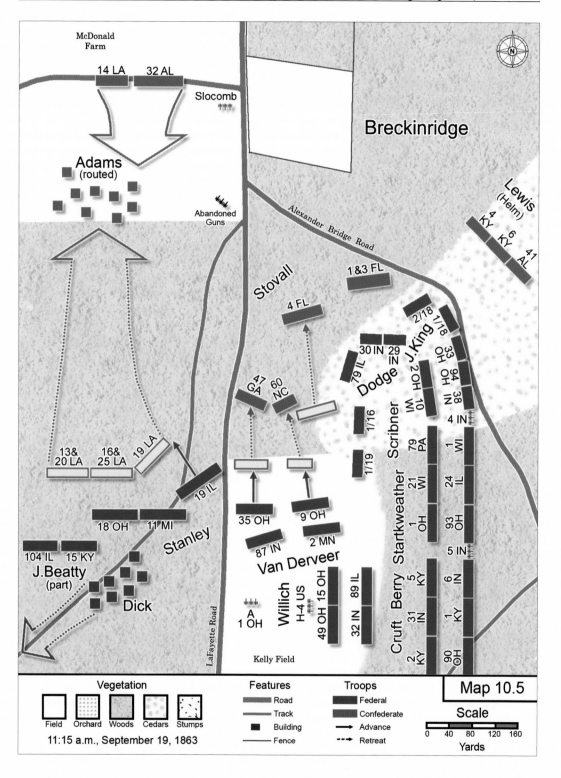

McDonald Farm

14 LA   32 AL

Slocomb

Breckinridge

Adams (routed)

Lewis (Helm)

4 KY   6 KY   41 AL

Abandoned Guns

Alexander Bridge Road

1 & 3 FL

Stovall

4 FL

2/18   1/18

30 IN   29 IN   33 OH   94 OH   38 IN

79 IL   2 OH

J. King

Dodge

10 WI

4 IN

13 & 20 LA   16 & 25 LA   19 LA

47 GA   60 NC

Scribner

1/16

79 PA

1 WI

19 IL

35 OH   9 OH

1/19

21 WI

1 IN

18 OH   11 MI

24 IL

1 OH   93 OH

Stanley

87 IN   2 MN

5 IN

104 IL   15 KY

Van Derveer

J. Beatty (part)

5 KY   6 IN

Dick

A 1 OH

Willich   H-4 US

49 OH   15 OH

32 IN   89 IL

Cruft   Berry   Startkweather

31 IN   1 KY

LaFayette Road

Kelly Field

2 KY   90 OH

Vegetation

Field   Orchard   Woods   Cedars   Stumps

11:15 a.m., September 19, 1863

Features

— Road
— Track
■ Building
— Fence

Troops

■ Federal
■ Confederate
→ Advance
⇢ Retreat

Map 10.5

Scale

0   40   80   120   160

Yards

10.6: Cleburne and Stewart Maneuver (10:15 a.m.)

While Breckinridge was sweeping over John Beatty's Federals near the McDonald House, the other half of D. H. Hill's Corps under Pat Cleburne was attempting to come to grips with the Federals farther south. His three brigades would encounter a much rockier experience.

Brig. Gen. Lucius Polk's Brigade held Cleburne's right, with orders to maintain contact with Benjamin Helm holding Breckinridge's left. Helm's advance signaled the start of Polk's own attack.[40] Brig. Gen. S.A.M. Wood held Cleburne's center, and Brig. Gen. James Deshler's regiments the left. Breckinridge's overall drift, however, was to the north or right, which pulled Lucius Polk in that direction. Wood couldn't keep up with this shift and, to make matters worse, lost contact with Deshler's advancing infantry on his left. Even worse, Deshler's line could not come to grips with the Federals because his front was blocked by A. P. Stewart's men, who had sidled north as earlier described (Map 9.3).[41]

Polk's men struck the Union line first, running up against the works held by Gens. Baird and Johnson. Lycurgus Sallee of the 1st Arkansas remembered the deadly encounter. The ground was open, he wrote, "a smooth ridge with very few trees." The entrenched Federals opened "fire at long range from three lines of log breast works and a battery."[42] Under a heavy fire the brigade shifted right, trying to keep up with Helm, but made no headway westward. Polk's men finally fell back and Sallee took cover behind an oak stump. The enemy, he recalled, "put possibly 50 lbs of lead into my stump in 1½ minutes." Polk's drive had stalled quickly. Cleburne, who was riding behind his right brigade, ordered Polk's regiments stopped about 175 yards from the Federal line. Confident they were under control, the division leader rode south to examine the rest of his division.[43]

Only Wood's right-most regiments, the 15th and combined 32nd/45th Mississippi, managed to keep contact with Polk's rightward drift, and they too was stopped dead in their tracks. The balance of Wood's Brigade halted in a shallow valley several hundred yards from the Yankee line. There, under "an artillery and desultory rifle fire," Wood awaited further instructions.[44] Given Wood's unsatisfactory performance the night before, Cleburne had reason to doubt his ability to lead a combat brigade. As of yet, he had not taken any steps to replace him. When he reached Wood's position, Cleburne "asked Wood why his men were not advancing, and Wood replied that he had lost contact with Polk on the right and that Deshler was blocked by Stewart's men on the left, leaving both of his flanks exposed."[45] It was a reasonable response, but Cleburne informed Wood that he must go forward, if only to help relieve the pressure along Polk's front. Cleburne promised Wood that he would personally make sure that Deshler closed up. Dutifully, Wood resumed his advance, this time drifting south, opening even more distance between himself and Polk.

With Wood moving forward anew, Cleburne rode to find Deshler. The Texans were stalled behind at least two battle lines of Rebels and could not advance to support Wood's left without becoming hopelessly intermingled. They would, however, serve to fill the growing gap in Cleburne's center. Cleburne ordered Deshler to shift his brigade northwest and hopefully come into action between Wood and Polk.[46] Cleburne's advance had been thoroughly disrupted, but he was doing all he could do to salvage his difficult situation.

Matters on A. P. Stewart's front were almost as confused. If Longstreet's shift north (Map 9.3) triggered the initial disruption, Bragg himself now lent a hand in compounding the problem. The army commander was so frustrated at the delay in his planned morning attack that by 10:00 a.m., he abandoned his scripted offensive and ordered Maj. Pollack Lee to ride the length of the battle line and order each division into action as he came to it, regardless of command structure or readiness. Stewart was the first recipient of this new directive.[47] Within minutes after receiving Lee's order, Stewart either met Cleburne or discovered Wood's advance and agreed to go forward alongside the Alabamian. In order to do so, Stewart brought Gen. William Bate's men up into line and directed Gen. John Brown's Brigade to attack across Poe Field when Wood started to move. It was a hasty and haphazard effort, but Stewart had no choice but to obey.

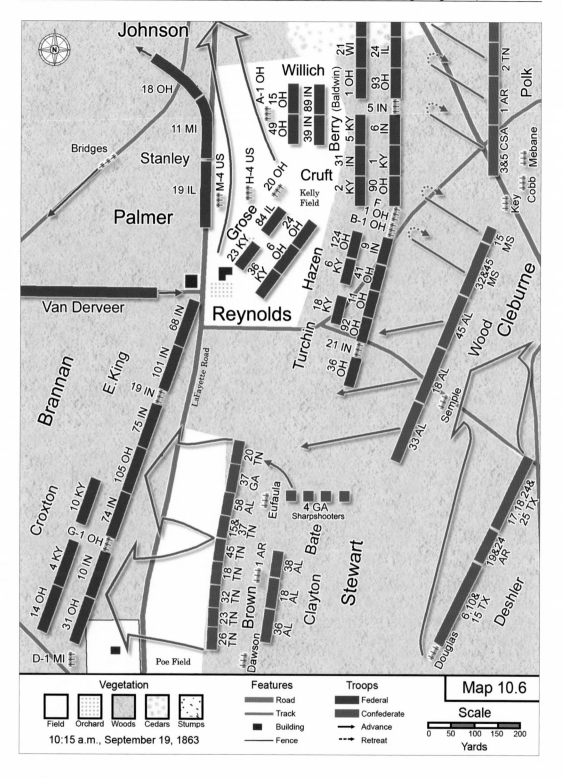

Johnson

18 OH

11 MI

Bridges

Stanley

19 IL

Palmer

Van Derveer

Willich

A-1 OH
49 OH
15 OH
39 IN 89 IN

Berry (Baldwin)

21 WI
24 IL
93 OH
1 OH
5 IN
6 IN
1 KY

Cruft

Kelly Field

31 IN
5 KY
2 KY
90 OH
F 1 OH
B-1 OH

Hazen

6 KY
124 OH
9 IN
41 OH
11 OH
92 OH
21 IN
36 OH

18 KY

Turchin

Reynolds

68 IN

LaFayette Road

101 IN

19 IN

E. King

75 IN

105 OH

74 IN

Brannan

Croxton

10 KY

G-1 OH

10 IN

4 KY

14 OH

31 OH

D-1 MI

Poe Field

M-4 US

H-4 US

20 OH

Grose

84 IL

24 OH

23 KY

6 OH

36 KY

21 WI
24 IL

Polk

1 AR
2 TN

3&5 CSA

Mebane

Cobb

Key

32&45 MS

15 MS

45 AL

Wood

Cleburne

18 AL

Semple

33 AL

20 TN
37 GA
58 AL
15& 37 TN
45 TN
18 TN
32 TN
23 TN
26 TN

Eufaula

4 GA
Sharpshooters

1 AR

Dawson

Brown

36 AL
18 AL
38 AL

Clayton

Stewart

Bate

17 18 24& 25 TX

19&24 AR

6 10& 15 TX

Deshler

Douglas

Vegetation

Field   Orchard   Woods   Cedars   Stumps

10:15 a.m., September 19, 1863

Features

Road
Track
Building
Fence

Troops

Federal
Confederate
Advance
Retreat

Map 10.6

Scale

0   50   100   150   200

Yards

10.7: Wood and Stewart Attack
(10:30 a.m.)

S.A.M. Wood's Rebel brigade struck the Federal line at an awkward place. As described previously (Map 9.2), John Turchin's Federal brigade extended George Thomas' line south along the slight ridge that paralleled the LaFayette Road, but in the vicinity of Poe Field, the ridge was in Rebel hands. Accordingly, Col. Edward King's brigade fell in west of the LaFayette Road, facing the narrow strip of open timber that separated Kelly and Poe fields, behind Turchin's right flank. Wood's men ran afoul of this deployment.

Wood had already lost part of his brigade when it followed Polk's line in the shift to the right. That fragment, the 15th and 32nd/45th Mississippi, struck Hazen's Federal brigade head-on and could go no farther. The rest of Wood's men (the 33rd and combined 16th and 18th Alabama) still had open ground in front of them. But with Polk no longer protecting the right flank and Deshler lagging well behind, Wood stopped them for a considerable time while confusion on the front was sorted out.[48] When Wood pushed his left regiments forward again, they advanced behind Turchin's right flank into the open woods in front of King's Yankees. Once there, however, they were subject to a "withering fire" from both front and flank.[49]

The trees here provided no cover. The combined line of the 16th/18th Alabama was especially exposed when its right flank brushed past Turchin's position. One Alabamian wrote that the 16th received a fire "so well directed that it compelled our regiment to seek protection in the bushes; [we] were ordered to lie down, but having no protection were killed by the dozen."[50] From brigade headquarters, Robert Bliss agreed: the 16th had the worst of it because its men "were subjected to an enfilading fire."[51]

To support Wood, Stewart ordered Brown to attack farther south across Poe Field, where the brigade suffered a similarly deadly fire. At first Brown thought his advance was going well, crossing 300 yards of "open woods" until his ranks stepped into the open field.[52] There, as he collided with the main Federal line, he reported that Wood's men broke in confusion, leaving his own right "wholly unsupported and receiving a

terrible cross-fire of musketry and artillery."[53] In fact there was a sizable gap between Wood's left and Brown's right, which allowed most of the Federals in Brannan's division to direct their full fire into Brown's ranks, which soon gave way. Pvt. N. J. Hampton of the 18th Tennessee recalled that the Yankees "threw such heavy volleys of musketry, grapeshot, and shells that we were compelled to fall back."[54] Brown admitted that it was impossible to rally either the 18th or the 45th Tennessee in front of the enemy guns, and let them go. His center and left made a little more progress, crossing the LaFayette Road and almost reaching the Federal lines, but without support this attack was doomed.

Bate's men advanced to the edge of Poe field when Wood's men moved out. Bate was still unsure what the signal was to trigger his advance. He thought he would be behind Wood, and expected Deshler to move up on his right and charge alongside Wood, which would signal his own attack. Bate was unaware that Cleburne had commandeered Deshler's Texans to fill the gap between Wood and Polk. When Wood's men came stumbling back, Stewart ordered Bate to go forward in an effort to bolster Brown's flank.[55] Leaving his battery and his sharpshooters in place, Bate took the rest of his men into the fight as Wood and Brown were coming out of it.

Alone in the north end of Poe field, Bate's fate was predictable. "My right" he reported, "became hotly engaged almost . . . [instantly] . . . subject to a most galling fire of grape and musketry from my right oblique."[56] Bate boldly rode ahead and lost his third mount of the battle here (a mouse-colored sorrel borrowed from the Eufala Artillery), but no amount of conspicuous personal bravery was going to wrest these breastworks from Federal hands.[57] Within a few minutes his brigade was also tumbling back into the trees.

The Yankees found the series of engagements here one of the easiest fights of the day. Their line was well-sited, protected by log breastworks and studded with artillery. All they had to do was load and fire, which they did with killing precision. Opposing Brown's men, Pvt. Sam McNeil of the 31st Ohio (whose fire was directed at Brown's left regiment, the 26th Tennessee) wrote that "with plenty of ammunition and food . . . the 17th and 31st Ohio could have held that position just so long as the enemy came up on our front."[58]

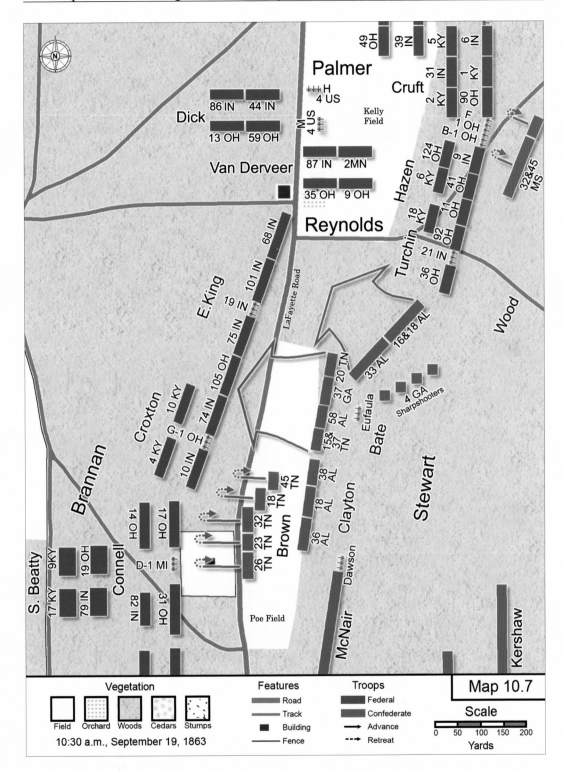

Palmer

Cruft

Dick

Kelly
Field

Van Derveer

Reynolds

Hazen

Turchin

Wood

E. King

LaFayette Road

Croxton

Bate

Eufaula

4 GA
Sharpshooters

Stewart

Brown

Clayton

Brannan

Connell

S. Beatty

Dawson

McNair

Poe Field

Kershaw

Vegetation

Field Orchard Woods Cedars Stumps

10:30 a.m., September 19, 1863

Features

Road

Track

Building

Fence

Troops

Federal

Confederate

Advance

Retreat

Map 10.7

Scale

0   50   100   150   200

Yards

10.8: Deshler Attacks (11:00 a.m.)

Pat Cleburne's attack had fallen apart completely. Polk's Brigade had already gone forward and been repulsed by the time Wood's men became seriously engaged, and now Wood's divided and confused regiments were staggering rearward.

On A. P. Stewart's front, advances by the brigades of Brown and Bate did little more than add to the casualty lists. The artillery had contributed almost nothing to the attack because there were no good fields of fire where they could drop trail and engage the Federal line. When he observed Wood's disordered retreat, Cleburne ordered his brigade, along with Semple's guns, farther to the rear to reform.[59]

As earlier noted, Deshler's men had experienced a frustrating morning even before coming into action. Just now they were swinging into line to replace Wood's right-most regiments (15th and 32nd/45th Mississippi). The Yankee artillery threw shells at the Texans as they advanced, but an effective fire did not ensue until after Deshler's men crested a ridge about 200 yards short of the Federal breastworks. "We were again ordered forward to regain and hold a place on the line from which three other brigades had [already] been driven in confusion," recalled Pvt. Jim Turner of the 6th Texas. "The enemy's fire was simply terrific."[60] R. M. Collins of the 15th Texas Cavalry (dismounted), which just moments before had been laughing at Wood's "mud-heads" as Deshler's line advanced, recalled how quickly the line of Texans was scythed down: "Company E . . . lost twenty-eight men . . . out of about fifty."[61] No one could venture beyond the ridge and live, so Cleburne ordered Deshler to halt his line just behind the crest and engage the Federals from that point.

The firefight was absolutely desperate from the Confederates' perspective, but the Yankees found it less so. William Hazen's men, opposing the right side of Deshler's line, made a pleasing discovery: even the rudimentary breastworks of fence rails, downed cedar, and hastily piled brush provided substantial cover. Hazen reported that he suffered only thirteen casualties during the morning fight. In similar actions on the 19th, at Shiloh, and again at Stones River, he had lost more than 400 men—in each engagement.[62]

Both sides learned a critical lesson: in future fights, men in blue and gray would dig in wherever there was time and opportunity to do so. It is important to recall that Cleburne's men were launching their fruitless attacks at the same time that Breckinridge's Division (Helm, Stovall, and Adams) were reaching the northern edge of Kelly Field, yet no one fighting along the Federal front felt so pressured they could not spare ample reserves to turn westward and face Adams and Stovall.

Loading and firing with a desperate fury, Deshler's men clung to the ridge for at least thirty minutes. Ammunition soon grew short, and then critically so. While examining cartridge boxes, Deshler was horribly mangled when a three-inch Federal artillery shell passed through his chest. "His heart was literally torn from his bosom," reported his successor, Col. Roger Q. Mills of the 10th Texas.[63]

Mills had little time to contemplate Deshler's death. By now Polk's Brigade had retired and, along with Wood's men, was recovering 400 yards to the rear. With but little idea of where the ammunition trains were situated, Mills ordered the men to resupply as best they could from the cartridge boxes of the fallen. Cleburne, not a commander who led from the rear, observed the Texans' difficulties. He rode the length of the line encouraging men to hold on, and dispatched members of his staff to help round up cartridges. Cleburne also realized the futility of pressing forward. Here, finally, Mills got a little relief when Cleburne ordered the brigade to hold its ground but stop advancing.[64] Mills let most of the men fall back behind the crest and take cover, leaving only a line of sharpshooters behind to harass the well-protected enemy.

Cleburne's attack had been a confused and costly failure for multiple reasons. Like Breckinridge's formation (Map 10.1), Cleburne's three brigades were deployed in a single line roughly one mile long, a formation too extended for a single general to control effectively in heavy terrain. Here, too, the lack of reserves was apparent. Even worse, coordination between the right and left wings was poorly handled. When Deshler's advance was blocked, it disrupted Cleburne's overall attack and his formation never fully recovered. Most importantly, there were too many well-protected Federals lining his front.

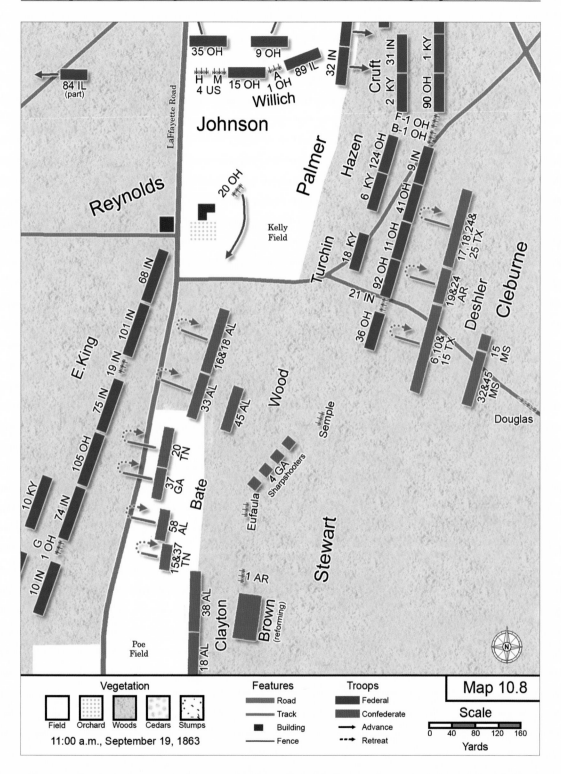

Map 10.8

Vegetation: Field, Orchard, Woods, Cedars, Stumps

Features: Road, Track, Building, Fence

Troops: Federal, Confederate, Advance, Retreat

Scale
0   40   80   120   160
Yards

11:00 a.m., September 19, 1863

10.9: Walker's Reserve Corps Reinforces Breckinridge (Noon)

While D. H. Hill's two divisions (Breckinridge and Cleburne) were struggling to break through George Thomas' powerful line, dissension among the Confederate commanders continued unabated.

Hill's available reserve consisted of Walker's Reserve Corps, which was standing idle instead of moving to support the first line. Walker and Hill disagreed about how to employ Walker's men to advantage. Hill was fixated on waiting for Walker's last brigade (Brig. Gen. States Rights Gist, just then arriving on the field) instead of relying just on Matt Ector's and Claudius Wilson's brigades (which were on hand), or using Brig. Gen. Liddell's Division (the brigades of Daniel Govan and Edward Walthall, all of which had already seen hard fighting on the 19th). Walker disagreed, arguing that his men were needed immediately. The squabble grew into "a high dispute," with both officers becoming loud and angry.[65] Leonidas Polk's effort to smooth things over only made matters worse and sent all three men, angry and perplexed, stomping off in different directions.[66] When news arrived of Breckinridge's repulse, followed by word that Cleburne had also failed, the trio of carping generals realized that reinforcements were needed urgently. There was no time to wait. Walker's men must go in at once.

Hill ordered Liddell to attack and recapture the ground lost by Adams, but left him only one brigade for the difficult task. Hill had personally detached Walthall to support Lucius Polk near the Alexander Bridge Road.[67] Walthall pushed his men south and west into a dense thicket but failed to find Polk. When his right flank was taken under a heavy fire (perhaps accidently from Ector's men), Walthall fell back. His effort to support Cleburne accomplished nothing.

Hill also committed State's Rights Gist's command to replace Ben Helm's (Lewis') line. Gist and part of his large brigade had just reached the field that morning. Because of his seniority, he assumed command of the division Ector had temporarily led the day before. Ector and Wilson's two brigades, however, had been so badly shot up the day before that they could barely scrape together a full brigade between

them. Gist's fresh brigade under its senior colonel, Peyton Colquitt took the lead, driving west above the Alexander Bridge Road. "Our brigade," recalled John H. Steinmeyer of the 24th South Carolina, "was rushed forward, without the opportunity to reconnoiter . . . and struck a concealed angle of the [enemy] works."[68] Under a vicious fire that tore into his exposed left, Gist attempted to have his former brigade change front south and charge the Yankees directly, but the effort failed. Too many officers were down, especially in the 24th. Colquitt was mortally wounded and the brigade, by this time badly scattered, retreated in disorder. The result was a slaughter similar to that suffered by the Orphans just two hours earlier.[69]

The repulse of Walthall and Gist (Colquitt) left Liddell with only Col. Daniel Govan's Brigade. Liddell protested that Govan was far too weak to replace Breckinridge's entire division, to no avail.[70] Moving in a long sweeping angle across the southeast corner of McDonald Field, Govan's line separated into two fragments, with two regiments (1st Louisiana and 6th/7th Arkansas) striking the end of Thomas's line north of Kelly Field, and the other three, Arkansans all (8th, 5th/13th, and 2nd/15th) swinging across the LaFayette Road to briefly reach the Union rear.[71] Without support, however, this drive was doomed to failure.

Realizing the exposed nature of his position, Govan's thoughts turned quickly from attack to retreat. "The enemy had succeeded in flanking the brigade on the left and were then in my rear," reported Lt. Col. John Murray of the combined 5th/13th Arkansas. Murray proposed an abrupt about-face so they could cut their way out, but as he soon discovered, "the men were opposed to this and somewhat demoralized on account of the enemy's being behind them."[72]

Fortunately for them, an alternative route was available. Maj. Watkins of the 8th Arkansas appeared from the right and was conferring with Murray when they were joined by Lt. Col. Rueben Harvey of the 2nd/15th. There was no enemy to the west, he reported. The three lost regiments could avoid capture by circling around in that direction and re-crossing the road farther north. Even better, one of Forrest's scouts was present and knew "the most practicable route."[73] And so the Arkansans slipped away, rejoining their division after an arduous march.

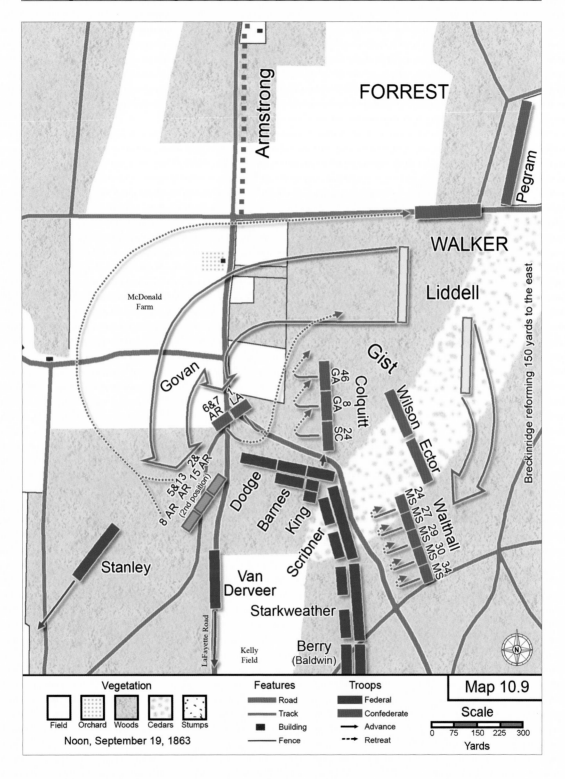

FORREST

Armstrong

Pegram

WALKER

Liddell

McDonald
Farm

Gist

Govan

46
GA
8
GA
24
SC

Colquitt

Wilson

Ector

6&7
AR LA

5&13 28&
AR AR 15 AR
8 AR (2nd position)

Dodge

Barnes

King

Scribner

Walthall

24 27 29 30 34
MS MS MS MS MS

Breckinridge reforming 150 yards to the east

Stanley

LaFayette Road

Van
Derveer

Starkweather

Kelly
Field

Berry
(Baldwin)

N

Vegetation					Features	Troops	Map 10.9

Field   Orchard   Woods   Cedars   Stumps

Noon, September 19, 1863

Road
Track
Building
Fence

Federal
Confederate
Advance
Retreat

Scale

0   75   150   225   300

Yards

Map Set 11: Longstreet Shatters the Union Right

(Midday, September 20)

11.1: Wood Departs (11:00 a.m.)

Thus far, the day's action had been confined to the Union left, where Maj. Gen. George Thomas struggled to drive back repeated Rebel thrusts. Maj. Gen. A. P. Stewart's attack into Poe Field, supporting Brig. Gen. S.A.M. Wood's assault, was the farthest south the fighting had spread. By late morning that action was winding down and the Rebels were in retreat. Throughout this fighting Thomas bombarded Maj. Gen. William Rosecrans and others with a steady stream of requests for reinforcements. The army commander shuffled as many troops as he could find toward Thomas' sector, often regardless of the chain of command or the integrity of his defensive line elsewhere. One of those requests was about to bear disastrous fruit.

About 10:30 a.m. Capt. Sanford Kellogg, Thomas' nephew and aide, instructed Brig. Gen. John Brannan in Poe Field to move the rest of the Third Division to Kelly Field. (Col. Ferdinand Van Derveer's brigade moved earlier.) Brannan consulted with Fourth Division commander Maj. Gen. Joseph J. Reynolds. In the wake of A. P. Stewart's repulse, Reynolds believed that he could hold on alone, but urged Kellogg to ride to Rosecrans and inform him that Brannan's move would leave Reynolds' right flank near Poe Field exposed.[1] After Kellogg left, Brannan and Reynolds changed their minds, but failed to recall Kellogg or send another courier to clarify matters. Kellogg wasted no time informing Rosecrans of the original decision, and Rosecrans reacted just as quickly by dictating an order (later referred to as the "fateful order of the day") instructing division commander Brig. Gen. Thomas J. Wood to "close up on Reynolds as fast as possible, and support him."[2]

Wood's front was quiet, but plenty of Rebels lurked in the timber to the east. Wood knew that Brannan's men were in line between his division and the position Reynolds occupied farther north, but he had no idea that Brannan had been ordered away. Puzzled by the order and seeking clarification, Wood showed it to XX

Corps commander Maj. Gen. Alexander McCook, who happened to be present. McCook insisted that it was peremptory, and that Wood must pull his brigades out of line, move north behind Brannan, find Reynolds, and report to him immediately.[3]

After the battle, Rosecrans partisans insisted that Wood knew his move would expose the army, but he followed the orders out of spite. Since the order was contradictory ("close up" suggested a move *laterally*, while "support" suggested that Wood move *behind* Reynolds' division) Wood should have remained in place and sought clarification. This line of argument glosses over the fact that Wood did seek clarification from McCook, who affirmed the move.

While the generals were conferring, Col. Frederic A. Bartleson of the 100th Illinois (Col. George Buell's brigade, Wood's division) set out on an unauthorized venture that bore out just how dangerous Wood's departure might be. Annoyed by Rebel skirmishers who had taken up residence in the Brotherton cabin, Bartleson advanced his entire regiment in what "turned out to be an unfortunate movement."[4] Bartleson led the 100th beyond the LaFayette Road until it stumbled into the front line of Lt. Gen. James Longstreet's massive attack column hidden in the woods beyond. Stung by enemy fire, the probing Illini staggered back to Union lines in disorder. Bartleson and two companies halted at the cabin, intending to hold it as a strong point.[5] The colonel was unaware that behind him, Wood's entire division—including Col. Sidney Barnes' brigade on loan from Brig. Gen. Horatio Van Cleve's division—was falling into column to scurry north.

Wood's first two brigades left without incident. Barnes, in the woods between Brotherton and Poe fields, moved first, and was already a considerable distance ahead before Harker's brigade started to move. Already confused by the impromptu advance of the 100th Illinois, Buell was considerably more nervous about abandoning his position in the front line. "Tell the General my skirmishers are actively engaged, and I cannot safely make the move," he insisted to one of Wood's aides.[6] The reply was unambiguous: orders were orders; his men must leave immediately. Thinking all of the wayward Illini of the 100th regiment had returned, Buell faced his regiments to the north and stepped off after Harker. His withdrawal set the stage for the most dramatic moment of the battle.

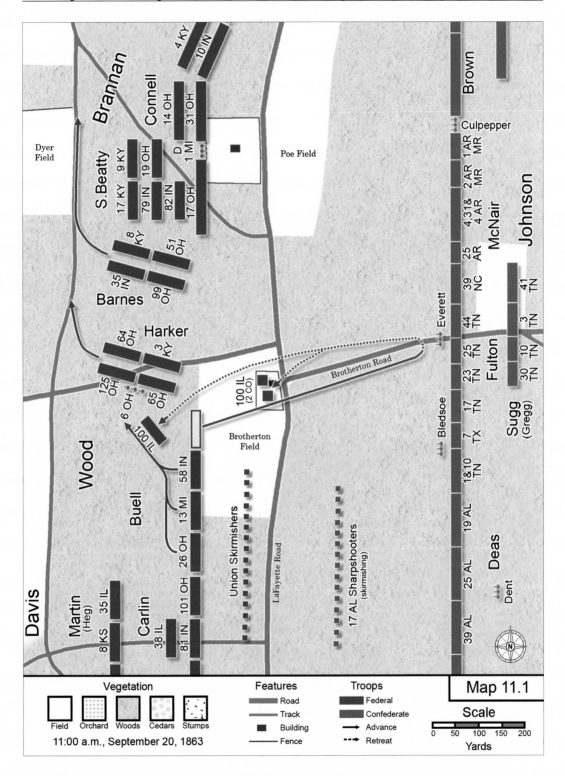

Map 11.1

Vegetation

Field Orchard Woods Cedars Stumps

11:00 a.m., September 20, 1863

Features

Road
Track
Building
Fence

Troops

Federal
Confederate
Advance
Retreat

Scale

0   50   100   150   200
Yards

11.2: The Confederates Attack (11:15 a.m.)

After ordering A. P. Stewart's men into action, Maj. Lee of Bragg's staff continued south, intent on delivering his orders to division after division as he was directed to do. Fortunately for the Rebels, Stewart informed Longstreet that "the battle had been put into the hands of the divisional commanders."[7] All morning the Left Wing commander expected to receive the order to engage. When word arrived instead of this piecemeal commitment, Longstreet sent word to Maj. Gen. John B. Hood to ignore Bragg's directive and wait for his instructions. A short time later, Longstreet ordered his entire assault column into motion.[8]

Unlike Leonidas Polk's efforts, Longstreet arranged his main attack in multiple lines. Three divisions were massed one behind the other, each with two brigades forward and one in support. Only the last line (Kershaw and Humphreys) lacked a supporting third brigade. In all, Longstreet massed eight brigades in five lines (Map 8.3).

Brig. Gen. Bushrod Johnson's Division led the attack. Holding the right flank, Brig. Gen. Evander McNair's command of mostly Arkansans and a regiment of North Carolinians struck the same Union line in Poe Field that had already proven to be invulnerable to frontal attack when John Brown's, William Bate's, and S.A.M. Wood's men had tried it. McNair suffered a similar repulse. Frank T. Ryan of the 1st Arkansas Mounted Infantry (fighting dismounted) described the Union defenses as "a solid line of breastworks, one log piled on top of another to the height of a man's waist."[9] Wounded early, Ryan looked on as his comrades staggered under the withering Union fire before halting in the timber on the east side of the field.

While McNair's men were being thrown back, Johnson's left was driving forward. The Tennessee brigade under Col. John Fulton thrust directly into the gap created by the withdrawal of Tom Wood's division at the Brotherton farm. Lt. Col. R. B. Snowden's 25th Tennessee overran Bartleson's hopelessly outnumbered Illinois detachment at the cabin, the 25th's officers happily reequipping themselves on the spot with captured Yankee accouterments.[10] Fulton's

Tennesseans next fell "like an avalanche" against Buell's unsuspecting regiments hurrying to catch up with the rest of Wood's Federals.[11]

Buell's men were wholly unprepared for the attack. Not only was he falling behind Wood's column, but Buell's own brigade was fragmenting. The 8th Indiana battery was finding it difficult to move through the woods, which in turn affected the speed at which the 13th Michigan and 26th Ohio behind them could march. When Fulton's Rebels appeared on Buell's right, the colonel and his two leading regiments (100th Illinois and 58th Indiana) were approaching Dyer Field, but the trailing regiments had scarcely moved more than 200 yards.

The 13th Michigan and 26th Ohio turned and fell into line, hoping to buy enough time for the 8th Indiana's battery to withdraw.[12] Seeking any avenue of escape, the guns rolled northward, crashing through (and thoroughly disrupting) the ranks of Sam Beatty's prone brigade behind the Poe House. The 13th and 26th were under-strength because both had suffered severely in the Viniard Field fight the day before. Within minutes their two commanders settled on different tactics. Lt. Col. William H. Young ordered his Buckeyes to fall back slowly, resisting as they went.[13] Maj. Willard G. Eaton, however, ordered his Wolverines to launch a counterattack into the teeth of Fulton's advancing ranks.[14] The surprising attack by this small body of Federals—no more than 150 men—may have been sufficient to check momentarily Fulton's Tennesseans, but there were simply not enough men to do more than that. Soon enough Eaton reversed course and ordered a retreat, joining Young in his move westward. Both regiments withdrew slowly northwest through the woods to Dyer Field, pausing briefly from time to time to fire at their pursuers.

Young's and Eaton's men might have suffered even more severely if not for the fact that Bushrod Johnson—despite the success in his center—still had problems on each flank. Col. John Connell's Federals would have to be pushed aside in Poe Field if McNair was to catch up, and Fulton's left was turning to deal with Federals from Brig. Gen. Jefferson C. Davis' division, which was trying to fulfill McCook's rash promise to replace Wood's line. Col. Cyrus Sugg's Brigade would help McNair, while Thomas Hindman's Division dealt with Davis.

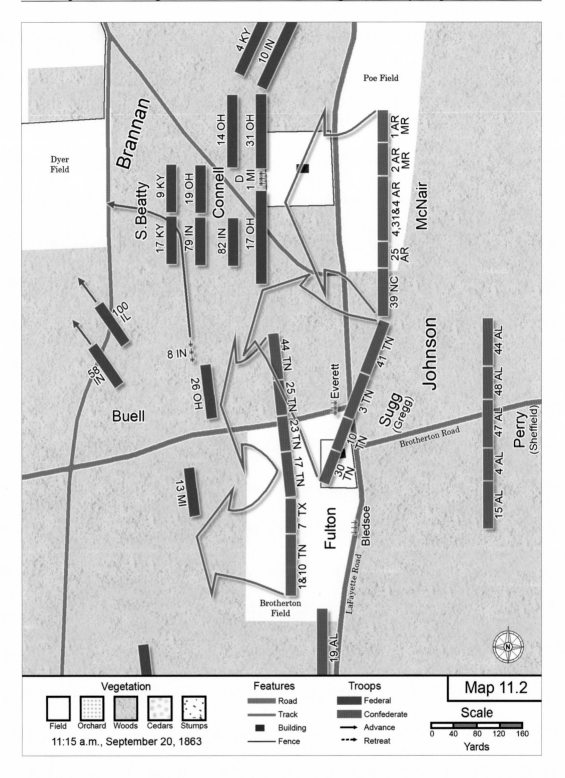

Poe Field

Dyer Field

Brannan

S.Beatty

Connell

Buell

Fulton

McNair

Johnson

Sugg (Gregg)

Perry (Sheffield)

Brotherton Road

LaFayette Road

Bledsoe

Brotherton Field

4 KY
10 IN
14 OH
31 OH
D 1 MI
9 KY
19 OH
17 KY
79 IN
82 IN
17 OH
1 AR MR
2 AR MR
4,31&4 AR
25 AR
39 NC
41 TN
44 TN
25 TN
23 TN
17 TN
13 MI
7 TN
1&10 TN
3 TN
10 TN
30 TN
44 AL
48 AL
47 AL
4 AL
15 AL
19 AL
100 IL
58 IN
8 IN
26 OH
Everett

Vegetation

Field   Orchard   Woods   Cedars   Stumps

11:15 a.m., September 20, 1863

Features

Road
Track
Building
Fence

Troops

Federal
Confederate
→ Advance
---▶ Retreat

Map 11.2

Scale

0   40   80   120   160

Yards

11.3: Davis is Overwhelmed (11:30 a.m.)

An impossible mission has just fallen onto the shoulders of Jefferson C. Davis. His two battered Federal brigades under Brig. Gen. William Carlin and Col. Hans Heg numbered fewer than 1,200 men, but they were about to face off against more than 6,000 bayonets under Thomas Hindman's command. Worse, McCook had just ordered Davis to move Heg's brigade (now under Col. John A. Martin), his sole reserve, into line to replace Wood's three larger brigades. Despite the odds against him, Davis struggled to comply.

Initially, the Federals mounted a surprisingly hearty resistance. Martin's fire swept through the ranks of Brig. Gen. Zachary Deas' Alabama brigade as it crossed the LaFayette Road, catching Lt. Col. Samuel McSpadden's 19th Alabama by surprise. Caught off-guard by Martin's last-minute rush into line, McSpadden's regiment, which held the right side of Deas' line, "exhibited a momentary hesitation and wavering."[15] The stunned Alabamians fell back to the road in search of cover.

Fulton's left regiments observed the repulse and responded. Fulton's line had been prolonged with the addition of two of Col. Sugg's regiments. (Sugg was in command of John Gregg's Brigade after the latter officer fell wounded the previous day.) The combined 1st/10th Tennessee and the 7th Texas, together with the 17th Tennessee, turned and delivered a raking fire against Martin's Federals.[16] The advancing Rebels quickly enveloped Martin's exposed left, allowing the 17th to push west and reconnect with the rest of Fulton's formation at the east edge of Dyer Field while Sugg's two regiments continued to aid Deas.

Thus supported, Deas renewed his attack, this time charging without halting to fire.[17] Observing this advance, Maj. Kleber Van Zandt and the 7th Texas went forward as well, clambering "over the rail fence" bordering the field and "driving the enemy."[18] Martin's line was completely shattered. The Kansas colonel recorded his frustration on October 18, 1863, when he wrote that the brigade was "simply crushed [emphasis in original] by overwhelming numbers. Our little Division, reduced by the first day's fight to less than 1,200 men, was confronted on the second day by at least two full divisions [emphasis in original] of the enemy's army, and both its flanks were left exposed by some one who moved the troops on our left [Wood's division] away."[19]

Carlin's four Midwestern regiments fared little better. They also gave Deas a sharp, if temporary, jab by laying down a solid field of fire into the advancing Rebels. Pvt. John Goodwin of the 22nd Alabama was struck twelve separate times here, evidence of the intensity of the Yankee musketry. One of Goodwin's comrades noted that the unfortunate foot soldier was "literally shot to pieces."[20] But as was usual at Chickamauga, a turned flank soon meant a routed line, and Carlin's flank was turned rather quickly. Struggling to hold Carlin's right, the 21st Illinois collapsed first. Illinois Pvt. Samuel Broughton had fallen out sick and was resting a little behind the line when the Southern hammer fell upon them. He watched in horror as his comrades stampeded. The regiment's commander, Col. John W. S. Alexander, was cut down in the act of ordering a retreat.[21]

The 81st Indiana was crushed almost as quickly. Maj. James E. Calloway watched the Rebels close to within twenty feet of the Union breastworks. When it became clear the attackers were not faltering, he ordered the 81st to withdraw. "As there was no support behind us," wrote the 81st's historian, "it was . . . impossible to form anything like a line," and the regiment retreated by squads, firing as they fell back.[22] Carlin attempted to commit his reserve regiment, the 38th Illinois, but it suffered the same fate. "With the attack in front and on both flanks simultaneously it was impossible for my troops to hold their position. The line melted away," Carlin recalled years later.[23] To their south, Thomas Hindman's other front rank brigade under Brig. Gen. Arthur Manigault swept past without meeting any opposition at all, driving toward Maj. Gen. Phil Sheridan's Federal division waiting several hundred yards to the west.

While Davis' command was being crushed, McCook—seeing that more troops were urgently needed—galloped for Sheridan's division. In just a handful of minutes, McCook's decisions had visited disastrous consequences upon Davis' troops. Now it was Sheridan's turn to experience McCook's meddling.

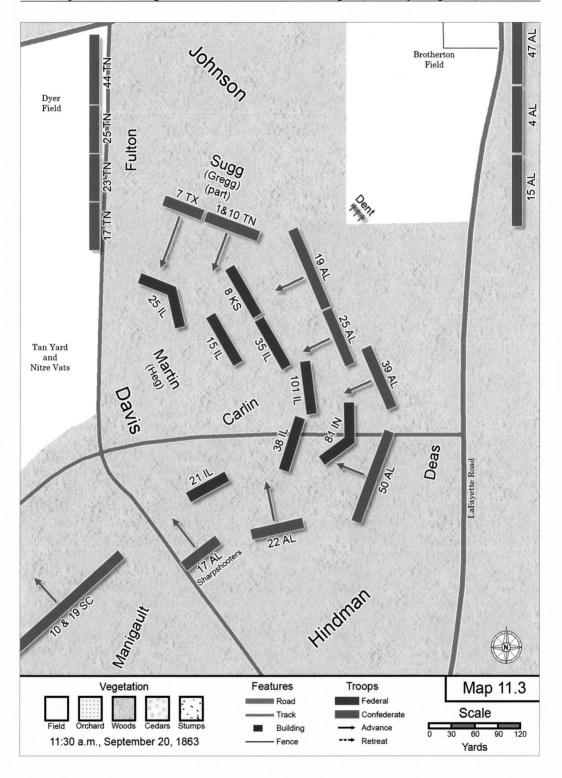

Map 11.3

11:30 a.m., September 20, 1863

11.4: Connell Outflanked, Beatty Routed (11:30 a.m.)

With Davis' Federals swept out of the way, the left flank of Longstreet's grand Confederate assault column had unimpeded access into the Federal rear. Brannan's obstinate Federals, however, still stymied McNair's Brigade, which composed the right side of Longstreet's assault force. Poe Field had to be cleared. Stalled in front of the Federal works, McNair needed support. Col. Sugg had the answer.

Stepping up to brigade command when Gregg fell wounded the night before, Sugg proved equal to the task. He watched as McNair's men were repulsed, reorganized, and repulsed a second time. Riding over to the Arkansan, Sugg suggested that McNair's men stand while his brigade passed through them and maneuvered to take Yankees in the flank. When Barnes' Federals left the front line before Longstreet's attack, Col. Connell worried about just such an attack against his exposed right. He threw out an additional line of skirmishers to alert him if Rebels appeared in that quarter. Those skirmishers, however, were no match for Sugg's regiments.[24]

The blow landed first on the 17th Ohio, which struggled to change front and face the new assault. The maneuver proved too difficult to accomplish under the pressure of the moment, and Ohio Capt. J. W. Stinchcomb watched "company after company break" as each tried to reorient, until "my company [is] the only one left; the battery is limbering; the Rebels are close enough to use the bayonet. . . . The Regiment is running for cover."[25] The routed Buckeyes swarmed through the prone 82nd Indiana (in reserve) and continued on, rushing through Brig. Gen. Sam Beatty's brigade. The Michigan gunners scrambled to draw off their pieces by hand, but the Southern attack was delivered so quickly that two guns had to be abandoned.[26]

The pandemonium spread like a contagion through the blue ranks. Packed tightly behind Connell's line, Beatty's four regiments had been subject to enemy fire through at least three assaults without being able to fire back. Now they were being run over and through by a routed battery (the 8th Indiana), which crushed men indiscriminately where they lay. These same men were facing the collapse of the Federal line immediately to their front. Not surprisingly, they also broke. Indiana Pvt. Leander Munhall recalled the moment: "We were just literally tore to pieces and scattered in every direction."[27]

Samuel Beatty was a plainspoken practical man, a Pennsylvania farmer twice elected sheriff of Stark County. His only military experience was as a lieutenant in the Mexican War, and his service thus far in this conflict. He had handled brigade command since Perryville, and had proven competent at that level. At Chickamauga, his brigade's experience had thus far been terribly unlucky. Flanked and routed on the 19th (Map 7.1), his command was shattered a second time on the 20th because of its unfortunate placement.

Not every Federal panicked and fled. After letting the routed 17th Ohio pass over his line, Col. Morton Hunter of the 82nd Indiana (Connell's brigade) ordered his Hoosiers to their feet. Their countercharge carried them back to their initial line of works.[28] Behind Hunter, fragments of several regiments tried to rally and follow, including soldiers from the Connell's 17th Ohio and Beatty's 19th Ohio and 9th Kentucky. Because Sugg's line was too strong and outflanked the Yankees, Hunter's valiant counterattack was unable to do more than buy a few minutes for the artillery to get away. Hunter's withdrawal exposed the right flanks of the 14th and 31st Ohio regiments, the other half of Connell's brigade. The prone 14th held the second line, lying "as flat as adders" while combat raged.[29] Sugg's attack fell on the Ohioans almost before they knew it, and now it was the 14th's Ohio's turn to be routed.[30] The 14th's rout pulled the 31st out of line, and with that Connell's collapse was complete.

Neither Sugg nor McNair (Bushrod Johnson's Division) turned north in an effort to roll up Brannan's divisional line. Fulton's Tennessee brigade was already into or through the trees separating Brotherton and Dyer Fields, so Sugg and McNair were hurried in that direction. Johnson was obeying Hood's orders to "go ahead, and keep ahead of everything."

Brannan's other brigade under Kentuckian Col. John Croxton was still in line and full of fight, but other Rebels would deal with him.[31]

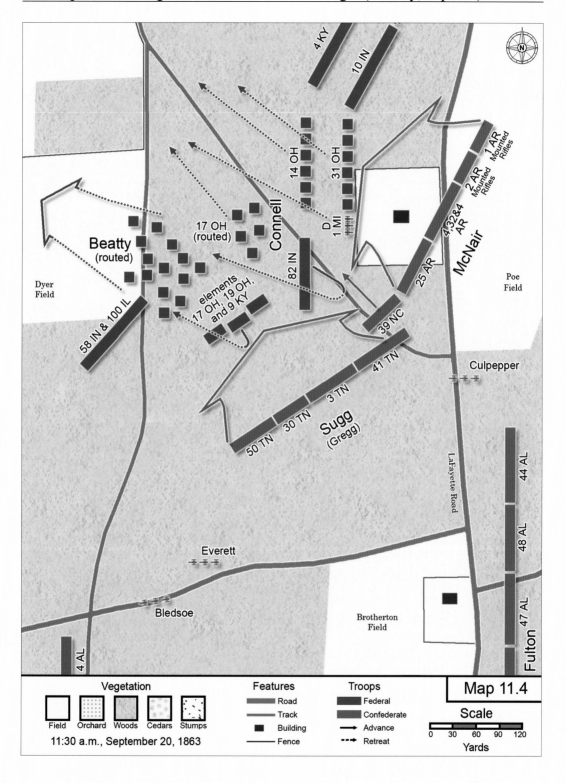

4 KY

10 IN

14 OH

31 OH

D.
1 MI

1 AR Mounted Rifles

2 AR Mounted Rifles

4,32&4 AR

25 AR

McNair

Poe Field

Connell

17 OH (routed)

Beatty (routed)

Dyer Field

82 IN

39 NC

58 IN & 100 IL

elements 17 OH, 19 OH, and 9 KY

41 TN

Culpepper

3 TN

30 TN

50 TN

Sugg (Gregg)

LaFayette Road

44 AL

48 AL

Everett

Bledsoe

47 AL

4 AL

Brotherton Field

Fulton

Vegetation

Field   Orchard   Woods   Cedars   Stumps

11:30 a.m., September 20, 1863

Features

Road
Track
Building
Fence

Troops

Federal
Confederate
Advance
Retreat

Map 11.4

Scale

0   30   60   90   120

Yards

11.5: Benning Attacks Croxton
(11:45 a.m.)

With Southern brigades under Sugg and McNair mauling his right flank, Brannan sought help anywhere he could find it. He dispatched Lt. Ira V. Germain to the rear, where he found Gen. Wood and Col. Harker. Wood was looking in vain for Gen. Reynolds, per Rosecrans' earlier order, but had not yet found him. Germain's news that Brannan's division was flanked and collapsing was quickly confirmed by the rush of panicked men pouring out of the timber to the south and across North Dyer Field. Wood directed Harker to move south.[32] Germain's message would have a significant impact on the course of the battle to come, but did little to help Brannan's unfolding situation.

For the Rebels, the wisdom of Longstreet's choice of a deep column formation was bearing fruit. Unlike the attacks along Leonidas Polk's front, Johnson's Division (McNair, Fulton and Sugg) continued driving forward while Law's Division finished the fight in Poe Field. James L. Sheffield's Brigade (led by Col. William F. Perry after Sheffield was injured in a fall from his horse on the 19th) was followed by Brig. Gens. Henry Benning and Jerome Robertson. All three of these commands under Law were moving into position to protect Johnson's flank. Perry was aware of the fighting to his right, but detached only one regiment, the 44th Alabama, to face north and screen his own flank.[33] The 44th fired several volleys at distant Federals, probably the 17th Ohio or 9th Kentucky, but the Yankees soon withdrew. The 44th did not follow them or try and catch up to the rest of the brigade; its fighting was largely done for the day.

Henry Benning, whose brigade initially trailed Perry's Alabamians, took the threat from the north more seriously. Benning, a veteran of the Army of Northern Virginia, faced his Georgians to the right (north) and marched his entire brigade toward the Poe farmstead in a single line four regiments abreast.[34] The Georgians could clearly see a new Federal line through the open woods west of Poe Field forming just 200 yards distant.

When Connell's line gave way, Col. Croxton (Brannan's division) was forced to turn his attention to his own right. He ordered part of

Battery C, 1st Ohio into the front line and had it fire south, enfilading the advancing Confederate lines. He ordered the 10th and 4th Kentucky regiments south in an effort to reoccupy Connell's works. This plan was foiled by Benning's sudden appearance, which forced the Kentuckians to halt facing south and square off against this new threat.[35]

The moment was a dramatic one. Casualties and the debris of war littered the narrow strip of ground between the two lines. The Poe cabin was ablaze, as were Connell's breastworks in places, casting a pall of smoke over the scene. A pair of guns from the 1st Michigan battery sat in no-mans-land, forlorn and abandoned.

The odds were about equal. Benning's four regiments numbered only about 600 men after their deadly ordeal in the "Ditch of Death" on the 19th, while the 4th and 10th Kentucky ranked about 500 bayonets.[36] They, too, had taken a beating on the 19th. The aggressive and capable Benning ordered his men to charge. The general led the right of the line and sent his adjutant, Capt. Ben Abbott, to lead the left. "The old Rebel yell broke out from every throat" remembered Abbott, only to be met by a "volcano of fire." Both Benning and Abbott were dismounted quickly when their horses were struck.[37] A scything fire and mounting losses did not initially dissuade the Georgians from their mission, and they closed to within "two rods" [about ten yards] of Capt. Marco B. Gary's 1st Ohio battery, whose gunners were beginning to fall.[38] When Croxton went down about this time with a leg wound, command devolved to Col. William Hays of the 10th Kentucky.[39] Neither side budged, and the fighting raged at brutally close range.

While first Croxton and then Hays struggled to reorient the brigade, John Brannan rode to rally Connell's shattered formations and hopefully find reinforcements. He moved west, spurring his mount north of Dyer Field to the high ground that rose so abruptly beyond. Brannan could no longer exert much control over events swirling in Poe Field, but his arrival on Horseshoe Ridge and efforts to reorganize his division there made him central to the next phase of the fight.

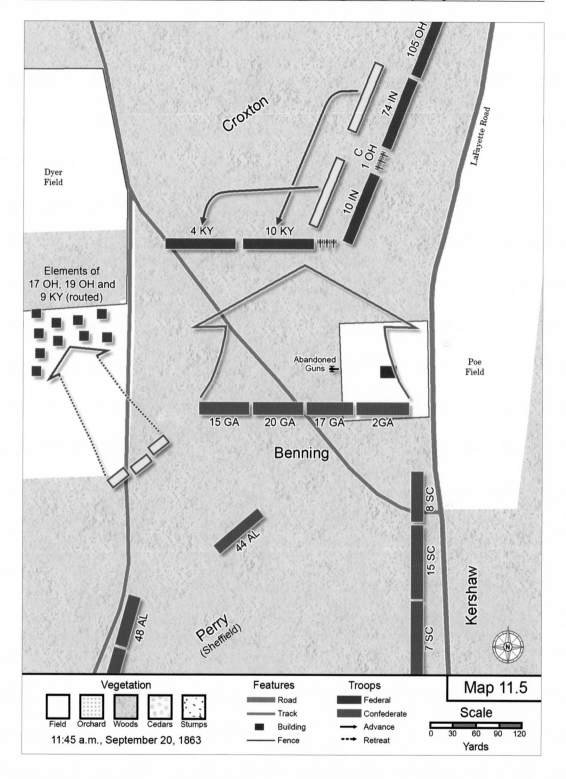

Map 11.5

11:45 a.m., September 20, 1863

11.6: Benning Repulsed (Noon)

With Benning's Georgians locked in a firefight with part of Croxton's (now Col. Hays') brigade, the rest of Law's Southern division moved swiftly to exploit the breakthrough.

Col. Perry's Alabamians had been drawn into following two of Bushrod Johnson's brigades (Sugg and McNair) driving to the west, but the Texas Brigade was still uncommitted. At their head rode Jerome Robertson, another veteran officer from the Army of Northern Virginia who had recently arrived in Georgia to support Bragg's Army of Tennessee. Robertson knew that Benning's change of front to the north had created a considerable gap between the Georgians and Longstreet's advancing front line. Because the growing distance posed a danger to Johnson's exposed right flank, Robertson decided to fill it.[40] He led his brigade at an angle northwest across the LaFayette Road into North Dyer Field in search of an enemy to fight.

As he absorbed his new command responsibilities at the head of Croxton's brigade, Hays might have believed he could hold off Benning's infantry. Robertson's advance to support Benning's left, however, changed the calculus of those odds. Realizing his right flank would be enveloped, Hays ordered the brigade to disengage and fall back to the northwest.[41]

Croxton's brigade had thus far fought with precision and displayed remarkable cohesion and coordination under very difficult tactical circumstances. After the loss of Croxton, however, the organization failed to perform at the same level of efficiency. Hays' order to retreat did not reach the left wing of the brigade (which was still fronting east), so only the two Kentucky regiments on the right—the 4th and 10th—fell back, and they did so in considerable disorder.[42] Their retreat exposed the 1st Ohio's Battery C, already badly mauled, to a dangerous retreat under fire. With thirteen men and twenty-five horses down, Capt. Gary believed it "impossible to save the battery" unless he acted immediately, so "without orders" he withdrew to the "left and rear."[43] With infantry help, the gunnery officer dragged five of his six guns far enough back to limber and leave; the sixth tube was removed from it's carriage by brute force and left in nearby brush.[44] The brigade's situation

further deteriorated when Col. Charles W. Chapman of the 74th Indiana, leading the left half of the brigade still facing east, broke his arm in a fall when his horse was shot out from under him. His injury severed yet another link in the brigade's chain of command.[45]

Benning's Georgians were well positioned to benefit from these Federal misfortunes. Two Indiana regiments, however, weren't ready to give up the contest. With Chapman down, Lt. Col. Marsh B. Taylor of the 10th Indiana took charge of what was left of the brigade. "In [his] shrill, piping voice," wrote regimental historian James B. Shaw, "[Taylor gave] the command, 'About face, fix bayonets, to the left oblique, charge!'"[46] Turning to face south, 250 Hoosiers plunged recklessly toward the middle of Benning's line.

The sudden charge proved too much for the Georgians. Decimated by earlier losses (officer casualties had been especially heavy) and with Benning dismounted and unable to exercise effective command, the brigade fell back in disorder. The retreat was shoved a little faster by the appearance of the 74th Indiana, which duplicated Taylor's move and took up a position in line on the 10th Indiana's right, prolonging the new Union line toward the Dry Valley Road. The chaotic retreat unnerved the usually dependable Benning. According to staff officer Lt. Col. Moxley Sorrell, he and Longstreet met Benning about this time mounted on a stray artillery horse. "I am ruined," Benning blurted. "My brigade was suddenly attacked and every man killed! Not one is to be found. Please give orders where I can do some fighting." The imperturbable Longstreet calmed down his subordinate: "Nonsense, General, you are not so badly hurt. Look about you. I know you will find at least one man, and with him on his feet report your brigade to me, and you two shall have a place in the fighting-line."[47]

After a short advance Col. Taylor halted his combined Hoosier command, unwilling to follow the retreating Rebels into an unknown and probably dangerous situation. He had no idea where to find either his division or his brigade commander. But he could see a strong Confederate brigade advancing across Dyer Field to his right front, menacing the rear of the entire Union position.

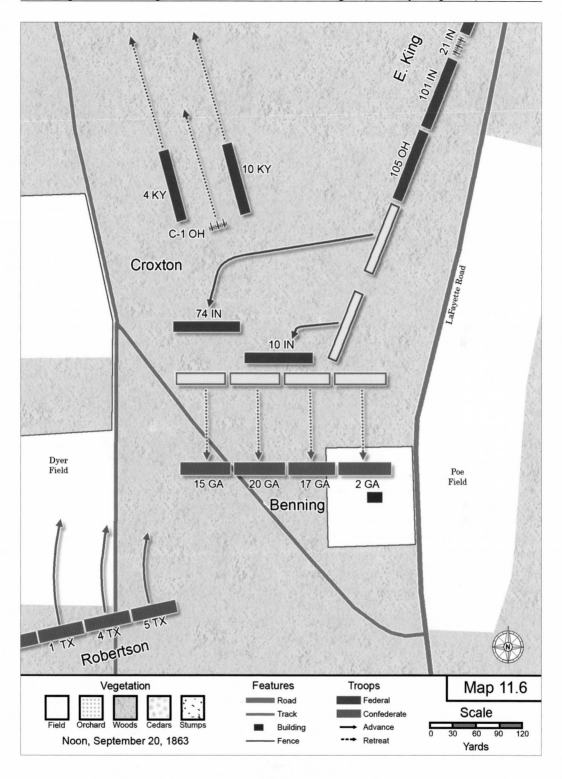

11.7: Reynolds and the 105th Ohio (12:15 p.m.)

By noon, Joseph Reynolds had reason to be alarmed. His morning confidence evaporated in the face of the rout and wreckage of Brannan's division. He became fully aware of the crisis only after Croxton fell wounded and his disordered brigade retreated to the northwest. Riding to investigate, Reynolds watched Col. Hays' chaotic retreat, and possibly witnessed Col. Taylor's dramatic shift to replace him. Only then did the major general fully grasp the mortal danger his division faced: his flank was compromised.

If Reynolds was aware of Taylor's advance, he issued no orders to the Hoosier. The 74th Indiana on Taylor's right could see into Dyer Field and had a fine view of Robertson's one Arkansas and three Texas infantry regiments. His roughly 1,000 infantry easily outnumbered Taylor's combined Hoosier commands—and there seemed to be no other Federals within supporting distance. Determined not to fall back without making some sort of a fight, the men from Indiana stood tall and opened fire at the advancing men in gray.

Robertson's regiments were in a good position, but they had problems of their own. Benning, whom Robertson intended to support, was in full retreat, and Law, in command of the division, was not close enough to offer guidance. Capt. J. S. Cleveland, elevated the day before to command the 5th Texas, witnessed Benning's retreat from the right side of Robertson's advancing brigade. As far as Cleveland could determine, the entire division was falling back. He retired his regiment a considerable distance before realizing that the rest of the brigade was not following suit.[48] While thus separated from the other three regiments, an enemy force of unknown size opened fire in the woods against Robertson's exposed right flank.

Col. Taylor of the 10th Indiana, of course, knew none of this. After firing for a short time into the diminished right flank of the Texas Brigade, he decided to retire northeast in search of someone to provide him with direction. The colonel retreated into Kelly Field and eventually brought the 10th and 74th Indiana to rest behind Hazen's brigade, peeling off stragglers along the way.[49] His momentary engagement with the Texans, however, so concerned Robertson that it would affect subsequent events.

Reynolds, meanwhile, his flank entirely exposed, had to craft a new defense. He had only two brigades, one under Col. Edward King, adjacent to Croxton's former line on the northwest side of Poe Field, and another under Brig. Gen. John Turchin, holding the extension of George Thomas' Kelly Field line in advance of King's position. Turchin would have to swing his regiments back to face south, while King shifted into position alongside him. If his line was reoriented, Reynolds believed he could hold his ground despite Brannan's collapse. The only question was whether the Rebels would give him enough time to complete his redeployment.

The solution, desperate as it was, was close at hand. King's reserve regiment was the 105th Ohio, 300 men strong. Returning from Croxton's fast-crumbling position, Reynolds rode directly to Maj. George T. Perkins and his Buckeyes and ordered them to charge.[50] The mission appeared suicidal. The men of the 105th realized the effort was a forlorn hope that would likely lead to their deaths, maiming, or a visit to a prisoner of war camp. Despite this grim prospect, Albion Tourgee of the 105th proudly recalled that not a man hesitated to do his duty.[51]

Benning's Georgians had already seen more than enough combat for the day. "When we struck their flank . . . they were already blown by their long charge through the woods," continued Tourgee. "Startled by our bold assault, they scattered; many surrendering."[52] In reality, the 105th only brushed past Benning's right flank as it charged down through Poe Field, overrunning wounded men and stragglers knocked out during earlier assaults by Brown's and McNair's brigades. The Ohioans struck deep, reaching (by their recollection) the Brotherton Road. The trick was to find a way out.

Many Rebels had fallen to the ground to let the 105th pass, meaning that in all likelihood that avenue of retreat would not be available to the Ohioans. Instead, maintained Tourgee, they made their way west, slipping between Rebel formations until the Buckeyes escaped up the Dry Valley Road. If true, the Ohioans were amazingly lucky, cutting their way through Longstreet's entire Left Wing without being noticed. Reynolds believed the Buckeyes were goners until he stumbled upon them at Rossville the next day.[53]

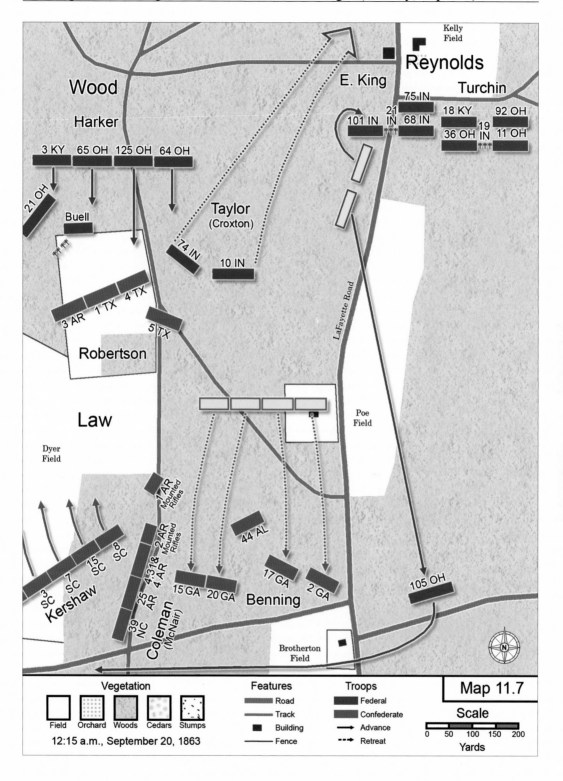

Kelly
Field

Wood

Reynolds

E. King

Turchin

Harker

75 IN

101 IN   21   68 IN
          IN

18 KY   92 OH
          19
36 OH   IN   11 OH

3 KY   65 OH   125 OH   64 OH

21 OH

Buell

Taylor
(Croxton)

74 IN

10 IN

3 AR   1 TX   4 TX

LaFayette Road

5 TX

Robertson

Law

Poe
Field

Dyer
Field

1 AR
Mounted
Rifles

2 AR
Mounted
Rifles

44 AL

8 SC
15 SC

4-31&
4 AR

17 GA   2 GA

7 SC

105 OH

3 SC

25
AR   15 GA   20 GA   Benning

Kershaw

39
NC   Coleman
      (McNair)

Brotherton
Field

N

| Vegetation | | | | | Features | Troops | Map 11.7 |

Field   Orchard   Woods   Cedars   Stumps

Road   Federal
Track   Confederate
Building   Advance
Fence   Retreat

Scale

12:15 a.m., September 20, 1863

0   50   100   150   200
Yards

Map Set 12: Sheridan Tries to Hold at Lytle Hill

(Midday, September 20)

12.1: Laiboldt Attacks (11:45 a.m.)

While John Brannan's Federals were fighting for time in Poe Field, Maj. Gen. Thomas Hindman's Rebels were chasing Brig. Gen. Jefferson C. Davis' broken division south and west of Brotherton Field. When his portion of the Federal battle line dissolved into chaos, Maj. Gen. Alexander McCook, commander of the XX Corps, cast about for any reinforcements he could find. Only his Third Division under Maj. Gen. Philip H. Sheridan stood in the path of the onrushing Rebels.

Like so many other troops that morning, Sheridan's three brigades were in transit. In the earlier scramble to replace Maj. Gen. Negley's shifting division, Sheridan sent Col. Bernard Laiboldt. Before he could take position, Davis' division moved north and Brig. Gen. Thomas Wood's division was fed into line. With nowhere to go, Laiboldt arranged his four regiments in a compact formation on the forward slope of the high ground overlooking West Dyer Field.[1] Laiboldt could now support Davis. Shortly thereafter—sometime after Wood received his order to find Reynolds and when Longstreet's attack stepped off—Sheridan was ordered to pull his remaining brigades away to help support Maj. Gen. George Thomas, whose left wing of the army was fighting farther north.

Davis found Laiboldt before Sheridan. Upset and excited by the unfolding disaster, Davis urged the colonel into action. Laiboldt demurred; after all, he had a strong position and preferred to let the Rebels come to him. Lt. Col. Horace Fisher of Rosecrans' staff appeared and urged similar action, to no avail. Finally, corps leader McCook appeared and ordered an assault.[2] Laiboldt deployed his men in column of regiments and reluctantly marched them eastward.

Laiboldt's stacked formation may have worked against a limited frontal assault, but his narrow front made it easier for Rebels to outflank him. He realized this and asked for time to redeploy, but McCook snapped back, "No, charge as you are."[3] As Laiboldt approached the foot of the hill, Rebels from several Alabama regiments appeared in a long line ahead of him. Brig. Gen. Zach Deas' Alabama brigade easily overlapped both of Laiboldt's flanks. At the same time, Brig. Gen. Arthur Manigault's Rebel brigade was advancing from the southeast into the Union rear, his right regiment (the 10th/19th South Carolina) moving through the woods south of Laiboldt.

The 73rd Illinois led Laiboldt's brigade and suffered heavily for the honor. The first obstacle was stragglers from Brig. Gen. William Carlin's brigade who swarmed through and disrupted its ranks. Then the Rebels appeared. The Illini managed a limited volley, but Deas' return fire ripped through them "in a shower of balls flying from our front, right and left."[4] The 73rd collapsed quickly, exposing the rest of the brigade to similar troubles. According to Col. Joseph Conrad, his 15th Missouri, "wheeling on the march to the right" to try and extend the brigade front, met "a murderous fire."[5] Bringing up the rear, the 2nd Missouri didn't even get off a round before it was shattered. Remnants of the other regiments (including from Carlin's and Heg's brigades), masked any chance they had to fight back.[6]

Col. Samuel McSpadden's 19th Alabama faced the 73rd Illinois near the small collection of shacks that marked the tan yard. Without "even a momentary hesitation," he boasted, "we drove the enemy with great slaughter . . . some 250 yards to an elevated skirt of heavy open woods."[7] There, a new line of Federals waited to receive them.

While Laiboldt was charging down the hill's eastern face, Brig. Gen. William H. Lytle's brigade (Sheridan) was hurrying into action from the west. Deploying astride the road at the foot of the hill and hustling troops to the crest, Lytle was about to plunge into the same maelstrom that brought Laiboldt to grief.

Days after the battle, Sheridan was still furious that Laiboldt had been sent forward so recklessly, "express[ing] himself . . . in language more forcible than elegant,"recalled Chauncy Castle of the 73rd Illinois.[8] McCook later claimed that the sacrifice was necessary in order to check the Rebel attack, and he committed the brigade to a desperate action in order to save three others. In fact, Laiboldt's troops accomplished very little. Deployed in the wrong formation and exposed to piecemeal destruction, they stood no chance at all.

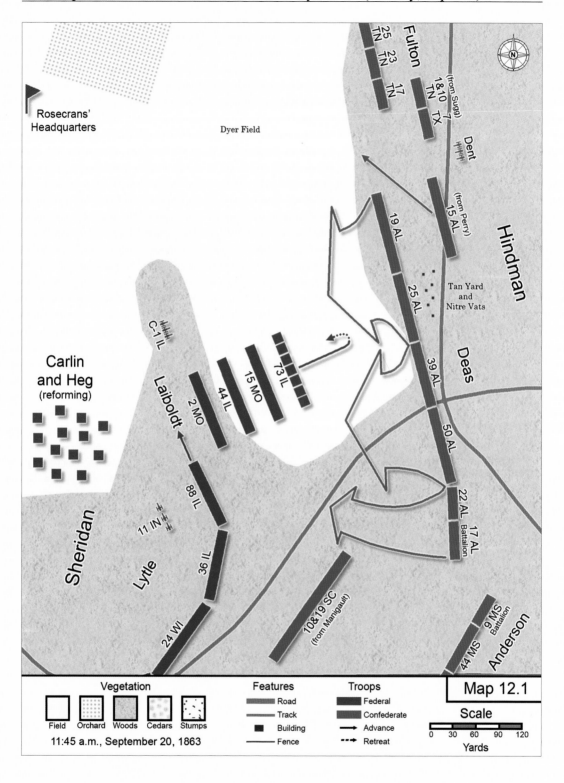

Rosecrans'
Headquarters

Dyer Field

25 TN
23 TN
Fulton
17 TN
1&10 TN
7 TX
(from Sugg)
Dent
(from Perry)
15 AL

Hindman

19 AL

Tan Yard
and
Nitre Vats

25 AL

C-1 IL

Carlin
and Heg
(reforming)

73 IL

Laiboldt

15 MO

2 MO

44 IL

39 AL

Deas

50 AL

Sheridan

88 IL

11 IN

22 AL

17 AL
Battalion

Lytle

36 IL

24 WI

10&19 SC
(from Manigault)

9 MS
Battalion

44 MS

Anderson

Vegetation

Field   Orchard   Woods   Cedars   Stumps

11:45 a.m., September 20, 1863

Features

Road
Track
Building
Fence

Troops

Federal
Confederate
Advance
Retreat

Map 12.1

Scale

0   30   60   90   120

Yards

12.2: Lytle and Walworth Stand (Noon)

While Laiboldt's men were advancing down the hill toward the approaching enemy, William Lytle's brigade was climbing up the wooded southeastern face to come into line on the crest. The guns of Capt. Mark H. Prescott's Battery C, 1st Illinois, were already present—the only Federal unit left to oppose Deas' Confederates. Laiboldt's earlier advance caught Capt. Prescott by surprise. No one had seen fit to tell him where the brigade was going or issue orders about what to do next.[9] Battery C opened fire as soon as its front was clear of friendly troops, but unaware of the approach of Lytle's men to their right-rear. Prescott was already looking to retreat.

Sheridan rushed Lytle's men into the fight. Pvt. Leonard W. Mann, Company A of the 36th Illinois, wrote in his diary that "our brigade [was] ordered [to] double-quick [a] half mile" and came into action "just as [Laiboldt's] line broke."[10] Daniel Bernard of the 88th Illinois recalled that "they took us into a very hot fire."[11] Col. Silas Miller, leading the 36th Illinois, reported that the brigade initially engaged in two lines, the 88th and 36th Illinois leading, with the 11th Indiana battery going into action at the base of the hill; the first line was forced back and allowed to rally by the timely arrival of Lytle's other two regiments, the 21st Michigan and 24th Wisconsin.[12] The 88th and 36th reformed and returned to the line at an oblique angle running up the crest of the hill toward Prescott's cannon. When fully deployed, Lytle's brigade formed a large semi-circle that created a dangerous convex angle allowing fire to come in from multiple directions. It was not an ideal deployment, but there was no time to make it better.

Lytle's aggressive appearance, however, was strong enough to halt the Rebels. Nearly worn out from overrunning two lines of Yankees and chasing the remnants half a mile or more, Deas' Alabamians failed to muster the nerve or wind for a third charge. Instead, they poured "a withering fire" into this newest Union line.[13] "Here took place a terrible conflict, which lasted about 20 minutes, in which we lost many brave spirits [including] our esteemed commander, Lt. Col. John Weedon," wrote Capt. Harry T. Toulmin of the 22nd Alabama.[14]

Another Alabama regiment appeared behind Deas' right and decided to lend a hand. Col. William C. Oates and his 15th Alabama, part of Law's former brigade now under Col. William F. Perry, was lost. The regiment that had earned undying fame just two months earlier at Gettysburg on the slopes of Little Round Top was nearly one-half mile off course when Oates spotted the conflict ahead. His leg bruised by a shell fragment, Oates hobbled after his impetuous regiment, warning his men not to shoot until they passed around Deas' line and had a clear field of fire. Unfortunately, the men failed to heed the warning and "began a heavy enfilading fire" directly into the backs of their fellow Alabamians in the 19th regiment.[15]

Behind Lytle hustled Col. Luther Bradley's brigade, now under the command of Col. Nathan Walworth. Severe fighting had been their lot on the 19th, and the all-Illinois command now numbered fewer than 1,000 muskets. Walworth's regiments had little time to get set for battle. Lt. Henry M. Weiss of the 27th Illinois recorded the frantic pace: "We are into it, and that before we can take a position. Bah! What can our brigade do against such odds?"[16]

The men filed into line along the Glenn-Kelly Road, a haphazard formation thrown up facing generally southeast to meet a new Rebel threat. Walworth ordered the 22nd Illinois, leading the advance, to face right "and check them if possible" while he brought up the other regiments.[17] In terms of commanders, at least, Walworth had a surfeit of help. Both McCook and Sheridan were active here, hand-placing the 42nd Illinois. Still, the brigade line was thin, elongated from the march and with no time to dress ranks.

Walworth's Illini were facing Brig. Gen. Patton Anderson's large 2,000-man brigade of six Mississippi regiments. Anderson ended up where he was because Hindman's Division (to which Anderson belonged) had opened a considerable gap between Deas' Alabamians (fighting their way through successive lines of Federals) and Manigault's men (advancing largely unopposed across Viniard Field). Anderson moved his line into this widening space. When the Alabamians paused, he brought his troops into action alongside Deas.[18]

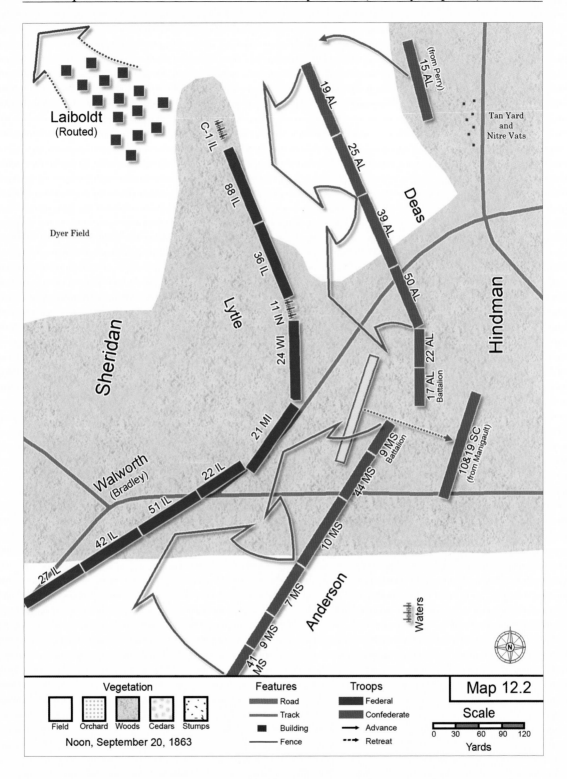

Laiboldt
(Routed)

Dyer Field

Tan Yard
and
Nitre Vats

C-1 IL

88 IL

36 IL

11 IN

24 WI

21 MI

22 IL

51 IL

42 IL

27 IL

Sheridan

Lytle

Walworth
(Bradley)

15 AL
(from Perry)

19 AL

25 AL

39 AL

Deas

50 AL

17 AL
Battalion

22 AL

Hindman

10&19 SC
(from Manigault)

9 MS
Battalion

44 MS

10 MS

7 MS

9 MS

41
MS

Anderson

Waters

Vegetation

Field Orchard Woods Cedars Stumps

Noon, September 20, 1863

Features

Road
Track
Building
Fence

Troops

Federal
Confederate
Advance
Retreat

Map 12.2

Scale

0   30   60   90   120

Yards

12.3: Rout of Lytle and Walworth (12:15 p.m.)

The arrival of Patton Anderson's large fresh Mississippi brigade (with one battery of Alabama guns) tipped the scales, the sheer weight of numbers driving the whole line forward. Anderson's right intermingled with the 22nd Alabama, the regiment holding Deas' left, but the brief disruption did not halt the renewed attack. The Rebels were encouraged to see the Yankee cannon atop the hill limber and leave at this critical moment of the assault.

Capt. Prescott's Battery C, 1st Illinois, was in a quandary. Laiboldt's sudden rout left him without orders, and he knew nothing of the arrival of William Lytle's brigade (which was tramping up the hill from the wooded southeast face). The only friendly troops Prescott could see were panicked stragglers pouring through his gun position and masking his field of fire. He managed to get off several rounds, but the rapidly approaching enemy convinced him to fall back to the next set of hills to save his guns.[19] The battery left in such a hurry that one limber, "swinging round with almost lightning speed struck a dead tree, which caused the top to come off," hitting two men in the 36th Illinois. Prescott's departure left Lytle without artillery support atop the hill, and allowed Deas' Alabama infantry to concentrate their fire against the infantry.[20]

Pvt. W. W. Gifford of the 36th Illinois, holding the left side of Lytle's brigade line, described the fighting that ensued: "After holding our position a short time we found the rebs too thick for us. We were getting sadly mixed up with them and were given the order to fall back."[21] Whether ordered to fall back or not, the Illini of the 36th and the 88th regiments were now both retiring in haste. The mounted Lytle was trying to rally the line and lead his regiments back to the crest when he was struck in the back with a bullet. He remained mounted with an aide next to him. A few moments later he was struck again, this time in the head, the bullet shattering his teeth and exiting his neck. "This was his third battle and his third wound," wrote the 36th's regimental historian. This time, however, the wound proved mortal.[22] The semi-conscious Lytle urged his aides to leave him on the field where he fell.

Matters were scarcely going better for the Federals at the foot of the hill. The 21st Michigan's Maj. Seymour Chase of Lytle's brigade reported that the fire delivered by his Wolverines checked the Alabamians for a good twenty minutes. If so, Company A's enhanced firepower in the form of five-shot Colt revolving rifles had something to do with it. At some point the 21st's right "was forced back, and the whole compelled to retire to escape capture."[23] This left the 24th Wisconsin and 11th Indiana battery alone at the apex of Lytle's unraveling line, where they were subjected to a terrible crossfire.[24] Within minutes the 24th was also gone. The Hoosiers manning the guns never heard orders to retreat, and when the Rebels closed to within 200 feet the gunners fell back, leaving two of their 3-inch rifles in Confederate hands.[25]

Farther south, Bradley's brigade under Col. Nathan Walworth (angled sharply northeast to southwest) was also overwhelmed as Anderson's Mississippians closed in. The 22nd Illinois, Walworth's left regiment, suffered the most, exposed to fire on its front and from its left flank and rear when Lytle's line crumbled away. According to Walworth, the 22nd and 42nd Illinois regiments lost "nearly half their men."[26] Walworth ordered his three left-most regiments to retreat, hoping to disengage and fall back to the next set of hills to the west. With his right intact, however, Walworth's line retired in better shape than did Lytle's command. In fact, Walworth's right was not only intact, but meeting with considerable success. The 27th Illinois and Schueler's Battery G, 1st Missouri Artillery, which combined to deliver an effective fire against the left side of Anderson's line, were also strongly reinforced.[27]

Col. John T. Wilder's brigade of Spencer-armed mounted infantry, along with other assortments of Federals including the 39th Indiana and Sheridan's divisional provost detachment, arrived in time to stop Manigault in his tracks. This left Anderson's flank unsupported and spared the 27th Illinois a fate similar to that suffered by the rest of the brigade. As Walworth's other three regiments fell back, the 27th remained near the Widow Glenn's, gathering up small squads of men from the other units. This stand also allowed Battery G to withdraw its guns safely, escaping in a more orderly fashion than the rest of the division's artillery.

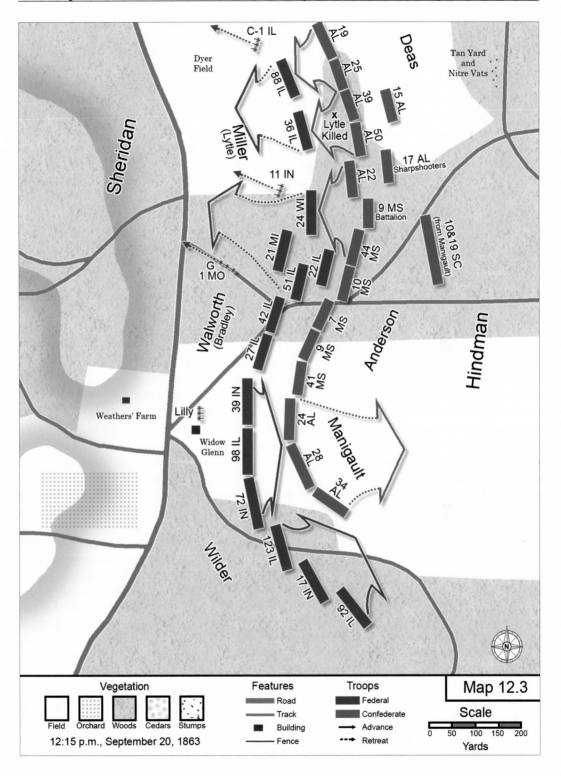

Map 12.3

Scale

0   50   100   150   200

Yards

12:15 p.m., September 20, 1863

Vegetation

Field   Orchard   Woods   Cedars   Stumps

Features

━━ Road
─── Track
■ Building
── Fence

Troops

■ Federal
■ Confederate
→ Advance
┅▶ Retreat

12.4: Sheridan Leaves the Field (12:30 p.m.)

For Patton Anderson and Zach Deas, the rout of Phil Sheridan's last line was the culmination of a glorious, if costly, charge that had begun well east of the LaFayette Road. Deas reported that his men, along with Anderson's troops, "captured several other pieces of artillery and scattered the enemy in our front so effectually that they never rallied or reformed again during the day on this part of the field."[28] In a letter home, Lt. William H. Moore of the 25th Alabama exulted, "we drove them with great slaughter, capturing over 900 prisoners and killing a Brig. Gen."[29] Anderson also claimed a large haul of captives, guns, and other trophies.

This success came at substantial cost. Over the course of the day, Anderson suffered 558 casualties, or thirty percent of his effective numbers. Deas' regiments suffered move heavily: 735 casualties, or a thirty-eight percent rate of attrition.[30] There was still fighting left to do, so not all of these losses were suffered here. However, the morning's work probably cost the two brigades between 800 and 1,000 men. The fighting winded the survivors and scattered them in every direction, with regiments and even brigades intermingled. Division leader Thomas Hindman called a halt to the pursuit short of the Dry Valley Road in order to reconstitute his command. Deas' men reformed on the reverse slope of the hill they fought so hard to possess; Anderson's men reorganized in the woods a little farther west.

The unfortunate William Lytle, meanwhile, remained on the field. The general had earned a measure of pre-war fame as a poet, and a number of Rebels claimed to have either helped him or later moved his body. Mindful of souvenir hunters, Hindman ordered a guard placed over the fallen Yankee and collected Lytle's side arms in order to send them back to his family in Cincinnati.[31] When Col. Oates and the 15th Alabama halted near the crest of the hill, Oates spotted Lytle and, in an effort to make him more comfortable, dragged the Federal under the shade of a tree.[32] He also ordered a company of the 15th to haul away one of the Union artillery pieces, staking the 15th regiment's claim for the honor of the capture.[33]

Hindman's decision to halt was reasonable, but it allowed large numbers of Sheridan's men to escape the collapsing front. Col. Silas Miller of the 36th Illinois, now in command of Lytle's brigade, set about rebuilding his command. Lt. Turnbull of the brigade staff collected about 100 men—some from every regiment in the brigade—and formed them into line. When Sheridan appeared, he praised Miller: "You are doing . . . good work. Have the men fall back to the next ridge and gather up every straggler."[34] Once there, some semblance of order appeared. Brigade commanders were found, regimental officers posted in specific locations, and the process of sorting out the survivors began. "My division . . . again formed on the ridge which overlooked the ground where this sanguinary contest had taken place," Sheridan reported, "the enemy manifesting no disposition to continue the engagement further."[35]

There remained the issue of what to do next. XIV Corps commander George Thomas, commanding the army's left wing, was still fighting. The logical course was to join him. The best route to do so was the Dry Valley Road, but it was menaced by Hindman's troops and cut off entirely by more Rebels farther north. By falling back behind Missionary Ridge, Sheridan reasoned, he should be able to find a way to circle around. By early that afternoon, after sweeping up all the loose Yankees he could find, Sheridan left the field.

After the battle, when accusations and recriminations flew thick and fast, a number of senior officers had their careers damaged or ended by departing the scene of the action before nightfall. Sheridan was not one of them, though rumors did swirl around him for a time. Sheridan, who could be difficult and even bullying, made his share of enemies in the army and this moment could have destroyed him. The fight his men put up went a long way toward dispelling any hints of dereliction, and to his credit, Sheridan made as good a fight as could be expected under very difficult circumstances.

Sheridan's were not the last Federals from this part of the field to abandon the fighting. In addition to the disorganization caused by his men's success, Hindman had other reasons for halting his advance. Anderson and Deas had met with success, but Manigault had not. In fact, his men were in full retreat and being chased by Wilder's Spencer-armed Federals.

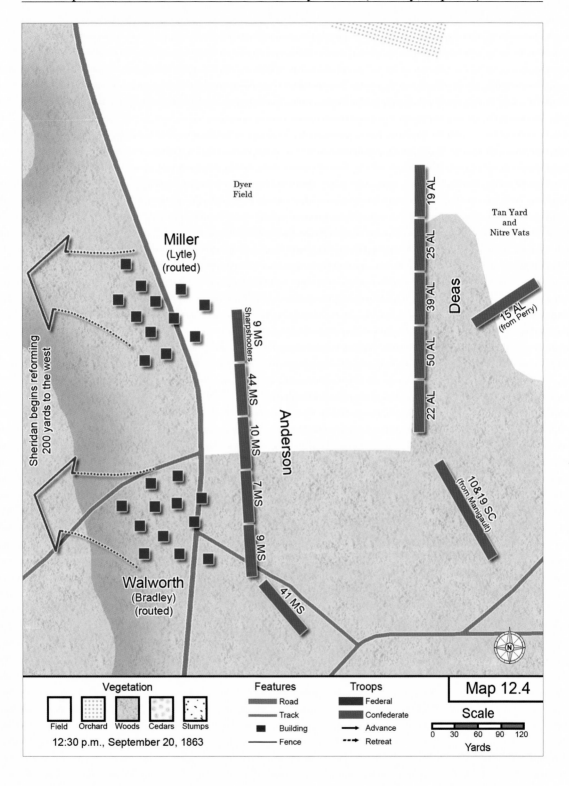

Dyer Field

Tan Yard and Nitre Vats

19 AL

25 AL

39 AL

Deas

50 AL

15 AL (from Perry)

22 AL

Miller
(Lytle)
(routed)

9 MS Sharpshooters

44 MS

Anderson

10 MS

7 MS

10&19 SC (from Manigault)

9 MS

Sheridan begins reforming 200 yards to the west

Walworth
(Bradley)
(routed)

41 MS

N

Vegetation

Field   Orchard   Woods   Cedars   Stumps

12:30 p.m., September 20, 1863

Features

━━━ Road
━━━ Track
■ Building
── Fence

Troops

■ Federal
■ Confederate
→ Advance
┅► Retreat

Map 12.4

Scale

0   30   60   90   120

Yards

12.5: Wilder Drives Manigault (12:30 p.m.)

A businessman before the war, Arthur Manigault had served in Mexico but had no formal training as a soldier. His first real combat was at Stone's River in late 1862, where as a colonel he led Patton Anderson's Brigade in a bloody attack that earned him a promotion to brigadier general. Chickamauga was his first battle at that rank with his own brigade.

At the start of the attack Manigault's front extended well beyond Carlin's Federal line, so he faced little opposition. Still, his progress was accomplished only with great difficulty. On the right, the combined 10th/19th South Carolina's advance was entirely through woods with limited visibility. His two center regiments had to cross nearly one mile of open ground (mostly cornfield) before striking any Federals, while the left-flank unit was at least partially in woods. With a front stretching about 700 yards, moving through such disparate terrain while maintaining alignment proved a challenge. Uncertainty compounded the problem because Manigault expected to encounter Yankees sooner than he did. However, he reported, "even their skirmish line retired, without discharging a rifle."[36] Soon enough the 10th/19th South Carolina separated from the brigade, veering to the right and coming into contact with Walworth's Federals.

The rest of Manigault's men (24th, 28th, and 34th Alabama) pressed on to the foot of the low ridge and the Widow Glenn cabin. Hours earlier it had served as Rosecrans' headquarters. Union troops had passed through here all morning. When Sheridan's last two brigades were sent north, it was left temporarily undefended. Had it remained so, Manigault might have swept behind Walworth's brigade, completing the destruction of Sheridan's division.

Fortunately for the Federals, when Alexander McCook ordered Sheridan away, he also sent word to Wilder to keep his brigade closed up to the XX Corps' right flank: "keep the line connected, and occupy the ground left vacant."[37] Manigault was ascending the eastern face of the rise when Wilder's brigade was dashing up the west side, the 92nd Illinois leading the way. The Federals crested the ridge to find the Rebels within 100 yards of their line. Wilder probably enjoyed a slight advantage in numbers, but his Spencer repeaters gave him a huge advantage in firepower. The 24th Alabama's Col. Ben F. Sawyer described the shock of the meeting: "they opened upon us with a continuous sheet of fire . . . we were in the very jaws of the monster . . . never before had I . . . seen such terrible execution."[38] As successive regiments came into action, the Yankee line extended beyond Manigault's left flank. To Lt. Joshua Callaway of the 28th Alabama, it suddenly seemed as if "all the enemies' fire was turned upon the 28th and 34th, which we didn't stand long. . . . Away we all went as fiercely as we had gone up."[39]

Col. Thomas J. Harrison's 39th Indiana Mounted Infantry also joined in. Technically, Harrison belonged to Willich's brigade of Brig. Gen. Richard Johnson's division. That spring, however, Harrison's Hoosiers were also detached, mounted, and equipped with Spencers. The 39th was hovering on Walworth's flank when Wilder appeared, and Harrison carried his men forward to join the 92nd's attack. "Neither party," Harrison reported, "discovered the other until within 30 paces. The struggle was brief, but desperate . . . [then] the enemy gave way, running in disorder."[40]

The sheer firepower blew holes through Manigault's lines and sent his Alabamians tumbling backward—just as Anderson and Deas were finishing off Lytle and most of Walworth. Manigault's men, with Wilder's troops following on their heels, were driven back all the way to the LaFayette Road. There, Manigault called for support from corps leader Maj. Gen. Simon Buckner, who was somewhere to his rear. Col. Robert Trigg's Brigade of William Preston's Division came forward in response, but did not become engaged. By this time the damage had been inflicted. Gens. Longstreet, Buckner, and Hindman expressed concern at this surprising Union counterstroke, delivered so masterfully at the moment of apparent Confederate triumph.

Manigault's problems highlighted some of the difficulties that plagued Hindman's Division. His was not a harmonious command. Hindman was unpopular with his brigadiers, had been sick for the last few days, and did not exert much personal control over this action. At least two of Hindman's brigadiers (Manigault and Anderson) had trouble handling their large brigades. Manigault's line advanced unopposed across largely open ground, and yet the 10th/19th lost contact with the Alabama regiments.

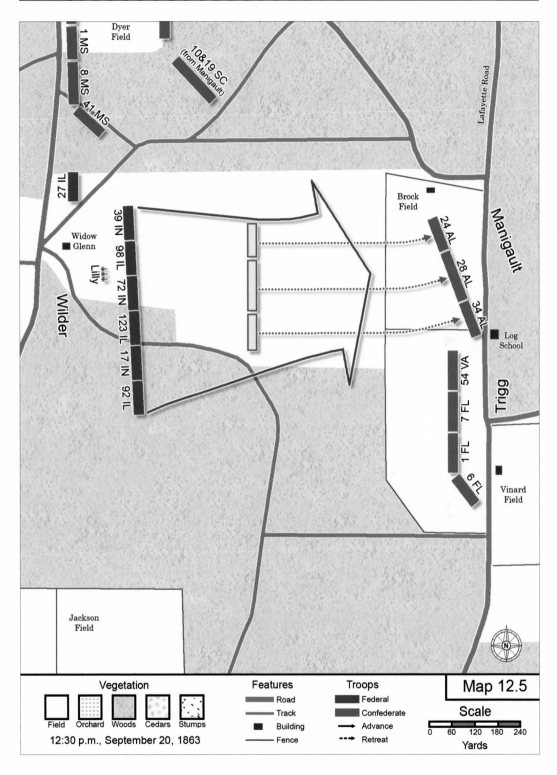

Map 12.5

Vegetation

Field   Orchard   Woods   Cedars   Stumps

12:30 p.m., September 20, 1863

Features

Road
Track
Building
Fence

Troops

Federal
Confederate
Advance
Retreat

Scale

0   60   120   180   240

Yards

12.6: Wilder's Proposed Counterattack (12:45 p.m.)

John Wilder had complete confidence in his brigade. With its weapons and training, he believed his "five lines of Spencer Rifles could break any line on earth."[41] The enemy in his front had fled. The question facing the colonel was obvious: what was coming next?

Wilder knew that Phil Sheridan's routed division was retreating behind Missionary Ridge. Gens. McCook and Rosecrans were nowhere to be found. Bodies of Confederates in significant strength were visible to the north. The distant noise, dust, and smoke from that direction suggested that at least some Yankees—Thomas and the XIV Corps, no doubt—remained on the field and were still fighting. From Wilder's perspective, he had two choices: fall back and cover what he could of the retreat, or attack "with his brigade through the center of the Confederate column, taking their regiments in flank, and pushing on to Thomas on the left." When asked for his opinion, Col. Smith Atkins of the 92nd Illinois replied that the latter option "was a desperate and bold movement . . . [but] might entirely change the result of the battle."[42]

According to Wilder, he arranged his brigade in a hollow square with Eli Lilly's artillery in the middle for an all-around defense should such a thing become necessary. Just how far this tactical scheme progressed from theory to reality is difficult to say. Many years later, Wilder insisted that he arrayed the brigade in this manner, but no contemporary report or private account mentions it.[43]

If the square formation was not utilized, one reason may have been the sudden appearance of a civilian traveling with the army. Assistant Secretary of War Charles A. Dana had been assigned to the army during the campaign as the War Department's representative (some would say "spy") to Rosecrans' headquarters. Now, in the wake of the rout, Dana was adrift on the field. Wilder later offered multiple accounts of this meeting, each more elaborate in detail but differing little in the basics. In his battle report, Wilder wrote that Dana told him "it was a worse rout than Bull Run," "Rosecrans [was] probably killed or captured," and that he "strongly advised me to fall back."[44] In later accounts, Wilder

portrayed Dana as more panicked, frantically ordering Wilder to escort him back to Chattanooga and suggesting that the distant firing was the Rebels finishing off Thomas. Dana had no authority to order soldiers do to anything on a battlefield, but Wilder wasn't sure of that.[45] Dana's memoirs offered a calmer view, including a carefully phrased explicit denial of issuing any orders to any officer. Instead, the assistant secretary claimed he advised Wilder to make for Thomas, and then rode for Chattanooga on his own.[46] In that last particular, at least, Dana was incorrect: Wilder provided him an escort to make sure he got through safely.

Instead of attacking, however, Wilder pulled back, first to the vicinity of the Widow Glenn's, and then into the foothills of Missionary Ridge west of the Dry Valley Road. The 39th Indiana joined with him there, as did some 600 of Sheridan's troops who coalesced around Col. Miles and the 27th Illinois.[47] Thus augmented, Wilder's men patrolled this area for several hours, collecting stragglers, wagons, and ambulances while looking for a way to avoid the Rebels. Late in the day, a staff officer brought word that Sheridan was falling back on Rossville and that Wilder should move his command farther west into the Chattanooga Valley.[48]

Could Wilder's plan to attack "through the center of the Confederate column" have succeeded? We know little about the route he might have taken, other than that he would have presumably ridden northeast toward the LaFayette Road, and then north to Kelly Field. This route would have moved Wilder behind Hindman's Confederate division. Bushrod Johnson's men were by this time far to the northwest. However, Longstreet still had Maj. Gen. William Preston's Confederate division in reserve, available to deal with just this kind of crisis. Elements of Law's Division were also available, regrouping in the vicinity of Brotherton Field.

In any case, Wilder never made his proposed attack. It would have been a desperate venture, and at worst would have cost the Army of the Cumberland an outstanding combat brigade for little or no gain.

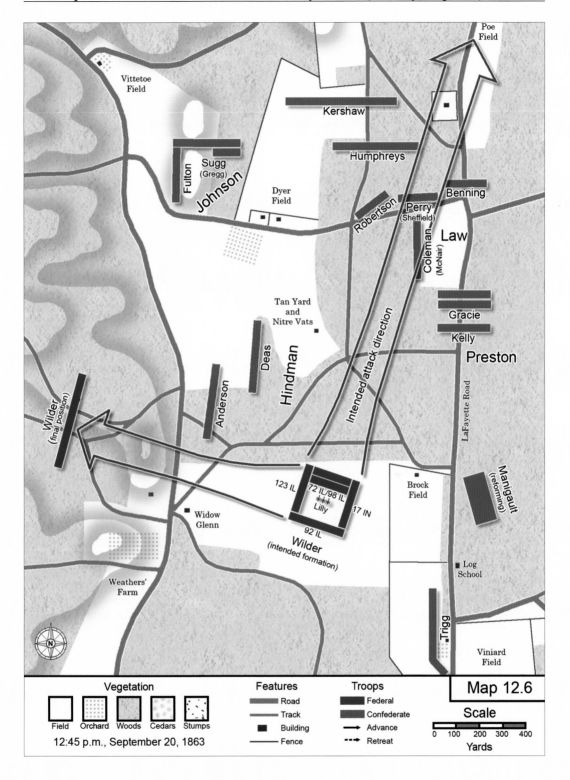

Poe
Field

Vittetoe
Field

Kershaw

Sugg
(Gregg)

Humphreys

Fulton

Johnson

Dyer
Field

Robertson

Perry
(Sheffield)

Benning

Coleman
(McNair)

Law

Gracie

Kelly

Tan Yard
and
Nitre Vats

Preston

Deas

Hindman

Intended attack direction

Anderson

LaFayette Road

Wilder
(final position)

Manigault
(reforming)

123 IL

72 IL/98 IL
Lilly

17 IN

Brock
Field

92 IL

Wilder
(intended formation)

Widow
Glenn

Weathers'
Farm

Log
School

Trigg

Viniard
Field

N

Vegetation

Field   Orchard   Woods   Cedars   Stumps

12:45 p.m., September 20, 1863

Features

— Road
— Track
■ Building
— Fence

Troops

Federal
Confederate
→ Advance
--▶ Retreat

Map 12.6

Scale

0   100   200   300   400
Yards

Map Set 13: Exploiting the Breakthrough: Clearing Dyer Field

(Midday, September 20)

13.1: Johnson Emerges into Dyer Field (11:45 a.m.)

Just before noon, Brig. Gen. Bushrod Johnson's three brigades (Fulton, Sugg, and McNair) were poised in the timber framing the eastern edge of the most significant stretch of cleared land on the battlefield. Dyer Field was a patchwork of various fields, interspersed with a couple of open woodlots and orchards. Maj. Gen. William Rosecrans chose the rising ground just southwest of the Dyer orchard as the site of his field headquarters because it offered the best view of the battle and was centrally located behind his lines. Now, just a few hundred yards distant, the Union commander could see long ranks of Confederates edging into the open.

In passing through and over the initial Union positions, Johnson's brigades had merged into a single battle line. Col. John Fulton's regiments angled slightly south after his attack on Brig. Gen. Jefferson C. Davis' Federal division line, while Col. Cyrus Sugg's advance left his men holding the division's center. After overrunning Col. John Connell's Federal brigade, Brig. Gen. Evander McNair's command caught up and resumed the advance on the division's right. A few Federal batteries crowned the high ground in the distance, while retreating Yankees—some organized, most not—filled the fields.

"The scene now presented was unspeakably grand," Johnson wrote. "The resolute and impetuous charge, the rush of our heavy columns sweeping out from the shadow and gloom of the forest into the open fields flooded with sunlight," he continued, "the glitter of arms, the onward dash of artillery and mounted men, the retreat of the foe . . . made up a battle scene of unsurpassed grandeur."[1] The 25th Tennessee's Lt. Col. R. B. Snowden echoed this fulsome rhetoric, describing it as the "most magnificent scene of the day, brigade after brigade emerging *en echelon* . . . and sweeping across [the field] with a wildness of enthusiasm."[2]

Rebel eyes were drawn to sixteen Federal guns lining the crest of the ridge opposite

Johnson's center. Heeding Brig. Gen. Thomas Wood's earlier warning against taking artillery into the woods, Maj. John Mendenhall held his pieces back until Maj. Gen. Thomas Crittenden directed him to gather whatever guns he could and establish a reserve position.[3] Mendenhall appropriated Brig. Gen. Horatio Van Cleve's three batteries, drawn up where they could support the division. As the morning fight progressed, these gunners watched Van Cleve's men shifting about until by midday there was no longer any infantry to support.[4]

John Mendenhall was a skilled artillerist. His most notable moment came at Stone's River, where in command of several Union batteries he contributed to the repulse—some would say the slaughter—of John Breckinridge's Division on January 2, 1863. Because the Army of the Cumberland still largely relied on outdated artillery doctrine calling for the dispersal of batteries to support individual infantry brigades, rather than massing them as larger formations, opportunities to repeat his Stone's River exploit were rare. Now Mendenhall controlled a similar grand battery, though under much different circumstances.

When the breakthrough occurred, routed Federals seemed to be everywhere. Hundreds and perhaps thousands streamed across Mendenhall's front toward the high ground of Horseshoe Ridge or directly through his position. Crittenden, who was caught up in the flood through the guns, tried to rally the mob, and was joined in the task by a desperate Van Cleve.[5]

Not every Federal unit had lost cohesion. Two batteries joined Mendenhall at this time. Capt. George Estep's 8th Indiana battery of Wood's division, after an almost miraculous escape from the grasp of Fulton's Tennesseans, added his six pieces to the southern end of the commanding gun line.[6] A more unusual arrival was Lt. Harry C. Cushing's Battery H, 4th U.S. Regulars. Cushing had expended his ammunition during the vigorous engagement in Kelly Field earlier that morning. When Thomas ordered him to find more, Cushing had to range much farther afield then either officer expected. Now, hours later, he found himself part of Mendenhall's patchwork gun line.[7]

Without any hope of finding their brigade commander or the balance of their comrades, the 26th Ohio and 13th Michigan regiments offered Mendenhall whatever meager infantry support they could provide.[8] Neither regiment numbered more than 100 or so bayonets.

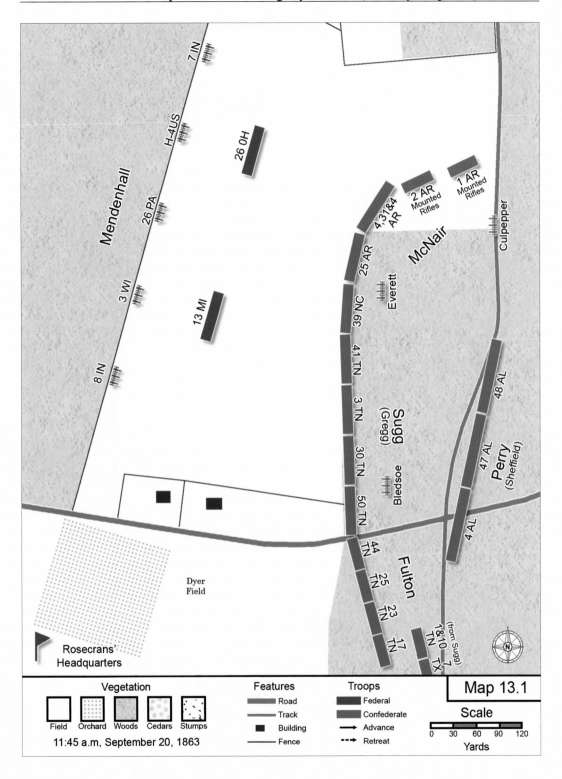

Dyer
Field

Rosecrans'
Headquarters

Vegetation

Field   Orchard   Woods   Cedars   Stumps

11:45 a.m, September 20, 1863

Features

Road
Track
Building
Fence

Troops

Federal
Confederate
Advance
Retreat

Map 13.1

Scale

0   30   60   90   120
Yards

13.2: Mendenhall's Line (Noon)

In keeping with Maj. Gen. John B. Hood's final directive, Bushrod Johnson decided that Maj. Mendenhall's array of guns would be his next objective.

Johnson, an Ohio Quaker who graduated from West Point in 1840 (with the Army of the Cumberland's XIV Corps leader George Thomas) and threw his lot in with the Confederacy two decades later, ordered Fulton's regiments to move south of the Dyer Road and turn west until they reached the Dyer peach orchard. From there, they would pivot north into the trees behind the artillery line.[9] Sugg's four regiments (the 1st/10th Tennessee and 7th Texas were still operating with Fulton) would make the same move on a shorter arc, "leaving [the Union artillery] on my right."[10] McNair's men would once again have the toughest task: launching a frontal attack up the slope to hold the enemy's attention. A trio of guns from Lt. William S. Everett's Company E, 9th Georgia Artillery Battalion, attempted to do their part, unlimbering at the edge of the tree line and opening fire. Three Rebel pieces, however, were no match for twenty-six Union guns. A member of the 3rd Wisconsin recalled that "our battery was trained on them so speedily and severely" that after getting only one gun unlimbered, the Rebels were soon "rushed back to the cover of the woods."[11] Union shells found other targets as well, pummeling McNair's men and wounding the brigadier severely enough for him to leave the field. Col. David Coleman of the 39th North Carolina assumed brigade command.[12]

Unbeknownst to Johnson, his line was about to be reinforced. Col. William Perry led the remaining three regiments of Brig. Gen. Evander Law's former brigade into the fight, forming on McNair's (now Coleman's) right flank. As noted previously (Map 11.5), Perry had already left the 44th Alabama back in the trees near Poe Field, while Col. William Oates and his 15th Alabama drifted far enough south to bedevil Zach Deas' Southern brigade (Map 12.2). The rest of the brigade, however, was ready for action. Perry was equally unaware of Johnson's plan, but when he spotted the Federal guns opening up, he decided that "the boldest policy was the safest" and

ordered a charge.[13] With his appearance, the field was alive with charging Rebel infantry.

Rosecrans, his headquarters, and his escort were directly in Fulton's path. Lt. William Moody reached Rosecrans about this time, delivering the now-fruitless request from Maj. Gen. James Negley for reinforcements. "I could see Gen. Rosecrans . . . endeavoring to check the avalanche of panic-stricken men," recalled Moody.[14] Shortly thereafter, Rosecrans was forced from the field.

With the enemy heading toward them, Mendenhall and his gunners knew there was little hope of saving their guns, but they continued firing anyway. Coleman's men faced a withering storm of shellfire, faltered, and finally scattered to take cover in the fence lines and trees.[15] The handful of blue infantry facing them also put up an impressive fight. Maj. Willard Eaton of the 13th Michigan estimated that he and his men held on for nearly fifteen minutes, a remarkable effort considering the odds.[16] Both the 26th Ohio and men of the 13th were doomed when Coleman's men began working their way along a fence separating the two regiments, threatening to flank both simultaneously. At the same time, Sugg's regiments had turned the corner on the gun line's flank.

The first to be overrun was the 8th Indiana battery. One of the gunners, P. I. Hubbard, recalled that the right-hand piece was still firing double canister into the faces of the oncoming Confederates while the left section was being smothered by enemy troops. In their haste to get away, the drivers cut horses loose from the limbers.[17] The loss of the Hoosier guns convinced the infantry of the 13th Michigan to break to the rear, followed by the Buckeyes of the 26th. Remarkably, both knots of infantry escaped with their colors, if not much else. Cushing's guns of Battery H managed to slip away in slightly better shape, but next to them the 3rd Wisconsin battery suffered severely. When Badger William Plackett wheeled up his limber, he saw "horses rearing and plunging, seemingly trying to extricate themselves from their fallen mates. Nothing short of a miracle could save the battery."[18]

No miracles were forthcoming. When Perry's Alabamians reached the line from the front, the last door of escape slammed shut. All told, fourteen of Mendenhall's guns were captured here, and every battery lost enough men and materiel to be considered completely wrecked.[19]

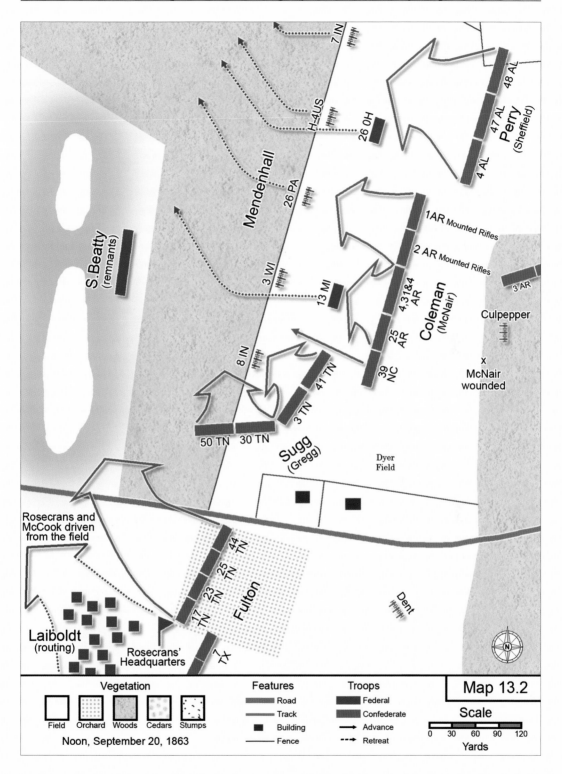

7 IN

48 AL

47 AL

Perry
(Sheffield)

4 AL

H 4 US

26 OH

Mendenhall

26 PA

1 AR Mounted Rifles

2 AR Mounted Rifles

S. Beatty
(remnants)

3 WI

3 AR

13 MI

4, 31 & 4
AR

Coleman
(McNair)

Culpepper

25
AR

x
McNair
wounded

8 IN

41 TN

39
NC

3 TN

Dyer
Field

50 TN   30 TN

Sugg
(Gregg)

Rosecrans and
McCook driven
from the field

44
TN

25
TN

Fulton

23
TN

Dent

Laiboldt
(routing)

Rosecrans'
Headquarters

17
TN

TX

Vegetation

| Field | Orchard | Woods | Cedars | Stumps |

Noon, September 20, 1863

Features

Road
Track
■ Building
—— Fence

Troops

Federal
Confederate
→ Advance
--→ Retreat

Map 13.2

Scale

0   30   60   90   120

Yards

13.3: Confederate Confusion in Dyer Field (12:15 p.m.)

To the south and west of Dyer Field, Federal resistance was either crumbling or already completely dispersed. The fight was still raging between Thomas Hindman's Division and Phil Sheridan's men, but by this time Hindman was gaining the upper hand. Mendenhall's gun line—the last Union effort to stem the tide flowing west—had failed. Only to the north (Thomas' XIV Corps) was there still a coherent Union defense.

By this time the overall cohesion of the Confederate attack was beginning to show signs of strain. Bushrod Johnson pressed west of the Dyer farm buildings to the next ridge with Cols. Fulton and Sugg, harassing the retreating Federals at every opportunity. McNair's (Coleman's) regiments, however, moved in the opposite direction, falling back to the Glenn-Kelly Road considerably disordered, their ammunition exhausted.[20] Johnson's other brigades also had ammunition problems, but among the detritus of the Union rout found wagons full of Federal cartridges that solved the problem.

More serious was the lack of control in the division led by Law. Originally comprising James Longstreet's third and fourth lines, Law's three brigades were now pulling in different directions. Brig. Gen. Henry Benning had been all but routed in Poe Field and would need some time to reform. For all practical purposes, his brigade was incapable of serious combat for the rest of the day. Col. William Perry's Alabama brigade was badly fragmented. The 15th and 44th Alabama were, for all practical purposes, adrift and lost for the day. Low on ammunition, Perry's remaining units (the 4th, 47th and 48th Alabama) stopped amid John Mendenhall's captured guns. Perry was uncertain of what to do next. He wanted to continue the attack, but not with just his own weakened regiments.[21]

Law's third brigade under Brig. Gen. Jerome Robertson was attacking northward without support on the west side of the LaFayette Road toward Federals gathered on Snodgrass Hill. The brigadier had sent repeated requests for help to the units on his right and left, to no avail.[22] The problems in Benning's command explain why

the Texans received no help from their right. Perry never mentioned appeals from Robertson for support, which would have come at exactly the time he was looking to renew his own advance. The officer who should have been coordinating these efforts was Law. But for reasons unknown, the veteran brigadier was nowhere to be found. None of the brigade commanders (Perry, Benning, or Robertson) mention seeing him at this stage of the fighting. Even Law's own battle report is silent about his activities during this period.

The fifth line of Longstreet's assault column was also in need of direction. Brig. Gen. Joe Kershaw's command, trailed by Brig. Gen. Ben Humphreys' Mississippi brigade, entered Dyer Field from the east but were wheeling north in response to Robertson's combat. Hood (who had direct charge of all these troops) was trying to coordinate the actions of his several divisions, but focused primarily on meeting threats against his right. Longstreet was with Maj. Gen. Simon Buckner near the Brotherton house trying to find support (Hindman's men) for Johnson's advance.

Off to the north, Snodgrass Hill still held organized bodies of Federals. Col. William Sirwell's brigade (Negley's division), as well as a number of artillery batteries, occupied the high ground, as did fragments from Brig. Gen. John Brannan's division and other Federals coalescing around them. On the knoll at the north end of Dyer Field, Capt. Frederick Schultz's Battery M, 1st Ohio Light Artillery, dispatched there earlier to protect Negley's flank, offered a rallying point.[23] Before too long Col. George Buell, the 58th Indiana, and members from the 100th Illinois gathered there after escaping the disaster in Brotherton Field.[24] The remnant of Capt. Josiah Church's Battery D, 1st Michigan, also reached Schultz's position to add his three surviving guns to its defense.[25] This scratch force was Robertson's target, and his Texans were closing fast.

The Confederates were unaware they were participating in a race that would have important consequences. Col. Charles Harker's brigade (Thomas Wood's division) had been halted a little more than half a mile to the north while Wood searched for Maj. Gen. Joseph Reynolds. When Wood was alerted about the crisis to the south, he led Harker's regiments back the way they had come in an effort to stave off complete disaster.

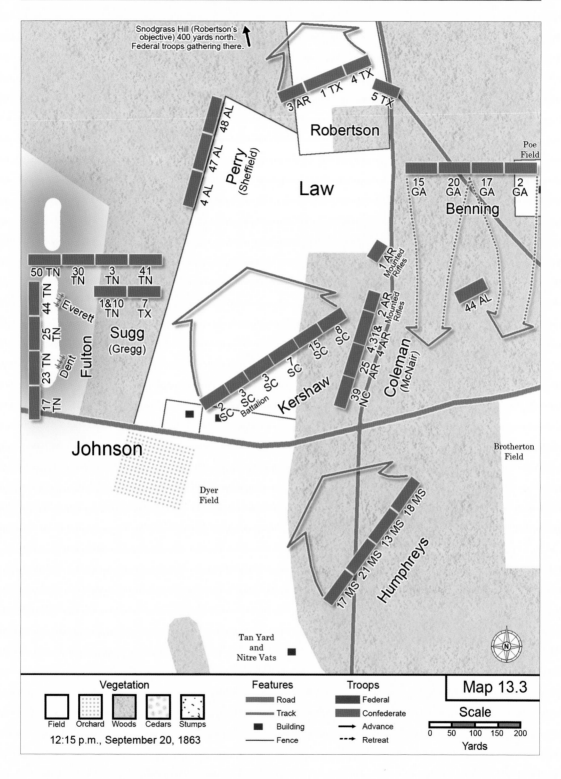

Snodgrass Hill (Robertson's objective) 400 yards north. Federal troops gathering there.

Robertson

3 AR   1 TX   4 TX   5 TX

Poe Field

48 AL   47 AL   4 AL

Perry (Sheffield)

Law

15 GA   20 GA   17 GA   2 GA

Benning

50 TN   30 TN   3 TN   41 TN

44 TN   Everett

1&10 TN   7 TX

25 TN   Sugg (Gregg)

23 TN   Dent   Fulton

17 TN

1 AR Mounted Rifles

2 AR Mounted Rifles

44 AL

8 SC   15 SC   7 SC   3 SC   3 SC Battalion   2 SC

Kershaw

4,31& 4 AR   25 AR   39 NC   Coleman (McNair)

Johnson

Brotherton Field

Dyer Field

18 MS   13 MS   21 MS   17 MS

Humphreys

Tan Yard and Nitre Vats

Vegetation

Field   Orchard   Woods   Cedars   Stumps

12:15 p.m., September 20, 1863

Features

Road
Track
■ Building
Fence

Troops

Federal
Confederate
→ Advance
--→ Retreat

Map 13.3

Scale

0   50   100   150   200

Yards

N

13.4: Robertson Charges the Knoll
(12:15 p.m.)

Jerome Robertson's Texas Brigade was beginning to experience problems. Capt. J. S. Cleveland's momentary retreat with the 5th Texas had pulled it out of line on the brigade's right (Map 11.7). After the earlier change of front to the north, Col. Van Manning of the 3rd Arkansas (on Robertson's left flank) observed "the deranged condition of the line" as it moved forward.[26] During a momentary halt at the fence line marking the field's southern border, Sgt. Valerius Giles of the 4th Texas remembered the intense enemy fire. "The Federal batteries beyond the old field were making our position a veritable hell on earth," he recorded.[27]

Angling to the northwest, Robertson's men crossed the field directly toward the Federals on the knoll with the 5th Texas lagging some distance behind the right rear. Cleveland's Texans were hurrying to catch up when the 10th and 74th Indiana regiments, still lingering in the woods framing the eastern edge of the field, caught sight of the Rebels. The woods here were open, and despite being inside the tree line, the Hoosiers could see well enough to open fire on Cleveland's command. The 5th wheeled to the right and answered with a volley, which seemed to disperse the Hoosiers.[28] In reality, the Yankees were retreating anyway, and that was enough for Cleveland. Leaving a company deployed as skirmishers to prevent similar attacks, he ordered the rest of the 5th Texas to hurry northwest to join the advancing brigade line.

The ferocity of the Federal defensive fire notwithstanding, victory appeared to be within Robertson's grasp. With a sudden commotion atop the knoll, Capt. Schultz's battery limbered and began to roll, ordered away at the worst possible minute by one of Negley's aides.[29] Exultant, the watching Rebels were sure they had won. Robertson reported that his brigade had "advanced to the top of the hill and drove the enemy from it."[30] Capt. James T. Hunter, leading Giles and the rest of the 4th Texas, concurred. "On our gaining the height," he wrote, "they deserted it."[31]

Just as quickly, fortunes reversed. Gen. Brannan rode into the Union ranks. He needed time to organize his men for a defense of the larger ridge just to the north. Schultz's guns had to stay put. The crews unlimbered and returned to their work. Without additional support, Brannan's order would have provided Robertson's men with several more artillery trophies to add to the Army of Tennessee's laurels. At this time, however, the Texans began taking fire from several directions—much of it, they were convinced, from friendly muzzles. Issued new uniforms on the long trip from Virginia, the Texans wore coats that "appeared more blue than gray."[32] Moreover, thought Lawrence Daffan in the 4th Texas, Bragg's men were more rag-a-muffin than the Eastern troops, and "had never seen a well-uniformed Confederate Regiment before."[33] Friendly or not, the fire was severe enough to convince Manning on the brigade's left that he was being flanked.[34]

Some of the fire almost certainly was of a friendly variety, but not all of it. On Robertson's left were 539 men of the 21st Ohio, who had stumbled on the action more by chance than design. The Buckeyes had been loaned to Brannan earlier by Negley, and had moved from point to point on Horseshoe Ridge as needed. They now moved ahead and down the ridge to a flat area, engaging the advancing Rebels as they did so.[35] The 21st didn't stay there long, and no other Yankees noted their presence, but their contribution came at just the right moment. "Before I could stop it," Robertson reported, "my line had been thrown into confusion, and I found it necessary to fall back to reform."[36] Seeing his beloved Texas Brigade in distress, Hood rode among the men to help Robertson put things right.

Yet another line of Yankees was about to add their weight to the struggle. While still in column, Thomas Wood had ordered Harker to change front to the rear of his brigade and deploy his four regiments in a single line. Now, Harker's Ohio and Kentucky troops were working their way south astride the Glenn-Kelly Road.[37] Peering through the trees, Wood spotted Robertson's line attempting to rally about 500 yards to the south, and ordered Harker forward.

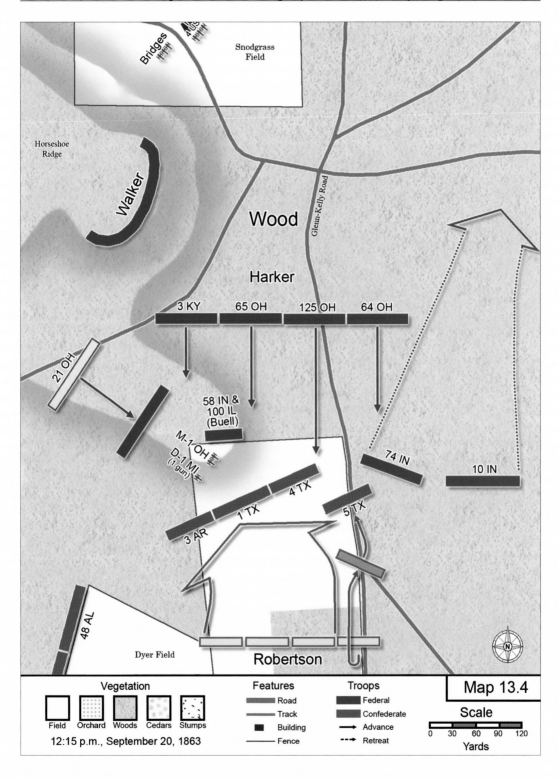

Snodgrass
Field

Bridges

Horseshoe
Ridge

Walker

Wood

Glenn-Kelly Road

Harker

3 KY   65 OH   125 OH   64 OH

21 OH

58 IN &
100 IL
(Buell)

M-1 OH
D-1 MI
(1 gun)

74 IN

10 IN

4 TX

1 TX

5 TX

3 AR

48 AL

Dyer Field

Robertson

Vegetation

Field   Orchard   Woods   Cedars   Stumps

12:15 p.m., September 20, 1863

Features

Road
Track
Building
Fence

Troops

Federal
Confederate
Advance
Retreat

Map 13.4

Scale

0   30   60   90   120

Yards

13.5: Harker Routs the Texas Brigade
(12:30 p.m.)

Harker's immediate objective was a fence line about midway between his men and Robertson's Texans. In order to win the footrace, Wood turned to Col. Emerson Opdyke, commander of the 125th Ohio, and ordered him to charge without waiting to dress ranks or work the chain of command. "The steel rattled in answer," Opdyke proudly wrote his wife. "[My horse] Barney galloped forward, and the 125th came after, with a yell that rose above the din of battle."[38] Reaching the fence, the Buckeyes pulled it down into a rude breastwork and returned fire. The rest of the brigade hurried after, coming into line to the right and left of the 125th. Harker's sudden appearance, wrote Wood, "seemed to take the enemy by surprise and disconcert his movements."[39]

Robertson's veterans were not so easily seen off. They stubbornly stood mid-field, trading fire with Harker's Yankees. Their disorder, however, suggested to Wood that the moment was ripe for a heavier counterattack. This time Wood ordered both the 64th and 125th Ohio regiments forward, employing the same unorthodox "Advance, Firing" tactic invented by Gen. August Willich and used so effectively by his brigade the day before against Maj. Gen. Benjamin Cheatham's men. Curiously, Willich's and Harker's brigades were not in the same division, or even in the same corps, but they seemed to be the only two commands in the army who knew the drill, let alone used it in combat. According to Capt. Charles T. Clark of the 125th, the Ohioans used it here with snap and precision, and to great and deadly effect.[40]

The fiery attack devastated the Texans. Sgt. Giles found North Dyer Field "the meanest, most unsatisfactory place I struck during the whole war." Around him, "men [were] staggering and stumbling to the rear covered in blood, some swearing and some calling on God to protect them in their blind endeavor to find shelter from the storm of iron hail, [it] made me feel like the world was coming to an end then and there."[41] Whatever semblance of order they had preserved was lost, and Robertson watched as his command melted away before his eyes.

Watching with pleasure as his victorious Buckeyes halted in a small knot of trees projecting into the field, Wood christened them with a nickname that stuck: "See the Tigers go in!"[42] Catching up to Adj. E. G. Whitesides of the 125th Ohio, Wood effused, "That was a glorious charge and if I live it shall be made official and go into history!"[43] The 125th and 64th regiments halted in the woodlot, leaving the other two regiments behind them along the northern boundary fence. From there, Capt. Clark had a splendid view as he watched one of the fateful moments of the battle unfold—had he but known it.

John Hood had just returned from redirecting Joseph Kershaw's South Carolinians to move to Robertson's support when he witnessed his old brigade streaming back in disorder. Hood rode amongst the Texans in an attempt to rally them and renew the attack. Hood and Robertson had just met at the southern end of the field when Hood was struck by a bullet in the upper right thigh that broke his femur. The general fell from the saddle into the arms of men he had led since he was a colonel. Texans of a superstitious bent noted that Hood was not riding "Jeff Davis," his favorite roan horse. At Gettysburg, Hood had been forced to ride another mount because Jeff was lame, and there he lost the use of an arm (paralyzed for the balance of his life from a shell fragment). Jeff Davis had been wounded the previous day, and now Hood would lose his leg to amputation.[44] With Hood down, the already chaotic Confederate command situation became much worse, and most of his brigades were left to fend for themselves.

It took some time before Longstreet learned of Hood's fall. As the attack commenced, Longstreet, accompanied by Simon Buckner, rode south to send in Hindman's Division, and probably watched some of the progress of his attack. Thereafter, Longstreet rode north along the LaFayette Road to Brotherton Field. He was there when Benning's men retreated from Poe Field (Map 11.7) sometime after noon. From there, after reassuring Benning, Longstreet rode west in Johnson's wake, witnessing the aftermath of the capture of John Mendenhall's Federal guns. While he was not far from where Hood fell, Longstreet's attention was focused more on pushing his men west than worrying about his right flank. That was about to change.

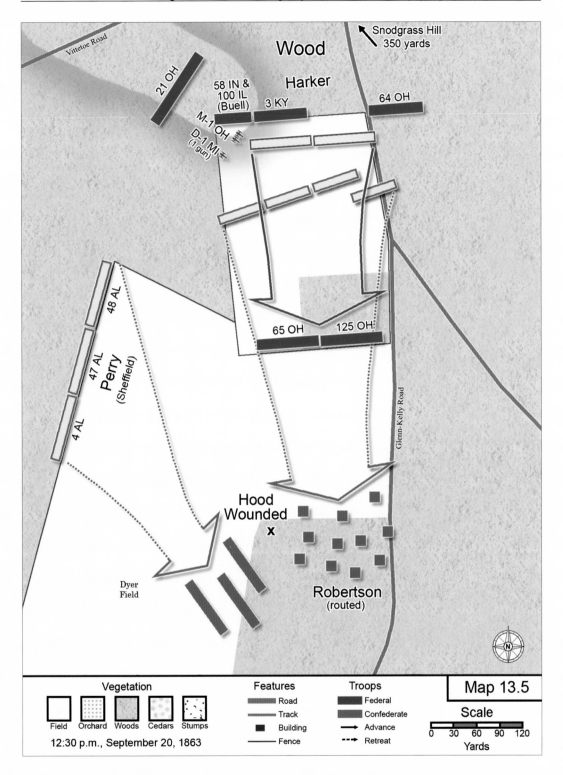

Vittetoe Road

Wood

Snodgrass Hill
350 yards

21 OH

Harker

58 IN &
100 IL
(Buell)

3 KY

64 OH

M-1 OH

D-1 MI
(1 gun)

48 AL

47 AL
Perry
(Sheffield)

65 OH   125 OH

4 AL

Glenn-Kelly Road

Hood
Wounded
X

Dyer
Field

Robertson
(routed)

N

Vegetation

Field   Orchard   Woods   Cedars   Stumps

12:30 p.m., September 20, 1863

Features

— Road
— Track
■ Building
— Fence

Troops

■ Federal
■ Confederate
→ Advance
---▶ Retreat

Map 13.5

Scale

0   30   60   90   120
Yards

13.6: Negley Retreats (12:30 p.m.)

Circumstances were little better on the Union side of the fighting. While men from Tom Wood's division were routing Robertson's Texas Brigade, another Federal commander was undergoing a crisis of confidence.

Maj. Gen. James Negley had already experienced a trying morning. His brigades had been ordered off to various points without him, and he was left with only vague orders to collect stray artillery and form a reserve, supported by his last brigade under Col. William Sirwell. The mass confusion brought about by the sudden Confederate breakthrough followed, including the dreadful spectacle of thousands of men flying rearward without any semblance of order or control. All this would have been a shock to the system of a healthy man, which James Negley was not. For much of the week before the battle He had been prostrate with diarrhea and was barely able to sit a saddle. By the time the battle began he was ambulatory, working on very little sleep, and completely exhausted.

By midday, the fragments of troops that joined Negley brought only bad news. The battered remnants of John Beatty's brigade only added to the gloomy picture.[45] The aides sent to Rosecrans returned with the horrifying news that the army commander had no troops to spare, and had been forced off the field himself. Brannan's arrival brought news of that division's collapse. When Brannan asked for the loan of the 21st Ohio Negley obliged, shifting the Buckeyes to the right where they played a hand in repulsing Robertson's Texans. (Negley was unaware of affairs on that front.)

Perhaps the final stroke was the appearance about noon of "a strong column of the enemy, who pressed forward rapidly between me and the troops on my left."[46] Frightened stragglers from Beatty's brigade, probably from either the 42nd or 88th Indiana regiments, confirmed this sighting when they reported that "they had counted 7 stands of [enemy] colors across the road in that direction."[47] To Negley, it now seemed that Thomas' XIV Corps line must have given way as well, and he was about to be outflanked from both sides. In reality, those Rebels were almost certainly men from that part of Daniel Govan's Brigade who found they

could not retreat to the east, and so sought a more roundabout way back to their own lines (Map 10.9.) Their appearance at just the wrong time, however, added greatly to Negley's fears.

A lingering mystery of the fighting on September 20 is why Negley failed to contact Thomas. In his after-action report and during a subsequent court of inquiry, Negley made much of his efforts to reach Rosecrans. He did not say much about trying to find Thomas, reporting only that he "was unable to communicate" with the XIV Corps commander.[48] Unlike with Rosecrans, however, there were no Rebels between Negley and Thomas. In fact, Thomas was only a few hundred yards distant, watching Wood's men drive back Robertson. Thomas, various staff officers, and even entire brigades of infantry would come and go between Kelly Field and Horseshoe Ridge that afternoon, largely unmolested by the enemy. There is no obvious reason why Negley could not have done the same.

Whatever the reasons, Negley believed he was on his own and ordered his command to retreat to Rossville, leaving the field via back roads and farm trails on his way to McFarland's Gap. Along the way he met Brannan. Each man carried away a different impression of that encounter. According to Brannan, Negley promised to extend the Union right atop Horseshoe Ridge, and he became enraged and embittered when he discovered that Negley had left.[49] According to Negley, Brannan was only confirming the loan of the 21st Ohio, and he dismissed the idea of the pledge to extend the Union right as "incredible."[50]

Although the troops who left did so in good order and without panic, the withdrawal itself was conducted haphazardly, with some units being ordered away, some following of their own volition, and others not realizing Negley had gone until they discovered they were alone. Negley took with him three full regiments of Sirwell's brigade, parts of several batteries amounting to roughly forty guns, and fragments of many other regiments and brigades—perhaps 2,600 men in all. Negley also took his own divisional ammunition trains and other such wagons, all of which would be sorely missed later that day.

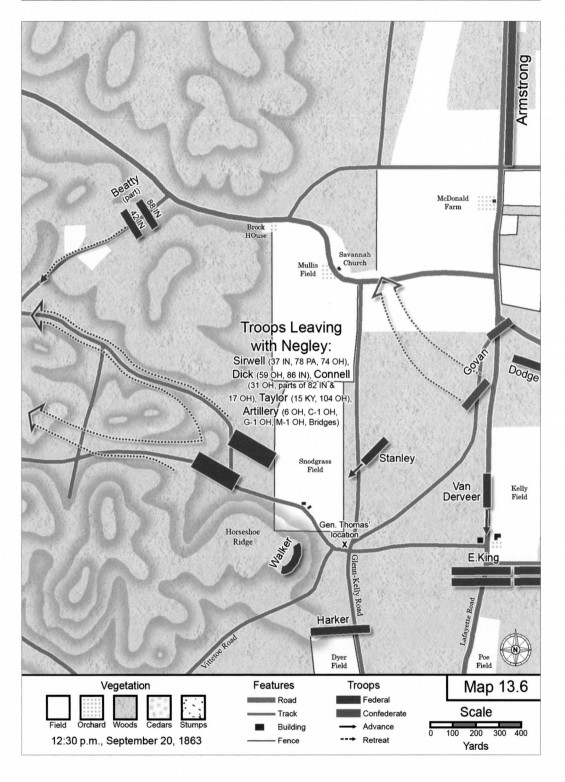

Troops Leaving with Negley:
Sirwell (37 IN, 78 PA, 74 OH),
Dick (59 OH, 86 IN), Connell
(31 OH, parts of 82 IN &
17 OH), Taylor (15 KY, 104 OH),
Artillery (6 OH, C-1 OH,
G-1 OH, M-1 OH, Bridges)

Beatty (part)
88 IN
42 IN

McDonald Farm

Brock HOuse

Savannah Church

Mullis Field

Govan

Dodge

Stanley

Snodgrass Field

Van Derveer

Kelly Field

Horseshoe Ridge

Walker

Gen. Thomas' location
X

Glenn-Kelly Road

E. King

Harker

Vittetoe Road

Dyer Field

Lafayette Road

Poe Field

Armstrong

Vegetation
Field Orchard Woods Cedars Stumps

12:30 p.m., September 20, 1863

Features
Road
Track
Building
Fence

Troops
Federal
Confederate
Advance
Retreat

Map 13.6

Scale
0   100   200   300   400
Yards

13.7: Kershaw Advances (12:45 p.m.)

John Bell Hood's crippling wound only served to exacerbate Confederate command confusion.

After the injured corps leader was carried away, Joe Kershaw and Bushrod Johnson met briefly in Dyer Field. Johnson urged Kershaw to support an attack against Horseshoe Ridge via the hill north of the Vittetoe House, a move that would outflank the nascent Federal line. Kershaw, however, wanted to go to Jerome Robertson's support, believing that Col. Harker's organized and belligerent Yankees posed the greater threat. Both men were brigadier generals newly thrust into acting divisional command and, having served in different armies, were unfamiliar with one another. When they were unable to settle on a single plan, Johnson demanded a comparison of date of rank to see who was senior. Kershaw had the advantage, which settled the question. The South Carolinians would attack Harker; Johnson would have to find support elsewhere. This "seemed to satisfy him," reported Kershaw.[51] Longstreet, who could have settled the matter definitively, was still back with Buckner, and likely not yet aware that Hood was even down.

Even after allowing for their heavy Gettysburg losses, Kershaw's South Carolina brigade was sizeable, with more than 1,500 men in the ranks. He could also call on Ben Humphreys' Mississippi regiments and he did just that, dispatching one of Hood's aides to bring them up on his right.[52] Kershaw, a prewar lawyer with Mexican War experience and an exceptionally good combat officer, knew there was no time to wait for the Mississippians; they would have to catch up on their own.

With his aide riding to find Humphreys, Kershaw's men (nicknamed the "Gamecocks") advanced toward Harker's line. They were joined by the 1st Arkansas Mounted Rifles of McNair's (Coleman's) Brigade, which had lost track of its own command and so fell in with Kershaw's infantry.[53]

Like Robertson's troops, Kershaw's men had also received a new issue of clothing en route to Georgia, and so presented a puzzling sight to Harker's Yankees. In addition to what looked like dark blue coats (these were of British make,

dyed a very dark steel gray) and light blue pants, their battle flags were also unfamiliar: the South Carolinians carried Army of Northern Virginia flags instead of the Polk or Hardee-pattern flags carried by the Army of Tennessee regiments. A debate of sorts erupted within the Union ranks: were these new troops friends or foes?[54] Gen. Thomas was also present. He believed the new arrivals might be some of Phil Sheridan's men, troops he had been expecting for the past hour. Even after they fired at Capt. Sanford Kellogg, Thomas remained unsure.[55] Meeting with Wood and Harker, both of whom were afraid they were about to open fire on friends, the commanders decided that the best thing to do was have the color guards in the various Federal regiments wave their flags ostentatiously. If the unknown force still fired at Harker, explained Thomas, he would have to shoot back no matter who they were.[56]

While the Federal commanders were debating the identity of the approaching infantry, Harker's defensive line was appreciably weakened by a pair of critical and ill-timed withdrawals. Schultz's battery received word to fall back and rejoin Negley, pulling away Harker's artillery support.[57] The 21st Ohio also fell back, climbing Horseshoe Ridge to rejoin Brannan. Its withdrawal left Harker without flank support on his right.[58] On Wood's orders, Harker pulled back the 64th and 125th Ohio to his main line, leaving skirmishers behind in the original position.[59]

Kershaw's men knew exactly who was waving Federal flags and took the wild shaking of the standards as a challenge, a taunt to come and try to take them. "As we were changing front to meet them they seemed to think we were wavering . . . so they waved their flags defiantly at us," wrote Lt. Col. Franklin Gaillard at the head of the 2nd South Carolina.[60] In a brilliant display of tactics and battlefield control, Kershaw instructed Gaillard to swing his regiment wide and outflank the Union line from its right, and the 8th South Carolina to do the same on the Union left; the rest of the brigade would make directly for the Federal line.

The South Carolinians advanced steadily while the bewildered Federals withheld from squeezing their triggers. When they closed within 100 yards, Kershaw's men opened a devastating fire. The storm of lead removed all doubts among the waiting Yankees.[61]

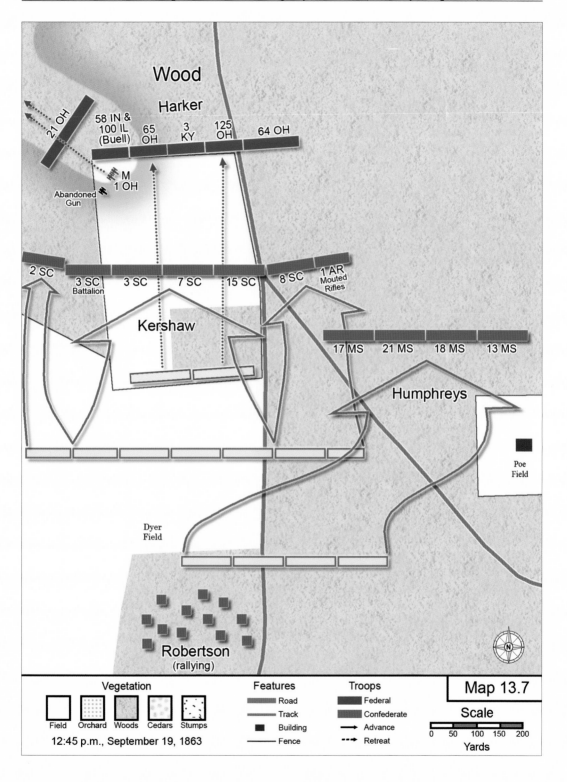

Wood

Harker

21 OH

58 IN &
100 IL
(Buell)

65
OH

3
KY

125
OH

64 OH

M
1 OH

Abandoned
Gun

2 SC

3 SC
Battalion

3 SC

7 SC

15 SC

8 SC

1 AR
Mouted
Rifles

Kershaw

17 MS

21 MS

18 MS

13 MS

Humphreys

Poe
Field

Dyer
Field

Robertson
(rallying)

Vegetation

Field Orchard Woods Cedars Stumps

12:45 p.m., September 19, 1863

Features

Road

Track

Building

Fence

Troops

Federal

Confederate

Advance

Retreat

Map 13.7

Scale

0   50   100   150   200

Yards

13.8: Harker Retreats
to Snodgrass Hill (1:00 p.m.)

The fighting between Joe Kershaw's regiments and Charles Harker's command raged with an intense fury. On the Union right, the combined 58th Indiana and 100th Illinois (Buell's brigade) suffered severely from the initial Rebel volley, but gamely managed a respectable return fire.[62]

These troops might have held if they were facing a threat only from their front, but a few minutes later Gaillard's 2nd South Carolina appeared on their right flank. Moving up a ravine through some woods, the 2nd swept up and over the ridge held earlier by the 21st Ohio to fall upon the Hoosier's exposed flank. The sudden attack overran the abandoned gun from Capt. Church's battery in the process.[63] "Another Rebel regiment advances with the red flag flying, dressed in our uniform," complained Sgt. George W. Holmes of the 100th Illinois. "Some of us open on them, and others say 'don't do it, they are our men.' While paying attention to this regiment," continued Holmes, "up comes a division [the 2nd South Carolina] on our right to flank us, so we have to 'skedaddle' again."[64]

When Col. Buell ordered the 58th to fall back, his retreat exposed the right flank of the 65th Ohio to Gaillard's onrushing Rebels. Bullets flew at the Buckeyes from the front, right flank, and right rear. The crossfire was crippling. Maj. Samuel C. Brown, who had taken command of the 65th the day before after Lt. Col. Horatio Whitbeck's wounding, was cut down here. The senior company leader also fell, leaving Capt. Thomas Powell in charge of the embattled Buckeyes. Powell (whose immediate predecessor was left unnamed when he penned his after-action report) wrote after the battle, "We held our position until the regiment on the right . . . broke in confusion, thus enabling the enemy to take possession of the hill. Our right being thus flanked," Powell continued, "we suffered a severe fire from the enemy and were forced to fall back."[65] The regiment retreated in considerable confusion, unable to rally until it reached the Snodgrass house.

Next to fall was the 3rd Kentucky. Col. Henry Dunlap recorded that the regiment suffered intensely from the crossfire, losing

"about 80 officers and men."[66] Capt. George W. McClure, who led company K on the regiment's left flank, remembered that Gen. Wood was directly behind the Kentuckians when the time to retreat arrived, and had just had a horse shot out from under him. "The brigade was just then driven back," related McClure. "Gen. Wood ran back afoot and made good speed but . . . [I] being young and muscular, outran and passed him."[67] Within minutes, half of Harker's brigade line was in full retreat. Only the 125th and 64th Ohio regiments remained in line.

While Kershaw's effort to envelop the Federal right succeeded brilliantly, things did not go as well on the left. With more woods to negotiate during its approach, and perhaps confused when Harker's line initially fell back under Gen. Wood's orders, the 8th South Carolina (with the 1st Arkansas Mounted Rifles on its right) did not keep pace with the rest of the regiments and drifted farther east than intended. The result was that the 64th Ohio holding Harker's left was not outflanked the way that Buell's 58th Indiana was on the opposite end of the line.

This did not mean that the Buckeyes of the 64th and 125th escaped unscathed. The 64th was aware of the threat posed by the approaching 8th South Carolina and fell back to avoid being surrounded.[68] Its withdrawal left Col. Emerson Opdyke's 125th Ohio to act as Harker's rearguard. It was up to these Buckeyes to cover the retreat and keep things from becoming a complete rout.

The 3rd Kentucky's withdrawal had already subjected Opdyke's men to the same crossfire from the right that had collapsed the rest of the line, but the 125th held its ground. An intense musketry duel ensued with the 7th and 15th South Carolina regiments. Three color bearers went down in quick succession. When the fourth, Cpl. John Warman, held the flag aloft, a ball shattered the shaft and left him clutching only the standard.[69]

The 125th seemed about to break, but Opdyke's cool presence rallied the men and allowed a controlled retreat. The Buckeyes gave ground grudgingly, "halting two or three times, facing to the rear and firing on the enemy directly south of us," recalled Capt. Clark, until the newly christened "Tigers" finally stopped "perhaps 200 feet" from the Snodgrass cabin.[70]

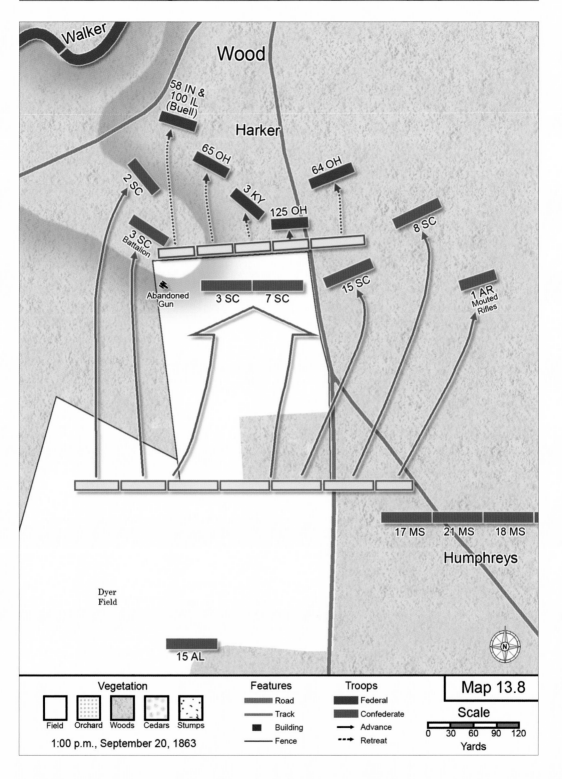

Walker

Wood

58 IN &
100 IL
(Buell)

Harker

65 OH

64 OH

2 SC

3 KY

8 SC

3 SC
Battalion

125 OH

Abandoned
Gun

3 SC   7 SC

15 SC

1 AR
Mouted
Rifles

17 MS   21 MS   18 MS

Humphreys

Dyer
Field

15 AL

Vegetation	Features	Troops	Map 13.8

Vegetation

Field   Orchard   Woods   Cedars   Stumps

1:00 p.m., September 20, 1863

Features

Road
Track
Building
Fence

Troops

Federal
Confederate
Advance
Retreat

Map 13.8

Scale

0   30   60   90   120

Yards

Map Set 14: The Federals Lose Horseshoe Ridge

(Afternoon, September 20)

14.1: Kershaw's First Assault (1:15 p.m.)

Despite suffering only relatively light losses in their fight against Col. Charles Harker's Federal brigade, Brig. Gen. Joseph Kershaw's South Carolina brigade was almost as disrupted by success as the Federals were by defeat. Gaps in Kershaw's line opened during the pursuit, one between the 3rd and 7th regiments, and another between the 15th and the 8th. The 7th also lost both Lt. Col. Elbert Bland and Maj. John S. Hard during the initial encounter, leaving the regiment without field officers for the rest of the battle. Kershaw intended to halt, reorganize, and wait for the Mississippians of Brig. Gen. Benjamin Humphreys' Brigade, but unfolding events dictated otherwise.[1]

Flushed with easy success during the outflanking of Harker's right, the men of Lt. Col. Franklin Gaillard's 2nd South Carolina barely paused when they caught sight of a new Federal line. "[We] followed up and met their second line at the summit ridge strongly posted. As we approached this we were met with a very destructive fire," Gaillard reported.[2] The 2nd was attempting to storm what is today known as Hill Three, a height that had been occupied only minutes before by the 21st Ohio of Col. William Sirwell's brigade.

After the repulse of Brig. Gen. Jerome Robertson's Texas Brigade, the Buckeyes of the 21st climbed up Hill Two in search of a mission. Brig. Gen. John Brannan ordered them into line to extend the Union right flank. The regiment lined the crest, "facing southward [and] adapting itself as best it . . . could to the irregularities . . . of the ground."[3] Deploying in a single rank to cover as much frontage as possible, the 21st's line snaked around the west face of Hill Two and along the east side of Hill Three, allowing the Ohioans to deliver a converging fire into the draw below. The Ohio troops packed an additional advantage with their five-shot Colt Revolving Rifles, which were carried by two-thirds of the regiment. Lt. William Vance described the effect of their weaponry: "At first

the charging Johnnies, reaching the proper distance and receiving a volley from the regiment, returned the same and then started on the keen jump, expecting to reach us before we could reload. Before they advanced ten paces . . . they would get another volley, and while they were pondering upon this circumstance, still a third; then they would scarcely get their backs turned [to retreat] . . . before the fourth would catch them, and [then] on a dead run, the fifth came singing about their ears." This was the "very destructive fire" the 2nd South Carolina's Gaillard recalled.[4]

Attacking Hill Two on the right of Gaillard's men were the pair of 3rd South Carolinas—one a battalion and the other a regiment. Both had lost most of their cohesion in the mad scramble through the woods. Lt. Augustus Dickert of Company H, 3rd South Carolina, wrote that the ranks "became for a moment a tangled, disorganized mass" as they moved up the slope, crowded together by circumstance.[5]

These South Carolinians met stubborn resistance from Brannan's newly cobbled line. The bulk of the defense on Hill Two was built around Col. William H. Hays, now in command of Col. John Croxton's brigade, and those fragments of the 14th Ohio and 4th and 10th Kentucky regiments that had followed him back from the fighting around Poe Field. Brannan reported Hays' movements during the retreat as being "accomplished with wonderful regularity under such circumstances."[6] These men provided a hard center around which others rallied, with several hundred rifles gathered atop the hill by the time the South Carolinians advanced.

Subjected to a crossfire from the 21st Ohio on its left flank, the 3rd Battalion (also known as the James Battalion) had a particularly difficult time making headway. On the battalion's right, Col. James Nance of the 3rd Regiment recalled that his men had barely started advancing when Kershaw ordered the entire line to halt.[7] Not all the Rebels obeyed. Federal Sgt. Harry Allspaugh, separated from the 31st Ohio, recalled that the Gamecocks chased him almost all the way up the hill before he fell in with some men of the 17th Ohio and helped drive Kershaw's men back from Hill One.[8]

Kershaw's first try at Horseshoe Ridge, more of an impromptu pursuit than an organized assault, had failed.

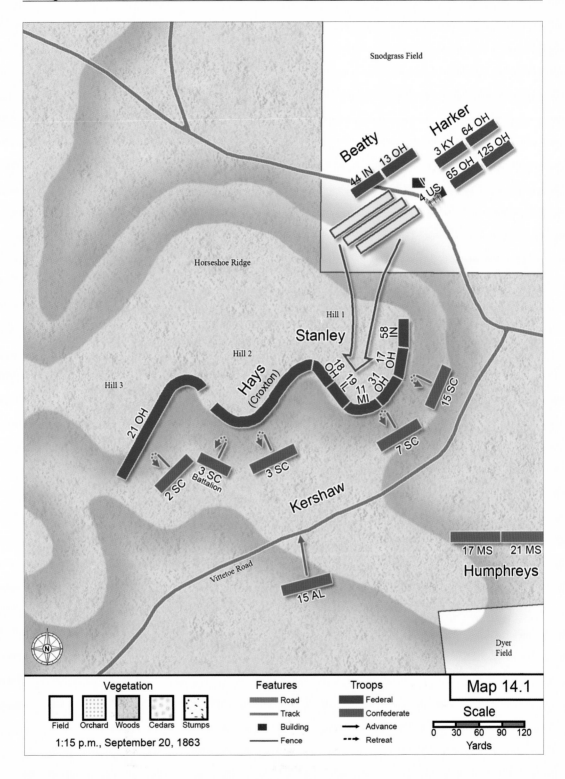

Snodgrass Field

Beatty

Harker

3 KY   64 OH

44 IN   13 OH

65 OH   125 OH

4 US

Horseshoe Ridge

Hill 1

Stanley

58 IN

Hill 2

Hays
(Croxton)

18 OH

19 IL

17 OH

31 OH

11 MI

15 SC

Hill 3

21 OH

7 SC

2 SC

3 SC
Battalion

3 SC

Kershaw

17 MS   21 MS

Humphreys

Vittetoe Road

15 AL

Dyer
Field

Vegetation

Field   Orchard   Woods   Cedars   Stumps

1:15 p.m., September 20, 1863

Features

▨ Road
— Track
■ Building
— Fence

Troops

■ Federal
■ Confederate
→ Advance
⇢ Retreat

Map 14.1

Scale

0   30   60   90   120

Yards

14.2: Humphreys Attacks, Johnson Deploys (1:30 p.m.)

As Kershaw's South Carolinians reformed along the Vittetoe Road, Humphreys' Mississippi brigade arrived, filling the interval between the 8th and 15th South Carolina. Humphreys inherited the brigade after Brig. Gen. William Barksdale was mortally wounded at Gettysburg. He was not yet fully comfortable in command, for Barksdale's ghost cast a long shadow: "A humiliating sense of my [own] incompetency," he admitted, "painfully oppressed me"[9] The brigade suffered terrible losses at Gettysburg, which induced Humphreys to act more cautiously in North Georgia.

These thoughts occupied Humphreys when he caught sight of the imposing line of Federals crowning the heights before him. In addition to Harker's and Brannan's survivors, the line included Col. Stanley's brigade. Stanley arrived looking for Maj. Gen. James Negley (who had left the field), and found instead fellow brigade leader Col. John Beatty, who had assumed command of this part of the line. Stanley fell in to support Lt. Smith's Battery I, 4th U.S. When Kershaw's men appeared, Stanley led the 11th Michigan and 19th Illinois forward. When he fell wounded, command passed to Col. William L. Stoughton of the 11th.[10]

For several minutes the 17th and 21st Mississippi endured a crossfire while halted at the foot of the ridge. They expected to attack, but the order never arrived. The Yankees, concluded Humphreys, appeared to be well entrenched and an effort to dislodge them would cost "half [his] brigade."[11] The Mississippian guided his men back to the north end of Dyer Field after suffering 152 killed and wounded to no purpose. His men were out of the fight for the rest of day. Humphreys sought guidance from Lt. Gen. James Longstreet, who agreed with his decision to fall back. Neither officer, however, informed Kershaw (nominally Humphrey's division commander), who was still expecting the Mississippians to join his South Carolinians in a coordinated effort to storm the ridge. Thus far, Longstreet had not taken a direct hand in organizing the assault on Horseshoe Ridge.[12]

Now Longstreet decided to outflank the new Union line rather than assault it directly.

One of Maj. Gen. Bushrod Johnson's many appeals for help had borne fruit when Longstreet ordered Maj. Gen. Thomas Hindman's Division to reinforce Johnson and attack the Union right. With this promised support, Johnson began to move his two remaining brigades under Cols. John Fulton and Cyrus Sugg. (Brig. Gen. Evander McNair's Brigade under Col. David Coleman had fallen back to Brotherton Field past the Vittetoe house.) From there, Johnson could ascend the ridge north of the farmstead and turn east, a position that should put his Tennesseans far beyond the Union right flank.

As they drew near the house, the Rebels were greeted exuberantly by its occupants. For the past two days Hiram Vittetoe, his wife, and their three daughters had hidden under the floorboards to avoid the "insults and dangers of the vandal foe." Now they stood outside, the women waving at the passing troops. Their presence stirred a flurry of chivalric romanticism. "Tear[s] of joyful sympathy started from many a soldier's eye," inspiring implied vows of "we will save you or die," effused Lt. Col. Watt Floyd of the 17th Tennessee.[13] From the ranks of the 17th, Pvt. Elijah Wiseman remembered that "the ladies of the house came out meeting us, waving their aprons and bonnets. We were almost worn out, but managed to give them a few cheers."[14] Thus heartened, Johnson's men began the difficult climb up Horseshoe Ridge.

While Humphreys was retreating and Johnson was advancing, reinforcements appeared in the middle of Kershaw's line. Col. William C. Oates and his wayward 15th Alabama slipped between the 3rd and 7th South Carolina regiments. Unable to find his own brigade, Oates decided to pitch into the closest available fight.

William C. Oates was a troubled man by the fall of 1863. He'd led a difficult violent early life, at one point fleeing his native Alabama for fear of a murder charge. He wandered through the South for years before coming home and studying law. His path to command of the 15th was also rocky, the result of a longstanding quarrel with fellow Capt. Alexander Lowther. After the death of his older brother John on the slopes of Little Round Top at Gettysburg, Oates became morose and withdrawn. His command decisions became more questionable. Thus far, his impact on the battle had been more negative than positive.

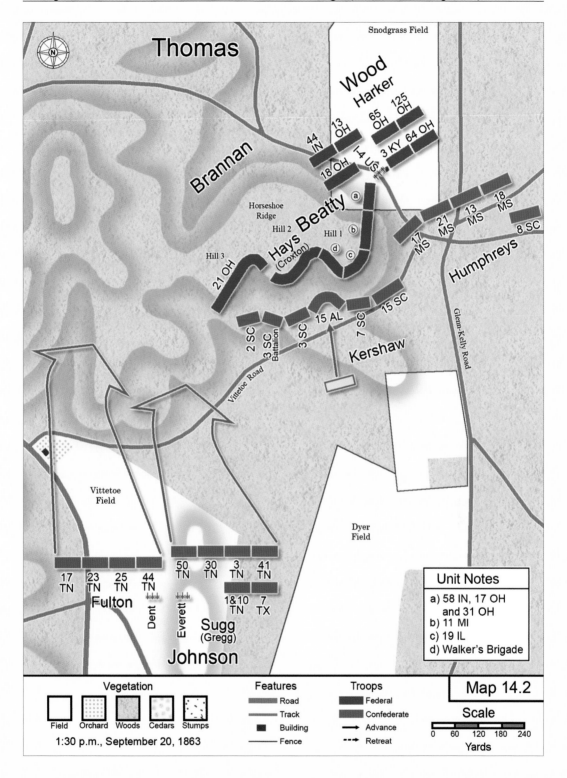

Snodgrass Field

Thomas

Wood

Harker

65 OH

125 OH

13 OH

44 IN

Brannan

18 OH

I 4 US

3 KY

64 OH

a)

21 MS

13 MS

18 MS

17 MS

8 SC

Horseshoe Ridge

Hays Beatty

Hill 2

Hill 1

b)

d)

c)

Humphreys

Hill 3

21 OH

15 SC

2 SC

3 SC Battalion

3 SC

15 AL

7 SC

15 SC

Glenn-Kelly Road

Kershaw

Vittetoe Road

Vittetoe Field

Dyer Field

Unit Notes

a) 58 IN, 17 OH and 31 OH
b) 11 MI
c) 19 IL
d) Walker's Brigade

17 TN

23 TN

25 TN

44 TN

50 TN

30 TN

3 TN

41 TN

Dent

Everett

1&10 TN

7 TX

Fulton

Sugg
(Gregg)

Johnson

Vegetation

Field   Orchard   Woods   Cedars   Stumps

1:30 p.m., September 20, 1863

Features

Road
Track
Building
Fence

Troops

Federal
Confederate
Advance
Retreat

Map 14.2

Scale

0   60   120   180   240

Yards

14.3: Steedman and Van Derveer Reinforce Thomas (1: 30 p.m.)

Fortunately for XIV Corps commander Maj. Gen. George Thomas, Federal troops were also hurrying toward Horseshoe Ridge, moving there without orders but welcome all the same. The largest contingent was Brig. Gen. James B. Steedman's First Division of the Union Reserve Corps, led by corps commander Maj. Gen. Gordon Granger.

Granger and Steedman had spent the morning at Rossville, several miles north of the battlefield, acting under the sketchiest of orders: hold Rossville and protect the direct route to Chattanooga, but also to be ready to support Thomas or Maj. Gen. Alexander McCook if needed.[15] With only three brigades and 6,000 men, Granger's command was more akin to a division than to a corps.

As the day wore on, Granger and Steedman grew more anxious. By noon, the fight raging several miles south of their position was clearly audible. Were they needed there? Abandoning Rossville, however, was out of the question. After some debate Granger decided to leave Col. Daniel McCook's brigade near McAfee's Church to defend the road to Chattanooga and take Steedman's two brigades to help Thomas.[16] With Brig. Gen. Walter C. Whitaker's brigade in the lead, followed by Col. John G. Mitchell's four regiments, Steedman's men marched south on the LaFayette Road.

Near Cloud Church, Steedman's command ran into Confederate cavalry. Earlier, Brig. Gen. Nathan Forrest had advanced a brigade to dispute the road and protect Maj. Gen. John C. Breckinridge's right flank when that officer turned his division south to attack Kelly Field. When Steedman ran into Forrest's picket line, he deployed his infantry and prepared to fight. At one point his lead regiment, the 96th Illinois, formed a square in anticipation of a Rebel charge.[17] Granger, who did not believe he had the luxury of time for skirmishing, dismissed the Rebel opposition as nothing more than "rag-a-muffin cavalry," and ordered Steedman to divert off the road, bypass the enemy, and head southwest across the fields.[18] During the move they ran a gauntlet of Rebel artillery Forrest had amassed several hundred yards farther east.[19]

Few of the men in the Reserve Corps had seen much action, and the cannonade offered a lively if largely ineffective initiation into the drama of combat. Watching the 89th Ohio traverse the most exposed portions of the route, Lt. Edward Scott of Company G, Whitaker's brigade, observed that "the shells made the boys dodge considerable. It was rather amusing to see them. They would be going along on the 'double-quick' when a shell would come howling along just above them and down they would go, flat on the ground as it passed, then jump up and trot along on the 'double-quick' again. No one was hurt, although some of them came pretty close."[20] As they drew closer to the fighting, however, the backwash of a great battle became readily obvious. "All around us were sickening signs of a contest," remembered Capt. William Boyd of the 84th Indiana, also of Whitaker's command. "The dead and wounded were lieing [sic] in every direction, mingled with all the implements of war . . . frightened women and children hastened through our lines."[21]

Another moment of high drama played out when Thomas first caught sight of Steedman's approaching column. If the men were Rebels, the Federals were doomed. Dust covered the troops, preventing easy identification. Even blue uniform coats did not guarantee friends, as Joe Kershaw's South Carolinians had so aptly demonstrated just an hour earlier in Dyer Field. The normally unflappable Thomas, so nervous he could not steady his field glasses, asked another to take them and look.[22] Within a few minutes it was clear the approaching troops were indeed Federals.

Col. Van Derveer's brigade rejoined Brannan's division about this same time. Van Derveer's men had been resting near the Kelly house after their morning exertions when Maj. Robert H. Kelly of the 3rd Kentucky retreated into their lines with news of the Federal rout in Poe Field (Map 11.4). Shortly thereafter, one of Thomas' aides arrived, confirmed Kelly's news, and added that Brannan's division had rallied on Horseshoe Ridge, where his men were even then fighting for their lives. Lacking other orders, Van Derveer set off with his men due west through the woods. He arrived in Snodgrass Field behind Harker's line and reported to Thomas directly.[23]

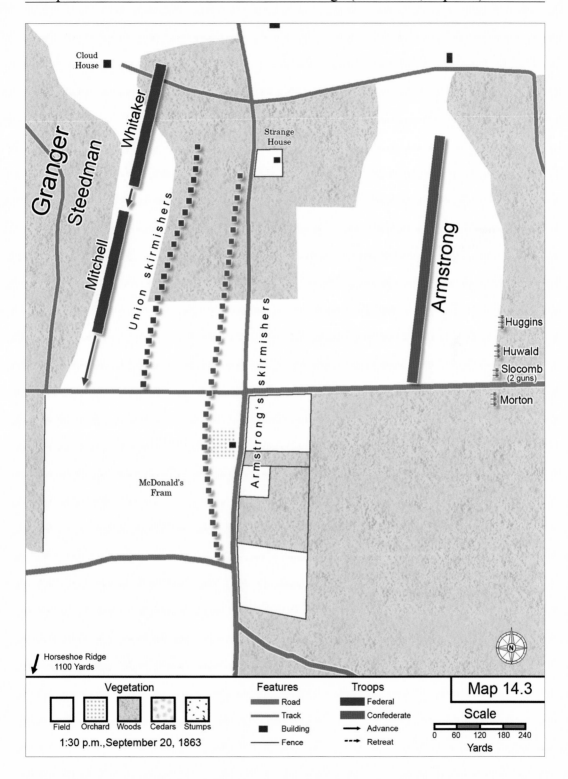

Cloud House

Whitaker

Granger

Steedman

Mitchell

Union skirmishers

Strange House

Armstrong

Huggins

Huwald

Slocomb (2 guns)

Morton

Armstrong's skirmishers

McDonald's Fram

Horseshoe Ridge 1100 Yards

Vegetation

Field Orchard Woods Cedars Stumps

1:30 p.m., September 20, 1863

Features

Road

Track

Building

Fence

Troops

Federal

Confederate

Advance

Retreat

Map 14.3

Scale

0   60   120   180   240

Yards

14.4: Oates and Kershaw Attack Again (1:45 p.m.)

When Col. Oates led his 15th Alabama into the ranks alongside the South Carolinians, he discovered that senior officers were in short supply. Earlier, Oates experienced a frustrating encounter with Bushrod Johnson, who could not tell him where his own brigade was, or even where Brig. Gen. Evander Law's Division might be found. Concluding (uncharitably) that Johnson was astonishingly ill-informed, Oates went his own way—despite that fact that it was Oates, and not Johnson, who was lost.[24]

Even though he had squeezed his Alabamians between the 3rd and 7th South Carolina regiments in Joe Kershaw's line of battle, Oates made little effort to locate the brigadier for further orders. Instead, he decided that he should attack, and tried to induce the units on his left and right to join him. Riding to the left, Oates found Col. Nance and asked for support from his 3rd South Carolina. When Nance refused, Oates ordered the colonel to join him. Since Nance ranked Oates by nearly a full year, the Alabamian's high-handed behavior failed. Oates left in disgust for a ride to the east to find the commander of the 7th South Carolina.[25]

By this stage of the fight the 7th was being led by a captain. Like Nance, he too balked at the idea, arguing that Kershaw had personally placed the regiment in line. Oates ignored the captain and addressed the entire regiment in an effort to shame them into an advance—a bold tactic that had some success. Initially, only a few companies stepped forward to join the 15th, but their forward motion triggered the rest of the 7th South Carolina to stumble ahead. Within a few minutes Oates had a sizable attack mounted against Hill One.[26]

Kershaw was father to the left with either the 2nd South Carolina or James' (3rd) Battalion, waiting for Ben Humphreys before signaling the next attack. The swell of firing from the right (Oates' unilateral assault) convinced Kershaw that the moment was at hand, and he ordered the brigade into action.[27] The 2nd South Carolina launched another bloody assault against Hill Three, where it once again met a devastating fire from the Colts wielded by the 21st Ohio. Lt. Debose Eggleston of the 2nd remembered that

they "reached the crest of the hill but were so broken, we could not hold it. Had our support been in its place we would have had no further trouble. . . . I was on the hill myself, but it was too hot to stay there long."[28] One of the fallen was Sgt. Richard Kirkland, made forever famous as the "Angel of Mayre's Heights" who had carried water to fallen Yankees at the battle of Fredericksburg in 1862.[29] Kirkland was killed as the regiment was falling back. His last words were recorded as, "Tell my pa, I died right."

Once ordered forward by Kershaw, Nance led his 3rd regiment up Hill Two. The men managed to close within fifty yards of the crest, where Nance reported "the fire became very deadly."[30] For all of Oates' pre-attack posturing, his own effort fell apart quickly, stripping support from Nance's right as the Alabamians and the 7th South Carolina tumbled down the hill in bloody confusion. Oates blamed the 7th for breaking first, claiming it "ingloriously fled."[31] Given that the regiment was largely leaderless, was assaulting the point of Hill One over difficult ground, and that its linear formation was disrupted during the early minutes of the advance, it isn't surprising that the South Carolinians failed to make much headway. Of course, neither did the 15th Alabama. Oates' men charged up the draw between Hills One and Two, and were exposed to the same kind of semi-circular crossfire the 2nd South Carolina had faced between Hills Two and Three. Oates watched his own men "start down the hill" and rushed into their dissolved ranks in an effort to rally them.[32] He partially succeeded, and managed to lead some—along with one company of the 7th—back into the draw far enough to establish a line and hold on, trading shots with the Yankees. The attack, however, had fizzled.

Once again, the length of Kershaw's line had precluded effective communication. Neither the 8th or 15th South Carolina joined in this attack. Only after this second effort was repulsed did Kershaw learn that instead of attacking, Humphreys had fallen back with his Mississippians to Dyer Field. Likely disgusted by the turn of events, Kershaw ordered his own brigade back about 250 yards to await reinforcements.[33]

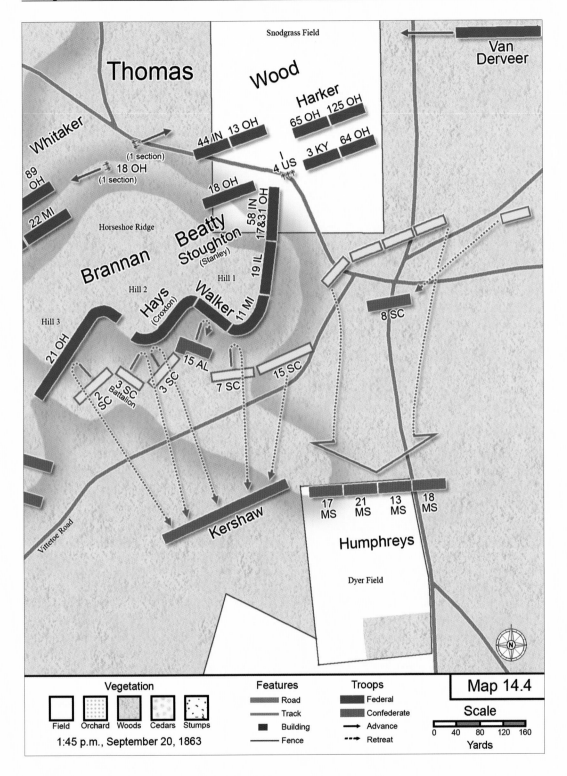

Snodgrass Field

Van Derveer

Thomas

Wood

Harker

65 OH   125 OH

44 IN   13 OH

3 KY   64 OH

I
4 US

Whitaker

89
OH

(1 section)
18 OH
(1 section)

18 OH

22 MI

Horseshoe Ridge

Beatty
Stoughton
(Stanley)

58 IN
177&31 OH

Brannan

Hill 1

19 IL

Hill 2

Hays
(Croxton)

Walker

11 MI

8 SC

Hill 3

21 OH

15 AL

3 SC

15 SC

2
SC

3 SC
Battalion

3 SC

7 SC

Kershaw

17
MS

21
MS

13
MS

18
MS

Vittetoe Road

Humphreys

Dyer Field

N

Vegetation

Field   Orchard   Woods   Cedars   Stumps

1:45 p.m., September 20, 1863

Features

Road
Track
Building
Fence

Troops

Federal
Confederate
Advance
Retreat

Map 14.4

Scale

0   40   80   120   160
Yards

14.5: Anderson and Johnson Attack (2:00 p.m.)

While Kershaw was recovering from his second repulse, Bushrod Johnson was reentering the fight. Johnson conferred with Hindman about Longstreet's support order (Map 14.2) and the two decided to cooperate as closely as possible. Brig. Gen. Patton Anderson's large Mississippi brigade would go forward with Johnson's own troops (Cols. John Fulton and Cyrus Sugg), with two other brigades under Gens. Zach Deas and Arthur Manigault following as soon as they finished drawing ammunition. Johnson would retain tactical control of both divisions (his own and Hindman's), which was probably a wise choice because he was more familiar with the terrain and Hindman had suffered a minor but painful neck wound earlier in the day.[34]

Fulton and Sugg advanced cautiously in search of the Union flank. The Tennesseans reached the spur above the Vittetoe house with their organizations considerably disrupted by the steep climb. Johnson took a few minutes to reform their lines. He also decided that the spur would make an excellent artillery platform, and ordered batteries under Capt. S. H. Dent and Lt. William S. Everett hauled up to unlimber there.[35]

While Johnson was preparing his command, Anderson's Mississippians arrived in his rear. James Patten Anderson had established a fine combat record at Shiloh and Murfreesboro. Hindman's recurring illnesses during the campaign often left Anderson in command of the division, and he would eventually be promoted to major general early in 1864. He was another self-taught soldier, having been a doctor, legislator, and even a U. S. Marshall for Washington Territory before following his adopted state of Florida out of the Union. Anderson was entering the fight with little understanding of the terrain or the opposition.

Johnson ordered Anderson to take up a position on his right, filling the space between his own division and Kershaw's left. With five regiments and a battalion of sharpshooters, he had more than enough men to fill the gap, so only the 10th and 44th Mississippi regiments comprised his front line. The remainder formed in support. The 9th Mississippi Battalion covered this deployment with a skirmish line, with orders to fall back and discourage stragglers when Anderson stepped off.[36]

From the top of the hill, the Buckeyes of the 21st Ohio watched the activity with growing concern. Lt. Col. Dwella Stoughton was shot by a sharpshooter about this time, and command devolved to Maj. Arnold McMahon. Word arrived that the regiment was about to be outflanked: heavy lines of Rebel infantry (Johnson) forming for battle overlapped the right.[37] Capt. Henry Alban requested permission to pull back Companies A and F and form them perpendicular to their current position.[38] This would be no more than a stopgap measure, however, unless Union reinforcements arrived soon.

When he finally advanced, Johnson did so cautiously. One reason was that his men were dog tired. Counting their actions at Reed's Bridge on September 18, this was their third straight day of combat. The wooded and hilly terrain limited reconnaissance, and he wasn't sure what kind of opposition he would find. Union stragglers fired at his line from all along the ridge west of the 21st Ohio, men unknown and unheralded to history, but in sufficient numbers to discourage Johnson from launching a charge. On the division's left, the 17th Tennessee's Col. Watt Floyd wrote, "I kept flankers well out on my left, as an occasional shot from the enemy's sharpshooters indicated danger from that quarter." Once the advance began, "we received the enemy's fire before we had gone 100 yards." Floyd halted his men where they could "make a standing fight," well short of the next rise.[39]

Anderson's advance was anything but cautious. His brigade rushed forward in what Johnson described as a "gallant and impetuous charge."[40] The ground was difficult here, too. The draw west of Hill Three angled northwest, exposing Anderson's front to raking fire from the 21st Ohio. The Mississippians turned to the right to meet the fire head-on.[41] Lt. Col. James Barr of the 10th Mississippi found his men between the Yankees on the crest and Sugg's Tennesseans moving up in his rear, while Everett's guns threw shells over his head. The 10th and 44th Mississippi regiments halted short of the crest, exchanging fire with the 21st Ohio. The 7th Mississippi moved up on the 44th's right to add its firepower to the attack.[42]

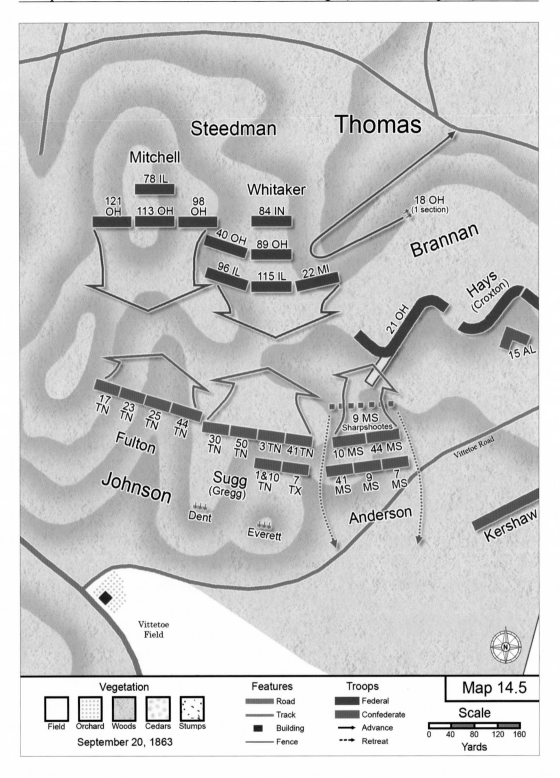

Steedman

Thomas

Mitchell

78 IL

Whitaker

121 OH   113 OH   98 OH   84 IN   18 OH
(1 section)

40 OH   89 OH   Brannan

96 IL   115 IL   22 MI

Hays
(Croxton)

21 OH

15 AL

17 TN   23 TN   25 TN   44 TN

Fulton

30 TN   50 TN   3 TN   41 TN

9 MS
Sharpshooters

10 MS   44 MS

Vittetoe Road

Johnson

Sugg
(Gregg)

1&10 TN   7 TX

41 MS   9 MS   7 MS

Dent

Everett

Anderson

Kershaw

Vittetoe
Field

N

Vegetation					Features	Troops		Map 14.5

Field   Orchard   Woods   Cedars   Stumps

Road
Track
Building
Fence

Federal
Confederate
Advance
Retreat

Scale

0   40   80   120   160
Yards

September 20, 1863

14.6: Steedman's Counterattack (2:15 p.m.)

When Gordon Granger's Federals arrived in Snodgrass Field, George Thomas' first impulse was to send them to fill the gaping hole in the line between Kelly Field and Snodgrass Hill. Before they could execute that order, however, John Brannan—who had caught wind of Johnson's and Anderson's deployments—sent word that the trouble on the Union right was more urgent. Reacting quickly, Thomas ordered Granger to shift Steedman's troops there.[43] "My men are fresh, and they are just the fellows for that work," snapped Granger, who anticipated a bloody job ahead. "They are raw troops, and they don't know any better than to charge up there."[44]

Walter Whitaker's six regiments led the way in a double column with a section of artillery trailing. The Midwesterners hurried west behind the 21st Ohio's line until they could front south, deploy, and start up the hill. Capt. William Boyd of the 84th Indiana recalled seeing Rebel skirmishers on the crest, their movements mirroring the Federals as the brigade turned and made ready to charge.[45] Concluding there was no time to spare, James Steedman deployed John Mitchell's regiments; they would have to close in behind, shift farther right, and follow Whitaker as best they could. Riding behind the 115th Illinois in Whitaker's center, Steedman ordered the charge.[46]

Whitaker's men moved with a cheer, their yells spreading from regiment to regiment until the sound drowned out everything else.[47] While they were rushing forward, Mitchell's four regiments passed behind them and deployed to their right. To extend his line, Mitchell shifted the 121st Ohio to the front, leaving only the 78th Illinois in support.[48] His deployment complete, Mitchell also started up the slope, chasing after their comrades in the First Brigade.

Whitaker's troops received the full attention of Johnson's two brigades of Tennesseans when they topped the ridge. "As our lines rolled over the crest," wrote Lt. Henry Royce of the 115th Illinois, "the Confederates were in plain view . . . scarcely more than sixty yards distant."[49] Whitaker's two right-front regiments halted and both sides exchanged deadly volleys at close range. Mounted officers proved especially

vulnerable. Whitaker and all but one of his staff were hit quickly (though the general's abdominal wound was a minor one).[50]

On Whitaker's left, Col. Heber Le Favour's 22nd Michigan barely paused. Marching up the ridge behind the 21st Ohio, the Wolverines passed through the Buckeye ranks and plunged down the draw, smashing into the exposed left flank of the 10th Mississippi, part of Anderson's Brigade. "Back [the rebels] went, pell-mell," recalled Michigan Pvt. Marvin Boget of the 22nd.[51]

With Whitaker's line fully engaged, Mitchell's regiments drew up alongside, his right stretching beyond Johnson's left flank. In the 23rd Tennessee, Capt. William Harder recalled "an overwhelming volley . . . in a semicircle completely infilading [sic] our line."[52] Exhausted, confused, outflanked, and outnumbered, Fulton's men began to fall back. On Fulton's right, Col. Sugg watched as his first line became disordered by the intense fire. The retreat he ordered exposed his second line to a severe fire.[53] Within a few minutes both of Johnson's brigades were in full retreat.

Seeing this, Col. Thomas Champion ordered his 96th Illinois forward after the running foe.[54] The Illini veered across Mitchell's left-front. Chasing Fulton's men out onto the spur, they ran into Rebel cannon that opened upon them at close range. The 96th attempted to stand for a few minutes, but broke under the intense fire.[55]

Whitaker's second line halted at or near the crest in some confusion that may have resulted from the general's wounding. The 89th Ohio veered in front of the 84th Indiana while trying to avoid some Union artillery, leaving both units just below the crest and behind the 115th Illinois.[56] The 40th Ohio halted behind where the 96th should have been, had Champion not struck out to his right.[57] Mitchell's line also stopped at the crest, brought to a halt there by Steedman.[58]

Battle was James Steedman's element. Federals from nearly every regiment recalled him in their amidst, rallying ranks or, as in the case of Mitchell's troops, heading off rash advances. A fall from his horse rendered Steedman hatless and bloody, but did not deter him from leading his division. At one point, fearing death would strike the general, an aide asked him if he had any last words. After a moment's reflection, Steedman shot back, "make sure they spell my name right."

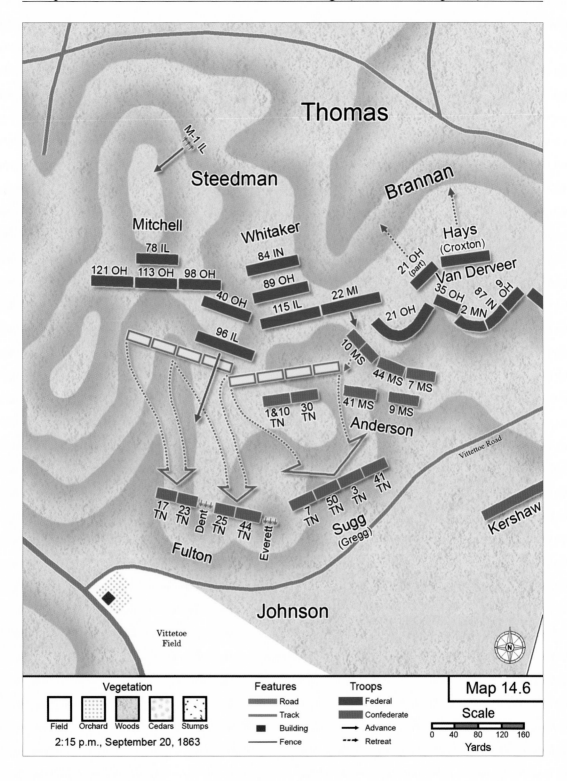

Map 14.6

2:15 p.m., September 20, 1863

14.7: Steedman's Line Stabilizes; Kershaw's Third Attack (2:30 p.m.)

Steedman's arrival completely disrupted the advance of Gens. Johnson and Anderson, shoving them back to their original lines. The Mississippians were especially hard-hit, the 22nd Michigan appearing like a thunderbolt on their left flank just as they were squaring off against the 21st Ohio. The attack was not intentional.

Col. Favour had ordered a halt atop the ridge so he could direct the 89th Ohio as well as his own 22nd Michigan, leaving the Wolverines in the hands of Lt. Col. William Sanborn. Unable to stop them, Sanborn and the 22nd plunged down the ridge's southern slope into the exposed 10th Mississippi.[59] The attack surprised and knocked Anderson back in confusion, but also exposed the Federals to a flanking fire from Johnson's artillery and Sugg's reforming Tennessee regiments.[60] Lead and iron swept through the 22nd's ranks, cutting down many men, including Sanborn and every man in the color guard.[61] Routed, the 22nd's survivors scrambled back up the slope and through part of the 21st Ohio's right flank.

The Michigan troops were not the only ones falling back. In fact, much of Whitaker's brigade retreated in a severely disordered state. Only the 40th and 89th Ohio remained in the front line after the charge. The balance ended up behind the ridge, where officers worked to rally the men. Mitchell's men suffered a kinder fate. Brought to a halt by Steedman's intervention, the brigade formed a hard shoulder on the army's right.

Fighting also intensified again east of Hill Three, where Joe Kershaw ordered his South Carolina brigade to make a third attack to support the arrival of Anderson and Johnson on his left. Had he faced the same scratch force of Federals—who by this time were exhausted and running low on ammunition—his effort may have succeeded. But just as Kershaw's regiments started forward, Col. Van Derveer's men filed into the front line to replace the 21st Ohio's left wing and the troops on Hill Two.[62]

On Kershaw's left, the 2nd South Carolina launched another spirited effort. To Pvt. Reginald Screvin, it was the "third and terrible charge. . . . Terrific fire, rifle bullets as thick as hail, crashing through trees, human flesh and bones—saw one man's foot lying by him completely shot off."[63] South Carolinian Lt. Dubose Eggleston came to believe that Patton Anderson's Mississippians played a hand in foiling their assault: "We were going up splendidly, when our support deliberately came in behind & poured a volley into us," he wrote with obvious disgust. "[O]f course it broke us."[64] Whether the fire was delivered from Mississippi rifled-muskets or from Wolverines wrapping around the hill during their countercharge, it was enough to send the 2nd tumbling back down the slope.

Not all of Kershaw's men went forward. Neither members of the 3rd Battalion nor Nance's 3rd South Carolina recorded a third effort. In the middle of the line Oates' Alabamians, still pinned down in the draw trading fire with the Yankees, were going nowhere. On their right, however, the 7th South Carolina launched one of the most desperate and dramatic efforts of the day. The regiment's gallant assault carried to the very crest of Hill One, where Rebels and Yankees grappled across the same hasty breastworks for control of the hill.

Ensign Alfred D. Clark of the 7th planted the regiment's Palmetto flag on the Union works, where it drew the eye of every man fighting for Hill One. For the briefest of moments, the Union line was ruptured. John Beatty, positioned down the slope some distance, rallied some of the withdrawing defenders and led them into a counterattack, "waving my hat and shouting like a madman."[65] At the same time Lt. Col. Charles H. Grosvenor led his 18th Ohio out of reserve, passing Beatty and aiming for Clark's colors. The rush of the Buckeyes and rallied men was enough to repulse the South Carolinians. Clark was cut down by multiple bullets, but in an act that even his opponents regarded as supremely courageous, with his last strength Clark hurled the flag back over his head into the arms of his comrades, saving it even as he died. Battered and bloodied, the survivors of the 7th fell back down the hill.[66]

This attack represented Kershaw's final effort. Exhausted by hours of fighting and heavy losses, the South Carolinians were simply played out. They would cling to the Vittetoe Road and continue a harassing fire at the enemy atop the ridge, but they could not muster the fortitude for another assault. Fresh troops would be needed to complete the job.

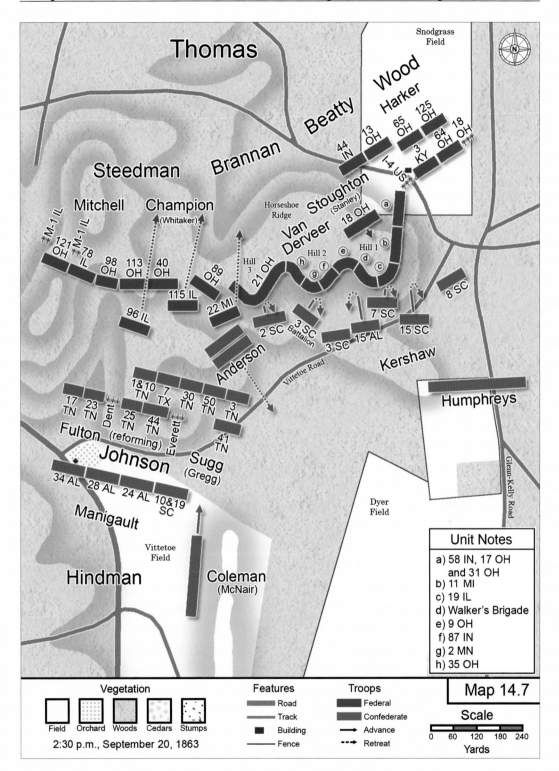

Thomas

Snodgrass Field

Wood

Harker

Beatty

Brannan

44 IN

13 OH

65 OH

125 OH

3 KY

64 OH

18 OH

14 US

Steedman

Mitchell

Champion

(Whitaker)

Horseshoe Ridge

Stoughton

(Stanley)

Van Derveer

18 OH

a

M-1 IL

M-1 IL

121 OH

78 IL

98 OH

113 OH

40 OH

89 OH

21 OH

Hill 3

Hill 2

h

g

f

e

Hill 1

d

c

b

8 SC

115 IL

96 IL

22 MI

2 SC

3 SC Battalion

3 SC

15 AL

7 SC

15 SC

Anderson

Vittetoe Road

Kershaw

Humphreys

1&10 TN

7 TX

30 TN

50 TN

3 TN

17 TN

23 TN

Dent

25 TN

44 TN

Everett

41 TN

Fulton

(reforming)

Sugg

(Gregg)

Johnson

34 AL

28 AL

24 AL

10&19 SC

Manigault

Vittetoe Field

Hindman

Coleman

(McNair)

Dyer Field

Glenn-Kelly Road

Unit Notes

a) 58 IN, 17 OH and 31 OH
b) 11 MI
c) 19 IL
d) Walker's Brigade
e) 9 OH
f) 87 IN
g) 2 MN
h) 35 OH

Map 14.7

Vegetation	Features	Troops
Field Orchard Woods Cedars Stumps	Road Track Building Fence	Federal Confederate Advance Retreat

2:30 p.m., September 20, 1863

Scale

0   60   120   180   240

Yards

14.8: Hindman and Johnson Try Again (3:00 to 3:30 p.m.)

Joseph Kershaw's third effort may have been his final attack of the day, but Bushrod Johnson was not yet ready to give up. Even as the brigades of Fulton, Sugg, and Anderson were being driven back by James Steedman's hammer-blows, the rest of Hindman's Division was filing behind Johnson's left-rear to extend the Rebel line farther west.

The brigades of Zach Deas and Arthur Manigault moved past the Vittetoe house and into line opposite some of the most daunting terrain on the battlefield. Deas' Alabamians faced a climb so steep that Deas had to dismount and lead his horse on foot.[67] Manigault's front straddled a gorge, making it impossible for him to keep a proper alignment. Johnson further complicated things when he decided that Hindman's men should wheel to the right as they advanced in an effort to find the elusive Union flank.[68]

Johnson bolstered the renewed effort by adding his own division to the attack, augmented by the recent return of McNair's Brigade (under Col. David Coleman), which one of Johnson's staff officers had found near the Brotherton House and redirected forward.[69] Johnson also intended for Anderson's Mississippians to add their weight, and hoped for cooperation from Kershaw. Anderson's organization was still thoroughly disrupted, leaving a break between his men and Kershaw's line.[70] Little help would come from the right.

The maneuver proved too complicated for the terrain. Deas and Manigault struck the Federal line at different times, dissipating much of their combined force. The Alabamians were sheltered from Union view until they crested the slope, where they encountered blasts of Federal fire at short range. Estimating the distance as close as eighty yards, Lt. James H. Frasier of the 50th Alabama recalled that "the men could go no farther, death reigned on every side."[71]

Col. Mitchell's Federals were reinforced by Union artillery, double-shotted with canister at pointblank range. "As fast as our canister would mow them down, they would close up & advance," recalled artillery Sgt. George Dolton. "We must have piled [emphasis in original] them

up."[72] On the 50th Alabama's left, the 19th Alabama met a similar storm of resistance and fell back below the brow of the hill to reform and try again, an effort that also met with no success.

Deas' line overlapped Mitchell's by a wide margin, and in normal circumstances he would have easily flanked the Yankees, but the terrain and confusion of the Confederate approach helped conceal that fact from the Alabamians. Aggressive thinking within the Union ranks helped hold the high ground. Finding the 96th Illinois still recovering behind Whitaker's line, Capt. Seth Moe of Steedman's staff rushed the Illini to the right to extend Mitchell's front.[73] At the same time, the 121st Ohio launched a counterattack that ripped into the advancing Rebels, routing them and capturing the colors of the 22nd Alabama.[74]

Manigault tried to slow his brigade's move to align with Deas, but fell behind, his efforts plagued by a host of problems. The 34th Alabama was quickly routed by Deas' stragglers, crippling Manigault's left.[75] On the right of the 34th, the 24th and 28th Alabama regiments struggled on, clambering up the draw until they too were toe-to-toe with the Yankees. Here they stopped and traded volleys for perhaps ten minutes until one member of the 28th recalled, "our whole line gave way and we went down the hill like a gang of sheep."[76] The counterattacking 98th Ohio lost four commanders in twenty minutes but drove the center of Manigault's disorganized effort back down the hill.[77] The large 10th/19th South Carolina on the right side of the brigade's line was also driven back, losing their colors temporarily until recovered by one of Fulton's regiments.[78] On Manigault's right, the advance offered by Johnson's weakened brigades was more cautious. It came to a complete stop with the collapse of Deas and Manigault on their left. The powerful high ground remained in Federal hands.

Poor deployment and difficult terrain combined to deny Manigault and Deas the success they so desperately sought. Johnson bears some of the blame for attempting to have both brigades wheel to the right as they moved, an impossible task on a steep slope carved by deep ravines. Hindman's men were also fought out. This was their third attack of the day, and in each instance they had suffered heavy losses.

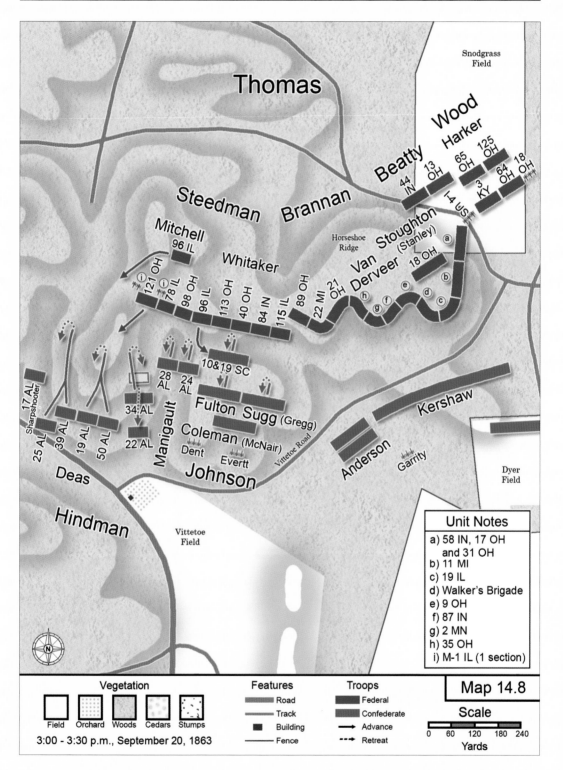

Snodgrass
Field

Thomas

Wood

Harker

Beatty

44
IN

13
OH

65
OH

125
OH

18
OH

3
KY

64
OH

I-4 US

Steedman   Brannan

Stoughton

Mitchell

96 IL

Horseshoe
Ridge

Van
Derveer (Stanley)

a

Whitaker

18 OH

b

121 OH

78 IL

98 OH

96 IL

113 OH

40 OH

84 IN

115 IL

89 OH

22 MI

21
OH

e

h

d

c

f

g

10&19 SC

28
AL

24
AL

Kershaw

17 AL

Sharpshooter

34 AL

Fulton Sugg (Gregg)

39 AL

19 AL

50 AL

22 AL

Manigault

Coleman (McNair)

Dent   Evertt

Vittetoe Road

Anderson

Garrity

Dyer
Field

25 AL

Deas

Johnson

Hindman

Vittetoe
Field

Unit Notes

a) 58 IN, 17 OH
   and 31 OH
b) 11 MI
c) 19 IL
d) Walker's Brigade
e) 9 OH
f) 87 IN
g) 2 MN
h) 35 OH
i) M-1 IL (1 section)

Vegetation

Field   Orchard   Woods   Cedars   Stumps

3:00 - 3:30 p.m., September 20, 1863

Features

Road
Track
Building
Fence

Troops

Federal
Confederate
Advance
Retreat

Map 14.8

Scale

0   60   120   180   240
Yards

14.9: Overall Situation (4:00 p.m.)

Three hours of constant (if disjointed) assaults against the hills that comprised the Horseshoe Ridge line had failed to dislodge the Federals, but James Longstreet, the commander of the Rebel "Left Wing," had no intention of stopping. There was still work to be done, regardless of the heavy confusion that ruled the field.

The division under Gen. Law seemed to be out of action, as was Joseph Kershaw's Brigade. Neither Thomas Hindman nor Bushrod Johnson had reported success in their last attacks on the far left. Throughout, Longstreet had been carefully hoarding his last reserve, William Preston's Division of Simon Buckner's Corps, which was now gathered just north of Brotherton Field.

About 3:00 p.m., Braxton Bragg summoned Longstreet to a very peculiar meeting somewhere east of the Brotherton cabin. Longstreet was ebullient, but to his surprise, Bragg appeared morose. Since the fighting on Leonidas Polk's front (the "Right Wing") had died down about midday, Longstreet argued, it was time to abandon the original plan and shift some of Polk's men to reinforce his own attack, or at least let them pursue the Federals up the Dry Valley Road while his own men attacked Horseshoe Ridge. Bragg's snappy reply—"[T]here is not a man in the Right Wing who has any fight in him"—caught Longstreet by surprise.[79] When Bragg left for his field headquarters near Jay's Mill, Longstreet realized that the army commander "thought . . . the battle was lost."[80]

Left to his own devices, Longstreet decided to commit Preston, whose division consisted of three brigades. Two of them, Brig. Gen. Archibald Gracie's and Col. John Kelly's, were close by. The third under Col. Robert Trigg was farther south, watching against Union cavalry forays (a valid concern since James Wilder's earlier attack there about midday). Trigg's men would have to catch up as best they could.

Guided by John Dyer, the son of the man who owned the Dyer farmstead, Gracie and Kelly advanced northwest across Dyer Field to form behind Kershaw's battered line.[81] What Longstreet did not do was replace Hood or appoint one overall commander to coordinate the attacks of what were by now four separate

divisions (Kershaw, Johnson, Hindman, and now Preston) from three different corps (Hood, Polk, and Buckner.) Since Preston was under Buckner's command, it might have made sense to give Buckner tactical control of these formations. Instead, Buckner remained at Longstreet's side throughout the afternoon, acting more like an aide than a corps commander.

On the Federal side of the hill, George Thomas grappled with myriad concerns, including what had happened to William Rosecrans and the rest of the army. About 3:45 p.m., he found out when Brig. Gen. James A. Garfield arrived to explain that the Union right had fallen back to Rossville. Rosecrans, he added, had ridden to Chattanooga and sent Garfield back to assess the situation.[82] Rosecrans' decision to send Garfield instead of riding back himself would be one of the most contentious of the war—and beyond. What mattered at the moment, however, was that Thomas finally knew with certainty that the rest of the army was not destroyed, but was rallying well behind him.

This news did little to alleviate his immediate concerns. The Kelly Field front seemed stable, and Horseshoe Ridge had thus far fought off every Rebel thrust, but the two positions remained isolated from one other, with a gaping hole more than 500 yards wide between them. Rebels controlled the LaFayette Road from the McDonald House northward, severing Thomas' direct connection with Rossville. Only scattered Union forces opposed that threat. With so many of his supply wagons swept off the field in the rout, ammunition was also becoming a critical concern. Even those troops replenished by the Reserve Corps supply Gordon Granger brought with him were running low once again.

Thomas was painfully aware that there were not enough troops and resources close at hand to alleviate these problems. August Willich shifted his brigade out of reserve east of Kelly Field to prolong Gen. Joseph Reynolds' line west of the LaFayette Road, but Willich didn't have enough troops to fill the entire gap to Horseshoe Ridge.

About this same time, with his own front quiet and the sounds of battle raging to the west, William Hazen requested permission to pull his brigade out of line and join Thomas on Horseshoe Ridge. Maj. Gen. John Palmer agreed, and Hazen's much-needed reinforcements marched away.[83]

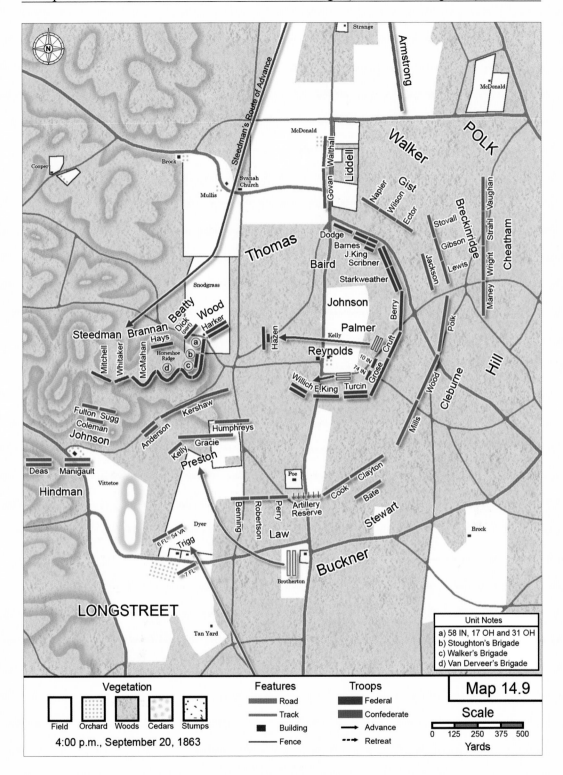

Unit Notes
a) 58 IN, 17 OH and 31 OH
b) Stoughton's Brigade
c) Walker's Brigade
d) Van Derveer's Brigade

Map 14.9

Vegetation

Field   Orchard   Woods   Cedars   Stumps

4:00 p.m., September 20, 1863

Features
▬ Road
— Track
■ Building
— Fence

Troops
▬ Federal
▬ Confederate
→ Advance
⇢ Retreat

Scale

0   125   250   375   500

Yards

14.10: Gracie attacks (4:30 p.m.)

Like many of the Confederate organizations that fought at Chickamauga, William Preston's Division was new to the Army of Tennessee. Comprised of troops brought from East Tennessee by Simon Buckner, it was of uncertain ability and temperament. Many of the division's regiments had never been in combat, and were recruited from regions that had not warmly embraced secession. Typical among them was Archibald Gracie's command, a large brigade with 1,927 officers and men consisting of the 63rd Tennessee, 43rd Alabama, and four battalions of Alabama infantry collectively known as Hilliard's Legion. After Chickamauga many of them would be accused of inciting treason and mutiny.[84] The 63rd Tennessee shed at least 150 men to desertion in the weeks leading up to the battle. Despite this, the regiment fought reasonably well.[85]

Gracie's command deployed first since it led the column. Preston intended to form Col. Kelly on Gracie's left, but before he could do so Gracie's line stepped off toward the enemy. The reason was Joseph Kershaw. When the South Carolinian spotted the large fresh brigade deploying in a long single line behind his right flank, he ordered Gracie into action immediately. Preston was furious, but the damage was done.[86] Kershaw later claimed he was trying to coordinate the actions of several brigades— McNair's (now under Coleman), Anderson's, Gracie's, and Kelly's—with his own. Even if this was true, it ignores the fact that he was interfering with the commands of no fewer than three other divisions. In any event, Kershaw's involvement had the opposite of its intended effect.[87]

Gracie discovered several difficulties as his line advanced. On his right, the 63rd Tennessee moved quickly into the fight, mostly against the open ridge of Snodgrass Hill. Hilliard's 4th Battalion near the opposite end of the line, however, was slowed by the abrupt departure of Col. Oates' 15th Alabama, which Law had finally located and recalled.[88] Disrupting Gracie's left-center was Oates' final contribution to the Confederate war effort that afternoon. Gracie's left flank lost continuity when the 43rd Alabama found its way blocked by Mississippians from Patton Anderson's Brigade. Instead of trying to pass through them, Gracie ordered the 43rd to halt, wait for rest of the brigade to pass on, and then fall in behind as a supporting line.[89]

Even if it had been perfectly orchestrated, Gracie's objective of carrying the high ground before him was a very difficult one. The 63rd Tennessee charged into Snodgrass Field, where it faced Col. Harker's merciless controlled volleys. William Hazen had just arrived from the Kelly Field sector to witness the attack. He deployed his command into line on Harker's left and added his fire to the defense of the hill.[90] Within minutes, the Tennesseans were hopelessly pinned down by a deadly crossfire.

The 1st and 2nd Alabama battalions on the 63rd's left assaulted Hill One from the east and south. The latter battalion, exposed to flanking fire when the Federals mauling the 63rd Tennessee shot in its direction, stopped at the foot of the hill, where the stymied Alabamians traded shots with the defenders.[91] The 1st Battalion assaulted the point of the hill held by the 19th Illinois, but even without much raking fire it fared little better. By now the slopes were slick and ghastly, churned to reddish mud by the spilling of so much Southern blood.[92] Gracie's right was completely stalled.

Gracie's two left battalions faced the same insurmountable difficulties. Disrupted by Oates' departure, the 4th Battalion paused to reform. When the 3rd Battalion on the far left noticed that the men on their right were absent, they too halted. When both units resumed their advance, they stepped into the draw west of Hill One, angling left and right to face the Union defenders. Once again, the curving nature of the Union lines exposed the Rebels to fire from multiple directions, sowing confusion and panic within the ranks. Maj. John D. McLennan, commanding the 4th Battalion, described the dire circumstances. "Fire pouring upon me from the front, right and left. . . . [T]o advance farther without support," he added, "would have been reckless in the extreme."[93] Men from the 3rd Battalion later claimed to have reached the crest of Hill Two in their attack, but in reality made it no farther than halfway up the slope. And there they remained, hugging the ground and unable to move forward, yet unwilling to retire.

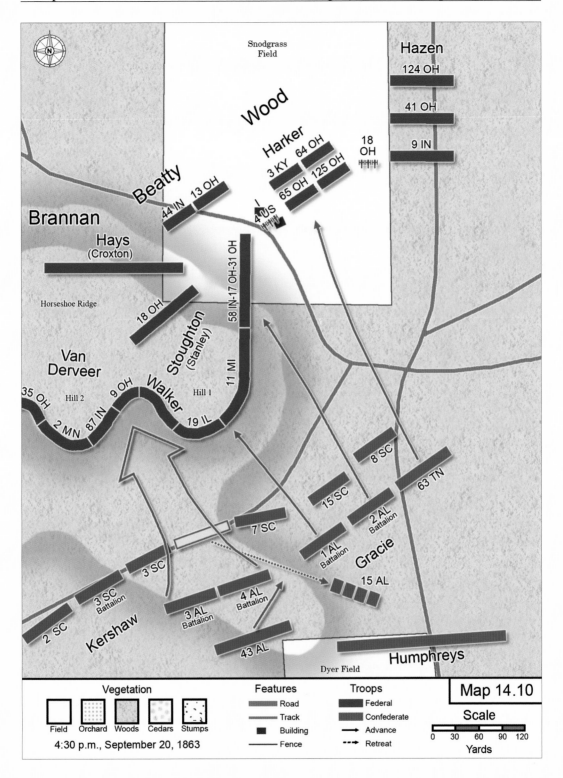

Snodgrass
Field

Hazen
124 OH
41 OH
9 IN

Wood

Harker   18
3 KY   64 OH   OH
65 OH 125 OH

Beatty   13 OH
44 IN

I
4 US

Brannan

Hays
(Croxton)

Horseshoe Ridge

18 OH

58 IN-17 OH-31 OH

Stoughton
(Stanley)

Van
Derveer

Hill 2   9 OH   Walker   Hill 1   11 MI

35 OH

2 MN   87 IN   19 IL

8 SC

15 SC   63 TN

7 SC   2 AL
Battalion

1 AL
Battalion   Gracie

3 SC   15 AL

2 SC   3 SC
Battalion

Kershaw   3 AL   4 AL
Battalion Battalion

43 AL   Humphreys

Dyer Field

Vegetation

Field   Orchard   Woods   Cedars   Stumps

4:30 p.m., September 20, 1863

Features
Road
Track
Building
Fence

Troops
Federal
Confederate
→ Advance
⇢ Retreat

Map 14.10

Scale

0   30   60   90   120
Yards

14.11: Gracie Falls Back; Kelly Takes Hill Three (4:30 p.m.)

With Gracie's left pinned down and taking heavy losses in front of Hills One and Two, the rest of his men began to retreat in confusion. Gracie rode along his lines in attempt to rally his troops, ordering the 43rd Alabama to move from his left to replace the 63rd Tennessee, on his right. Despite his earlier interference with Gracie's Brigade, Joe Kershaw's own attack never materialized. The South Carolinians were simply fought out. Other than hold their position and engage in long range firing, they were done for the day.

As Gracie's Alabamians were being beaten back, Col. John Kelly's Brigade stepped off to the attack. When Gracie's men had disappeared into the trees to begin their attack, Preston ordered Kelly to follow as best he could. Somewhere in this confusion Kelly ran into division commander Thomas Hindman and asked him for advice. Possessed of but a vague notion of the Union positions, Hindman vectored Kelly's four regiments northwest instead of straight north.[94] As the mixed brigade line of Virginians, Kentuckians, and North Carolinians approached Hill Three from the southeast, Hindman's mistake became apparent.

Col. John B. Palmer's 58th North Carolina, advancing on Kelly's right flank, suffered the most from this poor deployment. The Tar Heels' advance carried them across the front of Col. Van Derveer's Yankees atop Hill Two. The Rebels closed to within a mere handful of yards of the Union line before the 2nd Minnesota opened a killing flank fire that shattered Palmer's command. According to the colonel, fully two-thirds of his right flank company went down within seconds.[95] Stunned by the hammer blow, the men on the right instinctively fell back some distance, leaving Palmer with a regimental front shaped like a wide "L," with the long side facing generally north and the short side facing generally east. From this formation the North Carolinians opened a return fire. As this crisis was unfolding, Kelly ordered the 58th to cease firing because he believed they had stumbled into part of Gracie's advanced line. About two-thirds of Palmer's line stopped shooting. A frantic Palmer, who knew that Kelly was mistaken,

struggled unsuccessfully to correct the error, but the damage was done. Within a few minutes the 58th was in full retreat.[96]

Palmer's retreat caught Maj. James M. French's 63rd Virginia by surprise. He believed his Virginians were making headway to the left of the 58th because a line of Federals fell back at their approach. French ordered a volley and was preparing to charge when Kelly's mistaken order to stop shooting reached him. When the 58th gave way, French's line was exposed to the same flanking fire that had routed Palmer. Watching the unfolding action from atop Hill Two, Lt. Col. Judson Bishop of the 2nd Minnesota remembered that the Rebels "seemed to lose the reassuring touch of elbows, and as the vacancies rapidly increased, they began to hesitate . . . then they halted and commenced firing wildly into the tree tops, then turned and rushed madly down the slope, carrying the second line with them."[97]

The retreating line of Federals mentioned by French (above) was probably the 21st Ohio. The Buckeyes were virtually without ammunition, and their commanders had already begun to thin the lines by sending the men without bullets back into the ravine behind Hill Three to reform and wait until the entire regiment could fall back in search of rounds. By the time Kelly's final regiment, the 5th Kentucky, reached Hill Three, the 21st Ohio was largely gone.[98]

As Col. Hiram Hawkins led his 5th Kentucky through the scattered ranks of Anderson's Mississippians, one of Anderson's men offered some advice on how to proceed: "'don't stop when you sight them, but give a yell and rush them.'"[99] Hawkins intended to do just that. Facing just a smattering of fire, the Kentuckians holding Kelly's left flank broke into a yell and a run as they approached the crest, sweeping up and over Hill Three from southwest to northeast. They were brought to a halt when a robust fire from the 35th Ohio and the right side of the 2nd Minnesota—which, unlike the Buckeyes of the 21st Ohio, still had ammunition—greeted them.

The Kentuckians had achieved something significant. However tenuously, they were the first Rebel regiment to seize any of the high hills comprising Horseshoe Ridge.

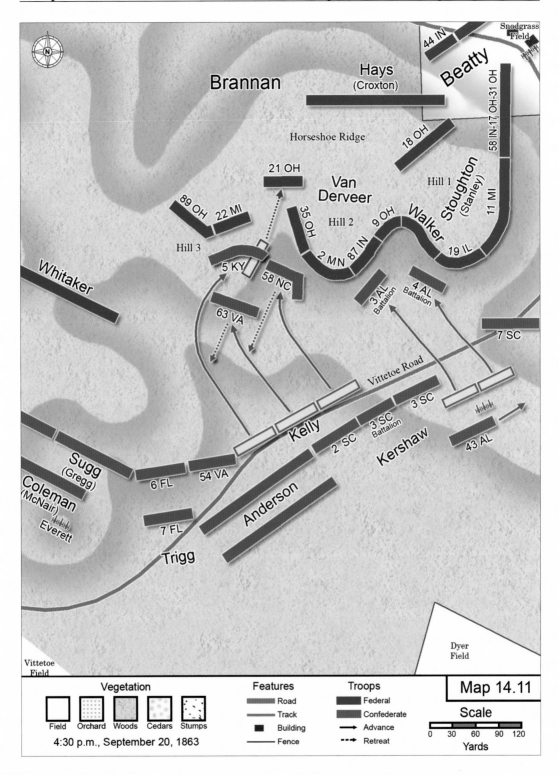

Snodgrass Field

44 IN

Beatty

Brannan

Hays
(Croxton)

58 IN-17, OH-31 OH

Horseshoe Ridge

18 OH

21 OH

Van
Derveer

Hill 1

Stoughton
(Stanley)

11 MI

89 OH   22 MI

35 OH

Hill 2

9 OH

Walker

Hill 3

2 MN   87 IN

19 IL

5 KY   58 NC

3 AL
Battalion

4 AL
Battalion

63 VA

7 SC

Whitaker

Vittetoe Road

Kelly

3 SC
Battalion   3 SC

Sugg
(Gregg)

6 FL   54 VA

2 SC

Kershaw

43 AL

Coleman
(McNair)

Everett

7 FL

Anderson

Trigg

Dyer
Field

Vittetoe
Field

Vegetation					Features	Troops	Map 14.11
					— Road	■ Federal	
					— Track	■ Confederate	Scale
Field	Orchard	Woods	Cedars	Stumps	■ Building	→ Advance	0 30 60 90 120
4:30 p.m., September 20, 1863					— Fence	◄--► Retreat	Yards

14.12: Gracie Takes Hill One (4:45 p.m.)

With Archibald Gracie's attack apparently repulsed (and not knowing about the 5th Kentucky clinging to Hill Two), George Thomas left Snodgrass Hill at 4:30 p.m., having concluded that he could not maintain his position past nightfall. The army would have to retreat to Rossville. He rode for Kelly Field to begin implementing plans for a withdrawal.

Gracie, however—a New York native who would survive Chickamauga only to die in the muddy trenches around Petersburg, Virginia— was not finished. His brigade had suffered losses, but he still had the fresh 43rd Alabama to commit to the offensive. As the officer who had helped raise the 43rd and serve as its first commander, Gracie had confidence that his Alabamians could restart his attack. He ordered the 43rd's commander, Col. Young M. Moody, to insert his men between the 63rd Tennessee and the 2nd Battalion and attack Hill One.

This approach, however, exposed the 43rd to the same fire that had brought the 2nd Battalion and Tennesseans to grief. Just as before, the volume of fire was staggering. Moody reported that every company commander in the right wing was cut down.[100] One member of the 43rd recalled that "a battery only a few hundred yards off was . . . pouring grape into us by the bushel."[101] The 63rd made a half-hearted effort to join in on the far right of the brigade line, but the Union fire drove them back quickly.[102]

When the 43rd Alabama fell back after suffering heavy losses, Gracie was there to meet them. The futility of sending them back up the hill in that location was obvious, so he ordered Moody to shift farther left, where his flank would be less exposed, and try again. In the face of a lighter fire, Moody drove his men upward. The 2nd Battalion, still fighting stubbornly from the foot of the slope, joined Moody's advance. Within minutes, a second point of Horseshoe Ridge, this time on Hill One, was in Rebel hands.

The successful piercing of the crest forced the 11th Michigan and 19th Illinois of Col. William Stoughton's brigade to fall back about twenty-five yards to the northern crest.[103] With Gracie's Alabamians utilizing the Yankee breastworks from the reverse side, the crown of Hill One became a no-mans land laced with fire.

This time there was no effort to drive the Confederates back. Ammunition shortages and a lack of reserves precluded it. Instead, both sides settled in and tried to maintain a steady fire.

Despite the shortage of bullets, few actively worked to conserve their last rounds. The 2nd Battalion's color bearer wedged his flag into the breastworks to keep it upright through the fighting. The next day he counted eighty-three bullet holes in the silk.[104] Despite the volume of fire aimed at his flag, Color Sgt. William H. Hiett received only a few cuts and scrapes during the heavy combat. When Confederate President Jefferson Davis visited the army two weeks later, Hiett presented the honored—if tattered—banner to Davis. The chief executive was impressed by the gesture, and Hiett was soon elevated to second lieutenant.

The left side of Gracie's Brigade had less success. What remained of the 1st Battalion followed the 2nd up the slope and clung to a foothold there, but with sixty percent casualties and heavy losses among its leaders, it was unfit and unable to continue. Pinned down on the slopes of Hill Two, the 3rd and 4th battalions were unable to reach the crest. Gracie rode up and down the lines in an effort to get the left organizations moving forward, to no avail.[105]

As parts of two of his brigades fought to hold lodgments along the Federal line, division leader William Preston scrambled to bring up his final brigade under Col. Robert Trigg. Like both Gracie and Kelly before him, Trigg's journey to the base of Horseshoe Ridge was laden with confusion. The colonel and three of his regiments worked their way west through the flotsam of battle in an attempt to enter the fight on Kelly's left. Col. G. Maxwell's 1st Florida Dismounted Cavalry, tardily recalled from picket duty, couldn't find Trigg and so advanced on Gracie's right. Gracie ordered the Floridians to charge across the same ground where the 43rd Alabama and 63rd Tennessee had already faltered. Maxwell was appalled, arguing, "It was hardly possible for my small regiment to do what [your] large brigade had failed to accomplish."[106] Gracie reconsidered and the 1st Florida was moved up to support his brigade's right flank. This move placed the 1st Florida 1,000 yards distant from the rest of Trigg's command, which was advancing on the division's left. Maxwell contributed little to the rest of the day's fighting.

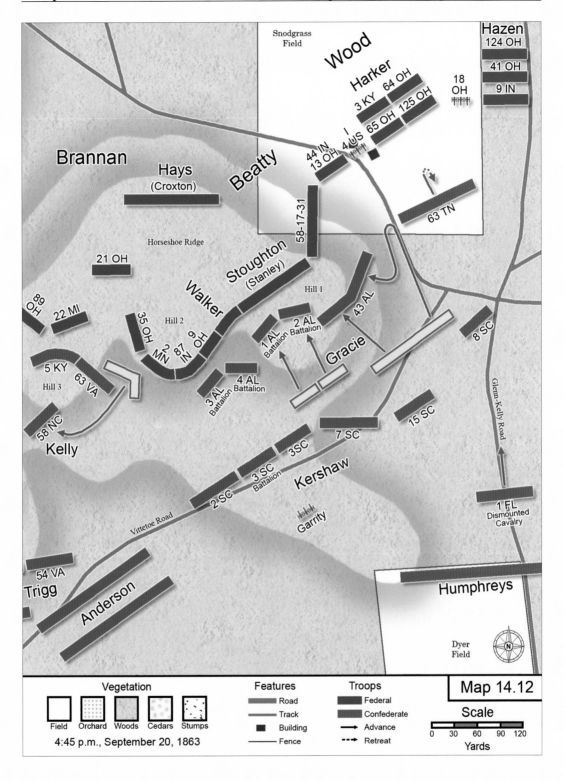

Snodgrass Field

Wood

Hazen
124 OH
41 OH
9 IN

Harker
3 KY 64 OH
65 OH 125 OH
44 IN 4 US
13 OH

18 OH

Brannan

Hays
(Croxton)

Beatty

58-17-31

63 TN

Horseshoe Ridge

21 OH

Stoughton
(Stanley)

Walker

Hill 1

89 OH

22 MI

35 OH

Hill 2

2 MN 87 IN 9 OH

1 AL
Battalion

2 AL
Battalion

43 AL

Gracie

8 SC

5 KY

63 VA

Hill 3

3 AL
Battalion

4 AL
Battalion

58 NC

Kelly

15 SC

7 SC

3SC

3 SC
Battalion

2 SC

Kershaw

Garrity

Vittetoe Road

Glenn-Kelly Road

1 FL
Dismounted
Cavalry

54 VA

Trigg

Anderson

Humphreys

Dyer
Field

N

Vegetation					Features	Troops	Map 14.12

Field Orchard Woods Cedars Stumps

Road
Track
Building
Fence

Federal
Confederate
Advance
Retreat

Scale

0   30   60   90   120
Yards

4:45 p.m., September 20, 1863

14.13: Johnson vs. Steedman (5:00 p.m.)

As Preston's brigades (Gracie and Kelly) assaulted the Federals on Hills One and Two, Bushrod Johnson continued pressing the enemy on his front farther west. It had been a long day for Johnson's men. Hindman's repulse had been a bitter disappointment, since many of Johnson's men believed that the involvement of Arthur Manigault's and Zach Deas' brigades would finally allow them to stand down. They were mistaken.

Johnson's post-battle report reflected his anger at Hindman's troops. Although his report was terse, Johnson included a statement from an aide, Lt. George Marchbanks, who had carried several dispatches to Hindman's reinforcing troops. These men, observed the lieutenant, "had scarcely gotten under fire when they began running back—one, two, and three together—until finally both brigades gave back in utter confusion. . . . I do not think these two brigades were under fire over twenty minutes."[107]

If the Union heights were going to be carried on the Confederate left, only Johnson's men were left to do it. Even with the arrival of Col. David Coleman's men (formerly McNair's Brigade), Johnson's three brigades mustered no more than 1,800 effectives (fewer than Gracie's single brigade). Linear headlong assaults were abandoned in favor of a loose order advance that pressed the Yankees cautiously and slowly while offering a less dense target mass.[108] Some of Manigault's men—parts of the 28th and 34th Alabama regiments—refused to be spectators and fought on Fulton's left, though Johnson failed to note their presence.[109]

It is easy to understand how Johnson could have missed them. Daylight was beginning to fade. Smoke from musketry and burning brush obscured visibility. Men advanced in clumps and in individual rushes instead of neat identifiable regimental battle lines. Hundreds of stragglers mixed indiscriminately from a wide assortment of regiments clogged the vales behind Johnson's position. The battle had slipped beyond the ability of any single officer to effectively shape it.

Most Confederates recalled this portion of the fight as a slow steady combat, so when the Yankees suddenly broke and ran it came as a surprise to everyone. Capt. John Lavender of the 4th Arkansas (Coleman) recalled that "our men had got on top of the Hill and give them such a Deadly Fire that they Broke Ranks and made a perfect stampede."[110] Col. R. H. Keeble of the 23rd Tennessee (Fulton) agreed: "the enemy . . . fled in the wildest confusion."[111]

James Steedman's Federals had little choice. Like so many of their comrades, they were out of ammunition or down to their final few rounds. Formations were disrupted, and command control had all but disappeared among the blue ranks. By this time, most of the defenders were fighting in small groups, clumped around a regimental flag or an officer of note. When the time to retreat arrived, the movement was made with little effort at coordination.

The unraveling of the position began on the right side of the crest with Col. John Mitchell's brigade. The 78th Illinois was the first to go, worried about being outflanked from the left. The Illini fell back about 300 yards, and with their last rounds prepared to make a final stand.[112] The 98th Ohio, without any ammunition at all, fell back, fixed bayonets, and fell in alongside the 78th.[113] This retreat exposed the 1st Illinois, Battery M, and the 121st Ohio, which also fell back. On the far right, when Capt. George Hicks' half of the 96th Illinois (part of Walter Whitaker's brigade) discovered the 121st gone, it moved east in an effort to find friendly troops and fill the gap. By chance, these men stumbled upon Col. Thomas Champion's fragment of the regiment that had been fighting farther left. With fewer than 100 men remaining and all semblance of organization gone, Champion herded them into a rough formation. "Never mind your companies, boys," he advised them. "Get into line somewhere."[114]

Similar stories played out all along the Federal front, where formal command at the regimental level was hit and miss at best. When Steedman met the retreating 115th Illinois, he ordered the men back up the hill. When its colonel, Jesse Moore, reported that his men were out of ammunition, Steedman told him to fix bayonets. Alone and exposed, the 115th made some effort to regain its former position, but was quickly driven back. When Moore's men retreated a second time, it was for good.[115] Bushrod Johnson's Rebels, now firmly in command of the crest, were content to let them go.

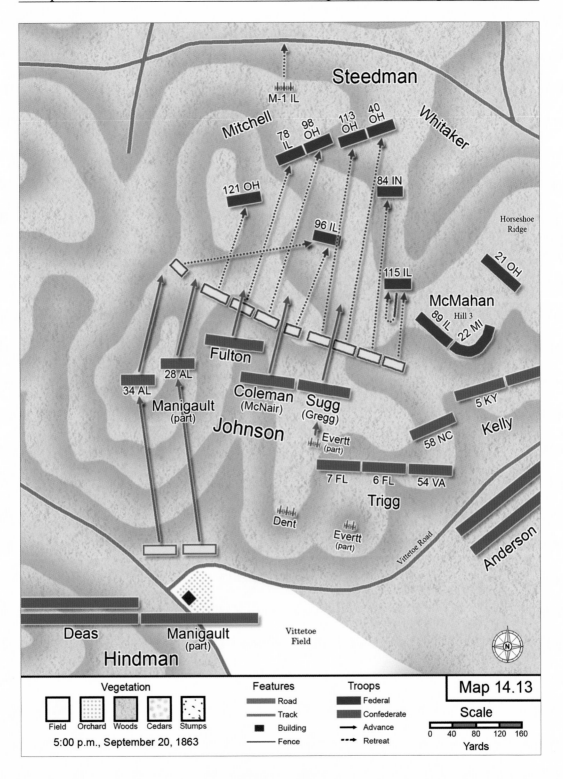

Steedman

M-1 IL

Mitchell

78 IL

98 OH

113 OH

40 OH

Whitaker

121 OH

84 IN

96 IL

Horseshoe Ridge

21 OH

115 IL

McMahan

89 IL   Hill 3

22 MI

Fulton

28 AL

34 AL

Manigault
(part)

Coleman
(McNair)

Sugg
(Gregg)

Johnson

Evertt
(part)

5 KY

58 NC

Kelly

7 FL   6 FL   54 VA

Trigg

Dent

Evertt
(part)

Vittetoe Road

Anderson

Deas   Manigault
(part)

Vittetoe
Field

N

Hindman

| Vegetation | | | | | Features | Troops | Map 14.13 |

Vegetation

Field   Orchard   Woods   Cedars   Stumps

5:00 p.m., September 20, 1863

Features

Road
Track
Building
Fence

Troops

Federal
Confederate
→ Advance
⇢ Retreat

Map 14.13

Scale

0   40   80   120   160

Yards

14.14: Gracie and Brannan Retreat (6:00 p.m.)

While Bushrod Johnson was gaining the crest of the ridge he had struggled much of the afternoon to capture, Archibald Gracie's Alabamians were giving up their hard-won toeholds on Hills One and Three. With his men out of ammunition, Gracie decided he could no longer wait to be relieved. Ironically, the Yankees opposite his regiments were reaching the same conclusion. And with George Thomas' retreat order now in place, they moved to implement it.

In the 43rd Alabama, Col. Moody reported that his men were out of bullets and their weapons had become so fouled from repeated use that they were no longer functional. As far as Moody was concerned, he had no choice but to fall back.[116] The other units in the brigade faced similar problems. Gracie bowed to the inevitable and ordered his men to fall back on line with the 1st Florida Cavalry, where they set to work reorganizing their formations. In the 1st Battalion, Pvt. John Davenport lamented the retreat: "if we onley had had a little more of that noisy kill dead [ammunition] we should have had the honer of [staying and] capturing the enemey's brigade."[117]

Gracie's withdrawal meant that Kelly's Brigade, on Gracie's left, was alone and vulnerable. After they had swept the crest of Hill Three, the Rebels of the 5th Kentucky went to ground and shot away all of their ammunition in a duel with Col. Van Derveer's Federals. The noisy exchange accomplished little except to empty cartridge boxes. By this time Col. Palmer's 58th North Carolina had switched flanks after its deadly encounter with Van Derveer, slipping behind the 63rd Virginia in an attempt to launch a new attack against Hill Three.

The Federals were also in motion. When the firing ceased on his right, Van Derveer pulled his brigade off Hill Two into the ravine behind it, leaving the 35th Ohio atop the hill to cover the move. The general completely missed the fact that the 22nd Michigan and 89th Ohio of Whitaker's brigade, both under command of the 22nd's Col. Le Favour, remained in line on the far side of Hill Three. This was not a surprising omission because the growing smoke and deepening gloom made a firm understanding of what was taking place quite difficult. Van Derveer's retreat triggered a larger withdrawal from Hill One. As Gracie's Rebels relinquished their hold on this peak, so too did the jumbled forces fighting under Col. William Stoughton and Gen. John Brannan. This mass of Federal regiments moved back (north) behind the Snodgrass cabin.

Not all the Federals were falling back. The 68th and 101st Indiana regiments of Ed King's brigade (part of Joseph Reynolds' division) arrived at this time. Looking for troops who still had ammunition, Thomas borrowed them after their own retreat from Kelly Field (Map 15.1) and sent them west to act as rearguard for the withdrawal toward Rossville.[118] Unaware of Thomas' efforts, Brannan sought out William Hazen to ask for the loan of a regiment for the same mission. His appeal produced the 9th Indiana, which one of Brannan's aides led up the hill to support the 35th Ohio.[119]

The 22nd Michigan and 89th Ohio were beginning to retreat when Le Favour encountered Maj. John Smith of Steedman's staff. The major immediately ordered Le Favour back up the hill to cover the rest of the retreat. "Ammunition and reinforcements" would be sent at once, Smith promised.[120] The reluctant colonel complied and returned the men to the hilltop.

Despite having been engaged all afternoon and running low on ammunition, the Buckeyes of the 21st Ohio were also ordered back into line. After their retreat from Hill Three, Maj. Arnold McMahan gathered what was left of his 21st regiment in the ravine and was about to lead it away when he met Van Derveer. After a frustrating exchange, Van Derveer ordered McMahan to fix bayonets and return to the crest.[121] With but one round apiece McMahan complied, though the regiment accidentally split into two factions. The Buckeyes moved past the 22nd Michigan, also just returning, only to bump into advancing Rebels belonging to the 58th North Carolina. The Buckeyes fired their last round and retreated again. Equally spooked in the smoky gloom, the Tar Heels opened an extended fusillade upon the now-empty hillside.[122]

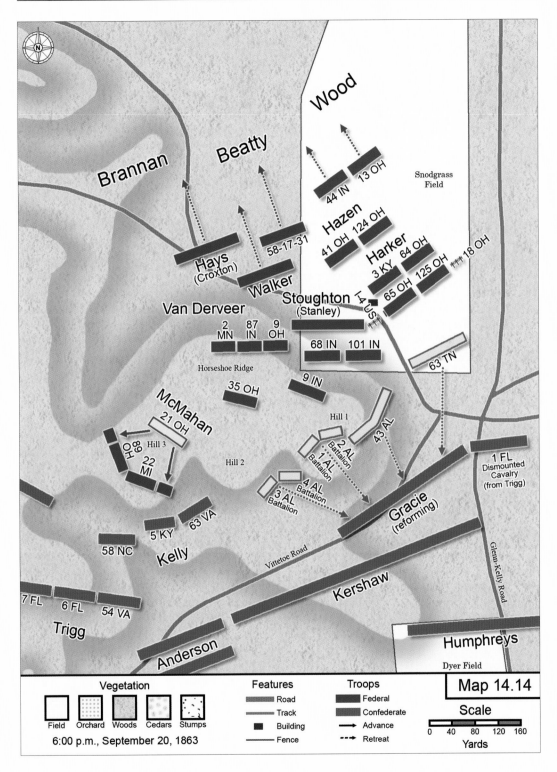

Wood

Brannan

Beatty

Snodgrass
Field

44 IN   13 OH

Hazen

41 OH   124 OH

58-17-31

Harker   64 OH

Hays
(Croxton)

3 KY

125 OH   18 OH

Walker

65 OH

Van Derveer

Stoughton
(Stanley)

14 US

2
MN

87
IN

9
OH

68 IN   101 IN

Horseshoe Ridge

63 TN

35 OH

9 IN

McMahan

21 OH

Hill 1

43 AL

89
OH

Hill 3

2 AL
Battalion

1 FL
Dismounted
Cavalry
(from Trigg)

22
MI

Hill 2

1 AL
Battalion

4 AL
Battalion

3 AL
Battalion

Gracie
(reforming)

5 KY   63 VA

58 NC

Kelly

Vittetoe Road

Kershaw

Glenn-Kelly Road

7 FL   6 FL   54 VA

Trigg

Anderson

Humphreys

Dyer Field

Vegetation					Features	Troops	Map 14.14

Field Orchard Woods Cedars Stumps

Road

Federal

Track

Confederate

Scale

Building

Advance

0   40   80   120   160

6:00 p.m., September 20, 1863

Fence

Retreat

Yards

14.15: Trigg Finally Advances (6:30 p.m.)

By 6:30 p.m., only five Union regiments (a de-facto rearguard) were in close proximity to the Confederates. Without the guidance of a single coherent hand in command, these troops were placed haphazardly and without a clear understanding of their overall deployment. They did, however, draw the focus of the remaining Southern effort to take Horseshoe Ridge.

When Col. Kelly shifted the 58th North Carolina to his left flank, he did so with the intention of renewing his assault. The 58th bumped into the 21st Ohio in an encounter that disrupted both commands. Kelly also sent the 5th Kentucky and 63rd Virginia forward in a joint effort that was equally confused. Kelly's men were once again warned to be on the lookout for friends, this time in the form of Trigg's men, who were coming into line on their left (west). Friendly fire was still on Kelly's mind.

All three of Kelly's regiments found Federals, but the encounter only served to increase the general sense of confusion. Catching sight of the 22nd Michigan atop Hill Three, Col. Hiram Hawkins of the 5th Kentucky (Confederate) demanded to know their identity. No less perplexed, the Wolverines replied "friends," hoping that any time purchased by the ruse would allow reinforcements to come to their relief.[123] A Rebel doubted the claim and shouted, "They are yanks!" At that point, reported Hawkins, "They treacherously fired into us."[124] The Yankees later disputed this accusation, claiming it was the Rebels who first tried to surrender and then opened fire.[125] Shaken by this encounter, the Kentuckians fell back.

This drama was playing out when Col. Trigg finally arrived with the 7th Florida. The 6th Florida and 54th Virginia were already in line on Kelly's left, so Trigg led the 7th farther west to prolong that flank, extending his line behind Bushrod Johnson's advanced position atop the ridge. Kelly and Trigg met and conferred. When the former officer argued they could outflank the Federals atop Hill Three, Trigg agreed to a joint advance, with the understanding that his line would swing around to the right while Kelly's men made another head-on advance up the hill.[126] Together, they believed, both commands

would be able to completely envelop the enemy. Before the new plan could be put in motion, one of Gen. Preston's aides arrived and called on Kelly to ride to the rear to consult with the division commander. Kelly departed at once, but failed to inform Trigg that he was leaving.

Kelly was new to brigade command. The Alabama native dropped out of West Point when war broke out, joined the Confederate Army as a lieutenant, and turned in a solid performance at Shiloh in April 1862 at the head of the 9th Arkansas Battalion. Promoted to colonel one month later, he led the 8th Arkansas Battalion during the Kentucky campaign and again at Stone's River. Just one week before this day, on September 13, he was appointed to command the brigade. At 23, he was the youngest brigade commander on the field, but his sterling combat record justified his promotion. Still, a more experienced brigadier might have declined to leave at such a critical moment in the fighting.

On Hill Two, meanwhile, another conference was unfolding, this one between Col. Isaac Suman of the 9th Indiana and Col. Henry Boynton of the 35th Ohio. Brannan's aide had led the Hoosiers to the position held by the Buckeyes, where Boynton ordered them farther forward to the southwestern face of Hill Two—considerably in advance of his own regiment. The Hoosiers were none to happy with this arrangement. "He is trying to work you, colonel," argued Maj. George H. Carter of the 9th. Suman agreed, replying to Boynton, "I don't know that I ought to take orders from you."[127] An angry exchange followed, with Boynton calling the 9th cowards. The epithet, coupled with the presence of Brannan's aide, convinced the Hoosiers to move to the southwestern face as directed. The regiment edged about thirty or forty yards ahead and lined the crest of Hill Two where it overlooked the draw between Hills Two and Three.[128]

On that next hilltop to the west, the 21st Ohio came to rest after its collision with the North Carolinians. The bulk of the 21st, now numbering only eighty or ninety men, according to Col. Caleb Carlton of the 89th, fell in alongside Carlton's right, facing west. Two companies of the 21st returned to their original position on the 22nd Michigan's left facing southeast.

The Federals had assumed their places for the closing act on Horseshoe Ridge.[129]

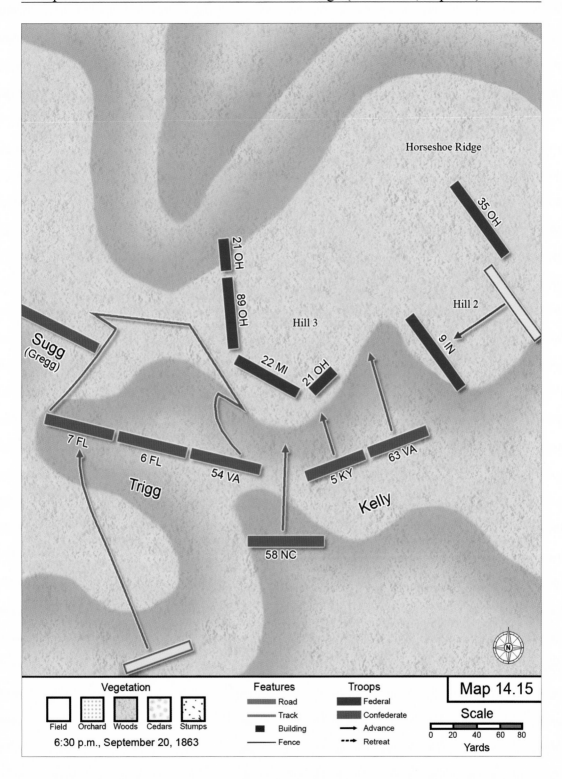

Horseshoe Ridge

35 OH

21 OH

89 OH

Hill 2

Hill 3

9 IN

Sugg
(Gregg)

22 MI

21 OH

7 FL

6 FL

54 VA

5 KY

63 VA

Trigg

Kelly

58 NC

Map 14.15

Scale

6:30 p.m., September 20, 1863

Vegetation	Features	Troops

Field   Orchard   Woods   Cedars   Stumps

Road
Track
Building
Fence

Federal
Confederate
Advance
Retreat

0   20   40   60   80
Yards

14.16: The Capture of Three Federal Regiments (7:00 p.m.)

Unaware of Kelly's absence, Trigg began advancing his brigade (6th and 7th Florida and 54th Virginia; the 1st Florida remained on the right of Archibald Gracie's line) as planned. He also attempted to get some of Bushrod Johnson's infantry involved, to no avail. Johnson's brigades had finally had enough fighting for the day.[130]

By now it was so dark that the advance was more of a grope than a charge, but the poor visibility worked to the Rebels' advantage. Trigg's activity drew enemy attention. From the ranks of the 7th Florida, Pvt. Robert Watson noted that the Floridians reached "the foot of the hill at dark. The enemy seeing us sent a man toward us to see whether we were their own men or not, with directions to fire if we were enemies but we took him before he could fire his gun, therefor [sic] the Yankees took it for granted that we were their own men."[131]

The captured soldier Watson recalled who had tried to determine their identity was Capt. Henry Alban of the 21st Ohio. A second man of the 21st was captured when Alban failed to return and he was sent to find him.[132] On the hill, Col. Le Favour of the 22nd Michigan undertook a similar mission. Col. Caleb Carlton of the 89th Ohio (Whitaker) rode to Le Favour, found him already gone, and elected to wait. When some of La Favour's men observed large numbers of men moving up the dark smoky slope, Carlton spurred his mount back to his own regiment. By now, Le Favour was also a prisoner.[133]

Despite Kelly's absence, his brigade followed Trigg's. Their combined regiments—exactly as the two Rebel colonels had conceived it—were converging on Hill Three from multiple directions, leaving the Federals little hope of escaping. The lack of Union ammunition didn't help matters. Lt. Edward Scott recalled the feeling of helplessness that swept through the ranks of the Buckeyes: "It was impossible to tell who they were until they got within ten feet of us, when through the gloom we could see that their uniforms were gray. It was too late then to do anything even if we had any ammunition."[134] The survivors of the 89th Ohio lay down their arms. Some members of the 21st Ohio

attempted to bolt, and a few got away, but most of the regiment still on the hill surrendered there, a bitter finish to their stubborn, day-long defense.[135]

The 22nd Michigan fared no better. "Just at dusk," recalled Wolverine Sgt. Marvin Boget, "our ammunition gave out, and the Johnnies had advanced on our right and left as we could tell by the yelling[.] Finally they closed in on us with guns pointing us in the face and a command to 'throw down your guns and lie down on the ground[.]' I tell you I wasn't long in obeying."[136] With that, more than 200 men from the 22nd regiment were added to growing roster of captives.

Members of Col. Suman's 9th Indiana (Hazen's brigade) witnessed the distressing climax of the hours-long fight for Horseshoe Ridge. Drawn by "an unnecessary amount of talking," Suman reported, "I went over to see what it meant, and to my surprise, I found the enemy demanding our troops to surrender."[137] Within moments Suman found himself a prisoner, but quick thinking saved him. After informing his captor that he had already surrendered once, the colonel slipped away and made it back to his regiment. Reunited with his Hoosiers, Suman ordered them to fire a volley and fall back on the 35th Ohio.

The volley fire from the 9th Indiana triggered more confusion. To the disgust of Suman, when he told Lt. Col. Boynton of what was taking place, the 35th Ohio commander scoffed at the idea that Rebels in any number were on top of the hill.[138] The Hoosier fire had missed its mark entirely, and the Rebels initially mistook it for another case of friendly fire. A Trigg aide named James Chenault was sent to put an end to the problem. When he rode up to the Union ranks, members of both the 35th Ohio and the 9th Indiana remember that he demanded their surrender and was promptly shot dead for his trouble.[139]

With that, both Federal regiments took to their heels, falling back toward the Snodgrass cabin. Trigg's and Kelly's men might have followed, had they not been busy recapturing the Federals who scattered when the volley rang out. Largely encircled, virtually all of them were rounded up. In addition to their dead and wounded, the three regiments reported a combined total of 563 men missing from their ranks the next day. After several bloody hours of fighting, Horseshoe Ridge was firmly in Rebel hands.

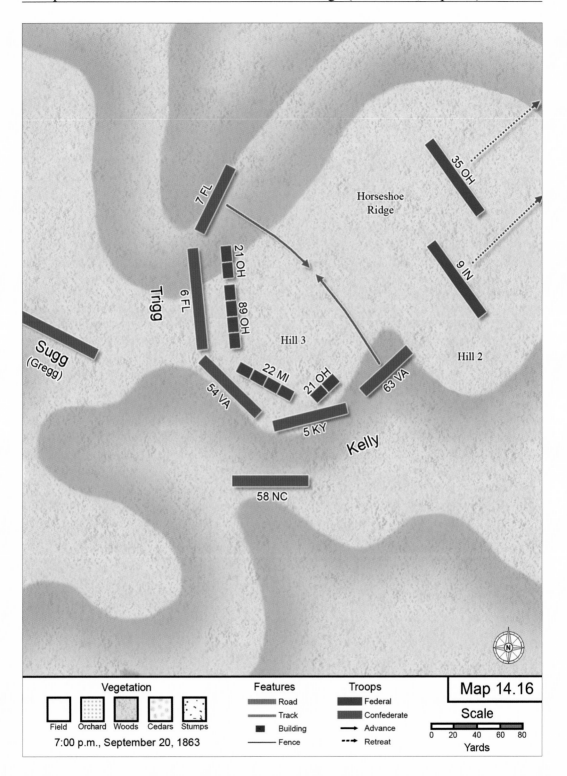

Horseshoe
Ridge

35 OH

7 FL

9 IN

21 OH

Trigg

6 FL

89 OH

Hill 3

Sugg
(Gregg)

Hill 2

22 MI

21 OH

63 VA

54 VA

5 KY

Kelly

58 NC

Vegetation

Field Orchard Woods Cedars Stumps

7:00 p.m., September 20, 1863

Features

Road
Track
Building
Fence

Troops

Federal
Confederate
Advance
Retreat

Map 14.16

Scale

0   20   40   60   80
Yards

Map Set 15: Thomas Retreats from Kelly Field

(Late Afternoon, September 20)

15.1: Orders to Retreat (4:30 p.m.)

As noted previously (Map 14.12), Maj. Gen. George Thomas left Snodgrass Hill about this time to return to Kelly Field. He played no further role in the defense of Horseshoe Ridge. Thomas, the leader of the army's "Left Wing," had not been present at Kelly Field since about noon. The repulse of the Confederate attacks that morning left this part of the line relatively quiet and stable. His return signified his intent to begin a difficult maneuver: the extrication of his command without alerting the Rebels and triggering a renewed assault.

Changes in Federal dispositions during his absence had been minor. The gap left by the departure of Brig. Gen. William Hazen's brigade was filled by Col. William Grose's brigade and some of Brig. Gen. Charles Cruft's men shifting to their right front.[1] These movements thinned Maj. Gen. John Palmer's defensive front to a single line, but this was a small concern considering how easily earlier Rebel attacks had been rebuffed. Some support was still at hand in the form of the 10th and 74th Indiana regiments, adrift from Col. John Croxton's brigade since the morning; they fell in behind Palmer's men.

The most significant changes took place at the southern end of the position. With John Brannan no longer on the field, Joseph Reynolds turned his division ninety degrees. The result was that John Turchin's brigade anchored the angle of this new line facing south, and Col. Edward King's brigade angled northwest back toward the LaFayette Road, facing southwest.[2] King's command was still short the 105th Ohio, and would be the rest of the day, but the other regiments were in good shape. About 4:00 p.m., Brig. Gen. August Willich, worried about the vulnerability of this refused flank, pulled his four regiments out of reserve and extended Reynolds' right across the LaFayette Road into the timber in an effort to bridge the gap to Horseshoe Ridge that so concerned Thomas.[3] The rest of the line remained as it had formed that morning, curving north around the end of Kelly Field to anchor in the woods east of the LaFayette Road, where Col. Joseph Dodge's men now held the flank. Despite his absence of several hours, Thomas had not designated a single commander for the Kelly Field sector. Each of the four division commanders present (Reynolds, Palmer, Johnson, Baird, from south to north) was responsible for his own sector.

Thomas' long absence, coupled with the sustained roar of battle in their rear on Horseshoe Ridge, preyed on the nerves of these Federals. Palmer was the senior commander on this part of the field, and the other division leaders turned to him for advice. About 4:00 p.m., Palmer noted that "the commander of one of the divisions near my own" rode up and urged immediate retreat. The rest of the army must be defeated, argued this officer, with both "Thomas and Rosecrans . . . killed or in the hands of the enemy."[4] Palmer was too circumspect to name the panicked officer, but other testimony reveals that it was Reynolds. Despite his staunch resistance that morning, Reynolds was by now rattled enough to remove his own rank insignia and talk of surrendering.[5]

John Palmer, a staunch anti-slavery prewar politician who played an important role in the nomination of Abraham Lincoln, was not prone to panic. The Kentucky native began the war as a Illinois colonel in May of 1861, making brigadier general that December. Palmer led a division at New Madrid and Island No. 10 and a brigade after Shiloh during the slow advance to Corinth, Mississippi, but his first hard combat came at Stone's River at the end of 1862, where he commanded a division under Tom Crittenden.

Reynolds' chatter about surrendering was not well received, and Palmer rejected such notions out of hand. He was confident Thomas would return soon, and he was right. When Thomas arrived, he determined that what was left of the army would retreat—but with discipline and care and not panic and chaos. The southern end would pull out first, with Reynolds leading. Only then would the remaining Federals pull out, division by division, crossing Kelly Field and using the woods to the west as cover. From there, they would fall back into McFarland's Gap, moving north behind the Horseshoe Ridge line until safely away. Once these troops were safely extricated, the Snodgrass defenders could pull out. It was a precarious plan, predicated on Leonidas Polk's Confederates remaining passive, but it was the best Thomas could manage under very difficult circumstances.

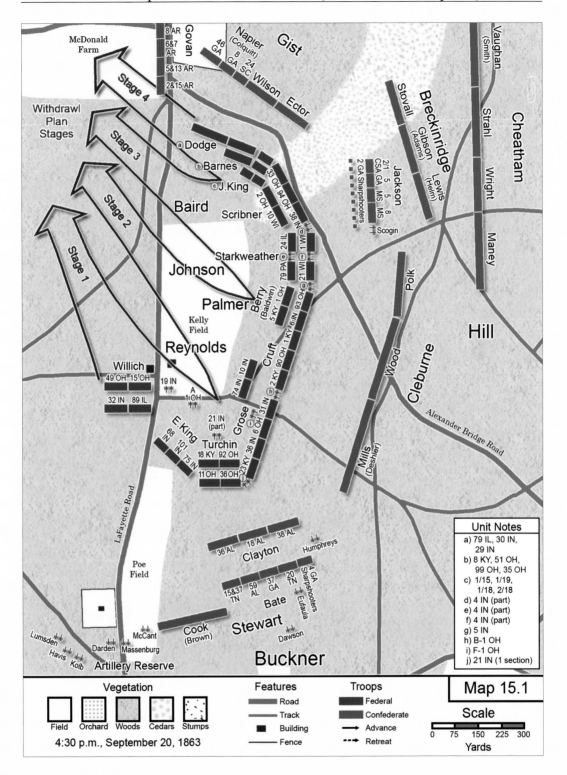

Map 15.1

4:30 p.m., September 20, 1863

Unit Notes
a) 79 IL, 30 IN, 29 IN
b) 8 KY, 51 OH, 99 OH, 35 OH
c) 1/15, 1/19, 1/18, 2/18
d) 4 IN (part)
e) 4 IN (part)
f) 4 IN (part)
g) 5 IN
h) B-1 OH
i) F-1 OH
j) 21 IN (1 section)

Vegetation
Field Orchard Woods Cedars Stumps

Features
Road
Track
Building
Fence

Troops
Federal
Confederate
Advance
Retreat

Scale
0   75   150   225   300
Yards

15.2: Confederates Renew the Attack (5:00 p.m.)

For several hours the Rebels wrapped around the Kelly Field sector had contented themselves with long range firing and harassing skirmishing. This fire proved much more annoying than it was damaging, although it managed to bring down Union brigade commander Edward King, who was shot and killed while dismounting near Palmer's position on the southeast corner of the line.[6] By 5:00 p.m., however, various Confederate units were evidencing a renewed interest in a fresh assault.[7]

After their midday repulse, Maj. Gen. A. P. Stewart's Division reformed in the woods east of Poe Field, supporting the gun line Maj. Gen. Simon Buckner assembled there to assail the Federals to their north. Buckner had held Stewart back for most of the afternoon, but now word arrived from Lt. Gen. James Longstreet, commander of the Confederate "Left Wing," to join in the advance.[8] Brig. Gen. John Brown's Brigade, led now by Col. Edmund C. Cook of the 32nd Tennessee, remained in support of the artillery while Brig. Gens. Henry Clayton and William Bate's commands advanced toward Turchin's position at the southeast corner of the Federal line.

Unbeknownst to Stewart, Thomas had already ordered Reynolds' men out of line. Moving in parallel columns, King's (now under Col. Milton Robinson) and Turchin's brigades hustled north along the LaFayette Road and filed into combat formation in the trees lining the southern end of McDonald Field. They occupied roughly the same line Brig. Gen. John Beatty's men had held at 8:00 a.m. on the morning of what must have seemed like an endless day.[9] Thomas intended to use Reynolds' command to clear McDonald Field, which was still swarming with Rebel infantry, keeping open the door for the escape of the rest of his men still waiting in the Kelly Field sector.

Clayton's Alabamians felt their way cautiously forward, wary when they did not meet the heavy resistance they expected. Instead, they witnessed Palmer's Federals beginning their own retreat, following in Reynolds' wake. Both Grose and Cruft were already in motion, their regiments running across the open field one at a time,

spaced so as to avoid presenting too tempting a target for Buckner's artillery at the Poe House.[10] The scene was a welcome contrast to previous fights. "The enemy [was] fleeing in wild disorder across a large open field," reported Clayton, "at the edge of which I ordered a halt, and the brigade continued to fire as long as the enemy could be seen."[11]

Opposite the Union center, skirmishing had been intensifying into a larger conflict for some time. About 2:00 p.m. Brig. Gen. John K. Jackson's Southern brigade was ordered forward to support the right side of Brig. Gen. Patrick Cleburne's Division, held by Brig. Gen. Lucius Polk's Brigade. Jackson arrived in front of Polk's line. Polk had fallen back in the wake of the failed attacks that morning and left a considerable gap on his left. Jackson sent the 2nd Georgia sharpshooters to cover this gap, a move that provoked a prolonged skirmish with the Brig. Gen. John Starkweather's Federals. In response to several queries Jackson made to Maj. Gen. D. H. Hill and Cleburne, Polk's men moved forward, angling northwest to connect with Jackson's line and support him.[12] All of this would take considerable time, but when the hour ticked to 5:00 p.m. Jackson's men advanced, triggering an action that quickly progressed beyond skirmishing.

Under heavy fire from front and flank (Polk's men had not yet closed the gap) Jackson asked for more support, this time from his own divisional commander, Maj. Gen. Frank Cheatham. The Tennessee division leader was already under orders to shift his line to the army's right in support of Brig. Gen. St. John Liddell; Jackson's request induced Cheatham to send two more brigades under Brig. Gens. Marcus Wright and George Maney to reinforce Jackson.[13] All of this activity was reigniting the battle on this long-quiet sector of the line.

Brig. Gen. Absalom Baird's Federals opposed Jackson's sortie. Baird was in a bit of a quandary. His regiments were holding their own, but Palmer's men on his right had already left the line, and Brig. Gen. Richard Johnson's troops (Col. William Berry's brigade, on Baird's right) were ordered to evacuate next. Thereafter it would be Baird's turn to follow Johnson—assuming he could successfully disengage from the new attack developing against his front.

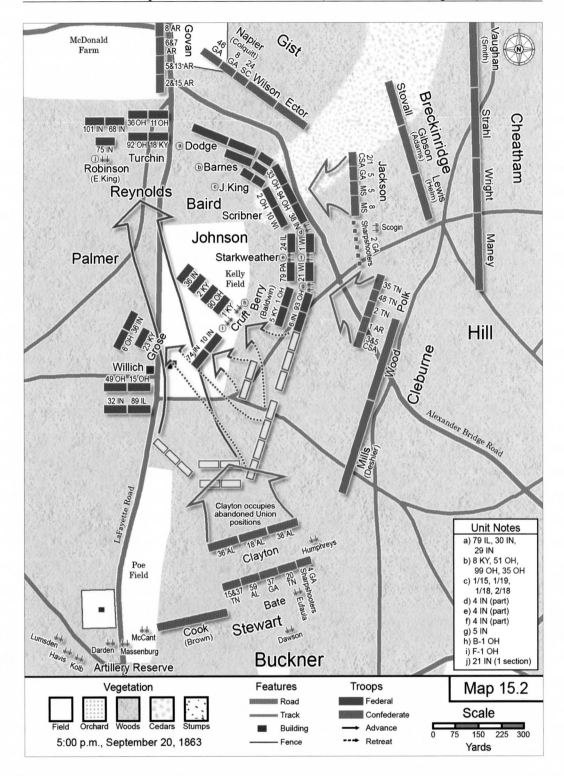

Unit Notes
a) 79 IL, 30 IN, 29 IN
b) 8 KY, 51 OH, 99 OH, 35 OH
c) 1/15, 1/19, 1/18, 2/18
d) 4 IN (part)
e) 4 IN (part)
f) 4 IN (part)
g) 5 IN
h) B-1 OH
i) F-1 OH
j) 21 IN (1 section)

Map 15.2

Scale

Vegetation
Field   Orchard   Woods   Cedars   Stumps

Features
Road
Track
Building
Fence

Troops
Federal
Confederate
Advance
Retreat

0   75   150   225   300
Yards

5:00 p.m., September 20, 1863

15.3 Reynolds Clears
McDonald Field (5:30 p.m.)

Unaware of Baird's unfolding dilemma, George Thomas remained focused on securing the area around McDonald Field. When he met Turchin, Thomas ordered him to take his brigade and clear the field. As a clear indication of just how confusing this battlefield was for the men who fought there, Turchin's troops initially formed facing south, unsure where the Rebels were located. Thomas realized the mistake and reoriented the men.[14] Col. Robinson's three regiments (King's brigade) angled to the left and came into a single line alongside Turchin.[15] After a brief hesitation to align their ranks, the Federals burst into the open, squarely on the left flank of Brig. Gen. Daniel Govan's combined Arkansas and Louisiana brigade.

Govan's men were sensitive to flanking efforts, having narrowly avoided an entrapment earlier (about midday). The sudden Federal attack had taken them completely by surprise, and they broke for the rear. "We issued from the woods and struck them a tremendous blow giving them the bayonet at close quarters," recalled Pvt. Rob Abney of the 36th Ohio (Turchin's brigade). "So sudden was our attack that we had our bayonets in their teeth before they knew it and in 15 seconds the whole plain was a mass of fleeing butternuts."[16]

Govan's division commander, St. John Liddell, had been expecting something like this. Earlier, corps leader D. H. Hill had directed Liddell to move his division forward in an effort to outflank the Kelly Field Federals from the north, essentially repeating the tactics that had failed that morning. Liddell well remembered the earlier failure and protested, "I will be exposed front and flank." Hill promised reinforcements, and dutifully Liddell moved his two brigades (Govan and Brig. Gen. Edward Walthall) forward into the field. Before Hill's promised support could materialize or Liddell could begin his own attack, Reynolds' division crushed his left flank. "The thing was done so suddenly that it was incomprehensible," lamented Liddell. "The enemy, passing my left flank in overwhelming numbers, took with him all of my men within reach."[17]

The Yankees weren't finished. With Govan's men swept away, Walthall's Mississippians found themselves equally exposed and badly out of position. Liddell's artillery was planted on the small rise around the McDonald House, shelling Federals in the direction of Snodgrass Hill, when Reynolds' men appeared. The gunners turned to face them and tried to engage the onrushing Federals, to no avail. "When the brigade to my left gave way," Walthall reported, " . . . my own soon followed, falling back in confusion under a furious cannonade."[18]

The Federal guns producing the cannonade mentioned by Walthall were firing from several directions. The closest (Capt. Charles M. Barnett's Battery I, 2nd Illinois) belonged to Col. Daniel McCook's brigade of the Union Reserve Corps, left behind by Granger to cover the rear and now in line along a wooded hillside several hundred yards to the northwest. Others must have been firing from the vicinity of the Snodgrass cabin when they weren't busy shooting at Archibald Gracie's Rebels. Liddell's two batteries were already enduring a hot fire when Reynolds' men appeared. When their infantry support melted away, Capts. Charles Swett's and William Fowler's batteries barely escaped ahead of the Federals.[19]

Turchin rode at the forefront of the dramatic Federal attack. It was at this point—the pinnacle of success—when the Federal effort disrupted itself. Thomas ordered Robinson and Turchin to swing their regiments to the left, intending to place them in line alongside Col. McCook's brigade, an effort to hold the door to McFarland's Gap open for the rest of the army. Reynolds, on the division's right, missed this change of direction. He, together with about 150 men intermingled from all four of Turchin's regiments, continued moving due north along the LaFayette Road. Once more seized with panic—this time he feared that he was about to be surrounded—Reynolds impulsively ordered the men not to fire for fear of antagonizing the Rebels, and told them they must surrender. Disgusted and outraged, the men refused. Within a few minutes cooler heads prevailed and the men rejoined their brigade now a quarter-mile distant. Their indignation at Reynolds' behavior would long linger.[20]

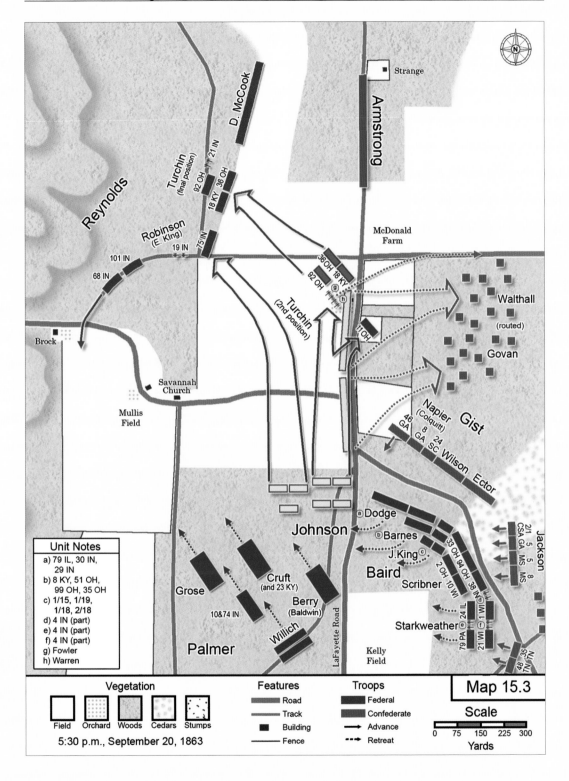

Map 15.3

Scale

5:30 p.m., September 20, 1863

15.4: Baird is Overrun (5:30 p.m.)

While Reynolds was losing his composure in McDonald Field, Baird's situation around the north end of Kelly Field was deteriorating. Two Rebel brigades (Gens. Jackson and Polk) were assailing his front, supported by Rebel guns raining shells along his line. When Col. William Berry's regiments withdrew, Gen. Starkweather's brigade of four regiments (part of Baird's division) was without flank support on his left. As the fighting intensified, a courier arrived with Thomas' order to retreat. Baird's first reaction was that "to fall back was more difficult than to remain."[21] Realistically, however, staying while the rest of the army left would only leave his men isolated and subject to mass capture.

Starkweather pulled out first. Not as confident as his division commander that he could hold his position, he ordered his reserve line to fall back into Kelly Field, halt there with the 5th Indiana battery, and await the first line. With all of his regiments on line, he intended to fall back fighting in order to cover the retreat of his guns. It didn't go as planned. His infantry was low on ammunition, and the Hoosier Battery had been mauled by two days of battle. Polk's Rebels pressed aggressively when the front line started falling back. Getting his men to halt again mid-field proved impossible. "[F]inding the troops retiring and retired . . . the enemy charging . . . with the bayonet . . . the troops gave way," admitted Starkweather."[22] "Gave way" really meant a rout that left Baird's next brigade under Col. Ben Scribner dangerously exposed.

Scribner's problems were compounded when Baird's withdrawal notice reached him. The order arrived with an officer from Brig. Gen. John King's Regular brigade instead of one of Baird's staff officers. Scribner dug in his heels and refused to retreat: "[I] called his attention to the supposed reinforcements and the fact that hitherto we had driven [the rebels] off."[23] Minutes later, Scribner watched with growing dismay as Starkweather's men on his right fell back in wild disorder. When Capt. Eugene Cary—who Scribner recognized as a divisional staffer—arrived and reiterated Baird's orders to fall back firing, Scribner struggled to comply. Polk's Rebels, however, were already turning to enfilade his lines from the right and rear. It was

now too late to affect an orderly retreat. Scribner's five regiments tried to fall back as best they could, but the clatter of combat and limited visibility fragmented formations and complicated the transmission of commands.

Pvt. August Bratnober described the scene in the 10th Wisconsin: "Suddenly we were charged from the [right] where we supposed our troops were . . . we gave way and made our best for the rear, only to discover we were completely surrounded. It was everyone for himself by this time."[24] Bratnober followed the regimental colors toward what he thought was escape, but both he and the colors were soon in enemy hands. Company leader James P. Mitchell, 94th Ohio, had a similar experience, though with a better outcome. "Very soon," he recalled, "I saw my company beginning to break away from the works and to fall back. . . . I looked to the right and I found all the troops had fled. My own company . . . obeyed the impulse to flee also."[25] Mitchell barely escaped, but wandered the rest of the evening trying to locate his regiment.

As Baird's Kelly Field line unraveled on the right, the Rebels increased pressure all along the front. In answer to earlier pleas from John Jackson, the brigades of Marcus Wright and George Maney arrived to add their weight to the attack. Passing through the prone formations of Maj. Gen. John Breckinridge's Division, both brigades advanced to support Jackson.[26] In addition, Brig. Gen. States R. Gist's three brigades (his own under Lt. Col. Leroy Napier, Brig. Gen. Matthew Ector, and Col. Claudius Wilson) were in line to the north across the Alexander's Bridge Road. Realizing the opportunity Baird's problems offered, Reserve Corps commander Maj. Gen. William Walker ordered Gist to attack Col. Joseph Dodge's and Col. Sidney Barnes' Federals, adding another jaw to the quickly-closing trap.[27]

Baird's retreat might have been managed more coherently if a senior officer had been coordinating the entire Kelly Field sector, but Thomas had already led Reynolds' division away. At the very least, Thomas should have directed one of the divisional officers—Palmer, since he was senior—to orchestrate the withdrawal. To some extent, Rosecrans must also carry some blame for this problem. Too often he ignored his corps commanders (Thomas excepted) and tended to fight his battles at the division level.

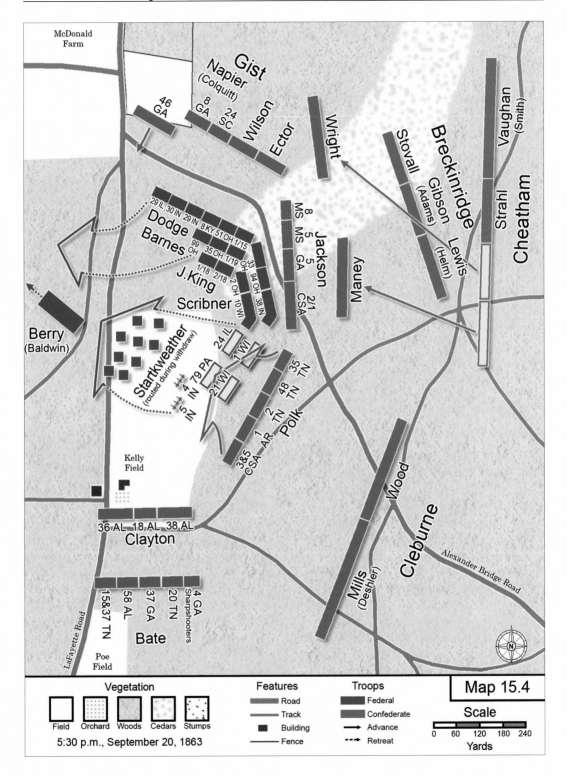

Map 15.4

5:30 p.m., September 20, 1863

Vegetation
Field Orchard Woods Cedars Stumps

Features
Road
Track
Building
Fence

Troops
Federal
Confederate
Advance
Retreat

Scale
0   60   120   180   240
Yards

15.5: Kelly Field is Cleared (6:00 p.m.)

Of Gist's three brigades, only the 46th Georgia regiment, led by Maj. A. M. Spear, was fresh and able to press forward aggressively. The rest of Lt. Col. Napier's (formerly Colquitt's) men had suffered heavily that morning, while Ector's and Wilson's infantry had suffered frightful losses on the 19th. Six companies of the 46th, however, arrived after the morning fighting ended and were anxious to engage the enemy. When the order to attack arrived they opened with a loud cheer and charged.[28] Napier's other regiments followed at a more sedate pace.

In the face of this overall tepid attack from the north Dodge's and Barnes' men managed to fall back in good order, fighting all the while but avoiding the collapse that swept through Starkweather's and Scribner's ranks. Still, their withdrawal from Kelly Field was barely in time to save their commands. The historian of the 8th Kentucky (part of Barnes' brigade) recorded that "our retreat was necessarily a running the gauntlet between two fires, while the enemy was trying to close on us and cut us off." Only about twenty Kentuckians fell into Rebel hands, and most of those were already wounded.[29] Thomas J. Kessler of the 51st Ohio (also of Barnes' command) noted similar losses. While the 51st managed to get most of its wounded off the field, "a good many fell into enemy hands."[30]

Dodge's three regiments required some prompting before departing. Detached from the rest of Gen. Richard Johnson's division, Dodge left Col. Allan Buckner of the 79th Illinois in command of the front while he remained with Johnson. When Buckner received the order to retreat he flatly refused, forcing Dodge to ride over and order the brigade off the field.[31] Dodge later recalled that the general scheme called for each regimental commander, "when the regiment on his right had gotten ten paces to the rear . . . should order his command back and reform on the Ringgold [LaFayette] road." The withdrawal did not go as smoothly as described, and there was a bit of a mad scramble across the northern reaches of Kelly Field, with "the troops . . . flying through on the double-quick, [toward] a wide gap in the fence."[32]

These retreats left King's Regulars holding the salient at the northeast corner of the line. It was now exposed on both flanks. In order to maintain a coherent front throughout the retreat, King intended to have his men fall back a battalion at a time, beginning with the first line. The 1/15th U.S., however, was just passing through the two battalions of the 18th when the second line—the combined 16th and 19th Regulars—gave way.[33]

The Regulars were now facing too many enemies from too many directions. Maney's Rebels passed through Jackson's stalled line to press home the attack, sweeping into the 1/15th's newly vacated position. A member of the 1st Tennessee recalled that his regiment stood astride the Federal breastworks, only to be confronted by "a solid mass of blue" at "short shooting range."[34] For a few minutes Maney's Tennesseans slugged it out with the Regulars in the 16th and 19th, but other Rebels pressing in from various directions rendered the Federal position untenable.

As the final Yankee line unraveled, the Confederate advance became general. As if to provide the final stroke, Breckinridge's three brigades (Adams', now led by Gibson, Stovall's, and Helm's, now commanded by Lewis) started forward. Plenty of Rebels already choked their path of advance, but Breckinridge's infantry line elbowed its way forward through them. Passing over Jackson's line, they followed Maney and Wright's men up and over the Union works and into Kelly Field, where they became further intermingled with Polk's troops scything in from the flank. Breckinridge reported that his command ultimately reached the LaFayette Road, taking prisoners and listing nine artillery pieces among the trophies. He also admitted that "most of [the enemy] escaped in the darkness."[35]

After the war, in a misguided and unnecessary effort to polish Thomas' reputation at Rosecrans' expense, several generals—Gordon Granger notable among them—suggested that when Thomas first received the retreat order from Rosecrans, he almost ignored it. Granger argued that retreat was unnecessary, and if they had only stayed, Chickamauga would have been a clear Union success. In fact, there is no contemporary evidence that Thomas considered staying. Ammunition was running low, and the Kelly Field and Horseshoe Ridge positions both lacked secure flanks.

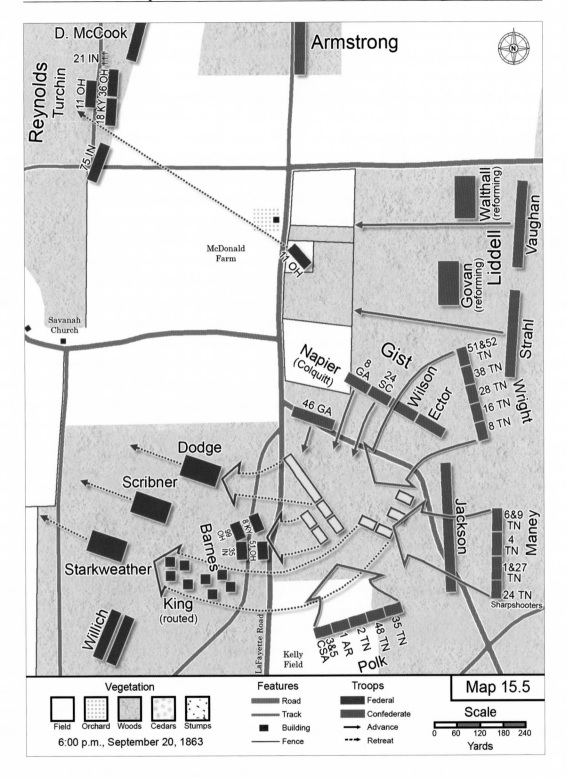

6:00 p.m., September 20, 1863

Map 15.5

Map Set 16: From Rossville to Chattanooga

September 21 to 23

16.1: The Retreat (Night of September 20-21)

The Army of the Cumberland's retreat to Rossville began as early as noon on September 20, when approximately one-third of the army was driven from the field by Lt. Gen. James Longstreet's assault. Three prominent officers participated in this departure: Maj. Gens. William Rosecrans, Thomas Crittenden, and Alexander McCook. Each left the field separately about midday via the Dry Valley Road and each eventually ended up in Chattanooga. While retreating as far as Rossville was inevitable, their decisions to ride to Chattanooga, made individually and for a variety of reasons, damaged each man's career.

Rosecrans' encounter with Chief of Staff James Garfield famously resulted in Rosecrans hurrying on to Chattanooga while Garfield returned to the battlefield to find the embattled Maj. Gen. George Thomas.[1] Unfamiliar with the local terrain, McCook forced a civilian guide to lead him, and ended up bypassing Rossville entirely.[2] Crittenden tried for a time to rally stragglers along the Dry Valley Road before telling a member of his staff, "I believe I have done all I can."[3]

Brig. Gen. Jefferson C. Davis and Maj. Gens. Phil Sheridan and James Negley, division commanders all, found one another at Rossville and held an impromptu conference. The trio decided that Davis would rally stragglers to protect Rossville from the south, Negley would post his command—including the huge artillery train he had accumulated—to defend Rossville's eastern approach, and Sheridan would try and reach Thomas via the LaFayette Road. Sheridan and his troops reached Cloud Church by dusk, but uncertain whether Thomas was still engaged, Sheridan reversed course and fell back to rejoin Negley's line after dark.[4]

The rest of the army held its ground until dark or shortly thereafter, when Thomas ordered a general retreat through McFarland's Gap. This movement consumed much of the night, troops finally coming to rest haphazardly in and around Rossville. Arriving around midnight, brigade commander John Beatty found that "the army is simply a mob. . . . The various commands are mixed up in what seems to be inextricable confusion."[5] In general, Crittenden's XXI Corps troops were directed to the left, extending the line along Missionary Ridge, while McCook's XX Corps men fell in with or behind Davis on the right. Thomas' own XIV Corps held the center. Granger's Reserve Corps was split: Steedman's battered command moved to Missionary Ridge, while Col. McCook's largely unengaged brigade joined Negley. One division, Van Cleve's of the XXI Corps, was so badly disrupted that it could not be reformed even in skeleton form until the next morning.

Denied the use of the Dry Valley Road, Col. John Wilder's brigade fell back overland into the valley of Chattanooga Creek. Finding Col. Sidney Post's detached brigade escorting a massive wagon train from Crawfish Spring, Wilder placed his formidable command across the valley as a screen, enabling Post to reach Chattanooga safely. Despite being unaware of Thomas' retreat, Wilder's instincts were sound. He performed an invaluable service protecting the trains as they fell back into the city and keeping any stray Rebels from outflanking the Rossville line from the west.[6]

Union cavalry performed much the same service on Thomas' more immediate front. Col. Robert Minty's brigade covered Rossville from the east along the Federal Road after falling back slowly from its advanced position at Red House Bridge. Well after dark, Minty halted at McAfee's Church.[7] Brig. Gen. Robert Mitchell and the rest of the Union cavalry departed Crawfish Springs at 5:00 p.m. after gathering as many wagons and ambulatory wounded as they could, falling back to a point just south of Gen. Davis' infantry line.[8]

When dawn on the 21st arrived, the Army of the Cumberland was in surprisingly good shape considering the disaster that had befallen it the day before. Most of its formations were intact, if still suffering from a lot of straggling, and Thomas was able to refill his cartridge boxes from ammunition found or moved to Rossville. The army also had an imposing defensive position in Missionary Ridge. Bragg would be hard-pressed to simply smash through Rossville Gap by sheer force. Any frontal attack there would likely cost the Confederates a great deal more men.

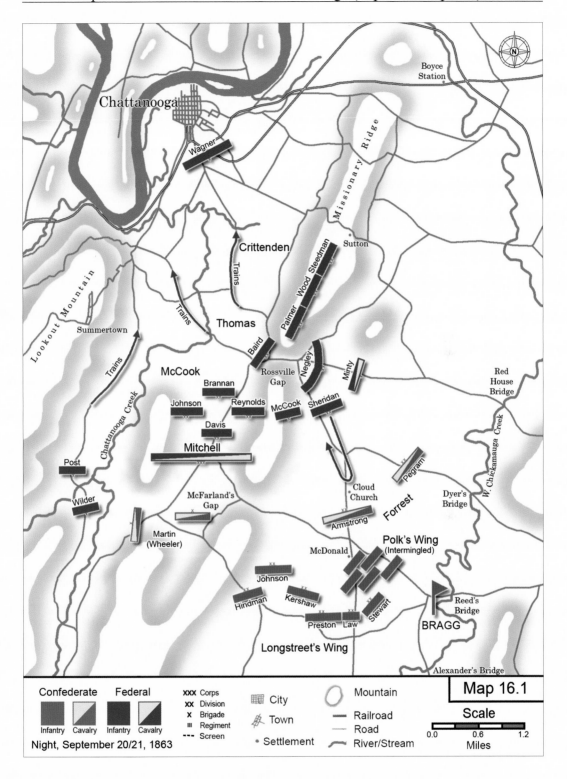

Chattanooga

Boyce
Station

Wagner

Missionary Ridge

Crittenden

Trains

Sutton

Palmer Wood Steedman

Lookout Mountain

Summertown

Trains

Thomas

Baird

Red
House
Bridge

Trains

McCook

Brannan

Rossville
Gap

Negley

Minty

W. Chickamauga Creek

Chattanooga Creek

Johnson

Reynolds

McCook

Sheridan

Davis

Mitchell

Pegram

Post

Wilder

McFarland's
Gap

Cloud
Church

Armstrong

Forrest

Dyer's
Bridge

Martin
(Wheeler)

McDonald

Polk's Wing
(Intermingled)

Johnson

Hindman

Kershaw

Stewart

Reed's
Bridge

Preston Law

BRAGG

Longstreet's Wing

Alexander's Bridge

Confederate	Federal		**xxx** Corps	City	Mountain		**Map 16.1**
			xx Division	Town	Railroad		**Scale**
			x Brigade				
Infantry Cavalry	Infantry Cavalry		**III** Regiment		Road		0.0 0.6 1.2
			- - - Screen	Settlement	River/Stream		Miles

Night, September 20/21, 1863

16.2. Confederate Movements (Afternoon, September 21)

Braxton Bragg has been almost universally condemned, both by his contemporaries and by posterity, for failing to follow up the shattering success of Chickamauga with a vigorous pursuit. Maj. Gen. D. H. Hill, who certainly bore Bragg a great deal of ill-will after the war, called Chickamauga a "barren victory" for that very reason. To the Rebel commanders at the time, however, the circumstances confronting both armies were much less obvious as September 21 dawned than they would be in hindsight.

As odd as it sounds today, few Confederates even realized that the enemy had left the field. When he was summoned for a pre-dawn conference at Bragg's headquarters, Longstreet declined to attend: he fully expected the combat to be renewed at any moment.[9] As the minutes ticked past without any contact, infantry and cavalry probes were ordered to fan out and find the enemy. In Leonidas Polk's sector, Bragg and Polk were already conferring when St. John Liddell reported the Federals had left his front around the McDonald House.[10] Bragg ordered the entire Rebel line to push skirmishers forward aggressively.

A little farther afield, Brig. Gen. Nathan B. Forrest left with some troopers on a reconnaissance patrol about 4:00 a.m. The Rebel horsemen engaged in a running fight with Minty's Union troopers for several hours, an action hot enough to cost Forrest another horse, this one shot in the neck.[11] Around 7:00 a.m. the Rebel mounted patrol scrambled up Missionary Ridge, where Forrest personally climbed a tree for a better view. The message he dispatched back to Bragg has been widely quoted. In part, Forrest noted that the Federals were "evacuating as hard as they can go," and urged Bragg to move forward immediately.[12] As electrifying as this news should have been, it provoked little immediate reaction from the Southern army commander.

In fact, Forrest was wrong. While he observed trains of wounded and wagons retreating across the Tennessee River or around the Point of Lookout Mountain, he did not mention a word about the entire Union army reforming around Rossville—something that should have been easily observable from his vantage point. The Federals were not evacuating but digging in, preparing to defend the city. This became more obvious later in the morning when one of Forrest's brigades tried to push directly through the Rossville Gap, only to find it held in force. Any direct pursuit would rapidly escalate into a frontal assault. Later in the day Forrest dispatched Brig. Gen. Frank Armstrong's Division farther north to try and outflank the Union line.[13]

Maj. Gen. Joseph Wheeler's cavalry, belatedly arriving from more distant camps near Lee and Gordon's Mills, encountered similar resistance in Chattanooga Valley. By midday, his two divisions were skirmishing with Mitchell's Federal cavalry, which was screening the front of McCook's Federal XX Corps. When Wheeler discovered an isolated Yankee column approaching his rear in an effort to sneak into Chattanooga, he led the bulk of his corps south to overwhelm Col. Louis Watkins' three regiments and supply train, inflicting considerable damage on the Federals.[14] None of this skirmishing, however, moved the Rebels any closer to Chattanooga.

That afternoon, Bragg finally ordered his entire army into motion, but his effort was limited by a severe lack of supply wagons. The recent reinforcements from Virginia, East Tennessee, and Mississippi had nearly doubled the size of his army, and many of these troops had moved by rail, leaving their own wagons behind. The lack of wheeled vehicles severely crippled Bragg's ability to move freely , and tied him closely to the railroad. About 2:00 p.m. Bragg ordered Polk's wing of the army not toward Chattanooga but northeast to Red House Bridge. Polk, now commanding both his reunited corps (Thomas Hindman's Division returned from Longstreet) and the "Right Wing," led with his own divisions. This move both shortened the distance back to Ringgold and protected Chickamauga Station so the railhead could be advanced that much closer to the army.[15]

Bragg could have pushed forward more aggressively than he did, and he should have kept a tighter leash on his cavalry, especially Joe Wheeler. It is highly unlikely, however, that he could have dealt a killing blow to the Army of the Cumberland at Rossville or stormed his way into Chattanooga.

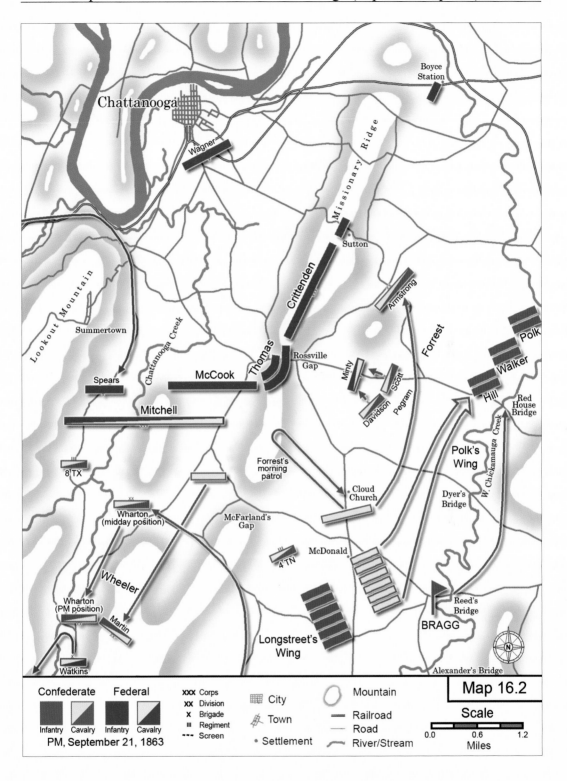

Boyce
Station

Chattanooga

Wagner

Missionary Ridge

Crittenden

Sutton

Lookout Mountain

Summertown

Spears

Chattanooga Creek

McCook

Thomas

Mitchell

Rossville
Gap

Minty

Armstrong

Forrest

Polk

Walker

Hill

Red
House
Bridge

Scott

Pegram

Davidson

8 TX

Polk's
Wing

W. Chickamauga Creek

Forrest's
morning
patrol

Cloud
Church

Dyer's
Bridge

Wharton,
(midday position)

McFarland's
Gap

McDonald

Wheeler

4 TN

Wharton
(PM position)

Martin

Reed's
Bridge

BRAGG

Longstreet's
Wing

Watkins

Alexander's Bridge

Confederate		Federal						Map 16.2

xxx Corps
xx Division
x Brigade
ııı Regiment
- - - Screen

City

Town

Settlement

Mountain

Railroad

Road

River/Stream

Scale

0.0   0.6   1.2
Miles

Infantry Cavalry   Infantry Cavalry
PM, September 21, 1863

16.3 Retreat to Chattanooga (Morning, September 22)

The Federals never intended to make Rossville a permanent defensive position because it was too easily outflanked from the north or west. By the night of September 21, the Army of the Cumberland had recovered some of its organization after the disaster of the previous day. The Army trains were either back in Chattanooga or on their way to Bridgeport, beyond immediate danger. Accordingly, after dark Rosecrans ordered Thomas to withdraw to Chattanooga, occupying the old defensive lines first erected by Bragg's men when the Rebels held the town.[16]

Once again the Yankees slipped away in the dead of night. By dawn the Army of the Cumberland occupied a tight line ringing the city and was working to greatly expand the original defenses. Atop Lookout Mountain, a Union cavalryman described the scene revealed in the morning light. Chattanooga, he wrote, was "encircled by yellow lines of earthworks, which extended unbrokenly from the mountains to the river. An inner circle of dark blue was still more apparent, from which the bayonets and the colors gleamed in the sunlight."[17] Only a handful of Federals remained outside those lines as a rearguard. Minty's cavalry covered Rossville Gap, infantry detachments watched Missionary Ridge to the north, and Brig. Gen James G. Spears' Federal East Tennessee brigade defended the northern end of Lookout Mountain. Other Union troops crossed over to the north bank of the Tennessee River to protect against Rebels crossing either upstream or downstream.

Just as before, Forrest's men led the pursuit, such as it was. About mid-morning he placed all four of his cavalry brigades in a single line facing Missionary Ridge and ordered their advance.[18] Skirmishes marked the movement as the Confederates pressed the Federal rearguard. On the southern end of this line, Col. George Dibrell's Brigade faced Minty's men. The two sides exchanged shots for several hours until the blue troopers fell back into George Thomas' line.[19] Col. Thomas Harrison's Brigade engaged the Union 39th and 44th Indiana regiments near the Moore house. The Hoosiers of the 39th used

their Spencer repeaters to good effect and rebuffed Harrison. Numbers soon told, however, and both Hoosier regiments fell back sometime around midday.[20] Farther north, Brig. Gen. John Pegram's two brigades, one each under Brig. Gen. Henry Davidson and Col. John Scott, advanced westward where the ridge disappeared as it neared the river. There, the 59th Ohio held the rail and road crossings over Chickamauga Creek. The Buckeyes were almost captured when Rebel cavalry pressed them in front and on both flanks, but a skillful retreat utilizing the raised portion of the rail bed as cover saved the men.[21]

Once atop Missionary Ridge, where they stopped to let the infantry catch up, Forrest's troopers had a magnificent view of the new Union defenses. South of town, however, Forrest pushed forward into Chattanooga Valley. Dibrell's men probed the Union line here but found it too strong to be swept aside. Characteristically, Forrest remained unconvinced until he saw it for himself. When he reached Col. Daniel W. Holman and the 11th Tennessee Cavalry, Forrest dismounted and faced the Union line astride the Rossville Road, demanding to know why Holman had stopped. Too many Federals, replied the colonel, who went on to write that Forrest replied: "There must be some mistake in that, and that he believed he could take Chattanooga with [just] his escort," and proceeded to try.[22] His effort, quickly rebuffed, cost Forrest several men and another horse.

Joe Wheeler's cavalry was notably absent on the 22nd. Having led the bulk of his corps against Col. Watkins' straggling Federal column the day before, Wheeler could have either pushed his command into Lookout Valley or turned north along the crest of Lookout Mountain in order to interdict the steady flow of Union wagons between Bridgeport and Chattanooga. Instead, Wheeler left Brig. Gen. William Martin's smaller division to picket Chattanooga Valley while he and Brig. Gen. John Wharton's much larger command retired to their former camps beyond Chickamauga Creek near Glass Mill—now many miles from the scene of any possible action.[23]

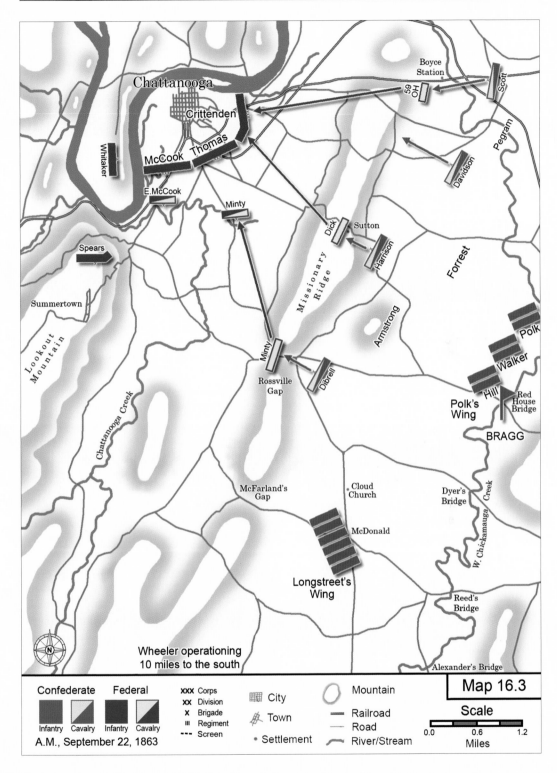

Map 16.3

Scale

0.0   0.6   1.2
Miles

Confederate   Federal

XXX Corps
XX   Division
X   Brigade
III Regiment
--- Screen

Infantry Cavalry Infantry Cavalry

City
Town
Settlement

Mountain
Railroad
Road
River/Stream

A.M., September 22, 1863

16.4: Rebel Pursuit
(Afternoon, Sept. 22, Morning, Sept. 23)

With the Federals retreating into a compact perimeter immediately around Chattanooga, Bragg ordered the bulk of his army to follow. The move was made with little urgency. On the 22nd, Bragg ordered that "Infantry outposts of not less than two brigades will be thrown forward from each wing," occupying Missionary Ridge, "if possible."[24] Instead of gathering for a killing blow, administrative details occupied much of Bragg's attention. The same order demanded casualty assessments, instructed commanders to repair or locate bridges and fords over the Chickamauga to their rear, and to cook three day's rations.

Worse still, at the moment of his greatest victory, Bragg had to return some of his borrowed troops. The first to leave was Matthew Ector's Brigade, heading back to Gen. Joe Johnston in Mississippi. Ector's loss was the first trickle of a slow but steady drain of the Army of Tennessee's strength that would occur over the next two months. The bleeding weakened Bragg just as he was preparing to face a renewed and rejuvenated Union force—and a new general named Ulysses S. Grant.

Fresh troops, however, were still arriving. Maj. Gen. Lafayette McLaws reached Ringgold on the 20th with the rest of his division, but played no role that day or the next. Longstreet assigned his division leader to lead the Left Wing's advance. Once he crossed Missionary Ridge, remembered McLaws, the skirmishing became constant. When he reached Thomas' well-entrenched main line, McLaws reported, "of course my advance was checked, as my force was entirely two small to risk an assault."[25]

McLaws encountered cavalry commander Forrest here, shortly after the latter's attempt to storm that same Union position with his escort. According to McLaws, Forrest advised him that the rest of the army had not yet crossed Missionary Ridge, that he was seven miles from the nearest Confederate infantry support, and that he risked capture if he remained in place. McLaws replied that he intended to hold his ground unless attacked.[26] Forrest partisans painted a much different picture of this meeting. They suggest that Forrest urged McLaws to

make an immediate attack while the Yankees were still demoralized, but that McLaws declined to do so because he had orders only to picket the Union line.[27] In either case McLaws (alone and unsupported) sensibly elected not to attack.

Maj. Gen. Benjamin Cheatham, commanding Polk's advance, moved even more cautiously. Cheatham's men crossed Missionary Ridge farther north, and once across faced active and aggressive Union skirmishing. In the face of this resistance, Cheatham fell back to the crest of the ridge to await the arrival of reinforcements. After dark, he and his staff rode to McLaws' headquarters to inform him of their orders to support him, if needed.[28]

The probes launched by McLaws and Cheatham represented the sum total of Bragg's infantry moves on the 22nd, but there was additional cavalry action. Once again, Wheeler's movements during the 22nd are unclear. His decision to return to his camps southeast of Glass Mill ensured that his command would spend most of its time riding to and fro rather than engaging the Federals. Bragg ordered Wheeler to move to Trenton, Georgia, that evening—apparently intending to throw Wheeler's troopers across the Tennessee River to disrupt the Yankee supply line—but late on September 23 abruptly ordered Wheeler to hurry back north and clear the crest of Lookout Mountain.[29] This he accomplished about dusk.

During the afternoon, however, Forrest sent Dibrell farther west to the foot of Lookout Mountain, where the Confederate Tennesseans encountered James Spears' brigade of Unionist Tennesseans. Dibrell dismounted his command and attacked with three regiments. The brisk skirmish lasted more than ninety minutes, drove Spears' men up the slope of the mountain, and closed the road around the base, severing Rosecrans' most direct link to Bridgeport.[30]

Spears' withdrawal into Chattanooga marked the final step of the Army of the Cumberland's retreat from Chickamauga. If Bragg wanted to complete his success over Rosecrans, a new campaign would be needed.

The cost of the campaign was frightful. Officially, Rosecrans reported 16,179 killed, wounded, and missing. Bragg reported 17,804, but 18,500 is probably a more accurate estimate for the Rebel army. (See Appendix 2, page 268.)

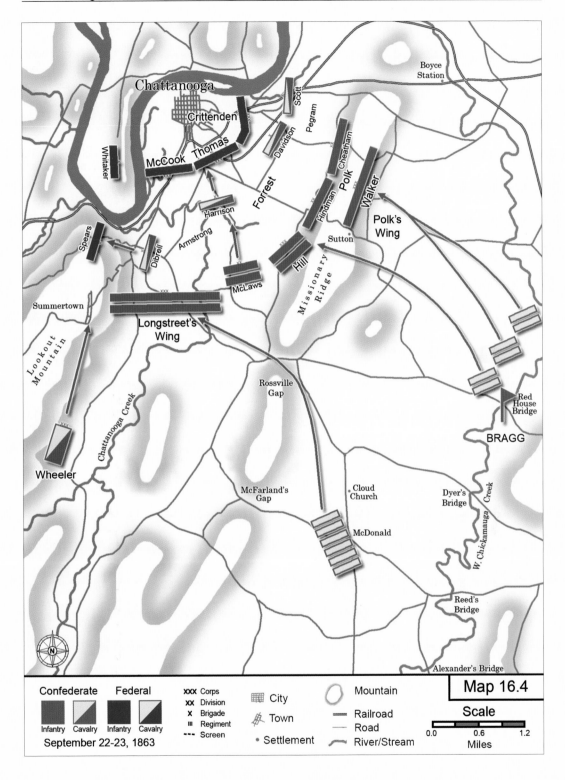

Map 16.4

The Chickamauga Campaign (Epilogue)

Braxton Bragg avoided a direct assault against the Union lines ringing Chattanooga, but he had too few troops to fully enforce an effective siege. As the days turned into weeks of continued stalemate, Southern home front morale, initially buoyed by the stunning Chickamauga victory, waned. In early October, Bragg authorized Joe Wheeler to launch a cavalry raid into Middle Tennessee in the hope of further crippling the flow of supplies into Chattanooga. The effort proved unsuccessful, running the Confederate horsemen ragged for little gain.

With his army stationary before a strong and protected enemy, Bragg focused his attention onto his lieutenants. As far as he was concerned, Gens. Leonidas Polk and Thomas Hindman had been derelict in their duties (Hindman at McLemore's Cove and Polk for failing to attack at dawn on September 20 as ordered). Both were sacked. In an effort to disrupt informal power blocks forming within the Army of Tennessee to oppose him, Bragg reorganized his command. For example, Cheatham's all-Tennessee division was broken up, its brigades swapped for troops from other states, and Simon B. Buckner was effectively demoted to divisional command. Many officers viewed Bragg's vindictiveness with growing dismay. Matters reached a head when a petition was organized to protest Bragg's continued tenure in command. This dangerous document (which verged on mutiny) was likely penned by Buckner, circulated by D. H. Hill, and supported by most of the other senior officers in the army, including James Longstreet.

In an effort to keep his main Western army from coming apart at the seams, Confederate President Jefferson Davis arrived in mid-October to try and reconcile the factions. Davis met with limited success. He sent Polk to another theater and re-instated Hindman, but sustained most of Bragg's decisions, leaving the army troubled and dangerously divided. Perhaps Bragg's greatest error was sending Longstreet and his men toward Knoxville in November, long after it was apparent that the strength of the Federals in Chattanooga was increasing. As would become obvious a few weeks later, the move fatally weakened the Rebel army.

Turmoil was not restricted to the Southern army, but the Yankees resolved their issues more decisively. William Rosecrans' decision to leave the battlefield on September 20 was too great a sin for an army commander to be overlooked. Despite the loyalty of many of his subordinates, Rosecrans was replaced by George Thomas. Gens. Thomas Crittenden (XXI Corps), Alexander McCook (XX Corps), and James Negley (Second Division, XIV Corps) were also sidelined. The most important change was Abraham Lincoln's appointment of Gen. Ulysses S. Grant to overall command of the Western Theater. Reinforcements were also hurried to the threatened point from Virginia and from Grant's own army in Mississippi, which had sat largely idle after the fall of Vicksburg that July. Quick action reopened supply lines to Chattanooga and the immediate crisis passed.

The result was both predictable and dramatic. During the final week of November Grant began moving his command out of its fortifications in a bold offensive. In just three days of maneuvering and fighting, Grant routed Bragg's army off Lookout Mountain and Missionary Ridge, lifting the quasi-siege and driving the enemy completely out of Tennessee. Whatever advantages the Rebels had gained at Chickamauga were squandered at Chattanooga. Southern morale, both within the army and at home, plummeted.

* * *

Braxton Bragg was finally relieved of command of the Army of Tennessee (replaced by Gen. Joseph E. Johnston) after the fiasco that was Chattanooga. Instead of being sent home, however, he became an advisor to President Davis. Bragg was reunited briefly with remnants of his old army at Bentonville, North Carolina, during the final days of the war. He later worked as an engineer and died in Texas in 1876.

Bragg's two "wing" commanders did not fare well after Chickamauga. Leonidas Polk was recalled by Joe Johnston to the Army of Tennessee to oppose Sherman's drive into Georgia in 1864. Polk was killed on June 14 outside Atlanta when an artillery shell nearly cut him in half.

After a failed campaign in East Tennessee, James Longstreet returned to Virginia and was badly wounded in the Wilderness. After the war he became a scapegoat for Southern defeat after he joined the Republican Party and attacked Lee for his generalship at Gettysburg. His memoirs were written largely as a response to criticism, but his pen was not as effective as his sword. Longstreet lived a long life before dying in 1904.

Bragg's corps leaders led interesting lives after Chickamauga. D. H. Hill was relieved in October 1863, before the Chattanooga debacle, and bumped down to major general. He became a college professor after the war but never lost his acerbic tongue and resentment for those who he felt had wronged him.

Simon Buckner advocated Bragg's removal after Chickamauga, and Bragg reduced him in command. Illness sidelined him, and a variety of bureaucratic assignments kept Buckner from the field and further combat. He achieved significant political success after the war, including serving as the governor of Kentucky and as the 1896 "Gold Democrats" nominee for vice president. He died near Munfordville in 1914.

William Walker's Reserve Corps was broken up after the battle. His division missed heavy fighting during the early stages of the Atlanta Campaign in 1864, but lost heavily at Peach Tree Creek on July 20. Two days later, Gen. William J. Hardee criticized Walker about his march and position before his attack against the left flank of the Union Army (Hardee later apologized). "I shall make him remember this insult—if I survive this battle he shall answer me for it," the cantankerous Walker told a staff officer. A short time later he was killed by a single rifle shot.

John Bell Hood recovered from his leg amputation to lead a corps in the Army of Tennessee under Joe Johnston during the Atlanta Campaign. He often disagreed with Johnston and openly criticized him. Some believe he was angling to command the army. If so, he got his wish on July 17 on the outskirts of Atlanta. Hood launched several unsuccessful assaults but the city fell on September 1. When an ill-advised invasion of Tennessee later that fall triggered a pair of crippling defeats at Franklin and Nashville, Hood was relieved from command. He contracted Yellow Fever and died in 1879. His memoir, *Attack and Retreat*, were posthumously published.

Cavalry leader Nathan Forrest emerged from Bragg's army with his reputation intact and lived to see it rise through the end of the war. A telling—if almost certainly apocryphal—account has Forrest confronting Bragg after

Chickamauga: "You have played the part of a damned scoundrel, and if you were any part of a man I would slap your jaws and force you to resent it. . . . If you ever try to interfere with me or cross my path it will be at the peril of your life." Forrest was made a major general that December and displayed brilliant military ability at Okolona and Brice's Cross Roads, but the controversial Fort Pillow massacre tarnished his reputation. In 1876 he was elected Grand Wizard of the Ku Klux Klan. He died of diabetes in 1877.

At the division level, William Preston's conniving against Bragg resulted in his being sent first to southwestern Virginia and then the Trans-Mississippi (by way of Europe). Preston refused to surrender at war's end and went abroad. He died in Kentucky in 1887.

A. P. Stewart fought with distinction during the Atlanta Campaign and in North Carolina, where he served as the last commander of the hard luck Army of Tennessee. He helped found the Chickamauga-Chattanooga National Military Park and died in Mississippi in 1908.

Bushrod Johnson ended up in Virginia, where he provided distinguished service before finally surrendering at Appomattox. Johnson lived an impoverished life on a small farm in Illinois, where he died in 1880.

Ben Cheatham fought well in the Missionary Ridge debacle and during the Atlanta Campaign. A longstanding dispute with John Hood (who assumed command of the army outside Atlanta) erupted at Spring Hill in November 1864 over a mistake that allowed the enemy to escape and set up the bloodshed at Franklin the following day. Cheatham died in Nashville in 1886.

Patrick Cleburne carved out one of the finest records of any combat commander in the war. He fell at the head of his division in the infamous attack at Franklin on November 30, 1864.

William Rosecrans remained in uniform and ended up in command of the Department of Missouri for the duration, where he served ably. After the war he moved to California and eventually served as a U.S. Senator. Had he not left the battlefield that Sunday afternoon, Rosecrans might have made a credible run for president.

Corps leader George Thomas lived up to the reputation he earned at Chickamauga by ably leading the Army of the Cumberland for the rest of the war. In December of 1864, his assault against Hood at Nashville effectively destroyed the Army of Tennessee. Sadly, his death in 1870 ended both a long career of public service and any chance at penning his memoirs. His wife burned his papers, much to the dismay of historians and biographers.

Tom Crittenden was offered a command in 1864 under Grant and George Meade in Virginia, but refused to waive his seniority. He resigned that December, but was appointed a colonel in the Regulars after the war. He died in 1881.

Alexander McCook reverted to his Regular Army rank of captain after the war. He served until 1895, by which time he was again a major general. McCook was instrumental in helping found the Army school that eventually became the Command and General Staff College at Fort Leavenworth, Kansas.

After helping save Rosecrans' army at Chickamauga, Gordon Granger alternated between division and corps command in East Tennessee and in operations along the Gulf coast, including the capture of Mobile. He remained in the Regular Army as colonel of the 25th Infantry and commanded the district of New Mexico in the 1870s. Often ill after the war, Granger died in Santa Fe in 1876 but was buried in Kentucky, his wife's native state.

Absalom Baird fought well for the rest of the war, driving with his division to Atlanta and then on the March to the Sea and through the Carolinas. He never reached corps command, a level he arguably deserved. He died in 1905.

Despite solid earlier service, James Negley's reputation didn't survive Chickamauga. Though a court of inquiry cleared him of charges of cowardice and desertion of his command, he was never led troops again. He resigned in 1865, arguing that the West Pointers had driven him, a civilian officer, out of the army. He was elected to Congress after the war and died in 1901.

John Brannan fought through the war and ended with the rank of brevet major general in both the volunteer and Regular services. He remained in the service until 1882 and died in New York ten years later.

Joseph Reynolds was made Thomas' chief of staff. In January of 1864, he was put in charge of the New Orleans defenses. That July he was given the XIX Corps and helped plan the campaign against Mobile. He remained in the army after the war. During an attack against a Sioux village along the Powder River, he ordered a premature retreat that left behind his dead and a wounded private, who was tortured to death. He was subjected (with others) to a general courts-martial and resigned. Reynolds died in 1899 and was buried in Arlington.

Phil Sheridan's men scaled the heights of Missionary Ridge around Chattanooga and helped drive away the Army of Tennessee, ending Bragg's tenure in the field. Sheridan went on to fame (and infamy) in the fighting in Virginia, where he led cavalry and then an army in the Shenandoah Valley. He held important posts in the west during the Indian Wars, and died in 1888.

Richard Johnson was badly wounded during the Atlanta Campaign, retired as a major general in 1867, and died thirty years later after a successful career as an author of military-related titles.

John Palmer resigned later in the war after arguing a petty matter regarding rank. He was elected Illinois governor in 1868 and U.S. Senator in 1891. He and former enemy Simon Buckner ran on the democratic ticket for president and vice president, respectively, in 1896. He died in 1900.

Horatio Van Cleve lost his command after the battle. He was assigned to lead troops in Murfreesboro, and died in 1891.

James "make sure they spell my name right" Steedman remained in the army but no opportunities like Chickamauga came his way again. He edited a paper and served in the state senate after the war, dying in Ohio in 1883.

Despite outstanding service as a division commander during the Atlanta Campaign and as a corps leader during the March to the Sea, Jefferson C. Davis achieved only brevet major general rank, perhaps because of his murder of fellow officer Gen. William Nelson in 1862.

John T. Wilder's "Lightning Brigade" continued to perform well, but its commander resigned from the army as a brevet brigadier general in late 1864 because of ill health. He lived a long life, dying in 1917.

Although his move out of line on September 20 left the hole through which James Longstreet's divisions poured, Thomas Wood remained in the army, performed distinguished service, and was promoted to major general. He died in 1906—the last survivor of his West Point class of 1845.

Appendix 1

Tullahoma Order of Battle

Army of the Cumberland
Maj. Gen. William S. Rosecrans

Gen. Headquarters

1st Battalion Ohio Sharpshooters
10th Ohio Infantry 15th Pennsylvania Cavalry

Pioneer Brigade: Brig. Gen. James St. Clair Morton

1st Battalion, 2nd Battalion,
3rd Battalion, 4th Battalion
Bridges' Illinois Battery, Capt. Lyman Bridges

Detached, serving as mounted infantry

(From First Brigade, Second Division, XX Corps)
39th Indiana: 4 wounded

*Wilder's Brigade (First Brigade,
Fourth Division, XIV Corps)*

98th Illinois: 1 killed, 4 wounded
123rd Illinois: 2 killed, 4 wounded
17th Indiana: 6 killed, 19 wounded
72nd Indiana: 2 killed, 12 wounded
18th Indiana Battery (10 guns)
Capt. Eli Lilly: 1 wounded

XIV Corps: Maj. Gen. George H. Thomas

Provost

9th Michigan
Co. L, 1st Ohio Cavalry

First Division: Brig. Gen. Lovell H. Rousseau

First Brigade: Col. Benjamin F. Scribner

38th Indiana: 1 wounded
2nd Ohio: 1 killed, 1 wounded
33rd Ohio: 4 wounded
94th Ohio
10th Wisconsin: 3 wounded

Second Brigade: Col. Henry A. Hambright

24th Illinois
79th Pennsylvania: 12 wounded
1st Wisconsin
21st Wisconsin

Third (Regular) Brigade: Brig. Gen. John H. King

1st Battalion, 15th U.S.: 3 killed, 2 wounded
1st Battalion, 16th U.S.
1st Battalion, 18th U.S.: 15 wounded
2nd Battalion, 18th U.S.
1st Battalion, 19th U.S.: 5 wounded

Artillery
4th Indiana (6 guns) Lt. David Flansburg: 1 wounded
A, 1st Michigan (6 guns) Lt. George W. Van Pelt:
1 wounded
H, 5th U.S. (6 guns) Capt. George A. Kensel

Second Division: Maj. Gen. James S. Negley

First Brigade: Brig. Gen. John Beatty
104th Illinois: 1 killed, 1 wounded
42nd Indiana: 1 wounded
88th Indiana: 1 wounded
15th Kentucky: 1 killed, 2 wounded
3rd Ohio

Second Brigade: William L. Stoughton

19th Illinois: 1 wounded
11th Michigan: 1 missing
18th Ohio: 2 wounded
69th Ohio: 1 wounded

Third Brigade: Col. William Sirwell

37th Indiana
21st Ohio
74th Ohio
78th Pennsylvania

Artillery
2nd Kentucky Battery (6 guns) Capt. John M. Hewett
G, 1st Ohio (6 guns) Capt. Alexander Marshall
M, 1st Ohio (6 guns) Capt. Frederick Schultz

Third Division: Brig. Gen. John M. Brannan

First Brigade: Col. Moses B. Walker

82nd Indiana: 1 killed, 1 wounded
17th Ohio: 2 killed, 20 wounded
31st Ohio: 2 killed, 13 wounded
38th Ohio: 6 wounded

Second Brigade: Brig. Gen. James B. Steedman

10th Indiana: 11 wounded
74th Indiana
4th Kentucky: 5 wounded
10th Kentucky: 1 wounded
14th Ohio: 2 wounded, 1 missing

Third Brigade: Col. Ferdinand Van Derveer

87th Indiana
2nd Minnesota: 2 wounded
9th Ohio
35th Ohio: 1 wounded

Artillery

D, 1st Michigan (6 guns) Capt. Josiah W. Church: 1
killed, 1 wounded
C, 1st Ohio (6 guns) Capt. Daniel K. Southwick
I, 4th U.S. (4 guns) Lt. Frank G. Smith

Fourth Division: Maj. Gen. Joseph J. Reynolds

First Brigade (Wilder) detached and serving
as mounted infantry

Second Brigade: Col. Albert S. Hall

80th Illinois
68th Indiana: 1 killed, 6 wounded
75th Indiana: 2 wounded
101st Indiana: 6 wounded
105th Ohio: 1 wounded

Third Brigade: Brig. Gen. George Crook

18th Kentucky: 2 killed, 3 wounded
11th Ohio
36th Ohio
89th Ohio
92nd Ohio: 1 killed, 1 wounded

Artillery

19th Indiana Battery (6 guns) Capt. Samuel J. Harris:
1 wounded

21st Indiana Battery (6 guns) Capt. William W.
Andrew

XX Corps: Maj. Gen. Alexander McDowell McCook

Provost

I, 2nd Kentucky Cavalry

First Division: Brig. Gen. Jefferson C. Davis

First Brigade: Col. P. Sidney Post

59th Illinois
74th Illinois
75th Illinois
22nd Indiana: 3 wounded

Second Brigade: Brig. Gen. William P. Carlin

21st Illinois: 1 wounded
38th Illinois: 3 killed, 19 wounded
81st Indiana
101st Ohio: 2 wounded

Third Brigade: Brig. Gen. Hans C. Heg

25th Illinois
35th Illinois: 1 missing
8th Kansas
15th Wisconsin

Artillery

2nd Minnesota Battery (6 guns) Lt. Albert Woodbury:
2 wounded
5th Wisconsin Battery (6 guns)
Capt. George Q. Gardner
8th Wisconsin Battery (6 guns) Capt. Henry E. Stiles

Second Division: Brig. Gen. Richard W. Johnson

First Brigade: Brig. Gen. August Willich

89th Illinois: 3 killed, 10 wounded
32nd Indiana: 7 killed, 19 wounded
15th Ohio: 8 killed, 24 wounded
49th Ohio: 5 killed, 15 wounded

Second Brigade: Col. John F. Miller

34th Illinois: 3 killed, 24 wounded
79th Illinois: 6 killed, 41 wounded
29th Indiana: 6 wounded
30th Indiana: 1 wounded
77th Pennsylvania: 4 killed, 35 wounded

Third Brigade: Col. Philemon P. Baldwin

6th Indiana: 13 wounded
5th Kentucky: 2 killed, 8 wounded
1st Ohio
93rd Ohio

Artillery
5th Indiana Battery (6 guns) Lt. Alfred Morrison
A, 1st Ohio Battery (6 guns)
Capt. Wilbur F. Goodspeed
20th Ohio Battery (6 guns) Capt. Edward Grosskopf
1 killed

Third Division: Maj. Gen. Philip H. Sheridan

First Brigade: Brig. Gen. William H. Lytle

36th Illinois, 88th Illinois
21st Michigan, 24th Wisconsin

Second Brigade: Col. Bernard Laiboldt

44th Illinois
73rd Illinois: 1 wounded
2nd Missouri: 1 wounded
15th Missouri: 1 wounded

Third Brigade: Col. Luther P. Bradley

22nd Illinois
27th Illinois: 1 wounded
42nd Illinois
51st Illinois

Artillery
C, 1st Illinois Battery (6 guns) Lt. Edward M. Wright
11th Indiana Battery (6 guns)
Capt. Arnold Sutermeister:
G, 1st Missouri Battery (6 guns) Capt. Henry Hescock

XXI Corps: Maj. Gen. Thomas L. Crittenden

Provost

K, 15th Illinois Cavalry

First Division: Brig. Gen. Thomas J. Wood

First Brigade: Col. George P. Buell

100th Illinois
58th Indiana
13th Michigan
26th Ohio

Second Brigade: Brig. Gen. George W. Wagner

15th Indiana
40th Indiana
57th Indiana
97th Ohio: 1 wounded

Third Brigade: Col. Charles G. Harker

3rd Kentucky, 64th Ohio
65th Ohio, 125th Ohio

Artillery
8th Indiana Battery (6 guns) Capt. George Estep:
10th Indiana Battery (6 guns) Lt. William A. Naylor
6th Ohio Battery (6 guns) Capt. Cullen Bradley

Second Division: Maj. Gen. John M. Palmer

First Brigade: Brig. Gen. Charles Cruft

31st Indiana, 1st Kentucky
2nd Kentucky, 90th Ohio

Second Brigade: Brig. Gen. William B. Hazen

9th Indiana, 6th Kentucky
41st Ohio, 124th Ohio

Third Brigade: Col. William Grose

84th Illinois, 36th Indiana, 23rd Kentucky,
6th Ohio, 24th Ohio

Artillery
B, 1st Ohio Battery (6 guns) Capt. William E. Standart
F, 1st Ohio Battery (6 guns) Capt. Daniel T. Cockerill
H, 4th U.S. (4 guns) Lt. Harry C. Cushing
M 4th U.S. (6 guns) Lt. Francis L. D. Russell

Third Division: Brig. Gen. Horatio P. Van Cleve

Provost

(Unable to confirm company)

First Brigade: Brig. Gen. Samuel Beatty

79th Indiana, 9th Kentucky
17th Kentucky, 19th Ohio

Second Brigade: Col. George F. Dick

44th Indiana, 86th Indiana
13th Ohio, 59th Ohio

Third Brigade: Col. Sidney M. Barnes

35th Indiana, 8th Kentucky
21st Kentucky, 51st Ohio
99th Ohio

Artillery
7th Indiana Battery (6 guns) Capt. George R. Swallow
26th Pennsylvania Battery (6 guns) Capt. A. J. Stevens
3rd Wisconsin (6 guns) Lt. Courtland Livingston

Reserve Corps: Maj. Gen. Gordon Granger

Gen. Headquarters

F, 1st Missouri Cavalry

First Division: Brig. Gen. Absalom Baird

First Brigade: Col. Smith D. Atkins

92nd Illinois, 96th Illinois
115th Illinois, 84th Indiana, 40th Ohio

Second Brigade: Col. William P. Reid

78th Illinois, 98th Ohio
113th Ohio, 121st Ohio

Third Brigade: Col. Henry C. Gilbert

33rd Indiana, 19th Michigan
85th Indiana (possibly*), 22nd Wisconsin (possibly*)

*Note: It is unclear from the various returns if these last
two regiments actually served with the brigade.

Artillery
M, 1st Illinois Battery (6 guns) Capt. George
W. Spencer
9th Ohio Battery (6 guns) Capt. Harrison B. York
18th Ohio Battery (6 guns) Capt. Charles C. Aleshire

Note: The remainder of the Reserve Corps is
garrisoning Nashville and other points on Rosecrans'
line of communications.

Cavalry Corps: Brig. Gen. David S. Stanley
First Division: Brig. Gen. Robert S. Mitchell
First Brigade: Col. Archibald P. Campbell

4th Kentucky: 2 wounded
6th Kentucky: 2 killed, 5 wounded

7th Kentucky
2nd Michigan: 2 wounded, 3 missing
9th Pennsylvania: 2 killed, 2 wounded
1st Tennessee: 2 killed, 1 wounded, 1 missing

Second Brigade: Col. Edward M. McCook

2nd Indiana
4th Indiana: 2 wounded
5th Kentucky: 6 wounded, 1 missing
2nd Tennessee: 1 wounded
1st Wisconsin: 2 wounded
D, 1st Ohio Battery (2 guns) Capt. Andrew J. Konkle

Second Division: Brig. Gen. John Turchin

First Brigade: Col. Robert H. G. Minty

3rd Indiana: 1 killed, 3 wounded
5th Iowa
4th Michigan: 8 wounded, 2 missing
7th Pennsylvania: 5 killed, 11 wounded
5th Tennessee: 2 killed, 1 missing
4th U.S.: 2 wounded
D, 1st Ohio Battery (2 guns) Lt. Nathaniel M. Newell

Second Brigade: Col. Eli Long

2nd Kentucky: 1 killed, 2 wounded, 2 missing
1st Ohio: 2 killed, 1 wounded
3rd Ohio: 6 wounded
4th Ohio: 5 wounded
10th Ohio
Chicago Board of Trade Battery (7 guns)
Capt. James H. Stokes

Army of Tennessee
Gen. Braxton Bragg

Note: This organization, with some modifications, is taken from the July 31, 1863, army returns found in the *Official Records*. There is no extant army-wide organizational chart for the end of June, when the Tullahoma Campaign occurred. In addition, there are no comprehensive casualty reports provided. Losses have been listed where known. In addition, desertions were rampant during the retreat and the Federals reported capturing more than 1,600 Confederates. For example, this shows up in some reports such as Brig. Gen. Bushrod Johnson's which reported 36 combat casualties in his four Tennessee regiments, and another three officers and 332 men left in Middle Tennessee for various reasons.

Gen. Headquarters

Druex Co. Louisiana Cavalry
K, 3rd Alabama Cavalry
Miners and Sappers

(Unable to confirm)

Artillery Reserve: Col. James Deshler
1st Louisiana Regulars, Infantry
Capt. Overton W. Barret's Missouri Battery (4 guns)
Havis' Georgia Battery: Lt. J. R. Duncan (4 guns)
Capt. Charles L. Lumsden's Alabama Battery (6 guns)
Capt. T. L. Massenberg's Georgia Battery (4 guns)

Jackson's Brigade: Brig. Gen. John K. Jackson

(Guarding rail communications at Chattanooga, Bridgeport, and Stevenson, Alabama.)
2nd Battalion, 1st Confederate
2nd Georgia Sharpshooters
5th Georgia
5th Mississippi, 8th Mississippi
Capt. E. E. Prichard's Georgia Battery (4 guns)
Capt. John Scogin's Georgia Battery (4 guns)

Polk's Corps: Lt. Gen. Leonidas Polk

Escort

Greenleaf's Co. Lousiana Cavalry

Cheatham's Division: Maj. Gen. Benjamin F. Cheatham

Escort

G, 2nd Georgia Cavalry

Maney's Brigade: Col. J. A. McMurry

1+27 Tennessee
4th Tennessee (Provisional Army)[1]
6+9 Tennessee
24th Tennessee Sharpshooters
Smith's Mississippi Battery (4 guns)
Lt. William B. Turner

Smith's Brigade: Brig. Gen. Preston Smith

11th Tennessee
12+47 Tennessee
13+154 Tennessee
29th Tennessee
Scott's Tennessee Battery (4 guns) Lt. A. T. Watson

Strahl's Brigade: Brig. Gen. Otho F. Strahl

4+5 Tennessee
19th Tennessee
24th Tennessee
31st Tennessee
33rd Tennessee
Capt. Thomas J. Stanford's Mississippi Battery (4 guns)

Wright's Brigade: Col. John H. Anderson

8th Tennessee
16th Tennessee
28th Tennessee
38th Tennessee
51+52 Tennessee
Capt. William W. Carnes' Tennessee Battery (4 guns)

Capt. John Scogin's Georgia Battery (4 guns)

Withers' Division: Maj. Gen. Jones M. Withers

Escort

Co. I, 3rd Alabama Cavalry

Anderson's Brigade: Brig. Gen. Patton Anderson

7th Mississippi
9th Mississippi
10th Mississippi
41st Mississippi
44th Mississippi
9th Mississippi Sharpshooters
Robertson's Alabama Battery: Capt. S. H. Dent (6 guns)

Deas' Brigade: Col. J. G. Coltart

19th Alabama

22nd Alabama

25th Alabama

39th Alabama

50th Alabama

17th Alabama Sharpshooters

Capt. James Garrity's Alabama Battery (4 guns)

Manigault's Brigade: Brig. Gen. Arthur M. Manigault

24th Alabama

28th Alabama

34th Alabama

10+19th South Carolina

Water's Alabama Battery (4 guns) Lt. W. F. Hamilton

Walthall's Brigade: Brig. Gen. Edward C. Walthall

24th Mississippi

27th Mississippi

29th Mississippi

30th Mississippi

34th Mississippi

Capt. William H. Fowler's Alabama Battery (4 guns)

Hardee's Corps: Lt. Gen. William J. Hardee

Escort

Raum's Co. Georgia Cavalry

Cleburne's Division: Maj. Gen. Patrick R. Cleburne

Escort

Sanders' Co. Tennessee Cavalry

Churchill's Brigade: Brig. Gen. Thomas J. Churchill

19+24 Arkansas

6+10+15 Texas

17+18+24+25 Texas

Capt. James P. Douglas' Texas Battery (4 guns)

Liddell's Brigade: Brig. Gen. St. John Liddell

2nd Arkansas: 14 killed, 35 wounded, 10 missing

5th Arkansas: 5 killed, 10 wounded, 7 missing

6+7th Arkansas: 1 killed, 12 wounded

8th Arkansas

13+15th Arkansas: 8 killed, 18 wounded

Warren Light Artillery Mississippi Battery, Capt.
Charles Swett (4 guns)

Polk's Brigade: Brig. Gen. Lucius E. Polk

1st Arkansas, 3+5th Confederate

2nd Tennessee, 35th Tennessee, 48th Tennessee

Calvert's Arkansas Battery, Lt. Thomas J. Key (4
guns)

Wood's Brigade: Col. Mark P. Lowrey

16th Alabama, 33rd Alabama,
45th Alabama, 32+45 Mississippi,
15th Mississippi Sharpshooters

Capt. Henry P. Semple's Alabama Battery (4 guns)

Stewart's Division

Escort

Foules' Co. Mississippi Cavalry

Bate's Brigade: Brig. Gen. William B. Bate

9th Alabama Battalion: 5 wounded

37th Georgia: 3 killed, 45 wounded

4th Georgia Sharpshooters: 4 killed, 39 wounded

15+37th Tennessee: 1 killed, 5 wounded

20th Tennessee: 9 killed, 24 wounded

Eufala Alabama Artillery (4 guns) Capt. McDonald
Oliver: 2 killed, 6 wounded

Capt. Frank Maney's Tennessee Battery (2 guns)

Brown's Brigade: Brig. Gen. John C. Brown

18th Tennessee

26th Tennessee

32nd Tennessee

45th Tennessee

23rd Tennessee Sharpshooters

Dawson's Georgia Battery (4 guns) Lt.
R. W. Anderson

Clayton's Brigade: Brig. Gen. Henry D. Clayton

18th Alabama

36th Alabama

38th Alabama

Capt. John T. Humphreys' 1st Arkansas Battery
(4 guns)

Johnson's Brigade: Brig. Gen. Bushrod R. Johnson

17th Tennessee: 1 killed, 16 wounded, 2 missing

23rd Tennessee: 1 killed, 4 wounded

25th Tennessee: 1 killed, 5 wounded, 1 missing

44th Tennessee: 2 wounded, 3 missing
Jefferson Mississippi Artillery (4 guns) Capt. Put.
Darden

Forrest's Cavalry Division:
Brig. Gen. Nathan B. Forrest (independent)

Escort

Jackson's Co. Tennessee Cavalry: 67 engaged,
losses unknown

First Brigade: Brig. Gen. Frank C. Armstrong

Escort

Bradley's Co. CSA Regular Cavalry

3rd Arkansas
2nd Kentucky
1st [6th] Tennessee
18th Tennessee Cavalry Battalion

Second Brigade: Col. Nicholas N. Cox

Escort

Capt. T. J. Gray's Company

4th Tennessee, 8th [13th] Tennessee
9th [19th] Tennessee, 10th Tennessee, 11th Tennessee

Artillery
Capt. A. L. Huggins' Tennessee Battery (4 guns)
Capt. John W. Morton's Tennessee Battery (4 guns)

Wheeler's Cavalry Corps

Martin's Division: Brig. Gen. William T. Martin

Escort

Co. A, 3rd Alabama: 34 engaged, losses unknown

First Brigade: Col. James Hogan

1st Alabama, 3rd Alabama
51st Alabama, 8th Confederate

Second Brigade: Col. A. A. Russell

4th Alabama, 1st Confederate

Artillery
Wiggins' Arkansas Battery, Lt. A. A. Blake (2 guns)

Morgan's Division: Brig. Gen. John H. Morgan

(detached, raiding into Ohio)

Wharton's Division: Brig. Gen. John A. Wharton

Escort

B, 8th Texas

First Brigade: Col. C. C. Crews

7th Alabama, 2nd Georgia
3rd Georgia, 4th Georgia

Second Brigade: Col. Thomas Harrison

3rd Confederate, 1st [3rd] Kentucky
4th [8th] Tennessee, 8th Texas, 11th Texas

Artillery
Capt. B. F. White's Tennessee Battery (4 guns)

Appendix 2

Chickamauga Order of Battle

Army of the Cumberland (Federal)
Maj. Gen. William S. Rosecrans

General Headquarters

1st Battalion Ohio SS (154)
10th Ohio Infantry (396): 1 missing
15th Pennsylvania Cavalry (438): 2 wounded,
3 missing

Detached (serving as mounted infantry)

39th Indiana (581): 5 killed,
35 wounded

Wilder's Brigade
(First Brigade, Fourth Division, XIV Corps)

92nd Illinois (383): 2 killed, 22 wounded, 2 missing
98th Illinois (485): 2 killed, 31 wounded, 2 missing
123rd Illinois (422): 1 killed, 13 wounded, 10 missing
17th Indiana (513): 4 killed, 10 wounded, 2 missing
72nd Indiana (480): 3 killed, 16 wounded, 2 missing
18th Indiana Battery (10 guns) Capt. Eli Lilly:
1 killed, 2 wounded

Brigade total: 2,283: 13 killed, 94 wounded,
18 missing = 125

XIV Corps: Maj. Gen. George H. Thomas

Provost

9th Michigan (384)
Co. L, 1st Ohio Cavalry

First Division: Brig. Gen. Absalom Baird

First Brigade: Col. Benjamin F. Scribner
38th Indiana (354): 13 killed, 57 wounded, 39 missing
2nd Ohio (412): 9 killed, 50 wounded, 122 missing
33rd Ohio (415): 14 killed, 63 wounded, 83 missing
94th Ohio (309): 2 killed, 22 wounded, 22 missing
10th Wisconsin (240): 11 killed, 55 wounded,
145 missing

Brigade total: 1,730: 49 killed, 247 wounded,
411 missing = 707

Second Brigade: Brig. Gen. John C. Starkweather

24th Illinois (362): 19 killed, 68 wounded, 56 missing
79th Pennsylvania (390): 16 killed,
67 wounded, 42 missing
1st Wisconsin (391): 27 killed, 84 wounded,
77 missing
21st Wisconsin (369): 2 killed, 43 wounded,
76 missing

Brigade total: 1,512: 64 killed, 262 wounded,
251 missing = 577

Third (Regular) Brigade: Brig. Gen. John H. King

1st Battalion, 15th U.S. (276): 9 killed,
49 wounded, 102 missing
1st Battalion, 16th U.S. (308): 3 killed,
19 wounded, 174 missing
1st Battalion, 18th U.S. (300): 19 killed,
71 wounded, 68 missing
2nd Battalion, 18th U.S. (287): 14 killed,
81 wounded, 50 missing
1st Battalion, 19th U.S. (204): 3 killed,
17 wounded, 116 missing

Brigade total: 1,375: 48 killed,
237 wounded, 510 missing = 795

Artillery
4th Indiana (6 guns) Lt. David Flansburg: 1 killed,
14 wounded, 5 missing
A, 1st Michigan (6 guns) Lt. George W. Van Pelt:
6 killed, 7 wounded, 12 missing
H, 5th U.S. (6 guns) Lt. Howard M. Burnham:
13 killed, 18 wounded, 13 missing

Second Division: Maj. Gen. James S. Negley

First Brigade: Brig. Gen. John Beatty

104th Illinois (299): 2 killed, 46 wounded, 16 missing
42nd Indiana (328): 1 killed, 52 wounded, 53 missing
88th Indiana (259): 3 killed, 33 wounded, 16 missing
15th Kentucky (305): 5 killed, 42 wounded, 15 missing

Brigade total: 1,191: 11 killed, 173 wounded,
100 missing = 2840

Second Brigade: Col. Timothy R. Stanley

19th Illinois (333): 10 killed, 45 wounded, 16 missing
11th Michigan (341): 5 killed, 42 wounded, 19 missing
18th Ohio (344): 5 killed, 55 wounded, 14 missing

Brigade Total: 1,018: 20 killed, 142 wounded,
49 missing = 211

Third Brigade: Col. William Sirwell

37th Indiana (361): 1 killed, 8 wounded, 2 missing
21st Ohio (561): 28 killed, 84 wounded, 131 missing
74th Ohio (300): 1 killed, 2 wounded, 6 missing
78th Pennsylvania (507): 2 wounded, 3 missing

Brigade total: 1,729: 30 killed, 96 wounded,
142 missing

Artillery
Bridges' Battery (6 guns) Capt. Lyman Bridges: 6
killed, 16 wounded, 4 missing
G, 1st Ohio (6 guns) Capt. Alexander Marshall
M, 1st Ohio (6 guns) Capt. Frederick Schultz:
4 wounded

Third Division: Brig. Gen. John M. Brannan

First Brigade: Col. John M. Connell

82nd Indiana (285): 20 killed, 68 wounded, 23 missing
17th Ohio (454): 16 killed, 114 wounded, 21 missing
31st Ohio (465): 13 killed, 134 wounded, 22 missing
38th Ohio (16) (regiment guarding trains)

Brigade total: 1,220: 49 killed, 316 wounded,
66 missing = 431

Second Brigade: Col. John T. Croxton

10th Indiana (366): 24 killed, 136 wounded, 6 missing
74th Indiana (400): 22 killed,
125 wounded, 10 missing
4th Kentucky (351): 25 killed, 157 wounded, 9 missing
10th Kentucky (421): 21 killed,
134 wounded, 11 missing
14th Ohio (460): 35 killed, 167 wounded, 43 missing

Brigade total: 1,998: 127 killed, 719 wounded,
79 missing = 925

Third Brigade: Col. Ferdinand Van Derveer

87th Indiana (366): 40 killed, 142 wounded, 8 missing

2nd Minnesota (384): 35 killed,
113 wounded, 14 missing
9th Ohio (502): 48 killed, 185 wounded, 16 missing
35th Ohio (391): 21 killed, 139 wounded, 27 missing

Brigade total: 1,643: 144 killed, 579 wounded,
65 missing = 788

Artillery
D, 1st Michigan (6 guns) Capt. Josiah W. Church:
7 wounded, 4 missing
C, 1st Ohio (6 guns) Lt. Marco B. Gary: 4 killed,
9 wounded
I, 4th U.S. (4 guns) Lt. Frank G. Smith: 1 killed,
21 wounded

Fourth Division: Maj. Gen. Joseph J. Reynolds

First Brigade (Wilder) detached and serving
as mounted infantry

Second Brigade: Col. Edward A. King

68th Indiana (356): 17 killed,
108 wounded, 12 missing
75th Indiana (360): 17 killed,
108 wounded, 13 missing
101st Indiana (400): 11 killed, 90 wounded, 18 missing
105th Ohio (382): 3 killed, 41 wounded, 26 missing

Brigade total: 1,476: 48 killed,
347 wounded, 69 missing

Third Brigade: Brig. Gen. John B. Turchin

Provost Guard: A, 18th Kentucky (29)
18th Kentucky (266): 7 killed, 46 wounded, 33 missing
11th Ohio (433): 5 killed, 36 wounded, 22 missing
36th Ohio (484): 12 killed, 65 wounded, 14 missing
92nd Ohio (400): 6 killed, 68 wounded, 17 missing

Brigade total: 1,612: 30 killed, 215 wounded,
86 missing = 331

Artillery
19th Indiana Battery (6 guns) Capt. Samuel J. Harris:
2 killed, 16 wounded, 2 missing
21st Indiana Battery (6 guns) Capt. William W.
Andrew: 12 wounded

XX Corps: Maj. Gen. Alexander McDowell McCook

Provost
I, 2nd Kentucky Cavalry (39)
D, 1st Ohio Infantry (41)

First Division: Brig. Gen. Jefferson C. Davis

First Brigade: Col. P. Sidney Post
(guarding trains, only lightly engaged)

59th Illinois (285): 1 wounded, 1 missing
74th Illinois (354): 1 wounded, 4 missing
75th Illinois (200): 10 missing
22nd Indiana (400): 1 killed, 2 wounded, 4 missing

Brigade total: 1,239: 1 killed, 4 wounded,
19 missing = 24

Second Brigade: Brig. Gen. William P. Carlin

21st Illinois (416): 22 killed, 70 wounded, 146 missing
38th Illinois (301): 15 killed, 87 wounded, 78 missing
81st Indiana (255): 4 killed, 60 wounded, 23 missing
101st Ohio (243): 13 killed, 82 wounded, 51 missing

Brigade total: 1,215: 54 killed, 299 wounded,
298 missing = 651

Third Brigade: Col. Hans C. Heg

25th Illinois (337): 10 killed, 171 wounded, 24 missing
35th Illinois (299): 17 killed, 130 wounded, 13 missing
8th Kansas (406): 30 killed, 165 wounded, 25 missing
15th Wisconsin (176): 13 killed,
53 wounded, 45 missing
Brigade total: 1,218: 70 killed, 519 wounded,
107 missing = 696

Artillery
2nd Minnesota Battery (6 guns) Lt. Albert Woodbury:
2 wounded
5th Wisconsin Battery (6 guns)
Capt. George Q. Gardner
8th Wisconsin Battery (6 guns) Lt. John D. McLean

Second Division: Brig. Gen. Richard W. Johnson

First Brigade: Brig. Gen. August Willich

89th Illinois (391): 14 killed, 88 wounded, 30 missing
32nd Indiana (378): 21 killed, 81 wounded, 20 missing
15th Ohio (325): 10 killed, 77 wounded, 33 missing
49th Ohio (405): 10 killed, 59 wounded, 30 missing

Brigade total: 1,499: 55 killed, 306 wounded,
114 missing = 475

Second Brigade: Col. Joseph B. Dodge

79th Illinois (263): 3 killed, 21 wounded, 97 missing
29th Indiana (315): 11 killed, 92 wounded, 69 missing
30th Indiana (299): 10 killed, 55 wounded, 61 missing
77th Pennsylvania (253): 3 killed, 28 wounded,
73 missing

Brigade total: 1,130: 27 killed, 198 wounded,
307 missing = 532

Third Brigade: Col. Philemon P. Baldwin

6th Indiana (467): 13 killed, 116 wounded, 31 missing
5th Kentucky (334): 14 killed, 79 wounded, 32 missing
1st Ohio (367): 13 killed, 96 wounded, 33 missing
93rd Ohio (459): 15 killed, 86 wounded, 29 missing

Brigade total: 1,627: 56 killed, 378 wounded,
125 missing = 559

Artillery
5th Indiana Battery (6 guns) Capt. Peter Simonson:
1 killed, 7 wounded, 1 missing
A, 1st Ohio Battery (6 guns) Capt. Wilbur F.
Goodspeed: 2 killed, 14 wounded, 4 missing
20th Ohio Battery (6 guns) Capt. Edward Grosskopf:
2 wounded, 2 missing

Third Division: Maj. Gen. Philip H. Sheridan

First Brigade: Brig. Gen. William H. Lytle

36th Illinois (358): 20 killed, 101 wounded, 20 missing
88th Illinois (449): 12 killed, 62 wounded, 14 missing
21st Michigan (299): 16 killed,
73 wounded, 17 missing
24th Wisconsin (487): 3 killed, 73 wounded,
29 missing

Brigade total: 1,593: 52 killed, 309 wounded,
80 missing = 441

Second Brigade: Col. Bernard Laiboldt

44th Illinois (269): 6 killed, 64 wounded, 34 missing
73rd Illinois (300): 13 killed, 57 wounded, 22 missing
2nd Missouri (281): 7 killed, 56 wounded, 29 missing
15th Missouri (250): 11 killed,
67 wounded, 22 missing

Brigade total: 1,100: 37 killed, 240 wounded,
107 missing = 384

Third Brigade: Col. Luther P. Bradley

22nd Illinois (314): 23 killed, 76 wounded, 31 missing
27th Illinois (463): 2 killed, 79 wounded, 10 missing
42nd Illinois (305): 15 killed, 123 wounded, 5 missing
51st Illinois (309): 18 killed, 93 wounded, 38 missing

Brigade total: 1,391: 58 killed, 372 wounded,
84 missing = 514

Artillery
C, 1st Illinois Battery (6 guns) Capt. Mark H. Prescott:
4 wounded
11th Indiana Battery (6 guns) Capt. Arnold
Sutermeister: 3 killed, 12 wounded, 4 missing
G, 1st Missouri Battery (6 guns) Lt. Gustavus
Schueler:1 killed, 3 wounded, 1 missing

XXI Corps: Maj. Gen. Thomas L. Crittenden

Provost:
K, 15th Illinois Cavalry (83): 3 wounded

First Division: Brig. Gen. Thomas J. Wood

First Brigade: Col. George P. Buell

100th Illinois (339): 23 killed
117 wounded, 24 missing
58th Indiana (397): 16 killed,
119 wounded, 34 missing
13th Michigan (220): 13 killed
67 wounded, 26 missing
26th Ohio (377): 27 killed, 140 wounded, 45 missing

Brigade total: 1,333: 79 killed, 443 wounded,
129 missing = 651

Second Brigade: stationed at Chattanooga

Third Brigade: Col. Charles G. Harker

3rd Kentucky (401): 13 killed, 78 wounded, 22 missing
64th Ohio (325): 8 killed, 50 wounded, 13 missing
65th Ohio (306): 14 killed, 71 wounded, 18 missing
125th Ohio (314): 16 killed, 84 wounded, 5 missing
Brigade total: 1,346: 51 killed, 283 wounded,
58 missing = 392

Artillery
8th Indiana Battery (6 guns) Capt. George Estep:
1 killed, 9 wounded, 7 missing
6th Ohio Battery (6 guns) Capt. Cullen Bradley:
1 killed, 8 wounded

Second Division: Maj. Gen. John M. Palmer

First Brigade: Brig. Gen. Charles Cruft

31st Indiana (380): 5 killed, 61 wounded, 17 missing
1st Kentucky (118): 2 killed, 26 wounded, 3 missing
2nd Kentucky (367): 10 killed,
64 wounded, 18 missing
90th Ohio (415): 7 killed, 62 wounded, 15 missing

Brigade total: 1,280: 24 killed, 213 wounded,
53 missing = 290

Second Brigade: Brig. Gen. William B. Hazen

9th Indiana (328): 13 killed, 91 wounded, 22 missing
6th Kentucky (302): 12 killed, 95 wounded, 11 missing
41st Ohio (360): 6 killed, 100 wounded, 9 missing
124th Ohio (453): 15 killed, 92 wounded, 34 missing

Brigade total: 1,443: 46 killed, 378 wounded,
76 missing = 500

Third Brigade: Col. William Grose

84th Illinois (382): 13 killed, 83 wounded, 9 missing
36th Indiana (347): 13 killed, 99 wounded, 17 missing
23rd Kentucky (263): 11 killed, 52 wounded, 6 missing
6th Ohio (362): 13 killed, 102 wounded, 17 missing
24th Ohio (277): 3 killed, 60 wounded, 16 missing

Brigade total: 1,631: 53 killed, 399 wounded,
65 missing = 517

Artillery
B, 1st Ohio Battery (6 guns) Lt. Norman A. Baldwin:
1 killed, 8 wounded, 4 missing
F, 1st Ohio Battery (6 guns) Lt. Giles J. Cockerill:
2 killed, 8 wounded, 2 missing
H, 4th U.S. (4 guns) Lt. Harry C. Cushing: 5 killed,
17 wounded
M, 4th U.S. (6 guns) Lt. Francis L. D. Russell:
2 killed, 6 wounded

Third Division: Brig. Gen. Horatio P. Van Cleve

Provost:
A, 9th Kentucky (30)

First Brigade: Brig. Gen. Samuel Beatty

79th Indiana (300): 1 killed, 44 wounded, 10 missing
9th Kentucky (213): 2 killed, 45 wounded, 13 missing
17th Kentucky (487): 6 killed
105 wounded, 15 missing
19th Ohio (384): 7 killed, 60 wounded, 23 missing

Brigade total: 1,384: 16 killed, 254 wounded,
61 missing = 331

Second Brigade: Col. George F. Dick

44th Indiana (229): 3 killed, 61 wounded, 10 missing
86th Indiana (261): 1 killed, 31 wounded, 21 missing
13th Ohio (304): 5 killed, 47 wounded, 22 missing
59th Ohio (290): 7 killed, 41 wounded, 30 missing

Brigade total: 1,084: 16 killed, 180 wounded,
83 missing = 279

Third Brigade: Col. Sidney M. Barnes

35th Indiana (229): 5 killed, 23 wounded, 37 missing
8th Kentucky (297): 4 killed, 47 wounded, 28 missing
51st Ohio (319): 8 killed, 35 wounded, 55 missing
99th Ohio (357): 3 killed, 30 wounded, 24 missing

Brigade total: 1,202: 20 killed, 135 wounded,
144 missing = 299

Artillery
7th Indiana Battery (6 guns) Capt. George R. Swallow:
8 wounded, 1 missing
26th Pennsylvania Battery (6 guns) Capt. A. J.
Stevens: 2 killed, 14 wounded, 1 missing
3rd Wisconsin (6 guns) Lt. Courtland Livingston:
2 killed, 13 wounded, 11 missing

Reserve Corps: Maj. Gen. Gordon Granger

First Division: Brig. Gen. James B. Steedman

First Brigade: Brig. Gen. Walter C. Whitaker

96th Illinois (419): 39 killed, 134 wounded, 52 missing
115th Illinois (426): 22 killed,
151 wounded, 10 missing
84th Indiana (374): 23 killed, 97 wounded, 13 missing
22nd Michigan (455): 32 killed
96 wounded, 261 missing
40th Ohio (537): 19 killed, 102 wounded, 11 missing
89th Ohio (389): 19 killed, 63 wounded, 171 missing

18th Ohio Battery (6 guns) Capt. Charles C. Aleshire:
10 wounded = 10

Brigade total: 2,695: 154 killed, 654 wounded,
518 missing = 1,326

Second Brigade: Col. John G. Mitchell

78th Illinois (353): 17 killed, 77 wounded, 62 missing
98th Ohio (181): 9 killed, 41 wounded, 13 missing
113th Ohio (355): 21 killed, 98 wounded, 12 missing
121st Ohio (235): 9 killed, 83 wounded, 7 missing
M, 1st Illinois Battery (6 guns) Lt. Thomas Burton:
2 killed, 9 wounded, 1 missing

Brigade Total: 1,124: 58 killed, 308 wounded,
95 missing = 461

Second Division: Commander not present

Second Brigade: Col. Daniel McCook

85th Illinois (371): 2 wounded
86 Illinois (420): 1 killed, 1 wounded, 5 missing
125th Illinois (439): 1 killed, 2 wounded, 4 missing
52nd Ohio (417): 5 wounded
69th Ohio (350): 13 missing
I, 2nd Illinois Battery (6 guns)
Capt. Charles M. Barnett

Cavalry Corps: Brig. Gen. Robert B. Mitchell

First Division: Col. Edward M. McCook

Escort:
Co. L, 4th Indiana (32)

First Brigade: Col. Archibald P. Campbell

2nd Michigan (273): 2 killed, 7 wounded, 2 missing
9th Pennsylvania (397): 3 missing
1st Tennessee (678): 1 missing

Brigade total: 1,384: 2 killed, 7 wounded,
6 missing = 15

Second Brigade: Col. Daniel M. Ray

2nd Indiana (388): 1 killed, 4 wounded
4th Indiana (316): 2 wounded, 7 missing
2nd Tennessee (476): 1 killed, 2 wounded
1st Wisconsin (384): 2 wounded, 4 missing

D, 1st Ohio Battery (2 guns) Lt. Nathaniel M. Newell:

Brigade total: 1,564: 2 killed, 10 wounded,
11 missing = 23

Third Brigade: Col. Louis D. Watkins

4th Kentucky (288): 1 wounded, 94 missing
5th Kentucky (363): 20 missing
6th Kentucky (524): 2 killed, 7 wounded, 122 missing

Brigade total: 1,175: 2 killed, 8 wounded,
236 missing = 246

Second Division: Brig. Gen. George Crook

First Brigade: Col. Robert H. G. Minty

3rd Indiana: detached to Chattanooga
4th Michigan (489): 1 killed, 12 wounded, 6 missing
7th Pennsylvania (496): 5 killed,
13 wounded, 1 missing
4th U.S. (711): 1 killed, 5 wounded, 1 missing

Brigade total: 1,696: 7 killed, 32 wounded,
8 missing = 47

Second Brigade: Col. Eli Long

2nd Kentucky (347): 11 killed, 50 wounded, 2 missing
1st Ohio (404): 2 killed, 13 wounded, 7 missing
3rd Ohio (550): 2 killed, 7 wounded, 8 missing
4th Ohio (545): 4 killed, 9 wounded, 21 missing

Brigade total: 1,846: 19 killed, 79 wounded,
38 missing = 136

Artillery
Chicago Board of Trade Battery (7 guns)
Capt. James H. Stokes

Army of Tennessee (Confederate)
Gen. Braxton Bragg

General Headquarters:

Druex Co. Louisiana Cavalry (68)
K, 3rd Alabama Cavalry (68)
Miners and Sappers (160)
C, 1st Louisiana Regulars, Infantry (48)

Right Wing and Polk's Corps: Lt. Gen. Leonidas Polk

Escort:
Greenleaf's Co. Louisiana Cavalry (33)

Cheatham's Division: Maj. Gen. Benjamin F. Cheatham

Escort:
G, 2nd Georgia Cavalry (32)

Jackson's Brigade: Brig. Gen. John K. Jackson

2nd Bn, 1st Confederate (194): 10 killed,
73 wounded
2nd Georgia SS (108): 3 killed, 27 wounded
5th Georgia (353): 27 killed, 165 wounded, 2 missing
5th Mississippi (252): 4 killed, 70 wounded, 1 missing
8th Mississippi (404): 10 killed, 84 wounded

Brigade total: 1,311: 54 killed, 419 wounded,
4 missing = 477

Maney's Brigade: Brig. Gen. George Maney

1+27 Tennessee (703): 14 killed, 75 wounded,
4th Tennessee (PA) (179): 10 killed
43 wounded, 12 missing
6+9 Tennessee (368): 26 killed
168 wounded, 17 missing
24th Tennessee SS (43) 19 wounded, 3 missing

Brigade total: 1,293: 50 killed, 305 wounded,
32 missing = 387

Smith's Brigade: Brig. Gen. Preston Smith

11th Tennessee (383): 8 killed, 44 wounded
12+47 Tennessee (351): 11 killed, 76 wounded
13+154 Tennessee (222): 8 killed, 67 wounded
29th Tennessee (413): 4 killed, 66 wounded, 1 missing
Dawson's Sharpshooter Bn (273): 7 killed,
49 wounded, 6 missing

Brigade total: 1,642: 38 killed, 302 wounded, 7 missing = 347

Strahl's Brigade: Brig. Gen. Otho F. Strahl

4+5 Tennessee (380): 3 killed, 30 wounded
19th Tennessee (266): 8 killed, 66 wounded, 20 missing
24th Tennessee (245): 43 total losses
31st Tennessee (168): 1 killed, 26 wounded
33rd Tennessee (122): 53 total losses

Brigade total: 1,181: 250 total losses

Wright's Brigade: Brig. Gen. Marcus J. Wright

8th Tennessee (285): 3 killed, 78 wounded, 1 missing
16th Tennessee (266): 1 killed, 67 wounded
28th Tennessee (279): 9 killed, 76 wounded
38th Tennessee (278): 4 killed, 56 wounded, 5 missing
51+52 Tennessee (255): 13 killed, 102 wounded,

Brigade total: 1,113: 30 killed, 379 wounded, 6 missing = 415

Artillery

Capt. William W. Carnes' Tennessee Battery (4 guns) 7 killed, 16 wounded
Capt. John Scogin's Georgia Battery (4 guns) 1 killed, 11 wounded, 1 missing
Scott's Tennessee Battery (4 guns) Lt. John H. Marsh: 2 killed, 14 wounded
Smith's Mississippi Battery (4 guns) Lt. William B. Turner: 2 wounded, 5 missing
Capt. Thomas J. Stanford's Mississippi Battery (4 guns), 4 wounded

Hindman's Division: Maj. Gen. Thomas C. Hindman

Escort:
I, 3rd Alabama Cavalry (65)

Anderson's Brigade: Brig. Gen. Patton Anderson

7th Mississippi (291): 10 killed, 64 wounded, 1 missing
9th Mississippi (355): 9 killed, 75 wounded, 9 missing
10th Mississippi (311): 17 killed, 59 wounded
41st Mississippi (502): 24 killed, 164 wounded, 9 missing
44th Mississippi (272): 81 total losses
9th Mississippi Sharpshooters (134): 36 total losses

Brigade total: 1,865: 80 killed, 454 wounded, 24 missing = 558

Deas' Brigade: Brig. Gen. Zach C. Deas

19th Alabama (515): 34 killed, 158 wounded, 12 missing
22nd Alabama (371): 44 killed, 161 wounded,
25th Alabama (330): 15 killed, 95 wounded, 2 missing
39th Alabama (340): 14 killed, 82 wounded
50th Alabama (500): 17 killed, 81 wounded, 8 missing
17th Alabama SS (76): 1 killed, 9 wounded, 2 missing

Brigade total: 2,132: 125 killed, 586 wounded, 24 missing = 735

Manigault's Brigade: Brig. Gen. Arthur M. Manigault

24th Alabama (381): 22 killed, 91 wounded, 3 missing
28th Alabama (629): 266 total losses
34th Alabama (329): 38 total losses
10+19th South Carolina (686): 26 killed, 210 wounded

Brigade total: 2,025: 656 total losses

Artillery

Capt. S. H. Dent's Alabama Battery (6 guns) 3 killed, 13 wounded
Capt. James Garrity's Alabama Battery (4 guns): 5 wounded
Water's Alabama Battery (4 guns)
Lt. Charles W. Watkins

Hill's Corps: Lt. Gen. Daniel H. Hill

Escort:
Raum's Co. Georgia Cavalry (51)

Breckinridge's Division:
Maj. Gen. John C. Breckinridge

Adams' Brigade: Brig. Gen. Daniel W. Adams

32nd Alabama (145): 4 wounded
13+20th Louisiana (309): 16 killed, 54 wounded, 44 missing
16+25 Louisiana (319): 21 killed, 49 wounded, 36 missing
19th Louisiana (349): 28 killed, 114 wounded, 11 missing
14th Louisiana SS (99): 7 wounded

Brigade total: 1,221: 65 killed, 238 wounded, 91 missing = 394

Helm's Brigade: Brig. Gen. Benjamin H. Helm

41st Alabama (357): 27 killed, 120 wounded, 11 missing
2nd Kentucky (302): 13 killed, 107 wounded, 25 missing
4th Kentucky (275): 7 killed, 51 wounded
6th Kentucky (220): 2 killed, 32 wounded
9th Kentucky (230): 11 killed, 89 wounded, 2 missing

Brigade total: 1,384: 60 killed, 399 wounded, 39 missing = 498

Stovall's Brigade: Brig. Gen. Marcellus A. Stovall

1+3rd Florida (298): 9 killed, 70 wounded, 13 missing
4th Florida (238): 9 killed, 67 wounded, 11 missing
47th Georgia (193): 11 killed, 59 wounded, 6 missing
60th North Carolina (168): 8 killed, 36 wounded, 16 missing

Brigade total: 897: 37 killed, 232 wounded, 46 missing = 315

Artillery

Capt. Robert Cobb's Kentucky Battery (5 guns) 3 killed, 7 wounded
Capt. John W. Mebane's Tennessee Battery (4 guns) 1 wounded
Capt. C. H. Slocomb's Louisiana Battery (6 guns) 11 killed, 22 wounded

Cleburne's Division: Maj. Gen. Patrick R. Cleburne

Escort:
Sanders' Co. Tennessee Cavalry: 1 wounded

Deshler's Brigade: Brig. Gen. James Deshler

19+24 Arkansas (226): 8 killed, 97 wounded, 1 missing
6+10+15 Texas (700): 20 killed, 95 wounded, 28 missing
17+18+24+25 Texas (767): 24 killed, 174 wounded

Brigade total: 1,693: 52 killed, 366 wounded, 29 missing = 447

Polk's Brigade: Brig. Gen. Lucius E. Polk

1st Arkansas (430): 13 killed, 180 wounded, 1 missing
3+5th Confederate (290): 13 killed, 104 wounded, 1 missing
2nd Tennessee (264): 13 killed, 145 wounded, 1 missing
35th Tennessee (236): 7 killed, 54 wounded
48th Tennessee (170): 10 killed, 65 wounded, 3 missing

Brigade total: 1390: 56 killed, 548 wounded, 6 missing = 610

Wood's Brigade: Brig. Gen. S. A. M. Wood

16th Alabama (414): 25 killed, 218 wounded,
33rd Alabama (459): 19 killed, 166 wounded,
45th Alabama (423): 22 killed, 95 wounded
18th Alabama Bn (87): 5 killed, 34 wounded,
32+45 Mississippi (541): 25 killed, 141 wounded
15th Mississippi SS (58): 3 killed, 23 wounded

Brigade total: 1,982: 96 killed, 680 wounded = 776

Artillery

Calvert's Arkansas Battery, Lt. Thomas J. Key (4 guns): 6 wounded
Capt. James P. Douglas' Texas Battery (4 guns)
Capt. Henry P. Semple's Alabama Battery (4 guns) 10 wounded

Reserve Corps: Maj. Gen. William H. T. Walker

Gist's Division: Brig. Gen. States Rights Gist

Colquitt's Brigade: Col. Peyton H. Colquitt

46th Georgia (591): 5 killed, 48 wounded, 19 missing
8th Georgia Bn (399): 14 killed, 59 wounded
24th South Carolina (410): 30 killed, 144 wounded, 17 missing

Brigade total: 1,400: 49 killed, 251 wounded, 36 missing = 336

Ector's Brigade: Brig. Gen. Matthew E. Ector

Stone's Alabama Bn (111): 5 killed, 17 wounded, 1 missing
Pound's Mississippi Bn (42): 1 killed, 8 wounded, 1 missing

29th North Carolina (215): 14 killed,
72 wounded, 25 missing
9th Texas (145): 6 killed, 36 wounded, 18 missing
10th Texas DC (272): 11 killed,
84 wounded, 24 missing
14th Texas DC (197): 10 killed,
47 wounded, 29 missing
32nd Texas DC (217): 13 killed,
65 wounded, 40 missing

Brigade total: 1,199: 60 killed, 329 wounded,
138 missing = 527

Wilson's Brigade: Col. Claudius C. Wilson

25th Georgia (383): 29 killed, 123 wounded
29th Georgia (220): 24 killed, 97 wounded, 8 missing
30th Georgia (334): 20 killed, 106 wounded
1st Georgia SS (152): 5 killed, 52 wounded, 4 missing
4th Louisiana Bn (228): 21 killed, 48 wounded,
68 missing

Brigade total: 1,317: 99 killed, 426 wounded,
80 missing = 605

Artillery
Capt. Evan P. Howell's Georgia Battery (6 guns)
7 wounded

Liddell's Division: Brig. Gen. St. John R. Liddell

Govan's Brigade: Col. Daniel C. Govan

2+15th Arkansas (349): 150 total losses
5+13th Arkansas (450): 38 killed,
131 wounded, 33 missing
6+7th Arkansas (388): 165 total losses
8th Arkansas (387): 14 killed, 92 wounded, 65 missing
1st Louisiana Regulars (401): 170 total losses

Brigade total: 1,975: 73 killed, 502 wounded,
283 missing = 858

Walthall's Brigade: Brig. Gen. Edward C. Walthall

24th Mississippi (428): 10 killed,
103 wounded, 19 missing
27th Mississippi (362): 10 killed,
88 wounded, 19 missing
29th Mississippi (368): 17 killed,
139 wounded, 38 missing
30th Mississippi (362): 5 killed
76 wounded, 38 missing

34th Mississippi (307): 15 killed
91 wounded, 19 missing

Brigade total: 1,827: 57 killed, 497 wounded,
133 missing = 687

Artillery: Capt. Charles Swett

Capt. William H. Fowler's Alabama Battery (4 guns)
6 killed, 17 wounded, 1 missing
Warren Light Artillery Mississippi Battery (4 guns)
Lt. H. Shannon: 2 killed, 6 wounded

Left Wing: Lt. Gen. James Longstreet
Escort:
A, 1st Louisiana Cavalry (30): losses unknown

Buckner's Corps: Maj. Gen. Simon B. Buckner
Escort:
Clark's Co. Tennessee Cavalry (20)
Train guard: 63rd Virginia/65th Georgia (80):

Preston's Division: Brig. Gen. William Preston

Gracie's Brigade: Brig. Gen. Archibald Gracie, Jr.

43rd Alabama (400): 16 killed, 83 wounded
1st Alabama/Hilliards (260): 24 killed, 144 wounded
2nd Alabama/Hilliards (230): 16 killed, 75 wounded
3rd Alabama/Hilliards (285): 5 killed, 45 wounded
4th Alabama/Hilliards (205): 15 killed, 87 wounded
63rd Tennessee (402): 16 killed, 184 wounded

Brigade total: 1,782: 92 killed, 618 wounded = 700

Kelly's Brigade: Col. John H. Kelly

65th Georgia (251): 4 wounded
5th Kentucky (377): 14 killed, 75 wounded, 2 missing
58th North Carolina (322): 46 killed,
114 wounded, 1 missing
63rd Virginia (196): 6 killed, 48 wounded

Brigade total: 1,145: 66 killed,
241 wounded, 3 missing = 310

Trigg's Brigade: Col. Robert C. Trigg

1st Florida DC (300): 3 killed, 24 wounded
6th Florida (470): 35 killed, 130 wounded
7th Florida (431): 4 killed, 34 wounded, 5 missing
54th Virginia (477): 4 killed, 43 wounded

Brigade total: 1,536 engaged, 46 killed,
231 wounded, 5 missing = 282

Artillery

Capt. William C. Jeffries' Virginia Battery (5 guns)

Capt. Tyler M. Peeples Georgia Battery (4 guns)
1 killed, 2 wounded

Capt. Andrew M. Wolihin's Georgia Battery (4 guns)

Stewart's Division: Maj. Gen. Alexander P. Stewart

Escort:

Foules' Co. Mississippi Cavalry (35):
1 killed, 1 missing

Bate's Brigade: Brig. Gen. William B. Bate

58th Alabama (287): 21 killed, 128 wounded

37th Georgia (425): 19 killed, 168 wounded, 7 missing

4th Georgia SS (92): 2 killed, 36 wounded

15+37th Tennessee (230): 15 killed,
102 wounded, 4 missing

20th Tennessee (183): 8 killed, 80 wounded

Brigade total: 1,211: 65 killed, 515 wounded,
11 missing = 591

Brown's Brigade: Brig. Gen. John C. Brown

18th Tennessee (362): 20 killed,
114 wounded, 1 missing

26th Tennessee (239): 12 killed,
79 wounded, 1 missing

32nd Tennessee (341): 9 killed,
112 wounded, 2 missing

45th Tennessee (254): 13 killed, 85 wounded

23rd Tennessee Sharpshooters (144): 3 killed,
29 wounded

Brigade total: 1,340: 57 killed,
419 wounded, 4 missing = 480

Clayton's Brigade: Brig. Gen. Henry D. Clayton

18th Alabama (527): 37 killed,
250 wounded, 8 missing

36th Alabama (429): 16 killed,
133 wounded, 3 missing

38th Alabama (490): 37 killed,
143 wounded, 5 missing

Brigade total: 1,446: 90 killed, 526 wounded,
16 missing = 634

Artillery

Capt. John T. Humphreys' 1st Arkansas Battery
(4 guns) 1 killed, 3 wounded

Dawson's Georgia Battery (4 guns) Lt. R. W.
Anderson: 1 killed, 6 wounded

Eufala Alabama Artillery (4 guns) Capt. McDonald
Oliver: 1 killed, 13 wounded

Buckner's Reserve Artillery: Maj. Samuel C. Williams

Capt. Edmund D. Baxter's Tennessee Battery
(2 guns)

Capt. Putnam Darden's Mississippi Battery (4 guns)
1 killed, 2 wounded

Capt. R. F. Kolb's Alabama Battery (4 guns)
2 killed, 1 wounded

Capt. Robert P. Mecants' Florida Battery (4 guns)
1 wounded

First Corps, Army of Northern Virginia:
Maj. Gen. John B. Hood

Escort:

Companies E and C, 1st Louisiana Cavalry (30):
losses unknown

Johnson's Provisional Division:
Brig. Gen. Bushrod R. Johnson

Fulton's Brigade: Col. John S. Fulton

17th Tennessee (249): 61 wounded, 69 missing

23rd Tennessee (186): 8 killed, 77 wounded, 13
missing 25th Tennessee (145): 10 killed, 45 wounded,
1 missing 44th Tennessee (294): 10 killed,
88 wounded, 15 missing

Brigade total: 874: 28 killed, 271 wounded,
98 missing = 397

Gregg's Brigade: Brig. Gen. John Gregg

3rd Tennessee (274): 22 killed, 87 wounded, 6 missing

10th Tennessee (190): 24 killed,
86 wounded, 4 missing

30th Tennessee (185): 21 killed,
73 wounded, 3 missing

41st Tennessee (325): 11 killed,
67 wounded, 1 missing

50th Tennessee (186): 9 killed, 46 wounded

1st Tennessee Bn (82): 13 killed,
24 wounded, 1 missing

7th Texas (177): 10 killed, 82 wounded

Brigade total: 1,419: 110 killed, 465 wounded,
15 missing = 590

McNair's Brigade: Brig. Gen. Evander McNair

1st Arkansas MR (273): 14 killed
76 wounded, 16 missing
2nd Arkansas MR (139): 6 killed
43 wounded, 3 missing
25th Arkansas (133): 7 killed, 51 wounded, 3 missing
4+31+4th Bn Arkansas (415): 14 killed
60 wounded, 29 missing
39th North Carolina (247): 10 killed
90 wounded, 3 missing

Brigade total: 1,207: 51 killed, 320 wounded,
54 missing = 425

Artillery
E, 9th Georgia Battery (4 guns) Lt .William S. Everett:
3 wounded
Bledsoe's Missouri Battery (4 guns) Lt. R. L. Wood:
1 killed, 1 wounded
Capt. James F. Culpeper's South Carolina Battery
(4 guns) 14 wounded

Hood's Division: Brig. Gen. Evander M. Law

Benning's Brigade: Brig. Gen. Henry L. Benning

2nd Georgia (427): 16 killed, 101 wounded
15th Georgia (285): 7 killed, 75 wounded
17th Georgia (250): 9 killed, 132 wounded, 8 missing
20th Georgia (238): 28 killed, 114 wounded

Brigade total: 1,200: 60 killed, 422 wounded,
8 missing = 490

Law's Brigade: Col. James L. Sheffield

4th Alabama (249): 12 killed, 45 wounded, 1 missing
15th Alabama (373): 11 killed, 121 wounded
44th Alabama (276): 10 killed, 71 wounded, 8 missing
47th Alabama (283): 7 killed, 56 wounded, 7 missing
48th Alabama (276): 19 killed, 67 wounded, 1 missing

Brigade total: 1,457: 59 killed, 360 wounded,
17 missing = 436

Robertson's Brigade: Brig. Gen. Jerome B. Robertson

3rd Arkansas (322): 25 killed,
120 wounded, 12 missing
1st Texas (409): 19 killed, 124 wounded, 12 missing
4th Texas (322): 26 killed, 102 wounded, 5 missing
5th Texas (247): 13 killed, 87 wounded, 12 missing

Brigade total: 1,300: 83 killed, 433 wounded,
41 missing = 557

*George "Tige" Anderson's and Micah Jenkins' Brigades
did not arrive in time to be engaged*

McLaw's Division: Brig. Gen. Joseph B. Kershaw

*Humphreys' Brigade: Brig. Gen.
Benjamin G. Humphreys*

13th Mississippi (300): 1 killed, 7 wounded
17th Mississippi (338): 12 killed, 76 wounded
18th Mississippi (260): 1 killed, 8 wounded
21st Mississippi (328): 7 killed, 43 wounded

Brigade total: 1,226: 21 killed,
134 wounded, = 155

Kershaw's Brigade: Brig. Gen. Joseph B. Kershaw

2nd South Carolina (225): 26 killed, 75 wounded,
3rd South Carolina (343): 51 killed, 115 wounded,
7th South Carolina (283): 10 killed,
76 wounded, 1 missing
8th South Carolina (215): 5 killed, 23 wounded,
15th South Carolina (343): 14 killed, 57 wounded,
3rd South Carolina Bn (182): 7 killed, 44 wounded,

Brigade total: 1,591: 113 killed, 390 wounded,
1 missing = 504

*Maj. Gen. Lafayette McLaws, William T. Wofford's
and Goode Bryan's brigades did not arrive in time
to be engaged*

*First Corps Artillery Battalion:
Col. E. Porter Alexander (not engaged)*

Reserve Artillery: Maj. Felix H. Robertson
Capt. Overton W. Barret's Missouri Battery (4 guns)
Capt. G. Le Gardeur's Louisiana Battery (4 guns)

Capt. M. W. Havis' Georgia Battery (3 guns) 1 killed,
1 wounded

Capt. Charles L. Lumsden's Alabama Battery (5 guns)
1 killed, 1 wounded

Capt. T. L. Massenberg's Georgia Battery (4 guns)
4 wounded

Forrest's Cavalry Corps: Brig. Gen. Nathan B. Forrest

Escort:

Jackson's Co. Tennessee Cavalry (67): losses unknown

Armstrong's Division: Brig. Gen. Frank C. Armstrong

Escort:
Bradley's Co. CSA Regular Cavalry (47):
losses unknown

Wheeler's Brigade: Col. James T. Wheeler

Escort:

E, 6th Tennessee (30 est.): losses unknown
3rd Arkansas (300): 2 killed, 2 wounded = 4
2nd Kentucky (427, est.) losses unknown
6th Tennessee (300): losses unknown
18th Tennessee Cavalry Battalion (164):
losses unknown

Brigade total: 1,221 (losses unknown)

Dibrell's Brigade: Col. George G. Dibrell

4th Tennessee (200): 2 killed, 16 wounded
8th Tennessee (300): 3 killed, 11 wounded
9th Tennessee (350): 8 wounded
10th Tennessee (474 engaged est.)
3 killed, 3 wounded
11th Tennessee (474 est.): 2 killed, 2 wounded,
Shaw's Tennessee Batl. (284 est.): losses unknown
Capt. A. L. Huggins' Tennessee Battery (4 guns)
losses unknown
Capt. John W. Morton's Tennessee Battery (4 guns)
losses unknown

Brigade total: 2,218: 10 killed,
40 wounded = 50

Pegram's Division: Brig. Gen. John Pegram

Davidson's Brigade: Brig. Gen. Henry B. Davidson

1st Georgia (295 engaged, est.): losses unknown
6th Georgia (400 est.): 12 killed, 72 wounded

6th North Carolina (520): 5 killed,
6 wounded, 18 missing

10th Confederate (250): 2 killed, 11 wounded
Rucker's Legion (385): 37 total losses
Capt. Gustave A. Huwald's Tennessee Battery
(4 guns) losses unknown

Brigade total: 1,900: 163 known losses

Scott's Brigade: Col. John S. Scott

Morgan's Detachment (240): 3 killed, 7 wounded
1st Louisiana (210 engaged est.):
10 killed, 42 wounded
2nd Tennessee (300 engaged est.):
5 killed, 14 wounded
5th Tennessee (300 engaged est.)
2 killed, 14 wounded
Lt. Winslow Robinson's Louisiana Battery (4 guns)
3 wounded

Brigade total: 1,100: 20 killed, 80 wounded = 100

Wheeler's Cavalry Corps: Maj. Gen. Joseph Wheeler

Wharton's Division: Brig. Gen. John A. Wharton

Escort:
B, 8th Texas (41 engaged est.): losses unknown

Crew's Brigade: Col. C. C. Crews

Malone's Alabama Regiment (502 engaged, est.)
losses unknown
2nd Georgia (600): losses unknown
3rd Georgia (418 engaged est.): losses unknown
4th Georgia (605): losses unknown

Brigade total: 2,125: losses unknown

Harrison's Brigade: Col. Thomas Harrison

3rd Confederate (550): losses unknown
3rd Kentucky (418 engaged est.): losses unknown
4th Tennessee (418 engaged est.): losses about 40, est.

8th Texas (412): losses unknown
11th Texas (398 engaged est.): losses unknown
Capt. B. F. White's Tennessee Battery (4 guns)
losses unknown

Brigade total: 2,273: losses unknown

Martin's Division: Brig. Gen. William T. Martin

Escort:
A, 3rd Alabama (34): losses unknown

Morgan's Brigade: Col. John T. Morgan

1st Alabama (418 engaged est.): losses unknown
3rd Alabama (279): losses unknown
51st Alabama (418 engaged est.): losses unknown
8th Confederate (418 engaged est.): losses unknown

Brigade total: 1,533: losses unknown

Russell's Brigade: Col. A. A. Russell
4th Alabama (418 engaged est.): losses unknown
1st Confederate (418 engaged est.): losses unknown
Wiggins' Arkansas Battery, Lt. J. P. Bryant (2 guns)
losses unknown

Brigade total: 836: losses unknown

Notes

Map Set 1

1. U.S. War Department, *The War of the Rebellion: A Compilation of the Official Records of the Union and Confederate Armies.* 128 Vols. Washington D.C.: U.S. Government Printing Office, 1880-1901. Series I, vol. 23, 2, 197, 733, hereinafter cited as *OR*.

2. William M. Lamers, *The Edge of Glory* (Baton Rouge, Louisiana State University Press, 1999. Reprint of 1961 edition), 272.

3. W. C. Dodson, ed. *Campaigns of Wheeler and His Cavalry, 1862-1865* (Memphis, TN, E. F. Williams and J. J. Fox, 1997. Reprint of 1899 edition), 85.

4. *OR* 23, 1, 543; and Dodson, *Campaigns of Wheeler*, 86.

5. *OR* 23, 1, 538.

6. *Ibid.*, 587-8.

7. *Ibid.*, 594.

8. *Ibid.*, 465.

9. Alexis Cope, *The 15th Ohio Volunteers and Its Campaigns, 1861-1865* (Columbus, OH, 1916), 286.

10. Craig L. Symonds, *Stonewall of the West: Patrick Cleburne and the Civil War* (Lawrence, KA., University Press of Kansas, 1997), 129.

11. Nathaniel Cheairs Hughes, Jr., and Gordon D. Whitney, *Jefferson Davis In Blue: The Life of Sherman's Relentless Warrior* (Baton Rouge, Louisiana State University Press, 2002), 159.

12. Cope, *15th Ohio*, 289-90.

13. Richard A. Baumgartner, *Blue Lightning* (Huntington, WV, Blue Acorn Press, 2007), 20, 22-23, 39-40, 51-2.

14. *OR* 23, 1, 458.

15. *Ibid.*, 611-13.

16. James A. Connelly, "Major James Austin Connelly," *Transactions of the Illinois State Historical Society for the Year 1928* (Springfield, Phillips Brothers, 1928), 268.

17. *OR* 23, 1, 521.

18. Helyn W. Tomlinson, ed. *"Dear Friends" The Civil War Letters and Diary of Charles Edwin Cort* (Minneapolis, 1962), 85.

19. Sam Davis Elliott, *Soldier of Tennessee: General Alexander Peter Stewart and the Civil War In The West* (Baton Rouge, Louisiana State University Press, 1999), 94-5.

20. As quoted in Judith Lee Hallock, *Braxton Bragg and Confederate Defeat: Vol. II* (Tuscaloosa, University of Alabama Press, 1991), 17.

21. Thomas Lawrence Connelly, *Autumn of Glory: The Army of Tennessee, 1862-1865* (Baton Rouge, LA, Louisiana State University Press, 1971), 128.

22. *OR* 23, 2, 888.

23. Jack Hurst, *Nathan Bedford Forrest* (Vintage books, NY, 1994), 128-30.

24. Thomas Jordan and J. Pryor, *The Campaigns of General Nathan Bedford Forrest and of Forrest's Cavalry* (New York, De Capo Press, 1996. Reprint of 1868 edition), 290-1.

25. *OR* 23, 1, 524.

26. Nathaniel Cheairs Hughes, ed. *Liddell's Record* (Baton Rouge, Louisiana State University Press, 1997, reprint of 1985 edition), 128.

27. Larry Daniel, *Days of Glory* (Baton Rouge, Louisiana State University Press, 2004), 273.

28. George S. Wilson, "Wilder's Brigade," *National Tribune*, October 19th, 1893.

29. Connelly, *Autumn of Glory*, 132-3.

Map Set 2

1. William S. Rosecrans, "The Chattanooga Campaign," *National Tribune*, March 25, 1882.

2. *OR* 30, 1, 485.

3. *Ibid.*, 245-6.

4. *Ibid.*, 52.

5. William S. Rosecrans, "The Chattanooga Campaign," *National Tribune*, March 25, 1882.

6. *OR* 30, 2, 136. D. H. Hill's report records his complete surprise when Wilder's troops showed up across the Tennessee River from Chattanooga. See also D. H. Hill, "Chickamauga—Great Battle of the West," *Battles and Leaders of the Civil War* (New York: Thomas Yoseloff, 1956), III, 639-40.

7. Entry for August 22, 1863, Brent Journal, Bragg Papers.

8. *Ibid.*, August 28, 1863.

9. *OR* 23, 2, 912, 930 mention the cavalry regiment at Bridgeport, and later identify it as the 3rd Confederate.

10. Entry for August 29, 1863, Brent Journal, Bragg Papers.

11. *Ibid.* See also *OR* 30, 4, 563-4.

12. *OR* 30, 4, 574.

13. Entry for September 1, 1863, W. B. Corbitt Diary, Emory University. Atlanta, GA.

14. *OR* 30, 4, 594. The dispatch from Bragg to Hill, dated 10:00 a.m. September 4, 1863, outlines Bragg's plan, the problems with the crossings, and Forrest's promise to find suitable fords.

15. William Robert Stevenson, "Robert Alexander Smith: A Southern Son." *Alabama Historical Quarterly*. Volume 20, 1958. 54, and Entry

for September 3, 1863, Brent Journal, Bragg Papers.

16. Entries for September 5-8, Corporal George Cooley Diary, Wisconsin Historical Society, Madison, WI.

17. David Sloane Stanley, *Personal Memoirs of Major General D. S. Stanley, U.S.A.* (Cambridge, MA, Harvard University Press, 1917), 158; *OR* 30, 3, 397.

18. XIV Corps positions by Day, Thomas File, Combat Studies Institute.

19. *OR* 30, 3, 370-1.

20. D. H. Hill, "Chickamauga—Great Battle of the West," III, 644.

21. *OR* 30, 4, 602, 614.

22. *Ibid.*, 610-11.

23. *Ibid.*, 621.

24. *OR* 30, 2, 523; Entry for September 8, 1863, Brent Journal, Bragg Papers; Gustave Huwald Letter, Leroy Moncure Nutt Papers, *Southern Historical Collection*, Wilson Library, University of North Carolina, Chapel Hill.

25. *Ninety-Second Illinois Volunteers* (Freeport, IL. Journal Steam Publishing House and Bookbindery, 1875), 100-101.

26. John Beatty, *The Citizen Soldier* (Lincoln, NE., University of Nebraska Press, 1998; Reprint of 1879 edition), 330.

27. Entry for September 8, 1863, Lt. James Thompson Diary, 4th Ohio Cavalry file, CCNMP; Entry for September 8, 1863, Captain William E. Crane Diary, 4th Ohio Cavalry, General Thomas' Papers, RG 94, NARA.

28. *OR* 30, 4, 591.

29. Nelson Gremillion, *Company G, 1st Louisiana Cavalry, CSA. A Narrative* (Lafayette: University of Southwestern Louisiana, 1986), 30.

30. Jordan and Pryor, *The Campaigns of Forrest*, 305-6.

31. *Ninety-Second Illinois Volunteers*, 102.

32. *OR* 30, 1, 497.

33. Hazen to Benson H. Lossing, August 23rd, 1866, William Palmer Collection, Western Reserve Historical Society, Cleveland, OH.

34. *OR* 30, 1, 852-3.

35. *Ibid.*, 603.

36. Summaries of News Received at Rosecrans Headquarters, RG 393, NARA.

37. *OR* 30, 3, 509-10.

38. Jordan and Pryor, *Campaigns of Forrest*, 306, and *OR* 30, 2, 28.

39. William T. Martin, "A Defense of General Bragg at Chickamauga." *Confederate Veteran.* Volume XI, number 4 (April, 1883) 205.

40. *OR* 30, 1, 723.

41. Gustave Huwald Letter, Leroy M. Nutt Papers, *Southern Historical Collection*, University of North Carolina, Chapel Hill.

42. *OR* 30, 2, 528.

43. *OR* 30, 1, 743.

44. Huwald Letter, Nutt Papers. UNC.

45. J. W. Minnich, "Unique Experiences in the Chickamauga Campaign," *Confederate Veteran*, 30, Issue 6 (June, 1922), 222.

46. Huwald letter, Nutt papers, *Southern Historical Collection*.

47. Entry for September 12, 1863, William H. Records Diary, Indiana State Library. Indianapolis, IN.

48. John M. Bernard to his wife and children, September 15, 1863, William Henry Smith Memorial Library, Indiana Historical Society, Indianapolis, IN.

49. *OR* 30, 1, 326.

50. William D. Ward Reminiscences, DePauw University, Greencastle, IN.

51. *OR* 30, 1, 326.

52. *Ibid.*, 326.

53. *Ibid.*, 285.

54. William Glenn Robertson, "The Chickamauga Campaign: McLemore's Cove," *Blue & Gray Magazine*, XXIII, Issue 6 (Spring 2007), 19.

55. Robertson, "The Chickamauga Campaign: McLemore's Cove," 19.

56. *OR* 30, 2, 307.

57. Connelly, *Autumn of Glory*, 183-4.

58. *OR* 30, 1, 327-8.

59. Entries for September 11 and 12, "Summaries of the news reaching Headquarters of General W. S. Rosecrans, 1863-64," NARA.

60. Daily locations of the XIV Corps, Combat Studies Institute, Fort Leavenworth, KS.

61. *OR* 30, 1, 853.

62. Entry for September 14, 1863, Samuel Pasco Diary, 3rd Florida File, CCNMP.

63. *OR* 30, 1, 486.

64. *OR* 30, 2, 30. The dispatch is not included, but mentioned in Bragg's orders to Polk.

65. *Ibid.*

66. *Ibid.*, 76.

67. The Union XXI Corps, reinforced by Wilder, numbered 14,500 men. Polk could count on Cheatham, 7,000; Walker added 6,500 more after 8:00 p.m., and if Hindman got into position by daylight, he would add another 6,000; giving Polk in all, 19,500 men, hardly overwhelming superiority. All numbers taken from Powell, *Numbers and Losses*, CCNMP.

68. *OR* 30, 2, 30.

69. Entry for September 13th, Brent Journal, Bragg Papers.

70. *OR* 30, 4, 643.

71. Entry for September 13th, Brent Journal, Bragg Papers.

72. Entry for September 15, 1863, W. B. Corbitt Diary, Emory University, Atlanta, GA.

73. Entry for September 15, 1863, William E. Sloan Diary, Tennessee State Library and Archives, Nashville, TN. This word probably did not reach Bragg until September 16th.

74. *OR* 30, 4, 645-9.

75. *OR* 30, 3, 627-9.

76. Robert H. G. Minty, "Minty's Saber Brigade," *National Tribune*, February 25, 1892; and Entry for September 17th, William H. Records Diary, Indiana State Library, Indianapolis, IN.

77. *OR* 30, 1, 853.

78. Order Book, Bragg Papers, WRHS.

79. William Glenn Robertson, "The Chickamauga Campaign: The Armies Collide," *Blue & Gray Magazine*, XXIV, No. 3 (Fall, 2007) 40.

Map Set 3

1. Powell, *Numbers and Losses*, CCNMP. This figure excludes Polk's Corps and about one-half of the First Corps, which was not yet present.

2. OR 30, 2, 31.

3. Robert H. G. Minty, "Minty's Saber Brigade," *National Tribune*, February 25th, 1892.

4. *Ibid.*

5. Joseph G. Vale, *Minty and The Cavalry, A History of Cavalry Campaigns In The Western Armies* (Harrisburg, PA: Edwin K. Meyers, Printer and Binder, 1886), 224-5. Today this is called Boynton Ridge, and should not be confused with another Peavine Ridge, about a mile to the east on the other side of the creek.

6. OR 30, 2, 451.

7. Captain William D. Harder Reminiscences, Combat Studies Institute, Fort Leavenworth, KS.

8. Henry Albert Potter, "Account of the Battle of Chickamauga and Wheeler's Raid." Bentley Historical Library, University of Michigan, Ann Arbor, MI.

9. *OR* 30, 1, 923; and Undated postwar statement of Lieutenant Sylvanus H. Stevens, Chicago Board Of Trade Battery File, CCNMP.

10. OR 30, 2, 479.

11. *Ibid.*, 452.

12. Vale, *Minty and The Cavalry*, 226.

13. Dale Edward Linville, *Battles, Skirmishes, Events and Scenes: The Letters and Memorandum of Ambrose Remley* (Crawfordsville, IN: Montgomery County Historical Society, 1997), 81.

14. *OR* 30, 1, 464.

15. B. F. McGee, *History of the 72d Indiana Volunteer Infantry of the Mounted Lightning Brigade* (Lafayette, IN, S. Vater & Co. 1882), 167.

16. McGee, *History of the 72nd Indiana*, 168.

17. "The Late Battle–Walthall's Brigade." *Memphis Daily Appeal*, October 1, 1863.

18. OR 30, 1, 458.

19. OR 30, 2, 272.

20. *Ibid.*, 251.

21. Magee, *History of the 72nd Indiana*, 168-9.

22. Vale, *Minty and the Cavalry*, 227.

23. *Ibid.*

24. Captain William H. Harder Reminiscences, Combat Studies Institute, Fort Leavenworth, KS.

25. E. Raymond Evans, *Chickamauga: Civil War Impact on an Area* (Chickamauga, GA, City of Chickamauga, 2002), 68. The Federals, naturally enough, assumed she was Mrs. Reed. None of the Reed family were present during the battle, however, and she remains unidentified.

26. John T. Goodrich, "Gregg's Brigade In The Battle of Chickamauga," *Confederate Veteran*, XXII (June, 1914), 264.

27. W. L. Gammage, *The Camp, The Bivouac, and The Battlefield* (Little Rock, AR., Arkansas Southern Press, 1958, reprint of 1864 edition), 90.

28. Braxton Bragg Papers, Western Reserve Historical Society, Cleveland, OH; and John Bell Hood, *Advance and Retreat* (Secausus, NJ, Blue and Grey Press, 1985. Reprint of 1880 edition), 61.

29. Bryam's Ford is also called Lambert's Ford.

30. OR 30, 2, 272.

31. Entry for September 18th, Edward Kitchell Diary, Lincoln Library, Springfield, IL.

32. J. W. Minnick, "Reminiscences of J. W. Minnick, 6th Georgia Cavalry," *Northwest Georgia Historical and Genealogical Society Quarterly*, 29, #3 (Summer, 1997), 20.

33. *OR* 30, 1, 923; and Vale, *Minty and The Cavalry*, 228.

34. Robert H. G. Minty, "Minty's Saber Brigade: Chickamauga," *National Tribune*, March 3, 1892; and Minty, *Remarks*, 5-6.

35. Baumgartner, *Blue Lightning*, 199-200.

36. OR 30, 2, 452.

37. *Ibid.*, 239.

38. *Ibid.*, 361, 413.

39. John T. Wilder supplemental report, 1888, CCNMP.

40. Minty, "Minty's Saber Brigade," *National Tribune*.

41. Goodrich, "Gregg's Brigade," *Confederate Veteran*, 264.

42. *OR* 30, 2, 452.

43. Minty, "Minty's Saber Brigade," *National Tribune*.

44. *OR* 30, 1, 822.

45. *Ibid.*, 832.

46. *OR* 30, 2, 453.

47. Powell, *Numbers and Losses*, CCNM.

48. *OR* 30, 1, 853.

49. Entry for September 18th, Levi Ross diary, Abraham Lincoln Library.

50. Henry J. Aten, *History of The Eighty-Fifth Regiment, Illinois Volunteer Infantry* (Hiawatha, KS, 1901), 103.

51. *Ibid.*, and Gammage, *The Camp, The Bivouac, and the Battlefield*, 95.

52. Gustave Huwald letter, October 7th, 1866, Leroy Monicure Nutt Papers, Southern Historical Collection, University of North Carolina.

53. W. F. Shropshire Reminiscences, *Confederate Veteran* Papers, Duke University, Durham, NC.

Map Set 4

1. *OR* 30, 1, 55.

2. Henry Fales Perry, *History of the Thirty-Eighth Regiment Indiana Volunteer Infantry* (Palo Alto, CA, A. Stuart, Printer, 1906), 87.

3. *OR* 30, 1, 871.

4. L. E. Chenoweth letter, Joseph H. Brigham Papers, Bowling Green State University, Bowling Green, OH.

5. J. W. Bishop, *The Story of a Regiment, Being a Narrative of the Service of the Second Regiment, Minnesota Veteran Volunteer Infantry, in the Civil War of 1861-1865* (St. Paul, MN, 1890), 99.

6. *OR* 30, 2, 524; Capt. H. B. Clay, "Concerning the Battle of Chickamauga," *Confederate Veteran*, XXI (February, 1905), 72.

7. *OR* 30, 1, 415.

8. J. W. Bishop, *Van Derveer's Brigade at Chicamauga* (St. Paul, MN, n. 1903), 6.

9. Albert Dickennan, "The Ninth Ohio At Chickamauga," *National Tribune*, October 18, 1906.

10. Report of M. B. Walker, Thomas Papers, Library of Congress; *OR* 30, 1, 400.

11. Clay, "Concerning the Battle of Chickamauga," 72.

12. Entry for September 19, Samuel F. Thompson Diary, Wisconsin Historical Society, Madison, WI; J. W. Minnich Manuscript, 6th Georgia Cavalry File, CCNMP.

13. Gustave Huwald letter, October 7th, 1866, Leroy Monicure Nutt Papers, Southern Historical Collection, University of North Carolina.

14. W. M. Marriner, "Chickamauga—The Opening," *Southern Bivouac*, III, No. 1 (September, 1884, Reprinted by Broadfoot Publishing Company, Wilmington, NC, 1992), 11.

15. *OR* 30, 2, 240, 248.

16. *OR* 30, 1, 419, 422; "My Dear Aunt," February 19, 1864, Henry G. Davidson Letters, Lincoln Library, Springfield, IL.

17. David V. Stroud, *Ector's Brigade and the Army of Tennessee, 1862-1865* (Longview, TX, Ranger Publishing, 2004), 132.

18. Jeremiah C. Dunahower Memoirs, Minnesota Historical Society, St. Paul, MN, 111.

19. Louis R. Smith and Andrew Quist, *Cush: A Civil War Memoir by Samuel H. Sprott* (Livingston, AL, Livingston Press, University of West Alabama, 1999), 50.

20. *OR* 30, 1, 408.

21. "Ector's Brigade in the Battle of Chickamauga," *Mobile Daily Register*, October 14, 1863.

22. *OR* 30, 1, 275.

23. John Allen Wyeth, *That Devil Forrest: Life of General Nathan Bedford Forrest* (Baton Rouge, LA, Louisiana State University Press, 1989), 227; Stroud, *Ector's Brigade*, 134.

24. Lucius D. Hinkley Memoir, Wisconsin Historical Society, Madison WI; James E. Edmonds Diary, United States Army Heritage and Education Center, Carlisle, PA. (hereafter AHEC).

25. Wyeth, *That Devil Forrest*, 227.

26. "D. G. Templeton, Sir," Oct. 13, 1863, Templeton Letters, Simpson History Complex, Hill College, Hillsboro, TX.; Casualty report, *Mobile Daily Register*, October 14, 1863.

27. Francis F. McKinney, *Education In Violence* (Chicago, IL, Americana House, 1991, reprint of 1961 edition), 232.

28. Richard W. Johnson, *A Soldier's Reminiscences in Peace and War* (Philadelphia, J. Lippincott Company, 1886), 226.

29. *OR* 30, 1, 56, 535; McKinney, *Education in Violence*, 232.

30. *OR* 30, 1, 440.

31. *Ibid.*, 923.

32. *OR* 30, 2, 32, 78.

33. Benjamin F. Scribner, *How Soldiers Were Made* (Huntington, WV., Blue Acorn Press, 1995. Reprint of 1887 edition), 144.

34. Nathaniel Chears Hughes, Jr., ed. *Liddell's Record* (Baton Rouge, LA, Louisiana State University Press, 1997), 140.

35. *Ibid.*

36. Scribner, *How Soldiers Were Made*, 145.

37. Captain J. D. Smith, "Walthall's Brigade at Chickamauga," *Confederate Veteran*, XX (October, 1904), 483.

38. Angus L. Waddle, *Three Years With the Armies of the Ohio and the Cumberland* (Chillicothe, OH, Scioto Gazette Book and Job Office, 1889), 51-2; August Bratnober Diary, 10th Wisconsin file, CCNMP.

39. Calvin L. Collier, *First In—Last Out* (Little Rock, AR., Pioneer Press, 1961), 82.

40. *OR* 30, 1, 299-301; Collier, *First In—Last Out*, 83.

41. *OR* 30, 1, 309; "Dear Pa," Thursday night, Sept 24, 1863, Henry H. Haymond Letters, Navarro College, Corsciana, TX.

42. *OR* 30, 1, 309.

43. Powell, *Numbers and Losses*, CCNMP.

44. "Letter of Sept. 24, 1863, W. B. Honnoll, Honnell Family Papers, Woodruff Library, Emory University, Atlanta GA.; Robert A. Jarman, "The History of Company K, 27th Mississippi Infantry, and its First and Last Muster Rolls," Williams Library, University of Mississippi, Oxford, MS.

45. *OR* 30, 1, 297.

46. Mark W. Johnson, *That Body of Brave Men* (Cambridge, MA, Da Capo Press, 2003), 133-41.

47. Bishop, *Van Derveer's Brigade at Chickamauga*, 7-8.

48. *OR* 30, 1, 428; Constantin Grebner, with Frederic Trautman, translator and ed., *We Were The Ninth* (Kent Ohio, Kent State University Press, 1987, originally published 1897), 142.

49. *OR* 30, 1, 428; and *OR* 30, 2, 273.

50. *OR* 30, 1, 416.

51. *Ibid.*

52. Floyd R. Barnhill, Sr. and Calvin L. Collier, *The Fighting Fifth: Pat Cleburne's Cutting Edge: The Fifth Arkansas Regiment, C.S.A.* (Jonesboro, AR., n.p. n.d.), 102.

53. "My Dear Aunt," Feb. 19, 1864, Henry G. Davidson Letters, Lincoln Library, Springfield, IL.

54. Jordan and Pryor, *The Campaigns of Forrest*, 319.

55. Dibrell Brigade Tablet, CCNMP.

56. *OR* 30, 1, 428; Jeremiah C. Dunahower Memoir, Minnesota Historical Society (hereafter Minnesota HS), 118.

57. Bishop, *Van Derveer's Brigade At Chickamauga*, 9.

58. Letter of September 23, 1863, *Rochester Chronicle*, October 15, 1863.

59. *OR* 30, 1, 434; Bishop, *The Story of A Regiment*, 103.

60. Memphis Daily Appeal, Friday October 9th, 1863.

Map Set 5

1. Powell, *Numbers and Losses*, CCNMP.

2. *OR* 30, 2, 77-8.

3. John M. Palmer, *Personal Recollections of John M. Palmer* (Cincinnati, The Robert Clarke Co, 1901), 174.

4. *OR* 30, 1, 713. Palmer says he was ordered to Thomas' aid at noon, but it was more likely before 11:00 a.m. At noon, his division was going into line on Johnson's flank.

5. Joseph B. Cumming Recollections, Southern Historical Collections, University of North Carolina (UNC) Chapel Hill, NC.

6. *OR* 30, 2, 89.

7. *OR* 30, 1, 416.

8. "A Sketch of Chickamauga," *Louisville Daily Journal*, October 6, 1863.

9. *OR* 30, 2, 83.

10. I. B. Webster, "Chickamauga," *National Tribune*, July 2, 1891.

11. *OR* 30, 1, 419.

12. *Ibid.*, 91.

13. Isaac K. Young, "Chickamauga," *National Tribune*, August 9, 1888.

14. *OR* 30, 1, 535.

15. Cope, *The Fifteenth Ohio*, 310.

16. *OR* 30, 1, 538.

17. *Ibid.*, 713.

18. *Ibid.*, 762.

19. Robert L. Kimberly and Ephraim S. Holloway, *The Forty-First Ohio Veteran Volunteer Infantry in the War of the Rebellion, 1861-1865* (Cleveland, OH, W.R. Smellie, Printer and Publisher, 1897), 49.

20. *OR* 30, 2, 111. Several of Smith's regiments were consolidated for tactical purposes, mostly due to their small numbers. Hazen's men had no time to entrench, but Brock Field was still in the process of being cleared. The Confederates mistook brush piles and felled trees for Union field works.

21. Entry for September 19, 1863, Alfred T. Fielder Diary, Chattanooga-Hamilton County Library, Chattanooga, TN.

22. Levi Wagner, "Recollections of an Enlistee, 1861-1864," AHEC, Carlisle, PA.

23. *OR* 30, 1, 730.

24. *OR* 30, 2, 118.

25. Carroll Henderson Clark Memoirs, TSLA.

26. *OR* 30, 2, 111.

27. *Ibid.*, 114.

28. *Ibid.*, 107.

29. *Ibid.*, 78.

30. Entry for September 19, 1863; William Sylvester Dillon Diary, Georgia Department of Archives and History, hereafter GDAH.

31. Entry for September 19, 1863; E. H. Reynolds Diary, 4th/5th Tennessee File, Combat Studies Institute.

32. OR 30, 2, 84.

33. Sam R. Watkins, *Co. "Aytch" First Tennessee Regiment: Or A Side Show of The Big Show* (Franklin, TN, Providence House Publishers, 2007), 107-8.

34. Capt. W. W. Carnes, "An Unusual Identification," *Confederate Veteran*, 37 (May, 1929), 188.

35. OR 30, 1, 607.

36. Kenneth W. Noe, ed. *A Southern Boy in Blue: The Memoir of Marcus Woodcock 9th Kentucky Infantry (U.S.A.)* (Knoxville, TN, University of Tennessee Press, 1996), 198.

37. OR 30, 1, 823.

38. T. L. Massenburg, "Captain W. W. Carnes' Battery At Chickamauga," *Confederate Veteran* (November, 1898), 517.

39. John B. Lindsley, Ed. *Military Annals of Tennessee*, II (Wilmington, NC, Broadfoot Publishing Co., 1995. Reprint of 1886 ed.), 822-3.

40. OR 30, 2, 361.

41. *Ibid.*

42. *Ibid.*, 30, 1, 473.

43. J. B. Dodge, "The Story of Chickamauga, as Told by an Eye-Witness," *Northern Indianian*, February 11, 1875.

44. S. J. A. Frazier, *The Lookout*, May 20, 1909; Clipping in the Hamilton County Bicentennial Library, Chattanooga, TN.

45. Cope, *The 15th Ohio Volunteers*, 279.

46. Watkins, *Co. Aytch*, 109.

47. OR 30, 2, 525.

48. Powell, *Numbers and Losses*, CCNMP.

49. OR 30, 2, 401.

50. Rev. Edgar W. Jones, "History of the 18th Alabama Regiment," 18th Alabama File, CCNMP.

51. "Dear Aunt," October 4th, 1863, John J Warbinton Letters, AHEC, Carlisle, PA.

52. OR 30, 1, 811.

53. OR 30, 2, 401.

54. *Ibid.*, 370.

55. T. I. Corn, "Brown's Brigade At Chickamauga," *Confederate Veteran*, XXI (March, 1913), 124.

56. OR 20, 2, 370.

57. N. J. Hampton, *An Eyewitness to the Dark Days of 1861-65* (Nashville, TN, np. 1898), 31.

58. Corn, "Brown's Brigade At Chickamauga," 124.

59. Statement of J. J. Reynolds, September 19, CCNMP.

60. See Reynolds Statement, CCNMP, and also Ebeneezer Hannaford, *The Story of a Regiment* (Cincinnati, OH, n. 1868), 463.

61. David Bittle Floyd, *History of the Seventy Fifth Regiment of Indiana Infantry Volunteers* (Philadelphia, Lutheran Publication Society, 1893), 138.

62. OR 30, 2, 371.

63. Edwin W. High, *History of the Sixty-Eighth Regiment Indiana Volunteer Infantry, 1862-1865* (Matamora, IN, np., 1902), 65.

64. OR 30, 1, 762.

65. OR 30, 2, 453.

Map Set 6

1. OR 30, 1, 498.

2. Charles Barney Dennis Memoir, Rutherford B. Hayes Presidential Center, Fremont, OH.

3. William Carlin, "Military Memoirs," *National Tribune*, April 16, 1885.

4. William E. Patterson Memoir, Western Historical Manuscript Collection, University of Missouri, Columbia, MO. 72-3.

5. Carlin, "Military Memoirs."

6. Chandler to H. V. Boynton, March 1, 1894, 35th Illinois File, CCNMP.

7. OR 30, 1, 498.

8. *Ibid.*, 515.

9. *Ibid.*

10. Ole C. Johnson Letter, November 3rd, 1863, Barton Papers, Wisconsin Historical Society.

11. William Henry Harder Reminiscences, TSLA.

12. "Dear Miss Florence," September 28, 1863, Clarence C. Malone Letter, Martha Harper Clayton Papers, Duke University, Chapel Hill, NC. While Malone's loss estimate was probably high for that first encounter, the regiment did lose 60% of its strength at Chickamauga.

13. Goodrich, "Gregg's Brigade in the Battle of Chickamauga," 264.

14. OR 30, 1, 533.

15. James E. Love Reminiscences, Missouri Historical Society, St. Louis, MO.

16. OR 30, 1, 533.

17. OR 30, 2, 453.

18. Herman, Ulmer, Jr. Ed. *The Correspondence of Will & JU Stockton, 1845-1869* (Auburn University, 1984), 225.

19. *OR* 30, 1, 521.

20. *Ibid.*, 447.

21. *Ibid.*, 839.

22. *Ibid.*, 519.

23. Gerald J. Miller, *Middletown Yank's "Journey to War and Back"* (Champaign, IL, n. 1985), 24.

24. William Glenn Robertson, "The Battle of Chickamauga, Day 1, September 19, 1863," *Blue & Gray Magazine*, XXIV, no. 6 (Spring 2008), 6-52, 44.

25. *OR* 30, 2, 454.

26. *Ibid.*, 511.

27. J. Gary Laine and Morris M. Penny, *Law's Alabama Brigade in the War Between the Union and the Confederacy* (Shippensburg, PA, White Mane Publishing, 1996), 145.

28. Calvin L. Collier, *"They'll Do to Tie To!" The Story of the Third Regiment, Arkansas Infantry, C.S.A* (Little Rock, AR, Pioneer Press, 1959), 157.

29. Patterson Memoir, 76.

30. *OR* 30, 1, 631.

31. *Ibid.*

32. A. C. Avery to E. A. Carman, August 5, 1905, 39th North Carolina File, CCNMP. Note that this site is sometimes identified as the location of the Brock House, but not the same Brock House in Brock Field, where Palmer's Division fought.

33. *OR* 30, 1, 691.

34. 50th Tennessee Miscellaneous File, Tennessee State Library and Archives, Nashville, TN.

35. T. J. Wright, "Battle of Chickamauga" *Estill County Historical and Genealogical Society Newsletter*, XVI, No, 12 (April, 1997), 104.

36. *OR* 30, 1, 516.

37. *OR* 30, 2, 414.

38. *OR* 30, 1, 839.

39. *OR* 30, 2, 438

40. Wright, "Battle of Chickamauga," 104.

41. "September 27, 1863, James M. Cole to Brother Jim," James M. Cole papers, Lincoln Library, Springfield, IL.

42. *OR* 30, 2, 436.

43. "Dear Father," September 27th, 1863, C. O. Bailey Papers, K. Yongue Library, University of Florida, Gainesville, FL.

44. *OR* 30, 2, 439.

45. George Woodruff, *Fifteen Years Ago, or the Patriotism of Will County* (Joliet, IL, Republican Book and Job Steam Printing House, 1876), 284.

46. *OR* 30, 1, 447.

47. Entry for September 19, Records Diary, Indiana State Library, 119.

48. *OR* 30, 1, 447.

49. *Wilmington Daily Journal,* October 1, 1863, Wilmington, NC.

50. Records' Diary, Indiana State Library, 119.

51. Carlin, "Military Memoirs."

52. "Dear Mary," October 2, 1863, B. I. Franklin Papers, Navarro College, Corsciana, TX.

53. Records Diary, Indiana State Library, 119.

54. *OR* 30, 1, 671.

55. *Ibid.*, 677.

56. *Ibid.*, 2, 511.

57. *Ibid.*, 1, 671.

58. William R. Houghton account, 2nd Georgia Infantry File, CCNMP.

59. *OR* 30, 2, 518.

60. Records Diary, Indiana State Library, 120.

61. *Indianapolis Daily Journal*, September 28, 1863. Wilder probably got an exaggerated view of how destructive this fire was from the number of casualties that were found in the ditch during earlier fighting.

62. McCook To Sheridan, Sept 19, 4 o'clock, 1863, Sheridan Papers, Library of Congress, Washington DC.

63. Luther Bradley Memoir, Bradley Papers, AHEC, Carlisle, PA.

64. *Ibid.*

65. "Dear James," September 29, 1863, John S. Glenn Letters, Lincoln Library, Springfield, IL.

66. Carlin, "Military Memoirs," *National Tribune,* April 16, 1885.

Map Set 7

1. Albion W. Tourgee, *The Story of A Thousand* (Buffalo, NY, S. McGerald & Son, 1896), 219.

2. James A. Barnes, James A. Carnahan, and Thomas H. B. McCain, *The Eighty-Sixth Regiment Indiana Volunteer Infantry* (Crawfordville, IN, the Journal Company, Printers, 1895), 181.

3. Kenneth W. Noe, ed., *A Southern Boy in Blue: The Memoir of Marcus Woodcock 9th Kentucky Infantry (U.S.A.)* (Knoxville, University of Tennessee Press, 1996), 199.

4. *OR* 30, 2, 371.

5. Anonymous, *Ninety-Second Illinois Volunteers* (Freeport, IL, Journal Steam Publishing House and Bookbindery, 1875), 109. Technically, the 92nd belonged to Reynolds' division, but Wilder acted independently throughout the campaign.

6. Reynolds Statement, September 19, CCNMP.

7. *Ninety-Second Illinois Volunteers*, 109.

8. Reynolds Statement, CCNMP.

9. High, *History of the Sixty-Eighth Indiana Volunteer Infantry, 1862-1865*, 67.

10. Jason Hurd Diary, Entry for September 19, 1863, Combat Studies Institute, Fort. Leavenworth, KS.

11. Peter Cozzens, *This Terrible Sound* (Urbana, IL, University of Illinois Press, 1992), 244-5.

12. Hurd Diary, CSI.

13. William B. Hazen, *A Narrative of Military Service* (Boston, Ticknor & Co. 1885), 128.

14. OR 30, 1, 762.

15. *Ibid.*, 2, 384.

16. *Ibid.*, 389.

17. Robert E. Berkenes, ed. *Private William Boddy's Civil War Journal: Empty Saddles . . . Empty Sleeves . . .* (Altoona, IA, Tiffcor Publishing House, 1996), 77-8.

18. OR 30, 1, 471.

19. "My Dear General," William E. Webber to General H. V. Boynton, December 3rd, 1900, 6th Ohio File, CCNMP.

20. OR 30, 1, 762.

21. *Ibid.*, 768.

22. Robert L. Kimberly, "At Chickamauga," *Lippincott's Magazine*, XVII (June, 1876), 716.

23. Entry for September 19, James Suiter Diary, Abraham Lincoln Presidential Library, Springfield, IL.

24. OR 30, 1, 780.

25. James L. Cooper Recollections, TSLA.

26. OR 30, 1, 786.

27. Suiter Diary, Lincoln Library.

28. Joab Goodson. "The Letters of Captain Joab Goodson 1862-62." Edited by W. Stanley Hoole, *The Alabama Review*, 10, April 1957, 150.

29. As quoted in Laine and Penny, *Law's Alabama Brigade*, 146.

30. OR 30, 1, 730-1.

31. OR 30, 2, 405.

32. Laine and Penny, *Law's Alabama Brigade*, 146-151.

33. Wilbur F. Hinman, *The Story of The Sherman Brigade* (Alliance, OH, Press of the Daily Review, 1897), 422.

34. William Henry Harder Reminiscences, TSLA.

35. OR 30, 2, 474.

36. William C. Oates, *The War Between The Union and The Confederacy* (New York, The Neale Publishing Co. 1905), 254-5.

37. OR 30, 1, 801.

38. OR 30, 2, 392.

39. "October 2nd, 1863," William L. Hilligos Letter, John Q. Thomas Collection, Indiana Historical Society.

40. Entry for September 19, James G. Essington Diary, Indiana Historical Society.

41. OR 30, 1, 440.

42. Ambrose Bierce, *Ambrose Bierce's Civil War* (Avenel, NJ, Wing Books, 1996), 33. Bierce served on Gen. Hazen's staff.

43. Hazen to Benson H. Lossing, August 23rd, 1866, William Palmer Collection, Western Reserve Historical Society, Cleveland, OH.

44. Bierce, *Civil War*, 33.

45. OR 30, 1, 801.

46. Dr. J. W. McMurray, "The Gap of Death at Chickamauga," *Confederate Veteran*, II (November, 1894), 329-30.

47. OR 30, 2, 392.

48. Brown reported 480 casualties for the two days. However, he reported only 827 officers and men ready for action on 9/20, and suffered roughly 100 losses on that day; all this leaves approximately 150 men unaccounted for. See *OR 30, 2*, 373.

49. OR 30, 2, 371. Note that Brown now seemed aware of Johnson's presence, but made no mention of Clayton at this time.

50. Rob Adney, "Account of the Battle of Chickamauga," 36th Ohio Unit File, CCNMP.

51. Curt Johnson, Ed. "A Forgotten Account of Chickamauga," *Civil War Times, Illustrated*, September-October, 1993, 54.

52. OR 30, 1, 474.

53. Laine and Penny, *Law's Brigade*, 154.

54. OR 30, 1, 474.

55. *Ibid.*, 401.

56. *Ibid.*, 408.

57. *Ibid.*, 441.

58. J. T. Gibson, *History of the Seventy-Eighth Pennsylvania Volunteer Infantry* (Pittsburg, PA, Pittsburg Printing Company, 1905), 97.

59. "Dear Parents," September 24, 1863, James A. Martin Letters, Bentley Library, University of Michigan, Ann Arbor, MI.

60. William D. Ward Recollections, Depauw University, Greencastle, IN.

Map Set 8

1. OR 30, 2, 252.

2. *Ibid.*, 274.

3. C. C. Briant, *History of The Sixth Regiment Indiana Infantry* (Indianapolis, IN, Wm. E. Burford, printer and binder, 1891), 239.

4. Hughes, *Liddell's Record*, 143.

5. Two of Cleburne's old brigades were those of Liddell, now Govan's, and Johnson's, now Fulton's; excellent troops that proved hard to replace.

6. Deanne Labenski, Ed., "Jim Turner Co. G, 6th Texas Infantry, C.S.A From 1861 to 1865," *Texana*, 162.

7. OR 30, 1, 250.

8. *Ibid.*, 535.

9. *Ibid.*, 276.

10. *Ibid.*, part 2, 154.

11. *Ibid.*, 167.

12. "Dear Father," October 2, 1863, Steiner Family Papers, Auburn University.

13. "Dear Arthur," October 9th, 1863, Robert L. Bliss Letters, Alabama Department of Archives and History, Montgomery, AL.

14. C. C. Briant, *History of the Sixth Regiment Indiana Volunteer Infantry* (Indianapolis, IN, William E. Burford, Printer and Binder, 1891), 233-4.

15. OR 30, 2, 154.

16. *Ibid.*, 291.

17. W. H. Springer Recollections, Indiana State Library, Indianapolis, IN.

18. OR 30, 1, 300-1.

19. "Dearest Ma," Sept 25, 1863, John Harris Letters, TSLA.

20. John Obreiter, *The Seventy-Seventh Pennsylvania At Shiloh: History of The Regiment* (Harrisburg, PA, Harrisburg Publishing Co. 1905), 129.

21. Harris Letters, TSLA.

22. OR 30, 1, 558.

Map Set 9

1. OR 30, 2, 33.

2. Interview with James Longstreet, *Cincinnati Enquirer*, April 1, 1883.

3. Polk to Bragg, September 28, 1863, Brent Papers, Perkins Library, Duke University, Durham, NC.

4. George Ratchford, "General D. H. Hill At Chickamauga," *Confederate Veteran*, XXIV, 121.

5. Hill, "Chickamauga," *Battles and Leaders*, 3, 653; T. Coleman Statement, D. H. Hill Papers, North Carolina Department of Archives and History, Raleigh, NC; James A. Reid letter, undated, D. H. Hill Papers, North Carolina Division of Archives and History.

6. James Longstreet, *From Manassas To Appomattox* (Philadelphia, J. Lippencott, 1896), 438-9.

7. OR 30, 1, 277.

8. Allen Buckner, *The Memoirs of Allen Buckner* (Lansing, MI, The Michigan Alcohol and Drug Information Foundation, 1982), 21.

9. OR 30, 1, 535.

10. John B. Turchin, *Chickamauga* (Chicago, Fergus Printing Co. 1888), 99-100.

11. OR 30, 1, 69-70.

12. *Ibid.*, 58.

13. OR 30, 2, 203.

14. Hill to Bragg, September 30th, 1863, D. H. Hill Papers, Virginia State Library, Richmond, VA.

15. William M. Polk, "General Polk at Chickamauga," *Battles and Leaders*, III (New York, Thomas Yoseloff, Inc. 1956), 662-3.

16. William Glenn Robertson, "Chickamauga: Day 2, September 20, 1863," *Blue and Gray Magazine*, XXV, No. 2 (Summer, 2008), 7.

17. John Bell Hood, *Advance and Retreat* (Secausus, NJ, Blue and Grey Press, 1985. Reprint of 1880 edition), 63.

18. OR 30, 1, 355.

19. *Ibid.*, 348.

20. *Ibid.*, 1014.

21. Sam Davis Elliott, *Soldier of Tennessee* (Baton Rouge, LA, Louisiana State University Press, 1999), 130; OR 30, 2, 288.

22. OR 30, 2, 288.

23. As quoted in Jeffry D. Wert, *General James Longstreet* (New York, Simon and Schuster, 1993), 312.

24. Interview with Longstreet, *Cincinnati Enquirer*, April 1, 1883.

25. OR 30, 1, 368.

26. Robertson, "Chickamauga, Day 2," 9.

27. OR 30, 1, 58.

28. OR 30, 1, 1014.

29. Robertson, "Chickamauga, Day 2," 9.

30. OR 30, 1, 500.

31. "My Darling Wife," October 7, 1863, Horatio Van Cleve Papers, Minnesota Historical Society, St. Paul, MN (hereafter Minnesota HS).

32. Robertson, "Chickamauga, Day 2," 7.

33. Hill, "Chickamauga," *Battles and Leaders*, 653.

34. Longstreet, *Manassas to Appomattox*, 440.

35. OR 30, 1, 358.

36. *Ibid.*, 329-30.

37. Powell, *Numbers and Losses*, CCNMP.

38. OR 30, 1, 840.

39. *Ibid.*, 803-4.

40. "My Darling Wife," Horatio Van Cleve Papers, Minnesota HS.

41. OR 30, 1, 610.

42. *Ibid.*, 763.

Map Set 10

1. William Wirt Calkins, *The History of the One Hundred and Fourth Regiment of Illinois Volunteer Infantry, War of the Great Rebellion, 1862-1865* (Chicago: Donohue and Hennenberry, 1895), 135-6.
2. OR 30, 2, 141.
3. Francis Carlisle Reminiscences, 42nd Indiana File, CCNMP.
4. Entry for September 20th, Douglas Hapeman Diary, Abraham Lincoln Library, Springfield, IL.
5. Fred Joyce, "Kentucky's Orphan Brigade At The Battle Of Chickamauga." *The Kentucky Explorer* (April 1994. Reprint of 1885 Reminiscences), 29.
6. OR 30, 1, 372.
7. *Ibid.* 375.
8. OR 30, 2, 199.
9. "Death of Gen. Ben Hardin Helm," William C. Leven Papers, Perkins Library, DU.
10. Robertson, "Chickamauga, Day 2," 19.
11. Kirk C. Jenkins, *The Battle Rages Higher: The Union's Fifteenth Kentucky Infantry* (Lexington, KY: University Press of Kentucky, 2003), 179.
12. OR 30, 1, 714.
13. "Statement of September 20th," Reynolds File, CCNMP.
14. OR 30, 1, 1021, 1026.
15. Ebeneezer Hannaford, *The Story of a Regiment* (Cincinnati, OH, n., 1968), 466.
16. *Ibid.*, 467.
17. Louis A. Simmons, *The History of the 84th Regt IL Vols.* (Macomb, IL, Hampton Brothers, Publishers, 1866), 97.
18. Entry for September 20, James Suiter Diary, Lincoln Library, Springfield, IL.
19. OR 30, 1, 787.
20. Buckner, *The Memoirs of Allen Buckner*, p. 21.
21. Robertson, "Chickamauga, Day 2," 20.
22. Entry for September 20th, E. John Ellis Diary, Louisiana State University, Baton Rouge, LA. Ellis attributed this error to the wounding of General Adams, and the resultant confusion of the change of command, but it is more likely that Adams fell later in the charge, leaving the order to halt unexplained.
23. "Dear Parents," September 24, 1863, James Martin Letters, Bentley Historical Library, University of Michigan, Ann Arbor, MI.
24. *Ibid.*
25. "Friend Dan," September 21, 1863, John McGrath Letters, Louisiana State University, Baton Rouge, LA.

26. OR 30, 1, 540.
27. *Ibid.*, 565.
28. Johnson, *That Body of Brave Men*, 403.
29. OR 30, 1, 429.
30. *Ibid.*, 379.
31. Entry for September 20, James Fenton Diary, Lincoln Library, Springfield, IL.
32. Beatty, *The Citizen-Soldier*, 337.
33. OR 30, 2, 216-17.
34. Fenton Diary, Lincoln Library.
35. Joseph A. Chalaron, "Memories of Major Rice E. Graves," *The Daviess County Historical Quarterly*, III, No. 1 (January, 1985), 13.
36. OR 30, 1, 430.
37. Judson Bishop, *Van Derveer's Brigade at Chickamauga* (St. Paul, MN., np. 1903), 13.
38. OR 30, 1, 828.
39. Chalaron, "Major Rice E. Graves," 13.
40. Craig L. Symonds, *Stonewall of the West: Patrick Cleburne and the Civil War* (Lawrence, KS, University of Kansas Press, 1997), 149.
41. OR 30, 2, 161.
42. Letter of May 2nd, 1910, Leonidas Polk Papers, University of North Carolina, Chapel Hill, NC.
43. OR 30, 2, 155.
44. W. E. Preston Memoir, 33, Alabama Department of Archives and History (ADAH) Montgomery, AL.
45. Symonds, *Stonewall of the West*, 149.
46. OR 30, 2, 155.
47. OR 30, 2, 363-4.
48. O. S. Palmer report, S.A.M. Wood papers, ADAH.
49. *Ibid.*
50. "Dear Father," October 2, 1863, Steiner Family Papers, Auburn University, Auburn, AL.
51. "Dearest Mother," September 27, 1863, Robert Lewis Bliss Papers, ADAH.
52. OR 30, 2, 372.
53. *Ibid.*
54. N. J. Hampton, *An Eyewitness to the Dark Days of 1861-65* (Nashville, TN, printed by the author, 1898), 32.
55. OR 30, 2, 385.
56. *Ibid.*
57. W. J. McMurray, *History of the Twentieth Tennessee Regiment Volunteer Infantry, C.S.A.* (Nashville, TN, publication committee of the Regiment, 1904), 291.
58. S. A. McNeil, "The 31st Ohio at Chickamauga," *National Tribune*, February 9, 1888.
59. OR 30, 2, 155.
60. Jim Turner, with Deanne Labenski, eds. "Jim Turner Co. G, 6th Texas Infantry, C.S.A From 1861 to 1865," *Texana*, 164.

61. R. M. Collins, *Chapters from the Unwritten History of the War Between the States* (Dayton, OH, Morningside House, 1988. Reprint of 1892 edition), 157-8.

62. *OR* 30, 1, 763.

63. *OR* 30, 2, 188.

64. *Ibid.*, 189.

65. St. John R. Liddell, *Liddell's Record* (Baton Rouge, LA, Louisiana State University Press, 1985), 145.

66. Extracts of William Watts Carnes Memoirs, 145, Combat Studies Institute, Fort Leavenworth, KS.

67. *OR* 30, 2, 274.

68. John Henry Steinmeyer Diary (Memoirs), 18. The South Caroliniana Library, University of South Carolina, Columbia, SC.

69. *Ibid.*

70. Liddell, *Liddell's Record*, 145.

71. Govan's Brigade Tablet, LaFayette Road, CCNMP.

72. *OR* 30, 2, 264-5.

73. *OR* 30, 2, 269.

Map Set 11

1. Statement of September 20th, Reynolds Papers, CCNMP.

2. *OR* 30, 1, 635.

3. Robertson, "Chickamauga, September 20th," 27-8. Traditionally, Wood has been cast as the villain in this incident, spitefully repaying Rosecrans for supposed slights earlier in the campaign. Dr. Robertson makes a convincing case that McCook not only insisted that Wood go immediately but also promised to fill the resultant gap.

4. George R. Woodruff, *Fifteen Years Ago: Or the Patriotism of Will County* (Joliet, IL, Joliet Republican Book and Job Steam Printing House, 1876), 285.

5. J. C. Lang letter, *Joliet Signal*, Joliet IL, October 27, 1863.

6. Woodruff, *Fifteen Years Ago,* 285-6.

7. Longstreet, *Manassas to Appomattox*, 447.

8. R. L. Dinardo and Albert A. Nofi, Eds. *James Longstreet: The Man, The Soldier, The Controversy* (Conshoshocken PA, Combined Publishing, 1998), 118.

9. Frank T. Ryan Reminiscences, Georgia Department of Archives and History (hereafter, GDAH.)

10. *OR* 30, 2, 490.

11. *OR* 30, 1, 656.

12. *OR* 30, 1, 673.

13. Captain Walden Kelly, *A Historic Sketch, Lest We Forget—Company "E," 26th Ohio Infantry in the War for the Union, 1861-65* (n.p., n.d), 15.

14. Letter to "Brother Rice, September 30, 1863" W. G. Eaton Papers, Western Michigan University, Kalamazoo, MI. (hereafter WMU.)

15. *OR* 30, 2, 334.

16. *Ibid.*, 482.

17. *Ibid.*, 336.

18. Sandra L. Myres, *Force Without Fanfare: The Autobiography of K. M. Van Zandt* (Fort Worth, TX, Texas Christian University Press, 1968), 102.

19. Martha B. Caldwell, Ed., "Some Notes On the Eighth Kansas Infantry and the Battle of Chickamauga: Letters of Colonel John A. Martin," *Kansas Historical Quarterly*, XIII, No. 2, May, 1944, 143.

20. Jim R. Martin Letter, 22nd Alabama Regiment. www.geocities.com/~bobjones/22nd–docs.htm. Yellowhammer was a nickname given to some Alabama soldiers.

21. Samuel Broughton Memoir and Journal, www.rootsweb.com/~ilcivilw/scrapbk/broughtjourn.html.

22. George W. Morris, *History of the Eighty-First Regiment of Indiana Volunteer Infantry in the Great War of the Rebellion 1861 to 1865* (Louisville, KY, Franklin Printing Co. 1901), 59.

23. William Carlin, "Military Memoirs," *National Tribune*, April 16, 1885.

24. *OR* 30, 2, 495.

25. "Letter from Captain Stinchcomb," *Lancaster Gazette*, October 8, 1863.

26. *OR* 30, 1, 414.

27. George A. Smyth, III, ed., *Leander Whitcomb Munhall's Letters Home, 1862-1865* (n.p., 1992), 45.

28. Alf G. Hunter, *History of the Eighty-Second Indiana Volunteer Infantry* (Indianapolis, Wm. B. Burford, Printer and Binder, 1893), 66.

29. "Dear Wife," Letter of September 27th, 1863, *Paulding Independent*, October 22, 1863.

30. "Beloved Wife and Family," Letter of September 27, 1863, B. B. Jackson Letters, Bowling Green State University, Bowling Green, OH.

31. *OR* 30, 2, 458.

32. *OR* 30, 1, 694.

33. Laine and Penny, *Law's Alabama Brigade*, 164.

34. *OR* 30, 2, 518.

35. I. B. Webster, "Chickamauga," *National Tribune*, July 2, 1891.

36. Powell, *Numbers and Losses*, CCNMP.

37. "Letter of September 26, 1863," Ben F. Abbott Papers, GDAH.

38. Rev. S. Hendrick, "Chickamauga," *National Tribune*, November 5, 1891.

39. *OR* 30, 1, 423.

40. *OR* 30, 2, 511.

41. *OR* 30, 1, 423.

42. Richard Boyle, "Chickamauga," *National Tribune*, January 10, 1907; and *OR* 30, 1, 1062.

43. *OR* 30, 1, 427.

44. Rev. S. Hendrick, "Chickamauga," *National Tribune*, November 5, 1891.

45. Gen. H. V. Boynton, November 26, 1895, Orville T. Chamberlain Letters, 74th Indiana File, CCNMP.

46. James Birney Shaw, *History of the Tenth Regiment Indiana Volunteer Infantry* (Lafayette, IN, 1912), 233.

47. Moxley Sorrell, *At The Right Hand of Longstreet, Recollections of A Confederate Staff Officer* (Lincoln, NE., University of Nebraska Press, 1999. Reprint of 1905 edition), 203.

48. *OR* 30, 2, 517.

49. Entry for September 20, 1863, Samuel Thompson Diary, WHS.

50. *OR* 30, 1, 441.

51. Albion W. Tourgee, *The Story of a Thousand: Being a History of the Service of the 105th Ohio Volunteer Infantry, in the War for the Union from August 21, 1862 to June 6, 1865* (Buffalo, NY, McGerald and Son, 1896), 223.

52. *Ibid.*, 224.

53. *Ibid.*, 226.

Map Set 12

1. *OR* 30, 1, 580.

2. Cozzens, *This Terrible Sound*, 379.

3. Chauncey H. Castle, "Comrade Castle's Address," *Minutes of Proceedings of the Fourteenth Annual Reunion, Survivors Seventy-Third Regiment Illinois Infantry Volunteers* (Gibson City, IL, Banner Print, n.d.), 13.

4. William H. Newlin, *A History of the Seventy-Third Regiment of Illinois Infantry Volunteers* (Springfield, IL, Regimental Reunion Association, 1890), 225.

5. *OR* 30, 1, 593.

6. *Ibid.*, 591.

7. *OR* 30, 2, 334.

8. Castle, "Comrade Castle's Address," 14.

9. *OR* 30, 1, 600.

10. Entry for September 20, Robert Sparks Waller Diary, *Chattanooga Times*, April 25, 1937.

11. "Dear Father," September 21, 1863, Howe- Bernard Family Papers, Newberry Library, Chicago.

12. *OR* 30, 1, 583.

13. "From the 36th," *Elgin Gazette*, October 14, 1863.

14. *OR* 30, 2, 336.

15. *OR* 30, 2, 334.

16. Excerpts of Letters from 2d. Lt. Henry M. Weiss to his wife in Shipman, IL, Combat Studies Institute, Fort Leavenworth, KS.

17. *OR* 30, 1, 595.

18. *OR* 30, 2, 318.

19. *OR* 30, 1, 600.

20. L.G. Bennett and William M. Haigh, *History of the Thirty-Sixth Regiment Illinois Volunteers During the War of the Rebellion* (Aurora, IL, Knickerbocker and Hodder), 1876, 468.

21. W. W. Gifford Letter, 36th Illinois File, CCNMP.

22. Bennett and Haigh, *Thirty-Sixth Illinois*, 469.

23. *OR* 30, 1, 383.

24. William J. K. Beaudot, *The 24th Wisconsin Infantry in the Civil War* (Mechanicsburg, PA, Stackpole Books, 2003), 239.

25. John Otto, *History of the 11th Indiana Battery During the War of the Rebellion, 1861 to 1865*, John Otto Papers, Smith Memorial Library, Indiana Historical Society, Indianapolis.

26. *OR* 30, 1, 595.

27. *OR* 30, 1, 597-8.

28. *OR* 30, 2, 330.

29. William H. Moore, "Writing Home To Talladega," *Civil War Times, Ill.*, XXIX, No. 5 (November/December, 1990), 71.

30. Powell, *Numbers and Losses*, CCNMP.

31. Anonymous, "The Death of General Lytle," *Confederate Veteran*, XXVI (June, 1918) 249.

32. William C. Oates, *The War Between the Union and the Confederacy* (New York, Neale Publishing Co. 1905), 258.

33. William C. Jordan, *Some Events and Incidents During the Civil War* (Montgomery AL, Paragon Press, 1909), 52.

34. Bennett and Haigh, *Thirty-Sixth Illinois*, 472.

35. *OR* 30, 1, 580.

36. Arthur M. Manigault, with R. Lockwood Tower, ed., *A Carolinian Goes to War* (Columbia, SC, University of South Carolina, 1983), 98.

37. *OR* 30, 1, 448.

38. Benjamin F. Sawyer, "Chickamauga," *Battles and Leaders*, 5 (Urbana IL, University of Illinois Press, 2002), 427.

39. Judith Lee Hallock, ed., *The Civil War Letters of Joshua K Callaway* (Athens, GA, University of Georgia Press, 1997), 136.

40. *OR* 30, 1, 548.

41. Revised Wilder Report, November 26, 1888, CCNMP.

42. Baumgartner, *Blue Lightning*, 180.

43. *Ibid.*, 181.

44. OR 30, 1, 449.

45. Baumgartner, *Blue Lightning*, 182-3.

46. Charles A. Dana, *Recollections of the Civil War* (New York, Collier Books, 1963 reprint of 1913 edition), 116.

47. OR 30, 1, 598.

48. OR 30, 1, 449.

Map Set 13

1. OR 30, 2, 457-8.

2. *Ibid.*, 490.

3. OR 30, 1, 610.

4. Anonymous, *History of the Services of the Third Battery, Wisconsin Light Artillery in the Civil War of the United States, 1861-65* (Berlin, WI, Courant Press, n.d.), 29.

5. "My Dear Sister," September 22nd, 1863, John J. McCook Letters, Gilder-Lehrman Collection.

6. OR 30, 1, 678.

7. *Ibid.*, 800, 851.

8. Anonymous, *History of the Services of the Third Battery*, 29.

9. Elijah Wiseman, "Tennesseans At Chickamauga," *Confederate Veteran* (July, 1894) 205.

10. OR 30, 2, 495.

11. Anonymous, *History of the Services of the Third Battery*, 29.

12. OR 30, 2, 500.

13. William F. Perry and Curt Johnson, ed. "A Forgotten Account of Chickamauga," *Civil War Times, Illus.* (September/October, 1983), 56.

14. OR 30, 1, 361.

15. John T. Goodrich, "Gregg's Brigade in the Battle of Chickamauga," *Confederate Veteran*, 22 (June, 1914), 264.

16. OR 30, 1, 667.

17. I. Hubbard, "The Capture of the 8th Ind. Battery," *National Tribune*, June 6, 1907.

18. Anonymous, *History of the Services of the Third Battery*, 29.

19. Traditionally, the loss generally attributed is fifteen cannon, not fourteen. A close reading of the reports, however, shows that Mendenhall mistakenly overlooks the fact that one of the 8th Indiana's guns escaped.

20. OR 30, 2, 500.

21. Perry, "A Forgotten Account of Chickamauga," 56.

22. OR 30, 2, 511.

23. Entry for September 20, 1863, Eben Sturges Diary, U.S. Army Heritage and Education Center, Carlisle, PA. (hereafter AHEC).

24. John R. Hight and Gilbert R.Stormont, *History of the Fifty-Eighth Regiment of Indiana Volunteer Infantry, Its Organization, Campaigns, and Battles from 1861 to 1865* (Princeton, IN, 1895), 193.

25. Position Marker for Church's battery, CCNMP.

26. OR 30, 2, 513.

27. Mary Lasswell, ed. *Rags and Hope: the Recollections of Val. C. Giles, Four Years with Hood's Texas Brigade, Fourth Texas Infantry, 1861-65* (New York, Coward-McCann Inc. 1961), 203.

28. OR 30, 2, 517.

29. Entry for September 20th, Sturges Diary, MHI.

30. OR 30, 2, 511-12.

31. *Ibid.*, 515.

32. Harold B. Simpson, *Hood's Texas Brigade: Lee's Grenadier Guard* (Fort Worth, TX, Landmark Publishing, 1999, reprint of 1970 edition), 324.

33. Kate Daffan, *My Father as I Remember Him* (Houston, Press of Gray and Dillaye, 1907), 41.

34. OR 30, 2, 513.

35. Silas S. Canfield, *History of the 21st Regiment Ohio Volunteer Infantry, in the War of the Rebellion* (Toledo, OH, Vrooman, Anderson and Bateman. 1893), 136.

36. OR 30, 2, 512.

37. OR 30, 1, 708.

38. Glenn V. Longacre and John V. Haas, eds. *The Battle for God and the Right: The Civil War Letterbooks of Emerson Opdyke* (Urbana, IL, University of Illinois Press, 2003), 100.

39. OR 30, 1, 636.

40. Charles T. Clark, *Opdyke Tigers: 125th O.V.I. A History of the Regiment and of the Campaigns and Battles of the Army of the Cumberland* (Columbus, OH, Spahr and Glenn, 1895), 107.

41. Lasswell, *Rags and Hope*, 203.

42. Richard A. Baumgartner and Larry M. Strayer, *Ralsa C. Rice, Yankee Tigers: Through the Civil War With The 125th Ohio* (Huntington, WV, Blue Acorn Press, 1992), 65.

43. Entry for September 20th, E. G. Whitesides Diary, USAMHI, Carlisle, PA.

44. John Bell Hood, *Advance and Retreat* (Secaucus, NJ, Blue and Gray Press, 1985. Reprint of 1880 edition), 63-65.

45. OR 30, 1, 369.

46. *Ibid.*, 330.

47. *Ibid.*, 343.

48. *Ibid.*, 331, 1022, 1028.

49. *Ibid.*, 402-3, 1041.

50. *Ibid.*, 1045.

51. *OR* 30, 2, 461, 503.

52. *Ibid.*, 503.

53. Entry for September 20th, Reynolds Diary, UARK.

54. Hight, *Fifty Eighth Regiment*, 192; Noe, *A Southern Boy in Blue*, 210.

55. *OR* 30, 1, 252.

56. Clark, *Opdyke Tigers*, 107.

57. September 20, Sturges Diary, AHEC.

58. Canfield, *History of the 21st Regiment*, 116.

59. *OR* 30, 1, 637.

60. "Dear Maria," October 5, 1863, Franklin Gaillard Papers, Southern Historical Collection, University of North Carolina, Chapel Hill, NC. (hereafter UNC).

61. *OR* 30, 2, 504.

62. Hight, *Fifty-Eighth Indiana*, 193.

63. "Dear Maria," Franklin Gaillard Papers, UNC.

64. Woodruff, *Fifteen Years Ago*, 291.

65. *OR* 30, 1, 704.

66. *Ibid.*, 700.

67. "Dear Sir," Anonymous Letter to H.V. Boynton, October 9, 1893, 3rd Kentucky File, CCNMP.

68. Charles G. Brown, ed. *The Sherman Brigade Marches South: The Civil War Memoirs of Colonel Robert Carson Brown* (Washington DC, n.p., 1995), 49.

69. Longacre and Haas, *Battle For God*, 100-102.

70. "Dear Sir," February 12, 1909, Charles T. Clark to Ezra E. Carmen, 125th Ohio Website, http://home.earthlink.net/~nhaldane/ctc-letter.html.

Map Set 14

1. *OR* 30, 2, 504.

2. "Dear Maria," Oct. 5, 1863. Franklin Gaillard Papers, SHC.

3. Canfield, *History of the Twenty-first Regiment*, 142.

4. Captain William J. Vance, "On Thomas' Right at Chickamauga," *Blue and Gray*, 1, No. 3, February 1893, 90.

5. D. Augustus Dickert, *History of Kershaw's Brigade* (Newberry, NC, Elbert H. Aull Company, 1899), 279.

6. *OR* 30, 1, 402.

7. *OR* 30, 2, 507-8.

8. Entry for September 20, Allspaugh Diary, University of Iowa.

9. Benjamin Humphreys, "History of the Sunflower Guards," John F. H. Claiborne Papers, UNC.

10. *OR* 30, 1, 380.

11. Archibald Gracie, *The Truth About Chickamauga* (Dayton, OH, Morningside Press, 1987, reprint of 1911 edition), 245.

12. *OR* 30, 2, 509.

13. *OR* 30, 2, 482-3.

14. Elijah Wiseman, "Tennesseans at Chickamauga," *Confederate Veteran* (July 1894), 205.

15. *OR* 30, 1, 69.

16. J. S. Fullerton, "Reinforcing Thomas at Chickamauga," *Battles and Leaders* (New York, Thomas Yoseloff, 1956), 3, 666.

17. Charles A. Partridge, "The Ninety-Sixth Illinois at Chickamauga," *Transactions of the Illinois State Historical Society*, Volume XI (1910), 75.

18. Cozzens, *This Terrible Sound*, 442; Fullerton, "Reinforcing Thomas," 666.

19. John Watson Morton, *The Artillery of Nathan Bedford Forrest's Cavalry* (Marietta, GA, R. Bemis Publishing, 1995. Reprint of 1909 ed.), 121.

20. Entry for September 20, 1863, Diary of Edward Scofield Scott, as quoted in Bryan Weaver and H. Lee Fenner, *Sacrifice at Chickamauga* (Palos Verdes Peninsula, CA., Moyweave Books, 2003), 103.

21. Entry for September 20, William A. Boyd Journal, University of California at Berkeley.

22. William Shanks, *Personal Recollections of Distinguished Generals* (New York, Harper, 1866), 69.

23. Judson W. Bishop, *The Story of a Regiment*, 108.

24. Oates, *War Between the Union and the Confederacy*, 259.

25. Oates, *War Between the Union and the Confederacy*, 259; and Wyckoff, *Third South Carolina*, 41.

26. Oates, *War Between the Union and the Confederacy*, 259.

27. *OR* 30, 2, 504.

28. "Before Chattanooga," September 27, 1863, Dubose Eggleston Papers, Southern Historical Collection, UNC Chapel Hill.

29. William D. Trantham, "Wonderful Story of Richard R. Kirkland," *Confederate Veteran*, 16, no. 3 (March, 1908), 105.

30. *OR* 30, 2, 508.

31. Oates, *War Between the Union and the Confederacy*, 262.

32. *Ibid.*

33. *OR* 30, 2, 508.

34. *Ibid.*, 304.

35. *Ibid.*, 461.

36. *Ibid.*, 328.

37. Canfield, *History of the Twenty-First Regiment*, 118.

38. H. H. Alban Letter, June 12, 1889, Sullivan Collection, BGSU.

39. *OR* 30, 2, 483.

40. *Ibid.*, 462.

41. *Ibid.*, 324.

42. *Ibid.*, 322.

43. Francis E. McKinney, *Education In Violence: The Life of George H. Thomas and the History of the Army of the Cumberland* (Chicago, Americana House, 1991. Reprint of 1961 edition), 249.

44. Fullerton, "Reinforcing Thomas," *Battles and Leaders*, III, 667.

45. Entry for September 20, 1863, William A. Boyd Journal, UC Berkeley.

46. John C. Smith, *Oration at the Unveiling of the Monument Erected to the Memory of Maj. Gen. James B. Steedman* (Chicago, Knight & Leonard Co. 1887), 29.

47. Isaac Henry Clay Royce, *History of the 115th Regiment Illinois Volunteer Infantry* (Terre Haute, IN, n.p., 1900), 128.

48. *OR* 30, 1, 867.

49. Royce, *History of the 115th Illinois*, 128.

50. "Dear sister Betsy," October 5, 1863. George Pepoon Letters, Northern Illinois University, Dekalb, IL.

51. Marvin Boget Letter, 22nd Michigan File, CCNMP.

52. William Henry Harder Reminiscences, TSLA.

53. *OR* 30, 2, 496.

54. Partridge, *History of the Ninety-Sixth Regiment*, 233.

55. *Ibid.*, 234.

56. "Dear Colonel," August 8, 1889, Carlton to Colonel Arnold McMahon, Sullivan Papers, BGSU.

57. Isaac Doan, *Reminiscences of the Chattanooga Campaign* (Richmond, IN, J. M. Coe, 1894).

58. George Dolton, *Capsule History of Battery M, 1st Illinois Light Artillery*, CCNMP.

59. Gracie, *The Truth About Chickamauga*, 433. n. 1. The 22nd and 89th were not normally of Whitaker's brigade. Instead they had been detached from their normal commands to perform guard duties, and then recently attached to the Reserve Corps when battle drew near. Le Favour acted as a demi-brigade commander for these two regiments, reporting to Whitaker—a command situation that would cause confusion later.

60. *OR* 30, 2, 324.

61. John Robertson, *Michigan in the War* (Lansing, MI, W. S. George & Co, State Printers, 1882), 424.

62. Report of M. B. Walker, Thomas Papers, RG 94, NARA.

63. Entry for September 20th, Reginald Screvin Diary, South Carolina Historical Society, Charleston, SC.

64. "Before Chattanooga," Sept 27, 1863, Dubose Eggleston Papers, UNC.

65. Beatty, *Citizen-Soldier*, 340.

66. J. S. Gilbert, "Ensign Clark's Courage," 7th South Carolina Unit file, CCNMP.

67. *Mobile Daily Register*, October 4, 1863.

68. Tower, *A Carolinian Goes to War*, 99.

69. "Entry for September 20, 1863," Reynolds Diary, University of Arkansas.

70. *OR* 30, 2, 462.

71. "Dear Pa," September 26, 1863, *Montgomery Daily Advertiser*, October 8, 1905, 17.

72. Theodore A. Dolton, ed. *The Path of Patriotism: Civil War Letters of George Edwin Dolton* (Booksurge, Palo Alto, CA., 2005), 78.

73. John C. Smith, *The Right of the Federal Army at Chickamauga* (Chicago, Knight, Leonard & Co, 1894), 12.

74. Letter of March 17, 1896, J. S. Gill to Chickamauga National Park Commission, 121st Ohio File, CCNMP.

75. *OR* 30, 2, 353.

76. Hallock, *The Civil War Letters of Joshua K. Calloway*, 137.

77. *Stuebenville Weekly Herald*, October 21, 1863.

78. *OR* 30, 2, 483.

79. Longstreet, *Manassas to Appomattox*, 451-2.

80. D. H. Hill, "Chickamauga—The Great Battle of the West," 3, 659.

81. *OR* 30, 2, 415.

82. See Cozzens, *This Terrible Sound*, 405, for a detailed discussion of the controversy.

83. *OR* 30, 1, 715. Palmer remembered that he ordered Hazen to go; Hazen recalled that he asked for and got permission to make the move. See Palmer, *Personal Recollections*, 183, and Hazen to Benson H. Lossing, August 23, 1866, William Palmer Collection, Western Reserve Historical Society, Cleveland, OH.

84. Georgia Lee Tatum, *Disloyalty in the Confederacy* (Lincoln, NE., University of Nebraska Press, 2000. Reprint of 1934 edition), 64-5.

85. Jeffrey Weaver, *63rd Virginia Infantry* (Lynchburg, VA, H. E. Howard, 1991), 34.

86. *OR* 30, 2, 415.

87. *Ibid.*, 505.

88. *Ibid.*, 427.

89. "Gracie's Brigade," *Mobile Advertiser and Register*, October 14, 1863.

90. Charles T. Clark to E. A. Carmen, February 12, 1909, Ezra Carmen Papers, New York Public Library.

91. OR 30, 2, 425.

92. J. Henry Haynie, *The Nineteenth Illinois* (Chicago, IL, Donahue, 1912), 225.

93. OR 30, 2, 427.

94. John B. Palmer, "The 58th North Carolina at the Battle of Chickamauga," *Our Living and Our Dead*, vol. 3 (1875), 454-5.

95. OR 30, 2, 445.

96. *Ibid.*

97. Bishop, *Van Derveer's Brigade at Chickamauga*, 17.

98. S. S. Canfield to Col. A. McMahan, June 7, 1889, Sullivan Collection, BGSU.

99. J. T. Gaines, "Recollections of Chickamauga," Confederate Veteran Papers, Duke.

100. OR 30, 2, 422.

101. "Gracie's Brigade," *Mobile Daily Register*, October 14, 1863.

102. OR 30, 2, 422.

103. "Dear Parents," September 24 1863, James Martin Letters, Bentley Historical Library, University of Michigan.

104. 2nd Alabama Battalion file, ADAH.

105. Anonymous, "The First Battalion Hilliard's Legion at Chickamauga," *Montgomery Advertiser*, May 5, 1907.

106. OR 30, 2, 434.

107. *Ibid.*, 470.

108. *Ibid.*, 464.

109. *Ibid.*, 350-3.

110. John W. Lavender, *They Never Came Back: The Story of Co. F. Fourth Arks. Infantry C.S.A (Originally Known as the Montgomery Hunters) as Told by Their Commanding Officer* (Pine Bluff, AR., The Perdue Co., 1956), 84.

111. OR 30, 2, 486.

112. OR 30, 1, 869.

113. J. L. Irwin, "Steedman at Snodgrass Hill," *National Tribune*, December 30, 1915.

114. Partridge, *History of the Ninety Sixth Regiment*, 240.

115. Royce, *History of the 115th Regiment*, 133-4.

116. OR 30, 2, 423.

117. "My Dear Wife and Children," Sept. 30, 1863, John F. Davenport letters, ADAH.

118. High, *History of the Sixty-Eighth Regiment Indiana Volunteer Infantry*, 97.

119. Hazen, *A Narrative*, 132.

120. John C. Smith, *The Right of the Federal Army at Chickamauga* (Chicago, Knight, Leonard & Co. 1894), 13.

121. Major McMahan's Response, Sullivan Collection, BGSU.

122. OR 30, 2, 446.

123. Hiram Hawkins Papers, Kentucky Historical Society, Frankfort, KY.

124. OR 30, 2, 444.

125. Carlton Papers, Library of Congress.

126. OR 30, 2, 441.

127. Gracie, *The Truth About Chickamauga*, 175. The resentment between Boynton and Suman lingered long after the battle ended. In the 1890s, the men of the 9th Indiana wanted to place their regimental monument on Hill Two, regarding this perilous evening advance as their most distinguished moment. Henry Boynton, however, by then the new park's chief historian, regarded Hill Two as the exclusive domain of the 35th Ohio. Boynton won again. The 35th's monument crowns Hill Two, and that of the 9th resides in Brotherton Field, marking its engagement there on September 19.

128. Carlton Papers, Library of Congress.

129. OR 30, 2, 432.

130. Entry for September 20, 1863, Robert Watson Diary, Florida State Archives.

131. Canfield, *History of the Twenty-First Regiment*, 144.

132. Carlton Papers, Library of Congress.

133. Turchin, *Chickamauga*, 207.

134. H. H. Van Camp, "Chickamauga: The Stubborn Fight made by the 21st Ohio," *National Tribune*, September 4, 1884.

135. Boget Letter, 22nd Michigan File, CCNMP.

136. OR 30, 1, 769.

137. *Ibid.*

138. Gracie, *The Truth About Chickamauga*, 447; OR 30, 1, 436.

Map Set 15

1. OR 30, 1, 732.

2. King's Brigade Tablet, Woods south of Kelly Field, Chickamauga Battlefield.

3. Willich Brigade Tablet, Southeast Corner of Kelly Field, Chickamauga Battlefield.

4. John M. Palmer, *Personal Recollections of John M. Palmer* (Cincinnati, OH, The Robert Clarke Company, 1901), 188.

5. Hiram F. Devol, *Biographical Sketch* (Kansas City, MO., Hudson-Kimberly Publishing Co, 1903), 38.

6. Palmer, *Personal Recollections*, 188.

7. Bragg takes credit for ordering this attack at 2:00 p.m., but that report puts him at odds with his statement to Longstreet at 3:00 p.m. that the right was fought out. Also, if Bragg did indeed give such an order at 2:00 p.m., it remains a mystery that only a single brigade of Polk's Wing instigated the fight, and three hours late to boot. It seems more likely that Bragg took credit for a developing situation not of his own making.

8. OR 30, 2, 364.

9. William F. Scott, *Philander Lane: Colonel of Volunteers in the Civil War, Eleventh Ohio Infantry* (privately printed, 1920), 254.

10. OR 30, 1, 733.

11. OR 30, 2, 402.

12. *Ibid.*, 85.

13. *Ibid.*, 80.

14. John B. Turchin, *Chickamauga* (Chicago, IL, Fergus Printing Co. 1888), 148.

15. Scott, *Philander Lane*, 254.

16. Rob Abney, *Account of the Battle of Chickamauga*, 36th Ohio File, CCNMP.

17. Hughes, ed., *Liddell's Record*, 145-6.

18. OR 30, 2, 275.

19. *Ibid.*, 271.

20. Rob Abney, *Account of the Battle of Chickamauga*, 36th Ohio File, CCNMP.

21. OR 30, 1, 279.

22. *Ibid.*, 279.

23. *Ibid.*, 288.

24. Extracts from the August Bratnober Diary, 10th Wisconsin File, CCNMP.

25. James Mitchell Reminiscences, Ohio Historical Society, Columbus, OH.

26. OR 30, 2, 80.

27. *Ibid.*, 241.

28. *Ibid.*, 246.

29. Thomas J. Wright, *History of the Eighth Regiment Kentucky Volunteer Infantry* (St. Joseph, MO., St. Joseph Steam Printing Company, 1880), 194.

30. "Dear Uncle," October 1, 1863, Thomas J. Kessler Papers, Navarro College, Corsiciana, TX.

31. OR 30, 1, 559.

32. Joseph B. Dodge, "The Story of Chickamauga," *Northern Indianian*, February 11, 1875.

33. Johnson, *That Body of Brave Men*, 416.

34. Anonymous, "Told by a Johnny Reb," *Portland Oregon Morning Organizer*, February 1, 1890.

35. OR 30, 2, 200.

Map Set 16

1. Cozzens, *This Terrible Sound,* 403-5.

2. William Glenn Robertson, "The Battle of Chickamauga, Day 2," 43.

3. OR 30, 1, 984.

4. OR 30, 1, 1036.

5. Beatty, *The Citizen-Soldier*, 345.

6. John T. Wilder, "Revised Report for the Battle of Chickamauga," Wilder File, CCNMP.

7. Robert H. G. Minty, "Chickamauga," *National Tribune*, March 3, 1892.

8. OR 30, 1, 393.

9. Longstreet to Bragg, September 21, 1863, Headquarters and Personal Papers, Folder 10, Bragg Papers, Western Reserve Historical Society.

10. OR 30, 2, 34.

11. Andrew Lytle, *Bedford Forrest and His Critter Company* (Seminole, FL., Green Key Press, 1984. Reprint of 1931 edition), 231.

12. OR 30, 4, 681.

13. Jordan and Pryor, *Forrest's Cavalry*, 351.

14. OR 30, 1, 915-16.

15. OR 30, 4, 680.

16. Francis F. McKinney, *Education in Violence* (Chicago, IL, Americana House, 1991, reprint of 1961 edition), 267.

17. John A. B. Williams, *Leaves From a Trooper's Diary* (Philadelphia, self-published, 1869), 72-3.

18. Jordan and Pryor, *Forrest's Cavalry*, 353.

19. R. H. G. Minty, "Rossville Gap," *The National Tribune*, March 8, 1894.

20. John H. Rerick, *The Forty-Fourth Indiana Volunteer Infantry: History of its Services in the War of the Rebellion and a Personal Record of its Members* (Lagrange, IN, n.p., 1880), 99.

21. OR 30, 1, 835.

22. Lindsey, *Military Annals of Tennessee*, II, 694.

23. *Rome Tri-Weekly Courier*, November 27, 1863.

24. OR 30, 4, 689.

25. Lafayette McLaws Letter, Cheves Family Papers, South Carolina Historical Society.

26. *Ibid.*

27. Jordan and Pryor, *Forrest's Cavalry*, 353-4.

28. Lafayette McLaws Letter, Cheves Family Papers, South Carolina Historical Society.

29. OR 30, 1, 552.

30. *Ibid.*, 2, 885.

Bibliography

This bibliography includes only sources directly cited in the text. Hundreds of additional sources have been consulted over the years, but space precludes their inclusion in this list. Sources cited with an asterisk (*) include transcripts prepared by William Glenn Robertson or his staff at the Command and General Staff College at Fort Leavenworth, Kansas. Every serious student of the battle of Chickamauga will benefit from the enormous work and insight Dr. Robertson has brought to this topic.

Manuscripts and Archival Sources

Alabama Department of Archives and History
  Robert Lewis Bliss Letters (S. A. M. Wood Staff)*
  John Davenport Letters (Hilliard's Legion)
  S.A.M. Wood Papers
  2nd/4th Alabama Infantry Battalion File*

Army Heritage and Education Center, Carlisle PA. (AHEC)
  Luther P. Bradley Papers
  James E. Edmonds Diary (94th Ohio Infantry)
  Eben P. Sturges Papers, (M, 1st Ohio Light Artillery)*
  Levi Wagner Recollections (1st Ohio Infantry)*
  John J. Warbinton Letters (59th Ohio Infantry)
  E. G. Whiteside Diary (125th Ohio Infantry)

Auburn University
  Steiner Family Papers (16th Alabama Infantry)

Bentley Historical Library, University of Michigan, Ann Arbor MI
  James Martin Letters (11th Michigan Infantry)

Bowling Green State University, Bowling Green Ohio (BGSU)
  Henry H. Alban Letter, (21st Ohio Infantry)
  Brigham Family Papers (69th Ohio Infantry)
  B. B. Jackson Letter (14th Ohio Infantry)
  Sullivan Collection, (21st Ohio Infantry)

Chattanooga-Hamilton County Library, Chattanooga Tennessee.
  Alfred Tyler Fielder Diary (12th Tennessee Infantry)
  Reminiscences of Chickamauga, by Capt. S.J.A. Frazier (19th Tennessee) 1909*

Chickamauga-Chattanooga National Military Park (CCNMP)
  Rob Adney, "Account of the Battle of Chickamauga," 36th Ohio File
  A. C. Avery Letters, 39th North Carolina File*
  Sergeant Marvin Boget Letter, 22nd Michigan File.
  August Bratnober Diary, 10th Wisconsin File
  Francis Carlyle Reminiscences, 42nd Indiana File*
  Orville T. Chamberlain Letters, 74th Indiana File
  William P. Chandler Letter, 35th Illinois File
  George Dolton, *Capsule History Of Battery M, 1st Illinois Light Artillery*
  W. W. Gifford Letter, 36th Illinois File
  J. S. Gilbert Letter, 7th South Carolina File*

J.S. Gill Letter, 121st Ohio File
History of the 18th Alabama Infantry, 18th Alabama Infantry File.
William R. Houghton Account, 2nd Georgia Infantry File
J. W. Minnich recollections, 6th Georgia Cavalry File
Samuel Pasco Diary, 3rd Florida File
David Powell, *Numbers and Losses at Chickamauga,* unpublished manuscript
J. J. Reynolds Statements, 19 and 20 September
James Thompson Diary, 4th Ohio Cavalry file
Unknown Letter, 3rd Kentucky US File
William G Webber letters, 6th Ohio File
John T. Wilder Supplemental Report

Combat Studies Institute, Command and General Staff College, Fort Leavenworth, (CSI)
William Watts Carnes Memoir
William Henry Harder Reminiscences (23rd Tennessee Infantry)*
Jason Hurd Diary, 19th Ohio File, Jason H. Moore Collection*
E. H. Reynolds Diary, 4th/5th Tennessee Infantry File
George H. Thomas File
Daily locations of the XIV Corps
Henry M Weiss Letter Excerpts, 27th Illinois Infantry File

Depauw University, Greencastle Indiana
William D. Ward Recollections (37th Indiana Infantry)

Emory University: Robert W. Woodruff Library Atlanta, GA
W. B. Corbitt Diary, Confederate Miscellany File (4th Tennessee Cavalry)*
Hannoll Family Collection, W. B. Hannoll letter (24th Mississippi Infantry)

Florida State Archives
Robert Watson Diary (7th Florida)

Georgia Department of Archives and History, Morrow, GA (GDAH)
Ben F. Abbott Letters, (2nd Georgia Infantry)
William Sylvester Dillon Diary (4th Tennessee Infantry)

Gilder-Lehrman Collection, New York Historical Society
John J. McCook Letter (Twenty-First Corps Staff)

Indiana State Library, Indianapolis
William H Records Diary, (72nd Indiana Mounted Infantry)
William H Springer Recollection, Springer-Brayton Papers (38th Indiana Infantry)

Illinois State Historical Library, Abraham Lincoln Presidential Library, Springfield
James M. Cole Letters (49th Ohio Infantry)
Henry G. Davidson Letters (10th Kentucky Infantry)
James Fenton Diary (19th Illinois Infantry)
John S. Glenn Papers (27th Illinois Infantry)*
Douglas Hapeman Diary (104th Illinois Infantry)
Edward Kitchell Diary (98th Illinois Infantry)*
James P. Suiter Diary (84th Illinois Infantry)
Levi A. Ross Diary (86th Illinois Infantry)

JD Williams Library, University of Mississippi, Oxford, MS
        Robert A. Jarman Manuscript, History of Company K, 27th Mississippi Infantry

Kentucky Historical Society, Frankfurt, KHS
        Hiram Hawkins Papers (5th Kentucky Infantry, CS)

Library of Congress (LOC)
        Caleb Henry Carlton Papers (89th Ohio Infantry)
        Philip H. Sheridan Papers

Louisiana State University, Hill Memorial Library, Baton Rouge
        John McGrath Papers (8th Texas Cavalry, 13th Louisiana Infantry)

Louisiana State University, Noel Memorial Library, Shreveport, LA
        John Harris Letter (19th Louisiana Infantry)

Minnesota Historical Society, St. Paul, MN (MinnHS)
        Jeremiah Chester Donahower Papers (2nd Minnesota Infantry)
        Horatio Van Cleve Papers

Missouri Historical Society, St. Louis Missouri.
        James Love Autobiography and Letters (8th Kansas Infantry)

National Archives (NARA)
        RG 94, General Thomas Papers, William E. Crane Diary, 4th Ohio Cavalry
        RG 94 Moses B. Walker Report
        RG 393, Summaries of News Received at Rosecrans Headquarters

Navarro College, Pearce Civil War Collection, Corsciana, Texas
        Benjamin I. Franklin Letters (5th Texas Infantry)
        Henry Heymond Letter (2/18th US Infantry
        Samuel Kessler Letter, Thomas J. Kessler Papers (15th Ohio Infantry)

Newberry Library, Chicago
        Daniel Emerson Bernard Letters, Howe-Bernard Family Papers (88th Illinois)

New York Public Library (NYPL)
        Ezra Carmen Papers

North Carolina Office of Archives and History, Raleigh NC, (NCAH)
        D. H. Hill Papers*

Northern Illinois University, DeKalb, IL, Regional History Center, Founder's Library
        George Pepoon Letters (96th Illinois Infantry)

Ohio Historical Society, Columbus OH (OHS)
        James P. Mitchell Reminiscences (94th Ohio Infantry)

Perkins Library, Duke University (DU)
        George Brent Papers (Bragg Staff)*
        William C. Leman Papers (Article on death of Helm)

Malone Letter, Martha Harper Clayton Papers (10th Tennessee Infantry)
Confederate Veteran Papers
      W. F. Shropshire Reminiscences (1st Georgia Cavalry)
      J. T. Gaines Recollections (5th Kentucky Infantry)*

Rutherford B. Hayes Presidential Center, Fremont, Ohio
    Charles Barney Dennis Memoir (101st Ohio Infantry)

Simpson History Complex, Hill College, Hillsboro, Texas
    John Templeton Letters (10th Texas Dismounted Cavalry)

Smith Memorial Library, Indiana Historical Society, Indianapolis
    John M. Barnard Letters (72nd Indiana Infantry)
    James G. Essington Diary (75th Indiana Infantry)
    John Otto Papers, (11th Indiana Battery)
    John Q. Thomas Collection
      W.L. Hilligos Letter, October 2nd,1863 (75th Indiana Infantry)

South Caroliniana Library, University of South Carolina, Columbia, SC
    John Henry Steinmeyer Diary (24th South Carolina Infantry)

South Carolina Historical Society (SCHS)
    Lafayette McLaws Letter, Cheves Family Papers*
    Reginald Screvin Diary (2nd South Carolina Infantry)*

Tennessee State Library and Archives, Nashville (TSLA)
    Carroll Henderson Clark Memoirs (16th Tennessee Infantry)
    Col. James L. Cooper Memoir (20th Tennessee Infantry)
    John Harris Letter (Staff of Preston Smith)
    William E. Sloan Diary (5th Tennessee Cavalry)*
    50th Tennessee Miscellaneous File

University of Arkansas, Fayetteville, Arkansas (UArk)
    Daniel Harris Reynolds Diary, (1st Ark. Mounted Rifles)

University of California, Berkeley, Bancroft Library
    Samuel S. Boyd Letters, Boyd Family Papers (84th Indiana Infantry)

University of Florida, Gainesville FL, Yongue Library
    C. O. Bailey Letters (7th Florida)

University of Iowa
    Harrison Allspaugh Diaries (31st Ohio Infantry)

University of Missouri—Rolla—Western Historical Manuscript Collection
    William Elwood. Patterson Memoir (38th Illinois Infantry)

University of North Carolina - Chapel Hill - Southern Historical Collection
    Ruffin, Roulhac & Hamilton Papers, DeBose Egleston Letter (2 South Carolina)*
    Benjamin Humphreys, "History of the Sunflower Guards," John F. H. Claiborne Papers
    Franklin Gaillard Papers (2nd South Carolina Infantry)*

Leonidas Polk Papers
Leroy Moncure Nutt Letters (Rucker's Legion)
Joseph B. Cummings Recollections (Walker's Staff)

Virginia State Library, Richmond VA (VSL)
D. H. Hill Papers*

Western Michigan University, Kalamazoo, Michigan. Regional History Collection
Lola J Warrick Collection, William G. Easton Letters (13th Michigan Infantry)

Western Reserve Historical Society, Cleveland OH (WRHS)
William Palmer Collection
Braxton Bragg Papers
William B. Hazen Papers*

Wisconsin Historical Society, Madison (WHS)
George F. Cooley Diary (24th Wisconsin Infantry)
Lucius Dwight Hinkley Papers (10th Wisconsin Infantry)
Ole C. Johnson Letter, Barton Papers (15th Wisconsin Infantry)
Samuel F. Thompson Diary (10th Indiana Infantry)

Government Publications:

U.S. War Department. *The War Of The Rebellion: A Compilation of the Official Records of the Union and Confederate Armies.* 128 Vols. Washington D.C.: U.S. Government Printing Office, 1880-1901

Newspapers

Elgin Gazette (IL)
Indianapolis Daily Journal (IN)
Joliet Signal (IL)
Lancaster Gazette (OH)
Louisville Daily Journal (KY)
Memphis Daily Appeal (TN)
Mobile Daily Register (AL)
Paulding Independent (OH)
Rochester Chronicle (IN)
Rome Tri-Weekly Courier (GA)
Stuebenville Weekly Herald (OH)
Wilmington Daily Journal (NC)

National Tribune Articles

Boyle, Robert E. "Chickamauga." January 10th, 1907. (10th Kentucky)
Carlin, William P. "Memoirs" April 2nd, April 16, and April 23, 1885.
Dickennan, Albert. "The 9th Ohio At Chickamauga." October 18th, 1906. (9th Ohio)
Hendrick, Rev. S. "Chickamauga." November 5, 1891. (C, 1st Ohio Light Artillery)
Hubbard, P. I. "The Capture Of The 8th Ind. Battery." June 6, 1907.
Irwin, J. L. "The 21st Ohio at Chickamauga." September 11th, 1884.
McNeil, S. A. "The 31st Ohio At Chickamauga." February 9, 1888.

Minty, Robert G. "Minty's Saber Brigade: The Part They Took in the Chattanooga Campaign. Part I." February 25, 1892.

———. "Minty's Saber Brigade: The Part They Took in the Chattanooga Campaign. Part II." March 3, 1892.

———. "Rossville Gap. Gen. Minty Has a Word to Say About Who Left it Last." March 8, 1894.

Rosecrans, William S. "Rosecrans' Accounts of Tullahoma and Chickamauga." March 11, March 18, March 25, 1882.

Van Camp, H. H. "Chickamauga." September 4th, 1884. (21st Ohio)

Webster, I. B. "Chickamauga." July 2nd, 1891. (10th Kentucky Infantry)

Wilson, George S. "Wilder's Brigade." October 19, 1893.

Young, Isaac K. "Chickamauga." August 9, 1888. (89th Illinois)

Other Articles

Anonymous, "The First Battalion Hilliard's Legion At Chickamauga," *Montgomery Advertiser,* May 5, 1907.

Anonymous. "Dear Pa," September 26, 1863. *Montgomery Daily Advertiser,* October 8, 1905, p. 17

Anonymous." Robert Sparks Waller Diary." *Chattanooga Times,* April 25, 1937.

Anonymous." Interview with James Longstreet." *Cincinnati Enquirer,* April 1, 1883

Anonymous, "The Death of General Lytle." *Confederate Veteran,* Vol. XXVI, (June, 1918) p. 249.

Anonymous, "Told by a Johnny Reb." *Portland Oregon Morning Organizer,* February 1, 1890.

Caldwell, Martha B. ed. "Some Notes on the Eighth Kansas Infantry and the Battle of Chickamauga; Letters of Col. John A. Martin." *Kansas Historical Quarterly.* May, 1944, pp. 139-45.

Clay, H. B. "Concerning the Battle of Chickamauga." *Confederate Veteran,* February, 1905. Vol. XIII p. 72. (Davidson's Staff)

Carnes, W. W. "An Unusual Identification." *Confederate Veteran* May, 1929. Vol. XXXVII, p. 188.

Chalaron. Joseph A. "Memories of Major Rice E. Graves, C.S.A." *Daviess County Historical Quarterly.* January, 1985, pp. 1- 13.

Castle, Chauncy H. "Comrade Castle's Address," *Minutes of Proceedings of the Fourteenth Annual Reunion, Survivors Seventy-Third Regiment Illinois Infantry Volunteers.* Gibson City, IL, Banner Print, n.d.

Corn, T.I. "Brown's Brigade at Chickamauga," *Confederate Veteran* March, 1913. Vol. XXI, pp. 124-5. (32nd Tennessee Infantry)

Dodge, J. B. "The Story of Chickamauga, as Told by an Eye-Witness, Part Two." *Northern Indianian,* February 11, 1875.

Fullerton, J. S. "Reinforcing Thomas at Chickamauga." *Battles and Leaders* (New York, Thomas Yoseloff, 1956). Vol. 3, p. 666.

Goodrich, John T. "Gregg's Brigade in the Battle of Chickamauga." *Confederate Veteran* June, 1914. Vol. XXII, pp. 263-4

Goodson, Joab. "The Letters of Captain Joab Goodson 1862-62." Edited by W. Stanley Hoole. *The Alabama Review.* Vol. 10, April 1957, pp. 149-153. (Law's Brigade)

Hill, Daniel Harvey, "Chickamauga—Great Battle of the West." *Battles and Leaders* (New York, Thomas Yoseloff, 1956), vol. 3, pp. 638-662.

Joyce, Fred. "Kentucky's Orphan Brigade at the Battle of Chickamauga." *The Kentucky Explorer,* April, 1994, pp. 27-9. (4th Kentucky Infantry)

Kimberly, Robert Lewis. "At Chickamauga." *Lippincott's Magazine.* Philadelphia, vol. XVII, June, 1876, pp. 713-722. (41st Ohio Infantry)

Labenski, Deanne, Ed. "Jim Turner Co. G, 6th Texas Infantry, C.S.A from 1861 to 1865." *Texana,* pp. 149-178.

Marriner, W. M. "Chickamauga: The Opening." *Southern Bivouac,* September, 1884.

Martin, William T. "A Defense of General Bragg's Conduct at Chickamauga." *Southern Historical Society Papers* Volume XI, Number 4, April 1883, pp. 201-6.

Massenburg, T. L. "Capt. W. W. Carnes' Battery at Chickamauga." *Confederate Veteran* November, 1898. Vol. VI, pp. 517-8.

McMurray, Dr. W. J. "The Gap of Death at Chickamauga." *Confederate Veteran* November, 1894. Vol. II, pp. 329-330. (20th Tennessee Infantry)

Minnich, J. W. "Unique Experiences in the Chickamauga Campaign." *Confederate Veteran, Vol. XXX* June, 1922, pp. 222-5 (6th Georgia Cavalry)

Minnick, J. W. (sic) "Reminiscences of J. W. Minnick, 6th Georgia Cavalry." *Northwest Georgia Historical and Genealogical Society Quarterly,* Vol. 29, #3, (Summer, 1997)

Moore, William. "Writing Home To Talladega." *Civil War Times Illustrated.* Vol. XXIX, number 5 (November/December, 1990), pp. 56, 71-4, 76-8. (25th Alabama Infantry)

Palmer, John B. "The 58th North Carolina at The Battle Of Chickamauga." *Our Living and Our Dead* Volume Three (1875), pp. 454-5.

Partridge, Charles A. "The Ninety-Sixth Illinois At Chickamauga." *Transactions of the Illinois State Historical Society for the Year 1910.* Springfield, IL, Illinois State Journal Publishing Company, 1912.

Perry, William F. Curt Johnson, ed. "A Forgotten Account of Chickamauga." *Civil War Times Illustrated,* Vol. XVII, No. 4 (September/October, 1983), pp. 53-6.

Polk, William M. "General Polk at Chickamauga." *Battles and Leaders, Vol. III.* New York, Thomas Yoseloff, Inc. 1956, pp. 662-3.

Ratchford, George, "General D. H. Hill At Chickamauga." *Confederate Veteran Vol. XXIV,* pp. 120-121

Robertson, William Glenn. "The Chickamauga Campaign: McLemore's Cove." *Blue & Gray Magazine,* Vol. XXIII, Issue 6 (Spring 2007).

Robertson, William Glenn. "The Chickamauga Campaign: The Armies Collide." *Blue & Gray Magazine,* Vol. XXIV, No. 3. (Fall, 2007)

Robertson, William Glenn, "The Battle of Chickamauga, Day 1, September 19, 1863." *Blue & Gray Magazine,* Vol. XXIV, no. 6 (Spring 2008).

Robertson, William Glenn, "Chickamauga: Day 2." *Blue & Gray Magazine,* Vol. XXV, No. 2 (Summer, 2008).

Sawyer, Benjamin F. "Chickamauga." *Battles and Leaders,* Vol. 5 (Urbana IL, University of Illinois Press, 2002), pp. 422-29.

Smith, J. D. "Walthall's Brigade at Chickamauga." *Confederate Veteran* October, 1904. Vol. XII, p. 483-4. (24th Mississippi Infantry)

Stevenson, William Robert. "Robert Alexander Smith: A Southern Son." *Alabama Historical Quarterly.* Vol. 20, 1958, pp. 35-60. (3rd Alabama Cavalry)

Trantham, William D. "Wonderful Story of Richard R. Kirkland." *Confederate Veteran,* Vol. 16, no. 3, (March, 1908) p. 105.

Vance, William J. "On Thomas' Right at Chickamauga." *Blue And Gray,* Vol. 1, No. 3, February 1893.

Wiseman, Elijah. "Tennesseans at Chickamauga." *Confederate Veteran* (July, 1894), p. 205.

Wright, T. J. "Battle of Chickamauga." *Estill County Historical and Genealogical Society Newsletter.* May, 1997. p. 5.

Regimental, Unit Histories, and Personal Memoirs

Anonymous, *Ninety-Second Illinois Volunteers.* Freeport, Illinois. Journal Steam Publishing House and Bookbindery, 1875.

Anonymous, *History of the Services of the Third Battery, Wisconsin Light Artillery In the Civil War of the United States, 1861-65* Berlin, WI, Courant Press, n.d.

Aten, Henry J. *History of The Eighty-Fifth Regiment, Illinois Volunteer Infantry.* Hiawatha KS, 1901.

Barnes, James A., James R. Carnahan, and Thomas H. B. McCain. *The Eighty-Sixth Regiment, Indiana Infantry. A Narrative of its Services in the Civil War of 1861-1865.* Crawfordsville, Indiana, The Journal Company Printers, 1895.

Barnhill, Floyd R. Sr. and Calvin L Collier *The Fighting Fifth: Pat Cleburne's Cutting Edge: The Fifth Arkansas Regiment, C.S.A.* Jonesboro Arkansas, n.d.

Baumgartner, Richard A. *Blue Lightning: Wilder's Mounted Infantry Brigade in the Battle of Chickamauga.* Huntington, WV. Blue Acorn Press, 1997. Revised edition, 2007.

Baumgartner, Richard A. and Larry M. Strayer, eds. *Ralsa C. Rice: Yankee Tigers Through The Civil War With The 125th Ohio.* Huntington, WV. Blue Acorn Press, 1992.

Beaudot, William J. K. *The 24th Wisconsin Infantry in the Civil War: The Biography of a Regiment.* Mechanicsburg, PA. Stackpole Books, 2003.

Beatty, John. *The Citizen-Soldier: The Memoirs of a Civil War Volunteer.* Lincoln, NE. University of Nebraska Press, 1998. Reprint of 1879 edition.

Berkenes, Robert E. ed. *Private William Boddy's Civil War Journal: Empty Saddles . . . Empty Sleeves . . .* Altoona, IA. TiffCor Publishing, 1996. (92nd Illinois Infantry)

Bennett, Lyman G. and William M Haigh. *History of the Thirty-Sixth Regiment Illinois Volunteers during the War of the Rebellion.* Aurora, IL Knickerbocker and Hodder, 1876.

Bierce, Ambrose. *Ambrose Bierce's Civil War.* Avenel, New Jersey. Wing Books, 1996.

Bishop, Judson W. *The Story of a Regiment, Being a Narrative of the Service of the Second Regiment, Minnesota Veteran Volunteer Infantry, in the Civil War of 1861-1865.* St. Paul, MN. 1890.

Bishop, Judson W. *Van Derveer's Brigade At Chicamauga.* St. Paul, MN, n.p. 1903.

Briant, C.C. *History of the Sixth Regiment Indiana Volunteer Infantry.* Indianapolis, 1891.

Brown, Robert Carson. *The Sherman Brigade Marches South: The Civil War Memoirs of Colonel Robert Carson Brown.* Edited by Charles G. Brown. Washington D.C. Charles G. Brown, publisher, 1995.

Buckner, Allen. *The Memoirs of Allen Buckner.* Lansing, MI. The Michigan Alcohol and Drug Information Foundation. 1982. (79th Illinois Infantry)

Calkins, William Wirt. *The History of the One Hundred and Fourth Regiment of Illinois Volunteer Infantry. War of the Great Rebellion 1862-1865.* Chicago, Donohue and Hennenberry, 1895.

Canfield, Silas S. *History of the 21st Regiment Ohio Volunteer Infantry, in the War of the Rebellion.* Toledo, OH. Vrooman, Anderson and Bateman. 1893

Clark, Charles T. *Opdyke Tigers: 125th O.V.I. A History of the Regiment and of the Campaigns and Battles of the Army of the Cumberland.* Columbus, OH. Spahr and Glenn, 1895.

Collier, Calvin L. *First In—Last Out: The Capitol Guards, Ark. Brigade.* Little Rock, Arkansas. Pioneer Press. 1961.

Collier, Calvin L. *They'll Do To Tie To! The Story of the Third Regiment, Arkansas Infantry, C.S.A.* Little Rock Arkansas, Pioneer Press, 1959.

Collins, R. M. *Unwritten Chapters of the War Between the States.* Dayton, OH. Morningside House, 1988. Reprint of 1892 edition. (Original title: *Chapters from the Unwritten History of the War Between the States.* 15th Texas Infantry)

Connelly, James A. "Major James Austin Connelly." *Transactions of the Illinois State Historical Society for the Year 1928.* Springfield, Phillips Brothers, 1928.

Cope, Alexis. *The Fifteenth Ohio Volunteers and its Campaigns War of 1861-5.* Columbus, OH. Self-Published, 1916.

Daffan, Katie. *My Father as I Remember Him.* Houston, Gray and Dillaye, 1907. (Autobiographical sketch of Lawrence A. Daffan, 4th Texas Infantry)

Dana, Charles A. *Recollections of the Civil War.* New York, Collier books, 1963 edition.

Devol, Hiram F. *Biographical Sketch.* Kansas City, Missouri. Hudson Kimberly Publishing Co. 1903 (36th Ohio Infantry, including marginalia by John Booth, copy from Abraham Lincoln Presidential Library, Springfield.)

Dickert, D Augustus. *History of Kershaw's Brigade,* Newberry, 1899.

Dodson, W. C. *Wheeler and His Cavalry, 1862-1865.* Atlanta, GA. Hudgins and Co. 1899.

Dolton, Theodore A, ed. *The Path of Patriotism: Civil War Letters of George Edwin Dolton.* Booksurge, Palo Alto, CA, 2005. (Battery M, 1st Illinois Artillery)

Floyd, David Bittle. *History of the Seventy-Fifth Regiment of Indiana Infantry Volunteers, its Organization, Campaigns, and Battles (1862-1865)* Philadelphia, 1983.

Gammage, W. L. *The Camp, The Bivouac, and The Battlefield* Selma, Little Rock, Arkansas, Arkansas Southern Press. 1958. Reprint of 1964 Edition. (4th Arkansas Infantry)

Gibson, J. T. *History of the Seventy-Eighth Pennsylvania Volunteer Infantry*. Pittsburg, PA Pittsburg Printing Company. 1905.

Grebner, Constantine. Translated and edited by Frederic Trautmann. *We Were The Ninth: A History of the Ninth Regiment, Ohio Volunteer Infantry, April 17, 1861 to June 7, 1864*. Kent, OH Kent State University Press, 1987. Translation and reprint of 1897 German edition.

Gremillion, Nelson. *Company G, 1st Regiment Louisiana Cavalry, CSA: A Narrative*. University of Southwestern Louisiana. 1986.

Hallock, Judith Lee, ed. *The Civil War Letters of Joshua K. Calloway*. Athens, GA University of Georgia Press, 1997. (28th Alabama Infantry)

Hampton, Noah J. *An Eyewitness to the Dark Days of 1861-1865, Or a private soldier's Adventures and Hardships during the War*. Nashville, n.p. 1898. (18th Tennessee Infantry)

Hannaford, Ebenezer. *The Story of A Regiment: A History of the Campaigns, and Associations in the Field of the Sixth Regiment Ohio Volunteer Infantry*. Cincinnati, published by the Author, 1868.

Haynie, J. Henry. *The Nineteenth Illinois: A Memoir of a Regiment of Volunteer Infantry Famous in the Civil War of Fifty Years Ago for its Drill, Bravery, and Distinguished Services*. Chicago, M.A. Donahue, 1912.

Hazen, William B. *A Narrative of Military Service*. Boston, Ticknor and Co, 1885.

High, Edwin W. *History of the Sixty-Eighth Regiment Indiana Volunteer Infantry, 1862-1865, with a Sketch of E. A. King's Brigade, Reynolds' Division, Thomas' Corps, in the Battle of Chickamauga*. Matamora, IN 1902.

Hight, John J, and Gilbert R. Stormont. *History of the Fifty-Eighth Regiment of Indiana Volunteer Infantry, Its Organization, Campaigns, and Battles from 1861 to 1865*. Princeton, Indiana. 1895.

Hinman, Wilbur F. *The Story of the Sherman Brigade. The Camp, the March, the Bivouac, the Battle, and How "The Boys" Lived and Died During Four Years of Active Service*. Alliance, OH. Press of Daily Review, 1897.

Hood, John Bell. *Advance and Retreat*. Secausus, NJ, Blue and Gray Press, 1985. Reprint of 1880 ed.

Hughes, Nathaniel Cheairs, Ed. *Liddell's Record: St. John Richardson Liddell*. Baton Rouge, LA Louisiana State University Press, 1985.

Hunter, Alf. G. *History of the Eighty-Second Indiana Volunteer Infantry, its Organization, Campaigns and Battles*. Indianapolis, Wm. B. Burford, Printer. 1983.

Jenkins, Kirk C. *The Battle Rages Higher: The Union's Fifteenth Kentucky Infantry*. Lexington, KY: University Press of Kentucky.

Johnson, Mark W. *That Body of Brave Men: The U.S. Regular Infantry and the Civil War in the West*. Cambridge, MA Da Capo Press, 2003.

Johnson, Robert W. *A Soldier's Reminiscences in Peace and War*. Philadelphia, J.P. Lippincott Company, 1886.

Jordan, William C. *Some Events and Incidents During the Civil War*. Montgomery, Alabama, The Paragon Press, 1909. (15th Alabama Infantry)

Jordan, Thomas, and J. P. Pryor. *The Campaigns of General Nathan Bedford Forrest and of Forrest's Cavalry*. New York, De Capo Press, 1996. Reprint of 1868 edition.

Kelly, Weldon. *A Historic Sketch, Lest We Forget—Company "E" 26th Ohio Infantry in the War for the Union 1861-65*. n.p. n.d.

Kimberly, Robert L. and Ephraim S. Holloway. *The Forty-First Ohio Veteran Volunteer Infantry in the War of the Rebellion 1861-1865*. Cleveland, OH W.R. Smellie, 1897.

Laine, J. Gary; and Morris M. Penny. *Law's Alabama Brigade in the War Between the Union and the Confederacy*. Shippensburg, PA. White Mane Publishing, 1996.

Lasswell, Mary, ed. *Rags and Hope: the Recollections of Val. C. Giles, Four Years with Hood's Texas Brigade, Fourth Texas Infantry 1861-65*. New York Cowar-McCann Inc. 1961.

Lavender, John W. *They Never Came Back: The Story of Co. F. Fourth Arks. Infantry C.S.A (Originally Known As The Montgomery Hunters) as Told by their Commanding Officer*. Pine Bluff, Arkansas. The Perdue Co. 1956.

Longacre, Glenn V. and John E. Haas, eds. *To Battle for God and the Right: The Civil War Letterbooks of Emerson Opdyke*. Champaign, Illinois, University of Illinois Press, 2003.

Longstreet, James. *From Manassas to Appomattox, Memoirs of the Civil War in America*. Philadelphia, P. J Lippincott, 1896.

Manigault, Arthur Middleton. *A Carolinian Goes To War: The Civil War Narrative of Arthur Middleton Manigault*. Charleston, South Carolina. University of South Carolina Press, 1983.

McMurray, W. J. *History of the Twentieth Tennessee Regiment Volunteer Infantry, C.S.A.* Nashville, TN, Publication Committee of the Regiment, 1904.

Miller, Gerald J. *Middletown Yank's "Journey to War And Back."* n.p. Champaign, IL 1985. (Diary of James G. Watson, 25th Illinois)

Minty, R. H.G . *Remarks of Brevet Major General R. H. G. Minty Made September 18th, 1895 at the Dedication of the Monument Erected to the Fourth Michigan Cavalry At Reed's Bridge, Chickamauga National Park*. Ogden Utah, 1896.

Morris, George W. *History of the Eighty-First Regiment of Indiana Volunteer Infantry in the Great War of the Rebellion 1861 To 1865*. Louisville, KY Franklin Printing Co. 1901.

Morton, John Watson. *The Artillery of Nathan Bedford Forrest's Cavalry*. Marietta, GA. R. Bemis Publishing, 1995. Reprint of 1909 edition.

Munhall, L. W. George A. Smyth, III Ed. *Leander Whitcomb Munhall's Letters Home 1862-1865* n. p. 1992.

Newlin, William H. *A History of the Seventy-Third Regiment of Illinois Infantry Volunteers*. Springfield, IL. Regimental Association, 1890.

Noe, Kenneth W. ed. *A Southern Boy in Blue: The Memoir of Marcus Woodcock, 9th Kentucky Infantry, U.S.A.* Knoxville, TN. University of Tennessee Press, 1996.

Myers, Sandra L., Ed. *Force Without Fanfare: The Autobiography of K. M. Van Zandt*. Fort Worth, Texas, Texas Christian University Press, 1968. (7th Texas Infantry)

Oates, William C. *The War Between the Union and the Confederacy and its Lost Opportunities with a History of the 15th Alabama Regiment and the Forty-eight Battles in which it was Engaged*. New York, Neale Publishing Co. 1905.

Obreiter, John. *The Seventy-Seventh Pennsylvania at Shiloh. History of the Regiment*. Harrisburg, PA. Harrisburg Publishing Company, 1905.

Palmer, John M. *Personal Recollections of John M. Palmer: The Story of an Earnest Life*. Cincinnati, OH. The Robert Clarke Co. 1901.

Partridge, Charles. *History of the Ninety-Sixth Regiment Illinois Volunteer Infantry*. Chicago, Brown, Pettibone and Company. 1887.

Perry, Henry Fales. *History of the Thirty-Eighth Regiment Indiana Volunteer Infantry: One of the Three Hundred Fighting Regiments of the Union Army*. Palo Alto, CA. 1906.

Rerick, John H. *The Forty-Fourth Indiana Volunteer Infantry: History of its Services in the War of the Rebellion and a Personal Record of its Members*. Lagrange, Indiana, 1880.

Robertson, John, Comp. *Michigan in the War*. Lansing, MI, W. S. George & Co, State Printers, 1882.

Royse, Isaac Henry Clay. *History of the 115th Regiment Illinois Volunteer Infantry*. Terre Haute, IN. Published by the Author, 1900.

Scribner, Benjamin F. *How Soldiers Were Made; Or the War as I Saw it Under Buell, Rosecrans, Thomas, Grant, and Sherman*. Chicago, Donohoe and Henneberry, Printers, 1887.

Shanks, William. *Personal Recollections of Distinguished Generals*. New York, Harper, 1866.

Shaw, James Birney. *History of the Tenth Regiment Indiana Volunteer Infantry*. Lafayette, Indiana 1912.

Simmons, L.A. *The History of the 84th Reg't Ill. Vols*. Macomb, IL. Hampton Bros. 1866.

Simpson, Col. Harold B. *Hood's Texas Brigade: Lee's Grenadier Guard*. Hillsboro TX 1970.

Smith, John C. *Oration at the Unveiling of the Monument Erected to the Memory of Maj. Gen. James B. Steedman*. Chicago, Knight & Leonard Co. 1887.

————. *The Right of the Federal Army at Chickamauga*. Chicago, Knight & Leonard Co. 1894.

Smith, Louis R. and Andrew Quist. *Cush: A Civil War Memoir by Samuel H. Sprott.* Livingston Press, University of West Alabama. 1999. (40th Alabama Infantry)

Sorrell, G. Moxley. *At The Right Hand of Longstreet: Recollections Of A Confederate Staff Officer.* Lincoln, NE, University of Nebraska Press, 1999. Reprint of 1905 edition.

Stanley, David S. *Personal Memoirs of Major General D. S. Stanley, U.S.A.* Cambridge, MA. Harvard University Press, 1917.

Stockton, Will and Ju. Herman Ulmer, ed. *The Correspondence of Will and Ju Stockton, 1845-1869.* Auburn University, 1984.

Stroud, David V. *Ector's Brigade and the Army of Tennessee, 1862-1865.* Longview, TX, Ranger Publishing, 2004.

Tomlinson, Helyn W. *"Dear Friends" The Civil War Letters and Diary Of Charles Edwin Cort.* n.p. 1962. (92nd Illinois Infantry)

Tourgee, Albion W. *The Story of a Thousand: Being a History of the Service of the 105th Ohio Volunteer Infantry, in the War for the Union from August 21, 1862 to June 6, 1865.* Buffalo, N. Y. McGerald and Son, 1896.

Turchin, John B. *Chickamauga.* Chicago, Fergus Printing Company, 1888.

Vale, Joseph G. *Minty and the Cavalry: A History of Cavalry Campaigns in the Western Armies.* Harrisburg, PA, Edwin K. Meyers, 1886.

Waddle, Angus. *Three Years with the Armies of the Ohio and the Cumberland.* Chillicothe, Ohio. Scioto Gazette Job and Book Office. 1889. (33rd Ohio)

Watkins, Sam R. and Ruth Hill Fulton McCallister, Ed. *Co. Aytch: Maury Grays, First Tennessee Regiment, or A Side Show of the Big Show.* Franklin, TN, Providence House Publishers, 2007.

Weaver, Bryan P. and H. Lee Fenner. *Sacrifice At Chickamauga: A History of the 89th Ohio Volunteer Infantry Regiment.* Palos Verdes Peninsula, California. MoyWeave Books, 2003.

Weaver, Jeffrey C. *63rd Virginia Infantry.* Lynchburg, VA, H. E. Howard, 1991.

Williams, John A.B. *Memoir of John A. B. Williams, or Leaves From a Trooper's Diary.* Philadelphia, Privately published, 1869. (15th Pennsylvania Cavalry)

Woodruff, George H. *Fifteen Years Ago: Or the Patriotism of Will County.* Joliet, IL. Joliet Republican Book and Job Steam Printing House, 1876. (100th Illinois Infantry)

Wright, T. J. *History Of The Eighth Regiment Kentucky Volunteer Infantry During its Three Years Campaigns Embracing Organization, Marches, Skirmishes, and Battles of the Command, With Much of the History of the Old Reliable Third Brigade, Commanded By Hon. Stanley Matthews, and Containing Many Interesting and Amusing Incidents of Army Life.* St. Joseph, MO. St. Joseph Steam Printing Co. 1880.

Wyckoff, Mac. *A History of the Third South Carolina Infantry 1861-1865.* Fredericksburg, VA. Sergeant Kirklands Museum and Historical Society, 1998.

Secondary Sources

Cozzens, Peter. *This Terrible Sound.* Urbana, IL, University Of Illinois Press, 1992.

Connelly, Thomas Lawrence. *Autumn of Glory: The Army Of Tennessee, 1862-1865.* Baton Rouge, LA, Louisiana State University Press, 1971.

Daniel, Larry. *Days of Glory: The Army of the Cumberland, 1861-1865.* Baton Rouge, Louisiana State University Press, 2004.

DiNardo, R. L. and Albert A. Nofi, *James Longstreet: The Man, The Soldier, The Controversy.* Conshohocken, PA. Combined Publishing, 1998.

Elliott, Sam Davis. *Soldier of Tennessee: General Alexander P. Stewart and the Civil War in the West.* Baton Rouge, Louisiana. Louisiana State University Press, 1999.

Evans, E. Raymond. *Chickamauga Civil War Impact on an Area: Tsikamagi, Crawfish Springs, Snow Hill, and Chickamauga.* City of Chickamauga, Walker County GA. 2002.

Gracie, Archibald. *The Truth About Chickamauga.* Dayton, Ohio, Morningside Press, 1987. Reprint of 1911 edition.

Hallock, Judith Lee. *Braxton Bragg and Confederate Defeat: Voume II.* Tuscaloosa, Alabama. University of Alabama Press. 1991.

Hughes, Nathaniel Cheairs, Jr., and Gordon D. Whitney, *Jefferson Davis in Blue: The Life of Sherman's Relentless Warrior.* Baton Rouge, Louisiana State University Press, 2002.

Hurst, Jack. *Nathan Bedford Forrest.* New York, Vantage Books, 1994.

Lamers, William M. *The Edge of Glory: A Biography of General William S. Rosecrans, U.S.A.* Baton Rouge, LA. Louisiana State University Press, 1999. Reprint of 1961 edition.

Lindsley, John. *The Military Annals of Tennessee. Confederate. First Series: Embracing a Review of Military Operations, with Regimental Histories and Memorial Rolls.* Nashville, J.M. Lindsley, 1886.

Lytle, Andrew. *Bedford Forrest and His Critter Company.* Seminole, FL, Green Key Press, 1984. Reprint of 1931 edition.

McKinney, Francis F. *Education on Violence.* Chicago, IL, Americana House, 1991, reprint of 1961 edition.

Scott, William Forse. *Philander P. Lane Colonel of Volunteers in the Civil War Eleventh Ohio Infantry.* n.p., 1920.

Symonds, Craig L. *Stonewall of the West: Patrick Cleburne and the Civil War.* Lawrence, Kansas, University of Kansas Press, 1997

Tatum, Georgia Lee. *Disloyalty in the Confederacy.* Lincoln, Nebraska, University of Nebraska Press, 2000. Reprint of 1934 edition.

Wert, Jeffry D. *General James Longstreet, The Confederacy's Most Controversial Soldier: A Biography.* New York, Simon and Schuster, 1993.

Wyeth, John A. *That Devil Forrest: Life of General Nathan Bedford Forrest.* Baton Rouge, LA, Louisiana State University Press, 1989.

Internet Sources

Samuel Broughton, 21st Illinois Infantry. Www.rootsweb.com/~ilcivilw/scrapk/broughtjourn.html.

"Dear Sir," February 12, 1909, Charles T. Clark to Ezra E. Carmen, 125th Ohio Website, www.home.earthlink.net/~nhaldane/ctc-letter.html

Jim R. Martin Letter, 22nd Alabama Regiment. www.geocities.com/~bobjones/22nd—docs.htm.

Index

About the Authors

David A. Powell is a graduate of the Virginia Military Institute, class of 1983, with a BA in history. After graduating he went to work in the family business, CBS Messenger, in the Chicago area. David has never lost his intense interest in military history in general, and in the American Civil War in particular. He has published a number of articles in various magazines, more than fifteen historical simulations of different battles, and regularly leads tours to historic sites. For the past decade David's focus has been the epic battle of Chickamauga, and he is nationally recognized for his tours of that important national battlefield. *The Maps of Chickamauga* is his first book.

David A. Friedrichs graduated from University of Wisconsin in 1982 and has worked since that time as a civil engineer. He is the author of many articles and papers on topics ranging from public asset management to military history. David's interest in military history began at a very early age. This interest, combined with a love of maps, resulted in the publication of several military simulations. *The Maps of Chickamauga* is his first book.